➤➤➤◄◄◄

THE COMPLETE POETRY AND PROSE OF

WALT WHITMAN

IN TWO VOLUMES: THIS IS

VOLUME TWO

➤➤➤◄◄◄

SPECIMEN DAYS, COLLECT, INCLUDING
NOTES LEFT OVER AND PIECES IN EARLY YOUTH
AND NOVEMBER BOUGHS

THE COMPLETE
POETRY AND PROSE OF

Walt Whitman

AS PREPARED BY HIM
FOR THE

DEATHBED EDITION

WITH AN INTRODUCTION BY

Malcolm Cowley

PELLEGRINI & CUDAHY · NEW YORK

CONTENTS

VOLUME TWO

→»» «««

SPECIMEN DAYS

COLLECT

Notes Left Over

COLLECT (APPENDIX)

Pieces in Early Youth 1834–'42

NOVEMBER BOUGHS

GOOD-BYE MY FANCY

VOLUME TWO

PROSE

Specimen Days

❈

A HAPPY HOUR'S COMMAND

Down in the Woods, July 2d, 1882.—If I do it at all I must delay no longer. Incongruous and full of skips and jumps as is that huddle of diary-jottings, war-memoranda of 1862–'65, Nature-notes of 1877–'81, with Western and Canadian observations afterwards, all bundled up and tied by a big string, the resolution and indeed mandate comes to me this day, this hour,—(and what a day! what an hour just passing! the luxury of riant grass and blowing breeze, with all the shows of sun and sky and perfect temperature, never before so filling me body and soul)—to go home, untie the bundle, reel out diary-scraps and memoranda, just as they are, large or small, one after another, into print-pages,[1] and let the melange's lackings and wants of connection take care of themselves. It will illustrate one phase of humanity anyhow; how few of life's days and hours (and they not by relative value or proportion, but by chance) are ever noted. Probably another point too, how we give long preparations for some object, planning and delving and fashioning, and then, when the actual hour for doing arrives, find ourselves still quite unprepared, and tumble the thing together, letting hurry and crudeness tell the story better than fine work. At any rate I obey my happy hour's command, which seems curiously imperative. May-be, if I don't do anything else, I shall send out the most wayward, spontaneous, fragmentary book ever printed.

3

ANSWER TO AN INSISTING FRIEND

You ASK for items, details of my early life—of genealogy and parentage, particularly of the women of my ancestry, and of its far back Netherlands stock on the maternal side—of the region where I was born and raised, and my father and mother before me, and theirs before them—with a word about Brooklyn and New York cities, the times I lived there as lad and young man. You say you want to get at these details mainly as the go-befores and embryons of "Leaves of Grass." Very good; you shall have at least some specimens of them all. I have often thought of the meaning of such things—that one can only encompass and complete matters of that kind by exploring behind, perhaps very far behind, themselves directly, and so into their genesis, antecedents, and cumulative stages. Then as luck would have it, I lately whiled away the tedium of a week's half-sickness and confinement, by collating these very items for another (yet unfulfill'd, probably abandon'd,) purpose; and if you will be satisfied with them, authentic in date-occurrence and fact simply, and told my own way, garrulous-like, here they are. I shall not hesitate to make extracts, for I catch at any thing to save labor; but those will be the best versions of what I want to convey.

GENEALOGY—VAN VELSOR AND WHITMAN

THE LATER years of the last century found the Van Velsor family, my mother's side, living on their own farm at Cold Spring, Long Island, New York State, near the eastern edge of Queens county, about a mile from the harbor.[2] My father's side—probably the fifth generation from the first English arrivals in New England—were at the same time farmers on their own land—(and a fine domain it was, 500 acres, all good soil, gently sloping east and south, about one-tenth woods, plenty of grand old trees,) two or three miles off, at West Hills, Suffolk county. The Whitman name in the Eastern States, and so branching West and South, starts undoubtedly from one John Whitman, born 1602, in Old England, where he grew up, married, and his eldest son was born in 1629. He came over in the "True Love" in 1640 to America, and lived in Weymouth, Mass., which place became the mother-hive of the New-Englanders of the name: he died in 1692. His brother, Rev. Zechariah Whitman, also came over in the "True Love," either at that time or soon after, and lived at Milford, Conn. A son of this Zechariah, named Joseph, migrated to Huntington, Long Island, and permanently settled there. Savage's "Genealogical Dictionary" (vol. iv, p. 524) gets the Whitman family establish'd at Huntington, per this Joseph, before 1664. It is quite certain that from that beginning, and from Joseph, the West Hill Whitmans, and all others in Suffolk county, have since radiated, myself among the number. John and Zechariah both went to England and back again divers times; they had large families, and several of their children were born in the old country. We hear of the father of John and Zechariah, Abijah Whitman, who goes over into the 1500's, but we know little about him, except that he also was for some time in America.

These old pedigree-reminiscences come up to me vividly from a visit I made not long since (in my 63d year) to West Hills, and to the burial grounds of my ancestry, both sides. I extract from notes of that visit, written there and then:

THE OLD WHITMAN AND VAN VELSOR CEMETERIES

July 29, 1881.—After more than forty years' absence, (except a brief visit, to take my father there once more, two years before he died,) went down Long Island on a week's jaunt to the place where I was born, thirty miles from New York city. Rode around the old familiar spots, viewing and pondering and dwelling long upon them, everything coming back to me. Went to the old Whitman homestead on the upland and took a view eastward, inclining south, over the broad and beautiful farm lands of my grandfather (1780,) and my father. There was the new house (1810,) the big oak a hundred and fifty or two hundred years old; there the well, the sloping kitchen-garden, and a little way off even the well-kept remains of the dwelling of my great-grandfather (1750-'60) still standing, with its mighty timbers and low ceilings. Near by, a stately grove of tall, vigorous black-walnuts, beautiful, Apollo-like, the sons or grandsons, no doubt, of black-walnuts during or before 1776. On the other side of the road spread the famous apple orchard, over twenty acres, the trees planted by hands long mouldering in the grave (my uncle Jesse's,) but quite many of them evidently capable of throwing out their annual blossoms and fruit yet.

I now write these lines seated on an old grave (doubtless of a century since at least) on the burial hill of the Whitmans of many generations. Fifty and more graves are quite plainly traceable, and as many more decay'd out of all form—depress'd mounds, crumbled and broken stones, cover'd with moss—the gray and sterile hill, the clumps of chestnuts outside, the silence, just varied by the soughing wind.

There is always the deepest eloquence of sermon or poem in any of these ancient graveyards of which Long Island has so many; so what must this one have been to me? My whole family history, with its succession of links, from the first settlement down to date, told here —three centuries concentrate on this sterile acre.

The next day, July 30, I devoted to the maternal locality, and if possible was still more penetrated and impress'd. I write this paragraph on the burial hill of the Van Velsors, near Cold Spring, the most significant depository of the dead that could be imagin'd, without the slightest help from art, but far ahead of it, soil sterile, a mostly bare plateau-flat of half an acre, the top of a hill, brush and well grown trees and dense woods bordering all around, very primitive, secluded, no visitors, no road (you cannot drive here, you have to bring the dead on foot, and follow on foot.) Two or three-score graves quite plain; as many more almost rubb'd out. My grandfather Cornelius and my grandmother Amy (Naomi) and numerous relatives nearer or remoter, on my mother's side, lie buried here. The scene as I stood or sat, the delicate and wild odor of the woods, a slightly drizzling rain, the emotional atmosphere of the place, and the inferr'd reminiscences, were fitting accompaniments.

THE MATERNAL HOMESTEAD

I WENT down from this ancient grave place eighty or ninety rods to the site of the Van Velsor homestead, where my mother was born (1795,) and where every spot had been familiar to me as a child and youth (1825–'40.) Then stood there a long rambling, dark-gray, shingle-sided house, with sheds, pens, a great barn, and much open road-space. Now of all those not a vestige left; all had been pull'd down, erased, and the plough and harrow pass'd over foundations, road-spaces and everything, for many summers; fenced in at present, and grain and clover growing like any other fine fields. Only a big hole from the cellar, with some little heaps of broken stone, green with grass and weeds, identified the place. Even the copious old brook and spring seem'd to have mostly dwindled away. The whole scene, with what it arous'd, memories of my young days there half a century ago, the vast kitchen and ample fireplace and the sitting-room adjoining, the plain furniture, the meals, the house full of merry people, my grandmother Amy's sweet old face in its Quaker cap, my grandfather "the Major," jovial, red, stout, with sonorous voice and characteristic physiognomy, with the actual sights themselves, made the most pronounc'd half-day's experience of my whole jaunt.

For there with all those wooded, hilly, healthy surroundings, my dearest mother, Louisa Van Velsor, grew up—(her mother, Amy Williams, of the Friends' or Quakers' denomination—the Williams family, seven sisters and one brother—the father and brother sailors, both of whom met their deaths at sea.) The Van Velsor people were noted for fine horses, which the men bred and train'd from blooded stock. My mother, as a young woman, was a daily and daring rider. As to the head of the family himself, the old race of the Netherlands, so deeply grafted on Manhattan island and in Kings and Queens counties, never yielded a more mark'd and full Americanized specimen than Major Cornelius Van Velsor.

TWO OLD FAMILY INTERIORS

OF THE domestic and inside life of the middle of Long Island, at and just before that time, here are two samples:

"The Whitmans, at the beginning of the present century, lived in a long story-and-a-half farm-house, hugely timber'd, which is still standing. A great smoke-canopied kitchen, with vast hearth and chimney, form'd one end of the house. The existence of slavery in New York at that time, and the possession by the family of some twelve or fifteen slaves, house and field servants, gave things quite a patriarchal look. The very young darkies could be seen, a swarm of them, toward sundown, in this kitchen, squatted in a circle on the floor, eating their supper of Indian pudding and milk. In the house, and in food and furniture, all was rude, but substantial. No carpets or stoves were known, and no coffee, and tea or sugar only for the women. Rousing wood fires gave both warmth and light on winter nights. Pork, poultry, beef, and all the ordinary vegetables and grains were plentiful. Cider was the men's common drink, and used at meals. The clothes were mainly homespun. Journeys were made by both men and women on horseback. Both sexes labor'd with their own hands—the men on the farm—the women in the house and around it. Books were scarce. The annual copy of the almanac was a treat, and was pored over through the long winter evenings. I must not forget to mention that both these families were near enough to the sea to behold it from the high places, and to hear in still hours the roar of the surf; the latter, after a storm, giving a peculiar sound at night. Then all hands, male and female, went down frequently on beach and bathing parties, and the men on practical expeditions for cutting salt hay, and for clamming and fishing."—John Burroughs's NOTES.

"The ancestors of Walt Whitman, on both the paternal and maternal sides, kept a good table, sustain'd the hospitalities, decorums, and an excellent social reputation in the county, and they were often of mark'd individuality. If space permitted, I should consider some of the men worthy special description; and still more some of the women. His great-grandmother on the paternal side, for instance, was a large swarthy

woman, who lived to a very old age. She smoked tobacco, rode on horse-back like a man, managed the most vicious horse, and, becoming a widow in later life, went forth every day over her farm-lands, frequently in the saddle, directing the labor of her slaves, with language in which, on exciting occasions, oaths were not spared. The two immediate grand-mothers were, in the best sense, superior women. The maternal one (Amy Williams before marriage) was a Friend, or Quakeress, of sweet, sensible character, housewifely proclivities, and deeply intuitive and spiritual. The other, (Hannah Brush,) was an equally noble, perhaps stronger char-acter, lived to be very old, had quite a family of sons, was a natural lady, was in early life a school-mistress, and had great solidity of mind. W. W. himself makes much of the women of his ancestry."—The same.

Out from these arrieres of persons and scenes, I was born May 31, 1819. And now to dwell awhile on the locality itself—as the successive growth stages of my infancy, childhood, youth and manhood were all pass'd on Long Island, which I sometimes feel as if I had incorpo-rated. I roam'd, as boy and man, and have lived in nearly all parts, from Brooklyn to Montauk point.

PAUMANOK, AND MY LIFE ON IT AS CHILD AND YOUNG MAN

Worth fully and particularly investigating indeed this Paumanok, (to give the spot its aboriginal name,[3]) stretching east through Kings, Queens and Suffolk counties, 120 miles altogether—on the north Long Island sound, a beautiful, varied and picturesque series of inlets, "necks" and sea-like expansions, for a hundred miles to Orient point. On the ocean side the great south bay dotted with countless hum-mocks, mostly small, some quite large, occasionally long bars of sand out two hundred rods to a mile-and-a-half from the shore. While now and then, as at Rockaway and far east along the Hamptons, the beach makes right on the island, the sea dashing up without intervention. Several light-houses on the shores east; a long history of wrecks trag-edies, some even of late years. As a youngster, I was in the atmosphere and traditions of many of these wrecks—of one or two almost an ob-server. Off Hempstead beach for example, was the loss of the ship "Mexico" in 1840, (alluded to in "the Sleepers" in L. of G.) And at Hampton, some years later, the destruction of the brig "Elizabeth," a fearful affair, in one of the worst winter gales, where Margaret Fuller went down, with her husband and child.

Inside the outer bars or beach this south bay is everywhere com-paratively shallow; of cold winters all thick ice on the surface. As a boy I often went forth with a chum or two, on those frozen fields, with hand-sled, axe and eel-spear, after messes of eels. We would cut holes in the ice, sometimes striking quite an eel-bonanza, and filling our baskets with great, fat, sweet, white-meated fellows. The scenes, the ice, drawing the hand-sled, cutting holes, spearing the eels, &c., were of course just such fun as is dearest to boyhood. The shores of this bay, winter and summer, and my doings there in early life, are woven all through L. of G. One sport I was very fond of was to go on a bay-party in summer to gather sea-gull's eggs. (The gulls lay two or three eggs, more than half the size of hen's eggs, right on the sand, and leave the sun's heat to hatch them.)

The eastern end of Long Island, the Peconic bay region, I knew quite well too—sail'd more than once around Shelter island, and down to Montauk—spent many an hour on Turtle hill by the old light-house, on the extreme point, looking out over the ceaseless roll of the Atlantic. I used to like to go down there and fraternize with the blue-fishers, or the annual squads of sea-bass takers. Sometimes, along Montauk peninsula, (it is some 15 miles long, and good grazing,) met the strange, unkempt, half-barbarous herdsmen, at that time living there entirely aloof from society or civilization, in charge, on those rich pasturages, of vast droves of horses, kine or sheep, own'd by farmers of the eastern towns. Sometimes, too, the few remaining Indians, or half-breeds, at that period left on Montauk peninsula, but now I believe altogether extinct.

More in the middle of the island were the spreading Hempstead plains, then (1830–'40) quite prairie-like, open, uninhabited, rather sterile, cover'd with kill-calf and huckleberry bushes, yet plenty of fair pasture for the cattle, mostly milch-cows, who fed there by hundreds, even thousands, and at evening, (the plains too were own'd by the towns, and this was the use of them in common,) might be seen taking their way home, branching off regularly in the right places. I have often been out on the edges of these plains toward sundown, and can yet recall in fancy the interminable cow processions, and hear the music of the tin or copper bells clanking far or near, and breathe the cool of the sweet and slightly aromatic evening air, and note the sunset.

Through the same region of the island, but further east, extended wide central tracts of pine and scrub-oak, (charcoal was largely made here,) monotonous and sterile. But many a good day or half-day did I have, wandering through those solitary cross-roads, inhaling the peculiar and wild aroma. Here, and all along the island and its shores, I spent intervals many years, all seasons, sometimes riding, sometimes boating, but generally afoot, (I was always then a good walker,) absorbing fields, shores, marine incidents, characters, the bay-men, farmers, pilots—always had a plentiful acquaintance with the latter, and with fishermen—went every summer on sailing trips—always liked the bare sea-beach, south side, and have some of my happiest hours on it to this day.

As I write, the whole experience comes back to me after the lapse of forty and more years—the soothing rustle of the waves, and the saline smell—boyhood's times, the clam-digging, barefoot, and with trowsers roll'd up—hauling down the creek—the perfume of the sedge-meadows—the hay-boat, and the chowder and fishing excursions;—or, of later years, little voyages down and out New York bay, in the pilot boats. Those same later years, also, while living in Brooklyn, (1836–'50) I went regularly every week in the mild seasons down to Coney island, at that time a long, bare unfrequented shore, which I had all to myself, and where I loved, after bathing, to race up and down the hard sand, and declaim Homer or Shakspere to the surf and sea-gulls by the hour. But I am getting ahead too rapidly, and must keep more in my traces.

MY FIRST READING—LAFAYETTE

FROM 1824 to '28 our family lived in Brooklyn in Front, Cranberry and Johnson streets. In the latter my father built a nice house for a home, and afterwards another in Tillary street. We occupied them, one after the other, but they were mortgaged, and we lost them. I yet remember Lafayette's visit.[4] Most of these years I went to the public schools. It must have been about 1829 or '30 that I went with my father and mother to hear Elias Hicks preach in a ball-room on Brooklyn heights. At about the same time employ'd as a boy in an office, lawyers', father and two sons, Clarke's, Fulton street, near Orange. I had a nice desk and window-nook to myself; Edward C. kindly help'd me at my handwriting and composition, and, (the signal event of my life up to that time,) subscribed for me to a big circulating library. For a time I now revel'd in romance-reading of all kinds; first, the "Arabian Nights," all the volumes, an amazing treat. Then, with sorties in very many other directions, took in Walter Scott's novels, one after another, and his poetry, (and continue to enjoy novels and poetry to this day.)

PRINTING OFFICE—OLD BROOKLYN

AFTER about two years went to work in a weekly newspaper and printing office, to learn the trade. The paper was the "Long Island Patriot," owned by S. E. Clements, who was also postmaster. An old printer in the office, William Hartshorne, a revolutionary character, who had seen Washington, was a special friend of mine, and I had many a talk with him about long past times. The apprentices, including myself, boarded with his grand-daughter. I used occasionally to go out riding with the boss, who was very kind to us boys; Sundays he took us all to a great old rough, fortress-looking stone church, on Joralemon street, near where the Brooklyn city hall now is—(at that time broad fields and country roads everywhere around.[5]) Afterward I work'd on the "Long Island Star," Alden Spooner's paper. My father all these years pursuing his trade as carpenter and builder, with varying fortune. There was a growing family of children—eight of us—my brother Jesse the oldest, myself the second, my dear sisters Mary and Hannah Louisa, my brothers Andrew, George, Thomas Jefferson, and then my youngest brother, Edward, born 1835, and always badly crippled, as I am myself of late years.

GROWTH—HEALTH—WORK

I developed (1833–4–5) into a healthy, strong youth (grew too fast, though, was nearly as big as a man at 15 or 16.) Our family at this period moved back to the country, my dear mother very ill for a long time, but recover'd. All these years I was down Long Island more or less every summer, now east, now west, sometimes months at a stretch. At 16, 17, and so on, was fond of debating societies, and had an active membership with them, off and on, in Brooklyn and one or two country towns on the island. A most omnivorous novel-reader, these and later years, devour'd everything I could get. Fond of the theatre, also, in New York, went whenever I could—sometimes witnessing fine performances.

1836–7, work'd as compositor in printing offices in New York city. Then, when little more than eighteen, and for a while afterwards, went to teaching country schools down in Queens and Suffolk counties, Long Island, and "boarded round." (This latter I consider one of my best experiences and deepest lessons in human nature behind the scenes, and in the masses.) In '39, '40, I started and publish'd a weekly paper in my native town, Huntington. Then returning to New York city and Brooklyn, work'd on as printer and writer, mostly prose, but an occasional shy at "poetry."

MY PASSION FOR FERRIES

Living in Brooklyn or New York city from this time forward, my life, then, and still more the following years, was curiously identified with Fulton ferry, already becoming the greatest of its sort in the world for general importance, volume, variety, rapidity, and pictur-esqueness. Almost daily, later, ('50 to '60,) I cross'd on the boats, often up in the pilot-houses where I could get a full sweep, absorbing shows, accompaniments, surroundings. What oceanic currents, eddies, under-neath—the great tides of humanity also, with ever-shifting movements. Indeed, I have always had a passion for ferries; to me they afford inimitable, streaming, never-failing, living poems. The river and bay scenery, all about New York island, any time of a fine day—the hurry-ing, splashing sea-tides—the changing panorama of steamers, all sizes, often a string of big ones outward bound to distant ports—the myriads of white-sail'd schooners, sloops, skiffs, and the marvellously beauti-ful yachts—the majestic sound boats as they rounded the Battery and came along towards 5, afternoon, eastward bound—the prospect off towards Staten island, or down the Narrows, or the other way up the Hudson—what refreshment of spirit such sights and experiences gave me years ago (and many a time since.) My old pilot friends, the Bal-sirs, Johnny Cole, Ira Smith, William White, and my young ferry friend, Tom Gere—how well I remember them all.

BROADWAY SIGHTS

Besides Fulton ferry, off and on for years, I knew and frequented Broadway—that noted avenue of New York's crowded and mixed hu-manity, and of so many notables. Here I saw, during those times, An-drew Jackson, Webster, Clay, Seward, Martin Van Buren, filibuster Walker, Kossuth, Fitz Greene Halleck, Bryant, the Prince of Wales, Charles Dickens, the first Japanese ambassadors, and lots of other celebrities of the time. Always something novel or inspiriting; yet mostly to me the hurrying and vast amplitude of those never-ending human currents. I remember seeing James Fenimore Cooper in a court-room in Chambers street, back of the city hall, where he was carrying on a law case—(I think it was a charge of libel he had brought against some one.) I also remember seeing Edgar A. Poe, and having a short interview with him, (it must have been in 1845 or '6,) in his office, second story of a corner building, (Duane or Pearl street.) He was editor and owner or part owner of "the Broadway Journal." The visit was about a piece of mine he had publish'd. Poe was very cor-dial, in a quiet way, appear'd well in person, dress, &c. I have a distinct and pleasing remembrance of his looks, voice, manner and matter; very kindly and human, but subdued, perhaps a little jaded. For an-other of my reminiscences, here on the west side, just below Houston street, I once saw (it must have been about 1832, of a sharp, bright

January day) a bent, feeble but stout-built very old man, bearded, swathed in rich furs, with a great ermine cap on his head, led and assisted, almost carried, down the steps of his high front stoop (a dozen friends and servants, emulous, carefully holding, guiding him) and then lifted and tuck'd in a gorgeous sleigh, envelop'd in other furs, for a ride. The sleigh was drawn by as fine a team of horses as I ever saw. (You needn't think all the best animals are brought up nowadays; never was such horseflesh as fifty years ago on Long Island, or south, or in New York city; folks look'd for spirit and mettle in a nag, not tame speed merely.) Well, I, a boy of perhaps thirteen or fourteen, stopp'd and gazed long at the spectacle of that fur-swathed old man, surrounded by friends and servants, and the careful seating of him in the sleigh. I remember the spirited, champing horses, the driver with his whip, and a fellow-driver by his side, for extra prudence. The old man, the subject of so much attention, I can almost see now. It was John Jacob Astor.

The years 1846, '47, and there along, see me still in New York city, working as writer and printer, having my usual good health, and a good time generally.

OMNIBUS JAUNTS AND DRIVERS

ONE phase of those days must by no means go unrecorded—namely, the Broadway omnibuses, with their drivers. The vehicles still (I write this paragraph in 1881) give a portion of the character of Broadway—the Fifth avenue, Madison avenue, and Twenty-third street lines yet running. But the flush days of the old Broadway stages, characteristic and copious, are over. The Yellow-birds, the Red-birds, the original Broadway, the Fourth avenue, the Knickerbocker, and a dozen others of twenty or thirty years ago, are all gone. And the men specially identified with them, and giving vitality and meaning to them —the drivers—a strange, natural, quick-eyed and wondrous race—(not only Rabelais and Cervantes would have gloated upon them, but Homer and Shakspere would)—how well I remember them, and must here give a word about them. How many hours, forenoons and afternoons—how many exhilarating night-times I have had—perhaps June or July, in cooler air—riding the whole length of Broadway, listening to some yarn, (and the most vivid yarns ever spun, and the rarest mimicry)—or perhaps I declaiming some stormy passage from Julius Cæsar or Richard, (you could roar as loudly as you chose in that heavy, dense, uninterrupted street-bass.) Yes, I knew all the drivers then, Broadway Jack, Dressmaker, Balky Bill, George Storms, Old Elephant, his brother Young Elephant (who came afterward,) Tippy,

Pop Rice, Big Frank, Yellow Joe, Pete Callahan, Patsy Dee, and dozens more; for there were hundreds. They had immense qualities, largely animal—eating, drinking, women—great personal pride, in their way —perhaps a few slouches here and there, but I should have trusted the general run of them, in their simple good-will and honor, under all circumstances. Not only for comradeship, and sometimes affection —great studies I found them also. (I suppose the critics will laugh heartily, but the influence of those Broadway omnibus jaunts and drivers and declamations and escapades undoubtedly enter'd into the gestation of "Leaves of Grass.")

PLAYS AND OPERAS TOO

AND certain actors and singers, had a good deal to do with the business. All through these years, off and on, I frequented the old Park, the Bowery, Broadway and Chatham-square theatres, and the Italian operas at Chambers-street, Astor-place or the Battery—many seasons was on the free list, writing for papers even as quite a youth. The old Park theatre—what names, reminiscences, the words bring back! Placide, Clarke, Mrs. Vernon, Fisher, Clara F., Mrs. Wood, Mrs. Seguin, Ellen Tree, Hackett, the younger Kean, Macready, Mrs. Richardson, Rice—singers, tragedians, comedians. What perfect acting! Henry Placide in "Napoleon's Old Guard" or "Grandfather Whitehead,"— or "the Provoked Husband" of Cibber, with Fanny Kemble as Lady Townley—or Sheridan Knowles in his own "Virginius"—or inimitable Power in "Born to Good Luck." These, and many more, the years of youth and onward. Fanny Kemble—name to conjure up great mimic scenes withal—perhaps the greatest. I remember well her rendering of Bianca in "Fazio," and Marianna in "the Wife." Nothing finer did ever stage exhibit—the veterans of all nations said so, and my boyish heart and head felt it in every minute cell. The lady was just matured, strong, better than merely beautiful, born from the footlights, had had three years' practice in London and through the British towns, and then she came to give America that young maturity and roseate power in all their noon, or rather forenoon, flush. It was my good luck to see her nearly every night she play'd at the old Park—certainly in all her principal characters.

I heard, these years, well render'd, all the Italian and other operas in vogue, "Sonnambula," "the Puritans," "Der Freischutz," "Huguenots," "Fille d'Regiment," "Faust," "Etoile du Nord," "Poliuto," and others. Verdi's "Ernani," "Rigoletto," and "Trovatore," with Donnizetti's "Lucia" or "Favorita" or "Lucrezia," and Auber's "Massaniello," or Rossini's "William Tell" and "Gazza Ladra," were among my special enjoyments. I heard Alboni every time she sang in New York and vicinity—also Grisi, the tenor Mario, and the baritone Badiali, the finest in the world.

This musical passion follow'd my theatrical one. As boy or young man I had seen, (reading them carefully the day beforehand,) quite all Shakspere's acting dramas, play'd wonderfully well. Even yet I cannot conceive anything finer than old Booth in "Richard Third," or "Lear," (I don't know which was best,) or Iago, (or Pescara, or Sir Giles Overreach, to go outside of Shakspere)—or Tom Hamblin in "Macbeth"—or old Clarke, either as the ghost in "Hamlet," or as Prospero in "the Tempest," with Mrs. Austin as Ariel, and Peter Richings as Caliban. Then other dramas, and fine players in them, Forrest as Metamora or Damon or Brutus—John R. Scott as Tom Cringle or Rolla —or Charlotte Cushman's Lady Gay Spanker in "London Assurance." Then of some years later, at Castle Garden, Battery, I yet recall the splendid seasons of the Havana musical troupe under Maretzek—the fine band, the cool sea-breezes, the unsurpass'd vocalism—Steffanone, Bosio, Truffi, Marini in "Marino Faliero," "Don Pasquale," or "Favorita." No better playing or singing ever in New York. It was here too I afterward heard Jenny Lind. (The Battery—its past associations— what tales those old trees and walks and sea-walls could tell!)

THROUGH EIGHT YEARS

In 1848, '49, I was occupied as editor of the "daily Eagle" newspaper, in Brooklyn. The latter year went off on a leisurely journey and working expedition (my brother Jeff with me) through all the middle States, and down the Ohio and Mississippi rivers. Lived awhile in New Orleans, and work'd there on the editorial staff of "daily Crescent," newspaper. After a time plodded back northward, up the Mississippi, and around to, and by way of the great lakes, Michigan, Huron, and Erie, to Niagara falls and lower Canada, finally returning through central New York and down the Hudson; traveling altogether probably 8000 miles this trip, to and fro. '51, '53, occupied in housebuilding in Brooklyn. (For a little of the first part of that time in printing a daily and weekly paper, "the Freeman.") '55, lost my dear father this year by death. Commenced putting "Leaves of Grass" to press for good, at the job printing office of my friends, the brothers Rome, in Brooklyn, after many MS. doings and undoings—(I had great trouble in leaving out the stock "poetical" touches, but succeeded at last.) I am now (1856-7) passing through my 37th year.

SOURCES OF CHARACTER—RESULTS—1860

To sum up the foregoing from the outset (and, of course, far, far more unrecorded,) I estimate three leading sources and formative stamps to my own character, now solidified for good or bad, and its subsequent literary and other outgrowth—the maternal nativity-stock brought hither from far-away Netherlands, for one, (doubtless the best)—the subterranean tenacity and central bony structure (obstinacy, wilfulness) which I get from my paternal English elements, for another—and the combination of my Long Island birth-spot, seashores, childhood's scenes, absorptions, with teeming Brooklyn and New York—with, I suppose, my experiences afterward in the secession outbreak, for the third.

For, in 1862, startled by news that my brother George, an officer in the 51st New York volunteers, had been seriously wounded (first Fredericksburg battle, December 13th,) I hurriedly went down to the field of war in Virginia. But I must go back a little.

OPENING OF THE SECESSION WAR

News of the attack on fort Sumter and *the flag* at Charleston harbor, S. C., was receiv'd in New York city late at night (13th April, 1861,) and was immediately sent out in extras of the newspapers. I had been to the opera in Fourteenth street that night, and after the performance was walking down Broadway toward twelve o'clock, on my way to Brooklyn, when I heard in the distance the loud cries of the newsboys, who came presently tearing and yelling up the street, rushing from side to side even more furiously than usual. I bought an extra and cross'd to the Metropolitan hotel (Niblo's) where the great lamps were still brightly blazing, and, with a crowd of others, who gather'd impromptu, read the news, which was evidently authentic. For the benefit of some who had no papers, one of us read the telegram aloud, while all listen'd silently and attentively. No remark was made by any of the crowd, which had increas'd to thirty or forty, but all stood a minute or two, I remember, before they dispers'd. I can almost see them there now, under the lamps at midnight again.

NATIONAL UPRISING AND VOLUNTEERING

I have said somewhere that the three Presidentiads preceding 1861 show'd how the weakness and wickedness of rulers are just as eligible here in America under republican, as in Europe under dynastic influences. But what can I say of that prompt and splendid wrestling with

secession slavery, the arch-enemy personified, the instant he unmistakably show'd his face? The volcanic upheaval of the nation, after
that firing on the flag at Charleston, proved for certain something
which had been previously in great doubt, and at once substantially
settled the question of disunion. In my judgment it will remain as the
grandest and most encouraging spectacle yet vouchsafed in any age,
old or new, to political progress and democracy. It was not for what
came to the surface merely—though that was important—but what it
indicated below, which was of eternal importance. Down in the
abysms of New World humanity there had form'd and harden'd a
primal hard-pan of national Union will, determin'd and in the majority, refusing to be tamper'd with or argued against, confronting all
emergencies, and capable at any time of bursting all surface bonds,
and breaking out like an earthquake. It is, indeed, the best lesson of
the century, or of America, and it is a mighty privilege to have been
part of it. (Two great spectacles, immortal proofs of democracy, unequall'd in all the history of the past, are furnish'd by the secession
war—one at the beginning, the other at its close. Those are, the general, voluntary, arm'd upheaval, and the peaceful and harmonious
disbanding of the armies in the summer of 1865.)

CONTEMPTUOUS FEELING

EVEN after the bombardment of Sumter, however, the gravity of the
revolt, and the power and will of the slave States for a strong and continued military resistance to national authority, were not at all realized at the North, except by a few. Nine-tenths of the people of the
free States look'd upon the rebellion, as started in South Carolina,
from a feeling one-half of contempt, and the other half composed of
anger and incredulity. It was not thought it would be join'd in by
Virginia, North Carolina, or Georgia. A great and cautious national
official predicted that it would blow over "in sixty days," and folks
generally believ'd the prediction. I remember talking about it on a
Fulton ferry-boat with the Brooklyn mayor, who said he only "hoped
the Southern fire-eaters would commit some overt act of resistance, as
they would then be at once so effectually squelch'd, we would never
hear of secession again—but he was afraid they never would have the
pluck to really do anything." I remember, too, that a couple of companies of the Thirteenth Brooklyn, who rendezvou'd at the city armory, and started thence as thirty days' men, were all provided with
pieces of rope, conspicuously tied to their musket-barrels, with which
to bring back each man a prisoner from the audacious South, to be
led in a noose, on our men's early and triumphant return!

BATTLE OF BULL RUN, JULY, 1861

ALL THIS sort of feeling was destin'd to be arrested and revers'd by a terrible shock—the battle of first Bull Run—certainly, as we now know it, one of the most singular fights on record. (All battles, and their results, are far more matters of accident than is generally thought; but this was throughout a casualty, a chance. Each side supposed it had won, till the last moment. One had, in point of fact, just the same right to be routed as the other. By a fiction, or series of fictions, the national forces at the last moment exploded in a panic and fled from the field.) The defeated troops commenced pouring into Washington over the Long Bridge at daylight on Monday, 22d—day drizzling all through with rain. The Saturday and Sunday of the battle (20th, 21st,) had been parch'd and hot to an extreme—the dust, the grime and smoke, in layers, sweated in, follow'd by other layers again sweated in, absorb'd by those excited souls—their clothes all saturated with the clay-powder filling the air—stirr'd up everywhere on the dry roads and trodden fields by the regiments, swarming wagons, artillery, &c.— all the men with this coating of murk and sweat and rain, now recoiling back, pouring over the Long Bridge—a horrible march of twenty miles, returning to Washington baffled, humiliated, panic-struck. Where are the vaunts, and the proud boasts with which you went forth? Where are your banners, and your bands of music, and your ropes to bring back your prisoners? Well, there isn't a band playing— and there isn't a flag but clings ashamed and lank to its staff.

The sun rises, but shines not. The men appear, at first sparsely and shame-faced enough, then thicker, in the streets of Washington— appear in Pennsylvania avenue, and on the steps and basement entrances. They come along in disorderly mobs, some in squads, stragglers, companies. Occasionally, a rare regiment, in perfect order, with its officers (some gaps, dead, the true braves,) marching in silence, with lowering faces, stern, weary to sinking, all black and dirty, but every man with his musket, and stepping alive; but these are the exceptions. Sidewalks of Pennsylvania avenue, Fourteenth street, &c., crowded, jamm'd with citizens, darkies, clerks, everybody, lookers-on; women in the windows, curious expressions from faces, as those swarms of dirt-cover'd return'd soldiers there (will they never end?) move by; but nothing said, no comments; (half our lookers-on secesh of the most venomous kind—they say nothing; but the devil snickers in their faces.) During the forenoon Washington gets all over motley with these defeated soldiers—queer-looking objects, strange eyes and faces, drench'd (the steady rain drizzles on all day) and fearfully worn, hungry, haggard, blister'd in the feet. Good people (but not over-many of them either,) hurry up something for their grub. They put wash-kettles on the fire, for soup, for coffee. They set tables on the side-walks—wagon-loads of bread are purchas'd, swiftly cut in stout chunks. Here are two aged ladies, beautiful, the first in the city for culture and charm, they stand with store of eating and drink at an improvis'd table of rough plank, and give food, and have the store re-plenish'd from their house every half-hour all that day; and there in the rain they stand, active, silent, white-hair'd, and give food, though the tears stream down their cheeks, almost without intermission, the whole time. Amid the deep excitement, crowds and motion, and desperate eagerness, it seems strange to see many, very many, of the soldiers sleeping—in the midst of all, sleeping sound. They drop down anywhere, on the steps of houses, up close by the basements or fences, on the sidewalk, aside on some vacant lot, and deeply sleep. A poor seventeen or eighteen year old boy lies there, on the stoop of a grand house; he sleeps so calmly, so profoundly. Some clutch their muskets firmly even in sleep. Some in squads; comrades, brothers, close to-gether—and on them, as they lay, sulkily drips the rain.

As afternoon pass'd, and evening came, the streets, the bar-rooms, knots everywhere, listeners, questioners, terrible yarns, bugaboo, mask'd batteries, our regiment all cut up, &c.—stories and story-tellers, windy, bragging, vain centres of street-crowds. Resolution, manliness, seem to have abandon'd Washington. The principal hotel, Willard's, is full of shoulder-straps—thick, crush'd, creeping with shoulder-straps. (I see them, and must have a word with them. There you are, shoul-der-straps!—but where are your companies? where are your men? Incompetents! never tell me of chances of battle, of getting stray'd, and the like. I think this is your work, this retreat, after all. Sneak, blow, put on airs there in Willard's sumptuous parlors and bar-rooms, or anywhere—no explanation shall save you. Bull Run is your work; had you been half or one-tenth worthy your men, this would never have happen'd.)

Meantime, in Washington, among the great persons and their en-tourage, a mixture of awful consternation, uncertainty, rage, shame, helplessness, and stupefying disappointment. The worst is not only imminent, but already here. In a few hours—perhaps before the next meal—the secesh generals, with their victorious hordes, will be upon us. The dream of humanity, the vaunted Union we thought so strong, so impregnable—lo! it seems already smash'd like a china plate. One bitter, bitter hour—perhaps proud America will never again know such an hour. She must pack and fly—no time to spare. Those white pal-aces—the dome-crown'd capitol there on the hill, so stately over the trees—shall they be left—or destroy'd first? For it is certain that the talk among certain of the magnates and officers and clerks and officials everywhere, for twenty-four hours in and around Washington after Bull Run, was loud and undisguised for yielding out and out, and substituting the southern rule, and Lincoln promptly abdicating and departing. If the secesh officers and forces had immediately follow'd, and by a bold Napoleonic movement had enter'd Washington the first day, (or even the second,) they could have had things their own way, and a powerful faction north to back them. One of our returning colonels express'd in public that night, amid a swarm of officers and gentlemen in a crowded room, the opinion that it was useless to fight, that the southerners had made their title clear, and that the best course for the national government to pursue was to desist from any further attempt at stopping them, and admit them again to the lead, on the best terms they were willing to grant. Not a voice was rais'd against this judgment, amid that large crowd of officers and gentlemen. (The fact is, the hour was one of the three or four of those crises we had then and afterward, during the fluctuations of four years, when human eyes appear'd at least just as likely to see the last breath of the Union as to see it continue.)

THE STUPOR PASSES—SOMETHING ELSE BEGINS

But the hour, the day, the night pass'd, and whatever returns, an hour, a day, a night like that can never again return. The President, recovering himself, begins that very night—sternly, rapidly sets about the task of reorganizing his forces, and placing himself in positions for future and surer work. If there were nothing else of Abraham Lincoln for history to stamp him with, it is enough to send him with his wreath to the memory of all future time, that he endured that hour, that day, bitterer than gall—indeed a crucifixion day—that it did not conquer him—that he unflinchingly stemm'd it, and resolv'd to lift himself and the Union out of it.

Then the great New York papers at once appear'd, (commencing that evening, and following it up the next morning, and incessantly through many days afterwards,) with leaders that rang out over the land with the loudest, most reverberating ring of clearest bugles, full of encouragement, hope, inspiration, unfaltering defiance. Those magnificent editorials! they never flagg'd for a fortnight. The "Herald" commenced them—I remember the articles well. The "Tribune" was equally cogent and inspiriting—and the "Times," "Evening Post," and other principal papers, were not a whit behind. They came in good time, for they were needed. For in the humiliation of Bull Run, the popular feeling north, from its extreme of superciliousness, recoil'd to the depth of gloom and apprehension.

(Of all the days of the war, there are two especially I can never forget. Those were the day following the news, in New York and Brooklyn, of that first Bull Run defeat, and the day of Abraham Lincoln's death. I was home in Brooklyn on both occasions. The day of the murder we heard the news very early in the morning. Mother prepared breakfast—and other meals afterward—as usual; but not a mouthful was eaten all day by either of us. We each drank half a cup of coffee; that was all. Little was said. We got every newspaper morning and evening, and the frequent extras of that period, and pass'd them silently to each other.)

DOWN AT THE FRONT

Falmouth, Va., *opposite Fredericksburgh, December 21, 1862.*— Begin my visits among the camp hospitals in the army of the Potomac. Spend a good part of the day in a large brick mansion on the banks of the Rappahannock, used as a hospital since the battle— seems to have receiv'd only the worst cases. Out doors, at the foot of a tree, within ten yards of the front of the house, I notice a heap of amputated feet, legs, arms, hands, &c., a full load for a one-horse cart. Several dead bodies lie near, each cover'd with its brown woolen blanket. In the door-yard, towards the river, are fresh graves, mostly of officers, their names on pieces of barrel-staves or broken boards, stuck in the dirt. (Most of these bodies were subsequently taken up and transported north to their friends.) The large mansion is quite crowded upstairs and down, everything impromptu, no system, all bad enough, but I have no doubt the best that can be done; all the wounds pretty bad, some frightful, the men in their old clothes, unclean and bloody. Some of the wounded are rebel soldiers and officers, prisoners. One, a Mississippian, a captain, hit badly in leg, I talk'd with some time; he ask'd me for papers, which I gave him. (I saw him three months afterward in Washington, with his leg amputated, doing well.) I went through the rooms, downstairs and up. Some of the men were dying. I had nothing to give at that visit, but wrote a few letters to folks home, mothers, &c. Also talk'd to three or four, who seem'd most susceptible to it, and needing it.

AFTER FIRST FREDERICKSBURG

December 23 to 31.—The results of the late battle are exhibited everywhere about here in thousands of cases, (hundreds die every day,) in the camp, brigade, and division hospitals. These are merely tents, and sometimes very poor ones, the wounded lying on the ground, lucky if their blankets are spread on layers of pine or hemlock twigs, or small leaves. No cots; seldom even a mattress. It is pretty cold. The ground is frozen hard, and there is occasional snow. I go around from one case to another. I do not see that I do much good to these wounded and dying; but I cannot leave them. Once in a while some youngster holds on to me convulsively, and I do what I can for him; at any rate, stop with him and sit near him for hours, if he wishes it.

Besides the hospitals, I also go occasionally on long tours through the camps, talking with the men, &c. Sometimes at night among the groups around the fires, in their shebang enclosures of bushes. These are curious shows, full of characters and groups. I soon get acquainted anywhere in camp, with officers or men, and am always well used. Sometimes I go down on picket with the regiment I know best. As to rations, the army here at present seems to be tolerably well supplied, and the men have enough, such as it is, mainly salt pork and hard tack. Most of the regiments lodge in the flimsy little shelter-tents. A few have built themselves huts of logs and mud, with fire-places.

BACK TO WASHINGTON

January, '63.—Left camp at Falmouth, with some wounded, a few days since, and came here by Aquia creek railroad, and so on government steamer up the Potomac. Many wounded were with us on the cars and boat. The cars were just common platform ones. The railroad journey of ten or twelve miles was made mostly before sunrise. The soldiers guarding the road came out from their tents or shebangs of bushes with rumpled hair and half-awake look. Those on duty were walking their posts, some on banks over us, others down far below the level of the track. I saw large cavalry camps off the road. At Aquia creek landing were numbers of wounded going north. While I waited some three hours, I went around among them. Several wanted word sent home to parents, brothers, wives, &c., which I did for them, (by mail the next day from Washington.) On the boat I had my hands full. One poor fellow died going up.

I am now remaining in and around Washington, daily visiting the hospitals. Am much in Patent-office, Eighth street, H street, Armory-square, and others. Am now able to do a little good, having money, (as almoner of others home,) and getting experience. To-day, Sunday afternoon and till nine in the evening, visited

Campbell hospital; attended specially to one case in ward 1, very sick with pleurisy and typhoid fever, young man, farmer's son, D. F. Russell, company E, 60th New York, downhearted and feeble; a long time before he would take any interest; wrote a letter home to his mother, in Malone, Franklin county, N. Y., at his request; gave him some fruit and one or two other gifts; envelop'd and directed his letter, &c. Then went thoroughly through ward 6, observ'd every case in the ward, without, I think, missing one; gave perhaps from twenty to thirty persons, each one some little gift, such as oranges, apples, sweet crackers, figs, &c.

Thursday, Jan. 21.—Devoted the main part of the day to Armory-square hospital; went pretty thoroughly through wards F, G, H, and I; some fifty cases in each ward. In ward F supplied the men throughout with writing paper and stamp'd envelope each; distributed in small portions, to proper subjects, a large jar of first-rate preserv'd berries, which had been donated to me by a lady—her own cooking. Found several cases I thought good subjects for small sums of money, which I furnish'd. (The wounded men often come up broke, and it helps their spirits to have even the small sum I give them.) My paper and envelopes all gone, but distributed a good lot of amusing reading matter; also, as I thought judicious, tobacco, oranges, apples, &c. Interesting cases in ward I; Charles Miller, bed 19, company D, 53d Pennsylvania, is only sixteen years of age, very bright, courageous boy, left leg amputated below the knee; next bed to him, another young lad very sick; gave each appropriate gifts. In the bed above, also, amputation of the left leg; gave him a little jar of raspberries; bed 1, this ward, gave a small sum; also to a soldier on crutches, sitting on his bed near. . . . (I am more and more surprised at the very great proportion of youngsters from fifteen to twenty-one in the army. I afterwards found a still greater proportion among the southerners.)

Evening, same day, went to see D. F. R., before alluded to; found him remarkably changed for the better; up and dress'd—quite a triumph; he afterwards got well, and went back to his regiment. Distributed in the wards a quantity of note-paper, and forty or fifty stamp'd envelopes, of which I had recruited my stock, and the men were much in need.

FIFTY HOURS LEFT WOUNDED ON THE FIELD

HERE is a case of a soldier I found among the crowded cots in the Patent-office. He likes to have some one to talk to, and we will listen to him. He got badly hit in his leg and side at Fredericksburgh that eventful Saturday, 13th of December. He lay the succeeding two days and nights helpless on the field, between the city and those grim terraces of batteries; his company and regiment had been compell'd to leave him to his fate. To make matters worse, it happen'd he lay with his head slightly down hill, and could not help himself. At the end of some fifty hours he was brought off, with other wounded, under a flag of truce. I ask him how the rebels treated him as he lay during those two days and nights within reach of them—whether they came to him—whether they abused him? He answers that several of the rebels, soldiers and others, came to him at one time and another. A couple of them, who were together, spoke roughly and sarcastically, but nothing worse. One middle-aged man, however, who seem'd to be moving around the field, among the dead and wounded, for benevolent purposes, came to him in a way he will never forget; treated our soldier kindly, bound up his wounds, cheer'd him, gave him a couple of biscuits and a drink of whiskey and water; asked him if he could eat some beef. This good secesh, however, did not change our soldier's position, for it might have caused the blood to burst from the wounds, clotted and stagnated. Our soldier is from Pennsylvania; has had a pretty severe time; the wounds proved to be bad ones. But he retains a good heart, and is at present on the gain. (It is not uncommon for the men to remain on the field this way, one, two, or even four or five days.)

HOSPITAL SCENES AND PERSONS

Letter Writing.—When eligible, I encourage the men to write, and myself, when called upon, write all sorts of letters for them, (including love letters, very tender ones.) Almost as I reel off these memoranda, I write for a new patient to his wife. M. de F., of the 17th Connecticut, company H, has just come up (February 17th) from Windmill point, and is received in ward H, Armory-square. He is an intelligent looking man, has a foreign accent, black-eyed and hair'd, a Hebraic appearance. Wants a telegraphic message sent to his wife, New Canaan, Conn. I agree to send the message—but to make things sure I also sit down and write the wife a letter, and despatch it to the post-office immediately, as he fears she will come on, and he does not wish her to, as he will surely get well.

Saturday, January 30th.—Afternoon, visited Campbell hospital. Scene of cleaning up the ward, and giving the men all clean clothes —through the ward (6) the patients dressing or being dress'd—the naked upper half of the bodies—the good-humor and fun—the shirts, drawers, sheets of beds, &c., and the general fixing up for Sunday. Gave J. L. 50 cents.

Wednesday, February 4th.—Visited Armory-square hospital, went pretty thoroughly through wards E and D. Supplied paper and envelopes to all who wish'd—as usual, found plenty of men who needed those articles. Wrote letters. Saw and talk'd with two or three members of the Brooklyn 14th regt. A poor fellow in ward D, with a fearful wound in a fearful condition, was having some loose splinters of bone taken from the neighborhood of the wound. The operation was long, and one of great pain—yet, after it was well commenced, the soldier bore it in silence. He sat up, propp'd—was much wasted—had lain a long time quiet in one position (not for days only but weeks,) a bloodless, brown-skinn'd face, with eyes full of determination—belong'd to a New York regiment. There was an unusual cluster of surgeons, medical cadets, nurses, &c., around his bed—I thought the whole thing was done with tenderness, and done well. In one case, the wife sat by the side of her husband, his sickness typhoid fever, pretty bad. In another, by the side of her son, a mother—she told me she had seven children, and this was the youngest. (A fine, kind, healthy, gentle mother, good-looking, not very old, with a cap on her head, and dress'd like home—what a charm it gave to the whole ward.) I liked the woman nurse in ward E—I noticed how she sat a long time by a poor fellow who just had, that morning, in addition to his other sickness, bad hemorrhage— she gently assisted him, reliev'd him of the blood, holding a cloth to his mouth, as he coughed it up—he was so weak he could only just turn his head over on the pillow.

One young New York man, with a bright, handsome face, had been lying several months from a most disagreeable wound, receiv'd at Bull Run. A bullet had shot him right through the bladder, hitting him front, low in the belly, and coming out back. He had suffer'd much—the water came out of the wound, by slow but steady quantities, for many weeks—so that he lay almost constantly in a sort of puddle—and there were other disagreeable circumstances. He was of good heart, however. At present comparatively comfortable, had a bad throat, was delighted with a stick of horehound candy I gave him, with one or two other trifles.

PATENT-OFFICE HOSPITAL

February 23.—I must not let the great hospital at the Patent-office pass away without some mention. A few weeks ago the vast area of the second story of that noblest of Washington buildings was crowded close with rows of sick, badly wounded and dying soldiers. They were placed in three very large apartments. I went there many times. It was a strange, solemn, and, with all its features of suffering and death, a sort of fascinating sight. I go sometimes at night to soothe and relieve particular cases. Two of the immense apartments are fill'd with high and ponderous glass cases, crowded with models in miniature of every kind of utensil, machine or invention, it ever enter'd into the mind of man to conceive; and with curiosities and foreign presents. Between these cases are lateral openings, perhaps eight feet wide and quite deep, and in these were placed the sick, besides a great long double row of them up and down through the middle of the hall. Many of them were very bad cases, wounds and amputations. Then there was a gallery running above the hall in which there were beds also. It was, indeed, a curious scene, especially at night when lit up. The glass cases, the beds, the forms lying there, the gallery above, and the marble pavement under foot—the suffering, and the fortitude to bear it in various degrees—occasionally, from some, the groan that could not be repress'd—sometimes a poor fellow dying, with emaciated face and glassy eye, the nurse by his side, the doctor also there, but no friend, no relative—such were the sights but lately in the Patent-office. (The wounded have since been removed from there, and it is now vacant again.)

THE WHITE HOUSE BY MOONLIGHT

February 24th.—A spell of fine soft weather. I wander about a good deal, sometimes at night under the moon. To-night took a long look at the President's house. The white portico—the palace-like, tall, round columns, spotless as snow—the walls also—the tender and soft moonlight, flooding the pale marble, and making peculiar faint languishing shades, not shadows—everywhere a soft transparent hazy, thin, blue moon-lace, hanging in the air—the brilliant and extra-plentiful clusters of gas, on and around the façade, columns, portico, &c.—everything so white, so marbly pure and dazzling, yet soft—the White House of future poems, and of dreams and dramas, there in the soft and copious moon—the gorgeous front, in the trees, under the lustrous flooding moon, full of reality, full of illusion—the forms of the trees, leafless, silent, in trunk and myriad-angles of branches, under the stars and sky—the White House of the land, and of beauty and night—sentries at the gates, and by the portico, silent, pacing there in blue overcoats—stopping you not at all, but eyeing you with sharp eyes, whichever way you move.

AN ARMY HOSPITAL WARD

LET me specialize a visit I made to the collection of barrack-like one-story edifices, Campbell hospital, out on the flats, at the end of the then horse railway route, on Seventh street. There is a long building appropriated to each ward. Let us go into ward 6. It contains to-day, I should judge, eighty or a hundred patients, half sick, half wounded. The edifice is nothing but boards, well whitewash'd inside, and the usual slender-framed iron bedsteads, narrow and plain. You walk down the central passage, with a row on either side, their feet towards you, and their heads to the wall. There are fires in large stoves, and the prevailing white of the walls is reliev'd by some ornaments, stars, circles, &c., made of evergreens. The view of the whole edifice and occupants can be taken at once, for there is no partition. You may hear groans or other sounds of unendurable suffering from two or three of the cots, but in the main there is quiet—almost a painful absence of demonstration; but the pallid face, the dull'd eye, and the moisture on the lip, are demonstration enough. Most of these sick or hurt are evidently young fellows from the country, farmers' sons, and such like. Look at the fine large frames, the bright and broad countenances, and the many yet lingering proofs of strong constitution and physique. Look at the patient and mute manner of our American wounded as they lie in such a sad collection; representatives from all New England, and from New York, and New Jersey, and Pennsylvania—indeed from all the States and all the cities—largely from the west. Most of them are entirely without friends or acquaintances here—no familiar face, and hardly a word of judicious sympathy or cheer, through their sometimes long and tedious sickness, or the pangs of aggravated wounds.

A CONNECTICUT CASE

THIS young man in bed 25 is H. D. B., of the 27th Connecticut, company B. His folks live at Northford, near New Haven. Though not more than twenty-one, or thereabouts, he has knock'd much around the world, on sea and land, and has seen some fighting on both. When I first saw him he was very sick, with no appetite. He declined offers of money—said he did not need anything. As I was quite anxious to do something, he confess'd that he had a hankering for a good home-made rice pudding—thought he could relish it better than anything. At this time his stomach was very weak. (The doctor, whom I consulted, said nourishment would do him more good than anything; but things in the hospital, though better than usual, revolted him.) I soon procured B. his rice-pudding. A Washington lady, (Mrs. O'C.), hearing his wish, made the pudding herself, and I took it up to him the next day. He subsequently told me he lived upon it for three or four days. This B. is a good sample of the American eastern young man—the typical Yankee. I took a fancy to him, and gave him a nice pipe, for a keepsake. He receiv'd afterwards a box of things from home, and nothing would do but I must take dinner with him, which I did, and a very good one it was.

TWO BROOKLYN BOYS

HERE in this same ward are two young men from Brooklyn, members of the 51st New York. I had known both the two as young lads at home, so they seem near to me. One of them, J. L., lies there with an amputated arm, the stump healing pretty well. (I saw him lying on the ground at Fredericksburgh last December, all bloody, just after the arm was taken off. He was very phlegmatic about it, munching away at a cracker in the remaining hand—made no fuss.) He will recover, and thinks and talks yet of meeting the Johnny Rebs.

A SECESH BRAVE

THE grand soldiers are not comprised in those of one side, any more than the other. Here is a sample of an unknown southerner, a lad of seventeen. At the War department, a few days ago, I witness'd a presentation of captured flags to the Secretary. Among others a soldier named Gant, of the 104th Ohio volunteers, presented a rebel battle-flag, which one of the officers stated to me was borne to the mouth of our cannon and planted there by a boy but seventeen years of age, who actually endeavor'd to stop the muzzle of the gun with fence-rails. He was kill'd in the effort, and the flag-staff was sever'd by a shot from one of our men.

THE WOUNDED FROM CHANCELLORSVILLE

May, '63.—As I write this, the wounded have begun to arrive from Hooker's command from bloody Chancellorsville. I was down among the first arrivals. The men in charge told me the bad cases were yet to come. If that is so I pity them, for these are bad enough. You ought to see the scene of the wounded arriving at the landing here at the foot of Sixth street, at night. Two boat loads came about half-past seven last night. A little after eight it rain'd a long and violent shower. The pale, helpless soldiers had been debark'd, and lay around on the wharf and neighborhood anywhere. The rain was, probably, grateful to them; at any rate they were exposed to it. The few torches light up the spectacle. All around—on the wharf, on the ground, out on side places—the men are lying on blankets, old quilts, &c., with bloody rags bound round heads, arms, and legs. The attendants are few, and at night few outsiders also—only a few hard-work'd transportation men and drivers. (The wounded are getting to be common, and people grow callous.) The men, whatever their condition, lie there, and patiently wait till their turn comes to be taken up. Near by, the ambulances are now arriving in clusters, and one after another is call'd to back up and take its load. Extreme cases are sent off on stretchers. The men generally make little or no ado, whatever their sufferings. A few groans that cannot be suppress'd, and occasionally a scream of pain as they lift a man into the ambulance. To-day, as I write, hundreds more are expected, and to-morrow and the next day more, and so on for many days. Quite often they arrive at the rate of 1000 a day.

A NIGHT BATTLE, OVER A WEEK SINCE

May 12.—There was part of the late battle at Chancellorsville, (second Fredericksburgh,) a little over a week ago, Saturday, Saturday night and Sunday, under Gen. Joe Hooker, I would like to give just a glimpse of—(a moment's look in a terrible storm at sea— of which a few suggestions are enough, and full details impossible.) The fighting had been very hot during the day, and after an intermission the latter part, was resumed at night, and kept up with furious energy till 3 o'clock in the morning. That afternoon (Saturday) an attack sudden and strong by Stonewall Jackson had gain'd a great advantage to the southern army, and broken our lines, entering us like a wedge, and leaving things in that position at dark. But Hooker at 11 at night made a desperate push, drove the secesh forces back, restored his original lines, and resumed his plans. This night scrimmage was very exciting, and afforded countless strange and fearful pictures. The fighting had been general both at Chancellorsville and northeast at Fredericksburgh. (We hear of some poor fighting, episodes, skedaddling on our part. I think not of it. I think of the fierce bravery, the general rule.) One corps, the 6th, Sedgewick's, fights four dashing and bloody battles in thirty-six hours, retreating in great jeopardy, losing largely but maintaining itself, fighting with the sternest desperation under all circumstances, getting over the Rappahannock only by the skin of its teeth, yet getting over. It lost many, many brave men, yet it took vengeance, ample vengeance.

But it was the tug of Saturday evening, and through the night and Sunday morning, I wanted to make a special note of. It was largely in the woods, and quite a general engagement. The night was very pleasant, at times the moon shining out full and clear, all Nature so calm in itself, the early summer grass so rich, and foliage of the trees—yet there the battle raging, and many good fellows lying helpless, with new accessions to them, and every minute amid the rattle of muskets and crash of cannon, (for there was an artillery contest too,) the red life-blood oozing out from heads or trunks or limbs upon that green and dew-cool grass. Patches of the woods take fire, and several of the wounded, unable to move, are consumed—quite large spaces are swept over, burning the dead also—some of the men have their hair and beards singed—some, burns on their faces and hands—others holes burnt in their clothing. The flashes of fire from the cannon, the quick flaring flames and smoke, and the immense roar—the musketry so general, the light nearly bright enough for each side to see the other—the crashing, tramping of men—the yelling—close quarters—we hear the secesh yells—our men cheer loudly back, especially if Hooker is in sight—hand to hand conflicts, each side stands up to it, brave, determin'd as demons, they often charge upon us—a thousand deeds are done worth to write newer greater poems on—and still the woods on fire—still many are not only scorch'd—too many, unable to move, are burn'd to death.

Then the camps of the wounded—O heavens, what scene is this? —is this indeed *humanity*—these butchers' shambles? There are several of them. There they lie, in the largest, in an open space in the woods, from 200 to 300 poor fellows—the groans and screams—the odor of blood, mixed with the fresh scent of the night, the grass, the trees—that slaughter-house! O well is it their mothers, their sisters cannot see them—cannot conceive, and never conceiv'd, these things. One man is shot by a shell, both in the arm and leg—both are amputated—there lie the rejected members. Some have their legs blown off—some bullets through the breast—some indescribably horrid wounds in the face or head, all mutilated, sickening, torn, gouged out —some in the abdomen—some mere boys—many rebels, badly hurt— they take their regular turns with the rest, just the same as any—the surgeons use them just the same. Such is the camp of the wounded —such a fragment, a reflection afar off of the bloody scene—while over all the clear, large moon comes out at times softly, quietly shining. Amid the woods, that scene of flitting souls—amid the crack and crash and yelling sounds—the impalpable perfume of the woods

—and yet the pungent, stifling smoke—the radiance of the moon, looking from heaven at intervals so placid—the sky so heavenly—the clear-obscure up there, those buoyant upper oceans—a few large placid stars beyond, coming silently and languidly out, and then disappearing—the melancholy, draperied night above, around. And there, upon the roads, the fields, and in those woods, that contest, never one more desperate in any age or land—both parties now in force—masses—no fancy battle, no semi-play, but fierce and savage demons fighting there—courage and scorn of death the rule, exceptions almost none.

What history, I say, can ever give—for who can know—the mad, determin'd tussle of the armies, in all their separate large and little squads—as this—each steep'd from crown to toe in desperate, mortal purports? Who know the conflict, hand-to-hand—the many conflicts in the dark, those shadowy-tangled, flashing-moonbeam'd woods—the writhing groups and squads—the cries, the din, the cracking guns and pistols—the distant cannon—the cheers and calls and threats and awful music of the oaths—the indescribable mix—the officers' orders, persuasions, encouragements—the devils fully rous'd in human hearts—the strong shout, *Charge, men, charge*—the flash of the naked sword, and rolling flame and smoke? And still the broken, clear and clouded heaven—and still again the moonlight pouring silvery soft its radiant patches over all. Who paint the scene, the sudden partial panic of the afternoon, at dusk? Who paint the irrepressible advance of the second division of the Third corps, under Hooker himself, suddenly order'd up—those rapid-filing phantoms through the woods? Who show what moves there in the shadows, fluid and firm—to save, (and it did save,) the army's name, perhaps the nation? as there the veterans hold the field. (Brave Berry falls not yet—but death has mark'd him—soon he falls.)

UNNAMED REMAINS THE BRAVEST SOLDIER

OF SCENES like these, I say, who writes—whoe'er can write the story? Of many a score—aye, thousands, north and south, of unwrit heroes, unknown heroisms, incredible, impromptu, first-class desperations—who tells? No history ever—no poem sings, no music sounds, those bravest men of all—those deeds. No formal general's report, nor book in the library, nor column in the paper, embalms the bravest, north or south, east or west. Unnamed, unknown, remain, and still remain, the bravest soldiers. Our manliest—our boys

—our hardy darlings; no picture gives them. Likely, the typic one of them (standing, no doubt, for hundreds, thousands,) crawls aside to some bush-clump, or ferny tuft, on receiving his death-shot— there sheltering a little while, soaking roots, grass and soil, with red blood—the battle advances, retreats, flits from the scene, sweeps by —and there, haply with pain and suffering (yet less, far less, than is supposed,) the last lethargy winds like a serpent round him—the eyes glaze in death—none recks—perhaps the burial-squads, in truce, a week afterwards, search not the secluded spot—and there, at last, the Bravest Soldier crumbles in mother earth, unburied and unknown.

SOME SPECIMEN CASES

June 18th.—In one of the hospitals I find Thomas Haley, company M, 4th New York cavalry—a regular Irish boy, a fine specimen of youthful physical manliness—shot through the lungs—inevitably dying—came over to this country from Ireland to enlist—has not a single friend or acquaintance here—is sleeping soundly at this moment, (but it is the sleep of death)—has a bullet-hole straight through the lung. I saw Tom when first brought here, three days since, and didn't suppose he could live twelve hours—(yet he looks well enough in the face to a casual observer.) He lies there with his frame exposed above the waist, all naked, for coolness, a fine built man, the tan not yet bleach'd from his cheeks and neck. It is useless to talk to him, as with his sad hurt, and the stimulants they give him, and the utter strangeness of every object, face, furniture, &c., the poor fellow, even when awake, is like some frighten'd, shy animal. Much of the time he sleeps, or half sleeps. (Sometimes I thought he knew more than he show'd.) I often come and sit by him in perfect silence; he will breathe for ten minutes as softly and evenly as a young babe asleep. Poor youth, so handsome, athletic, with profuse beautiful shining hair. One time as I sat looking at him while he lay asleep, he suddenly, without the least start, awaken'd, open'd his eyes, gave me a long steady look, turning his face very slightly to gaze easier—one long, clear, silent look—a slight sigh—then turn'd back and went into his doze again. Little he knew, poor death-stricken boy, the heart of the stranger that hover'd near.

W. H. E., Co. F., 2d N. J.—His disease is pneumonia. He lay sick at the wretched hospital below Aquia creek, for seven or eight days before brought here. He was detail'd from his regiment to go there and help as nurse, but was soon taken down himself. Is an elderly, sallow-faced, rather gaunt, gray-hair'd man, a widower, with children. He express'd a great desire for good, strong green tea. An excellent lady, Mrs. W., of Washington, soon sent him a package; also a small sum of money. The doctor said give him the tea at pleasure; it lay on the table by his side, and he used it every day. He slept a great deal; could not talk much, as he grew deaf. Occupied bed 15, ward I, Armory. (The same lady above, Mrs. W., sent the men a large package of tobacco.)

J. G. lies in bed 52, ward I; is of company B, 7th Pennsylvania. I gave him a small sum of money, some tobacco, and envelopes. To a man, adjoining also gave twenty-five cents; he flush'd in the face when I offer'd it—refused at first, but as I found he had not a cent, and was very fond of having the daily papers to read, I prest it on him. He was evidently very grateful, but said little.

J. T. L., of company F., 9th New Hampshire, lies in bed 37, ward I. Is very fond of tobacco. I furnish him some; also with a little money. Has gangrene of the feet; a pretty bad case; will surely have to lose three toes. Is a regular specimen of an old-fashion'd, rude, hearty, New England countryman, impressing me with his likeness to that celebrated singed cat, who was better than she look'd.

Bed 3, ward E, Armory, has a great hankering for pickles, something pungent. After consulting the doctor, I gave him a small bottle of horse-radish; also some apples; also a book. Some of the nurses are excellent. The woman-nurse in this ward I like very much. (Mrs. Wright—a year afterwards I found her in Mansion house hospital, Alexandria—she is a perfect nurse.)

In one bed a young man, Marcus Small, company K, 7th Maine—sick with dysentery and typhoid fever—pretty critical case—I talk with him often—he thinks he will die—looks like it indeed. I write a letter for him home to East Livermore, Maine—I let him talk to me a little, but not much, advise him to keep very quiet—do most of the talking myself—stay quite a while with him, as he holds on to my hand—talk to him in a cheering, but slow, low and measured manner—talk about his furlough, and going home as soon as he is able to travel.

Thomas Lindly, 1st Pennsylvania cavalry, shot very badly through the foot—poor young man, he suffers horribly, has to be constantly dosed with morphine, his face ashy and glazed, bright young eyes —I give him a large handsome apple, lay it in sight, tell him to have it roasted in the morning, as he generally feels easier then, and can eat a little breakfast. I write two letters for him.

Opposite, an old Quaker lady is sitting by the side of her son, Amer Moore, 2d U. S. artillery—shot in the head two weeks since, very low, quite rational—from hips down paralyzed—he will surely die. I speak a very few words to him every day and evening—he answers pleasantly—wants nothing—(he told me soon after he came about his home affairs, his mother had been an invalid, and he fear'd to let her know his condition.) He died soon after she came.

MY PREPARATIONS FOR VISITS

IN MY visits to the hospitals I found it was in the simple matter of personal presence, and emanating ordinary cheer and magnetism, that I succeeded and help'd more than by medical nursing, or delicacies, or gifts of money, or anything else. During the war I possess'd the perfection of physical health. My habit, when practicable, was to prepare for starting out on one of those daily or nightly tours of from .a couple to four or five hours, by fortifying myself with previous rest, the bath, clean clothes, a good meal, and as cheerful an appearance as possible.

AMBULANCE PROCESSIONS

June 25, Sundown.—As I sit writing this paragraph I see a train of about thirty huge four-horse wagons, used as ambulances, fill'd with wounded, passing up Fourteenth street, on their way, probably, to Columbian, Carver, and mount Pleasant hospitals. This is the way the men come in now, seldom in small numbers, but almost always in these long, sad processions. Through the past winter, while our army lay opposite Fredericksburgh, the like strings of ambulances were of frequent occurrence along Seventh street, passing slowly up from the steamboat wharf, with loads from Aquia creek.

BAD WOUNDS—THE YOUNG

THE soldiers are nearly all young men, and far more American than is generally supposed—I should say nine-tenths are native-born. Among the arrivals from Chancellorsville I find a large proportion of Ohio, Indiana, and Illinois men. As usual, there are all sorts of wounds. Some of the men fearfully burnt from the explosions of artillery caissons. One ward has a long row of officers, some with ugly hurts. Yesterday was perhaps worse than usual. Amputations are going on—the attendants are dressing wounds. As you pass by, you must be on your guard where you look. I saw the other day a gentleman, a visitor apparently from curiosity, in one of the wards, stop and turn a moment to look at an awful wound they were probing. He turn'd pale, and in a moment more he had fainted away and fallen on the floor.

THE MOST INSPIRITING OF ALL WAR'S SHOWS

June 29.—Just before sundown this evening a very large cavalry force went by—a fine sight. The men evidently had seen service. First came a mounted band of sixteen bugles, drums and cymbals, playing wild martial tunes—made my heart jump. Then the principal officers, then company after company, with their officers at their heads, making of course the main part of the cavalcade; then a long train of men with led horses, lots of mounted negroes with special horses—and a long string of baggage-wagons, each drawn by four horses—and then a motley rear guard. It was a pronouncedly warlike and gay show; the sabres clank'd, the men look'd young and healthy and strong; the electric tramping of so many horses on the hard road, and the gallant bearing, fine seat, and bright faced appearance of a thousand and more handsome young American men, were so good to see. An hour later another troop went by, smaller in numbers, perhaps three hundred men. They too look'd like serviceable men, campaigners used to field and fight.

July 3.—This forenoon, for more than an hour, again long strings of cavalry, several regiments, very fine men and horses, four or five abreast. I saw them in Fourteenth street, coming in town from north. Several hundred extra horses, some of the mares with colts, trotting along. (Appear'd to be a number of prisoners too.) How inspiriting always the cavalry regiments. Our men are generally well mounted, feel good, are young, gay on the saddle, their blankets in a roll behind them, their sabres clanking at their sides. This noise and movement and the tramp of many horses' hoofs has a curious effect upon one. The bugles play—presently you hear them afar off, deaden'd, mix'd with other noises. Then just as they had all pass'd, a string of ambulances commenc'd from the other way, moving up Fourteenth street north, slowly wending along, bearing a large lot of wounded to the hospitals.

BATTLE OF GETTYSBURG

July 4th.—The weather to-day, upon the whole, is very fine, warm, but from a smart rain last night, fresh enough, and no dust, which is a great relief for this city. I saw the parade about noon, Pennsylvania avenue, from Fifteenth street down toward the capitol. There were three regiments of infantry, (I suppose the ones doing patrol duty here,) two or three societies of Odd Fellows, a lot of children in barouches, and a squad of policemen. (A useless imposition upon the soldiers—they have work enough on their backs without piling the like of this.) As I went down the Avenue, saw a big flaring placard on the bulletin board of a newspaper office, announcing "Glorious Victory for the Union Army!" Meade had fought Lee at Gettysburg, Pennsylvania, yesterday and day before, and repuls'd him most signally, taken 3,000 prisoners, &c. (I afterwards saw Meade's despatch, very modest, and a sort of order of the day from the President himself, quite religious, giving thanks to the Supreme, and calling on the people to do the same.) I walk'd on to Armory hospital—took along with me several bottles of blackberry and cherry syrup, good and strong, but innocent. Went through several of the wards, announc'd to the soldiers the news from Meade, and gave them all a good drink of the syrups with ice water, quite refreshing—prepar'd it all myself, and serv'd it around. Meanwhile the Washington bells are ringing their sundown peals for Fourth of July, and the usual fusilades of boys' pistols, crackers, and guns.

A CAVALRY CAMP

I AM writing this, nearly sundown, watching a cavalry company (acting Signal service,) just come in through a shower, making their night's camp ready on some broad, vacant ground, a sort of hill, in full view opposite my window. There are the men in their yellow-striped jackets. All are dismounted; the freed horses stand with drooping heads and wet sides; they are to be led off presently in groups, to water. The little wall-tents and shelter tents spring up quickly. I see the fires already blazing, and pots and kettles over them. Some among the men are driving in tent-poles, wielding their axes with strong, slow blows. I see great huddles of horses, bundles of hay, groups of men (some with unbuckled sabres yet on their sides,) a few officers, piles of wood, the flames of the fires, saddles, harness, &c. The smoke streams upward, additional men arrive and dismount—some drive in stakes, and tie their horses to them; some go with buckets for water, some are chopping wood, and so on.

July 6th.—A steady rain, dark and thick and warm. A train of six-mule wagons has just pass'd bearing pontoons, great square-end flat-boats, and the heavy planking for overlaying them. We hear that the Potomac above here is flooded, and are wondering whether Lee will be able to get back across again, or whether Meade will indeed break him to pieces. The cavalry camp on the hill is a cease-less field of observation for me. This forenoon there stand the horses, tether'd together, dripping, steaming, chewing their hay.

The men emerge from their tents, dripping also. The fires are half quench'd.

July 10th.—Still the camp opposite—perhaps fifty or sixty tents. Some of the men are cleaning their sabres (pleasant to-day,) some brushing boots, some laying off, reading, writing—some cooking, some sleeping. On long temporary cross-sticks back of the tents are cavalry accoutrements—blankets and overcoats are hung out to air— there are the squads of horses tether'd, feeding, continually stamping and whisking their tails to keep off flies. I sit long in my third story window and look at the scene—a hundred little things going on—peculiar objects connected with the camp that could not be described, any one of them justly, without much minute drawing and coloring in words.

A NEW YORK SOLDIER

THIS afternoon, July 22d, I have spent a long time with Oscar F. Wilber, company G, 154th New York, low with chronic diarrhœa, and a bad wound also. He asked me to read him a chapter in the New Testament. I complied, and ask'd him what I should read. He said, "Make your own choice." I open'd at the close of one of the first books of the evangelists, and read the chapters describing the latter hours of Christ, and the scenes at the crucifixion. The poor, wasted young man ask'd me to read the following chapter also, how Christ rose again. I read very slowly, for Oscar was feeble. It pleased him very much, yet the tears were in his eyes. He ask'd me if I enjoy'd religion. I said, "Perhaps not, my dear, in the way you mean, and yet, may-be, it is the same thing." He said, "It is my chief reliance." He talk'd of death, and said he did not fear it. I said, "Why, Oscar, don't you think you will get well?" He said, "I may, but it is not probable." He spoke calmly of his condition. The wound was very bad, it discharg'd much. Then the diarrhœa had prostrated him, and I felt that he was even then the same as dying. He behaved very manly and affectionate. The kiss I gave him as I was about leaving he return'd fourfold. He gave me his mother's address, Mrs. Sally D. Wilber, Alleghany post-office, Cattaraugus county, N. Y. I had several such interviews with him. He died a few days after the one just described.

HOME-MADE MUSIC

August 8th.—To-night, as I was trying to keep cool, sitting by a wounded soldier in Armory-square, I was attracted by some pleasant singing in an adjoining ward. As my soldier was asleep, I left him, and entering the ward where the music was, I walk'd half-way down and took a seat by the cot of a young Brooklyn friend, S. R., badly wounded in the hand at Chancellorsville, and who has suffer'd much, but at that moment in the evening was wide awake and comparatively easy. He had turn'd over on his left side to get a better view of the singers, but the mosquito-curtains of the adjoining cots obstructed the sight. I stept round and loop'd them all up, so that he had a clear show, and then sat down again by him, and look'd and listen'd. The principal singer was a young lady-nurse of one of the wards, accompanying on a melodeon, and join'd by the lady-nurses of other wards. They sat there, making a charming group, with their handsome, healthy faces, and standing up a little behind them were some ten or fifteen of the convalescent soldiers, young men, nurses, &c., with books in their hands, singing. Of course it was not such a performance as the great soloists at the New York opera house take a hand in, yet I am not sure but I receiv'd as much pleasure under the circumstances, sitting there, as I have had from the best Italian compositions, express'd by world-famous performers. The men lying up and down the hospital, in their cots, (some badly wounded—some never to rise thence,) the cots themselves, with their drapery of white curtains, and the shadows down the lower and upper parts of the ward; then the silence of the men, and the attitudes they took—the whole was a sight to look around upon again and again. And there sweetly rose those voices up to the high, whitewash'd wooden roof, and pleasantly the roof sent it all back again. They sang very well, mostly quaint old songs and declamatory hymns, to fitting tunes. Here, for instance:

My days are swiftly gliding by, and I a pilgrim stranger,
Would not detain them as they fly, those hours of toil and danger;
For O we stand on Jordan's strand, our friends are passing over,
And just before, the shining shore we may almost discover.

We'll gird our loins my brethren dear, our distant home discerning,
Our absent Lord has left us word, let every lamp be burning,
For O we stand on Jordan's strand, our friends are passing over,
And just before, the shining shore we may almost discover.

ABRAHAM LINCOLN

August 12th.—I see the President almost every day, as I happen to live where he passes to or from his lodgings out of town. He never sleeps at the White House during the hot season, but has quarters at a healthy location some three miles north of the city, the Soldiers' home, a United States military establishment. I saw him this morning about 8½ coming in to business, riding on Vermont avenue, near L street. He always has a company of twenty-five or thirty cavalry, with sabres drawn and held upright over their shoulders. They say this guard was against his personal wish, but he let his counselors have their way. The party makes no great show in uniform or horses. Mr. Lincoln on the saddle generally rides a good-sized, easy-going gray horse, is dress'd in plain black, somewhat rusty and dusty, wears a black stiff hat, and looks about as ordinary in attire, &c., as the commonest man. A lieutenant, with yellow straps, rides at his left, and following behind, two by two, come the cavalry men, in their yellow-striped jackets. They are generally going at a slow trot, as that is the pace set them by the one they wait upon. The sabres and accoutrements clank, and the entirely unornamental *cortège* as it trots toward Lafayette square arouses no sensation, only some curious stranger stops and gazes. I see very plainly ABRAHAM LINCOLN's dark brown face, with the deep-cut lines, the eyes, always to me with a deep latent sadness in the expression. We have got so that we exchange bows, and very cordial ones. Sometimes the President goes and comes in an open barouche. The cavalry always accompany him, with drawn sabres. Often I notice as he goes out evenings—and sometimes in the morning, when he returns early—he turns off and halts at the large and handsome residence of the Secretary of War, on K street, and holds conference there. If in his barouche, I can see from my window he does not alight, but sits in his vehicle, and Mr. Stanton comes out to attend him. Sometimes one of his sons, a boy of ten or twelve, accompanies him, riding at his right on a pony. Earlier in the summer I occasionally saw the President and his wife, toward the latter part of the afternoon, out in a barouche, on a pleasure ride through the city. Mrs. Lincoln was dress'd in complete black, with a long crape veil. The equipage is of the plainest kind, only two horses, and they nothing extra. They pass'd me once very close, and I saw the President in the face fully, as they were moving slowly, and his look, though abstracted, happen'd to be directed steadily in my eye. He bow'd and smiled, but far beneath his smile I noticed well the expression I have alluded to. None of the artists or pictures has caught the deep, though subtle and indirect expression of this man's face. There is something else there. One of the great portrait painters of two or three centuries ago is needed.

HEATED TERM

THERE has lately been much suffering here from heat; we have had it upon us now eleven days. I go around with an umbrella and a fan. I saw two cases of sun-stroke yesterday, one in Pennsylvania avenue, and another in Seventh street. The City railroad company loses some horses every day. Yet Washington is having a livelier August, and is probably putting in a more energetic and satisfactory summer, than ever before during its existence. There is probably more human electricity, more population to make it, more business, more light-heartedness, than ever before. The armies that swiftly circumambiated from Fredericksburgh—march'd, struggled, fought, had out their mighty clinch and hurl at Gettysburg—wheel'd, circumambiated again, return'd to their ways, touching us not, either at their going or coming. And Washington feels that she has pass'd the worst; perhaps feels that she is henceforth mistress. So here she sits with her surrounding hills spotted with guns, and is conscious of a character and identity different from what it was five or six short weeks ago, and very considerably pleasanter and prouder.

SOLDIERS AND TALKS

SOLDIERS, soldiers, soldiers, you meet everywhere about the city, often superb-looking men, though invalids dress'd in worn uniforms, and carrying canes or crutches. I often have talks with them, occasionally quite long and interesting. One, for instance, will have been all through the peninsula under McClellan—narrates to me the fights, the marches, the strange, quick changes of that eventful campaign, and gives glimpses of many things untold in any official reports or books or journals. These, indeed, are the things that are genuine and precious. The man was there, has been out two years, has been through a dozen fights, the superfluous flesh of talking is long work'd off him, and he gives me little but the hard meat and sinew. I find it refreshing, these hardy, bright, intuitive, American young men, (experienc'd soldiers with all their youth.) The vocal play and significance moves one more than books. Then there hangs something majestic about a man who has borne his part in battles, especially if he is very quiet regarding it when you desire him to unbosom. I am continually lost at the absence of blowing and blowers among these old-young American militaires. I have found some man or other who has been in every battle since the war began, and have talk'd with them about each one in every part of the United States, and many of the engagements on the rivers and harbors too. I find men here from every State in the Union, without exception. (There are more Southerners, especially border State men, in the Union army than is generally supposed.[6]) I now doubt whether one can get a fair idea of what this war practically is, or what genuine America is, and her character, without some such experience as this I am having.

DEATH OF A WISCONSIN OFFICER

ANOTHER characteristic scene of that dark and bloody 1863, from notes of my visit to Armory-square hospital, one hot but pleasant summer day. In ward H we approach the cot of a young lieutenant of one of the Wisconsin regiments. Tread the bare board floor lightly here, for the pain and panting of death are in this cot. I saw the lieutenant when he was first brought here from Chancellorsville, and have been with him occasionally from day to day and night to night. He had been getting along pretty well till night before last, when a sudden hemorrhage that could not be stopt came upon him, and to-day it still continues at intervals. Notice that water-pail by the side of the bed, with a quantity of blood and bloody pieces of muslin, nearly full; that tells the story. The poor young man is struggling painfully for breath, his great dark eyes with a glaze already upon them, and the choking faint but audible in his throat. An attendant sits by him, and will not leave him till the last; yet little or nothing can be done. He will die here in an hour or two, without the presence of kith or kin. Meantime the ordinary chat and business of the ward a little way off goes on indifferently. Some of the inmates are laughing and joking, others are playing checkers or cards, others are reading, &c.

I have noticed through most of the hospitals that as long as there is any chance for a man, no matter how bad he may be, the surgeon and nurses work hard, sometimes with curious tenacity, for his life, doing everything, and keeping somebody by him to execute the doctor's orders, and minister to him every minute night and day. See that screen there. As you advance through the dusk of early candle-light, a nurse will step forth on tip-toe, and silently but imperiously forbid you to make any noise, or perhaps to come near at all. Some soldier's life is flickering there, suspended between recovery and death. Perhaps at this moment the exhausted frame has just fallen into a light sleep that a step might shake. You must retire. The neighboring patients must move in their stocking feet. I have been several times struck with such mark'd efforts—everything bent to save a life from the very grip of the destroyer. But when that grip is once firmly fix'd, leaving no hope or chance at all, the surgeon abandons the patient. If it is a case where stimulus is any relief, the nurse gives milk-punch or brandy, or whatever is wanted, *ad libitum*. There is no fuss made. Not a bit of sentimentalism or whining have I seen about a single death-bed in hospital or on the field, but generally impassive indifference. All is over, as far as any efforts can avail; it is useless to expend emotions or labors. While there is a prospect they strive hard—at least most surgeons do; but death certain and evident, they yield the field.

HOSPITALS ENSEMBLE

Aug., Sep., and Oct., '63.—I am in the habit of going to all, and to Fairfax seminary, Alexandria, and over Long bridge to the great Convalescent camp. The journals publish a regular directory of them—a long list. As a specimen of almost any one of the larger of these hospitals, fancy to yourself a space of three to twenty acres of ground, on which are group'd ten or twelve very large wooden barracks, with, perhaps, a dozen or twenty, and sometimes more than that number, small buildings, capable altogether of accommodating from five hundred to a thousand or fifteen hundred persons. Sometimes these wooden barracks or wards, each of them perhaps from a hundred to a hundred and fifty feet long, are rang'd in a straight row, evenly fronting the street; others are plann'd so as to form an immense V; and others again are ranged around a hollow square. They make altogether a huge cluster, with the additional tents, extra wards for contagious diseases, guard-houses, sutler's stores, chaplain's house; in the middle will probably be an edifice devoted to the offices of the surgeon in charge and the ward surgeons, principal attaches, clerks, &c. The wards are either letter'd alphabetically, ward G, ward K, or else numerically, 1, 2, 3, &c. Each has its ward surgeon and corps of nurses. Of course, there is, in the aggregate, quite a muster of employés, and over all the surgeon in charge. Here in Washington, when these army hospitals are all fill'd, (as they have been already several times,) they contain a population more numerous in itself than the whole of the Washington of ten or fifteen years ago. Within sight of the capitol, as I write, are some thirty or forty such collections, at times holding from fifty to seventy thousand men. Looking from any eminence and studying the topography in my rambles, I use them as landmarks. Through the rich August verdure of the trees, see that white group of buildings off yonder in the outskirts; then another cluster half a mile to the left of the first; then another a mile to the right, and another a mile beyond, and still another between us and the first. Indeed, we can hardly look in any direction but these clusters are dotting the landscape and environs. That little town, as you might suppose it, off there on the brow of a hill, is indeed a town, but of wounds, sickness, and death. It is Finley hospital, northeast of the city, on Kendall green, as it used to be call'd. That other is Campbell hospital. Both are large establishments. I have known these two alone to have from two thousand to twenty-five hundred inmates. Then there is Carver hospital, larger still, a wall'd and military city regularly laid out, and guarded by squads of sentries. Again, off east, Lincoln hospital, a still larger one; and half a mile further Emory hospital. Still sweeping the eye around down the river toward Alexandria, we see, to the right, the locality where the Convalescent camp stands, with its five, eight, or sometimes ten thousand inmates. Even all these are but a portion. The Harewood, Mount Pleasant, Armory-square, Judiciary hospitals, are some of the rest, and all large collections.

A SILENT NIGHT RAMBLE

October 20th.—To-night, after leaving the hospital at 10 o'clock, (I had been on self-imposed duty some five hours, pretty closely confined,) I wander'd a long time around Washington. The night was sweet, very clear, sufficiently cool, a voluptuous half-moon, slightly golden, the space near it of a transparent blue-gray tinge. I walk'd up Pennsylvania avenue, and then to Seventh street, and a long while around the Patent-office. Somehow it look'd rebukefully strong, majestic, there in the delicate moonlight. The sky, the planets, the constellations all so bright, so calm, so expressively silent, so soothing, after those hospital scenes. I wander'd to and fro till the moist moon set, long after midnight.

SPIRITUAL CHARACTERS AMONG THE SOLDIERS

EVERY now and then, in hospital or camp, there are beings I meet—specimens of unworldliness, disinterestedness, and animal purity and heroism—perhaps some unconscious Indianian, or from Ohio or Tennessee—on whose birth the calmness of heaven seems to have descended, and whose gradual growing up, whatever the circumstances of work-life or change, or hardship, or small or no education that attended it, the power of a strange spiritual sweetness, fibre and inward health, have also attended. Something veil'd and abstracted is often a part of the manners of these beings. I have met them, I say, not seldom in the army, in camp, and in the hospitals. The Western regiments contain many of them. They are often young men, obeying the events and occasions about them, marching, soldiering, fighting, foraging, cooking, working on farms or at some trade before the war—unaware of their own nature, (as to that, who is aware of his own nature?) their companions only understanding that they are different from the rest, more silent, "something odd about them," and apt to go off and meditate and muse in solitude.

CATTLE DROVES ABOUT WASHINGTON

AMONG other sights are immense droves of cattle with their drivers, passing through the streets of the city. Some of the men have a way of leading the cattle by a peculiar call, a wild, pensive hoot, quite musical, prolong'd, indescribable, sounding something between the cooing of a pigeon and the hoot of an owl. I like to stand and look at the sight of one of these immense droves—a little way off—(as the dust is great.) There are always men on horseback, cracking their whips and shouting—the cattle low—some obstinate ox or steer attempts to escape—then a lively scene—the mounted men, always excellent riders and on good horses, dash after the recusant, and wheel and turn—a dozen mounted drovers, their great slouch'd, broad-brim'd hats, very picturesque—another dozen on foot—everybody cover'd with dust—long goads in their hands—an immense drove of perhaps 1000 cattle—the shouting, hooting, movement, &c.

HOSPITAL PERPLEXITY

To ADD to other troubles, amid the confusion of this great army of sick, it is almost impossible for a stranger to find any friend or relative, unless he has the patient's specific address to start upon. Besides the directory printed in the newspapers here, there are one or two general directories of the hospitals kept at provost's headquarters, but they are nothing like complete; they are never up to date, and, as things are, with the daily streams of coming and going and changing, cannot be. I have known cases, for instance such as a farmer coming here from northern New York to find a wounded brother, faithfully hunting round for a week, and then compell'd to leave and go home without getting any trace of him. When he got home he found a letter from the brother giving the right address.

DOWN AT THE FRONT

CULPEPPER, VA., *Feb.* '64.—Here I am pretty well down toward
the extreme front. Three or four days ago General S., who is now in
chief command, (I believe Meade is absent, sick,) moved a strong
force southward from camp as if intending business. They went to
the Rapidan; there has since been some manœuvring and a little
fighting, but nothing of consequence. The telegraphic accounts
given Monday morning last, make entirely too much of it, I should
say. What General S. intended we here know not, but we trust in
that competent commander. We were somewhat excited, (but not
so very much either,) on Sunday, during the day and night, as orders were sent out to pack up and harness, and be ready to evacu-
ate, to fall back towards Washington. But I was very sleepy and
went to bed. Some tremendous shouts arousing me during the
night, I went forth and found it was from the men above mention'd, who were returning. I talk'd with some of the men; as usual
I found them full of gayety, endurance, and many fine little outshows, the signs of the most excellent good manliness of the world.
It was a curious sight to see those shadowy columns moving
through the night. I stood unobserv'd in the darkness and watch'd
them long. The mud was very deep. The men had their usual bur-
dens, overcoats, knapsacks, guns and blankets. Along and along
they filed by me, with often a laugh, a song, a cheerful word, but
never once a murmur. It may have been odd, but I never before so
realized the majesty and reality of the American people *en masse.*
It fell upon me like a great awe. The strong ranks moved neither
fast nor slow. They had march'd seven or eight miles already
through the slipping unctuous mud. The brave First corps stopt
here. The equally brave Third corps moved on to Brandy station.
The famous Brooklyn 14th are here, guarding the town. You see
their red legs actively moving everywhere. Then they have a theatre
of their own here. They give musical performances, nearly everything done capitally. Of course the audience is a jam. It is good
sport to attend one of these entertainments of the 14th. I like to
look around at the soldiers, and the general collection in front of
the curtain, more than the scene on the stage.

PAYING THE BOUNTIES

ONE of the things to note here now is the arrival of the paymaster
with his strong box, and the payment of bounties to veterans re-
enlisting. Major H. is here to-day, with a small mountain of green-

backs, rejoicing the hearts of the 2d division of the First corps. In the midst of a rickety shanty, behind a little table, sit the major and clerk Eldridge, with the rolls before them, and much moneys. A re-enlisted man gets in cash about $200 down, (and heavy instalments following, as the pay-days arrive, one after another.) The show of the men crowding around is quite exhilarating; I like to stand and look. They feel elated, their pockets full, and the ensuing furlough, the visit home. It is a scene of sparkling eyes and flush'd cheeks. The soldier has many gloomy and harsh experiences, and this makes up for some of them. Major H. is order'd to pay first all the re-enlisted men of the First corps their bounties and back pay, and then the rest. You hear the peculiar sound of the rustling of the new and crisp greenbacks by the hour, through the nimble fingers of the major and my friend clerk E.

RUMORS, CHANGES, &c.

ABOUT the excitement of Sunday, and the orders to be ready to start, I have heard since that the said orders came from some cautious minor commander, and that the high principalities knew not and thought not of any such move; which is likely. The rumor and fear here intimated a long circuit by Lee, and flank attack on our right. But I cast my eyes at the mud, which was then at its deepest and palmiest condition, and retired composedly to rest. Still it is about time for Culpepper to have a change. Authorities have chased each other here like clouds in a stormy sky. Before the first Bull Run this was the rendezvous and camp of instruction of the secession troops. I am stopping at the house of a lady who has witness'd all the eventful changes of the war, along this route of contending armies. She is a widow, with a family of young children, and lives here with her sister in a large handsome house. A number of army officers board with them.

VIRGINIA

DILAPIDATED, fenceless, and trodden with war as Virginia is, wherever I move across her surface, I find myself rous'd to surprise and admiration. What capacity for products, improvements, human life, nourishment and expansion. Everywhere that I have been in the Old Dominion, (the subtle mockery of that title now!) such thoughts have fill'd me. The soil is yet far above the average of any of the northern States. And how full of breadth the scenery, everywhere distant mountains, everywhere convenient rivers. Even yet prodigal in forest woods, and surely eligible for all the fruits, orchards, and flowers. The skies and atmosphere most luscious, as I feel certain, from more than a year's residence in the State, and movements hither and yon. I should say very healthy, as a general thing. Then a rich and elastic quality, by night and by day. The sun rejoices in his strength, dazzling and burning, and yet, to me, never unpleasantly weakening. It is not the panting tropical heat, but invigorates. The north tempers it. The nights are often unsurpassable. Last evening (Feb. 8,) I saw the first of the new moon, the outlined old moon clear along with it; the sky and air so clear, such transparent hues of color, it seem'd to me I had never really seen the new moon before. It was the thinnest cut crescent possible. It hung delicate just above the sulky shadow of the Blue mountains. Ah, if it might prove an omen and good prophecy for this unhappy State.

SUMMER OF 1864

I AM back again in Washington, on my regular daily and nightly rounds. Of course there are many specialties. Dotting a ward here and there are always cases of poor fellows, long-suffering under obstinate wounds, or weak and dishearten'd from typhoid fever, or the like; mark'd cases, needing special and sympathetic nourishment. These I sit down and either talk to, or silently cheer them up. They always like it hugely, (and so do I.) Each case has its peculiarities, and needs some new adaptation. I have learnt to thus conform—learnt a good deal of hospital wisdom. Some of the poor young chaps, away from home for the first time in their lives, hunger and thirst for affection; this is sometimes the only thing that will reach their condition. The men like to have a pencil, and something to write in. I have given them cheap pocket-diaries, and almanacs for 1864, interleav'd with blank paper. For reading I generally have some old pictorial magazines or story papers—they are always acceptable. Also the morning or evening papers of the day. The best books I do not give, but lend to read through the wards, and then take them to others, and so on; they are very punctual about returning the books. In these wards, or on the field, as I thus continue to go round, I have come to adapt myself to each emergency, after its kind or call, however trivial, however solemn, every one justified and made real under its circumstances—not only visits and cheering talk and little gifts—not only washing and dressing wounds, (I have some cases where the patient is unwilling any one should do this but me)—but passages from the Bible, expounding them, prayer at the bedside, explanations of doctrine, &c. (I think I see my friends smiling at this confession, but I was never more in earnest in my life.) In camp and everywhere, I was in the habit of reading or giving recitations to the men. They were very fond of it, and liked declamatory poetical pieces. We would gather in a large group by ourselves, after supper, and spend the time in such readings, or in talking, and occasionally by an amusing game called the game of twenty questions.

A NEW ARMY ORGANIZATION FIT FOR AMERICA

IT IS plain to me out of the events of the war, north and south, and out of all considerations, that the current military theory, practice, rules and organization, (adopted from Europe from the feudal institutes, with, of course, the "modern improvements," largely from the French,) though tacitly follow'd, and believ'd in by the officers generally, are not at all consonant with the United States, nor our people, nor our days. What it will be I know not—but I know that as entire an abnegation of the present military system, and the naval too, and a building up from radically different root-bases and centres appropriate to us, must eventually result, as that our political system has resulted and become establish'd, different from feudal Europe, and built up on itself from original, perennial, democratic premises. We have undoubtedly in the United States the greatest military power—an exhaustless, intelligent, brave and reliable rank and file—in the world, any land, perhaps all lands. The problem is to organize this in the manner fully appropriate to it, to the principles of the republic, and to get the best service out of it. In the present struggle, as already seen and review'd, probably three-fourths of the losses, men, lives, &c., have been sheer superfluity, extravagance, waste.

DEATH OF A HERO

I WONDER if I could ever convey to another—to you, for instance, reader dear—the tender and terrible realities of such cases, (many, many happen'd,) as the one I am now going to mention. Stewart C. Glover, company E, 5th Wisconsin—was wounded May 5, in one of those fierce tussles of the Wilderness—died May 21—aged about 20. He was a small and beardless young man—a splendid soldier—in fact almost an ideal American, of his age. He had serv'd nearly three years, and would have been entitled to his discharge in a few days. He was in Hancock's corps. The fighting had about ceas'd for the day, and the general commanding the brigade rode by and call'd for volunteers to bring in the wounded. Glover responded among the first—went out gayly—but while in the act of bearing in a wounded sergeant to our lines, was shot in the knee by a rebel sharpshooter; consequence, amputation and death. He had resided with his father, John Glover, an aged and feeble man, in Batavia, Genesee county, N. Y., but was at school in Wisconsin, after the war broke out, and there enlisted—soon took to soldier-life, liked it, was very manly, was belov'd by officers and comrades. He kept a little diary, like so many of the soldiers. On the day of his death he wrote the following in it, *to-day the doctor says I must die—all is over with me—ah, so young to die.* On another blank leaf he pencill'd to his brother, *dear brother Thomas, I have been brave but wicked—pray for me.*

HOSPITAL SCENES—INCIDENTS

It is Sunday afternoon, middle of summer, hot and oppressive, and very silent through the ward. I am taking care of a critical case, now lying in a half lethargy. Near where I sit is a suffering rebel, from the 8th Louisiana; his name is Irving. He has been here a long time, badly wounded, and lately had his leg amputated; it is not doing very well. Right opposite me is a sick soldier-boy, laid down with his clothes on, sleeping, looking much wasted, his pallid face on his arm. I see by the yellow trimming on his jacket that he is a cavalry boy. I step softly over and find by his card that he is named William Cone, of the 1st Maine cavalry, and his folks live in Skowhegan.

Ice Cream Treat.—One hot day toward the middle of June, I gave the inmates of Carver hospital a general ice cream treat, purchasing a large quantity, and, under convoy of the doctor or head nurse, going around personally through the wards to see to its distribution.

An Incident.—In one of the fights before Atlanta, a rebel soldier, of large size, evidently a young man, was mortally wounded top of the head, so that the brains partially exuded. He lived three days, lying on his back on the spot where he first dropt. He dug with his heel in the ground during that time a hole big enough to put in a couple of ordinary knapsacks. He just lay there in the open air, and with little intermission kept his heel going night and day. Some of our soldiers then moved him to a house, but he died in a few minutes.

Another.—After the battles at Columbia, Tennessee, where we repuls'd about a score of vehement rebel charges, they left a great many wounded on the ground, mostly within our range. Whenever any of these wounded attempted to move away by any means, generally by crawling off, our men without exception brought them down by a bullet. They let none crawl away, no matter what his condition.

A YANKEE SOLDIER

As I turn'd off the Avenue one cool October evening into Thirteenth street, a soldier with knapsack and overcoat stood at the corner inquiring his way. I found he wanted to go part of the road in my direction, so we walk'd on together. We soon fell into conversation. He was small and not very young, and a tough little fellow, as I judged in the evening light, catching glimpses by the lamps we pass'd. His answers were short, but clear. His name was Charles Carroll; he belong'd to one of the Massachusetts regiments, and was born in or near Lynn. His parents were living, but were very old. There were four sons, and all had enlisted. Two had died of starvation and misery in the prison at Andersonville, and one had been kill'd in the west. He only was left. He was now going home, and by the way he talk'd I inferr'd that his time was nearly out. He made great calculations on being with his parents to comfort them the rest of their days.

UNION PRISONERS SOUTH

MICHAEL STANSBURY, 48 years of age, a sea-faring man, a southerner by birth and raising, formerly captain of U. S. light ship Long Shoal, station'd at Long Shoal point, Pamlico sound—though a southerner, a firm Union man—was captur'd Feb. 17, 1863, and has been nearly two years in the Confederate prisons; was at one time order'd releas'd by Governor Vance, but a rebel officer re-arrested him; then sent on to Richmond for exchange—but instead of being exchanged was sent down (as a southern citizen, not a soldier,) to Salisbury, N. C., where he remain'd until lately, when he escap'd among the exchang'd by assuming the name of a dead soldier, and coming up via Wilmington with the rest. Was about sixteen months in Salisbury. Subsequent to October, '64, there were about 11,000 Union prisoners in the stockade; about 100 of them southern unionists, 200 U. S. deserters. During the past winter 1500 of the prisoners, to save their lives, join'd the confederacy, on condition of being assign'd merely to guard duty. Out of the 11,000 not more than 2500 came out; 500 of these were pitiable, helpless wretches—the rest were in a condition to travel. There were often 60 dead bodies to be buried in the morning; the daily average would be about 40. The regular food was a meal of corn, the cob and husk ground together, and sometimes once a week a ration of sorghum molasses. A diminutive ration of meat might possibly come once a month, not oftener. In the stockade, containing the 11,000 men, there was a partial show of tents, not enough for 2000. A large proportion of the men lived in holes in the ground, in the utmost wretchedness. Some froze to death, others had their hands and feet frozen. The rebel guards would occasionally, and on the least pretence, fire into the prison from mere demonism and wantonness. All the horrors that can be named, starvation, lassitude, filth, vermin, despair, swift loss of self-respect, idiocy, insanity, and frequent murder, were there. Stansbury has a wife and child living in Newbern—has written to them from here—is in the U. S. light-house employ still—(had been home to Newbern to see his family, and on his return to the ship was captured in his boat.) Has seen men brought there to Salisbury as hearty as you ever see in your life—in a few weeks completely dead gone, much of it from thinking on their condition—hope all gone. Has himself a hard, sad, strangely deaden'd kind of look, as of one chill'd for years in the cold and dark, where his good manly nature had no room to exercise itself.

DESERTERS

Oct. 24.—Saw a large squad of our own deserters, (over 300) surrounded with a cordon of arm'd guards, marching along Pennsylvania avenue. The most motley collection I ever saw, all sorts of rig, all sorts of hats and caps, many fine-looking young fellows, some of them shame-faced, some sickly, most of them dirty, shirts very dirty and long worn, &c. They tramp'd along without order, a huge huddling mass, not in ranks. I saw some of the spectators laughing, but I felt like anything else but laughing. These deserters are far more numerous than would be thought. Almost every day I see squads of them, sometimes two or three at a time, with a small guard; sometimes ten or twelve, under a larger one. (I hear that desertions from the army now in the field have often averaged 10,000 a month. One of the commonest sights in Washington is a squad of deserters.)

A GLIMPSE OF WAR'S HELL-SCENES

IN ONE of the late movements of our troops in the valley, (near Upperville, I think,) a strong force of Moseby's mounted guerillas attack'd a train of wounded, and the guard of cavalry convoying them. The ambulances contain'd about 60 wounded, quite a number of them officers of rank. The rebels were in strength, and the capture of the train and its partial guard after a short snap was effectually accomplish'd. No sooner had our men surrender'd, the rebels instantly commenced robbing the train and murdering their prisoners, even the wounded. Here is the scene or a sample of it, ten minutes after. Among the wounded officers in the ambulances were one, a lieutenant of regulars, and another of higher rank. These two were dragg'd out on the ground on their backs, and were now surrounded by the guerillas, a demoniac crowd, each member of which was stabbing them in different parts of their bodies. One of the officers had his feet pinn'd firmly to the ground by bayonets stuck through them and thrust into the ground. These two officers, as afterwards found on examination, had receiv'd about twenty such thrusts, some of them through the mouth, face, &c. The wounded had all been dragg'd (to give a better chance also for plunder,) out of their wagons; some had been effectually dispatch'd, and their bodies were lying there lifeless and bloody. Others, not yet dead, but horribly mutilated, were moaning or groaning. Of our men who surrender'd, most had been thus maim'd or slaughter'd.

At this instant a force of our cavalry, who had been following the train at some interval, charged suddenly upon the secesh captors, who proceeded at once to make the best escape they could. Most of them got away, but we gobbled two officers and seventeen men, in the very acts just described. The sight was one which admitted of little discussion, as may be imagined. The seventeen captur'd men and two officers were put under guard for the night, but it was decided there and then that they should die. The next morning the two officers were taken in the town, separate places, put in the centre of the street, and shot. The seventeen men were taken to an open ground, a little one side. They were placed in a hollow square, half-encompass'd by two of our cavalry regiments, one of which regiments had three days before found the bloody corpses of three of their men hamstrung and hung up by the heels to limbs of trees by Moseby's guerillas, and the other had not long before had twelve men, after surrendering, shot and then hung by the neck to limbs of trees, and jeering inscriptions pinn'd to the breast of one of the corpses, who had been a sergeant. Those three, and those twelve, had been found, I say, by these environing regiments. Now, with revolvers, they form'd the grim cordon of the seventeen prisoners. The latter were placed in the midst of the hollow square, unfasten'd, and the ironical remark made to them that they were now to be given "a chance for themselves." A few ran for it. But what use? From every side the deadly pills came. In a few minutes the seventeen corpses strew'd the hollow square. I was curious to know whether some of the Union soldiers, some few, (some one or two at least of the youngsters,) did not abstain from shooting on the helpless men. Not one. There was no exultation, very little said, almost nothing, yet every man there contributed his shot.

Multiply the above by scores, aye hundreds—verify it in all the forms that different circumstances, individuals, places, could afford —light it with every lurid passion, the wolf's, the lion's lapping thirst for blood—the passionate, boiling volcanoes of human revenge for comrades, brothers slain—with the light of burning farms, and heaps of smutting, smouldering black embers—and in the human heart everywhere black, worse embers—and you have an inkling of this war.

GIFTS—MONEY—DISCRIMINATION

As a very large proportion of the wounded came up from the front without a cent of money in their pockets, I soon discover'd that it was about the best thing I could do to raise their spirits, and show them that somebody cared for them, and practically felt a fatherly or brotherly interest in them, to give them small sums in such cases, using tact and discretion about it. I am regularly supplied with funds for this purpose by good women and men in Boston, Salem, Providence, Brooklyn, and New York. I provide myself with a quantity of bright new ten-cent and five-cent bills, and, when I think it incumbent, I give 25 or 30 cents, or perhaps 50 cents, and occasionally a still larger sum to some particular case. As I have started this subject, I take opportunity to ventilate the financial question. My supplies, altogether voluntary, mostly confidential, often seeming quite Providential, were numerous and varied. For instance, there were two distant and wealthy ladies, sisters, who sent regularly, for two years, quite heavy sums, enjoining that their names should be kept secret. The same delicacy was indeed a frequent condition. From several I had *carte blanche*. Many were entire strangers. From these sources, during from two to three years, in the manner described, in the hospitals, I bestowed, as almoner for others, many, many thousands of dollars. I learn'd one thing conclusively—that beneath all the ostensible greed and heartlessness of our times there is no end to the generous benevolence of men and women in the United States, when once sure of their object. Another thing became clear to me—while *cash* is not amiss to bring up the rear, tact and magnetic sympathy and unction are, and ever will be, sovereign still.

ITEMS FROM MY NOTE BOOKS

Some of the half-eras'd, and not over-legible when made, memoranda of things wanted by one patient or another, will convey quite a fair idea. D. S. G., bed 52, wants a good book; has a sore, weak throat; would like some horehound candy; is from New Jersey, 28th regiment. C. H. L., 145th Pennsylvania, lies in bed 6, with jaundice and erysipelas; also wounded; stomach easily nauseated; bring him some oranges, also a little tart jelly; hearty, full-blooded young fellow—(he got better in a few days, and is now home on a furlough.) J. H. G., bed 24, wants an undershirt, drawers, and socks; has not had a change for quite a while; is evidently a neat, clean boy from New England—(I supplied him; also with a comb, toothbrush, and some soap and towels; I noticed afterward he was the cleanest of the whole ward.) Mrs. G., lady-nurse, ward F, wants a bottle of brandy—has two patients imperatively requiring stimulus—low with wounds and exhaustion. (I supplied her with a bottle of first-rate brandy from the Christian commission rooms.)

A CASE FROM SECOND BULL RUN

Well, poor John Mahay is dead. He died yesterday. His was a painful and long-lingering case, (see p. 25 *ante*.) I have been with him at times for the past fifteen months. He belonged to company A, 101st New York, and was shot through the lower region of the abdomen at second Bull Run, August, '62. One scene at his bedside will suffice for the agonies of nearly two years. The bladder had been perforated by a bullet going entirely through him. Not long since I sat a good part of the morning by his bedside, ward E, Armory square. The water ran out of his eyes from the intense pain, and the muscles of his face were distorted, but he utter'd nothing except a low groan now and then. Hot moist cloths were applied, and reliev'd him somewhat. Poor Mahay, a mere boy in age, but old in misfortune. He never knew the love of parents, was placed in infancy in one of the New York charitable institutions, and subsequently bound out to a tyrannical master in Sullivan county, (the scars of whose cowhide and club remain'd yet on his back.) His wound here was a most disagreeable one, for he was a gentle, cleanly, and affectionate boy. He found friends in his hospital life, and, indeed, was a universal favorite. He had quite a funeral ceremony.

ARMY SURGEONS—AID DEFICIENCIES

I MUST bear my most emphatic testimony to the zeal, manliness, and professional spirit and capacity, generally prevailing among the surgeons, many of them young men, in the hospitals and the army. I will not say much about the exceptions, for they are few; (but I have met some of those few, and very incompetent and airish they were.) I never ceas'd to find the best men, and the hardest and most disinterested workers, among the surgeons in the hospitals. They are full of genius, too. I have seen many hundreds of them and this is my testimony. There are, however, serious deficiencies, wastes, sad want of system, in the commissions, contributions, and in all the voluntary, and a great part of the governmental nursing, edibles, medicines, stores, &c. (I do not say surgical attendance, because the surgeons cannot do more than human endurance permits.) Whatever puffing accounts there may be in the papers of the North, this is the actual fact. No thorough previous preparation, no system, no foresight, no genius. Always plenty of stores, no doubt, but never where they are needed, and never the proper application. Of all harrowing experiences, none is greater than that of the days following a heavy battle. Scores, hundreds of the noblest men on earth, uncomplaining, lie helpless, mangled, faint, alone, and so bleed to death, or die from exhaustion, either actually untouch'd at all, or merely the laying of them down and leaving them, when there ought to be means provided to save them.

THE BLUE EVERYWHERE

THIS city, its suburbs, the capitol, the front of the White House, the places of amusement, the Avenue, and all the main streets, swarm with soldiers this winter, more than ever before. Some are out from the hospitals, some from the neighboring camps, &c. One source or another, they pour plenteously, and make, I should say, the mark'd feature in the human movement and costume-appearance of our national city. Their blue pants and overcoats are everywhere. The clump of crutches is heard up the stairs of the paymasters' offices, and there are characteristic groups around the doors of the same, often waiting long and wearily in the cold. Toward the latter part of the afternoon, you see the furlough'd men, sometimes singly, sometimes in small squads, making their way to the Baltimore depot. At all times, except early in the morning, the patrol detachments are moving around, especially during the earlier hours of evening, examining passes, and arresting all soldiers without them. They do not question the one-legged, or men badly disabled or maim'd, but all others are stopt. They also go around evenings through the auditoriums of the theatres, and make officers and all show their passes, or other authority, for being there.

A MODEL HOSPITAL

Sunday, January 29th, 1865.—Have been in Armory-square this afternoon. The wards are very comfortable, new floors and plaster walls, and models of neatness. I am not sure but this is a model hospital after all, in important respects. I found several sad cases of old lingering wounds. One Delaware soldier, William H. Millis, from Bridgeville, whom I had been with after the battles of the Wilderness, last May, where he receiv'd a very bad wound in the chest, with another in the left arm, and whose case was serious (pneumonia had set in) all last June and July, I now find well enough to do light duty. For three weeks at the time mention'd he just hovered between life and death.

BOYS IN THE ARMY

As I walk'd home about sunset, I saw in Fourteenth street a very young soldier, thinly clad, standing near the house I was about to enter. I stopt a moment in front of the door and call'd him to me. I knew that an old Tennessee regiment, and also an Indiana regiment, were temporarily stopping in new barracks, near Fourteenth street. This boy I found belonged to the Tennessee regiment. But I could hardly believe he carried a musket. He was but 15 years old, yet had been twelve months a soldier, and had borne his part in several battles, even historic ones. I ask'd him if he did not suffer from the cold, and if he had no overcoat. No, he did not suffer from cold, and had no overcoat, but could draw one whenever he wish'd. His father was dead, and his mother living in some part of East Tennessee; all the men were from that part of the country. The next forenoon I saw the Tennessee and Indiana regiments marching down the Avenue. My boy was with the former, stepping along with the rest. There were many other boys no older. I stood and watch'd them as they tramp'd along with slow, strong, heavy, regular steps. There did not appear to be a man over 30 years of age, and a large proportion were from 15 to perhaps 22 or 23. They had all the look of veterans, worn, stain'd, impassive, and a certain unbent, lounging gait, carrying in addition to their regular arms and knapsacks, frequently a frying-pan, broom, &c. They were all of pleasant physiognomy; no refinement, nor blanch'd with intellect, but as my eye pick'd them, moving along, rank by rank, there did not seem to be a single repulsive, brutal or markedly stupid face among them.

BURIAL OF A LADY NURSE

HERE is an incident just occurr'd in one of the hospitals. A lady named Miss or Mrs. Billings, who has long been a practical friend of soldiers, and nurse in the army, and had become attached to it in a way that no one can realize but him or her who has had experience, was taken sick, early this winter, linger'd some time, and finally died in the hospital. It was her request that she should be buried among the soldiers, and after the military method. This request was fully carried out. Her coffin was carried to the grave by soldiers, with the usual escort, buried, and a salute fired over the grave. This was at Annapolis a few days since.

FEMALE NURSES FOR SOLDIERS

THERE are many women in one position or another, among the hospitals, mostly as nurses here in Washington, and among the military stations; quite a number of them young ladies acting as volunteers. They are a help in certain ways, and deserve to be mention'd with respect. Then it remains to be distinctly said that few or no young ladies, under the irresistible conventions of society, answer the practical requirements of nurses for soldiers. Middle-aged or healthy and good condition'd elderly women, mothers of children, are always best. Many of the wounded must be handled. A hundred things which cannot be gainsay'd, must occur and must be done. The presence of a good middle-aged or elderly woman, the magnetic touch of hands, the expressive features of the mother, the silent soothing of her presence, her words, her knowledge and privileges arrived at only through having had children, are precious and final qualifications. It is a natural faculty that is required; it is not merely having a genteel young woman at a table in a ward. One of the finest nurses I met was a red-faced illiterate old Irish

woman; I have seen her take the poor wasted naked boys so tenderly up in her arms. There are plenty of excellent clean old black
women that would make tip-top nurses.

SOUTHERN ESCAPEES

Feb. 23, '65.—I saw a large procession of young men from the rebel
army, (deserters they are call'd, but the usual meaning of the word
does not apply to them,) passing the Avenue to-day. There were
nearly 200, come up yesterday by boat from James river. I stood
and watch'd them as they shuffled along, in a slow, tired, worn sort
of way; a large proportion of light-hair'd, blonde, light gray-eyed
young men among them. Their costumes had a dirt-stain'd uniformity; most had been originally gray; some had articles of our uniform, pants on one, vest or coat on another; I think they were
mostly Georgia and North Carolina boys. They excited little or no
attention. As I stood quite close to them, several good looking
enough youths, (but O what a tale of misery their appearance told,)
nodded or just spoke to me, without doubt divining pity and father-
liness out of my face, for my heart was full enough of it. Several
of the couples trudg'd along with their arms about each other, some
probably brothers, as if they were afraid they might somehow get
separated. They nearly all look'd what one might call simple, yet
intelligent, too. Some had pieces of old carpet, some blankets, and
others old bags around their shoulders. Some of them here and there
had fine faces, still it was a procession of misery. The two hundred
had with them about half a dozen arm'd guards. Along this week
I saw some such procession, more or less in numbers, every day, as
they were brought up by the boat. The government does what it can
for them, and sends them north and west.

Feb. 27.—Some three or four hundred more escapees from the
confederate army came up on the boat. As the day has been very
pleasant indeed, (after a long spell of bad weather,) I have been
wandering around a good deal, without any other object than to be
out-doors and enjoy it; have met these escaped men in all directions. Their apparel is the same ragged, long-worn motley as before
described. I talk'd with a number of the men. Some are quite bright
and stylish, for all their poor clothes—walking with an air, wearing
their old head-coverings on one side, quite saucily. I find the old,
unquestionable proofs, as all along the past four years, of the un-
scrupulous tyranny exercised by the secession government in con-
scripting the common people by absolute force everywhere, and
paying no attention whatever to the men's time being up—keeping

them in military service just the same. One gigantic young fellow, a Georgian, at least six feet three inches high, broad-sized in proportion, attired in the dirtiest, drab, well-smear'd rags, tied with strings, his trousers at the knees all strips and streamers, was complacently standing eating some bread and meat. He appear'd contented enough. Then a few minutes after I saw him slowly walking along. It was plain he did not take anything to heart.

Feb. 28.—As I pass'd the military headquarters of the city, not far from the President's house, I stopt to interview some of the crowd of escapees who were lounging there. In appearance they were the same as previously mention'd. Two of them, one about 17, and the other perhaps 25 or '6, I talk'd with some time. They were from North Carolina, born and rais'd there, and had folks there. The elder had been in the rebel service four years. He was first conscripted for two years. He was then kept arbitrarily in the ranks. This is the case with a large proportion of the secession army. There was nothing downcast in these young men's manners; the younger had been soldiering about a year; he was conscripted; there were six brothers (all the boys of the family) in the army, part of them as conscripts, part as volunteers; three had been kill'd; one had escaped about four months ago, and now this one had got away; he was a pleasant and well-talking lad, with the peculiar North Carolina idiom (not at all disagreeable to my ears.) He and the elder one were of the same company, and escaped together— and wish'd to remain together. They thought of getting transportation away to Missouri, and working there; but were not sure it was judicious. I advised them rather to go to some of the directly northern States, and get farm work for the present. The younger had made six dollars on the boat, with some tobacco he brought; he had three and a half left. The elder had nothing; I gave him a trifle. Soon after, met John Wormley, 9th Alabama, a West Tennessee rais'd boy, parents both dead—had the look of one for a long time on short allowance—said very little—chew'd tobacco at a fearful rate, spitting in proportion—large clear dark-brown eyes, very fine— didn't know what to make of me—told me at last he wanted much to get some clean underclothes, and a pair of decent pants. Didn't care about coat or hat fixings. Wanted a chance to wash himself well, and put on the underclothes. I had the very great pleasure of helping him to accomplish all those wholesome designs.

March 1st.—Plenty more butternut or clay-color'd escapees every day. About 160 came in to-day, a large portion South Carolinians. They generally take the oath of allegiance, and are sent north, west, or extreme south-west if they wish. Several of them told me that the desertions in their army, of men going home, leave or no leave, are far more numerous than their desertions to our side. I saw a very forlorn looking squad of about a hundred, late this afternoon, on their way to the Baltimore depot.

THE CAPITOL BY GAS-LIGHT

To-night I have been wandering awhile in the capitol, which is all lit up. The illuminated rotunda looks fine. I like to stand aside and look a long, long while, up at the dome; it comforts me somehow. The House and Senate were both in session till very late. I look'd in upon them, but only a few moments; they were hard at work on tax and appropriation bills. I wander'd through the long and rich corridors and apartments under the Senate; an old habit of mine, former winters, and now more satisfaction than ever. Not many persons down there, occasionally a flitting figure in the distance.

THE INAUGURATION

March 4.—The President very quietly rode down to the capitol in his own carriage, by himself, on a sharp trot, about noon, either because he wish'd to be on hand to sign bills, or to get rid of marching in line with the absurd procession, the muslin temple of liberty, and pasteboard monitor. I saw him on his return, at three o'clock, after the performance was over. He was in his plain two-horse barouche, and look'd very much worn and tired; the lines, indeed, of vast responsibilities, intricate questions, and demands of life and death, cut deeper than ever upon his dark brown face; yet all the old goodness, tenderness, sadness, and canny shrewdness, underneath the furrows. (I never see that man without feeling that he is one to become personally attach'd to, for his combination of purest, heartiest tenderness, and native western form of manliness.) By his side sat his little boy, of ten years. There were no soldiers, only a lot of civilians on horseback, with huge yellow scarfs over their shoulders, riding around the carriage. (At the inauguration for years ago, he rode down and back again surrounded by a dense mass of arm'd cavalrymen eight deep, with drawn sabres; and there were sharp-shooters station'd at every corner on the route.) I ought to make mention of the closing levee of Saturday night last. Never before was such a compact jam in front of the White House—all the grounds fill'd, and away out to the spacious sidewalks. I was there, as I took a notion to go—was in the rush inside with the crowd—surged along the passage-ways, the blue and other rooms, and through the great east room. Crowds of country people, some very funny. Fine music from the Marine band, off in a side place. I saw Mr. Lincoln, drest all in black, with white kid gloves and a claw-hammer coat, receiving, as in duty bound, shaking hands, looking very disconsolate, and as if he would give anything to be somewhere else.

ATTITUDE OF FOREIGN GOVERNMENTS DURING THE WAR

LOOKING over my scraps, I find I wrote the following during 1864. The happening to our America, abroad as well as at home, these years, is indeed most strange. The democratic republic has paid her to-day the terrible and resplendent compliment of the united wish of all the nations of the world that her union should be broken, her future cut off, and that she should be compell'd to descend to the level of kingdoms and empires ordinarily great. There is certainly not one government in Europe but is now watching the war in this country, with the ardent prayer that the United States may be effectually split, crippled, and dismember'd by it. There is not one but would help toward that dismemberment, if it dared. I say such is the ardent wish to-day of England and of France, as governments, and of all the nations of Europe, as governments. I think indeed it is to-day the real, heartfelt wish of all the nations of the world, with the single exception of Mexico—Mexico, the only one to whom we have ever really done wrong, and now the only one who prays for us and for our triumph, with genuine prayer. Is it not indeed strange? America, made up of all, cheerfully from the beginning opening her arms to all, the result and justifier of all, of Britain, Germany, France and Spain—all here—the accepter, the friend, hope, last resource and general house of all—she who has harm'd none, but been bounteous to so many, to millions, the mother of strangers and exiles, all nations—should now I say be paid this dread compliment of general governmental fear and hatred. Are we indignant? alarm'd? Do we feel jeopardized? No; help'd, braced, concentrated, rather. We are all too prone to wander from ourselves, to affect Europe, and watch her frowns and smiles. We need this hot lesson of general hatred, and henceforth must never forget it. Never again will we trust the moral sense nor abstract friendliness of a single *government* of the old world.

THE WEATHER—DOES IT SYMPATHIZE
WITH THESE TIMES?

Whether the rains, the heat and cold, and what underlies them all, are affected with what affects man in masses, and follow his play of passionate action, strain'd stronger than usual, and on a larger scale than usual—whether this, or no, it is certain that there is now, and has been for twenty months or more, on this American continent north, many a remarkable, many an unprecedented expression of the subtile world of air above us and around us. There, since this war, and the wide and deep national agitation, strange analogies, different combinations, a different sunlight, or absence of it; different products even out of the ground. After every great battle, a great storm. Even civic events the same. On Saturday last, a forenoon like whirling demons, dark, with slanting rain, full of rage; and then the afternoon, so calm, so bathed with flooding splendor from heaven's most excellent sun, with atmosphere of sweetness; so clear, it show'd the stars, long, long before they were due. As the President came out on the capitol portico, a curious little white cloud, the only one in that part of the sky, appear'd like a hovering bird, right over him.

Indeed, the heavens, the elements, all the meteorological influences, have run riot for weeks past. Such caprices, abruptest alternation of frowns and beauty, I never knew. It is a common remark that (as last summer was different in its spells of intense heat from any preceding it,) the winter just completed has been without parallel. It has remain'd so down to the hour I am writing. Much of the daytime of the past month was sulky, with leaden heaviness, fog, interstices of bitter cold, and some insane storms. But there have been samples of another description. Nor earth nor sky ever knew spectacles of superber beauty than some of the nights lately here. The western star, Venus, in the earlier hours of evening, has never been so large, so clear; it seems as if it told something, as if it held rapport indulgent with humanity, with us Americans. Five or six nights since, it hung close by the moon, then a little past its first quarter. The star was wonderful, the moon like a young mother. The sky, dark blue, the transparent night, the planets, the moderate west wind, the elastic temperature, the miracle of that great star, and the young and swelling moon swimming in the west, suffused the soul. Then I heard, slow and clear, the deliberate notes of a bugle come up out of the silence, sounding so good through the night's mystery, no hurry, but firm and faithful, floating along, rising, falling leisurely, with here and there a long-drawn note; the bugle, well play'd, sounding tattoo, in one of the army hospitals near here, where the wounded (some of them personally so dear to me,) are lying in their cots, and many a sick boy come down to the war from Illinois, Michigan, Wisconsin, Iowa, and the rest.

INAUGURATION BALL

March 6.—I have been up to look at the dance and supper-rooms, for the inauguration ball at the Patent office; and I could not help thinking, what a different scene they presented to my view a while since, fill'd with a crowded mass of the worst wounded of the war, brought in from second Bull Run, Antietam, and Fredericksburgh. To-night, beautiful women, perfumes, the violins' sweetness, the polka and the waltz; then the amputation, the blue face, the groan, the glassy eye of the dying, the clotted rag, the odor of wounds and blood, and many a mother's son amid strangers, passing away untended there, (for the crowd of the badly hurt was great, and much for nurse to do, and much for surgeon.)

SCENE AT THE CAPITOL

I MUST mention a strange scene at the capitol, the hall of Representatives, the morning of Saturday last, (March 4th.) The day just dawn'd, but in half-darkness, everything dim, leaden, and soaking. In that dim light, the members nervous from long drawn duty, exhausted, some asleep, and many half asleep. The gas-light, mix'd with the dingy day-break, produced an unearthly effect. The poor little sleepy, stumbling pages, the smell of the hall, the members with heads leaning on their desks, the sounds of the voices speaking, with unusual intonations—the general moral atmosphere also of the close of this important session—the strong hope that the war is approaching its close—the tantalizing dread lest the hope may be a false one—the grandeur of the hall itself, with its effect of vast shadows up toward the panels and spaces over the galleries—all made a mark'd combination.

In the midst of this, with the suddenness of a thunderbolt, burst one of the most angry and crashing storms of rain and hail ever heard. It beat like a deluge on the heavy glass roof of the hall, and the wind literally howl'd and roar'd. For a moment, (and no wonder,) the nervous and sleeping Representatives were thrown into confusion. The slumberers awaked with fear, some started for the doors, some look'd up with blanch'd cheeks and lips to the roof, and the little pages began to cry; it was a scene. But it was over almost as soon as the drowsied men were actually awake. They recover'd themselves; the storm raged on, beating, dashing, and with loud noises at times. But the House went ahead with its business then, I think, as calmly and with as much deliberation as at any time in its career. Perhaps the shock did it good. (One is not without impression, after all, amid these members of Congress, of both the Houses, that if the flat routine of their duties should ever be broken in upon by some great emergency involving real danger, and calling for first-class personal qualities, those qualities would be found generally forthcoming, and from men not now credited with them.)

A YANKEE ANTIQUE

March 27, 1865.—Sergeant Calvin F. Harlowe, company C, 29th Massachusetts, 3d brigade, 1st division, Ninth corps—a mark'd sample of heroism and death, (some may say bravado, but I say *heroism,* of grandest, oldest order)—in the late attack by the rebel troops, and temporary capture by them, of fort Steadman, at night. The fort was surprised at dead of night. Suddenly awaken'd from their sleep, and rushing from their tents, Harlowe, with others, found himself in the hands of the secesh—they demanded his surrender—he answer'd, *Never while I live.* (Of course it was useless. The others surrender'd; the odds were too great.) Again he was ask'd to yield, this time by a rebel captain. Though surrounded, and quite calm, he again refused, call'd sternly to his comrades to fight on, and himself attempted to do so. The rebel captain then shot him—but at the same instant he shot the captain. Both fell together mortally wounded. Harlowe died almost instantly. The rebels were driven out in a very short time. The body was buried next day, but soon taken up and sent home, (Plymouth county, Mass.) Harlowe was only 22 years of age—was a tall, slim, dark-hair'd, blue-eyed young man—had come out originally with the 29th; and that is the way he met his death, after four years' campaign. He was in the Seven Days fight before Richmond, in second Bull Run, Antietam, first Fredericksburgh, Vicksburgh, Jackson, Wilderness, and the campaigns following—was as good a soldier as ever wore the blue, and every old officer in the regiment will bear that testimony. Though so young, and in a common rank, he had a spirit as resolute and brave as any hero in the books, ancient or modern—It was too great to say the words "I surrender"—and so he died. (When I think of such things, knowing them well, all the vast and complicated events of the war, on which history dwells and makes its volumes, fall aside, and for the moment at any rate I see nothing but young Calvin Harlowe's figure in the night, disdaining to surrender.)

WOUNDS AND DISEASES

THE war is over, but the hospitals are fuller than ever, from former and current cases. A large majority of the wounds are in the arms and legs. But there is every kind of wound, in every part of the body. I should say of the sick, from my observation, that the prevailing maladies are typhoid fever and the camp fevers generally, diarrhœa, catarrhal affections and bronchitis, rheumatism and pneumonia. These forms of sickness lead; all the rest follow. There are twice as many sick as there are wounded. The deaths range from seven to ten per cent. of those under treatment.[7]

DEATH OF PRESIDENT LINCOLN

April 16, '65.—I find in my notes of the time, this passage on the death of Abraham Lincoln: He leaves for America's history and biography, so far, not only its most dramatic reminiscence—he leaves, in my opinion, the greatest, best, most characteristic, artistic, moral personality. Not but that he had faults, and show'd them in the Presidency; but honesty, goodness, shrewdness, conscience, and (a new virtue, unknown to other lands, and hardly yet really known here, but the foundation and tie of all, as the future will grandly develop,) UNIONISM, in its truest and amplest sense, form'd the hard-pan of his character. These he seal'd with his life. The tragic splendor of his death, purging, illuminating all, throws round his form, his head, an aureole that will remain and will grow brighter through time, while history lives, and love of country lasts. By many has this Union been help'd; but if one name, one man, must be pick'd out, he, most of all, is the conservator of it, to the future. He was assassinated—but the Union is not assassinated—*ça ira!* One falls, and another falls. The soldier drops, sinks like a wave—but the ranks of the ocean eternally press on. Death does its work, obliterates a hundred, a thousand—President, general, captain, private —but the Nation is immortal.

SHERMAN'S ARMY'S JUBILATION—ITS SUDDEN STOPPAGE

WHEN Sherman's armies, (long after they left Atlanta,) were marching through South and North Carolina—after leaving Savannah, the news of Lee's capitulation having been receiv'd—the men never mov'd a mile without from some part of the line sending up continued, inspiriting shouts. At intervals all day long sounded out the wild music of those peculiar army cries. They would be commenc'd by one regiment or brigade, immediately taken up by others, and at length whole corps and armies would join in these wild triumphant choruses. It was one of the characteristic expressions of the western troops, and became a habit, serving as a relief and outlet to the men—a vent for their feelings of victory, returning peace, &c. Morning, noon, and afternoon, spontaneous, for occasion or without occasion, these huge, strange cries, differing from any other, echoing through the open air for many a mile, expressing youth, joy, wildness, irrepressible strength, and the ideas of advance and conquest, sounded along the swamps and uplands of the South, floating to the skies. ('There never were men that kept in better spirits in danger or defeat—what then could they do in victory?'—said one of the 15th corps to me, afterwards.) This exuberance continued till the armies arrived at Raleigh. There the news of the President's murder was receiv'd. Then no more shouts or yells, for a week. All the marching was comparatively muffled. It was very significant—hardly a loud word or laugh in many of the regiments. A hush and silence pervaded all.

NO GOOD PORTRAIT OF LINCOLN

PROBABLY the reader has seen physiognomies (often old farmers, sea-captains, and such) that, behind their homeliness, or even ugliness, held superior points so subtle, yet so palpable, making the real life of their faces almost as impossible to depict as a wild perfume or fruit-taste, or a passionate tone of the living voice—and such was Lincoln's face, the peculiar color, the lines of it, the eyes, mouth, expression. Of technical beauty it had nothing—but to the eye of a great artist it furnished a rare study, a feast and fascination. The current portraits are all failures—most of them caricatures.

RELEAS'D UNION PRISONERS FROM SOUTH

THE releas'd prisoners of war are now coming up from the southern prisons. I have seen a number of them. The sight is worse than any sight of battle-fields, or any collection of wounded, even the bloodiest. There was, (as a sample,) one large boat load, of several hundreds, brought about the 25th, to Annapolis; and out of the whole number only three individuals were able to walk from the boat. The rest were carried ashore and laid down in one place or another. Can those be *men*—those little livid brown, ash-streak'd, monkey-looking dwarfs?—are they really not mummied, dwindled corpses?

They lay there, most of them, quite still, but with a horrible look in their eyes and skinny lips (often with not enough flesh on the lips to cover their teeth.) Probably no more appalling sight was ever seen on this earth. (There are deeds, crimes, that may be forgiven; but this is not among them. It steeps its perpetrators in blackest, escapeless, endless damnation. Over 50,000 have been compell'd to die the death of starvation—reader, did you ever try to realize what *starvation* actually is?—in those prisons—and in a land of plenty.) An indescribable meanness, tyranny, aggravating course of insults, almost incredible—was evidently the rule of treatment through all the southern military prisons. The dead there are not to be pitied as much as some of the living that come from there—if they can be call'd living—many of them are mentally imbecile, and will never recuperate.[8]

DEATH OF A PENNSYLVANIA SOLDIER

Frank H. Irwin, company E, 93d Pennsylvania—died May 1, '65— My letter to his mother.—Dear madam: No doubt you and Frank's friends have heard the sad fact of his death in hospital here, through his uncle, or the lady from Baltimore, who took his things. (I have not seen them, only heard of them visiting Frank.) I will write you a few lines—as a casual friend that sat by his death-bed. Your son, corporal Frank H. Irwin, was wounded near fort Fisher, Virginia, March 25th, 1865—the wound was in the left knee, pretty bad. He was sent up to Washington, was receiv'd in ward C, Armory-square hospital, March 28th—the wound became worse, and on the 4th of April the leg was amputated a little above the knee— the operation was perform'd by Dr. Bliss, one of the best surgeons in the army—he did the whole operation himself—there was a good deal of bad matter gather'd—the bullet was found in the knee. For a couple of weeks afterwards he was doing pretty well. I visited and sat by him frequently, as he was fond of having me. The last ten or twelve days of April I saw that his case was critical. He previously had some fever, with cold spells. The last week in April he was much of the time flighty—but always mild and gentle. He died first of May. The actual cause of death was pyæmia, (the absorption of the matter in the system instead of its discharge.) Frank, as far as I saw, had everything requisite in surgical treatment, nursing, &c. He had watches much of the time. He was so good and well-behaved and affectionate, I myself liked him very much. I was in the habit of coming in afternoons and sitting by him, and soothing him, and he liked to have me—liked to put his arm out and lay his hand on my knee—would keep it so a long while. Toward the last he was more restless and flighty at night—often fancied himself with his regiment—by his talk sometimes seem'd as if his feelings were hurt by being blamed by his officers for something he was entirely innocent of—said, "I never in my life was thought capable of such a thing, and never was." At other times he would fancy himself talking as it seem'd to children or such like, his relatives I suppose, and giving them good advice; would talk to them a long while. All the time he was out of his head not one single bad word or idea escaped him. It was remark'd that many a man's conversation in his senses was not half as good as Frank's delirium. He seem'd quite willing to die—he had become very weak and had suffer'd a good deal, and was perfectly resign'd, poor boy. I do not know his past life, but I feel as if it must have been good. At any rate what I saw of him here, under the most trying circumstances, with a painful wound, and among strangers, I can say that he behaved so brave, so composed, and so sweet and affectionate, it could not be surpass'd. And now like many other noble and good men, after serving his country as a soldier, he has yielded up his young life at the very outset in her service. Such things are gloomy—yet there is a text, "God doeth all things well"—the meaning of which, after due time, appears to the soul.

I thought perhaps a few words, though from a stranger, about your son, from one who was with him at the last, might be worth while—for I loved the young man, though I but saw him immediately to lose him. I am merely a friend visiting the hospitals occasionally to cheer the wounded and sick.   W. W.

THE ARMIES RETURNING

May 7.—Sunday.—To-day as I was walking a mile or two south of Alexandria, I fell in with several large squads of the returning Western army, (*Sherman's men* as they call'd themselves) about a thousand in all, the largest portion of them half sick, some convalescents, on their way to a hospital camp. These fragmentary excerpts, with the unmistakable Western physiognomy and idioms, crawling along slowly—after a great campaign, blown this way, as it were, out of their latitude—I mark'd with curiosity, and talk'd with off and on for over an hour. Here and there was one very sick; but all were able to walk, except some of the last, who had given out, and were seated on the ground, faint and despondent. These I tried to cheer, told them the camp they were to reach was only a little way further over the hill, and so got them up and started, accompanying some of the worst a little way, and helping them, or putting them under the support of stronger comrades.

May 21.—Saw General Sheridan and his cavalry to-day; a strong, attractive sight; the men were mostly young, (a few middle-aged,) superb-looking fellows, brown, spare, keen, with well-worn clothing, many with pieces of water-proof cloth around their shoulders, hanging down. They dash'd along pretty fast, in wide close ranks, all spatter'd with mud; no holiday soldiers; brigade after brigade. I could have watch'd for a week. Sheridan stood on a balcony, under a big tree, coolly smoking a cigar. His looks and manner impress'd me favorably.

May 22.—Have been taking a walk along Pennsylvania avenue and Seventh street north. The city is full of soldiers, running around loose. Officers everywhere, of all grades. All have the weather-beaten look of practical service. It is a sight I never tire of. All the armies are now here (or portions of them,) for to-morrow's review. You see them swarming like bees everywhere.

THE GRAND REVIEW

FOR two days now the broad spaces of Pennsylvania avenue along to Treasury hill, and so by detour around to the President's house, and so up to Georgetown, and across the aqueduct bridge, have been alive with a magnificent sight, the returning armies. In their wide ranks stretching clear across the Avenue, I watch them march or ride along, at a brisk pace, through two whole days—infantry, cavalry, artillery—some 200,000 men. Some days afterwards one or two other corps; and then, still afterwards, a good part of Sherman's immense army, brought up from Charleston, Savannah, &c.

WESTERN SOLDIERS

May 26-7.—The streets, the public buildings and grounds of Washington, still swarm with soldiers from Illinois, Indiana, Ohio, Missouri, Iowa, and all the Western States. I am continually meeting and talking with them. They often speak to me first, and always show great sociability, and glad to have a good interchange of chat. These Western soldiers are more slow in their movements, and in their intellectual quality also; have no extreme alertness. They are larger in size, have a more serious physiognomy, are continually looking at you as they pass in the street. They are largely animal, and handsomely so. During the war I have been at times with the Fourteenth, Fifteenth, Seventeenth, and Twentieth Corps. I always feel drawn toward the men, and like their personal contact when we are crowded close together, as frequently these days in the street-cars. They all think the world of General Sherman; call him "old Bill," or sometimes "uncle Billy."

A SOLDIER ON LINCOLN

May 28.—As I sat by the bedside of a sick Michigan soldier in hospital to-day, a convalescent from the adjoining bed rose and came to me, and presently we began talking. He was a middle-aged man, belonged to the 2d Virginia regiment, but lived in Racine, Ohio, and had a family there. He spoke of President Lincoln, and said: "The war is over, and many are lost. And now we have lost the best, the fairest, the truest man in America. Take him altogether, he was the best man this country ever produced. It was quite a while I thought very different; but some time before the murder, that's the way I have seen it." There was deep earnestness in the soldier. (I found upon further talk he had known Mr. Lincoln personally, and quite closely, years before.) He was a veteran; was now in the fifth year of his service; was a cavalry man, and had been in a good deal of hard fighting.

TWO BROTHERS, ONE SOUTH, ONE NORTH

May 28-9.—I staid to-night a long time by the bedside of a new patient, a young Baltimorean, aged about 19 years, W. S. P., (2d Maryland, southern,) very feeble, right leg amputated, can't sleep hardly at all—has taken a great deal of morphine, which, as usual, is costing more than it comes to. Evidently very intelligent and well bred—very affectionate—held on to my hand, and put it by his face, not willing to let me leave. As I was lingering, soothing him in his pain, he says to me suddenly, "I hardly think you know who I am— I don't wish to impose upon you—I am a rebel soldier." I said I did not know that, but it made no difference. Visiting him daily for about two weeks after that, while he lived, (death had mark'd him, and he was quite alone,) I loved him much, always kiss'd him, and he did me. In an adjoining ward I found his brother, an officer of rank, a Union soldier, a brave and religious man, (Col. Clifton K. Prentiss, sixth Maryland infantry, Sixth corps, wounded in one of the engagements at Petersburgh, April 2—linger'd, suffer'd much, died in Brooklyn, Aug. 20, '65.) It was in the same battle both were hit. One was a strong Unionist, the other Secesh; both fought on their respective sides, both badly wounded, and both brought together here after a separation of four years. Each died for his cause.

SOME SAD CASES YET

May 31.—James H. Williams, aged 21, 3d Virginia cavalry.—About as mark'd a case of a strong man brought low by a complication of diseases, (laryngitis, fever, debility and diarrhœa,) as I have ever seen—has superb physique, remains swarthy yet, and flushed and red with fever—is altogether flighty—flesh of his great breast and arms tremulous, and pulse pounding away with treble quickness— lies a good deal of the time in a partial sleep, but with low muttering and groans—a sleep in which there is no rest. Powerful as he is, and so young, he will not be able to stand many more days of the strain and sapping heat of yesterday and to-day. His throat is in a bad way, tongue and lips parch'd. When I ask him how he feels, he is able just to articulate, "I feel pretty bad yet, old man," and looks at me with his great bright eyes. Father, John Williams, Millensport, Ohio.

June 9-10.—I have been sitting late to-night by the bedside of a wounded captain, a special friend of mine, lying with a painful fracture of left leg in one of the hospitals, in a large ward partially vacant. The lights were put out, all but a little candle, far from where I sat. The full moon shone in through the windows, making long, slanting silvery patches on the floor. All was still, my friend too was silent, but could not sleep; so I sat there by him, slowly wafting the fan, and occupied with the musings that arose out of the scene, the long shadowy ward, the beautiful ghostly moonlight on the floor, the white beds, here and there an occupant with huddled form, the bed-clothes thrown off. The hospitals have a number of cases of sun-stroke and exhaustion by heat, from the late reviews. There are many such from the Sixth corps, from the hot parade of day before yesterday. (Some of these shows cost the lives of scores of men.)

Sunday, Sep. 10.—Visited Douglas and Stanton hospitals. They are quite full. Many of the cases are bad ones, lingering wounds, and old sickness. There is a more than usual look of despair on the countenances of many of the men; hope has left them. I went through the wards, talking as usual. There are several here from the confederate army whom I had seen in other hospitals, and they recognized me. Two were in a dying condition.

CALHOUN'S REAL MONUMENT

IN ONE of the hospital tents for special cases, as I sat to-day tending a new amputation, I heard a couple of neighboring soldiers talking to each other from their cots. One down with fever, but improving, had come up belated from Charleston not long before. The other was what we now call an "old veteran," (*i.e.*, he was a Connecticut youth, probably of less than the age of twenty-five years, the four last of which he had spent in active service in the war in all parts of the country.) The two were chatting of one thing and another. The fever soldier spoke of John C. Calhoun's monument, which he had seen, and was describing it. The veteran said: "I have seen Calhoun's monument. That you saw is not the real monument. But I have seen it. It is the desolated, ruined south; nearly the whole generation of young men between seventeen and thirty destroyed or maim'd; all the old families used up—the rich impoverish'd, the plantations cover'd with weeds, the slaves unloos'd and become the masters, and the name of southerner blacken'd with every shame—all that is Calhoun's real monument."

HOSPITALS CLOSING

October 3.—There are two army hospitals now remaining. I went to the largest of these (Douglas) and spent the afternoon and evening. There are many sad cases, old wounds, incurable sickness, and some of the wounded from the March and April battles before Richmond. Few realize how sharp and bloody those closing battles were. Our men exposed themselves more than usual; press'd ahead without urging. Then the southerners fought with extra desperation. Both sides knew that with the successful chasing of the rebel cabal from Richmond, and the occupation of that city by the national troops, the game was up. The dead and wounded were unusually many. Of the wounded the last lingering driblets have been brought to hospital here. I find many rebel wounded here, and have been extra busy to-day 'tending to the worst cases of them with the rest.

Oct., Nov. and Dec., '65—Sundays.—Every Sunday of these months visited Harewood hospital out in the woods, pleasant and recluse, some two and a half or three miles north of the capitol. The situation is healthy, with broken ground, grassy slopes and patches of oak woods, the trees large and fine. It was one of the most extensive of the hospitals, now reduced to four or five partially occupied wards, the numerous others being vacant. In November, this became the last military hospital kept up by the government, all the others being closed. Cases of the worst and most incurable wounds, obstinate illness, and of poor fellows who have no homes to go to, are found here.

Dec. 10—Sunday.—Again spending a good part of the day at Hare-

wood. I write this about an hour before sundown. I have walk'd out
for a few minutes to the edge of the woods to soothe myself with
the hour and scene. It is a glorious, warm, golden-sunny, still afternoon. The only noise is from a crowd of cawing crows, on some
trees three hundred yards distant. Clusters of gnats swimming and
dancing in the air in all directions. The oak leaves are thick under
the bare trees, and give a strong and delicious perfume. Inside the
wards everything is gloomy. Death is there. As I enter'd, I was confronted by it the first thing; a corpse of a poor soldier, just dead,
of typhoid fever. The attendants had just straighten'd the limbs,
put coppers on the eyes, and were laying it out.

The roads.—A great recreation, the past three years, has been in
taking long walks out from Washington, five, seven, perhaps ten
miles and back; generally with my friend Peter Doyle, who is as
fond of it as I am. Fine moonlight nights, over the perfect military
roads, hard and smooth—or Sundays—we had these delightful walks,
never to be forgotten. The roads connecting Washington and the
numerous forts around the city, made one useful result, at any rate,
out of the war.

TYPICAL SOLDIERS

EVEN the typical soldiers I have been personally intimate with,—
it seems to me if I were to make a list of them it would be like
a city directory. Some few only have I mention'd in the foregoing
pages—most are dead—a few yet living. There is Reuben Farwell,
of Michigan, (little 'Mitch;') Benton H. Wilson, color-bearer, 185th
New York; Wm. Stansberry; Manvill Winterstein, Ohio; Bethuel
Smith; Capt. Simms, of 51st New York, (kill'd at Petersburgh mine
explosion,) Capt. Sam. Pooley and Lieut. Fred. McReady, same
reg't. Also, same reg't., my brother, George W. Whitman—in active
service all through, four years, re-enlisting twice—was promoted,
step by step, (several times immediately after battles,) lieutenant,
captain, major and lieut. colonel—was in the actions at Roanoke,
Newbern, 2d Bull Run, Chantilly, South Mountain, Antietam, Fredericksburgh, Vicksburgh, Jackson, the bloody conflicts of the Wilderness, and at Spottsylvania, Cold Harbor, and afterwards around
Petersburgh; at one of these latter was taken prisoner, and pass'd
four or five months in secesh military prisons, narrowly escaping
with life, from a severe fever, from starvation and half-nakedness in
the winter. (What a history that 51st New York had! Went out
early—march'd, fought everywhere—was in storms at sea, nearly
wreck'd—storm'd forts—tramp'd hither and yon in Virginia, night

and day, summer of '62—afterwards Kentucky and Mississippi—
re-enlisted—was in all the engagements and campaigns, as above.)
I strengthen and comfort myself much with the certainty that the
capacity for just such regiments, (hundreds, thousands of them)
is inexhaustible in the United States, and that there isn't a county
nor a township in the republic—nor a street in any city—but could
turn out, and, on occasion, would turn out, lots of just such typical
soldiers, whenever wanted.

"CONVULSIVENESS"

As I have look'd over the proof-sheets of the preceding pages, I have
once or twice fear'd that my diary would prove, at best, but a
batch of convulsively written reminiscences. Well, be it so. They
are but parts of the actual distraction, heat, smoke and excitement
of those times. The war itself, with the temper of society preceding
it, can indeed be best described by that very word *convulsiveness*.

THREE YEARS SUMM'D UP

DURING those three years in hospital, camp or field, I made over
six hundred visits or tours, and went, as I estimate, counting all,
among from eighty thousand to a hundred thousand of the wounded
and sick, as sustainer of spirit and body in some degree, in time
of need. These visits varied from an hour or two, to all day or night;
for with dear or critical cases I generally watch'd all night. Sometimes I took up my quarters in the hospital, and slept or watch'd
there several nights in succession. Those three years I consider
the greatest privilege and satisfaction, (with all their feverish excitements and physical deprivations and lamentable sights,) and,
of course, the most profound lesson of my life. I can say that in my
ministerings I comprehended all, whoever came in my way, northern
or southern, and slighted none. It arous'd and brought out and
decided undream'd-of depths of emotion. It has given me my most
fervent views of the true *ensemble* and extent of the States. While
I was with wounded and sick in thousands of cases from the New
England States, and from New York, New Jersey, and Pennsylvania,
and from Michigan, Wisconsin, Ohio, Indiana, Illinois, and all the
Western States, I was with more or less from all the States, North
and South, without exception. I was with many from the border
States, especially from Maryland and Virginia, and found, during
those lurid years 1862–63, far more Union southerners, especially
Tennesseans, than is supposed. I was with many rebel officers and

men among our wounded, and gave them always what I had, and
tried to cheer them the same as any. I was among the army teamsters considerably, and, indeed, always found myself drawn to
them. Among the black soldiers, wounded or sick, and in the contra-
band camps, I also took my way whenever in their neighborhood,
and did what I could for them.

THE MILLION DEAD, TOO, SUMM'D UP

THE dead in this war—there they lie, strewing the fields and woods
and valleys and battle-fields of the south—Virginia, the Peninsula—
Malvern hill and Fair Oaks—the banks of the Chickahominy—the
terraces of Fredericksburgh—Antietam bridge—the grisly ravines of
Manassas—the bloody promenade of the Wilderness—the varieties
of the *strayed* dead, (the estimate of the War department is 25,000
national soldiers kill'd in battle and never buried at all, 5,000
drown'd—15,000 inhumed by strangers, or on the march in haste, in
hitherto unfound localities—2,000 graves cover'd by sand and mud
by Mississippi freshets, 3,000 carried away by caving-in of banks,
&c.,)—Gettysburgh, the West, Southwest—Vicksburgh—Chattanooga
—the trenches of Petersburgh—the numberless battles, camps, hospitals everywhere—the crop reap'd by the mighty reapers, typhoid,
dysentery, inflammations—and blackest and loathesomest of all, the
dead and living burial-pits, the prison-pens of Andersonville, Salisbury, Belle-Isle, &c., (not Dante's pictured hell and all its woes, its
degradations, filthy torments, excell'd those prisons)—the dead, the
dead, the dead—*our* dead—or South or North, ours all, (all, all, all,
finally dear to me)—or East or West—Atlantic coast or Mississippi
valley—somewhere they crawl'd to die, alone, in bushes, low gullies,
or on the sides of hills—(there, in secluded spots, their skeletons,
bleach'd bones, tufts of hair, buttons, fragments of clothing, are
occasionally found yet)—our young men once so handsome and so
joyous, taken from us—the son from the mother, the husband from
the wife, the dear friend from the dear friend—the clusters of camp
graves, in Georgia, the Carolinas, and in Tennessee—the single
graves left in the woods or by the road-side, (hundreds, thousands,
obliterated)—the corpses floated down the rivers, and caught and
lodged, (dozens, scores, floated down the upper Potomac, after the
cavalry engagements, the pursuit of Lee, following Gettysburgh)
—some lie at the bottom of the sea—the general million, and the
special cemeteries in almost all the States—the infinite dead—(the
land entire saturated, perfumed with their impalpable ashes' exhala-
tion in Nature's chemistry distill'd, and shall be so forever, in every

future grain of wheat and ear of corn, and every flower that grows, and every breath we draw)—not only Northern dead leavening Southern soil—thousands, aye tens of thousands, of Southerners, crumble to-day in Northern earth.

And everywhere among these countless graves—everywhere in the many soldiers Cemeteries of the Nation, (there are now, I believe, over seventy of them)—as at the time in the vast trenches, the depositories of slain, Northern and Southern, after the great battles—not only where the scathing trail passed those years, but radiating since in all the peaceful quarters of the land—we see, and ages yet may see, on monuments and gravestones, singly or in masses, to thousands or tens of thousands, the significant word Unknown.

(In some of the cemeteries nearly *all* the dead are unknown. At Salisbury, N. C., for instance, the known are only 85, while the unknown are 12,027, and 11,700 of these are buried in trenches. A national monument has been put up here, by order of Congress, to mark the spot—but what visible, material monument can ever fittingly commemorate that spot?)

THE REAL WAR WILL NEVER GET IN THE BOOKS

And so good-bye to the war. I know not how it may have been, or may be, to others—to me the main interest I found, (and still, on recollection, find,) in the rank and file of the armies, both sides, and in those specimens amid the hospitals, and even the dead on the field. To me the points illustrating the latent personal character and eligibilities of these States, in the two or three millions of American young and middle-aged men, North and South, embodied in those armies—and especially the one-third or one-fourth of their number, stricken by wounds or disease at some time in the course of the contest—were of more significance even than the political interests involved. (As so much of a race depends on how it faces death, and how it stands personal anguish and sickness. As, in the glints of emotions under emergencies, and the indirect traits and asides in Plutarch, we get far profounder clues to the antique world than all its more formal history.)

Future years will never know the seething hell and the black infernal background of countless minor scenes and interiors, (not the official surface-courteousness of the Generals, not the few great battles) of the Secession war; and it is best they should not—the real war will never get in the books. In the mushy influences of current times, too, the fervid atmosphere and typical events of those years are in danger of being totally forgotten. I have at night watch'd by the side of a sick man in the hospital, one who could not live many hours. I have seen his eyes flash and burn as he raised himself and recurr'd to the cruelties on his surrender'd brother, and mutilations of the corpse afterward. (See, in the preceding pages, the incident at Upperville—the seventeen kill'd as in the description, were left there on the ground. After they dropt dead, no one touch'd them—all were made sure of, however. The carcasses were left for the citizens to bury or not, as they chose.)

Such was the war. It was not a quadrille in a ball-room. Its interior history will not only never be written—its practicality, minutiæ of deeds and passions, will never be even suggested. The actual soldier of 1862–'65, North and South, with all his ways, his incredible dauntlessness, habits, practices, tastes, language, his fierce friendship, his appetite, rankness, his superb strength and animality, lawless gait, and a hundred unnamed lights and shades of camp, I say, will never be written—perhaps must not and should not be.

The preceding notes may furnish a few stray glimpses into that life, and into those lurid interiors, never to be fully convey'd to the future. The hospital part of the drama from '61 to '65, deserves indeed to be recorded. Of that many-threaded drama, with its sudden and strange surprises, its confounding of prophecies, its moments of despair, the dread of foreign interference, the interminable campaigns, the bloody battles, the mighty and cumbrous and green armies, the drafts and bounties—the immense money expenditure, like a heavy-pouring constant rain—with, over the whole land, the last three years of the struggle, an unending, universal mourning-wail of women, parents, orphans—the marrow of the tragedy concentrated in those Army Hospitals—(it seem'd sometimes as if the whole interest of the land, North and South, was one vast central hospital, and all the rest of the affair but flanges)— those forming the untold and unwritten history of the war—infinitely greater (like life's) than the few scraps and distortions that are ever told or written. Think how much, and of importance, will be —how much, civic and military, has already been—buried in the grave, in eternal darkness.

AN INTERREGNUM PARAGRAPH

SEVERAL years now elapse before I resume my diary. I continued at Washington working in the Attorney-General's department through

'66 and '67, and some time afterward. In February '73 I was stricken down by paralysis, gave up my desk, and migrated to Camden, New Jersey, where I lived during '74 and '75, quite unwell—but after that began to grow better; commenc'd going for weeks at a time, even for months, down in the country, to a charmingly recluse and rural spot along Timber creek, twelve or thirteen miles from where it enters the Delaware river. Domicil'd at the farm-house of my friends, the Staffords, near by, I lived half the time along this creek and its adjacent fields and lanes. And it is to my life here that I, perhaps, owe partial recovery (a sort of second wind, or semi-renewal of the lease of life) from the prostration of 1874–'75. If the notes of that outdoor life could only prove as glowing to you, reader dear, as the experience itself was to me. Doubtless in the course of the following, the fact of invalidism will crop out, (I call myself *a half-Paralytic* these days, and reverently bless the Lord it is no worse,) between some of the lines—but I get my share of fun and healthy hours, and shall try to indicate them. (The trick is, I find, to tone your wants and tastes low down enough, and make much of negatives, and of mere daylight and the skies.)

NEW THEMES ENTERED UPON

1876, '77.—I find the woods in mid-May and early June my best places for composition.[9] Seated on logs or stumps there, or resting on rails, nearly all the following memoranda have been jotted down. Wherever I go, indeed, winter or summer, city or country, alone at home or traveling, I must take notes—(the ruling passion strong in age and disablement, and even the approach of—but I must not say it yet.) Then underneath the following excerpta—crossing the *t*'s and dotting the *i*'s of certain moderate movements of late years— I am fain to fancy the foundations of quite a lesson learn'd. After you have exhausted what there is in business, politics, conviviality, love, and so on—have found that none of these finally satisfy, or permanently wear—what remains? Nature remains; to bring out from their torpid recesses, the affinities of a man or woman with the open air, the trees, fields, the changes of seasons—the sun by day and the stars of heaven by night. We will begin from these convictions. Literature flies so high and is so hotly spiced, that our notes may seem hardly more than breaths of common air, or draughts of water to drink. But that is part of our lesson.

Dear, soothing, healthy, restoration-hours—after three confining years of paralysis—after the long strain of the war, and its wounds and death.

ENTERING A LONG FARM-LANE

As EVERY man has his hobby-liking, mine is for a real farm-lane fenced by old chestnut-rails gray-green with dabs of moss and lichen, copious weeds and briers growing in spots athwart the heaps of stray-pick'd stones at the fence bases—irregular paths worn between, and horse and cow tracks—all characteristic accompaniments marking and scenting the neighborhood in their seasons—apple-tree blossoms in forward April—pigs, poultry, a field of August buckwheat, and in another the long flapping tassels of maize—and so to the pond, the expansion of the creek, the secluded-beautiful, with young and old trees, and such recesses and vistas.

TO THE SPRING AND BROOK

So, STILL sauntering on, to the spring under the willows—musical as soft clinking glasses—pouring a sizeable stream, thick as my neck, pure and clear, out from its vent where the bank arches over like a great brown shaggy eyebrow or mouth-roof—gurgling, gurgling ceaselessly—meaning, saying something, of course (if one could only translate it)—always gurgling there, the whole year through —never giving out—oceans of mint, blackberries in summer—choice of light and shade—just the place for my July sun-baths and water-baths too—but mainly the inimitable soft sound-gurgles of it, as I sit there hot afternoon. How they and all grow into me, day after day—everything in keeping—the wild, just-palpable perfume, and the dapple of leaf-shadows, and all the natural-medicinal, elemental-moral influences of the spot.

Babble on, O brook, with that utterance of thine! I too will express what I have gather'd in my days and progress, native, sub-terranean, past—and now thee. Spin and wind thy way—I with thee, a little while, at any rate. As I haunt thee so often, season by season, thou knowest reckest not me, (yet why be so certain? who can tell?)—but I will learn from thee, and dwell on thee—receive, copy, print from thee.

AN EARLY SUMMER REVEILLE

AWAY then to loosen, to unstring the divine bow, so tense, so long. Away, from curtain, carpet, sofa, book—from "society"—from city house, street, and modern improvements and luxuries—away to the primitive winding, aforementioned wooded creek, with its untrimm'd bushes and turfy banks—away from ligatures, tight boots, buttons, and the whole cast-iron civilizee life—from entourage of artificial store, machine, studio, office, parlor—from tailordom and fashion's clothes—from any clothes, perhaps, for the nonce, the summer heats advancing, there in those watery, shaded solitudes. Away, thou soul, (let me pick thee out singly, reader dear, and talk in perfect freedom, negligently, confidentially,) for one day and night at least, returning to the naked source-life of us all—to the breast of the great silent savage all-acceptive Mother. Alas! how many of us are so sodden—how many have wander'd so far away, that return is almost impossible.

But to my jottings, taking them as they come, from the heap, without particular selection. There is little consecutiveness in dates. They run any time within nearly five or six years. Each was carelessly pencilled in the open air, at the time and place. The printers will learn this to some vexation perhaps, as much of their copy is from those hastily-written first notes.

BIRDS MIGRATING AT MIDNIGHT

Did you ever chance to hear the midnight flight of birds passing through the air and darkness overhead, in countless armies, changing their early or late summer habitat? It is something not to be forgotten. A friend called me up just after 12 last night to mark the peculiar noise of unusually immense flocks migrating north (rather late this year.) In the silence, shadow and delicious odor of the hour, (the natural perfume belonging to the night alone,) I thought it rare music. You could *hear* the characteristic motion— once or twice "the rush of mighty wings," but oftener a velvety rustle, long drawn out—sometimes quite near—with continual calls and chirps, and some song-notes. It all lasted from 12 till after 3. Once in a while the species was plainly distinguishable; I could make out the bobolink, tanager, Wilson's thrush, white-crown'd sparrow, and occasionally from high in the air came the notes of the plover.

BUMBLE-BEES

May-month—month of swarming, singing, mating birds—the bumble-bee month—month of the flowering lilac—(and then my own birth-month.) As I jot this paragraph, I am out just after sunrise, and down towards the creek. The lights, perfumes, melodies—the blue birds, grass birds and robins, in every direction— the noisy, vocal, natural concert. For undertones, a neighboring wood-pecker tapping his tree, and the distant clarion of chanticleer. Then the fresh earth smells—the colors, the delicate drabs and thin blues of the perspective. The bright green of the grass has receiv'd an added tinge from the last two days' mildness and moisture. How the sun silently mounts in the broad clear sky, on his day's journey! How the warm beams bathe all, and come streaming kissingly and almost hot on my face.

A while since the croaking of the pond-frogs and the first white of the dog-wood blossoms. Now the golden dandelions in endless profusion, spotting the ground everywhere. The white cherry and pear-blows—the wild violets, with their blue eyes looking up and saluting my feet, as I saunter the wood-edge—the rosy blush of budding apple-trees—the light-clear emerald hue of the wheat-fields —the darker green of the rye—a warm elasticity pervading the air— the cedar-bushes profusely deck'd with their little brown apples— the summer fully awakening—the convocation of black birds, garrulous flocks of them, gathering on some tree, and making the hour and place noisy as I sit near.

Later.—Nature marches in procession, in sections, like the corps of an army. All have done much for me, and still do. But for the last two days it has been the great wild bee, the humble-bee, or "bumble," as the children call him. As I walk, or hobble, from the farm-house down to the creek, I traverse the before-mention'd lane, fenced by old rails, with many splits, splinters, breaks, holes, &c., the choice habitat of those crooning, hairy insects. Up and down and by and between these rails, they swarm and dart and fly in countless myriads. As I wend slowly along, I am often accompanied with a moving cloud of them. They play a leading part in my morning, midday or sunset rambles, and often dominate the landscape in a way I never before thought of—fill the long lane, not by scores or hundreds only, but by thousands. Large and vivacious and swift, with wonderful momentum and a loud swelling perpetual hum, varied now and then by something almost like a shriek, they dart to and fro, in rapid flashes, chasing each other, and (little things as they are,) conveying to me a new and pronounc'd sense of strength, beauty, vitality and movement. Are they in their mating season? or what is the meaning of this plenitude, swiftness, eagerness, display? As I walk'd, I thought I was follow'd by a particular swarm, but upon observation I saw that it was a rapid succession of changing swarms, one after another.

As I write, I am seated under a big wild-cherry tree—the warm day temper'd by partial clouds and a fresh breeze, neither too heavy nor light—and here I sit long and long, envelop'd in the deep musical drone of these bees, flitting, balancing, darting to and fro about me by hundreds—big fellows with light yellow jackets, great glistening swelling bodies, stumpy heads and gauzy wings—humming their perpetual rich mellow boom. (Is there not a hint in it for a musical composition, of which it should be the back-ground? some bumble-bee symphony?) How it all nourishes, lulls me, in the way most needed; the open air, the rye-fields, the apple orchards. The last two days have been faultless in sun, breeze, temperature and everything; never two more perfect days, and I have enjoy'd them wonderfully. My health is somewhat better, and my spirit at peace. (Yet the anniversary of the saddest loss and sorrow of my life is close at hand.)

Another jotting, another perfect day: forenoon, from 7 to 9, two hours envelop'd in sound of bumble-bees and bird-music. Down in the apple-trees and in a neighboring cedar were three or four russet-back'd thrushes, each singing his best, and roulading in ways I never heard surpass'd. Two hours I abandon myself to hearing them, and indolently absorbing the scene. Almost every bird I notice has a special time in the year—sometimes limited to a few days—when it sings its best; and now is the period of these russet-backs. Meanwhile, up and down the lane, the darting, droning, musical bumble-bees. A great swarm again for my entourage as I return home, moving along with me as before.

As I write this, two or three weeks later, I am sitting near the brook under a tulip tree, 70 feet high, thick with the fresh verdure of its young maturity—a beautiful object—every branch, every leaf perfect. From top to bottom, seeking the sweet juice in the blossoms, it swarms with myriads of these wild bees, whose loud and steady humming makes an undertone to the whole, and to my mood and the hour. All of which I will bring to a close by extracting the following verses from Henry A. Beers's little volume:

> "As I lay yonder in tall grass
> A drunken bumble-bee went past
> Delirious with honey toddy.
> The golden sash about his body
> Scarce kept it in his swollen belly
> Distent with honeysuckle jelly.
> Rose liquor and the sweet-pea wine
> Had fill'd his soul with song divine;
> Deep had he drunk the warm night through,
> His hairy thighs were wet with dew.
> Full many an antic he had play'd
> While the world went round through sleep and shade.

Oft had he lit with thirsty lip
Some flower-cup's nectar'd sweets to sip,
When on smooth petals he would slip,
Or over tangled stamens trip,
And headlong in the pollen roll'd,
Crawl out quite dusted o'er with gold;
Or else his heavy feet would stumble
Against some bud, and down he'd tumble
Amongst the grass; there lie and grumble
In low, soft bass—poor maudlin bumble!"

CEDAR-APPLES

As I journey'd to-day in a light wagon ten or twelve miles through
the country, nothing pleas'd me more, in their homely beauty and
novelty (I had either never seen the little things to such advantage,
or had never noticed them before) than that peculiar fruit, with its
profuse clear-yellow dangles of inch-long silk or yarn, in boundless
profusion spotting the dark-green cedar bushes—contrasting well
with their bronze tufts—the flossy shreds covering the knobs all
over, like a shock of wild hair on elfin pates. On my ramble afterward down by the creek I pluck'd one from its bush, and shall keep
it. These cedar-apples last only a little while however, and soon
crumble and fade.

SUMMER SIGHTS AND INDOLENCES

June 10th.—As I write, 5½ P.M., here by the creek, nothing can
exceed the quiet splendor and freshness around me. We had a
heavy shower, with brief thunder and lightning, in the middle of
the day; and since, overhead, one of those not uncommon yet indescribable skies (in quality, not details or forms) of limpid blue,
with rolling silver-fringed clouds, and a pure-dazzling sun. For
underlay, trees in fulness of tender foliage—liquid, reedy, long-
drawn notes of birds—based by the fretful mewing of a querulous
cat-bird, and the pleasant chippering-shriek of two kingfishers. I
have been watching the latter the last half hour, on their regular
evening frolic over and in the stream; evidently a spree of the
liveliest kind. They pursue each other, whirling and wheeling
around, with many a jocund downward dip, splashing the spray in
jets of diamonds—and then off they swoop, with slanting wings and
graceful flight, sometimes so near me I can plainly see their dark-
gray feather-bodies and milk-white necks.

SUNDOWN PERFUME—QUAIL-NOTES— THE HERMIT-THRUSH

June 19th, 4 to 6½, P.M.—Sitting alone by the creek—solitude here, but the scene bright and vivid enough—the sun shining, and quite a fresh wind blowing (some heavy showers last night,) the grass and trees looking their best—the clare-obscure of different greens, shadows, half-shadows, and the dappling glimpses of the water, through recesses—the wild flageolet-note of a quail near by—the just-heard fretting of some hylas down there in the pond—crows cawing in the distance—a drove of young hogs rooting in soft ground near the oak under which I sit—some come sniffing near me, and then scamper away, with grunts. And still the clear notes of the quail—the quiver of leaf-shadows over the paper as I write— the sky aloft, with white clouds, and the sun well declining to the west—the swift darting of many sand-swallows coming and going, their holes in a neighboring marl-bank—the odor of the cedar and oak, so palpable, as evening approaches—perfume, color, the bronze- and-gold of nearly ripen'd wheat—clover-fields, with honey-scent— the well-up maize, with long and rustling leaves—the great patches of thriving potatoes, dusky green, fleck'd all over with white blos- soms—the old, warty, venerable oak above me—and ever, mix'd with the dual notes of the quail, the soughing of the wind through some near-by pines.

As I rise for return, I linger long to a delicious song-epilogue (is it the hermit-thrush?) from some bushy recess off there in the swamp, repeated leisurely and pensively over and over again. This, to the circle-gambols of the swallows flying by dozens in concentric rings in the last rays of sunset, like flashes of some airy wheel.

A JULY AFTERNOON BY THE POND

THE fervent heat, but so much more endurable in this pure air— the white and pink pond-blossoms, with great heart-shaped leaves; the glassy waters of the creek, the banks, with dense bushery, and the picturesque beeches and shade and turf; the tremulous, reedy call of some bird from recesses, breaking the warm, indolent, half- voluptuous silence; an occasional wasp, hornet, honey-bee or bumble (they hover near my hands or face, yet annoy me not, nor I them, as they appear to examine, find nothing, and away they go) —the vast space of the sky overhead so clear, and the buzzard up there sailing his slow whirl in majestic spirals and discs; just over the surface of the pond, two large slate-color'd dragon-flies, with wings of lace, circling and darting and occasionally balancing themselves quite still, their wings quivering all the time, (are they not showing off for my amusement?)—the pond itself, with the sword-shaped calamus; the water snakes—occasionally a flitting blackbird, with red dabs on his shoulders, as he darts slantingly by—the sounds that bring out the solitude, warmth, light and shade—the quawk of some pond duck—(the crickets and grasshoppers are mute in the noon heat, but I hear the song of the first cicadas;)—then at some distance the rattle and whirr of a reaping machine as the horses draw it on a rapid walk through a rye field on the opposite side of the creek—(what was the yellow or light-brown bird, large as a young hen, with short neck and long-stretch'd legs I just saw, in flapping and awkward flight over there through the trees?) the prevailing delicate, yet palpable, spicy, grassy, clovery perfume to my nostrils; and over all, encircling all, to my sight and soul, the free space of the sky, transparent and blue—and hovering there in the west, a mass of white-gray fleecy clouds the sailors call "shoals of mackerel"—the sky, with silver swirls like locks of toss'd hair, spreading, expanding—a vast voiceless, formless simulacrum—yet may-be the most real reality and formulator of everything—who knows?

LOCUSTS AND KATYDIDS

Aug. 22.—Reedy monotones of locust, or sounds of katydid—I hear the latter at night, and the other both day and night. I thought the morning and evening warble of birds delightful; but I find I can listen to these strange insects with just as much pleasure. A single locust is now heard near noon from a tree two hundred feet off, as I write—a long whirring, continued, quite loud noise graded in distinct whirls, or swinging circles, increasing in strength and rapidity up to a certain point, and then a fluttering, quietly tapering fall. Each strain is continued from one to two minutes. The locust-song is very appropriate to the scene—gushes, has meaning, is masculine, is like some fine old wine, not sweet, but far better than sweet.

But the katydid—how shall I describe its piquant utterances? One sings from a willow-tree just outside my open bedroom window, twenty yards distant; every clear night for a fortnight past has sooth'd me to sleep. I rode through a piece of woods for a hundred rods the other evening, and heard the katydids by myriads—very curious for once; but I like better my single neighbor on the tree.

Let me say more about the song of the locust, even to repetition; a long, chromatic, tremulous crescendo, like a brass disk whirling round and round, emitting wave after wave of notes, beginning with a certain moderate beat or measure, rapidly increasing in speed and emphasis, reaching a point of great energy and significance, and then quickly and gracefully dropping down and out. Not the melody of the singing-bird—far from it; the common musician might think without melody, but surely having to the finer ear a harmony of its own; monotonous—but what a swing there is in that brassy drone, round and round, cymbal-line—or like the whirling of brass quoits.

THE LESSON OF A TREE

Sept. 1.—I should not take either the biggest or the most picturesque tree to illustrate it. Here is one of my favorites now before me, a fine yellow poplar, quite straight, perhaps 90 feet high, and four thick at the butt. How strong, vital, enduring! how dumbly eloquent! What suggestions of imperturbability and *being*, as against the human trait of mere *seeming*. Then the qualities, almost emotional, palpably artistic, heroic, of a tree; so innocent and harmless, yet so savage. It *is*, yet says nothing. How it rebukes by its tough and equable serenity all weathers, this gusty-temper'd little whiffet, man, that runs indoors at a mite of rain or snow. Science (or rather half-way science) scoffs at reminiscence of dryad and hamadryad, and of trees speaking. But, if they don't, they do as well as most speaking, writing, poetry, sermons—or rather they do a great deal better. I should say indeed that those old dryad-reminiscences are quite as true as any, and profounder than most reminiscences we get. ("Cut this out," as the quack mediciners say, and keep by you.) Go and sit in a grove or woods, with one or more of those voiceless companions, and read the foregoing, and think.

One lesson from affiliating a tree—perhaps the greatest moral lesson anyhow from earth, rocks, animals, is that same lesson of inherency, of *what is*, without the least regard to what the looker on (the critic) supposes or says, or whether he likes or dislikes. What worse—what more general malady pervades each and all of us, our literature, education, attitude toward each other, (even toward ourselves,) than a morbid trouble about *seems*, (generally temporarily seems too,) and no trouble at all, or hardly any, about the sane, slow-growing, perennial, real parts of character, books, friendship, marriage—humanity's invisible foundations and hold-together? (As the all-basis, the nerve, the great-sympathetic, the plenum within humanity, giving stamp to everything, is necessarily invisible.)

Aug. 4, 6 P.M.—Lights and shades and rare effects on tree-foliage and grass—transparent greens, grays, &c., all in sunset pomp and dazzle. The clear beams are now thrown in many new places, on the quilted, seam'd, bronze-drab, lower tree-trunks, shadow'd except at this hour—now flooding their young and old columnar ruggedness with strong light, unfolding to my sense new amazing features of silent, shaggy charm, the solid bark, the expression of harmless impassiveness, with many a bulge and gnarl unreck'd before. In the revealings of such light, such exceptional hour, such mood, one does not wonder at the old story fables, (indeed, why fables?) of people falling into love-sickness with trees, seiz'd extatic with the mystic realism of the resistless silent strength in them—*strength,* which after all is perhaps the last, completest, highest beauty.

Trees I am familiar with here

Oaks, (many kinds—one sturdy old fellow, vital, green, bushy, five feet thick at the butt, I sit under every day.)

Cedars, plenty.

Tulip trees, (*Liriodendron,* is of the magnolia family—I have seen it in Michigan and southern Illinois, 140 feet high and 8 feet thick at the butt [10]; does not transplant well; best rais'd from seeds—the lumbermen call it yellow poplar.)

Sycamores.

Gum-trees, both sweet and sour.

Beeches.

Black-walnuts.

Sassafras.

Willows.

Catalpas.

Persimmons.

Mountain-ash

Hickories.

Maples, many kinds.

Locusts.

Birches.

Dogwood.

Pine.

the Elm.

Chestnut.

Linden.

Aspen.

Spruce.

Hornbeam.

Laurel.

Holly.

AUTUMN SIDE-BITS

Sept. 20.—Under an old black oak, glossy and green, exhaling aroma —amid a grove the Albic druids might have chosen—envelop'd in the warmth and light of the noonday sun, and swarms of flitting insects —with the harsh cawing of many crows a hundred rods away—here I sit in solitude, absorbing, enjoying all. The corn, stack'd in its cone-shaped stacks, russet-color'd and sere—a large field spotted thick with scarlet-gold pumpkins—an adjoining one of cabbages, showing well in their green and pearl, mottled by much light and shade—melon patches, with their bulging ovals, and great silver-streak'd, ruffled,

broad-edged leaves—and many an autumn sight and sound beside—
the distant scream of a flock of guinea-hens—and pour'd over all the
September breeze, with pensive cadence through the tree tops.

Another Day.—The ground in all directions strew'd with *debris* from
a storm. Timber creek, as I slowly pace its banks, has ebb'd low, and
shows reaction from the turbulent swell of the late equinoctial. As I
look around, I take account of stock—weeds and shrubs, knolls, paths,
occasional stumps, some with smooth'd tops, (several I use as seats
of rest, from place to place, and from one I am now jotting these lines,)
—frequent wild-flowers, little white, star-shaped things, or the cardinal
red of the lobelia, or the cherry-ball seeds of the perennial rose, or
the many-threaded vines winding up and around trunks of trees.

Oct. 1, 2 and 3.—Down every day in the solitude of the creek. A
serene autumn sun and westerly breeze to-day (3d) as I sit here, the
water surface prettily moving in wind-ripples before me. On a stout
old beech at the edge, decayed and slanting, almost fallen to the
stream, yet with life and leaves in its mossy limbs, a gray squirrel,
exploring, runs up and down, flirts his tail, leaps to the ground, sits
on his haunches upright as he sees me, (a Darwinian hint?) and then
races up the tree again.

Oct. 4.—Cloudy and coolish; signs of incipient winter. Yet pleasant
here, the leaves thick-falling, the ground brown with them already;
rich coloring, yellows of all hues, pale and dark-green, shades from
lightest to richest red—all set in and toned down by the prevailing
brown of the earth and gray of the sky. So, winter is coming; and I
yet in my sickness. I sit here amid all these fair sights and vital influences, and abandon myself to that thought, with its wandering trains
of speculation.

THE SKY—DAYS AND NIGHTS—HAPPINESS

Oct. 20.—A clear, crispy day—dry and breezy air, full of oxygen. Out
of the sane, silent, beauteous miracles that envelope and fuse me—
trees, water, grass, sunlight, and early frost—the one I am looking at
most to-day is the sky. It has that delicate, transparent blue, peculiar
to autumn, and the only clouds are little or larger white ones, giving
their still and spiritual motion to the great concave. All through the
earlier day (say from 7 to 11) it keeps a pure, yet vivid blue. But as
noon approaches the color gets lighter, quite gray for two or three
hours—then still paler for a spell, till sun-down—which last I watch
dazzling through the interstices of a knoll of big trees—darts of fire
and a gorgeous show of light-yellow, liver-color and red, with a vast
silver glaze askant on the water—the transparent shadows, shafts,

sparkle, and vivid colors beyond all the paintings ever made.

I don't know what or how, but it seems to me mostly owing to these skies, (every now and then I think, while I have of course seen them every day of my life, I never really saw the skies before,) I have had this autumn some wondrously contented hours—may I not say perfectly happy ones? As I've read, Byron just before his death told a friend that he had known but three happy hours during his whole existence. Then there is the old German legend of the king's bell, to the same point. While I was out there by the wood, that beautiful sunset through the trees, I thought of Byron's and the bell story, and the notion started in me that I was having a happy hour. (Though perhaps my best moments I never jot down; when they come I cannot afford to break the charm by inditing memoranda. I just abandon myself to the mood, and let it float on, carrying me in its placid extasy.)

What is happiness, anyhow? Is this one of its hours, or the like of it?—so impalpable—a mere breath, an evanescent tinge? I am not sure —so let me give myself the benefit of the doubt. Hast Thou, pellucid, in Thy azure depths, medicine for case like mine? (Ah, the physical shatter and troubled spirit of me the last three years.) And dost Thou subtly mystically now drip it through the air invisibly upon me?

Night of Oct. 28.—The heavens unusually transparent—the stars out by myriads—the great path of the Milky Way, with its branch, only seen of very clear nights—Jupiter, setting in the west, looks like a huge hap-hazard splash, and has a little star for companion.

> *Clothed in his white garments,*
> *Into the round and clear arena slowly entered the brahmin,*
> *Holding a little child by the hand,*
> *Like the moon with the planet Jupiter in a cloudless night-sky.*
> Old Hindu Poem.

Early in November.—At its farther end the lane already described opens into a broad grassy upland field of over twenty acres, slightly sloping to the south. Here I am accustom'd to walk for sky views and effects, either morning or sundown. To-day from this field my soul is calm'd and expanded beyond description, the whole forenoon by the clear blue arching over all, cloudless, nothing particular, only sky and daylight. Their soothing accompaniments, autumn leaves, the cool dry air, the faint aroma—crows cawing in the distance—two great buzzards wheeling gracefully and slowly far up there—the occasional murmur of the wind, sometimes quite gently, then threatening through the trees—a gang of farm-laborers loading corn-stalks in a field in sight, and the patient horses waiting.

COLORS—A CONTRAST

Such a play of colors and lights, different seasons, different hours of the day—the lines of the far horizon where the faint-tinged edge of the landscape loses itself in the sky. As I slowly hobble up the lane toward day-close, an incomparable sunset shooting in molten sapphire and gold, shaft after shaft, through the ranks of the long-leaved corn, between me and the west.

Another day.—The rich dark green of the tulip-trees and the oaks, the gray of the swamp-willows, the dull hues of the sycamores and black-walnuts, the emerald of the cedars (after rain,) and the light yellow of the beeches.

NOVEMBER 8, '76

The forenoon leaden and cloudy, not cold or wet, but indicating both. As I hobble down here and sit by the silent pond, how different from the excitement amid which, in the cities, millions of people are now waiting news of yesterday's Presidential election, or receiving and discussing the result—in this secluded place uncared-for, unknown.

CROWS AND CROWS

Nov. 14.—As I sit here by the creek, resting after my walk, a warm languor bathes me from the sun. No sound but a cawing of crows, and no motion but their black flying figures from overhead, reflected in the mirror of the pond below. Indeed a principal feature of the scene to-day is these crows, their incessant cawing, far or near, and their countless flocks and processions moving from place to place, and at times almost darkening the air with their myriads. As I sit a moment writing this by the bank, I see the black, clear-cut reflection of them far below, flying through the watery looking-glass, by ones, twos, or long strings. All last night I heard the noises from their great roost in a neighboring wood.

A WINTER DAY ON THE SEA-BEACH

One bright December mid-day lately I spent down on the New Jersey sea-shore, reaching it by a little more than an hour's railroad trip over the old Camden and Atlantic. I had started betimes, fortified by nice strong coffee and a good breakfast (cook'd by the hands I love, my dear sister Lou's—how much better it makes the victuals taste, and then assimilate, strengthen you, perhaps make the whole day comfortable afterwards.) Five or six miles at the last, our track enter'd a broad region of salt grass meadows, intersected by lagoons, and cut up everywhere by watery runs. The sedgy perfume, delightful to my nostrils, reminded me of "the mash" and south bay of my native island. I could have journey'd contentedly till night through these flat and odorous sea-prairies. From half-past 11 till 2 I was nearly all the time along the beach, or in sight of the ocean, listening to its hoarse murmur, and inhaling the bracing and welcome breezes. First, a rapid five-mile drive over the hard sand—our carriage wheels hardly made dents in it. Then after dinner (as there were nearly two hours to spare) I walk'd off in another direction, (hardly met or saw a person,) and taking possesion of what appear'd to have been the reception-room of an old bath-house range, had a broad expanse of view all to myself —quaint, refreshing, unimpeded—a dry area of sedge and Indian grass immediately before and around me—space, simple, unornamented space. Distant vessels, and the far-off, just visible trailing smoke of an inward bound steamer; more plainly, ships, brigs, schooners, in sight, most of them with every sail set to the firm and steady wind.

The attractions, fascinations there are in sea and shore! How one dwells on their simplicity, even vacuity! What is it in us, arous'd by those indirections and directions? That spread of waves and gray-white beach, salt, monotonous, senseless—such an entire absence of art, books, talk, elegance—so indescribably comforting, even this winter day—grim, yet so delicate-looking, so spiritual—striking emotional, impalpable depths, subtler than all the poems, paintings, music, I have ever read, seen, heard. (Yet let me be fair, perhaps it is because I have read those poems and heard that music.)

SEA-SHORE FANCIES

EVEN as a boy, I had the fancy, the wish, to write a piece, perhaps a poem, about the sea-shore—that suggesting, dividing line, contact, junction, the solid marrying the liquid—that curious, lurking something, (as doubtless every objective form finally becomes to the subjective spirit,) which means far more than its mere first sight, grand as that is—blending the real and ideal, and each made portion of the other. Hours, days, in my Long Island youth and early manhood, I haunted the shores of Rockaway or Coney island, or away east to the Hamptons or Montauk. Once, at the latter place, (by the old lighthouse, nothing but sea-tossings in sight in every direction as far as the eye could reach,) I remember well, I felt that I must one day write a book expressing this liquid, mystic theme. Afterward, I recollect, how it came to me that instead of any special lyrical or epical or literary attempt, the sea-shore should be an invisible *influence*, a pervading gauge and tally for me, in my composition. (Let me give a hint here to young writers. I am not sure but I have unwittingly follow'd out the same rule with other powers besides sea and shores—avoiding them, in the way of any dead set at poetizing them, as too big for formal handling—quite satisfied if I could indirectly show that we have met and fused, even if only once, but enough—that we have really absorb'd each other and understand each other.)

There is a dream, a picture, that for years at intervals, (sometimes quite long ones, but surely again, in time,) has come noiselessly up before me, and I really believe, fiction as it is, has enter'd largely into my practical life—certainly into my writings, and shaped and color'd them. It is nothing more or less than a stretch of interminable white-brown sand, hard and smooth and broad, with the ocean perpetually, grandly, rolling in upon it, with slow-measured sweep, with rustle and hiss and foam, and many a thump as of low bass drums. This scene, this picture, I say, has risen before me at times for years. Sometimes I wake at night and can hear and see it plainly.

IN MEMORY OF THOMAS PAINE

*Spoken at Lincoln Hall, Philadelphia, Sunday, Jan. 28, '77, for
140th anniversary of T. P.'s birth-day*

SOME thirty-five years ago, in New York city, at Tammany hall, of which place I was then a frequenter, I happen'd to become quite well acquainted with Thomas Paine's perhaps most intimate chum, and certainly his later years' very frequent companion, a remarkably fine old man, Col. Fellows, who may yet be remember'd by some stray relics of that period and spot. If you will allow me, I will first give a description of the Colonel himself. He was tall, of military bearing, aged about 78 I should think, hair white as snow, clean-shaved on the face, dress'd very neatly, a tail-coat of blue cloth with metal buttons, buff vest, pantaloons of drab color, and his neck, breast and wrists showing the whitest of linen. Under all circumstances, fine manners; a good but not profuse talker, his wits still fully about him, balanced and live and undimm'd as ever. He kept pretty fair health, though so old. For employment—for he was poor—he had a post as constable of some of the upper courts. I used to think him very picturesque on the fringe of a crowd holding a tall staff, with his erect form, and his superb, bare, thick-hair'd, closely-cropt white head. The judges and young lawyers, with whom he was ever a favorite, and the subject of respect, used to call him Aristides. It was the general opinion among them that if manly rectitude and the instincts of absolute justice remain'd vital anywhere about New York City Hall, or Tammany, they were to be found in Col. Fellows. He liked young men, and enjoy'd to leisurely talk with them over a social glass of toddy, after his day's work, (he on these occasions never drank but one glass,) and it was at reiterated meetings of this kind in old Tammany's back parlor of those days, that he told me much about Thomas Paine. At one of our interviews he gave me a minute account of Paine's sickness and death. In short, from those talks, I was and am satisfied that my old friend, with his mark'd advantages, had mentally, morally and emotionally gauged the author of "Common Sense," and besides giving me a good portrait of his appearance and manners, had taken the true measure of his interior character.

Paine's practical demeanor, and much of his theoretical belief, was a mixture of the French and English schools of a century ago, and the best of both. Like most old-fashion'd people, he drank a glass or two every day, but was no tippler, nor intemperate, let alone being a drunkard. He lived simply and economically, but quite well—was always cheery and courteous, perhaps occasionally a little blunt, having very positive opinions upon politics, religion, and so forth. That he labor'd well and wisely for the States in the trying period of their parturition, and in the seeds of their character, there seems to me no question. I dare not say how much of what our Union is owning and enjoying to-day—its independence—its ardent belief in, and substantial practice of, radical human rights—and the severance of its government from all ecclesiastical and superstitious dominion—I dare not say how much of all this is owing to Thomas Paine, but I am inclined to think a good portion of it decidedly is.

But I was not going either into an analysis or eulogium of the man. I wanted to carry you back a generation or two, and give you by indirection a moment's glance—and also to ventilate a very earnest and I believe authentic opinion, nay conviction, of that time, the fruit of the interviews I have mention'd, and of questioning and cross-questioning, clench'd by my best information since, that Thomas Paine had a noble personality, as exhibited in presence, face, voice, dress, manner, and what may be call'd his atmosphere and magnetism, especially the later years of his life. I am sure of it. Of the foul and foolish fictions yet told about the circumstances of his decease, the absolute fact is that as he lived a good life, after its kind, he died calmly and philosophically, as became him. He served the embryo Union with most precious service—a service that every man, woman and child in our thirty-eight States is to some extent receiving the benefit of to-day —and I for one here cheerfully, reverently throw my pebble on the cairn of his memory. As we all know, the season demands—or rather, will it ever be out of season?—that America learn to better dwell on her choicest possession, the legacy of her good and faithful men—that she well preserve their fame, if unquestion'd—or, if need be, that she fail not to dissipate what clouds have intruded on that fame, and burnish it newer, truer and brighter, continually.

A TWO HOURS' ICE-SAIL

Feb. 3, '77.—From 4 to 6 P. M. crossing the Delaware, (back again at my Camden home,) unable to make our landing, through the ice; our boat stanch and strong and skilfully piloted, but old and sulky, and poorly minding her helm. (*Power,* so important in poetry and war, is also first point of all in a winter steam-boat, with long stretches of ice-packs to tackle.) For over two hours we bump'd and beat about, the invisible ebb, sluggish but irresistible, often carrying us long distances against our will. In the first tinge of dusk, as I look'd around, I thought there could not be presented a more chilling, arctic, grim-extended, depressing scene. Everything was yet plainly visible; for miles north and south, ice, ice, ice, mostly broken, but some big cakes, and no clear water in sight. The shores, piers, surfaces, roofs, shipping, mantled with snow. A faint winter vapor hung a fitting accompaniment around and over the endless whitish spread, and gave it just a tinge of steel and brown.

Feb. 6.—As I cross home in the 6 P. M. boat again, the transparent shadows are filled everywhere with leisurely falling, slightly slanting, curiously sparse but very large, flakes of snow. On the shores, near and far, the glow of just-lit gas-clusters at intervals. The ice, sometimes in hummocks, sometimes floating fields, through which our boat goes crunching. The light permeated by that peculiar evening haze, right after sunset, which sometimes renders quite distant objects so distinctly.

SPRING OVERTURES—RECREATIONS

Feb. 10.—The first chirping, almost singing, of a bird to-day. Then I noticed a couple of honey-bees spirting and humming about the open window in the sun.

Feb. 11.—In the soft rose and pale gold of the declining light, this beautiful evening, I heard the first hum and preparation of awakening spring—very faint—whether in the earth or roots, or starting of insects, I know not—but it was audible, as I lean'd on a rail (I am down in my country quarters awhile,) and look'd long at the western horizon.

Turning to the east, Sirius, as the shadows deepen'd, came forth in dazzling splendor. And great Orion; and a little to the north-east the big Dipper, standing on end.

Feb. 20.—A solitary and pleasant sundown hour at the pond, exercising arms, chest, my whole body, by a tough oak sapling thick as my wrist, twelve feet high—pulling and pushing, inspiring the good air. After I wrestle with the tree awhile, I can feel its young sap and virtue welling up out of the ground and tingling through me from crown to toe, like health's wine. Then for addition and variety I launch forth in my vocalism; shout declamatory pieces, sentiments, sorrow, anger, &c., from the stock poets or plays—or inflate my lungs and sing the wild tunes and refrains I heard of the blacks down south, or patriotic songs I learn'd in the army. I make the echoes ring, I tell you! As the twilight fell, in a pause of these ebullitions, an owl somewhere the other side of the creek sounded *too-oo-oo-oo-oo*, soft and pensive (and I fancied a little sarcastic) repeated four or five times. Either to applaud the negro songs—or perhaps an ironical comment on the sorrow, anger, or style of the stock poets.

ONE OF THE HUMAN KINKS

How is it that in all the serenity and lonesomeness of solitude, away off here amid the hush of the forest, alone, or as I have found in prairie wilds, or mountain stillness, one is never entirely without the instinct of looking around, (I never am, and others tell me the same of themselves, confidentially,) for somebody to appear, or start up out of the earth, or from behind some tree or rock? Is it a lingering, inherited remains of man's primitive wariness, from the wild animals? or from his savage ancestry far back? It is not at all nervousness or fear. Seems as if something unknown were possibly lurking in those bushes, or solitary places. Nay, it is quite certain there is—some vital unseen presence.

AN AFTERNOON SCENE

Feb. 22.—Last night and to-day rainy and thick, till mid-afternoon, when the wind chopp'd round, the clouds swiftly drew off like curtains, the clear appear'd, and with it the fairest, grandest, most wondrous rainbow I ever saw, all complete, very vivid at its earth-ends, spreading vast effusions of illuminated haze, violet, yellow, drab-green, in all directions overhead, through which the sun beam'd—an indescribable utterance of color and light, so gorgeous yet so soft, such as I had never witness'd before. Then its continuance: a full hour pass'd before the last of those earth-ends disappear'd. The sky behind was all spread in translucent blue, with many little white clouds and edges. To these a sunset, filling, dominating the esthetic and soul senses, sumptuously, tenderly, full. I end this note by the pond, just light enough to see, through the evening shadows, the western reflections in its water-mirror surface, with inverted figures of trees. I hear now and then the *flup* of a pike leaping out, and rippling the water.

THE GATES OPENING

April 6.—Palpable spring indeed, or the indications of it. I am sitting in bright sunshine, at the edge of the creek, the surface just rippled by the wind. All is solitude, morning freshness, negligence. For companions my two kingfishers sailing, winding, darting, dipping, sometimes capriciously separate, then flying together. I hear their guttural twittering again and again; for awhile nothing but that peculiar sound. As noon approaches other birds warm up. The reedy notes of the robin, and a musical passage of two parts, one a clear delicious gurgle, with several other birds I cannot place. To which is join'd, (yes, I just hear it,) one low purr at intervals from some impatient hylas at the pond-edge. The sibilant murmur of a pretty stiff breeze now and then through the trees. Then a poor little dead leaf, long frost-bound, whirls from somewhere up aloft in one wild escaped freedom-spree in space and sunlight, and then dashes down to the waters, which hold it closely and soon drown it out of sight. The bushes and trees are yet bare, but the beeches have their wrinkled yellow leaves of last season's foliage largely left, frequent cedars and pines yet green, and the grass not without proofs of coming fulness. And over all a wonderfully fine dome of clear blue, the play of light coming and going, and great fleeces of white clouds swimming so silently.

THE COMMON EARTH, THE SOIL

THE soil, too—let others pen-and-ink the sea, the air, (as I sometimes try)—but now I feel to choose the common soil for theme—naught else. The brown soil here, (just between winter-close and opening spring and vegetation)—the rain-shower at night, and the fresh smell next morning—the red worms wriggling out of the ground—the dead leaves, the incipient grass, and the latent life underneath—the effort to start something—already in shelter'd spots some little flowers—the distant emerald show of winter wheat and the rye-fields—the yet naked trees, with clear interstices, giving prospects hidden in summer—the tough fallow and the plow-team, and the stout boy whistling to his horses for encouragement—and there the dark fat earth in long slanting stripes upturn'd.

BIRDS AND BIRDS AND BIRDS

A little later—bright weather.—An unusual melodiousness, these days, (last of April and first of May) from the blackbirds; indeed all sorts of birds, darting, whistling, hopping or perch'd on trees. Never before have I seen, heard, or been in the midst of, and got so flooded and saturated with them and their performances, as this current month. Such oceans, such successions of them. Let me make a list of those I find here:

Black birds (plenty,)	Meadow-larks (plenty,)
Ring doves,	Cat-birds (plenty,)
Owls,	Cuckoos,
Woodpeckers,	Pond snipes (plenty,)
King-birds,	Cheewinks,
Crows (plenty,)	Quawks,
Wrens,	Ground robins,
Kingfishers,	Ravens,
Quails,	Gray snipes,
Turkey-buzzards,	Eagles,
Hen-hawks,	High-holes,
Yellow birds,	Herons,
Thrushes,	Tits,
Reed birds,	Woodpigeons.

Early came the

Blue birds,	Meadow lark,
Killdeer,	White-bellied swallow,
Plover,	Sandpiper,
Robin,	Wilson's thrush,
Woodcock,	Flicker.

FULL-STARR'D NIGHTS

May 21.—Back in Camden. Again commencing one of those unusually transparent, full-starr'd, blue-black nights, as if to show that however lush and pompous the day may be, there is something left in the not-day that can outvie it. The rarest, finest sample of long-drawn-out clear-obscure, from sundown to 9 o'clock. I went down to the Delaware, and cross'd and cross'd. Venus like blazing silver well up in the west. The large pale thin crescent of the new moon, half an hour high, sinking languidly under a bar-sinister of cloud, and then emerging. Arcturus right overhead. A faint fragrant sea-odor wafted up from the south. The gloaming, the temper'd coolness, with every feature of the scene, indescribably soothing and tonic—one of those hours that give hints to the soul, impossible to put in a statement. (Ah, where would be any food for spirituality without night and the stars?) The vacant spaciousness of the air, and the veil'd blue of the heavens, seem'd miracles enough.

As the night advanc'd it changed its spirit and garments to ampler stateliness. I was almost conscious of a definite presence, Nature silently near. The great constellation of the Water-Serpent stretch'd its coils over more than half the heavens. The Swan with outspread wings was flying down the Milky Way. The northern Crown, the Eagle, Lyra, all up there in their places. From the whole dome shot down points of light, rapport with me, through the clear blue-black. All the usual sense of motion, all animal life, seem'd discarded, seem'd a fiction; a curious power, like the placid rest of Egyptian gods, took possession, none the less potent for being impalpable. Earlier I had seen many bats, balancing in the luminous twilight, darting their black forms hither and yon over the river; but now they altogether disappear'd. The evening star and the moon had gone. Alertness and peace lay calmly couching together through the fluid universal shadows.

Aug. 26.—Bright has the day been, and my spirits an equal *forzando*. Then comes the night, different, inexpressibly pensive, with its own tender and temper'd splendor. Venus lingers in the west with a voluptuous dazzle unshown hitherto this summer. Mars rises early, and the red sulky moon, two days past her full; Jupiter at night's meridian, and the long curling-slanted Scorpion stretching full view in the south, Aretus-neck'd. Mars walks the heavens lord-paramount now; all through this month I go out after supper and watch for him; sometimes getting up at midnight to take another look at his unparallel'd lustre. (I see lately an astronomer has made out through the new Washington telescope that Mars has certainly one moon, perhaps two.) Pale and distant, but near in the heavens, Saturn precedes him.

MULLEINS AND MULLEINS

LARGE, placid mulleins, as summer advances, velvety in texture, of a light greenish-drab color, growing everywhere in the fields—at first earth's big rosettes in their broad-leav'd low cluster-plants, eight, ten, twenty leaves to a plant—plentiful on the follow twenty-acre lot, at the end of the lane, and especially by the ridge-sides of the fences— then close to the ground, but soon springing up—leaves as broad as

my hand, and the lower ones twice as long—so fresh and dewy in the
morning—stalks now four or five, even seven or eight feet high. The
farmers, I find, think the mullein a mean unworthy weed, but I have
grown to a fondness for it. Every object has its lesson, enclosing the
suggestion of everything else—and lately I sometimes think all is concentrated for me in these hardy, yellow-flower'd weeds. As I come
down the lane early in the morning, I pause before their soft wool-like
fleece and stem and broad leaves, glittering with countless diamonds.
Annually for three summers now, they and I have silently return'd
together; at such long intervals I stand or sit among them, musing—
and woven with the rest, of so many hours and moods of partial
rehabilitation—of my sane or sick spirit, here as near at peace as it
can be.

DISTANT SOUNDS

THE axe of the wood-cutter, the measured thud of a single threshing-
flail, the crowing of chanticleer in the barn-yard, (with invariable responses from other barn-yards,) and the lowing of cattle—but most of
all, or far or near, the wind—through the high tree-tops, or through
low bushes, laving one's face and hands so gently, this balmy-bright
noon, the coolest for a long time, (Sept. 2)—I will not call it *sighing*,
for to me it is always a firm, sane, cheery expression, though a monotone, giving many varieties, or swift or slow, or dense or delicate. The
wind in the patch of pine woods off there—how sibilant. Or at sea, I
can imagine it this moment, tossing the waves, with spirts of foam
flying far, and the free whistle, and the scent of the salt—and that vast
paradox somehow with all its action and restlessness conveying a sense
of eternal rest.

Other adjuncts.—But the sun and moon here and these times. As
never more wonderful by day, the gorgeous orb imperial, so vast, so
ardently, lovingly hot—so never a more glorious moon of nights, especially the last three or four. The great planets too—Mars never before
so flaming bright, so flashing-large, with slight yellow tinge, (the
astronomers say—is it true?—nearer to us than any time the past century)—and well up, lord Jupiter, (a little while since close by the
moon)—and in the west, after the sun sinks, voluptuous Venus, now
languid and shorn of her beams, as if from some divine excess.

A SUN-BATH—NAKEDNESS

Sunday, Aug. 27.—Another day quite free from mark'd prostration and
pain. It seems indeed as if peace and nutriment from heaven subtly

filter into me as I slowly hobble down these country lanes and across fields, in the good air—as I sit here in solitude with Nature—open, voiceless, mystic, far removed, yet palpable, eloquent Nature. I merge myself in the scene, in the perfect day. Hovering over the clear brook-water, I am sooth'd by its soft gurgle in one place, and the hoarser murmurs of its three-foot fall in another. Come, ye disconsolate, in whom any latent eligibility is left—come get the sure virtues of creek-shore, and wood and field. Two months (July and August, '77,) have I absorb'd them, and they begin to make a new man of me. Every day, seclusion—every day at least two or three hours of freedom, bathing, no talk, no bonds, no dress, no books, no *manners*.

Shall I tell you, reader, to what I attribute my already much-restored health? That I have been almost two years, off and on, without drugs and medicines, and daily in the open air. Last summer I found a particularly secluded little dell off one side by my creek, originally a large dug-out marl-pit, now abandon'd, fill'd with bushes, trees, grass, a group of willows, a straggling bank, and a spring of delicious water running right through the middle of it, with two or three little cascades. Here I retreated every hot day, and follow it up this summer. Here I realize the meaning of that old fellow who said he was seldom less alone than when alone. Never before did I get so close to Nature; never before did she come so close to me. By old habit, I pencill'd down from time to time, almost automatically, moods, sights, hours, tints and outlines, on the spot. Let me specially record the satisfaction of this current forenoon, so serene and primitive, so conventionally exceptional, natural.

An hour or so after breakfast I wended my way down to the recesses of the aforesaid dell, which I and certain thrushes, catbirds, &c., had all to ourselves. A light south-west wind was blowing through the tree-tops. It was just the place and time for my Adamic air-bath and flesh-brushing from head to foot. So hanging clothes on a rail near by, keeping old broadbrim straw on head and easy shoes on feet, havn't I had a good time the last two hours! First with the stiff-elastic bristles rasping arms, breast, sides, till they turn'd scarlet—then partially bathing in the clear waters of the running brook—taking everything very leisurely, with many rests and pauses—stepping about barefooted every few minutes now and then in some neighboring black ooze, for unctuous mud-bath to my feet—a brief second and third rinsing in the crystal running waters—rubbing with the fragrant towel —slow negligent promenades on the turf up and down in the sun, varied with occasional rests, and further frictions of the bristle-brush —sometimes carrying my portable chair with me from place to place, as my range is quite extensive here, nearly a hundred rods, feeling quite secure from intrusion, (and that indeed I am not at all nervous about, if it accidentally happens.)

As I walk'd slowly over the grass, the sun shone out enough to show the shadow moving with me. Somehow I seem'd to get identity with each and every thing around me, in its condition. Nature was naked, and I was also. It was too lazy, soothing, and joyous-equable to speculate about. Yet I might have thought somehow in this vein: Perhaps the inner never lost rapport we hold with earth, light, air, trees, &c., is not to be realized through eyes and mind only, but through the whole corporeal body, which I will not have blinded or bandaged any more than the eyes. Sweet, sane, still Nakedness in Nature!—ah if poor, sick, prurient humanity in cities might really know you once more! Is not nakedness then indecent? No, not inherently. It is your thought, your sophistication, your fear, your respectability, that is indecent. There come moods when these clothes of ours are not only too irksome to wear, but are themselves indecent. Perhaps indeed he or she to whom the free exhilarating extasy of nakedness in Nature has never been eligible (and how many thousands there are!) has not really known what purity is—nor what faith or art or health really is. (Probably the whole curriculum of first-class philosophy, beauty, heroism, form, illustrated by the old Hellenic race— the highest height and deepest depth known to civilization in those departments—came from their natural and religious idea of Nakedness.)

Many such hours, from time to time, the last two summers—I attribute my partial rehabilitation largely to them. Some good people may think it a feeble or half-crack'd way of spending one's time and thinking. May-be it is.

THE OAKS AND I

Sept. 5, '77.—I write this, 11 A. M., shelter'd under a dense oak by the bank, where I have taken refuge from a sudden rain. I came down here, (we had sulky drizzles all the morning, but an hour ago a lull,) for the before-mention'd daily and simple exercise I am fond of—to pull on that young hickory sapling out there—to sway and yield to its tough-limber upright stem—haply to get into my old sinews some of its elastic fibre and clear sap. I stand on the turf and take these health-pulls moderately and at intervals for nearly an hour, inhaling great draughts of fresh air. Wandering by the creek, I have three or four naturally favorable spots where I rest—besides a chair I lug with me and use for more deliberate occasions. At other spots convenient I have selected, besides the hickory just named, strong and limber boughs of beech or holly, in easy-reaching distance, for my natural gymnasia, for arms, chest, trunk-muscles. I can soon feel the sap and sinew rising through me, like mercury to heat. I hold on boughs or slender trees caressingly there in the sun and shade, wrestle with their innocent stalwartness—and *know* the virtue thereof passes from them into me. (Or may-be we interchange—may-be the trees are more aware of it all than I ever thought.)

But now pleasantly imprison'd here under the big oak—the rain dripping, and the sky cover'd with leaden clouds—nothing but the pond on one side, and the other a spread of grass, spotted with the milky blossoms of the wild carrot—the sound of an axe wielded at some distant wood-pile—yet in this dull scene, (as most folks would call it,) why am I so (almost) happy here and alone? Why would any intrusion, even from people I like, spoil the charm? But am I alone? Doubtless there comes a time—perhaps it has come to me—when one feels through his whole being, and pronouncedly the emotional part, that identity between himself subjectively and Nature objectively which Schelling and Fichte are so fond of pressing. How it is I know not, but I often realize a presence here—in clear moods I am certain of it, and neither chemistry nor reasoning nor esthetics will give the least explanation. All the past two summers it has been strengthening and nourishing my sick body and soul, as never before. Thanks, invisible physician, for thy silent delicious medicine, the day and night, thy waters and thy airs, the banks, the grass, the trees, and e'en the weeds!

A QUINTETTE

WHILE I have been kept by the rain under the shelter of my great oak, (perfectly dry and comfortable, to the rattle of the drops all around,) I have pencill'd off the mood of the hour in a little quintette, which I will give you:

> At vacancy with Nature,
> Acceptive and at ease,
> Distilling the present hour,
> Whatever, wherever it is,
> And over the past, oblivion.

Can you get hold of it, reader dear? and how do you like it anyhow?

THE FIRST FROST—MEMS

WHERE I was stopping I saw the first palpable frost, on my sunrise walk, October 6; all over the yet-green spread a light blue-gray veil, giving a new show to the entire landscape. I had but little time to notice it, for the sun rose cloudless and mellow-warm, and as I returned along the lane it had turn'd to glittering patches of wet. As I walk I notice the bursting pods of wild-cotton, (Indian hemp they call it here,) with flossy-silky contents, and dark red-brown seeds—a startled rabbit—I pull a handful of the balsamic life-everlasting and stuff it down in my trowsers-pocket for scent.

THREE YOUNG MEN'S DEATHS

December 20.—Somehow I got thinking to-day of young men's deaths —not at all sadly or sentimentally, but gravely, realistically, perhaps a little artistically. Let me give the following three cases from budgets of personal memoranda, which I have been turning over, alone in my room, and resuming and dwelling on, this rainy afternoon. Who is there to whom the theme does not come home? Then I don't know how it may be to others, but to me not only is there nothing gloomy or depressing in such cases—on the contrary, as reminiscences, I find them soothing, bracing, tonic.

ERASTUS HASKELL.—[I just transcribe verbatim from a letter written by myself in one of the army hospitals, 16 years ago, during the secession war.] *Washington, July 28, 1863.*—Dear M.,—I am writing this in the hospital, sitting by the side of a soldier, I do not expect to last many hours. His fate has been a hard one—he seems to be only about 19 or 20—Erastus Haskell, company K, 141st N.Y.—has been out about a year, and sick or half-sick more than half that time—has been down on the peninsula—was detail'd to go in the band as fifer-boy. While sick, the surgeon told him to keep up with the rest—(probably work'd and march'd too long.) He is a shy, and seems to me a very sensible boy—has fine manners—never complains—was sick down on the peninsula in an old storehouse—typhoid fever. The first week this July was brought up here—journey very bad, no accommodations, no nourishment, nothing but hard jolting, and exposure enough to make a well man sick; (these fearful journeys do the job for many)—arrived here July 11th—a silent dark-skinn'd Spanish-looking youth, with large very dark blue eyes, peculiar looking. Doctor F. here made light of his sickness—said he would recover soon, &c.; but I thought very different, and told F. so repeatedly; (I came near quarreling with him about it from the first)—but he laugh'd, and would not listen to me. About four days ago, I told Doctor he would in my opinion lose the boy without doubt—but F. again laugh'd at me. The next day he changed his opinion—I brought the head surgeon of the post—he said the boy would probably die, but they would make a hard fight for him.

The last two days he has been lying panting for breath—a pitiful sight. I have been with him some every day or night since he arrived. He suffers a great deal with the heat—says little or nothing—is flighty the last three days, at times—knows me always, however—calls me "Walter"—(sometimes calls the name over and over and over again, musingly, abstractedly, to himself.) His father lives at Breesport, Chemung county, N. Y., is a mechanic with large family—is a steady, religious man; his mother too is living. I have written to them, and shall write again today—Erastus has not receiv'd a word from home for months.

As I sit here writing to you, M., I wish you could see the whole scene. This young man lies within reach of me, flat on his back, his hands clasp'd across his breast, his thick black hair cut close; he is dozing, breathing hard, every breath a spasm—it looks so cruel. He is a noble youngster,—I consider him past all hope. Often there is no one with him for a long while. I am here as much as possible.

WILLIAM ALCOTT, fireman. *Camden, Nov., 1874.*—Last Monday afternoon his widow, mother, relatives, mates of the fire department, and his other friends, (I was one, only lately it is true, but our love grew fast and close, the days and nights of those eight weeks by the chair of rapid decline, and the bed of death,) gather'd to the funeral of this young man, who had grown up, and was well-known here. With nothing special, perhaps, to record, I would give a word or two to his memory. He seem'd to me not an inappropriate specimen in character and elements, of that bulk of the average good American race that ebbs and flows perennially beneath this scum of eructations on the surface. Always very quiet in manner, neat in person and dress, good temper'd—punctual and industrious at his work, till he could work no longer—he just lived his steady, square, unobtrusive life, in its own humble sphere, doubtless unconscious of itself. (Though I think there were currents of emotion and intellect undevelop'd beneath, far deeper than his acquaintances ever suspected—or than he himself ever did.) He was no talker. His troubles, when he had any, he kept to himself. As there was nothing querulous about him in life, he made no complaints during his last sickness. He was one of those persons that while his associates never thought of attributing any particular talent or grace to him, yet all insensibly, really, liked Billy Alcott.

I, too, loved him. At last, after being with him quite a good deal—after hours and days of panting for breath, much of the time unconscious, (for though the consumption that had been lurking in his system, once thoroughly started, made rapid progress, there was still great vitality in him, and indeed for four or five days he lay dying, before the close,) late on Wednesday night, Nov. 4th, where we surrounded his bed in silence, there came a lull—a longer drawn breath, a pause, a faint sigh—another—a weaker breath, another sigh—a pause again and just a tremble—and the face of the poor wasted young man (he was just 26,) fell gently over, in death, on my hand, on the pillow.

CHARLES CASWELL.—[I extract the following, verbatim, from a letter to me dated September 29, from my friend John Burroughs, at Esopus-on-Hudson, New York State.] S. was away when your picture came, attending his sick brother, Charles—who has since died—an event that has sadden'd me much. Charlie was younger than S., and a most attractive young fellow. He work'd at my father's, and had done so for two years. He was about the best specimen of a young country farm-hand I ever knew. You would have loved him. He was like one of your poems. With his great strength, his blond hair, his cheerfulness and contentment, his universal good will, and his silent manly ways, he was a youth hard to match. He was murder'd by an old doctor. He had typhoid fever, and the old fool bled him twice. He lived to wear out the fever, but had not strength to rally. He was out of his head nearly all the time. In the morning, as he died in the afternoon. S. was standing over him, when Charlie put up his arms around S.'s neck, and pull'd his face down and kiss'd him. S. said he knew then the end was near. (S. stuck to him day and night to the last.) When I was home in August, Charlie was cradling on the hill, and it was a picture to see him walk through the grain. All work seem'd play to him. He had no vices, any more than Nature has, and was belov'd by all who knew him.

I have written thus to you about him, for such young men belong to you; he was of your kind. I wish you could have known him. He had the sweetness of a child, and the strength and courage and readiness of a young Viking. His mother and father are poor; they have a rough, hard farm. His mother works in the field with her husband when the work presses. She has had twelve children.

FEBRUARY DAYS

February 7, 1878.—Glistening sun to-day, with slight haze, warm enough, and yet tart, as I sit here in the open air, down in my country retreat, under an old cedar. For two hours I have been idly wandering around the woods and pond, lugging my chair, picking out choice spots to sit awhile—then up and slowly on again. All is peace here. Of course, none of the summer noises or vitality; to-day hardly even the winter ones. I amuse myself by exercising my voice in recitations, and in ringing the changes on all the vocal and alphabetical sounds. Not even an echo; only the cawing of a solitary crow, flying at some distance. The pond is one bright, flat spread, without a ripple—a vast Claude Lorraine glass, in which I study the sky, the light, the leafless trees, and an occasional crow, with flapping wings, flying overhead. The brown fields have a few white patches of snow left.

Feb. 9.—After an hour's ramble, now retreating, resting, sitting close by the pond, in a warm nook, writing this, shelter'd from the breeze, just before noon. The *emotional* aspects and influences of Nature! I, too, like the rest, feel these modern tendencies (from all the prevailing intellections, literature and poems,) to turn everything to pathos, ennui, morbidity, dissatisfaction, death. Yet how clear it is to me that those are not the born results, influences of Nature at all, but of one's own distorted, sick or silly soul. Here, amid this wild, free scene, how healthy, how joyous, how clean and vigorous and sweet!

Mid-afternoon.—One of my nooks is south of the barn, and here I am sitting now, on a log, still basking in the sun, shielded from the wind. Near me are the cattle, feeding on corn-stalks. Occasionally a cow or the young bull (how handsome and bold he is!) scratches and munches the far end of the log on which I sit. The fresh milky odor is quite perceptible, also the perfume of hay from the barn. The perpetual rustle of dry corn-stalks, the low sough of the wind round the barn gables, the grunting of pigs, the distant whistle of a locomotive, and occasional crowing of chanticleers, are the sounds.

Feb. 19.—Cold and sharp last night—clear and not much wind— the full moon shining, and a fine spread of constellations and little and big stars—Sirius very bright, rising early, preceded by many-orb'd Orion, glittering, vast, sworded, and chasing with his dog. The earth hard frozen, and a stiff glare of ice over the pond. Attracted by the calm splendor of the night, I attempted a short walk, but was driven back by the cold. Too severe for me also at 9 o'clock, when I came out this morning, so I turn'd back again. But now, near noon, I have walk'd down the lane, basking all the way in the sun (this farm has a pleasant southerly exposure,) and here I am, seated under the lee of a bank, close by the water. There are blue-birds already flying about, and I hear much chirping and twittering and two or three real songs, sustain'd quite awhile, in the mid-day brilliance and warmth. (There! that is a true carol, coming out boldly and repeatedly, as if the singer meant it.) Then as the noon strengthens, the reedy trill of the robin—to my ear the most cheering of bird-notes. At intervals, like bars and breaks (out of the low murmur that in any scene, however quiet, is never entirely absent to a delicate ear,) the occasional crunch and cracking of the ice-glare congeal'd over the creek, as it gives way to the sunbeams—sometimes with low sigh—sometimes with indignant, obstinate tug and snort.

(Robert Burns says in one of his letters: "There is scarcely any earthly object gives me more—I do not know if I should call it pleasure—but something which exalts me—something which enraptures me—than to walk in the shelter'd side of a wood in a cloudy winter day, and hear the stormy wind howling among the trees, and raving over the plain. It is my best season of devotion." Some of his most characteristic poems were composed in such scenes and seasons.)

A MEADOW LARK

March 16.—Fine, clear, dazzling morning, the sun an hour high, the air just tart enough. What a stamp in advance my whole day receives from the song of that meadow lark perch'd on a fence-stake twenty rods distant! Two or three liquid-simple notes, repeated at intervals, full of careless happiness and hope. With its peculiar shimmering-slow progress and rapid-noiseless action of the wings, it flies on a ways, lights on another stake, and so on to another, shimmering and singing many minutes.

SUNDOWN LIGHTS

May 6, 5 P. M.—This is the hour for strange effects in light and shade—enough to make a colorist go delirious—long spokes of molten silver sent horizontally through the trees (now in their brightest tenderest green,) each leaf and branch of endless foliage a lit-up miracle, then lying all prone on the youthful-ripe, interminable grass, and giving the blades not only aggregate but individual splendor, in ways unknown to any other hour. I have particular spots where I get these effects in their perfection. One broad splash lies on the water, with many a rippling twinkle, offset by the rapidly deepening black-green murky-transparent shadows behind, and at intervals all along the banks. These, with great shafts of horizontal fire thrown among the trees and along the grass as the sun lowers, give effects more and more peculiar, more and more superb, unearthly, rich and dazzling.

THOUGHTS UNDER AN OAK—A DREAM

June 2.—This is the fourth day of a dark northeast storm, wind and rain. Day before yesterday was my birthday. I have now enter'd on my 60th year. Every day of the storm, protected by overshoes and a waterproof blanket, I regularly come down to the pond, and ensconce myself under the lee of the great oak; I am here now writing these lines. The dark smoke-color'd clouds roll in furious silence athwart the sky; the soft green leaves dangle all round me; the wind steadily keeps up its hoarse, soothing music over my head—Nature's mighty whisper. Seated here in solitude I have been musing over my life—connecting events, dates, as links of a chain, neither sadly nor cheerily, but somehow, to-day here under the oak, in the rain, in an unusually matter-of-fact spirit.

But my great oak—sturdy, vital, green—five feet thick at the butt. I sit a great deal near or under him. Then the tulip tree near by—the Apollo of the woods—tall and graceful, yet robust and sinewy, inimitable in hang of foliage and throwing-out of limb; as if the beauteous, vital, leafy creature could walk, if it only would. (I had a sort of dream-trance the other day, in which I saw my favorite trees step out and promenade up, down and around, very curiously —with a whisper from one, leaning down as he pass'd me, *We do all this on the present occasion, exceptionally, just for you.*)

CLOVER AND HAY PERFUME

July 3d, 4th, 5th.—Clear, hot, favorable weather—has been a good summer—the growth of clover and grass now generally mow'd. The familiar delicious perfume fills the barns and lanes. As you go along you see the fields of grayish white slightly tinged with yellow, the loosely stack'd grain, the slow-moving wagons passing, and farmers in the fields with stout boys pitching and loading the sheaves. The corn is about beginning to tassel. All over the middle and southern states the spear-shaped battalia, multitudinous, curving, flaunting— long, glossy, dark-green plumes for the great horseman, earth. I hear the cheery notes of my old acquaintance Tommy quail; but too late for the whip-poor-will, (though I heard one solitary lingerer night before last.) I watch the broad majestic flight of a turkey-buzzard, sometimes high up, sometimes low enough to see the lines of his form, even his spread quills, in relief against the sky. Once or twice lately I have seen an eagle here at early candle-light flying low.

AN UNKNOWN

June 15.—To-day I noticed a new large bird, size of a nearly grown hen—a haughty, white-bodied dark-wing'd hawk—I suppose a hawk from his bill and general look—only he had a clear, loud, quite musical, sort of bell-like call, which he repeated again and again, at intervals, from a lofty dead tree-top, overhanging the water. Sat there a long time, and I on the opposite bank watching him. Then he darted down, skimming pretty close to the stream—rose slowly, a magnificent sight, and sail'd with steady wide-spread wings, no flapping at all, up and down the pond two or three times, near me, in circles in clear sight, as if for my delectation. Once he came quite close over my head; I saw plainly his hook'd bill and hard restless eyes.

BIRD-WHISTLING

How much music (wild, simple, savage, doubtless, but so tart-sweet,) there is in mere whistling. It is four-fifths of the utterance of birds. There are all sorts and styles. For the last half-hour, now, while I have been sitting here, some feather'd fellow away off in the bushes has been repeating over and over again what I may call a kind of throbbing whistle. And now a bird about the robin size has just appear'd, all mulberry red, flitting among the bushes—head, wings, body, deep red, not very bright—no song, as I have heard. *4 o'clock:* There is a real concert going on around me—a dozen different birds pitching in with a will. There have been occasional rains, and the growths all show its vivifying influences. As I finish this, seated on a log close by the pond-edge, much chirping and trilling in the distance, and a feather'd recluse in the woods near by is singing deliciously—not many notes, but full of music of almost human sympathy—continuing for a long, long while.

HORSE-MINT

Aug. 22.—Not a human being, and hardly the evidence of one, in sight. After my brief semi-daily bath, I sit here for a bit, the brook musically brawling, to the chromatic tones of a fretful cat-bird somewhere off in the bushes. On my walk hither two hours since, through fields and the old lane, I stopt to view, now the sky, now the mile-off woods on the hill, and now the apple orchards. What a contrast from New York's or Philadelphia's streets! Everywhere great patches of dingy-blossom'd horse-mint wafting a spicy odor through the air, (especially evenings.) Everywhere the flowering boneset, and the rose-bloom of the wild bean.

THREE OF US

July 14.—My two kingfishers still haunt the pond. In the bright sun and breeze and perfect temperature of to-day, noon, I am sitting here by one of the gurgling brooks, dipping a French water-pen in the limpid crystal, and using it to write these lines, again watching the feather'd twain, as they fly and sport athwart the water, so close, almost touching into its surface. Indeed there seem to be three of us. For nearly an hour I indolently look and join them while they dart and turn and take their airy gambols, sometimes far up the creek disappearing for a few moments, and then surely returning again, and performing most of their flight within sight of me, as if they knew I appreciated and absorb'd their vitality, spirituality, faithfulness, and the rapid, vanishing, delicate lines of moving yet quiet electricity they draw for me across the spread of the grass, the trees, and the blue sky. While the brook babbles, babbles, and the shadows of the boughs dapple in the sunshine around me, and the cool west by-nor'-west wind faintly soughs in the thick bushes and tree tops.

Among the objects of beauty and interest now beginning to appear quite plentifully in this secluded spot, I notice the humming-bird, the dragon-fly with its wings of slate-color'd gauze, and many varieties of beautiful and plain butterflies, idly flapping among the plants and wild posies. The mullein has shot up out of its nest of broad leaves, to a tall stalk towering sometimes five or six feet high, now studded with knobs of golden blossoms. The milk-weed, (I see a great gorgeous creature of gamboge and black lighting on one as I write,) is in flower, with its delicate red fringe; and there are profuse clusters of a feathery blossom waving in the wind on taper stems. I see lots of these and much else in every direction, as I saunter or sit. For the last half hour a bird has persistently kept up a simple, sweet, melodious song, from the bushes. (I have a positive conviction that some of these birds sing, and others fly and flirt about here, for my especial benefit.)

DEATH OF WILLIAM CULLEN BRYANT

New York City.—Came on from West Philadelphia, June 13, in the 2 P.M. train to Jersey city, and so across and to my friends, Mr. and Mrs. J. H. J., and their large house, large family (and large hearts,) amid which I feel at home, at peace—away up on Fifth avenue, near Eighty-sixth street, quiet, breezy, overlooking the dense woody fringe of the park—plenty of space and sky, birds chirping, and air comparatively fresh and odorless. Two hours before starting, saw the announcement of William Cullen Bryant's funeral, and felt a strong desire to attend. I had known Mr. Bryant over thirty years ago, and he had been markedly kind to me. Off and on, along that time for years as they pass'd, we met and chatted together. I thought him very sociable in his way, and a man to become attach'd to. We were both walkers, and when I work'd in Brooklyn he several times came over, middle of afternoons, and we took rambles miles long, till dark, out towards Bedford or Flatbush, in company. On these occasions he gave me clear accounts of scenes in Europe—the cities, looks, architecture, art, especially Italy—where he had travel'd a good deal.

June 14.—The Funeral.—And so the good, stainless, noble old citizen and poet lies in the closed coffin there—and this is his funeral. A solemn, impressive, simple scene, to spirit and senses. The remarkable gathering of gray heads, celebrities—the finely render'd anthem, and other music—the church, dim even now at approaching noon, in its light from the mellow-stain'd windows—the pronounc'd eulogy on the bard who loved Nature so fondly, and sung so well her shows and seasons—ending with these appropriate well-known lines:

> *I gazed upon the glorious sky,*
>   *And the green mountains round,*
> *And thought that when I came to lie*
>   *At rest within the ground,*
> *'Twere pleasant that in flowery June,*
> *When brooks send up a joyous tune,*
>   *And groves a cheerful sound,*
> *The sexton's hand, my grave to make,*
> *The rich green mountain turf should break.*

JAUNT UP THE HUDSON

June 20th.—On the "Mary Powell," enjoy'd everything beyond precedent. The delicious tender summer day, just warm enough—the constantly changing but ever beautiful panorama on both sides of the river—(went up near a hundred miles)—the high straight walls of the stony Palisades—beautiful Yonkers, and beautiful Irvington—the never-ending hills, mostly in rounded lines, swathed with verdure,—the distant turns, like great shoulders in blue veils—the frequent gray and brown of the tall-rising rocks—the river itself, now narrowing, now expanding—the white sails of the many sloops, yachts, &c., some near, some in the distance—the rapid succession of handsome villages and cities, (our boat is a swift traveler, and makes few stops)—the Race—picturesque West Point, and indeed all along—the costly and often turreted mansions forever showing in some cheery light color, through the woods—make up the scene.

HAPPINESS AND RASPBERRIES

June 21.—Here I am, on the west bank of the Hudson, 80 miles north of New York, near Esopus, at the handsome, roomy, honey-suckle-and-rose-embower'd cottage of John Burroughs. The place, the perfect June days and nights, (leaning toward crisp and cool,) the hospitality of J. and Mrs. B., the air, the fruit, (especially my favorite dish, currants and raspberries, mixed, sugar'd, fresh and ripe from the bushes—I pick 'em myself)—the room I occupy at night, the perfect bed, the window giving an ample view of the Hudson and the opposite shores, so wonderful toward sunset, and the rolling music of the RR. trains, far over there—the peaceful rest —the early Venus-heralded dawn—the noiseless splash of sunrise, the light and warmth indescribably glorious, in which, (soon as the sun is well up,) I have a capital rubbing and rasping with the flesh-brush—with an extra scour on the back by Al. J., who is here with us—all inspiriting my invalid frame with new life, for the day. Then, after some whiffs of morning air, the delicious coffee of Mrs. B., with the cream, strawberries, and many substantials, for break-fast.

A SPECIMEN TRAMP FAMILY

June 22.—This afternoon we went out (J. B., Al. and I) on quite a drive around the country. The scenery, the perpetual stone fences, (some venerable old fellows, dark-spotted with lichens)—the many fine locust-trees—the runs of brawling water, often over descents of rock—these, and lots else. It is lucky the roads are first-rate here, (as they are,) for it is up or down hill everywhere, and sometimes steep enough. B. has a tip-top horse, strong, young, and both gentle and fast. There is a great deal of waste land and hills on the river edge of Ulster county, with a wonderful luxuriance of wild flowers and bushes—and it seems to me I never saw more vitality of trees— eloquent hemlocks, plenty of locusts and fine maples, and the balm of Gilead, giving out aroma. In the fields and along the road-sides unusual crops of the tall-stemm'd wild daisy, white as milk and yellow as gold.

We pass'd quite a number of tramps, singly or in couples—one squad, a family in a rickety one-horse wagon, with some baskets evidently their work and trade—the man seated on a low board, in front, driving—the gauntish woman by his side, with a baby well bundled in her arms, its little red feet and lower legs sticking out right towards us as we pass'd—and in the wagon behind, we saw two (or three) crouching little children. It was a queer, taking, rather sad picture. If I had been alone and on foot, I should have stopp'd and held confab. But on our return nearly two hours afterward, we found them a ways further along the same road, in a lonesome open spot, haul'd aside, unhitch'd, and evidently going to camp for the night. The freed horse was not far off, quietly cropping the grass. The man was busy at the wagon, the boy had gather'd some dry wood, and was making a fire—and as we went a little further we met the woman afoot. I could not see her face, in its great sun-bonnet, but somehow her figure and gait told misery, terror, destitution. She had the rag-bundled, half-starv'd infant still in her arms, and in her hands held two or three baskets, which she had evidently taken to the next house for sale. A little barefoot five-year old girl-child, with fine eyes, trotted behind her, clutching her gown. We stopp'd, asking about the baskets, which we bought. As we paid the money, she kept her face hidden in the recesses of her bonnet. Then as we started, and stopp'd again, Al., (whose sympathies were evidently arous'd,) went back to the camping group to get another basket. He caught a look of her face, and talk'd with her a little. Eyes, voice and manner were those of a corpse, animated by electricity. She was quite young—the man she was traveling with, middle-aged. Poor woman—what story was it, out of her fortunes, to account for that inexpressibly scared way, those glassy eyes, and that hollow voice?

MANHATTAN FROM THE BAY

June 25.—Returned to New York last night. Out to-day on the waters for a sail in the wide bay, southeast of Staten island—a rough, tossing ride, and a free sight—the long stretch of Sandy Hook, the highlands of Navesink, and the many vessels outward and inward bound. We came up through the midst of all, in the full sun. I especially enjoy'd the last hour or two. A moderate sea-breeze had set in; yet over the city, and the waters adjacent, was a thin haze, concealing nothing, only adding to the beauty. From my point of view, as I write amid the soft breeze, with a sea-temperature, surely nothing on earth of its kind can go beyond this show. To the left the North river with its far vista—nearer, three or four war-ships, anchor'd peacefully—the Jersey side, the banks of Weehawken, the Palisades, and the gradually receding blue, lost in the distance—to the right the East river—the mast-hemm'd shores—the grand obelisk-like towers of the bridge, one on either side, in haze, yet plainly defin'd, giant brothers twain, throwing free graceful interlinking

loops high across the tumbled tumultuous current below—(the tide
is just changing to its ebb)—the broad water-spread everywhere
crowded—no, not crowded, but thick as stars in the sky—with all
sorts and sizes of sail and steam vessels, plying ferry-boats, arriving
and departing coasters, great ocean Dons, iron-black, modern, magnificent in size and power, fill'd with their incalculable value of
human life and precious merchandise—with here and there, above
all, those daring, careening things of grace and wonder, those white
and shaded swift-darting fish-birds, (I wonder if shore or sea elsewhere can outvie them,) ever with their slanting spars, and fierce,
pure, hawk-like beauty and motion—first-class New York sloop or
schooner yachts, sailing, this fine day, the free sea in a good wind.
And rising out of the midst, tall-topt, ship-hemm'd, modern, American, yet strangely oriental, V-shaped Manhattan, with its compact
mass, its spires, its cloud-touching edifices, group'd at the centre—
the green of the trees, and all the white, brown and gray of the
architecture well blended, as I see it, under a miracle of limpid sky,
delicious light of heaven above, and June haze on the surface below.

HUMAN AND HEROIC NEW YORK

THE general subjective view of New York and Brooklyn—(will not
the time hasten when the two shall be municipally united in one,
and named Manhattan?)—what I may call the human interior and
exterior of these great seething oceanic populations, as I get it in
this visit, is to me best of all. After an absence of many years, (I
went away at the outbreak of the secession war, and have never
been back to stay since,) again I resume with curiosity the crowds,
the streets I knew so well, Broadway, the ferries, the west side of
the city, democratic Bowery—human appearances and manners as
seen in all these, and along the wharves, and in the perpetual travel
of the horse-cars, or the crowded excursion steamers, or in Wall and
Nassau streets by day—in the places of amusement at night—bub-
bling and whirling and moving like its own environment of waters—
endless humanity in all phases—Brooklyn also—taken in for the last
three weeks. No need to specify minutely—enough to say that (making all allowances for the shadows and side-streaks of a million-
headed-city) the brief total of the impressions, the human qualities,
of these vast cities, is to me comforting, even heroic, beyond statement. Alertness, generally fine physique, clear eyes that look straight
at you, a singular combination of reticence and self-possession, with
good nature and friendliness—a prevailing range of according manners, taste and intellect, surely beyond any elsewhere upon earth—

and a palpable outcropping of that personal comradeship I look forward to as the subtlest, strongest future hold of this many-item'd Union—are not only constantly visible here in these mighty channels of men, but they form the rule and average. To-day, I should say—defiant of cynics and pessimists, and with a full knowledge of all their exceptions—an appreciative and perceptive study of the current humanity of New York gives the directest proof yet of successful Democracy, and of the solution of that paradox, the eligibility of the free and fully developed individual with the paramount aggregate. In old age, lame and sick, pondering for years on many a doubt and danger for this republic of ours—fully aware of all that can be said on the other side—I find in this visit to New York, and the daily contact and rapport with its myriad people, on the scale of the oceans and tides, the best, most effective medicine my soul has yet partaken—the grandest physical habitat and surroundings of land and water the globe affords—namely, Manhattan island and Brooklyn, which the future shall join in one city—city of superb democracy, amid superb surroundings.

HOURS FOR THE SOUL

July 22d, 1878.—Living down in the country again. A wonderful conjunction of all that goes to make those sometime miracle-hours after sunset—so near and yet so far. Perfect, or nearly perfect days, I notice, are not so very uncommon; but the combinations that make perfect nights are few, even in a life time. We have one of those perfections to-night. Sunset left things pretty clear; the larger stars were visible soon as the shades allow'd. A while after 8, three or four great black clouds suddenly rose, seemingly from different points, and sweeping with broad swirls of wind but no thunder, underspread the orbs from view everywhere, and indicated a violent heat-storm. But without storm, clouds, blackness and all, sped and vanish'd as suddenly as they had risen; and from a little after 9 till 11 the atmosphere and the whole show above were in that state of exceptional clearness and glory just alluded to. In the northwest turned the Great Dipper with its pointers round the Cynosure. A little south of east the constellation of the Scorpion was fully up, with red Antares glowing in its neck; while dominating, majestic Jupiter swam, an hour and a half risen, in the east—(no moon till after 11.) A large part of the sky seem'd just laid in great splashes of phosphorus. You could look deeper in, farther through, than usual; the orbs thick as heads of wheat in a field. Not that there was any special brilliancy either—nothing near as sharp as I have seen of keen winter nights, but a curious general luminousness throughout to sight, sense, and soul. The latter had much to do with it. (I am convinced there are hours of Nature, especially of the atmosphere, mornings and evenings, address'd to the soul. Night transcends, for that purpose, what the proudest day can do.) Now, indeed, if never before, the heavens declared the glory of God. It was to the full the sky of the Bible, of Arabia, of the prophets, and of the oldest poems. There, in abstraction and stillness, (I had gone off by myself to absorb the scene, to have the spell unbroken,) the copiousness, the removedness, vitality, loose-clear-crowdedness, of that stellar concave spreading overhead, softly absorb'd into me, rising so free, interminably high, stretching east, west, north, south— and I, though but a point in the centre below, embodying all.

As if for the first time, indeed, creation noiselessly sank into and through me its placid and untellable lesson, beyond—O, so infinitely beyond!—anything from art, books, sermons, or from science, old or new. The spirit's hour—religion's hour—the visible suggestion of God in space and time—now once definitely indicated, if never again. The untold pointed at—the heavens all paved with it. The Milky Way, as if some superhuman symphony, some ode of universal vagueness, disdaining syllable and sound—a flashing glance of Deity, address'd to the soul. All silently—the indescribable night and stars—far off and silently.

THE DAWN.—*July 23.*—This morning, between one and two hours before sunrise, a spectacle wrought on the same background, yet of quite different beauty and meaning. The moon well up in the heavens, and past her half, is shining brightly—the air and sky of that cynical-clear, Minerva-like quality, virgin cool—not the weight of sentiment or mystery, or passion's ecstasy indefinable—not the religious sense, the varied All, distill'd and sublimated into one, of the night just described. Every star now clear-cut, showing for just what it is, there in the colorless ether. The character of the heralded morning, ineffably sweet and fresh and limpid, but for the esthetic sense alone, and for purity without sentiment. I have itemized the night—but dare I attempt the cloudless dawn? (What subtle tie is this between one's soul and the break of day? Alike, and yet no two nights or morning shows ever exactly alike.) Preceded by an immense star, almost unearthly in its effusion of white splendor, with two or three long unequal spoke-rays of diamond radiance, shedding down through the fresh morning air below—an hour of this, and then the sunrise.

THE EAST.—What a subject for a poem! Indeed, where else a more pregnant, more splendid one? Where one more idealistic-real, more subtle, more sensuous-delicate? The East, answering all lands, all ages, peoples; touching all senses, here, immediate, now—and yet so indescribably far off—such retrospect! The East—long-stretching —so losing itself—the orient, the gardens of Asia, the womb of history and song—forth-issuing all those strange, dim cavalcades—

Florid with blood, pensive, rapt with musings, hot with passion,
Sultry with perfume, with ample and flowing garments,
With sunburnt visage, intense soul and glittering eyes.

Always the East—old, how incalculably old! And yet here the same—ours yet, fresh as a rose, to every morning, every life, to-day —and always will be.

Sept. 17.—Another presentation—same theme—just before sunrise again, (a favorite hour with me.) The clear gray sky, a faint glow in the dull liver-color of the east, the cool fresh odor and the moisture—the cattle and horses off there grazing in the fields—the star Venus again, two hours high. For sounds, the chirping of crickets in the grass, the clarion of chanticleer, and the distant cawing of an early crow. Quietly over the dense fringe of cedars and pines rises that dazzling, red, transparent disk of flame, and the low sheets of white vapor roll and roll into dissolution.

THE MOON.—*May 18.*—I went to bed early last night, but found myself waked shortly after 12, and, turning awhile sleepless and mentally feverish, I rose, dress'd myself, sallied forth and walk'd down the lane. The full moon, some three or four hours up—a sprinkle of light and less-light clouds just lazily moving—Jupiter an hour high in the east, and here and there throughout the heavens a random star appearing and disappearing. So, beautifully veil'd and varied—the air, with that early-summer perfume, not at all damp or raw—at times Luna languidly emerging in richest brightness for minutes, and then partially envelop'd again. Far off a whip-poor-will plied his notes incessantly. It was that silent time between 1 and 3.

The rare nocturnal scene, how soon it sooth'd and pacified me! Is there not something about the moon, some relation or reminder, which no poem or literature has yet caught? (In very old and primitive ballads I have come across lines or asides that suggest it.) After a while the clouds mostly clear'd, and as the moon swam on, she carried, shimmering and shifting, delicate color-effects of pellucid green and tawny vapor. Let me conclude this part with an extract, (some writer in the "Tribune," May 16, 1878:)

No one ever gets tired of the moon. Goddess that she is by dower of her eternal beauty, she is a true woman by her tact—knows the charm of being seldom seen, of coming by surprise and staying but a little while; never wears the same dress two nights running, nor all night the same way; commends herself to the matter-of-fact people by her usefulness, and makes her uselessness adored by poets, artists, and all lovers in all lands; lends herself to every symbolism and to every emblem; is Diana's bow and Venus's mirror and Mary's throne; is a sickle, a scarf, an eyebrow, his face or her face, as look'd at by her or by him; is the madman's hell, the poet's heaven, the baby's toy, the philosopher's study; and while her admirers follow her footsteps, and hang on her lovely looks, she knows how to keep her woman's secret—her other side—unguess'd and unguessable.

Furthermore.—February 19, 1880.—Just before 10 P.M. cold and entirely clear again, the show overhead, bearing southwest, of wonderful and crowded magnificence. The moon in her third quarter—the clusters of the Hyades and Pleiades, with the planet Mars between—in full crossing sprawl in the sky the great Egyptian X, (Sirius, Procyon, and the main stars in the constellations of the Ship, the Dove, and of Orion;) just north of east Bootes, and in his knee Arcturus, an hour high, mounting the heaven, ambitiously large and sparkling, as if he meant to challenge with Sirius the stellar supremacy.

With the sentiment of the stars and moon such nights I get all the free margins and indefiniteness of music or poetry, fused in geometry's utmost exactness.

STRAW-COLOR'D AND OTHER PSYCHES

Aug. 4.—A pretty sight! Where I sit in the shade—a warm day, the sun shining from cloudless skies, the forenoon well advanc'd—I look over a ten-acre field of luxuriant clover-hay, (the second crop)— the livid-ripe red blossoms and dabs of August brown thickly spotting the prevailing dark-green. Over all flutter myriads of light-yellow butterflies, mostly skimming along the surface, dipping and oscillating, giving a curious animation to the scene. The beautiful, spiritual insects! straw-color'd Psyches! Occasionally one of them leaves his mates, and mounts, perhaps spirally, perhaps in a straight line in the air, fluttering up, up, till literally out of sight. In the lane as I came along just now I noticed one spot, ten feet square or so, where more than a hundred had collected, holding a revel, a gyration-dance, or butterfly good-time, winding and circling, down and across, but always keeping within the limits. The little creatures have come out all of a sudden the last few days, and are now very plentiful. As I sit outdoors, or walk, I hardly look around without somewhere seeing two (always two) fluttering through the air in amorous dalliance. Then their inimitable color, their fragility, peculiar motion—and that strange, frequent way of one leaving the crowd and mounting up, up in the free ether, and apparently never returning. As I look over the field, these yellow-wings everywhere mildly sparkling, many snowy blossoms of the wild carrot gracefully bending on their tall and taper stems—while for sounds, the distant guttural screech of a flock of guinea-hens comes shrilly yet somehow musically to my ears. And now a faint growl of heat-thunder in the north—and ever the low rising and falling wind-purr from the tops of the maples and willows.

Aug. 20.—Butterflies and butterflies, (taking the place of the bumble-bees of three months since, who have quite disappear'd,) continue to flit to and fro, all sorts, white, yellow, brown, purple—now and then some gorgeous fellow flashing lazily by on wings like artists' palettes dabb'd with every color. Over the breast of the pond I notice many white ones, crossing, pursuing their idle capricious flight. Near where I sit grows a tall-stemm'd weed topt with a profusion of rich scarlet blossoms, on which the snowy insects alight and dally, sometimes four or five of them at a time. By-and-by a humming-bird visits the same, and I watch him coming and going, daintily balancing and shimmering about. These white butterflies give new beautiful contrasts to the pure greens of the August foliage, (we have had some copious rains lately,) and over the glistening bronze of the pond-surface. You can tame even such insects; I have one big and handsome moth down here, knows and comes to me, likes me to hold him up on my extended hand.

Another Day, later.—A grand twelve-acre field of ripe cabbages with their prevailing hue of malachite green, and floating-flying over and among them in all directions myriads of these same white butterflies. As I came up the lane to-day I saw a living globe of the same, two to three feet in diameter, many scores cluster'd together and rolling along in the air, adhering to their ball-shape, six or eight feet above the ground.

A NIGHT REMEMBRANCE

Aug. 25, 9–10 a. m.—I sit by the edge of the pond, everything quiet, the broad polish'd surface spread before me—the blue of the heavens and the white clouds reflected from it—and flitting across, now and then, the reflection of some flying bird. Last night I was down here with a friend till after midnight; everything a miracle of splendor—the glory of the stars, and the completely rounded moon—the passing clouds, silver and luminous-tawny—now and then masses of vapory illuminated scud—and silently by my side my dear friend. The shades of the trees, and patches of moonlight on the grass—the softly blowing breeze, and just-palpable odor of the neighboring ripening corn—the indolent and spiritual night, inexpressibly rich, tender, suggestive—something altogether to filter through one's soul, and nourish and feed and soothe the memory long afterwards.

WILD FLOWERS

THIS has been and is yet a great season for wild flowers; oceans of them line the roads through the woods, border the edges of the water-runlets, grow all along the old fences, and are scatter'd in profusion over the fields. An eight-petal'd blossom of gold-yellow, clear and bright, with a brown tuft in the middle, nearly as large as a silver half-dollar, is very common; yesterday on a long drive I noticed it thickly lining the borders of the brooks everywhere. Then there is a beautiful weed cover'd with blue flowers, (the blue of the old Chinese teacups treasur'd by our grand-aunts,) I am continually stopping to admire—a little larger than a dime, and very plentiful. White, however, is the prevailing color. The wild carrot I have spoken of; also the fragrant life-everlasting. But there are all hues and beauties, especially on the frequent tracts of half-open scrub-oak and dwarf-cedar hereabout—wild asters of all colors. Notwithstanding the frost-touch the hardy little chaps maintain themselves in all their bloom. The tree-leaves, too, some of them are beginning to turn yellow or drab or dull green. The deep wine-color of the sumachs and gum-trees is already visible, and the straw-color of the dog-wood and beech. Let me give the names of some of these perennial blossoms and friendly weeds I have made acquaintance with hereabout one season or another in my walks:

wild azalea,	scented marjoram,
wild honeysuckle,	snakeroot,
wild roses,	Solomon's seal,
golden rod,	sweet balm,
larkspur,	mint, (great plenty,)
early crocus,	wild geranium,
sweet flag, (great patches of it,)	wild heliotrope,
creeper, trumpet-flower,	burdock,

dandelions,
yarrow,
coreopsis,
wild pea,
woodbine,
elderberry,
poke-weed,
sun-flower,

chamomile,
violets,
clematis,
bloodroot,
swamp magnolia,
milk-weed,
wild daisy, (plenty,)
wild chrysanthemum.

A CIVILITY TOO LONG NEGLECTED

THE foregoing reminds me of something. As the individualities I
would mainly portray have certainly been slighted by folks who
make pictures, volumes, poems, out of them—as a faint testimonial
of my own gratitude for many hours of peace and comfort in half-
sickness, (and not by any means sure but they will somehow get
wind of the compliment,) I hereby dedicate the last half of these
Specimen Days to the

bees,
black-birds,
dragon-flies,
pond-turtles,
mulleins, tansy, peppermint,
moths (great and little, some
    splendid fellows,)
glow-worms, (swarming millions
    of them indescribably strange
    and beautiful at night over the
    pond and creek,)

water-snakes,
crows,
millers,
mosquitoes,
butterflies,
wasps and hornets,
cat birds (and all other birds,)
cedars,
tulip-trees (and all other trees,)
and to the spots and memories of
    those days, and of the creek.

DELAWARE RIVER—DAYS AND NIGHTS

April 5, 1879.—With the return of spring to the skies, airs, waters
of the Delaware, return the sea-gulls. I never tire of watching their
broad and easy flight, in spirals, or as they oscillate with slow un-
flapping wings, or look down with curved beak, or dipping to the
water after food. The crows, plenty enough all through the winter,
have vanish'd with the ice. Not one of them now to be seen. The
steamboats have again come forth—bustling up, handsome, freshly
painted, for summer work—the Columbia, the Edwin Forrest, (the
Republic not yet out,) the Reybold, the Nelly White, the Twilight,
the Ariel, the Warner, the Perry, the Taggart, the Jersey Blue—even
the hulky old Trenton—not forgetting those saucy little bull-pups
of the current, the steamtugs.

But let me bunch and catalogue the affair—the river itself, all the way from the sea—cape Island on one side and Henlopen light on the other—up the broad bay north, and so to Philadelphia, and on further to Trenton;—the sights I am most familiar with, (as I live a good part of the time in Camden, I view matters from that out-look)—the great arrogant, black, full-freighted ocean steamers, in-ward or outward bound—the ample width here between the two cities, intersected by Windmill island—an occasional man-of-war, sometimes a foreigner, at anchor, with her guns and port-holes, and the boats, and the brown-faced sailors, and the regular oar-strokes, and the gay crowds of "visiting day"—the frequent large and hand-some three-masted schooners, (a favorite style of marine build, hereabout of late years,) some of them new and very jaunty, with their white-gray sails and yellow pine spars—the sloops dashing along in a fair wind—(I see one now, coming up, under broad canvas, her gaff-topsail shining in the sun, high and picturesque—what a thing of beauty amid the sky and waters!)—the crowded wharf-slips along the city—the flags of different nationalities, the sturdy English cross on its ground of blood, the French tricolor, the banner of the great North German empire, and the Italian and the Spanish colors—sometimes, of an afternoon, the whole scene enliven'd by a fleet of yachts, in a half calm, lazily returning from a race down at Gloucester;—the neat, rakish, revenue steamer "Hamil-ton" in mid-stream, with her perpendicular stripes flaunting aft—and, turning the eyes north, the long ribands of fleecy-white steam, or dingy-black smoke, stretching far, fan-shaped, slanting diagonally across from the Kensington or Richmond shores, in the west-by-south-west wind.

SCENES ON FERRY AND RIVER—LAST WINTER'S NIGHTS

THEN the Camden ferry. What exhilaration, change, people, busi-ness, by day. What soothing, silent, wondrous hours, at night, cross-ing on the boat, most all to myself—pacing the deck, alone, forward or aft. What communion with the waters, the air, the exquisite *chiaroscuro*—the sky and stars, that speak no word, nothing to the intellect, yet so eloquent, so communicative to the soul. And the ferry men—little they know how much they have been to me, day and night—how many spells of listlessness, ennui, debility, they and their hardy ways have dispell'd. And the pilots—captains Hand, Walton, and Giberson by day, and captain Olive at night; Eugene Crosby, with his strong young arm so often supporting, circling, convoying me over the gaps of the bridge, through impediments, safely aboard. Indeed all my ferry friends—captain Frazee the super-intendent, Lindell, Hiskey, Fred Rauch, Price, Watson, and a dozen more. And the ferry itself, with its queer scenes—sometimes children suddenly born in the waiting-houses (an actual fact—and more than once)—sometimes a masquerade party, going over at night, with a band of music, dancing and whirling like mad on the broad deck, in their fantastic dresses; sometimes the astronomer, Mr. Whitall, (who posts me up in points about the stars by a living lesson there and then, and answering every question)—sometimes a prolific family group, eight, nine, ten, even twelve! (Yesterday, as I cross'd, a mother, father, and eight children, waiting in the ferry-house, bound westward somewhere.)

I have mention'd the crows. I always watch them from the boats. They play quite a part in the winter scenes on the river, by day. Their black splatches are seen in relief against the snow and ice everywhere at that season—sometimes flying and flapping—some-times on little or larger cakes, sailing up or down the stream. One day the river was mostly clear—only a single long ridge of broken ice making a narrow stripe by itself, running along down the cur-rent for over a mile, quite rapidly. On this white stripe the crows were congregated, hundreds of them—a funny procession—("half mourning" was the comment of some one.)

Then the reception room, for passengers waiting—life illustrated thoroughly. Take a March picture I jotted there two or three weeks since. Afternoon, about 3½ o'clock, it begins to snow. There has been a matinee performance at the theater—from 4¼ to 5 comes a stream of homeward bound ladies. I never knew the spacious room to present a gayer, more lively scene—handsome, well-drest Jersey women and girls, scores of them, streaming in for nearly an hour—the bright eyes and glowing faces, coming in from the air—a sprin-kling of snow on bonnets or dresses as they enter—the five or ten minutes' waiting—the chatting and laughing—(women can have capital times among themselves, with plenty of wit, lunches, jovial abandon)—Lizzie, the pleasant-manner'd waiting-room woman—for sound, the bell-taps and steam-signals of the departing boats with their rhythmic break and undertone—the domestic pictures, mothers with bevies of daughters, (a charming sight)—children, countrymen —the railroad men in their blue clothes and caps—all the various characters of city and country represented or suggested. Then out-side some belated passenger frantically running, jumping after the boat. Towards six o'clock the human stream gradually thickening—now a pressure of vehicles, drays, piled railroad crates—now a drove of cattle, making quite an excitement, the drovers with heavy sticks, belaboring the steaming sides of the frighten'd brutes. Inside the reception room, business bargains, flirting, love-making, *eclaircisse-ments,* proposals—pleasant, sober-faced Phil coming in with his burden of afternoon papers—or Jo, or Charley (who jump'd in the dock last week, and saved a stout lady from drowning,) to replenish the stove, after clearing it with long crow-bar poker.

Besides all this "comedy human," the river affords nutriment of a higher order. Here are some of my memoranda of the past winter, just as pencill'd down on the spot.

A January Night.—Fine trips across the wide Delaware to-night. Tide pretty high, and a strong ebb. River, a little after 8, full of ice, mostly broken, but some large cakes making our strong-timber'd steamboat hum and quiver as she strikes them. In the clear moonlight they spread, strange, unearthly, silvery, faintly glistening, as far as I can see. Bumping, trembling, sometimes hissing like a thousand snakes, the tide-procession, as we wend with or through it, affording a grand undertone, in keeping with the scene. Overhead, the splendor indescribable; yet something haughty, almost supercilious, in the night. Never did I realize more latent sentiment, almost *passion,* in those silent interminable stars up there. One can understand, such a night, why, from the days of the Pharaohs or Job, the dome of heaven, sprinkled with planets, has supplied the subtlest, deepest criticism on human pride, glory, ambition.

Another Winter Night.—I don't know anything more *filling* than to be on the wide firm deck of a powerful boat, a clear, cool, extra-moonlight night, crushing proudly and resistlessly through this thick, marbly, glistening ice. The whole river is now spread with it —some immense cakes. There is such weirdness about the scene— partly the quality of the light, with its tinge of blue, the lunar twilight—only the large stars holding their own in the radiance of the moon. Temperature sharp, comfortable for motion, dry, full of oxygen. But the sense of power—the steady, scornful, imperious urge of our strong new engine, as she ploughs her way through the big and little cakes.

Another.—For two hours I cross'd and recross'd, merely for pleasure—for a still excitement. Both sky and river went through several changes. The first for awhile held two vast fan-shaped echelons of light clouds, through which the moon waded, now radiating, carrying with her an aureole of tawny transparent brown, and now flooding the whole vast with clear vapory light-green, through which, as through an illuminated veil, she moved with measur'd womanly motion. Then, another trip, the heavens would be absolutely clear, and Luna in all her effulgence. The big Dipper in the north, with the double star in the handle much plainer than common. Then the sheeny track of light in the water, dancing and rippling. Such transformations; such pictures and poems, inimitable.

Another.—I am studying the stars, under advantages, as I cross to-night. (It is late in February, and again extra clear.) High toward the west, the Pleiades, tremulous with delicate sparkle, in the soft heavens. Aldebaran, leading the V-shaped Hyades—and overhead Capella and her kids. Most majestic of all, in full display in the high south, Orion, vast-spread, roomy, chief histrion of the stage, with his shiny yellow rosette on his shoulder, and his three Kings—and a little to the east, Sirius, calmly arrogant, most wondrous single star. Going late ashore, (I couldn't give up the beauty and soothingness of the night,) as I staid around, or slowly wander'd, I heard the echoing calls of the railroad men in the West Jersey depot yard, shifting and switching trains, engines, &c.; amid the general silence otherways, and something in the acoustic quality of the air, musical, emotional effects, never thought of before. I linger'd long and long, listening to them.

Night of March 18, '79.—One of the calm, pleasantly cool, exquisitely clear and cloudless, early spring nights—the atmosphere again that rare vitreous blue-black, welcom'd by astronomers. Just at 8, evening, the scene overhead of certainly solemnest beauty, never surpass'd. Venus nearly down in the west, of a size and lustre as if trying to outshow herself, before departing. Teeming, maternal orb—I take you again to myself. I am reminded of that spring preceding Abraham Lincoln's murder, when I, restlessly haunting the Potomac banks, around Washington city, watch'd you, off there, aloof, moody as myself:

As we walk'd up and down in the dark blue so mystic,
As we walk'd in silence the transparent shadowy night,
As I saw you had something to tell, as you bent to me night after night,
As you droop from the sky low down, as if to my side, (while the other
*   stars all look'd on,)*
As we wander'd together the solemn night.

With departing Venus, large to the last, and shining even to the edge of the horizon, the vast dome presents at this moment, such a spectacle! Mercury was visible just after sunset—a rare sight. Arcturus is now risen, just north of east. In calm glory all the stars of Orion hold the place of honor, in meridian, to the south—with the Dog-star a little to the left. And now, just rising, Spica, late, low, and slightly veil'd. Castor, Regulus and the rest, all shining unusually clear, (no Mars or Jupiter or moon till morning.) On the edges of the river, many lamps twinkling—with two or three huge chimneys, a couple of miles up, belching forth molten, steady flames, volcano-like, illuminating all around—and sometimes an electric or calcium, its Dante-Inferno gleams, in far shafts, terrible, ghastly-powerful. Of later May nights, crossing, I like to watch the fishermen's little buoy-lights—so pretty, so dreamy—like corpse candles—undulating delicate and lonesome on the surface of the shadowy waters, floating with the current.

THE FIRST SPRING DAY ON CHESTNUT STREET

WINTER relaxing its hold, has already allow'd us a foretaste of spring. As I write, yesterday afternoon's softness and brightness, (after the morning fog, which gave it a better setting, by contrast,) show'd Chestnut street—say between Broad and Fourth—to more advantage in its various asides, and all its stores, and gay-dress'd crowds generally, than for three months past. I took a walk there between one and two. Doubtless, there were plenty of hard-up folks along the pavements, but nine-tenths of the myriad-moving human panorama to all appearance seem'd flush, well-fed, and fully-provided. At all events it was good to be on Chestnut street yesterday. The peddlers on the sidewalk—("sleeve-buttons, three for five cents")—the handsome little fellow with canary-bird whistles—the cane men, toy men, toothpick men—the old woman squatted in a heap on the cold stone flags, with her basket of matches, pins and tape—the young negro mother, sitting, begging, with her two little coffee-color'd twins on her lap—the beauty of the cramm'd conservatory of rare flowers, flaunting reds, yellows, snowy lilies, incredible orchids, at the Baldwin mansion near Twelfth street—the show of fine poultry, beef, fish, at the restaurants—the china stores, with glass and statuettes—the luscious tropical fruits—the street cars plodding along, with their tintinnabulating bells—the fat, cab-looking, rapidly driven one-horse vehicles of the post-office, squeez'd full of coming or going letter-carriers, so healthy and handsome and manly-looking, in their gray uniforms—the costly books, pictures, curiosities, in the windows—the gigantic policemen at most of the corners—will all be readily remember'd and recognized as features of this principal avenue of Philadelphia. Chestnut street, I have discover'd, is not without individuality, and its own points, even when compared with the great promenade-streets of other cities. I

have never been in Europe, but acquired years' familiar experience
with New York's, (perhaps the world's,) great thoroughfare, Broadway, and possess to some extent a personal and saunterer's knowledge of St. Charles street in New Orleans, Tremont street in Boston,
and the broad trottoirs of Pennsylvania avenue in Washington. Of
course it is a pity that Chestnut were not two or three times wider;
but the street, any fine day, shows vividness, motion, variety, not
easily to be surpass'd. (Sparkling eyes, human faces, magnetism,
well-dress'd women, ambulating to and fro—with lots of fine things
in the windows—are they not about the same, the civilized world
over?)

> *How fast the flitting figures come!*
> *The mild, the fierce, the stony face;*
> *Some bright with thoughtless smiles—and some*
> *Where secret tears have left their trace.*

A few days ago one of the six-story clothing stores along here
had the space inside its plate-glass show-window partition'd into a
little corral, and litter'd deeply with rich clover and hay, (I could
smell the odor outside,) on which reposed two magnificent fat
sheep, full-sized but young—the handsomest creatures of the kind
I ever saw. I stopp'd long and long, with the crowd, to view them—
one lying down chewing the cud, and one standing up, looking out,
with dense-fringed patient eyes. Their wool, of a clear tawny color,
with streaks of glistening black—altogether a queer sight amidst
that crowded promenade of dandies, dollars and drygoods.

UP THE HUDSON TO ULSTER COUNTY

April 23.—Off to New York on a little tour and visit. Leaving the
hospitable, home-like quarters of my valued friends, Mr. and Mrs.
J. H. Johnston—took the 4 P.M. boat, bound up the Hudson, 100
miles or so. Sunset and evening fine. Especially enjoy'd the hour
after we passed Cozzens's landing—the night lit by the crescent
moon and Venus, now swimming in tender glory, and now hid by
the high rocks and hills of the western shore, which we hugg'd
close. (Where I spend the next ten days is in Ulster county and its
neighborhood, with frequent morning and evening drives, observations of the river, and short rambles.)

April 24—Noon.—A little more and the sun would be oppressive.
The bees are out gathering their bread from willows and other
trees. I watch them returning, darting through the air or lighting

on the hives, their thighs covered with the yellow forage. A solitary
robin sings near. I sit in my shirt sleeves and gaze from an open
bay-window on the indolent scene—the thin haze, the Fishkill hills
in the distance—off on the river, a sloop with slanting mainsail, and
two or three little shad-boats. Over on the railroad opposite, long
freight trains, sometimes weighted by cylinder-tanks of petroleum,
thirty, forty, fifty cars in a string, panting and rumbling along in
full view, but the sound soften'd by distance.

DAYS AT J.B.'s—TURF FIRES—SPRING SONGS

April 26.—At sunrise, the pure clear sound of the meadow lark. An
hour later, some notes, few and simple, yet delicious and perfect,
from the bush-sparrow—towards noon the reedy trill of the robin.
To-day is the fairest, sweetest yet—penetrating warmth—a lovely
veil in the air, partly heat-vapor and partly from the turf-fires everywhere in patches on the farms. A group of soft maples near by
silently bursts out in crimson tips, buzzing all day with busy bees.
The white sails of sloops and schooners glide up or down the river;
and long trains of cars, with ponderous roll, or faint bell notes, almost constantly on the opposite shore. The earliest wild flowers in
the woods and fields, spicy arbutus, blue liverwort, frail anemone,
and the pretty white blossoms of the bloodroot. I launch out in slow
rambles, discovering them. As I go along the roads I like to see the
farmers' fires in patches, burning the dry brush, turf, debris. How
the smoke crawls along, flat to the ground, slanting, slowly rising,
reaching away, and at last dissipating. I like its acrid smell—whiffs
just reaching me—welcomer than French perfume.

The birds are plenty; of any sort, or of two or three sorts, curiously, not a sign, till suddenly some warm, gushing, sunny April
(or even March) day—lo! there they are, from twig to twig, or
fence to fence, flirting, singing, some mating, preparing to build.
But most of them *en passant*—a fortnight, a month in these parts,
and then away. As in all phases, Nature keeps up her vital, copious,
eternal procession. Still, plenty of the birds hang around all or most
of the season—now their love-time, and era of nest-building. I find
flying over the river, crows, gulls and hawks. I hear the afternoon
shriek of the latter, darting about, preparing to nest. The oriole
will soon be heard here, and the twanging *meoeow* of the cat-bird;
also the king-bird, cuckoo and the warblers. All along, there are
three peculiarly characteristic spring songs—the meadow-lark's, so
sweet, so alert and remonstrating (as if he said, "don't you see?" or,

"can't you understand?")—the cheery, mellow, human tones of the robin—(I have been trying for years to get a brief term, or phrase, that would identify and describe that robin-call)—and the amorous whistle of the high-hole. Insects are out plentifully at midday.

April 29.—As we drove lingering along the road we heard, just after sundown, the song of the wood-thrush. We stopp'd without a word, and listen'd long. The delicious notes—a sweet, artless, voluntary, simple anthem, as from the flute-stops of some organ, wafted through the twilight—echoing well to us from the perpendicular high rock, where, in some thick young trees' recesses at the base, sat the bird—fill'd our senses, our souls.

MEETING A HERMIT

I FOUND in one of my rambles up the hills a real hermit, living in a lonesome spot, hard to get at, rocky, the view fine, with a little patch of land two rods square. A man of youngish middle age, city born and raised, had been to school, had travel'd in Europe and California. I first met him once or twice on the road, and pass'd the time of day, with some small talk; then, the third time, he ask'd me to go along a bit and rest in his hut (an almost unprecedented compliment, as I heard from others afterwards.) He was of Quaker stock, I think; talk'd with ease and moderate freedom, but did not unbosom his life, or story, or tragedy, or whatever it was.

AN ULSTER COUNTY WATERFALL

I JOT this mem. in a wild scene of woods and hills, where we have come to visit a waterfall. I never saw finer or more copious hemlocks, many of them large, some old and hoary. Such a sentiment to them, secretive, shaggy—what I call weather-beaten and let-alone— a rich underlay of ferns, yew sprouts and mosses, beginning to be spotted with the early summer wild-flowers. Enveloping all, the monotone and liquid gurgle from the hoarse impetuous copious fall —the greenish-tawny, darkly transparent waters, plunging with velocity down the rocks, with patches of milk-white foam—a stream of hurrying amber, thirty feet wide, risen far back in the hills and woods, now rushing with volume—every hundred rods a fall, and sometimes three or four in that distance. A primitive forest, druidical, solitary and savage—not ten visitors a year—broken rocks everywhere—shade overhead, thick underfoot with leaves—a just palpable wild and delicate aroma.

WALTER DUMONT AND HIS MEDAL

As I saunter'd along the high road yesterday, I stopp'd to watch a
man near by, ploughing a rough stony field with a yoke of oxen.
Usually there is much geeing and hawing, excitement, and continual noise and expletives, about a job of this kind. But I noticed
how different, how easy and wordless, yet firm and sufficient, the
work of this young ploughman. His name was Walter Dumont, a
farmer, and son of a farmer, working for their living. Three years
ago, when the steamer "Sunnyside" was wreck'd of a bitter icy night
on the west bank here, Walter went out in his boat—was the first
man on hand with assistance—made a way through the ice to shore,
connected a line, perform'd work of first-class readiness, daring,
danger, and saved numerous lives. Some weeks after, one evening
when he was up at Esopus, among the usual loafing crowd at the
country store and post-office, there arrived the gift of an unexpected
official gold medal for the quiet hero. The impromptu presentation
was made to him on the spot, but he blush'd, hesitated as he took
it, and had nothing to say.

HUDSON RIVER SIGHTS

IT WAS a happy thought to build the Hudson river railroad right
along the shore. The grade is already made by nature; you are sure
of ventilation one side—and you are in nobody's way. I see, hear,
the locomotives and cars, rumbling, roaring, flaming, smoking, constantly, away off there, night and day—less than a mile distant, and
in full view by day. I like both sight and sound. Express trains
thunder and lighten along; of freight trains, most of them very long,
there cannot be less than a hundred a day. At night far down you
see the headlight approaching, coming steadily on like a meteor.
The river at night has its special character-beauties. The shad
fishermen go forth in their boats and pay out their nets—one sitting
forward, rowing, and one standing up aft dropping it properly—
marking the line with little floats bearing candles, conveying, as
they glide over the water, an indescribable sentiment and doubled
brightness. I like to watch the tows at night, too, with their twinkling lamps, and hear the husky panting of the steamers; or catch
the sloops' and schooners' shadowy forms, like phantoms, white,
silent, indefinite, out there. Then the Hudson of a clear moonlight
night.

But there is one sight the very grandest. Sometimes in the fiercest
driving storm of wind, rain, hail or snow, a great eagle will appear
over the river, now soaring with steady and now overhended wings

—always confronting the gale, or perhaps cleaving into, or at times literally *sitting* upon it. It is like reading some first-class natural tragedy or epic, or hearing martial trumpets. The splendid bird enjoys the hubbub—is adjusted and equal to it—finishes it so artistically. His pinions just oscillating—the position of his head and neck—his resistless, occasionally varied flight—now a swirl, now an upward movement—the black clouds driving—the angry wash below —the hiss of rain, the wind's piping (perhaps the ice colliding, grunting)—he tacking or jibing—now, as it were, for a change, abandoning himself to the gale, moving with it with such velocity— and now, resuming control, he comes up against it, lord of the situation and the storm—lord, amid it, of power and savage joy.

Sometimes (as at present writing,) middle of sunny afternoon, the old "Vanderbilt" steamer stalking ahead—I plainly hear her rhythmic, slushing paddles—drawing by long hawsers an immense and varied following string, ("an old sow and pigs," the river folks call it.) First comes a big barge, with a house built on it, and spars towering over the roof; then canal boats, a lengthen'd, clustering train, fasten'd and link'd together—the one in the middle, with high staff, flaunting a broad and gaudy flag—others with the almost invariable lines of new-wash'd clothes, drying; two sloops and a schooner aside the tow—little wind, and that adverse—with three long, dark, empty barges bringing up the rear. People are on the boats: men lounging, women in sun-bonnets, children, stovepipes with streaming smoke.

TWO CITY AREAS, CERTAIN HOURS

NEW YORK, *May 24*, '79.—Perhaps no quarters of this city (I have return'd again for awhile,) make more brilliant, animated, crowded, spectacular human presentations these fine May afternoons than the two I am now going to describe from personal observation. First: that area comprising Fourteenth street (especially the short range between Broadway and Fifth avenue) with Union square, its adjacencies, and so retrostretching down Broadway for half a mile. All the walks here are wide, and the spaces ample and free—now flooded with liquid gold from the last two hours of powerful sunshine. The whole area at 5 o'clock, the days of my observations, must have contain'd from thirty to forty thousand finely-dress'd people, all in motion, plenty of them good-looking, many beautiful women, often youths and children, the latter in groups with their nurses—the trottoirs everywhere close-spread, thick-tangled, (yet no collision, no trouble,) with masses of bright color, action, and tasty toilets; (surely the women dress better than ever before, and the men do too.) As if New York would show these afternoons what it can do in its humanity, its choicest physique and physiognomy, and its countless prodigality of locomotion, dry goods, glitter, magnetism, and happiness.

Second: also from 5 to 7 P.M. the stretch of Fifth avenue, all the way from the Central Park exits at Fifty-ninth street, down to Fourteenth, especially along the high grade by Fortieth street, and down the hill. A Mississippi of horses and rich vehicles, not by dozens and scores, but hundreds and thousands—the broad avenue filled and cramm'd with them—a moving, sparkling, hurrying crush, for more than two miles. (I wonder they don't get block'd, but I believe they never do.) Altogether it is to me the marvel sight of New York. I like to get in one of the Fifth avenue stages and ride up, stemming the swift-moving procession. I doubt if London or Paris or any city in the world can show such a carriage carnival as I have seen here five or six times these beautiful May afternoons.

CENTRAL PARK WALKS AND TALKS

May 16 to 22.—I visit Central Park now almost every day, sitting, or slowly rambling, or riding around. The whole place presents its very best appearance this current month—the full flush of the trees, the plentiful white and pink of the flowering shrubs, the emerald green of the grass spreading everywhere, yellow dotted still with dandelions—the specialty of the plentiful gray rocks, peculiar to these grounds, cropping out, miles and miles—and over all the beauty and purity, three days out of four, of our summer skies. As I sit, placidly, early afternoon, off against Ninetieth street, the policeman, C. C., a well-form'd sandy-complexion'd young fellow, comes over and stands near me. We grow quite friendly and chatty forthwith. He is a New Yorker born and raised, and in answer to my questions tells me about the life of a New York Park policeman, (while he talks keeping his eyes and ears vigilantly open, occasionally pausing and moving where he can get full views of the vistas of the road, up and down, and the spaces around.) The pay is $2.40 a day (seven days to a week)—the men come on and work eight hours straight ahead, which is all that is required of them out of the twenty-four. The position has more risks than one might suppose—for instance if a team or horse runs away (which happens daily) each man is expected not only to be prompt, but to waive safety and stop wildest nag or nags—(*do it,* and don't be thinking of your bones or face)—give the alarm-whistle too, so that other guards

may repeat, and the vehicles up and down the tracks be warn'd.
Injuries to the men are continually happening. There is much alertness and quiet strength. (Few appreciate, I have often thought, the
Ulyssean capacity, derring do, quick readiness in emergencies,
practicality, unwitting devotion and heroism, among our American
young men and working-people—the firemen, the railroad employés,
the steamer and ferry men, the police, the conductors and drivers—
the whole splendid average of native stock, city and country.) It is
good work, though; and upon the whole, the Park force members
like it. They see life, and the excitement keeps them up. There is
not so much difficulty as might be supposed from tramps, roughs,
or in keeping people "off the grass." The worst trouble of the regular Park employé is from malarial fever, chills, and the like.

A FINE AFTERNOON, 4 TO 6

TEN thousand vehicles careering through the Park this perfect afternoon. Such a show! and I have seen all—watch'd it narrowly, and
at my leisure. Private barouches, cabs and coupés, some fine horseflesh—lapdogs, footmen, fashions, foreigners, cockades on hats, crests
on panels—the full oceanic tide of New York's wealth and "gentility." It was an impressive, rich, interminable circus on a grand
scale, full of action and color in the beauty of the day, under the
clear sun and moderate breeze. Family groups, couples, single
drivers—of course dresses generally elegant—much "style," (yet perhaps little or nothing, even in that direction, that fully justified
itself.) Through the windows of two or three of the richest carriages I saw faces almost corpse-like, so ashy and listless. Indeed
the whole affair exhibited less of sterling America, either in spirit or
countenance, than I had counted on from such a select mass-
spectacle. I suppose, as a proof of limitless wealth, leisure, and the
aforesaid "gentility," it was tremendous. Yet what I saw those hours
(I took two other occasions, two other afternoons to watch the
same scene,) confirms a thought that haunts me every additional
glimpse I get of our top-loftical general or rather exceptional phases
of wealth and fashion in this country—namely, that they are ill at
ease, much too conscious, cased in too many cerements, and far
from happy—that there is nothing in them which we who are poor
and plain need at all envy, and that instead of the perennial smell
of the grass and woods and shores, their typical redolence is of
soaps and essences, very rare may be, but suggesting the barber
shop—something that turns stale and musty in a few hours anyhow.
Perhaps the show on the horseback road was prettiest. Many

groups (threes a favorite number,) some couples, some singly—many ladies—frequently horses or parties dashing along on a full run—fine riding the rule—a few really first-class animals. As the afternoon waned, the wheel'd carriages grew less, but the saddle-riders seemed to increase. They linger'd long—and I saw some charming forms and faces.

DEPARTING OF THE BIG STEAMERS

May 15.—A three hours' bay-trip from 12 to 3 this afternoon, accompanying "the City of Brussels" down as far as the Narrows, in behoof of some Europe-bound friends, to give them a good send off. Our spirited little tug, the "Seth Low," kept close to the great black "Brussels," sometimes one side, sometimes the other, always up to her, or even pressing ahead, (like the blooded pony accompanying the royal elephant.) The whole affair, from the first, was an animated, quick-passing, characteristic New York scene; the large, good-looking, well-dress'd crowd on the wharf-end—men and women come to see their friends depart, and bid them God-speed—the ship's sides swarming with passengers—groups of bronze-faced sailors, with uniform'd officers at their posts—the quiet directions, as she quickly unfastens and moves out, prompt to a minute—the emotional faces, adieus and fluttering handkerchiefs, and many smiles and some tears on the wharf—the answering faces, smiles, tears and fluttering handkerchiefs, from the ship—(what can be subtler and finer than this play of faces on such occasions in these responding crowds?—what go more to one's heart?)—the proud, steady, noiseless cleaving of the grand oceaner down the bay—we speeding by her side a few miles, and then turning, wheeling, amid a babel of wild hurrahs, shouted partings, ear-splitting steam whistles, kissing of hands and waving of handkerchiefs.

This departing of the big steamers, noons or afternoons—there is no better medicine when one is listless or vapory. I am fond of going down Wednesdays and Saturdays—their more special days—to watch them and the crowds on the wharves, the arriving passengers, the general bustle and activity, the eager looks from the faces, the clear-toned voices, (a travel'd foreigner, a musician, told me the other day she thinks an American crowd has the finest voices in the world,) the whole look of the great, shapely black ships themselves, and their groups and lined sides—in the setting of our bay with the blue sky overhead. Two days after the above I saw the "Britannic," the "Donau," the "Helvetia" and the "Schiedam" steam out, all off for Europe—a magnificent sight.

TWO HOURS ON THE MINNESOTA

FROM 7 to 9, aboard the United States school-ship Minnesota, lying up the North river. Captain Luce sent his gig for us about sundown, to the foot of Twenty-third street, and receiv'd us aboard with officer-like hospitality and sailor heartiness. There are several hundred youths on the Minnesota to be train'd for efficiently manning the government navy. I like the idea much; and, so far as I have seen to-night, I like the way it is carried out on this huge vessel. Below, on the gun-deck, were gather'd nearly a hundred of the boys, to give us some of their singing exercises, with a melodeon accompaniment, play'd by one of their number. They sang with a will. The best part, however, was the sight of the young fellows themselves. I went over among them before the singing began, and talk'd a few minutes informally. They are from all the States; I asked for the Southerners, but could only find one, a lad from Baltimore. In age, apparently, they range from about fourteen years to nineteen or twenty. They are all of American birth, and have to pass a rigid medical examination; well-grown youths, good flesh, bright eyes, looking straight at you, healthy, intelligent, not a slouch among them, nor a menial—in every one the promise of a man. I have been to many public aggregations of young and old, and of schools and colleges, in my day, but I confess I have never been so near satisfied, so comforted, (both from the fact of the school itself, and the splendid proof of our country, our composite race, and the sample-promises of its good average capacities, its future,) as in the collection from all parts of the United States on this navy training ship. ("Are there going to be *any men* there?" was the dry and pregnant reply of Emerson to one who had been crowding him with the rich material statistics and possibilities of some western or Pacific region.)

May 26.—Aboard the Minnesota again. Lieut. Murphy kindly came for me in his boat. Enjoy'd specially those brief trips to and fro—the sailors, tann'd, strong, so bright and able-looking, pulling their oars in long side-swing, man-of-war style, as they row'd me across. I saw the boys in companies drilling with small arms; had a talk with Chaplain Rawson. At 11 o'clock all of us gathered to breakfast around a long table in the great ward room—I among the rest—a genial, plentiful, hospitable affair every way—plenty to eat, and of the best; became acquainted with several new officers. This second visit, with its observations, talks, (two or three at random with the boys,) confirm'd my first impressions.

MATURE SUMMER DAYS AND NIGHTS

Aug. 4.—Forenoon—as I sit under the willow shade, (have retreated down in the country again,) a little bird is leisurely dousing and flirting himself amid the brook almost within reach of me. He evidently fears me not—takes me for some concomitant of the neighboring earthy banks, free bushery and wild weeds. *6 p. m.*—The last three days have been perfect ones for the season, (four nights ago copious rains, with vehement thunder and lightning.) I write this sitting by the creek watching my two kingfishers at their sundown sport. The strong, beautiful, joyous creatures! Their wings glisten in the slanted sunbeams as they circle and circle around, occasionally dipping and dashing the water, and making long stretches up and down the creek. Wherever I go over fields, through lanes, in by-places, blooms the white-flowering wild-carrot, its delicate pat of snow-flakes crowning its slender stem, gracefully oscillating in the breeze.

EXPOSITION BUILDING—NEW CITY HALL— RIVER TRIP

PHILADELPHIA, *Aug. 26.*—Last night and to-night of unsurpass'd clearness, after two days' rain; moon splendor and star splendor. Being out toward the great Exposition building, West Philadelphia, I saw it lit up, and thought I would go in. There was a ball, democratic but nice; plenty of young couples waltzing and quadrilling— music by a good string-band. To the sight and hearing of these— to moderate strolls up and down the roomy spaces—to getting off aside, resting in an arm-chair and looking up a long while at the grand high roof with its graceful and multitudinous work of iron rods, angles, gray colors, plays of light and shade, receding into dim outlines—to absorbing (in the intervals of the string band,) some capital voluntaries and rolling caprices from the big organ at the other end of the building—to sighting a shadow'd figure or group or couple of lovers every now and then passing some near or farther aisle—I abandon'd myself for over an hour.

Returning home, riding down Market street in an open summer car, something detain'd us between Fifteenth and Broad, and I got out to view better the new, three-fifths-built marble edifice, the City Hall, of magnificent proportions—a majestic and lovely show there in the moonlight—flooded all over, façades, myriad silver-white lines and carv'd heads and mouldings, with the soft dazzle—silent, weird, beautiful—well, I know that never when finish'd will that

magnificent pile impress one as it impress'd me those fifteen minutes.

To-night, since, I have been long on the river. I watch the
C-shaped Northern Crown, (with the star Alshacca that blazed out
so suddenly, alarmingly, one night a few years ago.) The moon in
her third quarter, and up nearly all night. And there, as I look eastward, my long-absent Pleiades, welcome again to sight. For an hour
I enjoy the soothing and vital scene to the low splash of waves—new
stars steadily, noiselessly rising in the east.

As I cross the Delaware, one of the deck-hands, F. R., tells me
how a woman jump'd overboard and was drown'd a couple of hours
since. It happen'd in mid-channel—she leap'd from the forward part
of the boat, which went over her. He saw her rise on the other side
in the swift running water, throw her arms and closed hands high
up, (white hands and bare forearms in the moonlight like a flash,)
and then she sank. (I found out afterwards that this young fellow
had promptly jump'd in, swam after the poor creature, and made,
though unsuccessfully, the bravest efforts to rescue her; but he
didn't mention that part at all in telling me the story.)

SWALLOWS ON THE RIVER

Sept. 3.—Cloudy and wet, and wind due east; air without palpable
fog, but very heavy with moisture—welcome for a change. Forenoon, crossing the Delaware, I noticed unusual numbers of swallows in flight, circling, darting, graceful beyond description, close
to the water. Thick, around the bows of the ferry-boat as she lay
tied in her slip, they flew; and as we went out I watch'd beyond the
pier-heads, and across the broad stream, their swift-winding loop-
ribands of motion, down close to it, cutting and intersecting. Though
I had seen swallows all my life, seem'd as though I never before
realized their peculiar beauty and character in the landscape.
(Some time ago, for an hour, in a huge old country barn, watching
these birds flying, recall'd the 22d book of the Odyssey, where
Ulysses slays the suitors, bringing things to *eclaircissement,* and
Minerva, swallow-bodied, darts up through the spaces of the hall,
sits high on a beam, looks complacently on the show of slaughter,
and feels in her element, exulting, joyous.)

BEGIN A LONG JAUNT WEST

THE following three or four months (Sept. to Dec. '79) I made
quite a western journey, fetching up at Denver, Colorado, and

penetrating the Rocky Mountain region enough to get a good notion of it all. Left West Philadelphia after 9 o'clock one night, middle of September, in a comfortable sleeper. Oblivious of the two or three hundred miles across Pennsylvania; at Pittsburgh in the morning to breakfast. Pretty good view of the city and Birmingham—fog and damp, smoke, coke-furnaces, flames, discolor'd wooden houses, and vast collections of coal-barges. Presently a bit of fine region, West Virginia, the Panhandle, and crossing the river, the Ohio. By day through the latter State—then Indiana—and so rock'd to slumber for a second night, flying like lightning through Illinois.

IN THE SLEEPER

WHAT a fierce weird pleasure to lie in my berth at night in the luxurious palace-car, drawn by the mighty Baldwin—embodying, and filling me, too, full of the swiftest motion, and most resistless strength! It is late, perhaps midnight or after—distances join'd like magic—as we speed through Harrisburg, Columbus, Indianapolis. The element of danger adds zest to it all. On we go, rumbling and flashing, with our loud whinnies thrown out from time to time, or trumpet-blasts, into the darkness. Passing the homes of men, the farms, barns, cattle—the silent villages. And the car itself, the sleeper, with curtains drawn and lights turn'd down—in the berths the slumberers, many of them women and children—as on, on, on, we fly like lightning through the night—how strangely sound and sweet they sleep! (They say the French Voltaire in his time designated the grand opera and a ship of war the most signal illustrations of the growth of humanity's and art's advance beyond primitive barbarism. Perhaps if the witty philosopher were here these days, and went in the same car with perfect bedding and feed from New York to San Francisco, he would shift his type and sample to one of our American sleepers.)

MISSOURI STATE

WE SHOULD have made the run of 960 miles from Philadelphia to St. Louis in thirty-six hours, but we had a collision and bad loco-motive smash about two-thirds of the way, which set us back. So merely stopping over night that time in St. Louis, I sped on westward. As I cross'd Missouri State the whole distance by the St. Louis and Kansas City Northern Railroad, a fine early autumn day, I thought my eyes had never looked on scenes of greater pastoral beauty. For over two hundred miles successive rolling prairies, agriculturally perfect view'd by Pennsylvania and New Jersey eyes, and dotted here and there with fine timber. Yet fine as the land is, it isn't the finest portion; (there is a bed of impervious clay and hard-pan beneath this section that holds water too firmly, "drowns the land in wet weather, and bakes it in dry," as a cynical farmer told me.) South are some richer tracts, though perhaps the beauty-spots of the State are the northwestern counties. Altogether, I am clear, (now, and from what I have seen and learn'd since,) that Missouri, in climate, soil, relative situation, wheat, grass, mines, railroads, and every important materialistic respect, stands in the front rank of the Union. Of Missouri averaged politically and socially I have heard all sorts of talk, some pretty severe—but I should have no fear myself of getting along safely and comfortably anywhere among the Missourians. They raise a good deal of tobacco. You see at this time quantities of the light greenish-gray leaves pulled and hanging out to dry on temporary frameworks or rows of sticks. Looks much like the mullein familiar to eastern eyes.

LAWRENCE AND TOPEKA, KANSAS

WE THOUGHT of stopping in Kansas City, but when we got there we found a train ready and a crowd of hospitable Kansians to take us on to Lawrence, to which I proceeded. I shall not soon forget my good days in L., in company with Judge Usher and his sons, (especially John and Linton,) true westerners of the noblest type. Nor the similar days in Topeka. Nor the brotherly kindness of my RR. friends there, and the city and State officials. Lawrence and Topeka are large, bustling, half-rural, handsome cities. I took two or three long drives about the latter, drawn by a spirited team over smooth roads.

THE PRAIRIES
And an Undelivered Speech

AT A large popular meeting at Topeka—the Kansas State Silver Wedding, fifteen or twenty thousand people—I had been erroneously bill'd to deliver a poem. As I seem'd to be made much of, and wanted to be good-natured, I hastily pencill'd out the following little speech. Unfortunately, (or fortunately,) I had such a good time and rest, and talk and dinner, with the U. boys, that I let the hours slip away and didn't drive over to the meeting and speak my piece. But here it is just the same:

"My friends, your bills announce me as giving a poem; but I have no poem—have composed none for this occasion. And I can honestly say I am now glad of it. Under these skies resplendent in September beauty—amid the peculiar landscape you are used to, but which is new to me—these interminable and stately prairies—in the freedom and vigor and sane enthusiasm of this perfect western air and autumn sunshine—it seems to me a poem would be almost an impertinence. But if you care to have a word from me, I should speak it about these very prairies; they impress me most, of all the objective shows I see or have seen on this, my first real visit to the West. As I have roll'd rapidly hither for more than a thousand miles, through fair Ohio, through bread-raising Indiana and Illinois—through ample Missouri, that contains and raises everything; as I have partially explor'd your charming city during the last two days, and, standing on Oread hill, by the university, have launch'd my view across broad expanses of living green, in every direction—I have again been most impress'd, I say, and shall remain for the rest of my life most impress'd, with that feature of the topography of your western central world—that vast Something, stretching out on its own unbounded scale, unconfined, which there is in these prairies, combining the real and ideal, and beautiful as dreams.

"I wonder indeed if the people of this continental inland West know how much of first-class art they have in these prairies—how original and all your own—how much of the influences of a character for your future humanity, broad, patriotic, heroic and new? how entirely they tally on land the grandeur and superb monotony of the skies of heaven, and the ocean with its waters? how freeing, soothing, nourishing they are to the soul?

"Then is it not subtly they who have given us our leading modern Americans, Lincoln and Grant?—vast-spread, average men—their foregrounds of character altogether practical and real, yet (to those who have eyes to see) with finest backgrounds of the ideal, towering high as any. And do we not see, in them, foreshadowings of the future races that shall fill these prairies?

"Not but what the Yankee and Atlantic States, and every other part— Texas, and the States flanking the south-east and the Gulf of Mexico—the Pacific shore empire—the Territories and Lakes, and the Canada line (the day is not yet, but it will come, including Canada entire)—are equally and integrally and indissolubly this Nation, the sine qua non of the human, political and commercial New World. But this favor'd central area of (in round numbers) two thousand miles square seems fated to be the home both of what I would call America's distinctive ideas and distinctive realities."

ON TO DENVER—A FRONTIER INCIDENT

The jaunt of five or six hundred miles from Topeka to Denver took me through a variety of country, but all unmistakably prolific, western, American, and on the largest scale. For a long distance we follow the line of the Kansas river, (I like better the old name, Kaw,) a stretch of very rich, dark soil, famed for its wheat, and call'd the Golden Belt—then plains and plains, hour after hour—Ellsworth county, the centre of the State—where I must stop a moment to tell a characteristic story of early days—scene the very spot where I am passing—time 1868. In a scrimmage at some public gathering in the town, A. had shot B. quite badly, but had not kill'd him. The sober men of Ellsworth conferr'd with one another and decided that A. deserv'd punishment. As they wished to set a good example and establish their reputation the reverse of a Lynching town, they open an informal court and bring both men before them for deliberate trial. Soon as this trial begins the wounded man is led forward to give his testimony. Seeing his enemy in durance and unarm'd, B. walks suddenly up in a fury and shoots A. through the head—shoots him dead. The court is instantly adjourn'd, and its unanimous members, without a word of debate, walk the murderer B. out, wounded as he is, and hang him.

In due time we reach Denver, which city I fall in love with from the first, and have that feeling confirm'd, the longer I stay there. One of my pleasantest days was a jaunt, via Platte cañon, to Leadville.

AN HOUR ON KENOSHA SUMMIT

JOTTINGS from the Rocky Mountains, mostly pencill'd during a day's trip over the South Park RR., returning from Leadville, and especially the hour we were detain'd, (much to my satisfaction,) at Kenosha summit. As afternoon advances, novelties, far-reaching splendors, accumulate under the bright sun in this pure air. But I had better commence with the day.

The confronting of Platte cañon just at dawn, after a ten miles' ride in early darkness on the rail from Denver—the seasonable stoppage at the entrance of the cañon, and good breakfast of eggs, trout, and nice griddle-cakes—then as we travel on, and get well in the gorge, all the wonders, beauty, savage power of the scene—the wild stream of water, from sources of snows, brawling continually in sight one side—the dazzling sun, and the morning lights on the rocks—such turns and grades in the track, squirming around corners, or up and down hills—far glimpses of a hundred peaks, titanic necklaces, stretching north and south—the huge rightly-named Dome-rock—and as we dash along, others similar, simple, monolithic, elephantine.

AN EGOTISTICAL "FIND"

"I HAVE found the law of my own poems," was the unspoken but more-and-more decided feeling that came to me as I pass'd, hour after hour, amid all this grim yet joyous elemental abandon—this plenitude of material, entire absence of art, untrammel'd play of primitive Nature—the chasm, the gorge, the crystal mountain stream, repeated scores, hundreds of miles—the broad handling and absolute uncrampedness—the fantastic forms, bathed in transparent browns, faint reds and grays, towering sometimes a thousand, sometimes two or three thousand feet high—at their tops now and then huge masses pois'd, and mixing with the clouds, with only their outlines, hazed in misty lilac, visible. ("In Nature's grandest shows," says an old Dutch writer, an ecclesiastic, "amid the ocean's depth, if so might be, or countless worlds rolling above at night, a man thinks of them, weighs all, not for themselves or the abstract, but with reference to his own personality, and how they may affect him or color his destinies.")

NEW SENSES—NEW JOYS

WE FOLLOW the stream of amber and bronze brawling along its bed, with its frequent cascades and snow-white foam. Through the cañon we fly—mountains not only each side, but seemingly, till we get near right in front of us—every rood a new view flashing, and each flash defying description—on the almost perpendicular sides, clinging pines, cedars, spruces, crimson sumach bushes, spots of wild grass—but dominating all, those towering rocks, rocks, rocks, bathed in delicate vari-colors, with the clear sky of autumn overhead. New senses, new joys, seem develop'd. Talk as you like, a typical Rocky Mountain cañon, or a limitless sea-like stretch of the great Kansas or Colorado plains, under favoring circumstances, tallies, perhaps expresses, certainly awakes, those grandest and subtlest element-emotions in the human soul, that all the marble temples and sculptures from Phidias to Thorwaldsen—all paintings, poems, reminiscences, or even music, probably never can.

STEAM-POWER, TELEGRAPHS, &c.

I GET out on a ten minutes' stoppage at Deer creek, to enjoy the unequal'd combination of hill, stone and wood. As we speed again, the yellow granite in the sunshine, with natural spires, minarets, castellated perches far aloft—then long stretches of straight-upright palisades, rhinoceros color—then gamboge and tinted chromos. Ever the best of my pleasures the cool-fresh Colorado atmosphere, yet sufficiently warm. Signs of man's restless advent and pioneerage, hard as Nature's face is—deserted dug-outs by dozens in the side-hills—the scantling-hut, the telegraph-pole, the smoke of some impromptu chimney or outdoor fire—at intervals little settlements of log-houses, or parties of surveyors or telegraph builders, with their comfortable tents. Once, a canvas office where you could send a message by electricity anywhere around the world! Yes, pronounc'd signs of the man of latest dates, dauntlessly grappling with these grisliest shows of the old kosmos. At several places steam saw-mills, with their piles of logs and boards, and the pipes puffing. Occasionally Platte cañon expanding into a grassy flat of a few acres. At one such place, toward the end, where we stop, and I get out to stretch my legs, as I look skyward, or rather mountain-top-ward, a huge hawk or eagle (a rare sight here) is idly soaring, balancing along the ether, now sinking low and coming quite near, and then up again in stately-languid circles—then higher, higher, slanting to the north, and gradually out of sight.

AMERICA'S BACK-BONE

I JOT these lines literally at Kenosha summit, where we return, afternoon, and take a long rest, 10,000 feet above sea-level. At this immense height the South Park stretches fifty miles before me. Mountainous chains and peaks in every variety of perspective, every hue of vista, fringe the view, in nearer, or middle, or far-dim distance, or fade on the horizon. We have now reach'd, penetrated the Rockies, (Hayden calls it the Front Range,) for a hundred miles or so; and though these chains spread away in every direction, specially north and south, thousands and thousands farther, I have seen specimens of the utmost of them, and know henceforth at least what they are, and what they look like. Not themselves alone, for they typify stretches and areas of half the globe—are, in fact, the vertebræ or back-bone of our hemisphere. As the anatomists say a man is only a spine, topp'd, footed, breasted and radiated, so the whole Western world is, in a sense, but an expansion of these mountains. In South America they are the Andes, in Central America and Mexico the Cordilleras, and in our States they go under different names—in California the Coast and Cascade ranges—thence more eastwardly the Sierra Nevadas—but mainly and more centrally here the Rocky Mountains proper, with many an elevation such as Lincoln's, Grey's, Harvard's, Yale's, Long's and Pike's peaks, all over 14,000 feet high.

(East, the highest peaks of the Alleghanies, the Adirondacks, the Catskills, and the White Mountains, range from 2000 to 5500 feet—only Mount Washington, in the latter, 6300 feet.)

THE PARKS

IN THE midst of all here, lie such beautiful contrasts as the sunken basins of the North, Middle, and South Parks, (the latter I am now on one side of, and overlooking,) each the size of a large, level, almost quadrangular, grassy, western county, wall'd in by walls of hills, and each park the source of a river. The ones I specify are the largest in Colorado, but the whole of that State, and of Wyoming, Utah, Nevada and western California, through their sierras and ravines, are copiously mark'd by similar spreads and openings, many of the small ones of paradisiac loveliness and perfection, with their offsets of mountains, streams, atmosphere and hues beyond compare.

ART FEATURES

TALK, I say again, of going to Europe, of visiting the ruins of feudal castles, or Coliseum remains, or kings' palaces—when you can come *here.* The alternations one gets, too; after the Illinois and Kansas prairies of a thousand miles—smooth and easy areas of the corn and wheat of ten million democratic farms in the future—here start up in every conceivable presentation of shape, these non-utilitarian piles, coping the skies, emanating a beauty, terror, power, more than Dante or Angelo ever knew. Yes, I think the chyle of not only poetry and painting, but oratory, and even the metaphysics and music fit for the New World, before being finally assimilated, need first and feeding visits here.

Mountain streams.—The spiritual contrast and etheriality of the whole region consist largely to me in its never-absent peculiar streams—the snows of inaccessible upper areas melting and running down through the gorges continually. Nothing like the water of pastoral plains, or creeks with wooded banks and turf, or anything of the kind elsewhere. The shapes that element takes in the shows of the globe cannot be fully understood by an artist until he has studied these unique rivulets.

Aerial effects.—But perhaps as I gaze around me the rarest sight of all is in atmospheric hues. The prairies—as I cross'd them in my journey hither—and these mountains and parks, seem to me to afford new lights and shades. Everywhere the aerial gradations and sky-effects inimitable; nowhere else such perspectives, such transparent lilacs and grays. I can conceive of some superior landscape painter, some fine colorist, after sketching awhile out here, discarding all his previous work, delightful to stock exhibition amateurs, as muddy, raw and artificial. Near one's eye ranges an infinite variety; high up, the bare whitey-brown, above timber line; in certain spots afar patches of snow any time of year; (no trees, no flowers, no birds, at those chilling altitudes.) As I write I see the Snowy Range through the blue mist, beautiful and far off. I plainly see the patches of snow.

DENVER IMPRESSIONS

THROUGH the long-lingering half-light of the most superb of evenings we return'd to Denver, where I staid several days leisurely exploring, receiving impressions, with which I may as well taper off this memorandum, itemizing what I saw there. The best was the men, three-fourths of them large, able, calm, alert, American. And cash! why they create it here. Out in the smelting works, (the biggest and most improv'd ones, for the precious metals, in the world,) I saw long rows of vats, pans, cover'd by bubbling-boiling water, and fill'd with pure silver, four or five inches thick, many thousand dollars' worth in a pan. The foreman who was showing me shovel'd it carelessly up with a little wooden shovel, as one might toss beans. Then large silver bricks, worth $2000 a brick, dozens of piles, twenty in a pile. In one place in the mountains, at a mining camp, I had a few days before seen rough bullion on the ground in the open air, like the confectioner's pyramids at some swell dinner in New York. (Such a sweet morsel to roll over with a poor author's pen and ink —and appropriate to slip in here—that the silver product of Colorado and Utah, with the gold product of California, New Mexico, Nevada and Dakota, foots up an addition to the world's coin of considerably over a hundred millions every year.)

A city, this Denver, well-laid out—Laramie street, and 15th and 16th and Champa streets, with others, particularly fine—some with tall storehouses of stone or iron, and windows of plate-glass—all the streets with little canals of mountain water running along the sides —plenty of people, "business," modernness—yet not without a certain racy wild smack, all its own. A place of fast horses, (many mares with their colts,) and I saw lots of big greyhounds for antelope hunting. Now and then groups of miners, some just come in, some starting out, very picturesque.

One of the papers here interview'd me, and reported me as saying off-hand: "I have lived in or visited all the great cities on the Atlantic third of the republic—Boston, Brooklyn with its hills, New Orleans, Baltimore, stately Washington, broad Philadelphia, teeming Cincinnati and Chicago, and for thirty years in that wonder, wash'd by hurried and glittering tides, my own New York, not only the New World's but the world's city—but, newcomer to Denver as I am, and threading its streets, breathing its air, warm'd by its sunshine, and having what there is of its human as well as aerial ozone flash'd upon me now for only three or four days, I am very much like a man feels sometimes toward certain people he meets with, and warms to, and hardly knows why. I, too, can hardly tell why, but as I enter'd the city in the slight haze of a late September afternoon, and have breath'd its air, and slept well o' nights, and have roam'd or rode leisurely, and watch'd the comers and goers at the hotels, and absorb'd the climatic magnetism of this curiously attractive region, there has steadily grown upon me a feeling of affection for the spot, which, sudden as it is, has become so definite and strong that I must put it on record."

So much for my feeling toward the Queen city of the plains and peaks, where she sits in her delicious rare atmosphere, over 5000 feet above sea-level, irrigated by mountain streams, one way looking east over the prairies for a thousand miles, and having the other, westward, in constant view by day, draped in their violet haze, mountain tops innumerable. Yes, I fell in love with Denver, and even felt a wish to spend my declining and dying days there.

I TURN SOUTH—AND THEN EAST AGAIN

LEAVE Denver at 8 A. M. by the Rio Grande RR. going south. Mountains constantly in sight in the apparently near distance, veil'd slightly, but still clear and very grand—their cones, colors, sides, distinct against the sky—hundreds, it seem'd thousands, interminable necklaces of them, their tops and slopes hazed more or less slightly in that blue-gray, under the autumn sun, for over a hundred miles—the most spiritual show of objective Nature I ever beheld, or ever thought possible. Occasionally the light strengthens, making a contrast of yellow-tinged silver on one side, with dark and shaded gray on the other. I took a long look at Pike's peak, and was a little disappointed. (I suppose I had expected something stunning.) Our view over plains to the left stretches amply, with corrals here and there, the frequent cactus and wild sage, and herds of cattle feeding. Thus about 120 miles to Pueblo. At that town we board the comfortable and well-equipt Atchison, Topeka and Santa Fe RR., now striking east.

UNFULFILL'D WANTS—THE ARKANSAS RIVER

I HAD wanted to go to the Yellowstone river region—wanted specially to see the National Park, and the geysers and the "hoodoo" or goblin land of that country; indeed, hesitated a little at Pueblo, the turning point—wanted to thread the Veta pass—wanted to go over the Santa Fe trail away southwestward to New Mexico—but turn'd and set my face eastward—leaving behind me whetting glimpse-tastes of southeastern Colorado, Pueblo, Bald mountain, the Spanish peaks, Sangre de Christos, Mile-Shoe-curve (which my veteran friend on the locomotive told me was "the boss railroad curve of the universe,") fort Garland on the plains, Veta, and the three great peaks of the Sierra Blancas.

The Arkansas river plays quite a part in the whole of this region—I see it, or its high-cut rocky northern shore, for miles, and cross and recross it frequently, as it winds and squirms like a snake. The plains vary here even more than usual—sometimes a long sterile stretch of scores of miles—then green, fertile and grassy, an equal length. Some very large herds of sheep. (One wants new words in writing about these plains, and all the inland American West—the terms, *far, large, vast,* &c., are insufficient.)

A SILENT LITTLE FOLLOWER— THE COREOPSIS

HERE I must say a word about a little follower, present even now before my eyes. I have been accompanied on my whole journey from Barnegat to Pike's Peak by a pleasant floricultural friend, or rather millions of friends—nothing more or less than a hardy little yellow five-petal'd September and October wild-flower, growing I think everywhere in the middle and northern United States. I had seen it on the Hudson and over Long Island, and along the banks of the Delaware and through New Jersey, (as years ago up the Connecticut, and one fall by Lake Champlain.) This trip it follow'd me regularly, with its slender stem and eyes of gold, from Cape May to the Kaw valley, and so through the cañons and to these plains. In Missouri I saw immense fields all bright with it. Toward western Illinois I woke up one morning in the sleeper and the first thing when I drew the curtain of my berth and look'd out was its pretty countenance and bending neck.

Sept. 25th.—Early morning—still going east after we leave Sterling, Kansas, where I stopp'd a day and night. The sun up about half an hour; nothing can be fresher or more beautiful than this time, this region. I see quite a field of my yellow flower in full bloom. At intervals dots of nice two-story houses, as we ride swiftly by. Over the immense area, flat as a floor, visible for twenty miles in every direction in the clear air, a prevalence of autumn-drab and reddish-tawny herbage—sparse stacks of hay and enclosures, breaking the landscape—as we rumble by, flocks of prairie-hens starting up. Between Sterling and Florence a fine country. (Remembrances to E. L., my old-young soldier friend of war times, and his wife and boy at S.)

THE PRAIRIES AND GREAT PLAINS IN POETRY

(After traveling Illinois, Missouri, Kansas and Colorado)

GRAND as the thought that doubtless the child is already born who will see a hundred millions of people, the most prosperous and advanc'd of the world, inhabiting these Prairies, the great Plains, and the valley of the Mississippi, I could not help thinking it would be grander still to see all those inimitable American areas fused in the alembic of a perfect poem, or other esthetic work, entirely western, fresh and limitless—altogether our own, without a trace or taste of Europe's soil, reminiscence, technical letter or spirit. My days and nights, as I travel here—what an exhilaration!—not the air alone, and the sense of vastness, but every local sight and feature. Everywhere something characteristic—the cactuses, pinks, buffalo grass, wild sage—the receding perspective, and the far circle-line of the horizon all times of day, especially forenoon—the clear, pure, cool, rarefied nutriment for the lungs, previously quite unknown—the black patches and streaks left by surface-conflagrations—the deep-plough'd furrow of the "fire-guard"—the slanting snow-racks built all along to shield the railroad from winter drifts—the prairie-dogs and the herds of antelope—the curious "dry rivers"—occasionally a "dug-out" or corral—Fort Riley and Fort Wallace—those towns of the northern plains, (like ships on the sea,) Eagle-Tail, Coyotè, Cheyenne, Agate, Monotony, Kit Carson—with ever the ant-hill and the buffalo-wallow—ever the herds of cattle and the cow-boys ("cow-punchers") to me a strangely interesting class, bright-eyed as hawks, with their swarthy complexions and their broad-brimm'd hats—apparently always on horseback, with loose arms slightly raised and swinging as they ride.

THE SPANISH PEAKS—EVENING ON THE PLAINS

BETWEEN Pueblo and Bent's fort, southward, in a clear afternoon sun-spell I catch exceptionally good glimpses of the Spanish peaks. We are in southeastern Colorado—pass immense herds of cattle as our first-class locomotive rushes us along—two or three times crossing the Arkansas, which we follow many miles, and of which river I get fine views, sometimes for quite a distance, its stony, upright, not very high, palisade banks, and then its muddy flats. We pass Fort Lyon—lots of adobie houses—limitless pasturage, appropriately fleck'd with those herds of cattle—in due time the declining sun in the west—a sky of limpid pearl over all—and so evening on the great plains. A calm, pensive, boundless landscape—the perpendicular rocks of the north Arkansas, hued in twilight—a thin line of violet on the southwestern horizon—the palpable coolness and slight aroma—a belated cow-boy with some unruly member of his herd—an emigrant wagon toiling yet a little further, the horses slow and tired—two men, apparently father and son, jogging along on foot—and around all the indescribable *chiaroscuro* and sentiment, (profounder than anything at sea,) athwart these endless wilds.

AMERICA'S CHARACTERISTIC LANDSCAPE

SPEAKING generally as to the capacity and sure future destiny of that plain and prairie area (larger than any European kingdom) it is the inexhaustible land of wheat, maize, wool, flax, coal, iron, beef and pork, butter and cheese, apples and grapes—land of ten million virgin farms—to the eye at present wild and unproductive—yet experts say that upon it when irrigated may easily be grown enough wheat to feed the world. Then as to scenery (giving my own thought and feeling,) while I know the standard claim is that Yosemite, Niagara falls, the upper Yellowstone and the like, afford the greatest natural shows, I am not so sure but the Prairies and Plains, while less stunning at first sight, last longer, fill the esthetic sense fuller, precede all the rest, and make North America's characteristic landscape.

Indeed through the whole of this journey, with all its shows and varieties, what most impress'd me, and will longest remain with me, are these same prairies. Day after day, and night after night, to my eyes, to all my senses—the esthetic one most of all—they silently and broadly unfolded. Even their simplest statistics are sublime.

EARTH'S MOST IMPORTANT STREAM

THE valley of the Mississippi river and its tributaries, (this stream and its adjuncts involve a big part of the question,) comprehends more than twelve hundred thousand square miles, the greater part prairies. It is by far the most important stream on the globe, and would seem to have been marked out by design, slow-flowing from north to south, through a dozen climates, all fitted for man's healthy occupancy, its outlet unfrozen all the year, and its line forming a safe, cheap continental avenue for commerce and passage from the north temperate to the torrid zone. Not even the mighty Amazon (though larger in volume) on its line of east and west—not the Nile in Africa, nor the Danube in Europe, nor the three great rivers of China, compare with it. Only the Mediterranean sea has play'd some such part in history, and all through the past, as the Mississippi is destined to play in the future. By its demesnes, water'd and welded by its branches, the Missouri, the Ohio, the Arkansas, the Red, the Yazoo, the St. Francis and others, it already compacts twenty-five millions of people, not merely the most peaceful and money-making, but the most restless and warlike on earth. Its valley, or reach, is rapidly concentrating the political power of the American Union. One almost thinks it *is* the Union—or soon will be. Take it out, with its radiations, and what would be left? From the car windows through Indiana, Illinois, Missouri, or stopping some days along the Topeka and Santa Fe road, in southern Kansas, and indeed wherever I went, hundreds and thousands of miles through this region, my eyes feasted on primitive and rich meadows, some of them partially inhabited, but far, immensely far more untouch'd, unbroken—and much of it more lovely and fertile in its unplough'd innocence than the fair and valuable fields of New York's, Pennsylvania's, Maryland's or Virginia's richest farms.

PRAIRIE ANALOGIES—THE TREE QUESTION

THE word Prairie is French, and means literally meadow. The cosmical analogies of our North American plains are the Steppes of Asia, the Pampas and Llanos of South America, and perhaps the Saharas of Africa. Some think the plains have been originally lakebeds; others attribute the absence of forests to the fires that almost annually sweep over them—(the cause, in vulgar estimation, of Indian summer.) The tree question will soon become a grave one. Although the Atlantic slope, the Rocky mountain region, and the southern portion of the Mississippi valley, are well wooded, there are here stretches of hundreds and thousands of miles where either not a tree grows, or often useless destruction has prevail'd; and the matter of the cultivation and spread of forests may well be press'd upon thinkers who look to the coming generations of the prairie States.

MISSISSIPPI VALLEY LITERATURE

Lying by one rainy day in Missouri to rest after quite a long exploration—first trying a big volume I found there of "Milton, Young, Gray, Beattie and Collins," but giving it up for a bad job—enjoying however for awhile, as often before, the reading of Walter Scott's poems, "Lay of the Last Minstrel," "Marmion," and so on—I stopp'd and laid down the book, and ponder'd the thought of a poetry that should in due time express and supply the teeming region I was in the midst of, and have briefly touch'd upon. One's mind needs but a moment's deliberation anywhere in the United States to see clearly enough that all the prevalent book and library poets, either as imported from Great Britain, or follow'd and *doppel-gang'd* here, are foreign to our States, copiously as they are read by us all. But to fully understand not only how absolutely in opposition to our times and lands, and how little and cramp'd, and what anachronisms and absurdities many of their pages are, for American purposes, one must dwell or travel awhile in Missouri, Kansas and Colorado, and get rapport with their people and country.

Will the day ever come—no matter how long deferr'd—when those models and lay-figures from the British islands—and even the precious traditions of the classics—will be reminiscences, studies only? The pure breath, primitiveness, boundless prodigality and amplitude, strange mixture of delicacy and power, of continence, of real and ideal, and of all original and first-class elements, of these prairies, the Rocky mountains, and of the Mississippi and Missouri rivers—will they ever appear in, and in some sort form a standard for our poetry and art? (I sometimes think that even the ambition of my friend Joaquin Miller to put them in, and illustrate them, places him ahead of the whole crowd.)

Not long ago I was down New York bay, on a steamer, watching the sunset over the dark green heights of Navesink, and viewing all that inimitable spread of shore, shipping and sea, around Sandy hook. But an intervening week or two, and my eyes catch the shadowy outlines of the Spanish peaks. In the more than two thousand miles between, though of infinite and paradoxical variety, a curious and absolute fusion is doubtless steadily annealing, compacting, identifying all. But subtler and wider and more solid, (to produce such compaction,) than the laws of the States, or the common ground of Congress or the Supreme Court, or the grim welding of our national wars, or the steel ties of railroads, or all the kneading and fusing processes of our material and business history, past or present, would in my opinion be a great throbbing, vital, imaginative work, or series of works, or literature, in constructing which the Plains, the Prairies, and the Mississippi river, with the demesnes of its varied and ample valley, should be the concrete background, and America's humanity, passions, struggles, hopes, there and now —an *eclaircissement* as it is and is to be, on the stage of the New World, of all Time's hitherto drama of war, romance and evolution —should furnish the lambent fire, the ideal.

AN INTERVIEWER'S ITEM

Oct. 17, '79.—To-day one of the newspapers of St. Louis prints the following informal remarks of mine on American, especially Western literature: "We called on Mr. Whitman yesterday and after a somewhat desultory conversation abruptly asked him: 'Do you think we are to have a distinctively American literature?' 'It seems to me,' said he, 'that our work at present is to lay the foundations of a great nation in products, in agriculture, in commerce, in networks of intercommunication, and in all that relates to the comforts of vast masses of men and families, with freedom of speech, ecclesiasticism, &c. These we have founded and are carrying out on a grander scale than ever hitherto, and Ohio, Illinois, Indiana, Missouri, Kansas and Colorado, seem to me to be the seat and field of these very facts and ideas. Materialistic prosperity in all its varied forms, with those other points that I mentioned, intercommunication and freedom, are first to be attended to. When those have their results and get settled, then a literature worthy of us will begin to be defined. Our American superiority and vitality are in the bulk of our people, not in a gentry like the old world. The greatness of our army during the secession war, was in the rank and file, and so with the nation. Other lands have their vitality in a few, a class, but we have it in the bulk of the people. Our leading men are not of much account and never have been, but the average of the people is immense, beyond all history. Sometimes I think in all departments, literature and art included, that will be the way our superiority will exhibit itself. We will not have great individuals or great leaders, but a great average bulk, unprecedentedly great.'"

THE WOMEN OF THE WEST

Kansas City.—I am not so well satisfied with what I see of the women of the prairie cities. I am writing this where I sit leisurely in a store in Main street, Kansas city, a streaming crowd on the sidewalks flowing by. The ladies (and the same in Denver) are all fashionably drest, and have the look of "gentility" in face, manner and action, but they do *not* have, either in physique or the mentality appropriate to them, any high native originality of spirit or body, (as the men certainly have, appropriate to them.) They are "intellectual" and fashionable, but dyspeptic-looking and generally doll-like; their ambition evidently is to copy their eastern sisters. Something far different and in advance must appear, to tally and complete the superb masculinity of the West, and maintain and continue it.

THE SILENT GENERAL

Sept. 28, '79.—So General Grant, after circumambiating the world, has arrived home again—landed in San Francisco yesterday, from the ship City of Tokio from Japan. What a man he is! what a history! what an illustration—his life—of the capacities of that American individuality common to us all. Cynical critics are wondering "what the people can see in Grant" to make such a hubbub about. They aver (and it is no doubt true) that he has hardly the average of our day's literary and scholastic culture, and absolutely no pronounc'd genius or conventional eminence of any sort. Correct: but he proves how an average western farmer, mechanic, boatman, carried by tides of circumstances, perhaps caprices, into a position of incredible military or civic responsibilities, (history has presented none more trying, no born monarch's, no mark more shining for attack or envy,) may steer his way fitly and steadily through them all, carrying the country and himself with credit year after year—command over a million armed men—fight more than fifty pitch'd battles—rule for eight years a land larger than all the kingdoms of Europe combined—and then, retiring, quietly (with a cigar in his mouth) make the promenade of the whole world, through its courts and coteries, and kings and czars and mikados, and splendidest glitters and etiquettes, as phlegmatically as he ever walk'd the portico of a Missouri hotel after dinner. I say all this is what people like—and I am sure I like it. Seems to me it transcends Plutarch. How those old Greeks, indeed, would have seized on him! A mere plain man—no art, no poetry—only practical sense, ability to do, or try his best to do, what devolv'd upon him. A common trader, money-maker, tanner, farmer of Illinois—general for the republic, in its terrific struggle with itself, in the war of attempted secession—President following, (a task of peace, more difficult than the war itself)—nothing heroic, as the authorities put it—and yet the greatest hero. The gods, the destinies, seem to have concentrated upon him.

PRESIDENT HAYES'S SPEECHES

Sept. 30.—I see President Hayes has come out West, passing quite informally from point to point, with his wife and a small cortege of big officers, receiving ovations, and making daily and sometimes double-daily addresses to the people. To these addresses—all impromptu, and some would call them ephemeral—I feel to devote a memorandum. They are shrewd, good-natur'd, face-to-face speeches, on easy topics not too deep; but they give me some revised ideas of oratory—of a new, opportune theory and practice of that art, quite changed from the classic rules, and adapted to our days, our occasions, to American democracy, and to the swarming populations of the West. I hear them criticised as wanting in dignity, but to me they are just what they should be, considering all the circumstances, who they come from, and who they are address'd to. Underneath, his objects are to compact and fraternize the States, encourage their materialistic and industrial development, soothe and expand their self-poise, and tie all and each with resistless double ties not only of inter-trade barter, but human comradeship.

From Kansas city I went on to St. Louis, where I remain'd nearly three months, with my brother T. J. W., and my dear nieces.

ST. LOUIS MEMORANDA

Oct., Nov., and Dec., '79.—The points of St. Louis are its position, its absolute wealth, (the long accumulations of time and trade, solid riches, probably a higher average thereof than any city,) the unrivall'd amplitude of its well-laid out environage of broad plateaus, for future expansion—and the great State of which it is the head. It fuses northern and southern qualities, perhaps native and foreign ones, to perfection, rendezvous the whole stretch of the Mississippi and Missouri rivers, and its American electricity goes well with its German phlegm. Fourth, Fifth and Third streets are store-streets, showy, modern, metropolitan, with hurrying crowds, vehicles, horse-cars, hubbub, plenty of people, rich goods, plate-glass windows, iron fronts often five or six stories high. You can purchase anything in St. Louis (in most of the big western cities for the matter of that) just as readily and cheaply as in the Atlantic marts. Often in going about the town you see reminders of old, even decay'd civilization. The water of the west, in some places, is not good, but they make it up here by plenty of very fair wine, and inexhaustible quantities of the best beer in the world. There are immense establishments for slaughtering beef and pork— and I saw flocks of sheep, 5000 in a flock. (In Kansas city I had visited a packing establishment that kills and packs an average of 2500 hogs a day the whole year round, for export. Another in Atchison, Kansas, same extent; others nearly equal elsewhere. And just as big ones here.)

NIGHTS ON THE MISSISSIPPI

Oct. 29th, 30th, and 31st.—Wonderfully fine, with the full harvest moon, dazzling and silvery. I have haunted the river every night lately, where I could get a look at the bridge by moonlight. It is indeed a structure of perfection and beauty unsurpassable, and I never tire of it. The river at present is very low; I noticed to-day it had much more of a blue-clear look than usual. I hear the slight ripples, the air is fresh and cool, and the view, up or down, wonderfully clear, in the moonlight. I am out pretty late: it is so fascinating, dreamy. The cool night-air, all the influences, the silence, with those far-off eternal stars, do me good. I have been quite ill of late. And so, well-near the centre of our national demesne, these night views of the Mississippi.

UPON OUR OWN LAND

"ALWAYS, after supper, take a walk half a mile long," says an old proverb, dryly adding, "and if convenient let it be upon your own land." I wonder does any other nation but ours afford opportunity for such a jaunt as this? Indeed has any previous period afforded it? No one, I discover, begins to know the real geographic, democratic, indissoluble American Union in the present, or suspect it in the future, until he explores these Central States, and dwells awhile observantly on their prairies, or amid their busy towns, and the mighty father of waters. A ride of two or three thousand miles, "on one's own land," with hardly a disconnection, could certainly be had in no other place than the United States, and at no period before this. If you want to see what the railroad is, and how civilization and progress date from it—how it is the conqueror of crude nature, which it turns to man's use, both on small scales and on the largest—come hither to in-land America.

I return'd home, east, Jan. 5, 1880, having travers'd, to and fro and across, 10,000 miles and more. I soon resumed my seclusions down in the woods, or by the creek, or gaddings about cities, and an occasional disquisition, as will be seen following.

EDGAR POE'S SIGNIFICANCE

Jan. 1, '80.—In diagnosing this disease called humanity—to assume for the nonce what seems a chief mood of the personality and writings of my subject—I have thought that poets, somewhere or other on the list, present the most mark'd indications. Comprehending artists in a mass, musicians, painters, actors, and so on, and considering each and all of them as radiations or flanges of that furious whirling wheel, poetry, the centre and axis of the whole, where else indeed may we so well investigate the causes, growths, tally-marks of the time—the age's matter and malady?

By common consent there is nothing better for man or woman than a perfect and noble life, morally without flaw, happily balanced in activity, physically sound and pure, giving its due proportion, and no more, to the sympathetic, the human emotional element—a life, in all these, unhasting, unresting, untiring to the end. And yet there is another shape of personality dearer far to the artist-sense, (which likes the play of strongest lights and shades,) where the perfect character, the good, the heroic, although never attain'd, is never lost sight of, but through failures, sorrows, temporary downfalls, is return'd to again and again, and while often violated, is passionately adhered to as long as mind, muscles, voice, obey the power we call volition. This sort of personality we see more or less in Burns, Byron, Schiller, and George Sand. But we do not see it in Edgar Poe. (All this is the result of reading at intervals the last three days a new volume of his poems —I took it on my rambles down by the pond, and by degrees read it all through there.) While to the character first outlined the service Poe renders is certainly that entire contrast and contradiction which is next best to fully exemplifying it.

Almost without the first sign of moral principle, or of the concrete or its heroisms, or the simpler affections of the heart, Poe's verses illustrate an intense faculty for technical and abstract beauty, with the rhyming art to excess, an incorrigible propensity toward nocturnal themes, a demoniac undertone behind every page—and, by final judgment, probably belong among the electric lights of imaginative literature, brilliant and dazzling, but with no heat. There is an indescribable magnetism about the poet's life and reminiscences, as well as the poems. To one who could work out their subtle retracing and retrospect, the latter would make a close tally no doubt between the author's birth and antecedents, his childhood and youth, his physique, his so-call'd education, his studies and associates, the literary and social Baltimore, Richmond, Philadelphia and New York, of those times —not only the places and circumstances in themselves, but often, very often, in a strange spurning of, and reaction from them all.

The following from a report in the Washington "Star" of November 16, 1875, may afford those who care for it something further of my point of view toward this interesting figure and influence of our era. There occurr'd about that date in Baltimore a public reburial of Poe's remains, and dedication of a monument over the grave:

"Being in Washington on a visit at the time, 'the old gray' went over to Baltimore, and though ill from paralysis, consented to hobble up and silently take a seat on the platform, but refused to make any speech, saying, 'I have felt a strong impulse to come over and be here to-day myself in memory of Poe, which I have obey'd, but not the slightest impulse to make a speech, which, my dear friends, must also be obeyed.' In an informal circle, however, in conversation after the ceremonies, Whitman said: 'For a long while, and until lately, I had a distaste for Poe's writings. I wanted, and still want for poetry, the clear sun shining, and fresh air blowing—the strength and power of health, not of delirium, even amid the stormiest passions—with always the background of the eternal moralities. Non-complying with these requirements, Poe's genius has yet conquer'd a special recognition for itself, and I too have come to fully admit it, and appreciate it and him.

" 'In a dream I once had, I saw a vessel on the sea, at midnight, in a storm. It was no great full-rigg'd ship, nor majestic steamer, steering firmly through the gale, but seem'd one of those superb little schooner yachts I had often seen lying anchor'd, rocking so jauntily, in the waters around New York, or up Long Island sound—now flying uncontroll'd with torn sails and broken spars through the wild sleet and winds and waves of the night. On the deck was a slender, slight, beautiful figure, a dim man, apparently enjoying all the terror, the murk, and the dislocation of which he was the centre and the victim. That figure of my lurid dream might stand for Edgar Poe, his spirit, his fortunes, and his poems—themselves all lurid dreams.' "

Much more may be said, but I most desired to exploit the idea put at the beginning. By its popular poets the calibres of an age, the weak spots of its embankments, its sub-currents, (often more significant than the biggest surface ones,) are unerringly indicated. The lush and the weird that have taken such extraordinary possession of Nineteenth century verse-lovers—what mean they? The inevitable tendency of poetic culture to morbidity, abnormal beauty—the sickliness of all technical thought or refinement in itself—the abnegation of the perennial and democratic concretes at first hand, the body, the earth and sea, sex and the like—and the substitution of something for them at second or third hand—what bearings have they on current pathological study?

BEETHOVEN'S SEPTETTE

Feb. 11, '80.—At a good concert to-night in the foyer of the opera house, Philadelphia—the band a small but first-rate one. Never did music more sink into and soothe and fill me—never so prove its soul-rousing power, its impossibility of statement. Especially in the rendering of one of Beethoven's master septettes by the well-chosen and perfectly-combined instruments (violins, viola, clarionet, horn, 'cello and contrabass,) was I carried away, seeing, absorbing many wonders. Dainty abandon, sometimes as if Nature laughing on a hillside in the sunshine; serious and firm monotonies, as of winds; a horn sounding through the tangle of the forest, and the dying echoes; soothing floating of waves, but presently rising in surges, angrily lashing, muttering, heavy; piercing peals of laughter, for interstices; now and then weird, as Nature herself is in certain moods—but mainly spontaneous, easy, careless—often the sentiment of the postures of naked children playing or sleeping. It did me good even to watch the violinists drawing their bows so masterly—every motion a study. I allow'd myself, as I sometimes do, to wander out of myself. The conceit came to me of a copious grove of singing birds, and in their midst a simple harmonic duo, two human souls, steadily asserting their own pensiveness, joyousness.

A HINT OF WILD NATURE

Feb. 13.—As I was crossing the Delaware to-day, saw a large flock of wild geese, right overhead, not very high up, ranged in V-shape, in relief against the noon clouds of light smoke-color. Had a capital though momentary view of them, and then of their course on and on southeast, till gradually fading—(my eyesight yet first rate for the open air and its distances, but I use glasses for reading.) Queer thoughts melted into me the two or three minutes, or less, seeing these creatures cleaving the sky—the spacious, airy realm—even the prevailing smoke-gray color everywhere, (no sun shining)—the waters below—the rapid flight of the birds, appearing just for a minute—flashing to me such a hint of the whole spread of Nature, with her eternal unsophisticated freshness, her never-visited recesses of sea, sky, shore—and then disappearing in the distance.

LOAFING IN THE WOODS

March 8.—I write this down in the country again, but in a new spot, seated on a log in the woods, warm, sunny, midday. Have been loafing here deep among the trees, shafts of tall pines, oak, hickory, with a thick undergrowth of laurels and grapevines—the ground cover'd everywhere by debris, dead leaves, breakage, moss—everything solitary, ancient, grim. Paths (such as they are) leading hither and yon—(how made I know not, for nobody seems to come here, nor man nor cattle-kind.) Temperature to-day about 60, the wind through the pine-tops; I sit and listen to its hoarse sighing above (and to the *stillness*) long and long, varied by aimless rambles in the old roads and paths, and by exercise-pulls at the young saplings, to keep my joints from getting stiff. Blue-birds, robins, meadow-larks begin to appear.

Next day, 9th.—A snowstorm in the morning, and continuing most of the day. But I took a walk over two hours, the same woods and paths, amid the falling flakes. No wind, yet the musical low murmur through the pines, quite pronounced, curious, like waterfalls, now still'd, now pouring again. All the senses, sight, sound, smell, delicately gratified. Every snowflake lay where it fell on the evergreens, holly-trees, laurels, &c., the multitudinous leaves and branches piled, bulging-white, defined by edge-lines of emerald—the tall straight columns of the plentiful bronze-topt pines—a slight resinous odor blending with that of the snow. (For there is a scent to everything, even the snow, if you can only detect it—no two places, hardly any two hours, anywhere, exactly alike. How different the odor of noon from midnight, or winter from summer, or a windy spell from a still one.)

A CONTRALTO VOICE

May 9, Sunday.—Visit this evening to my friends the J.'s—good supper, to which I did justice—lively chat with Mrs. J. and I. and J. As I sat out front on the walk afterward, in the evening air, the church-choir and organ on the corner opposite gave Luther's hymn, *Ein feste berg*, very finely. The air was borne by a rich contralto. For nearly half an hour there in the dark, (there was a good string of English stanzas,) came the music, firm and unhurried, with long pauses. The full silver star-beams of Lyra rose silently over the church's dim roof-ridge. Vari-color'd lights from the stain'd glass windows broke through the tree-shadows. And under all—under the Northern Crown up there, and in the fresh breeze below, and the *chiaroscuro* of the night, that liquid-full contralto.

SEEING NIAGARA TO ADVANTAGE

June 4, '80.—For really seizing a great picture or book, or piece of music, or architecture, or grand scenery—or perhaps for the first time even the common sunshine, or landscape, or may-be even the mystery of identity, most curious mystery of all—there comes some lucky five minutes of a man's life, set amid a fortuitous concurrence of circumstances, and bringing in a brief flash the culmination of years of reading and travel and thought. The present case about two o'clock this afternoon, gave me Niagara, its superb severity of action and color and majestic grouping, in one short, indescribable show. We were very slowly crossing the Suspension bridge—not a full stop anywhere, but next to it—the day clear, sunny, still—and I out on the platform. The falls were in plain view about a mile off, but very distinct, and no roar—hardly a murmur. The river tumbling green and white, far below me; the dark high banks, the plentiful umbrage, many bronze cedars, in shadow; and tempering and arching all the immense materiality, a clear sky overhead, with a few white clouds, limpid, spiritual, silent. Brief, and as quiet as brief, that picture—a remembrance always afterwards. Such are the things, indeed, I lay away with my life's rare and blessed bits of hours, reminiscent, past—the wild sea-storm I once saw one winter day, off Fire island—the elder Booth in Richard, that famous night forty years ago in the old Bowery—or Alboni in the children's scene in Norma—or night-views, I remember, on the field, after battles in Virginia—or the peculiar sentiment of moonlight and stars over the great Plains, western Kansas—or scooting up New York bay, with a stiff breeze and a good yacht, off Navesink. With these, I say, I henceforth place that view, that afternoon, that combination complete, that five minutes' perfect absorption of Niagara—not the great majestic gem alone by itself, but set complete in all its varied, full, indispensable surroundings.

JAUNTING TO CANADA

To GO back a little, I left Philadelphia, 9th and Green streets, at 8 o'clock P.M., June 3, on a first-class sleeper, by the Lehigh Valley (North Pennsylvania) route, through Bethlehem, Wilkesbarre, Waverly, and so (by Erie) on through Corning to Hornellsville, where we arrived at 8, morning, and had a bounteous breakfast. I must say I never put in such a good night on any railroad track— smooth, firm, the minimum of jolting, and all the swiftness compatible with safety. So without change to Buffalo, and thence to

Clifton, where we arrived early afternoon; then on to London, Ontario, Canada, in four more—less than twenty-two hours altogether. I am domiciled at the hospitable house of my friends Dr. and Mrs. Bucke, in the ample and charming garden and lawns of the asylum.

SUNDAY WITH THE INSANE

June 6.—Went over to the religious services (Episcopal) main Insane asylum, held in a lofty, good-sized hall, third story. Plain boards, whitewash, plenty of cheap chairs, no ornament or color, yet all scrupulously clean and sweet. Some three hundred persons present, mostly patients. Everything, the prayers, a short sermon, the firm, orotund voice of the minister, and most of all, beyond any portraying or suggesting, *that audience*, deeply impress'd me. I was furnish'd with an arm-chair near the pulpit, and sat facing the motley, yet perfectly well-behaved and orderly congregation. The quaint dresses and bonnets of some of the women, several very old and gray, here and there like the heads in old pictures. O the looks that came from those faces! There were two or three I shall probably never forget. Nothing at all markedly repulsive or hideous— strange enough I did not see one such. Our common humanity, mine and yours, everywhere:

> *"The same old blood—the same red, running blood;"*

yet behind most, an inferr'd arriere of such storms, such wrecks, such mysteries, fires, love, wrong, greed for wealth, religious problems, crosses—mirror'd from those crazed faces (yet now temporarily so calm, like still waters,) all the woes and sad happenings of life and death—now from every one the devotional element radiating—was it not, indeed, *the peace of God that passeth all understanding*, strange as it may sound? I can only say that I took long and searching eye-sweeps as I sat there, and it seem'd so, rousing unprecedented thoughts, problems unanswerable. A very fair choir, and melodeon accompaniment. They sang "Lead, kindly light," after the sermon. Many join'd in the beautiful hymn, to which the minister read the introductory text, *"In the daytime also He led them with a cloud, and all the night with a light of fire."* Then the words:

> *Lead, kindly light, amid the encircling gloom,*
> *Lead thou me on.*
> *The night is dark, and I am far from home;*
> *Lead thou me on.*
> *Keep thou my feet; I do not ask to see*
> *The distant scene; one step enough for me.*

I was not ever thus, nor pray'd that thou
  Should'st lead me on;
I lov'd to choose and see my path; but now
  Lead thou me on.
I loved the garish day, and spite of fears
Pride ruled my will; remember not past years.

A couple of days after, I went to the "Refractory building," under special charge of Dr. Beemer, and through the wards pretty thoroughly, both the men's and women's. I have since made many other visits of the kind through the asylum, and around among the detach'd cottages. As far as I could see, this is among the most advanced, perfected, and kindly and rationally carried on, of all its kind in America. It is a town in itself, with many buildings and a thousand inhabitants.

I learn that Canada, and especially this ample and populous province, Ontario, has the very best and plentiest benevolent institutions in all departments.

REMINISCENCE OF ELIAS HICKS

June 8.—To-day a letter from Mrs. E. S. L., Detroit, accompanied in a little post-office roll by a rare old engraved head of Elias Hicks, (from a portrait in oil by Henry Inman, painted for J. V. S., must have been 60 years or more ago, in New York)—among the rest the following excerpt about E. H. in the letter:

"I have listen'd to his preaching so often when a child, and sat with my mother at social gatherings where he was the centre, and every one so pleas'd and stirr'd by his conversation. I hear that you contemplate writing or speaking about him, and I wonder'd whether you had a picture of him. As I am the owner of two, I send you one."

GRAND NATIVE GROWTH

IN A few days I go to lake Huron, and may have something to say of that region and people. From what I already see, I should say the young native population of Canada was growing up, forming a hardy, democratic, intelligent, radically sound, and just as American, good-natured and *individualistic* race, as the average range of best specimens among us. As among us, too, I please myself by considering that this element, though it may not be the majority, promises to be the leaven which must eventually leaven the whole lump.

A ZOLLVEREIN BETWEEN THE U. S. AND CANADA

SOME of the more liberal of the presses here are discussing the question of a zollverein between the United States and Canada. It is proposed to form a union for commercial purposes—to altogether abolish the frontier tariff line, with its double sets of custom house officials now existing between the two countries, and to agree upon one tariff for both, the proceeds of this tariff to be divided between the two governments on the basis of population. It is said that a large proportion of the merchants of Canada are in favor of this step, as they believe it would materially add to the business of the country, by removing the restrictions that now exist on trade between Canada and the States. Those persons who are opposed to the measure believe that it would increase the material welfare of the country, but it would loosen the bonds between Canada and England; and this sentiment overrides the desire for commercial prosperity. Whether the sentiment can continue to bear the strain put upon it is a question. It is thought by many that commercial considerations must in the end prevail. It seems also to be generally agreed that such a zollverein, or common customs union, would bring practically more benefits to the Canadian provinces than to the United States. (It seems to me a certainty of time, sooner or later, that Canada shall form two or three grand States, equal and independent, with the rest of the American Union. The St. Lawrence and lakes are not for a frontier line, but a grand interior or mid-channel.)

THE ST. LAWRENCE LINE

August 20.—Premising that my three or four months in Canada were intended, among the rest, as an exploration of the line of the St. Lawrence, from lake Superior to the sea, (the engineers here insist upon considering it as one stream, over 2000 miles long, including lakes and Niagara and all)—that I have only partially carried out my programme; but for the seven or eight hundred miles so far fulfill'd, I find that the *Canada question* is absolutely control'd by this vast water line, with its first-class features and points of trade, humanity, and many more—here I am writing this nearly a thousand miles north of my Philadelphia starting-point (by way of Montreal and Quebec) in the midst of regions that go to a further extreme of grimness, wildness of beauty, and a sort of still and pagan *scaredness*, while yet Christian, inhabitable, and partially fertile, than perhaps any other on earth. The weather remains perfect; some might call it a little cool, but I wear my old gray overcoat and find it just right. The days are full of sunbeams and oxygen. Most of the forenoons and afternoons I am on the forward deck of the steamer.

THE SAVAGE SAGUENAY

Up these black waters, over a hundred miles—always strong, deep, (hundreds of feet, sometimes thousands,) ever with high, rocky hills for banks, green and gray—at times a little like some parts of the Hudson, but much more pronounc'd and defiant. The hills rise higher—keep their ranks more unbroken. The river is straighter and of more resolute flow, and its hue, though dark as ink, exquisitely polish'd and sheeny under the August sun. Different, indeed, this Saguenay from all other rivers—different effects—a bolder, more vehement play of lights and shades. Of a rare charm of singleness and simplicity. (Like the organ-chant at midnight from the old Spanish convent, in "Favorita"—one strain only, simple and monotonous and unornamented—but indescribably penetrating and grand and masterful.) Great place for echoes: while our steamer was tied at the wharf at Tadousac (taj-oo-sac) waiting, the escape-pipe letting off steam, I was sure I heard a band at the hotel up in the rocks —could even make out some of the tunes. Only when our pipe stopp'd, I knew what caused it. Then at cape Eternity and Trinity rock, the pilot with his whistle producing similar marvellous results, echoes indescribably weird, as we lay off in the still bay under their shadows.

CAPES ETERNITY AND TRINITY

But the great, haughty, silent capes themselves; I doubt if any crack points, or hills, or historic places of note, or anything of the kind elsewhere in the world, outvies these objects—(I write while I am before them face to face.) They are very simple, they do not startle—at least they did not me—but they linger in one's memory forever. They are placed very near each other, side by side, each a mountain rising flush out of the Saguenay. A good thrower could throw a stone on each in passing—at least it seems so. Then they are as distinct in form as a perfect physical man or a perfect physical woman. Cape Eternity is bare, rising, as just said, sheer out of the water, rugged and grim (yet with an indescribable beauty) nearly two thousand feet high. Trinity rock, even a little higher, also rising flush, top-rounded like a great head with close-cut verdure of hair.

I consider myself well repaid for coming my thousand miles to get the sight and memory of the unrivall'd duo. They have stirr'd me more profoundly than anything of the kind I have yet seen. If Europe or Asia had them, we should certainly hear of them in all sorts of sent-back poems, rhapsodies, &c., a dozen times a year through our papers and magazines.

CHICOUTIMI AND HA-HA BAY

No INDEED—life and travel and memory have offer'd and will preserve to me no deeper-cut incidents, panorama, or sights to cheer my soul, than these at Chicoutimi and Ha-ha bay, and my days and nights up and down this fascinating savage river—the rounded mountains, some bare and gray, some dull red, some draped close all over with matted green verdure or vines—the ample, calm, eternal rocks everywhere—the long streaks of motley foam, a milk-white curd on the glistening breast of the stream—the little two-masted schooner, dingy yellow, with patch'd sails, set wing-and-wing, nearing us, coming saucily up the water with a couple of swarthy, black-hair'd men aboard—the strong shades falling on the light gray or yellow outlines of the hills all through the forenoon, as we steam within gunshot of them—while ever the pure and delicate sky spreads over all. And the splendid sunsets, and the sights of evening —the same old stars, (relatively a little different, I see, so far north) Arcturus and Lyra, and the Eagle, and great Jupiter like a silver globe, and the constellation of the Scorpion. Then northern lights nearly every night.

THE INHABITANTS—GOOD LIVING

GRIM and rocky and black-water'd as the demesne hereabout is, however, you must not think genial humanity, and comfort, and good-living are not to be met. Before I began this memorandum I made a first-rate breakfast of sea-trout, finishing off with wild raspberries. I find smiles and courtesy everywhere—physiognomies in general curiously like those in the United States—(I was astonish'd to find the same resemblance all through the province of Quebec.) In general the inhabitants of this rugged country (Charlevoix, Chicoutimi and Tadousac counties, and lake St. John region) a simple, hardy population, lumbering, trapping furs, boating, fishing, berry-picking and a little farming. I was watching a group of young boatmen eating their early dinner—nothing but an immense loaf of bread, had apparently been the size of a bushel measure, from which they cut chunks with a jack-knife. Must be a tremendous winter country this, when the solid frost and ice fully set in.

CEDAR-PLUMS LIKE—NAMES

(Back again in Camden and down in Jersey)

ONE time I thought of naming this collection "Cedar-Plums Like" (which I still fancy wouldn't have been a bad name, nor inappropriate.) A melange of loafing, looking, hobbling, sitting, traveling— a little thinking thrown in for salt, but very little—not only summer but all seasons—not only days but nights—some literary meditations —books, authors examined, Carlyle, Poe, Emerson tried, (always under my cedar-tree, in the open air, and never in the library)— mostly the scenes everybody sees, but some of my own caprices, meditations, egotism—truly an open air and mainly summer formation—singly, or in clusters—wild and free and somewhat acrid— indeed more like cedar-plums than you might guess at first glance.

But do you know what they are? (To city man, or some sweet parlor lady, I now talk.) As you go along roads, or barrens, or across country, anywhere through these States, middle, eastern, western, or southern, you will see, certain seasons of the year, the thick woolly tufts of the cedar mottled with bunches of china-blue berries, about as big as fox-grapes. But first a special word for the tree itself: everybody knows that the cedar is a healthy, cheap, democratic wood, streak'd red and white—an evergreen—that it is not a *cultivated* tree—that it keeps away moths—that it grows inland or seaboard, all climates, hot or cold, any soil—in fact rather prefers sand and bleak side spots—content if the plough, the fertilizer and the trimming-axe, will but keep away and let it alone. After a long rain, when everything looks bright, often have I stopt in my wood-saunters, south or north, or far west, to take in its dusky green, wash'd clean and sweet, and speck'd copiously with its fruit of clear, hardy blue. The wood of the cedar is of use—but what profit on earth are those sprigs of acrid plums? A question impossible to answer satisfactorily. True, some of the herb doctors give them for stomachic affections, but the remedy is as bad as the disease. Then in my rambles down in Camden county I once found an old crazy woman gathering the clusters with zeal and joy. She show'd, as I was told afterwards, a sort of infatuation for them, and every year placed and kept profuse bunches high and low about her room. They had a strange charm on her uneasy head, and effected docility and peace. (She was harmless, and lived near by with her well-off married daughter.) Whether there is any connection between those bunches, and being out of one's wits, I cannot say, but I myself entertain a weakness for them. Indeed, I love the cedar, anyhow—its naked ruggedness, its just palpable odor, (so different from the perfumer's best,) its silence, its equable acceptance of winter's cold and summer's heat, of rain or drouth—its shelter to me from those, at times—its associations—(well, I never could explain *why* I love anybody, or anything.) The service I now specially owe to the cedar is, while I cast around for a name for my proposed collection, hesitating, puzzled—after rejecting a long, long string, I lift my eyes, and lo! the very term I want. At any rate, I go no further—I tire in the search. I take what some invisible kind spirit has put before me. Besides, who shall say there is not affinity enough between (at least the bundle of sticks that produced) many of these pieces, or granulations, and those blue berries? their uselessness growing wild—a certain aroma of Nature I would so like to have in my pages—the thin soil whence they come—their content in being let alone—their stolid and deaf repugnance to answering questions, (this latter the nearest, dearest trait affinity of all.)

Then reader dear, in conclusion, as to the point of the name for the present collection, let us be satisfied to *have* a name—something to identify and bind it together, to concrete all its vegetable, mineral, personal memoranda, abrupt raids of criticism, crude gossip of philosophy, varied sands and clumps—without bothering ourselves because certain pages do not present themselves to you or me as coming under their own name with entire fitness or amiability. (It is a profound, vexatious, never-explicable matter—this of names. I have been exercised deeply about it my whole life.[11])

After all of which the name "Cedar-Plums Like" got its nose put out of joint; but I cannot afford to throw away what I pencill'd down the lane there, under the shelter of my old friend, one warm October noon. Besides, it wouldn't be civil to the cedar tree.

DEATH OF THOMAS CARLYLE

Feb. 10, '81.—And so the flame of the lamp, after long wasting and flickering, has gone out entirely.

As a representative author, a literary figure, no man else will bequeath to the future more significant hints of our stormy era, its fierce paradoxes, its din, and its struggling parturition periods, than Carlyle. He belongs to our own branch of the stock too; neither Latin nor Greek, but altogether Gothic. Rugged, mountainous, volcanic, he was himself more a French revolution than any of his volumes. In some respects, so far in the Nineteenth century, the best equipt, keenest mind, even from the college point of view, of all Britain; only he had an ailing body. Dyspepsia is to be traced in every page, and now and then fills the page. One may include among the lessons of his life—even though that life stretch'd to amazing length—how behind the tally of genius and morals stands the stomach, and gives a sort of casting vote.

Two conflicting agonistic elements seem to have contended in the man, sometimes pulling him different ways like wild horses. He was a cautious, conservative Scotchman, fully aware what a fœtid gas-bag much of modern radicalism is; but then his great heart demanded reform, demanded change—often terribly at odds with his scornful brain. No author ever put so much wailing and despair into his books, sometimes palpable, oftener latent. He reminds me of that passage in Young's poems where as death presses closer and closer for his prey, the soul rushes hither and thither, appealing, shrieking, berating, to escape the general doom.

Of short-comings, even positive blur-spots, from an American point of view, he had serious share.

Not for his merely literary merit, (though that was great)—not as "maker of books," but as launching into the self-complacent atmosphere of our days a rasping, questioning, dislocating agitation and shock, is Carlyle's final value. It is time the English-speaking peoples had some true idea about the verteber of genius, namely power. As if they must always have it cut and bias'd to the fashion, like a lady's cloak! What a needed service he performs! How he shakes our comfortable reading circles with a touch of the old Hebraic anger and prophecy—and indeed it is just the same. Not Isaiah himself more scornful, more threatening: "The crown of pride, the drunkards of Ephraim, shall be trodden under feet: And the glorious beauty which is on the head of the fat valley shall be a fading flower." (The word prophecy is much misused; it seems narrow'd to prediction merely. That is not the main sense of the Hebrew word translated "prophet;" it means one whose mind bubbles up and pours forth as a fountain, from inner, divine spontaneities revealing God. Prediction is a very minor part of prophecy. The great matter is to reveal and outpour the God-like suggestions pressing for birth in the soul. This is briefly the doctrine of the Friends or Quakers.)

Then the simplicity and amid ostensible frailty the towering strength of this man—a hardy oak knot, you could never wear out—an old farmer dress'd in brown clothes, and not handsome—his very foibles fascinating. Who cares that he wrote about Dr. Francia, and "Shooting Niagara"—and "the Nigger Question,"—and didn't at all admire our United States? (I doubt if he ever thought or said half as bad words about us as we deserve.) How he splashes like leviathan in the seas of modern literature and politics! Doubtless, respecting the latter, one needs first to realize, from actual observation, the squalor, vice and doggedness ingrain'd in the bulk-population of the British Islands, with the red tape, the fatuity, the flunkeyism everywhere, to understand the last meaning in his pages. Accordingly, though he was no chartist or radical, I consider Carlyle's by far the most indignant comment or protest anent the fruits of feudalism to-day in Great Britain—the increasing poverty and degradation of the homeless, landless twenty millions, while a few thousands, or rather a few hundreds, possess the entire soil, the money, and the fat berths. Trade and shipping, and clubs and culture, and prestige, and guns, and a fine select class of gentry and aristocracy, with every modern improvement, cannot begin to salve or defend such stupendous hoggishness.

The way to test how much he has left his country were to consider, or try to consider, for a moment, the array of British thought, the resultant *ensemble* of the last fifty years, as existing to-day, *but with Carlyle left out.* It would be like an army with no artillery. The show were still a gay and rich one—Byron, Scott, Tennyson, and many more—horsemen and rapid infantry, and banners flying— but the last heavy roar so dear to the ear of the train'd soldier, and that settles fate and victory, would be lacking.

For the last three years we in America have had transmitted glimpses of a thin-bodied, lonesome, wifeless, childless, very old man, lying on a sofa, kept out of bed by indomitable will, but, of late, never well enough to take the open air. I have noted this news from time to time in brief descriptions in the papers. A week ago I read such an item just before I started out for my customary evening stroll between eight and nine. In the fine cold night, unusually clear, (Feb. 5, '81,) as I walk'd some open grounds adjacent, the condition of Carlyle, and his approaching—perhaps even then actual— death, filled me with thoughts eluding statement, and curiously blending with the scene. The planet Venus, an hour high in the west, with all her volume and lustre recover'd, (she has been shorn and languid for nearly a year,) including an additional sentiment I never noticed before—not merely voluptuous, Paphian, steeping, fascinating—now with calm commanding seriousness and hauteur—the Milo Venus now. Upward to the zenith, Jupiter, Saturn, and the moon past her quarter, trailing in procession, with the Pleiades following, and the constellation Taurus, and red Aldebaran. Not a cloud in heaven. Orion strode through the southeast, with his glittering belt—and a trifle below hung the sun of the night, Sirius. Every star dilated, more vitreous, nearer than usual. Not as in some clear nights when the larger stars entirely outshine the rest. Every little star or cluster just as distinctly visible, and just as nigh. Berenice's hair showing every gem, and new ones. To the northeast and north the Sickle, the Goat and kids, Cassiopea, Castor and Pollux, and the two Dippers. While through the whole of this silent indescribable show, inclosing and bathing my whole receptivity, ran the thought of Carlyle dying. (To soothe and spiritualize, and, as far as may be, solve the mysteries of death and genius, consider them under the stars at midnight.)

And now that he has gone hence, can it be that Thomas Carlyle, soon to chemically dissolve in ashes and by winds, remains an identity still? In ways perhaps eluding all the statements, lore and speculations of ten thousand years—eluding all possible statements to mortal sense—does he yet exist, a definite, vital being, a spirit, an individual—perhaps now wafted in space among those stellar systems, which, suggestive and limitless as they are, merely edge more limitless, far more suggestive systems? I have no doubt of it. In silence, of a fine night, such questions are answer'd to the soul, the best answers that can be given. With me, too, when depress'd by some specially sad event, or tearing problem, I wait till I go out under the stars for the last voiceless satisfaction.

Later Thoughts and Jottings

CARLYLE FROM AMERICAN POINTS OF VIEW

THERE is surely at present an inexplicable *rapport* (all the more piquant from its contradictoriness) between that deceas'd author and our United States of America—no matter whether it lasts or not.[12] As we Westerners assume definite shape, and result in formations and fruitage unknown before, it is curious with what a new sense our eyes turn to representative outgrowths of crises and personages in the Old World. Beyond question, since Carlyle's death, and the publication of Froude's memoirs, not only the interest in his books, but every personal bit regarding the famous Scotchman—his dyspepsia, his buffetings, his parentage, his paragon of a wife, his career in Edinburgh, in the lonesome nest on Craigenputtock moor, and then so many years in London—is probably wider and livelier to-day in this country than in his own land. Whether I succeed or no, I, too, reaching across the Atlantic and taking the man's dark fortune-telling of humanity and politics, would offset it all, (such is the fancy that comes to me,) by a far more profound horoscope-casting of those themes—G. F. Hegel's.[13]

First, about a chance, a never-fulfill'd vacuity of this pale cast of thought—this British Hamlet from Cheyne row, more puzzling than the Danish one, with his contrivances for settling the broken and spavin'd joints of the world's government, especially its democratic dislocation. Carlyle's grim fate was cast to live and dwell in, and largely embody, the parturition agony and qualms of the old order, amid crowded accumulations of ghastly morbidity, giving birth to the new. But conceive of him (or his parents before him) coming to America, recuperated by the cheering realities and activity of our people and country—growing up and delving face-to-face resolutely among us here, especially at the West—inhaling and exhaling our limitless air and eligibilities—devoting his mind to the theories and developments of this Republic amid its practical facts as exemplified in Kansas, Missouri, Illinois, Tennessee, or Louisiana. I say *facts*, and face-to-face confrontings—so different from books, and all those quiddities and mere reports in the libraries, upon which the man (it was wittily said of him at the age of thirty, that there was no one in Scotland who had glean'd so much and seen so little,) almost wholly fed, and which even his sturdy and vital mind but reflected at best.

Something of the sort narrowly escaped happening. In 1835, after more than a dozen years of trial and non-success, the author of "Sartor Resartus" removing to London, very poor, a confirmed hypochondriac, "Sartor" universally scoffed at, no literary prospects ahead, deliberately settled on one last casting-throw of the literary dice— resolv'd to compose and launch forth a book on the subject of *the French Revolution*—and if that won no higher guerdon or prize than hitherto, to sternly abandon the trade of author forever, and emigrate for good to America. But the venture turn'd out a lucky one, and there was no emigration.

Carlyle's work in the sphere of literature as he commenced and carried it out, is the same in one or two leading respects that Immanuel Kant's was in speculative philosophy. But the Scotchman had none of the stomachic phlegm and never-perturb'd placidity of the Konigsberg sage, and did not, like the latter, understand his own limits, and stop when he got to the end of them. He clears away jungle and poison-vines and underbrush—at any rate hacks valiantly at them, smiting hip and thigh. Kant did the like in his sphere, and it was all he profess'd to do; his labors have left the ground fully prepared ever since—and greater service was probably never perform'd by mortal man. But the pang and hiatus of Carlyle seem to me to consist in the evidence everywhere that amid a whirl of fog and fury and cross-purposes, he firmly believ'd he had a clue to the medication of the world's ills, and that his bounden mission was to exploit it.[14]

There were two anchors, or sheet-anchors, for steadying, as a last resort, the Carlylean ship. One will be specified presently. The other, perhaps the main, was only to be found in some mark'd form of personal force, an extreme degree of competent urge and will, a man or men "born to command." Probably there ran through every vein and current of the Scotchman's blood something that warm'd up to this kind of trait and character above aught else in the world, and which makes him in my opinion the chief celebrator and promulger of it in literature—more than Plutarch, more than Shakspere. The great masses of humanity stand for nothing—at least nothing but nebulous raw material; only the big planets and shining suns for him. To ideas almost invariably languid or cold, a number-one forceful personality was sure to rouse his eulogistic passion and savage joy. In such case, even the standard of duty hereinafter rais'd, was to be instantly lower'd and vail'd. All that is comprehended under the terms republicanism and democracy were distasteful to him from the first, and as he grew older they became hateful and contemptible. For an undoubtedly candid and penetrating faculty such as his, the bearings he persistently ignored were marvellous. For instance, the promise, nay certainty of the democratic principle, to each and every State of the current world, not so much of helping it to perfect legislators and executives, but as the only effectual method for surely, however slowly, training people on a large scale toward voluntarily ruling and managing themselves (the ultimate aim of political and all other development)—to gradually reduce the fact of *governing* to its minimum, and to subject all its staffs and their doings to the telescopes and microscopes of committees and parties—and greatest of all, to afford (not stagnation and obedient content, which went well enough with the feudalism and ecclesiasticism of the antique and medieval world, but) a vast and sane and recurrent ebb and tide action for those floods of the great deep that have henceforth palpably burst forever their old bounds—seem never to have enter'd Carlyle's thought. It was splendid how he refus'd any compromise to the last. He was curiously antique. In that harsh, picturesque, most potent voice and figure, one seems to be carried back from the present of the British islands more than two thousand years, to the range between Jerusalem and Tarsus. His fullest best biographer justly says of him:

"He was a teacher and a prophet, in the Jewish sense of the word. The prophecies of Isaiah and Jeremiah have become a part of the permanent spiritual inheritance of mankind, because events proved that they had

*interpreted correctly the signs of their own times, and their prophecies
were fulfill'd. Carlyle, like them, believ'd that he had a special message
to deliver to the present age. Whether he was correct in that belief, and
whether his message was a true message, remains to be seen. He has
told us that our most cherish'd ideas of political liberty, with their corol-
laries, are mere illusions, and that the progress which has seem'd to go
along with them is a progress towards anarchy and social dissolution.
If he was wrong, he has misused his powers. The principles of his teachings are false. He has offer'd himself as a guide upon a road of which
he had no knowledge; and his own desire for himself would be the
speediest oblivion both of his person and his works. If, on the other hand,
he has been right; if, like his great predecessors, he has read truly the
tendencies of this modern age of ours, and his teaching is authenticated
by facts, then Carlyle, too, will take his place among the inspired seers."*

To which I add an amendment that under no circumstances, and
no matter how completely time and events disprove his lurid vatici-
nations, should the English-speaking world forget this man, nor fail
to hold in honor his unsurpass'd conscience, his unique method, and
his honest fame. Never were convictions more earnest and genuine.
Never was there less of a flunkey or temporizer. Never had political
progressivism a foe it could more heartily respect.

The second main point of Carlyle's utterance was the idea of *duty
being done.* (It is simply a new codicil—if it be particularly new, which
is by no means certain—on the time-honor'd bequest of dynasticism,
the mould-eaten rules of legitimacy and kings.) He seems to have
been impatient sometimes to madness when reminded by persons who
thought at least as deeply as himself, that this formula, though precious, is rather a vague one, and that there are many other considerations to a philosophical estimate of each and every department either
in general history or individual affairs.

Altogether, I don't know anything more amazing than these persistent strides and throbbings so far through our Nineteenth century of
perhaps its biggest, sharpest, and most erudite brain, in defiance and
discontent with everything; contemptuously ignoring, (either from
constitutional inaptitude, ignorance itself, or more likely because he
demanded a definite cure-all here and now,) the only solace and
solvent to be had.

There is, apart from mere intellect, in the make-up of every superior
human identity, (in its moral completeness, considered as *ensemble*,
not for that moral alone, but for the whole being, including physique,)
a wondrous something that realizes without argument, frequently
without what is called education, (though I think it the goal and apex
of all education deserving the name)—an intuition of the absolute

balance, in time and space, of the whole of this multifarious, mad chaos of fraud, frivolity, hoggishness—this revel of fools, and incredible make-believe and general unsettledness, we call *the world;* a soul-sight of that divine clue and unseen thread which holds the whole congeries of things, all history and time, and all events, however trivial, however momentous, like a leash'd dog in the hand of the hunter. Such soul-sight and root-centre for the mind—mere optimism explains only the surface or fringe of it—Carlyle was mostly, perhaps entirely without. He seems instead to have been haunted in the play of his mental action by a spectre, never entirely laid from first to last, (Greek scholars, I believe, find the same mocking and fantastic apparition attending Aristophanes, his comedies,)—the spectre of world-destruction.

How largest triumph or failure in human life, in war or peace, may depend on some little hidden centrality, hardly more than a drop of blood, a pulse-beat, or a breath of air! It is certain that all these weighty matters, democracy in America, Carlyleism, and the temperament for deepest political or literary exploration, turn on a simple point in speculative philosophy.

The most profound theme that can occupy the mind of man—the problem on whose solution science, art, the bases and pursuits of nations, and everything else, including intelligent human happiness, (here to-day, 1882, New York, Texas, California, the same as all times, all lands,) subtly and finally resting, depends for competent outset and argument, is doubtless involved in the query: What is the fusing explanation and tie—what the relation between the (radical, democratic) Me, the human identity of understanding, emotions, spirit, &c., on the one side, of and with the (conservative) Not Me, the whole of the material objective universe and laws, with what is behind them in time and space, on the other side? Immanuel Kant, though he explain'd, or partially explain'd, as may be said, the laws of the human understanding, left this question an open one. Schelling's answer, or suggestion of answer, is (and very valuable and important, as far as it goes,) that the same general and particular intelligence, passion, even the standards of right and wrong, which exist in a conscious and formulated state in man, exist in an unconscious state, or in perceptible analogies, throughout the entire universe of external Nature, in all its objects large or small, and all its movements and processes—thus making the impalpable human mind, and concrete Nature, notwithstanding their duality and separation, convertible, and in centrality and essence one. But G. F. Hegel's fuller statement of the matter probably remains the last best word that has been said upon it, up to date. Substantially adopting the scheme just epitomized, he so carries it out and fortifies it and merges everything in it, with certain serious gaps now for the first time fill'd, that it becomes a coherent metaphysical system, and substantial answer (as far as there can be any answer) to the foregoing question—a system which, while I distinctly admit that the brain of the future may add to, revise, and even entirely reconstruct, at any rate beams forth to-day, in its entirety, illuminating the thought of the universe, and satisfying the mystery thereof to the human mind, with a more consoling scientific assurance than any yet.

According to Hegel the whole earth, (an old nucleus-thought, as in the Vedas, and no doubt before, but never hitherto brought so absolutely to the front, fully surcharged with modern scientism and facts, and made the sole entrance to each and all,) with its infinite variety, the past, the surroundings of to-day, or what may happen in the future, the contrarieties of material with spiritual, and of natural with artificial, are all, to the eye of the *ensemblist*, but necessary sides and unfoldings, different steps or links, in the endless process of Creative thought, which amid numberless apparent failures and contradictions, is held together by central and never-broken unity—not contradictions or failures at all, but radiations of one consistent and eternal purpose; the whole mass of everything steadily, unerringly tending and flowing toward the permanent *utile* and *morale*, as rivers to oceans. As life is the whole law and incessant effort of the visible universe, and death only the other or invisible side of the same, so the *utile*, so truth, so health, are the continuous-immutable laws of the moral universe, and vice and disease, with all their perturbations, are but transient, even if ever so prevalent expressions.

To politics throughout, Hegel applies the like catholic standard and faith. Not any one party, or any one form of government, is absolutely and exclusively true. Truth consists in the just relations of objects to each other. A majority or democracy may rule as outrageously and do as great harm as an oligarchy or despotism—though far less likely to do so. But the great evil is either a violation of the relations just referr'd to, or of the moral law. The specious, the unjust, the cruel, and what is called the unnatural, though not only permitted but in a certain sense, (like shade to light,) inevitable in the divine scheme, are by the whole constitution of that scheme, partial, inconsistent, temporary, and though having ever so great an ostensible majority, are certainly destin'd to failure, after causing great suffering.

Theology, Hegel translates into science.[15] All apparent contradictions in the statement of the Deific nature by different ages, nations, churches, points of view, are but fractional and imperfect expressions of one essential unity, from which they all proceed—crude endeavors or distorted parts, to be regarded both as distinct and united. In short (to put it in our own form, or summing up,) that thinker or analyzer or overlooker who by an inscrutable combination of train'd wisdom and natural intuition most fully accepts in perfect faith the moral unity and sanity of the creative scheme, in history, science, and all life and time, present and future, is both the truest cosmical devotee or religioso, and the profoundest philosopher. While he who, by the spell of himself and his circumstance, sees darkness and despair in the sum of the workings of God's providence, and who, in that, denies or prevaricates, is, no matter how much piety plays on his lips, the most radical sinner and infidel.

I am the more assured in recounting Hegel a little freely here,[16] not only for offsetting the Carlylean letter and spirit—cutting it out all and several from the very roots, and below the roots—but to counterpoise, since the late death and deserv'd apotheosis of Darwin, the tenets of the evolutionists. Unspeakably precious as those are to biology, and henceforth indispensable to a right aim and estimate in study, they neither comprise or explain everything—and the last word or whisper still remains to be breathed, after the utmost of those claims, floating high and forever above them all, and above technical metaphysics. While the contributions which German Kant and Fichte and Schelling and Hegel have bequeath'd to humanity—and which English Darwin has also in his field—are indispensable to the erudition of America's future, I should say that in all of them, and the best of them, when compared with the lightning flashes and flights of the old prophets and *exaltés,* the spiritual poets and poetry of all lands, (as in the Hebrew Bible,) there seems to be, nay certainly is, something lacking—something cold, a failure to satisfy the deepest emotions of the soul—a want of living glow, fondness, warmth, which the old *exaltés* and poets supply, and which the keenest modern philosophers so far do not.

Upon the whole, and for our purposes, this man's name certainly belongs on the list with the just-specified, first-class moral physicians of our current era—and with Emerson and two or three others—though his prescription is drastic, and perhaps destructive, while theirs is assimilating, normal and tonic. Feudal at the core, and mental offspring and radiation of feudalism as are his books, they afford ever-valuable lessons and affinities to democratic America. Nations or individuals, we surely learn deepest from unlikeness, from a sincere opponent, from the light thrown even scornfully on dangerous spots and liabilities. (Michel Angelo invoked heaven's special protection against his friends and affectionate flatterers; palpable foes he could manage for himself.) In many particulars Carlyle was indeed, as Froude terms him, one of those far-off Hebraic utterers, a new Micah or Habbakuk. His words at times bubble forth with abysmic inspiration. Always precious, such men; as precious now as any time. His rude, rasping, taunting, contradictory tones—what ones are more wanted amid the supple, polish'd, money-worshipping, Jesus-and-Judas-equalizing, suffrage-sovereignty echoes of current America? He has lit up our Nineteenth century with the light of a powerful, penetrating, and perfectly honest intellect of the first-class, turn'd on British and European politics, social life, literature, and representative personages—thoroughly dissatisfied with all, and mercilessly exposing the illness of all. But while he announces the malady, and scolds and raves about it, he himself, born and bred in the same atmosphere, is a mark'd illustration of it.

A COUPLE OF OLD FRIENDS—A COLERIDGE BIT

Latter April.—Have run down in my country haunt for a couple of days, and am spending them by the pond. I had already discover'd my kingfisher here (but only one—the mate not here yet.) This fine bright morning, down by the creek, he has come out for a spree, circling, flirting, chirping at a round rate. While I am writing these lines he is disporting himself in scoots and rings over the wider parts of the pond, into whose surface he dashes, once or twice making a loud *souse*—the spray flying in the sun—beautiful! I see his white and dark-gray plumage and peculiar shape plainly, as he has deign'd to come very near me. The noble, graceful bird! Now he is sitting on the limb of an old tree, high up, bending over the water—seems to be looking at me while I memorandize. I almost fancy he knows me. *Three days later.*—My second kingfisher is here with his (or her) mate. I saw the two together flying and whirling around. I had heard, in the distance, what I thought was the clear rasping staccato of the birds several times already—but I couldn't be sure the notes came from both until I saw them together. To-day at noon they appear'd, but apparently either on business, or for a little limited exercise only. No wild frolic now, full of free fun and motion, up and down for an hour. Doubtless, now they have cares, duties, incubation responsibilities. The frolics are deferr'd till summer-close.

I don't know as I can finish to-day's memorandum better than with Coleridge's lines, curiously appropriate in more ways than one:

"All Nature seems at work—slugs leave their lair,
The bees are stirring—birds are on the wing,
And winter, slumbering in the open air,
Wears on his smiling face a dream of spring;
And I, the while, the sole unbusy thing,
Nor honey make, nor pair, nor build, nor sing."

A WEEK'S VISIT TO BOSTON

May 1, '81.—Seems as if all the ways and means of American travel to-day had been settled, not only with reference to speed and directness, but for the comfort of women, children, invalids, and old fellows like me. I went on by a through train that runs daily from Washington to the Yankee metropolis without change. You get in a sleeping-car soon after dark in Philadelphia, and after ruminating an hour or two, have your bed made up if you like, draw the curtains, and go to sleep in it—fly on through Jersey to New York—hear in your half-slumbers a dull jolting and bumping sound or two—are unconsciously toted from Jersey city by a midnight steamer around the Battery and under the big bridge to the track of the New Haven road—resume your flight eastward, and early the next morning you wake up in Boston. All of which was my experience. I wanted to go to the Revere house. A tall unknown gentleman, (a fellow-passenger on his way to Newport he told me, I had just chatted a few moments before with him,) assisted me out through the depot crowd, procured a hack, put me in it with my traveling bag, saying smilingly and quietly, "Now I want you to let this be *my* ride," paid the driver, and before I could remonstrate bow'd himself off.

The occasion of my jaunt, I suppose I had better say here, was for a public reading of "the death of Abraham Lincoln" essay, on the sixteenth anniversary of that tragedy; which reading duly came off, night of April 15. Then I linger'd a week in Boston—felt pretty well (the mood propitious, my paralysis lull'd)—went around everywhere, and saw all that was to be seen, especially human beings. Boston's immense material growth—commerce, finance, commission stores, the plethora of goods, the crowded streets and sidewalks—made of course the first surprising show. In my trip out West, last year, I thought the wand of future prosperity, future empire, must soon surely be wielded by St. Louis, Chicago, beautiful Denver, perhaps San Francisco; but I see the said wand stretch'd out just as decidedly in Boston, with just as much certainty of staying; evidences of copious capital—indeed no centre of the New World ahead of it, (half the big railroads in the West are built with Yankees' money, and they take the dividends.)

Old Boston with its zigzag streets and multitudinous angles, (crush up a sheet of letter-paper in your hand, throw it down, stamp it flat, and that is a map of old Boston)—new Boston with its miles upon miles of large and costly houses—Beacon street, Commonwealth avenue, and a hundred others. But the best new departures and expansions of Boston, and of all the cities of New England, are in another direction.

THE BOSTON OF TO-DAY

In the letters we get from Dr. Schliemann (interesting but fishy) about his excavations there in the far-off Homeric area, I notice cities, ruins, &c., as he digs them out of their graves, are certain to be in layers—that is to say, upon the foundation of an old concern, very far down indeed, is always another city or set of ruins, and upon that another superadded—and sometimes upon that still another—each representing either a long or rapid stage of growth and development, different from its predecessor, but unerringly growing out of and resting on it. In the moral, emotional, heroic, and human growths, (the main of a race in my opinion,) something of this kind has certainly taken place in Boston. The New England metropolis of to-day may be described as sunny, (there is something else that makes warmth, mastering even winds and meteorologies, though those are not to be sneez'd at,) joyous, receptive, full of ardor, sparkle, a certain element of yearning, magnificently tolerant, yet not to be fool'd; fond of good eating and drinking—costly in costume as its purse can buy; and all through its best average of houses, streets, people, that subtle something (generally thought to be climate, but it is not—it is something indefinable in the *race*, the turn of its development) which effuses behind the whirl of animation, study, business, a happy and joyous public spirit, as distinguish'd from a sluggish and saturnine one. Makes me think of the glints we get (as in Symonds's books) of the jolly old Greek cities. Indeed there is a good deal of the Hellenic in B., and the people are getting handsomer too—padded out, with freer motions, and with color in their faces. I never saw (although this is not Greek) so many *fine-looking gray hair'd women*. At my lecture I caught myself pausing more than once to look at them, plentiful everywhere through the audience—healthy and wifely and motherly, and wonderfully charming and beautiful—I think such as no time or land but ours could show.

MY TRIBUTE TO FOUR POETS

April 16.—A short but pleasant visit to Longfellow. I am not one of the calling kind, but as the author of "Evangeline" kindly took the trouble to come and see me three years ago in Camden, where I was ill, I felt not only the impulse of my own pleasure on that occasion, but a duty. He was the only particular eminence I called on in Boston, and I shall not soon forget his lit-up face and glowing warmth and courtesy, in the modes of what is called the old school.

And now just here I feel the impulse to interpolate something about the mighty four who stamp this first American century with its birthmarks of poetic literature. In a late magazine one of my reviewers, who ought to know better, speaks of my "attitude of contempt and scorn and intolerance" toward the leading poets—of my "deriding" them, and preaching their "uselessness." If anybody cares to know what I think—and have long thought and avow'd—about them, I am entirely willing to propound. I can't imagine any better luck befalling these States for a poetical beginning and initiation than has come from Emerson, Longfellow, Bryant, and Whittier. Emerson, to me, stands unmistakably at the head, but for the others I am at a loss where to give any precedence. Each illustrious, each rounded, each distinctive. Emerson for his sweet, vital-tasting melody, rhym'd philosophy, and poems as amber-clear as the honey of the wild bee he loves to sing. Longfellow for rich color, graceful forms and incidents —all that makes life beautiful and love refined—competing with the singers of Europe on their own ground, and, with one exception, better and finer work than that of any of them. Bryant pulsing the first interior verse-throbs of a mighty world—bard of the river and the wood, ever conveying a taste of open air, with scents as from hayfields, grapes, birch-borders—always lurkingly fond of threnodies— beginning and ending his long career with chants of death, with here and there through all, poems, or passages of poems, touching the highest universal truths, enthusiasms, duties—morals as grim and eternal, if not as stormy and fateful, as anything in Eschylus. While in Whittier, with his special themes—(his outcropping love of heroism and war, for all his Quakerdom, his verses at times like the measur'd step of Cromwell's old veterans)—in Whittier lives the zeal, the moral energy, that founded New England—the splendid rectitude and ardor of Luther, Milton, George Fox—I must not, dare not, say the wilfulness and narrowness—though doubtless the world needs now, and always will need, almost above all, just such narrowness and wilfulness.

MILLET'S PICTURES—LAST ITEMS

April 18.—Went out three or four miles to the house of Quincy Shaw, to see a collection of J. F. Millet's pictures. Two rapt hours. Never before have I been so penetrated by this kind of expression. I stood long and long before "the Sower." I believe what the picture-men designate "the first Sower," as the artist executed a second copy, and a third, and, some think, improved in each. But I doubt it. There is something in this that could hardly be caught again—a sublime murkiness and original pent fury. Besides this masterpiece, there were many others, (I shall never forget the simple evening scene, "Watering the Cow,") all inimitable, all perfect as pictures, works of mere art; and then it seem'd to me, with that last impalpable ethic purpose from the artist (most likely unconscious to himself) which I am always looking for. To me all of them told the full story of what went before and necessitated the great French revolution—the long precedent crushing of the masses of a heroic people into the earth, in abject poverty, hunger—every right denied, humanity attempted to be put back for generations—yet Nature's force, titanic here, the stronger and hardier for that repression—waiting terribly to break forth, revengeful—the pressure on the dykes, and the bursting at last—the storming of the Bastile—the execution of the king and queen—the tempest of massacres and blood. Yet who can wonder?

> *Could we wish humanity different?*
> *Could we wish the people made of wood or stone?*
> *Or that there be no justice in destiny or time?*

The true France, base of all the rest, is certainly in these pictures. I comprehend "Field-People Reposing," "the Diggers," and "the Angelus" in this opinion. Some folks always think of the French as a small race, five or five and a half feet high, and ever frivolous and smirking. Nothing of the sort. The bulk of the personnel of France, before the revolution, was large-sized, serious, industrious as now, and simple. The revolution and Napoleon's wars dwarf'd the standard of human size, but it will come up again. If for nothing else, I should dwell on my brief Boston visit for opening to me the new world of Millet's pictures. Will America ever have such an artist out of her own gestation, body, soul?

Sunday, April 17.—An hour and a half, late this afternoon, in silence and half light, in the great nave of Memorial hall, Cambridge, the walls thickly cover'd with mural tablets, bearing the names of students and graduates of the university who fell in the secession war.

April 23.—It was well I got away in fair order, for if I had staid another week I should have been killed with kindness, and with eating and drinking.

BIRDS—AND A CAUTION

May 14.—Home again; down temporarily in the Jersey woods. Between 8 and 9 A. M. a full concert of birds, from different quarters, in keeping with the fresh scent, the peace, the naturalness all around me. I am lately noticing the russet-back, size of the robin or a trifle less, light breast and shoulders, with irregular dark stripes—tail long—sits hunch'd up by the hour these days, top of a tall bush, or some tree, singing blithely. I often get near and listen, as he seems tame; I like to watch the working of his bill and throat, the quaint sidle of his body, and flex of his long tail. I hear the woodpecker, and night and early morning the shuttle of the whip-poor-will—noons, the gurgle of thrush delicious, and *meo-o-ow* of the cat-bird. Many I cannot name; but I do not very particularly seek information. (You must not know too much, or be too precise or scientific about birds and trees and flowers and water-craft; a certain free margin, and even vagueness—perhaps ignorance, credulity—helps your enjoyment of these things, and of the sentiment of feather'd, wooded, river, or marine Nature generally. I repeat it—don't want to know too exactly, or the reasons why. My own notes have been written off-hand in the latitude of middle New Jersey. Though they describe what I saw—what appear'd to me—I dare say the expert ornithologist, botanist or entomologist will detect more than one slip in them.)

SAMPLES OF MY COMMON-PLACE BOOK

I OUGHT not to offer a record of these days, interests, recuperations, without including a certain old, well-thumb'd common-place book,[17] filled with favorite excerpts, I carried in my pocket for three summers, and absorb'd over and over again, when the mood invited. I find so much in having a poem or fine suggestion sink into me (a little then goes a great ways) prepar'd by these vacant-sane and natural influences.

MY NATIVE SAND AND SALT ONCE MORE

July 25, '81.—Far Rockaway, L. I.—A good day here, on a jaunt, amid the sand and salt, a steady breeze setting in from the sea, the sun shining, the sedge-odor, the noise of the surf, a mixture of hissing and booming, the milk-white crests curling over. I had a leisurely bath and naked ramble as of old, on the warm-gray shore-sands, my companions off in a boat in deeper water—(I shouting to them Jupiter's menaces against the gods, from Pope's Homer.)

July 28—to Long Branch.—8½ A. M., on the steamer "Plymouth Rock," foot of 23d Street, New York, for Long Branch. Another fine day, fine sights, the shores, the shipping and bay—everything comforting to the body and spirit of me. (I find the human and objective atmosphere of New York city and Brooklyn more affiliative to me than any other.) *An hour later*—Still on the steamer, now sniffing the salt very plainly—the long pulsating *swash* as our boat steams seaward—the hills of Navesink and many passing vessels—the air the best part of all. At Long Branch the bulk of the day, stopt at a good hotel, took all very leisurely, had an excellent dinner, and then drove for over two hours about the place, especially Ocean avenue, the finest drive one can imagine, seven or eight miles right along the beach. In all directions costly villas, palaces, millionaires—(but few among them I opine like my friend George W. Childs, whose personal integrity, generosity, unaffected simplicity, go beyond all worldly wealth.)

HOT WEATHER NEW YORK

August.—In the big city awhile. Even the height of the dog-days, there is a good deal of fun about New York, if you only avoid fluster, and take all the buoyant wholesomeness that offers. More comfort, too, than most folks think. A middle-aged man, with plenty of money in his pocket, tells me that he has been off for a month to all the swell places, has disburs'd a small fortune, has been hot and out of kilter everywhere, and has return'd home and lived in New York city the last two weeks quite contented and happy. People forget when it is hot here, it is generally hotter still in other places. New York is so situated, with the great ozonic brine on both sides, it comprises the most favorable health-chances in the world. (If only the suffocating crowding of some of its tenement houses could be broken up.) I find I never sufficiently realized how beautiful are the upper two-thirds of Manhattan island. I am stopping at Mott Haven, and have been familar now for ten days with the region above One-hundredth street, and along the Harlem river and Washington heights. Am dwelling a few days with my friends, Mr. and Mrs. J. H. J., and a merry housefull of young ladies. Am putting the last touches on the printer's copy of my new volume of "Leaves of Grass"—the completed book at last. Work at it two or three hours, and then go down and loaf along the Harlem river; have just had a good spell of this recreation. The sun sufficiently veil'd, a soft south breeze, the river full of small or large shells (light taper boats) darting up and down, some singly, now and then long ones with six or eight young fellows practicing—very inspiriting sights. Two fine yachts lie anchor'd off the shore. I linger long, enjoying the sundown, the glow, the streak'd sky, the heights, distances, shadows.

Aug. 10.—As I haltingly ramble an hour or two this forenoon by the more secluded parts of the shore, or sit under an old cedar half way up the hill, the city near in view, many young parties gather to bathe or swim, squads of boys, generally twos or threes, some larger ones, along the sand-bottom, or off an old pier close by. A peculiar and pretty carnival—at its height a hundred lads or young men, very democratic, but all decent behaving. The laughter, voices, calls, responses —the springing and diving of the bathers from the great string-piece of the decay'd pier, where climb or stand long ranks of them, naked, rose-color'd, with movements, postures ahead of any sculpture. To all this, the sun, so bright, the dark-green shadow of the hills the other side, the amber-rolling waves, changing as the tide comes in to a transparent tea-color—the frequent splash of the playful boys, sousing —the glittering drops sparkling, and the good western breeze blowing.

"CUSTER'S LAST RALLY"

WENT to-day to see this just-finish'd painting by John Mulvany, who has been out in far Dakota, on the spot, at the forts, and among the frontiersmen, soldiers and Indians, for the last two years, on purpose to sketch it in from reality, or the best that could be got of it. Sat for over an hour before the picture, completely absorb'd in the first view. A vast canvas, I should say twenty or twenty-two feet by twelve, all crowded, and yet not crowded, conveying such a vivid play of color, it takes a little time to get used to it. There are no tricks; there is no throwing of shades in masses; it is all at first painfully real, overwhelming, needs good nerves to look at it. Forty or fifty figures, perhaps more, in full finish and detail in the mid-ground, with three times that number, or more, through the rest—swarms upon swarms of savage Sioux, in their war-bonnets, frantic, mostly on ponies, driving through the background, through the smoke, like a hurricane of demons. A dozen of the figures are wonderful. Altogether a western, autochthonic phase of America, the frontiers, culminating, typical, deadly, heroic to the uttermost—nothing in the books like it, nothing in Homer, nothing in Shakspere; more grim and sublime than either, all native, all our own, and all a fact. A great lot of muscular, tan-faced men, brought to bay under terrible circumstances—death ahold of them, yet every man undaunted, not one losing his head, wringing out every cent of the pay before they sell their lives. Custer (his hair cut short) stands in the middle, with dilated eye and extended arm, aiming a huge cavalry pistol. Captain Cook is there, partially wounded, blood on the white handkerchief around his head, aiming his carbine coolly, half kneeling—(his body was afterwards found close by Custer's.) The slaughter'd or half-slaughter'd horses, for breastworks, make a peculiar feature. Two dead Indians, herculean, lie in the foreground, clutching their Winchester rifles, very characteristic. The many soldiers, their faces and attitudes, the carbines, the broadbrimm'd western hats, the powder-smoke in puffs, the dying horses with their rolling eyes almost human in their agony, the clouds of war-bonneted Sioux in the background, the figures of Custer and Cook—with indeed the whole scene, dreadful, yet with an attraction and beauty that will remain in my memory. With all its color and fierce action, a certain Greek continence pervades it. A sunny sky and clear light envelop all. There is an almost entire absence of the stock traits of European war pictures. The physiognomy of the work is realistic and Western. I only saw it for an hour or so; but it needs to be seen many times—needs to be studied over and over again. I could look on such a work at brief intervals all my life without tiring; it is very tonic to me; then it has an ethic purpose below all, as all great art must have. The artist said the sending of the picture abroad, probably to London, had been talk'd of. I advised him if it went abroad to take it to Paris. I think they might appreciate it there—nay, they certainly would. Then I would like to show Messieur Crapeau that some things can be done in America as well as others.

SOME OLD ACQUAINTANCES—MEMORIES

Aug. 16.—"Chalk a big mark for to-day," was one of the sayings of an old sportsman-friend of mine, when he had had unusually good luck—come home thoroughly tired, but with satisfactory results of fish or birds. Well, to-day might warrant such a mark for me. Everything propitious from the start. An hour's fresh stimulation, coming down ten miles of Manhattan island by railroad and 8 o'clock stage. Then an excellent breakfast at Pfaff's restaurant, 24th street. Our host himself, an old friend of mine, quickly appear'd on the scene to welcome me and bring up the news, and, first opening a big fat bottle of the best wine in the cellar, talk about ante-bellum times, '59 and '60, and the jovial suppers at his then Broadway place, near Bleecker street. Ah, the friends and names and frequenters, those times, that place. Most are dead—Ada Clare, Wilkins, Daisy Sheppard, O'Brien, Henry Clapp, Stanley, Mullin, Wood, Brougham, Arnold—all gone. And there Pfaff and I, sitting opposite each other at the little table, gave a remembrance to them in a style they would have themselves fully confirm'd, namely, big, brimming, fill'd-up champagne-glasses, drain'd in abstracted silence, very leisurely, to the last drop. (Pfaff is a generous German *restaurateur,* silent, stout, jolly, and I should say the best selector of champagne in America.)

A DISCOVERY OF OLD AGE

PERHAPS the best is always cumulative. One's eating and drinking one wants fresh, and for the nonce, right off, and have done with it —but I would not give a straw for that person or poem, or friend, or city, or work of art, that was not more grateful the second time than the first—and more still the third. Nay, I do not believe any grandest eligibility ever comes forth at first. In my own experience, (persons, poems, places, characters,) I discover the best hardly ever at first, (no absolute rule about it, however,) sometimes suddenly bursting forth, or stealthily opening to me, perhaps after years of unwitting familiarity, unappreciation, usage.

A VISIT, AT THE LAST, TO R. W. EMERSON

Concord, Mass.—Out here on a visit—elastic, mellow, Indian-summery weather. Came to-day from Boston, (a pleasant ride of 40 minutes by steam, through Somerville, Belmont, Waltham, Stony Brook, and other lively towns,) convoy'd by my friend F. B. Sanborn, and to his ample house, and the kindness and hospitality of Mrs. S. and their fine family. Am writing this under the shade of some old hickories and elms, just after 4 P.M., on the porch, within a stone's throw of the Concord river. Off against me, across stream, on a meadow and side-hill, haymakers are gathering and wagoning-in probably their second or third crop. The spread of emerald-green and brown, the knolls, the score or two of little haycocks dotting the meadow, the loaded-up wagons, the patient horses, the slow-strong action of the men and pitchforks—all in the just-waning afternoon, with patches of yellow sun-sheen, mottled by long shadows—a cricket shrilly chirping, herald of the dusk—a boat with two figures noiselessly gliding along the little river, passing under the stone bridge-arch—the slight settling haze of aerial moisture, the sky and the peacefulness expanding in all directions and overhead—fill and soothe me.

Same evening.—Never had I a better piece of luck befall me: a long and blessed evening with Emerson, in a way I couldn't have wish'd better or different. For nearly two hours he has been placidly sitting where I could see his face in the best light, near me. Mrs. S.'s back-parlor well fill'd with people, neighbors, many fresh and charming faces, women, mostly young, but some old. My friend A. B. Alcott and his daughter Louisa were there early. A good deal of talk, the subject Henry Thoreau—some new glints of his life and fortunes, with letters to and from him—one of the best by Margaret Fuller, others by Horace Greeley, Channing, &c.—one from Thoreau himself, most quaint and interesting. (No doubt I seem'd very stupid to the room-full of company, taking hardly any part in the conversation; but I had "my own pail to milk in," as the Swiss proverb puts it.) My seat and the relative arrangement were such that, without being rude, or anything of the kind, I could just look squarely at E., which I did a good part of the two hours. On entering, he had spoken very briefly and politely to several of the company, then settled himself in his chair, a trifle push'd back, and, though a listener and apparently an alert one, remain'd silent through the whole talk and discussion. A lady friend quietly took a seat next him, to give special attention. A good color in his face, eyes clear, with the well-known expression of sweetness, and the old clear-peering aspect quite the same.

Next Day.—Several hours at E.'s house, and dinner there. An old familiar house, (he has been in it thirty-five years,) with surroundings, furnishment, roominess, and plain elegance and fullness, signifying democratic ease, sufficient opulence, and an admirable old-fashioned simplicity—modern luxury, with its mere sumptuousness and affectation, either touch'd lightly upon or ignored altogether. Dinner the same. Of course the best of the occasion (Sunday, September 18, '81) was the sight of E. himself. As just said, a healthy color in the cheeks, and good light in the eyes, cheery expression, and just the amount of talking that best suited, namely, a word or short phrase only where needed, and almost always with a smile. Besides Emerson himself, Mrs. E., with their daughter Ellen, the son Edward and his wife, with my friend F. S. and Mrs. S., and others, relatives and intimates. Mrs. Emerson, resuming the subject of the evening before, (I sat next to her,) gave me further and fuller information about Thoreau, who, years ago, during Mr. E.'s absence in Europe, had lived for some time in the family, by invitation.

OTHER CONCORD NOTATIONS

THOUGH the evening at Mr. and Mrs. Sanborn's, and the memorable family dinner at Mr. and Mrs. Emerson's, have most pleasantly and permanently fill'd my memory, I must not slight other notations of

Concord. I went to the old Manse, walk'd through the ancient garden, enter'd the rooms, noted the quaintness, the unkempt grass and
bushes, the little panes in the windows, the low ceilings, the spicy
smell, the creepers embowering the light. Went to the Concord
battle ground, which is close by, scann'd French's statue, "the Minute Man," read Emerson's poetic inscription on the base, linger'd a
long while on the bridge, and stopp'd by the grave of the unnamed
British soldiers buried there the day after the fight in April '75. Then
riding on, (thanks to my friend Miss M. and her spirited white
ponies, she driving them,) a half hour at Hawthorne's and Thoreau's
graves. I got out and went up of course on foot, and stood a long
while and ponder'd. They lie close together in a pleasant wooded
spot well up the cemetery hill, "Sleepy Hollow." The flat surface
of the first was densely cover'd by myrtle, with a border of arbor-
vitæ, and the other had a brown headstone, moderately elaborate,
with inscriptions. By Henry's side lies his brother John, of whom
much was expected, but he died young. Then to Walden pond, that
beautifully embower'd sheet of water, and spent over an hour there.
On the spot in the woods where Thoreau had his solitary house is
now quite a cairn of stones, to mark the place; I too carried one and
deposited on the heap. As we drove back, saw the "School of Philosophy," but it was shut up, and I would not have it open'd for me.
Near by stopp'd at the house of W. T. Harris, the Hegelian, who
came out, and we had a pleasant chat while I sat in the wagon. I
shall not soon forget those Concord drives, and especially that
charming Sunday forenoon one with my friend Miss M., and the
white ponies.

BOSTON COMMON—MORE OF EMERSON

Oct. 10–13.—I spend a good deal of time on the Common, these
delicious days and nights—every mid-day from 11.30 to about 1—
and almost every sunset another hour. I know all the big trees, especially the old elms along Tremont and Beacon streets, and have
come to a sociable-silent understanding with most of them, in the
sunlit air, (yet crispy-cool enough,) as I saunter along the wide
unpaved walks. Up and down this breadth by Beacon street, between these same old elms, I walk'd for two hours, of a bright sharp
February mid-day twenty-one years ago, with Emerson, then in his
prime, keen, physically and morally magnetic, arm'd at every point,
and when he chose, wielding the emotional just as well as the intellectual. During those two hours he was the talker and I the listener.

It was an argument-statement, reconnoitring, review, attack, and pressing home, (like an army corps in order, artillery, cavalry, infantry,) of all that could be said against that part (and a main part) in the construction of my poems, "Children of Adam." More precious than gold to me that dissertation—it afforded me, ever after, this strange and paradoxical lesson; each point of E.'s statement was unanswerable, no judge's charge ever more complete or convincing, I could never hear the points better put—and then I felt down in my soul the clear and unmistakable conviction to disobey all, and pursue my own way. "What have you to say then to such things?" said E., pausing in conclusion. "Only that while I can't answer them at all, I feel more settled than ever to adhere to my own theory, and exemplify it," was my candid response. Whereupon we went and had a good dinner at the American House. And thenceforward I never waver'd or was touch'd with qualms, (as I confess I had been two or three times before).

AN OSSIANIC NIGHT—DEAREST FRIENDS

Nov. '81.—Again back in Camden. As I cross the Delaware in long trips to-night, between 9 and 11, the scene overhead is a peculiar one—swift sheets of flitting vapor-gauze, follow'd by dense clouds throwing an inky pall on everything. Then a spell of that transparent steel-gray black sky I have noticed under similar circumstances, on which the moon would beam for a few moments with calm lustre, throwing down a broad dazzle of highway on the waters; then the mists careering again. All silently, yet driven as if by the furies they sweep along, sometimes quite thin, sometimes thicker—a real Ossianic night—amid the whirl, absent or dead friends, the old, the past, somehow tenderly suggested—while the Gael-strains chant themselves from the mists—["Be thy soul blest, O Carril! in the midst of thy eddying winds. O that thou would'st come to my hall when I am alone by night! And thou dost come, my friend. I hear often thy light hand on my harp, when it hangs on the distant wall, and the feeble sound touches my ear. Why dost thou not speak to me in my grief, and tell me when I shall behold my friends? But thou passest away in thy murmuring blast; the wind whistles through the gray hairs of Ossian."]

But most of all, those changes of moon and sheets of hurrying vapor and black clouds, with the sense of rapid action in weird silence, recall the far-back Erse belief that such above were the preparations for receiving the wraiths of just-slain warriors—["We sat that night in Selma, round the strength of the shell. The wind was abroad in the oaks. The spirit of the mountain roar'd. The blast came rustling through the hall, and gently touch'd my harp. The sound was mournful and low, like the song of the tomb. Fingal heard it the first. The crowded sighs of his bosom rose. Some of my heroes are low, said the gray-hair'd king of Morven. I hear the sound of death on the harp. Ossian, touch the trembling string. Bid the sorrow rise, that their spirits may fly with joy to Morven's woody hills. I touch'd the harp before the king; the sound was mournful and low. Bend forward from your clouds, I said, ghosts of my fathers! bend. Lay by the red terror of your course. Receive the falling chief; whether he comes from a distant land, or rises from the rolling sea. Let his robe of mist be near; his spear that is form'd of a cloud. Place a half-extinguish'd meteor by his side, in the form of a hero's sword. And oh! let his countenance be lovely, that his friends may delight in his presence. Bend from your clouds, I said, ghosts of my fathers, bend. Such was my song in Selma, to the lightly trembling harp."]

How or why I know not, just at the moment, but I too muse and think of my best friends in their distant homes—of William O'Connor, of Maurice Bucke, of John Burroughs, and of Mrs. Gilchrist—friends of my soul—stanchest friends of my other soul, my poems.

ONLY A NEW FERRY BOAT

Jan. 12, '82.—Such a show as the Delaware presented an hour before sundown yesterday evening, all along between Philadelphia and Camden, is worth weaving into an item. It was full tide, a fair breeze from the southwest, the water of a pale tawny color, and just enough motion to make things frolicsome and lively. Add to these an approaching sunset of unusual splendor, a broad tumble of clouds, with much golden haze and profusion of beaming shaft and dazzle. In the midst of all, in the clear drab of afternoon light, there steam'd up the river the large, new boat, "the Wenonah," as pretty an object as you could wish to see, lightly and swiftly skimming along, all trim and white, cover'd with flags, transparent red and blue, streaming out in the breeze. Only a new ferry-boat, and yet in its fitness comparable with the prettiest product of Nature's cunning, and rivaling it. High up in the transparent ether gracefully balanced and circled four or five great sea hawks, while here below, amid the pomp and picturesqueness of sky and river, swam this creation of artificial beauty and motion and power, in its way no less perfect.

DEATH OF LONGFELLOW

Camden, April 3, '82.—I have just return'd from an old forest haunt, where I love to go occasionally away from parlors, pavements, and the newspapers and magazines—and where, of a clear forenoon, deep in the shade of pines and cedars and a tangle of old laurel-trees and vines, the news of Longfellow's death first reach'd me. For want of anything better, let me lightly twine a sprig of the sweet ground-ivy trailing so plentifully through the dead leaves at my feet, with reflections of that half hour alone, there in the silence, and lay it as my contribution on the dead bard's grave.

Longfellow in his voluminous works seems to me not only to be eminent in the style and forms of poetical expression that mark the present age, (an idiosyncrasy, almost a sickness, of verbal melody,) but to bring what is always dearest as poetry to the general human heart and taste, and probably must be so in the nature of things. He is certainly the sort of bard and counteractant most needed for our materialistic, self-assertive, money-worshipping, Anglo-Saxon races, and especially for the present age in America—an age tyrannically regulated with reference to the manufacturer, the merchant, the financier, the politician and the day workman—for whom and among whom he comes as the poet of melody, courtesy, deference—poet of the mellow twilight of the past in Italy, Germany, Spain, and in Northern Europe—poet of all sympathetic gentleness—and universal poet of women and young people. I should have to think long if I were ask'd to name the man who has done more, and in more valuable directions, for America.

I doubt if there ever was before such a fine intuitive judge and selecter of poems. His translations of many German and Scandinavian pieces are said to be better than the vernaculars. He does not urge or lash. His influence is like good drink or air. He is not tepid either, but always vital, with flavor, motion, grace. He strikes a splendid average, and does not sing exceptional passions, or humanity's jagged escapades. He is not revolutionary, brings nothing offensive or new, does not deal hard blows. On the contrary, his songs soothe and heal, or if they excite, it is a healthy and agreeable excitement. His very anger is gentle, is at second hand, (as in the "Quadroon Girl" and the "Witnesses.")

There is no undue element of pensiveness in Longfellow's strains. Even in the early translation, the Manrique, the movement is as of strong and steady wind or tide, holding up and buoying. Death is not avoided through his many themes, but there is something almost

winning in his original verses and renderings on that dread subject
—as, closing "the Happiest Land" dispute,

> And then the landlord's daughter
> Up to heaven rais'd her hand,
> And said, "Ye may no more contend,
> There lies the happiest land."

To the ungracious complaint-charge of his want of racy nativity
and special originality, I shall only say that America and the world
may well be reverently thankful—can never be thankful enough—
for any such singing-bird vouchsafed out of the centuries, without
asking that the notes be different from those of other songsters;
adding what I have heard Longfellow himself say, that ere the New
World can be worthily original, and announce herself and her own
heroes, she must be well saturated with the originality of others,
and respectfully consider the heroes that lived before Agamemnon.

STARTING NEWSPAPERS

Reminiscences—(From the "Camden Courier.")—As I sat taking my
evening sail across the Delaware in the staunch ferryboat "Beverly,"
a night or two ago, I was join'd by two young reporter friends. "I
have a message for you," said one of them; "the C. folks told me
to say they would like a piece sign'd by your name, to go in their
first number. Can you do it for them?" "I guess so," said I; "what
might it be about?" "Well, anything on newspapers, or perhaps
what you've done yourself, starting them." And off the boys went,
for we had reach'd the Philadelphia side. The hour was fine and
mild, the bright half-moon shining; Venus, with excess of splendor,
just setting in the west, and the great Scorpion rearing its length
more than half up in the southeast. As I cross'd leisurely for an hour
in the pleasant night-scene, my young friend's words brought up
quite a string of reminiscences.

I commenced when I was but a boy of eleven or twelve writing
sentimental bits for the old "Long Island Patriot," in Brooklyn; this
was about 1832. Soon after, I had a piece or two in George P.
Morris's then celebrated and fashionable "Mirror," of New York
city. I remember with what half-suppress'd excitement I used to
watch for the big, fat, red-faced, slow-moving, very old English
carrier who distributed the "Mirror" in Brooklyn; and when I got
one, opening and cutting the leaves with trembling fingers. How it
made my heart double-beat to see *my piece* on the pretty white
paper, in nice type.

My first real venture was the "Long Islander," in my own beautiful town of Huntington, in 1839. I was about twenty years old. I had
been teaching country school for two or three years in various parts
of Suffolk and Queens counties, but liked printing; had been at it
while a lad, learn'd the trade of compositor, and was encouraged
to start a paper in the region where I was born. I went to New
York, bought a press and types, hired some little help, but did most
of the work myself, including the press-work. Everything seem'd
turning out well; (only my own restlessness prevented me gradually establishing a permanent property there.) I bought a good
horse, and every week went all round the country serving my papers,
devoting one day and night to it. I never had happier jaunts—going
over to south side, to Babylon, down the south road, across to Smith-
town and Comac, and back home. The experiences of those jaunts,
the dear old-fashion'd farmers and their wives, the stops by the hayfields, the hospitality, nice dinners, occasional evenings, the girls,
the rides through the brush, come up in my memory to this day.

I next went to the "Aurora" daily in New York city—a sort of free
lance. Also wrote regularly for the "Tattler," an evening paper.
With these and a little outside work I was occupied off and on,
until I went to edit the "Brooklyn Eagle," where for two years I had
one of the pleasantest sits of my life—a good owner, good pay, and
easy work and hours. The troubles in the Democratic party broke
forth about those times (1848–'49) and I split off with the radicals,
which led to rows with the boss and "the party," and I lost my
place.

Being now out of a job, I was offer'd impromptu, (it happen'd
between the acts one night in the lobby of the old Broadway theatre
near Pearl street, New York city,) a good chance to go down to
New Orleans on the staff of the "Crescent," a daily to be started
there with plenty of capital behind it. One of the owners, who was
north buying material, met me walking in the lobby, and though
that was our first acquaintance, after fifteen minutes' talk (and a
drink) we made a formal bargain, and he paid me two hundred
dollars down to bind the contract and bear my expenses to New
Orleans. I started two days afterwards; had a good leisurely time,
as the paper wasn't to be out in three weeks. I enjoy'd my journey
and Louisiana life much. Returning to Brooklyn a year or two afterward I started the "Freeman," first as a weekly, then daily. Pretty
soon the secession war broke out, and I, too, got drawn in the current southward, and spent the following three years there, (as
memorandized preceding.)

Besides starting them as aforementioned, I have had to do, one time or another, during my life, with a long list of papers, at divers places, sometimes under queer circumstances. During the war, the hospitals at Washington, among other means of amusement, printed a little sheet among themselves, surrounded by wounds and death, the "Armory Square Gazette," to which I contributed. The same long afterward, casually, to a paper—I think it was call'd the "Jim-plecute"—out in Colorado where I stopp'd at the time. When I was in Quebec province, in Canada, in 1880, I went into the queerest little old French printing office near Tadousac. It was far more primitive and ancient than my Camden friend William Kurtz's place up on Federal street. I remember, as a youngster, several characteristic old printers of a kind hard to be seen these days.

THE GREAT UNREST OF WHICH WE ARE PART

My THOUGHTS went floating on vast and mystic currents as I sat to-day in solitude and half-shade by the creek—returning mainly to two principal centres. One of my cherish'd themes for a never-achiev'd poem has been the two impetuses of man and the universe —in the latter, creation's incessant unrest,[18] exfoliation. (Darwin's evolution, I suppose.) Indeed, what is Nature but change, in all its visible, and still more its invisible processes? Or what is humanity in its faith, love, heroism, poetry, even morals, but *emotion?*

BY EMERSON'S GRAVE

May 6, '82.—We stand by Emerson's new-made grave without sadness—indeed a solemn joy and faith, almost hauteur—our soul-benison no mere

"Warrior, rest, thy task is done,"

for one beyond the warriors of the world lies surely symboll'd here. A just man, poised on himself, all-loving, all-inclosing, and sane and clear as the sun. Nor does it seem so much Emerson himself we are here to honor—it is conscience, simplicity, culture, humanity's attributes at their best, yet applicable if need be to average affairs, and eligible to all. So used are we to suppose a heroic death can only come from out of battle or storm, or mighty personal contest, or amid dramatic incidents or danger, (have we not been taught so for ages by all the plays and poems?) that few even of those who most sympathizingly mourn Emerson's late departure will fully appreciate the ripen'd grandeur of that event, with its play of calm and fitness, like evening light on the sea.

How I shall henceforth dwell on the blessed hours when, not long since, I saw that benignant face, the clear eyes, the silently smiling mouth, the form yet upright in its great age—to the very last, with so much spring and cheeriness, and such an absence of decrepitude, that even the term *venerable* hardly seem'd fitting.

Perhaps the life now rounded and completed in its mortal development, and which nothing can change or harm more, has its most illustrious halo, not in its splendid intellectual or esthetic products, but as forming in its entirety one of the few, (alas! how few!) perfect and flawless excuses for being, of the entire literary class.

We can say, as Abraham Lincoln at Gettysburg, It is not we who come to consecrate the dead—we reverently come to receive, if so it may be, some consecration to ourselves and daily work from him.

AT PRESENT WRITING—PERSONAL
A letter to a German friend—extract

May 31, '82.—"From to-day I enter upon my 64th year. The paralysis that first affected me nearly ten years ago, has since remain'd, with varying course—seems to have settled quietly down, and will probably continue. I easily tire, am very clumsy, cannot walk far; but my spirits are first-rate. I go around in public almost every day— now and then take long trips, by railroad or boat, hundreds of miles —live largely in the open air—am sun-burnt and stout, (weigh 190) —keep up my activity and interest in life, people, progress, and the questions of the day. About two-thirds of the time I am quite comfortable. What mentality I ever had remains entirely unaffected; though physically I am a half-paralytic, and likely to be so, long as I live. But the principal object of my life seems to have been accomplish'd—I have the most devoted and ardent of friends, and affectionate relatives—and of enemies I really make no account."

AFTER TRYING A CERTAIN BOOK

I TRIED to read a beautifully printed and scholarly volume on "the Theory of Poetry," received by mail this morning from England— but gave it up at last for a bad job. Here are some capricious pencillings that follow'd, as I find them in my notes:

In youth and maturity Poems are charged with sunshine and varied pomp of day; but as the soul more and more takes precedence, (the sensuous still included,) the Dusk becomes the poet's atmosphere. I too have sought, and ever seek, the brilliant sun, and make my songs according. But as I grow old, the half-lights of evening are far more to me.

The play of Imagination, with the sensuous objects of Nature for symbols, and Faith—with Love and Pride as the unseen impetus and moving-power of all, make up the curious chess-game of a poem.

Common teachers or critics are always asking "What does it mean?" Symphony of fine musician, or sunset, or sea-waves rolling up the beach—what do they mean? Undoubtedly in the most subtle-elusive sense they mean something—as love does, and religion does, and the best poems;—but who shall fathom and define those meanings? (I do not intend this as a warrant for wildness and frantic escapades—but to justify the soul's frequent joy in what cannot be defined to the intellectual part, or to calculation.)

At its best, poetic lore is like what may be heard of conversation in the dusk, from speakers far or hid, of which we get only a few broken murmurs. What is not gather'd is far more—perhaps the main thing.

Grandest poetic passages are only to be taken at free removes, as we sometimes look for stars at night, not by gazing directly toward them, but off one side.

(*To a poetic student and friend.*)—I only seek to put you in rapport. Your own brain, heart, evolution, must not only understand the matter, but largely supply it.

FINAL CONFESSIONS—LITERARY TESTS

So DRAW near their end these garrulous notes. There have doubtless occurr'd some repetitions, technical errors in the consecutiveness of dates, in the minutiæ of botanical, astronomical, &c., exactness, and perhaps elsewhere;—for in gathering up, writing, peremptorily dispatching copy, this hot weather, (last of July and through August, '82,) and delaying not the printers, I have had to hurry along, no time to spare. But in the deepest veracity of all—in reflections of objects, scenes, Nature's outpourings, to my senses and receptivity, as they seem'd to me—in the work of giving those who care for it, some authentic glints, specimen-days of my life—and in the *bona fide* spirit and relations, from author to reader, on all the subjects design'd, and as far as they go, I feel to make unmitigated claims.

The synopsis of my early life, Long Island, New York city, and so forth, and the diary-jottings in the Secession war, tell their own story. My plan in starting what constitutes most of the middle of the book, was originally for hints and data of a Nature-poem that should carry one's experiences a few hours, commencing at noon-flush, and so through the after-part of the day—I suppose led to such idea by my own life-afternoon now arrived. But I soon found I could move at more ease, by giving the narrative at first hand. (Then there is a humiliating lesson one learns, in serene hours, of a fine day or night. Nature seems to look on all fixed-up poetry and art as something almost impertinent.)

Thus I went on, years following, various seasons and areas, spinning forth my thought beneath the night and stars, (or as I was confined to my room by half-sickness,) or at midday looking out upon the sea, or far north steaming over the Saguenay's black breast, jotting all down in the loosest sort of chronological order, and here printing from my impromptu notes, hardly even the seasons group'd together, or anything corrected—so afraid of dropping what smack of outdoors or sun or starlight might cling to the lines, I dared not try to meddle with or smooth them. Every now and then, (not often, but for a foil,) I carried a book in my pocket—or perhaps tore out from some broken or cheap edition a bunch of loose leaves; most always had something of the sort ready, but only took it out when the mood demanded. In that way, utterly out of reach of literary conventions, I re-read many authors.

I cannot divest my appetite of literature, yet I find myself eventually trying it all by Nature—*first premises* many call it, but really the crowning results of all, laws, tallies and proofs. (Has it never occurr'd to any one how the last deciding tests applicable to a book are entirely outside of technical and grammatical ones, and that any truly first-class production has little or nothing to do with the rules and calibres of ordinary critics? or the bloodless chalk of Allibone's Dictionary? I have fancied the ocean and the daylight, the mountain and the forest, putting their spirit in a judgment on our books. I have fancied some disembodied human soul giving its verdict.)

NATURE AND DEMOCRACY—MORALITY

DEMOCRACY most of all affiliates with the open air, is sunny and hardy and sane only with Nature—just as much as Art is. Something is required to temper both—to check them, restrain them from excess, morbidity. I have wanted, before departure, to bear special testimony to a very old lesson and requisite. American Democracy, in its myriad personalities, in factories, work-shops, stores, offices—through the dense streets and houses of cities, and all their manifold sophisticated life—must either be fibred, vitalized, by regular contact with out-door light and air and growths, farm-scenes, animals, fields, trees, birds, sun-warmth and free skies, or it will certainly dwindle and pale. We cannot have grand races of mechanics, work people, and commonalty, (the only specific purpose of America,) on any less terms. I conceive of no flourishing and heroic elements of Democracy in the United States, or of Democracy maintaining itself at all, without the Nature-element forming a main part —to be its health-element and beauty-element—to really underlie the whole politics, sanity, religion and art of the New World.

Finally, the morality: "Virtue," said Marcus Aurelius, "what is it, only a living and enthusiastic sympathy with Nature?" Perhaps indeed the efforts of the true poets, founders, religions, literatures, all ages, have been, and ever will be, our time and times to come, essentially the same—to bring people back from their persistent strayings and sickly abstractions, to the costless average, divine, original concrete.

NOTES

1. The pages from 4 to 15 are nearly verbatim an off-hand letter of mine in January, 1882, to an insisting friend. Following, I give some gloomy experiences. The war of attempted secession has, of course, been the distinguishing event of my time. I commenced at the close of 1862, and continued steadily through '63, '64, and '65, to visit the sick and wounded of the army, both on the field and in the hospitals in and around Washington city. From the first I kept little note-books for impromptu jottings in pencil to refresh my memory of names and circumstances, and what was specially wanted, &c. In these I brief'd cases, persons, sights, occurrences in camp, by the bedside, and not seldom by the corpses of the dead. Some were scratch'd down from narratives I heard and itemized while watching, or waiting, or tending somebody amid those scenes. I have dozens of such little note-books left, forming a special history of those years, for myself alone, full of associations never to be possibly said or sung. I wish I could convey to the reader the associations that attach to these soil'd and creas'd livraisons, each composed of a sheet or two of paper, folded small to carry in the pocket, and fasten'd with a pin. I leave them just as I threw them by after the war, blotch'd here and there with more than one blood-stain, hurriedly written, sometimes at the clinique, not seldom amid the excitement of uncertainty, or defeat, or of action, or getting ready for it, or a march. Most of the pages from 26 to 81 are verbatim copies of those lurid and blood-smutch'd little note-books.

Very different are most of the memoranda that follow. Some time after the war ended I had a paralytic stroke, which prostrated me for several years. In 1876 I began to get over the worst of it. From this date, portions of several seasons, especially summers, I spent at a secluded haunt down in Camden county, New Jersey—Timber creek, quite a little river (it enters from the great Delaware, twelve miles away)—with primitive solitudes, winding stream, recluse and woody banks, sweet-feeding springs, and all the charms that birds, grass, wild-flowers, rabbits and squirrels, old oaks, walnut trees, &c., can bring. Through these times, and on these spots, the diary from page 83 onward was mostly written.

The COLLECT afterward gathers up the odds and ends of whatever pieces I can now lay hands on, written at various times past, and swoops all together like fish in a net.

I suppose I publish and leave the whole gathering, first, from that eternal tendency to perpetuate and preserve which is behind all Nature, authors included; second, to symbolize two or three specimen interiors, personal and other, out of the myriads of my time, the middle range of the Nineteenth century in the New World; a strange, unloosen'd, wondrous time. But the book is probably without any definite purpose that can be told in a statement.

199

2. Long Island was settled first on the west end by the Dutch, from Holland, then on the east end by the English—the dividing line of the two nationalities being a little west of Huntington, where my father's folks lived, and where I was born.

3. "Paumanok, (or Paumanake, or Paumanack, the Indian name of Long Island,) over a hundred miles long; shaped like a fish—plenty of sea shore, sandy, stormy, uninviting, the horizon boundless, the air too strong for invalids, the bays a wonderful resort for aquatic birds, the south-side meadows cover'd with salt hay, the soil of the island generally tough, but good for the locust-tree, the apple orchard, and the blackberry, and with numberless springs of the sweetest water in the world. Years ago, among the bay-men—a strong, wild race, now extinct, or rather entirely changed—a native of Long Island was called a *Paumanacker*, or *Creole-Paumanacker*."—*John Burroughs*.

4. "On the visit of General Lafayette to this country, in 1824, he came over to Brooklyn in state, and rode through the city. The children of the schools turn'd out to join in the welcome. An edifice for a free public library for youths was just then commencing, and Lafayette consented to stop on his way and lay the corner-stone. Numerous children arriving on the ground, where a huge irregular excavation for the building was already dug, surrounded with heaps of rough stone, several gentlemen assisted in lifting the children to safe or convenient spots to see the ceremony. Among the rest, Lafayette, also helping the children, took up the five-year-old Walt Whitman, and pressing the child a moment to his breast, and giving him a kiss, handed him down to a safe spot in the excavation." —*John Burroughs*.

5. Of the Brooklyn of that time (1830–40) hardly anything remains, except the lines of old streets. The population was then between ten and twelve thousand. For a mile Fulton street was lined with magnificent elm trees. The character of the place was thoroughly rural. As a sample of comparative values, it may be mention'd that twenty-five acres in what is now the most costly part of the city, bounded by Flatbush and Fulton avenues, were then bought by Mr. Parmentier, a French *emigré*, for $4,000. Who remembers the old places as they were? Who remembers the old citizens of that time? Among the former were Smith & Wood's, Coe Downing's and other public houses at the ferry, the old Ferry itself, Love lane, the Heights as then, the Wallabout with the wooden bridge, and the road out beyond Fulton street to the old toll-gate. Among the latter were the majestic and genial General Jeremiah Johnson, with others, Gabriel Furman, Rev. E. M. Johnson, Alden Spooner, Mr. Pierrepont, Mr. Joralemon, Samuel Willoughby, Jonathan Trotter, George Hall, Cyrus P. Smith, N. B. Morse, John Dikeman, Adrian Hegeman, William Udall, and old Mr. Duflon, with his military garden.

6. MR. GARFIELD (*In the House of Representatives, April 15, '79.*) "Do gentlemen know that (leaving out all the border States) there were fifty regiments and seven companies of white men in our army fighting for the Union from the States that went into rebellion? Do they know that from the single State of Kentucky more Union soldiers fought under our flag than Napoleon took into the battle of Waterloo? more than Wellington took with all the allied armies against Napoleon? Do they remember that 186,000 color'd men fought under our flag against the rebellion and for

the Union, and that of that number 90,000 were from the States which went into rebellion?"

7. In the U. S. Surgeon-General's office since, there is a formal record and treatment of 253,142 cases of wounds by government surgeons. What must have been the number unofficial, indirect—to say nothing of the Southern armies?

8. *From a review of* "ANDERSONVILLE, A STORY OF SOUTHERN MILITARY PRISONS," *published serially in the "Toledo Blade," in 1879, and afterwards in book form.*

"There is a deep fascination in the subject of Andersonville—for that Golgotha, in which lie the whitening bones of 13,000 gallant young men, represents the dearest and costliest sacrifice of the war for the preservation of our national unity. It is a type, too, of its class. Its more than hundred hecatombs of dead represent several times that number of their brethren, for whom the prison gates of Belle Isle, Danville, Salisbury, Florence, Columbia, and Cahaba open'd only in eternity. There are few families in the North who have not at least one dear relative or friend among these 60,000 whose sad fortune it was to end their service for the Union by lying down and dying for it in a southern prison pen. The manner of their death, the horrors that cluster'd thickly around every moment of their existence, the loyal, unfaltering steadfastness with which they endured all that fate had brought them, has never been adequately told. It was not with them as with their comrades in the field, whose every act was perform'd in the presence of those whose duty it was to observe such matters and report them to the world. Hidden from the view of their friends in the north by the impenetrable veil which the military operations of the rebels drew around the so-called confederacy, the people knew next to nothing of their career or their sufferings. Thousands died there less heeded even than the hundreds who perish'd on the battle-field. Grant did not lose as many men kill'd outright, in the terrible campaign from the Wilderness to the James river—43 days of desperate fighting—as died in July and August at Andersonville. Nearly twice as many died in that prison as fell from the day that Grant cross'd the Rapidan, till he settled down in the trenches before Petersburg. More than four times as many Union dead lie under the solemn soughing pines about that forlorn little village in southern Georgia, than mark the course of Sherman from Chattanooga to Atlanta. The nation stands aghast at the expenditure of life which attended the two bloody campaigns of 1864, which virtually crush'd the confederacy, but no one remembers that more Union soldiers died in the rear of the rebel lines than were kill'd in the front of them. The great military events which stamp'd out the rebellion drew attention away from the sad drama which starvation and disease play'd in those gloomy pens in the far recesses of sombre southern forests."

From a letter of "Johnny Bouquet," in N. Y. Tribune, March 27, '81.
"I visited at Salisbury, N. C., the prison pen or the site of it, from which nearly 12,000 victims of southern politicians were buried, being confined in a pen without shelter, exposed to all the elements could do, to all the disease herding animals together could create, and to all the starvation and cruelty an incompetent and intense caitiff government could accomplish. From the conversation and almost from the recollection of the northern people this place has dropp'd, but not so in the gossip of the

Salisbury people, nearly all of whom say that the half was never told; that such was the nature of habitual outrage here that when Federal prisoners escaped the townspeople harbor'd them in their barns, afraid the vengeance of God would fall on them, to deliver even their enemies back to such cruelty. Said one old man at the Boyden House, who join'd in the conversation one evening: 'There were often men buried out of that prison pen alive. I have the testimony of a surgeon that he has seen them pull'd out of the dead cart with their eyes open and taking notice, but too weak to lift a finger. There was not the least excuse for such treatment, as the confederate government had seized every sawmill in the region, and could just as well have put up shelter for these prisoners as not, wood being plentiful here. It will be hard to make any honest man in Salisbury say that there was the slightest necessity for those prisoners having to live in old tents, caves and holes half-full of water. Representations were made to the Davis government against the officers in charge of it, but no attention was paid to them. Promotion was the punishment for cruelty there. The inmates were skeletons. Hell could have no terrors for any man who died there, except the inhuman keepers.' "

9. Without apology for the abrupt change of field and atmosphere—after what I have put in the preceding fifty or sixty pages—temporary episodes, thank heaven!—I restore my book to the bracing and buoyant equilibrium of concrete outdoor Nature, the only permanent reliance for sanity of book or human life.

Who knows, (I have it in my fancy, my ambition,) but the pages now ensuing may carry ray of sun, or smell of grass or corn, or call of bird, or gleam of stars by night, or snow-flakes falling fresh and mystic, to denizen of heated city house, or tired workman or workwoman?—or may-be in sick-room or prison—to serve as cooling breeze, or Nature's aroma, to some fever'd mouth or latent pulse.

10. There is a tulip poplar within sight of Woodstown, which is twenty feet around, three feet from the ground, four feet across about eighteen feet up the trunk, which is broken off about three or four feet higher up. On the south side an arm has shot out from which rise two stems, each to about ninety-one or ninety-two feet from the ground. Twenty-five (or more) years since the cavity in the butt was large enough for, and nine men at one time, ate dinner therein. It is supposed twelve to fifteen men could now, at one time, stand within its trunk. The severe winds of 1877 and 1878 did not seem to damage it, and the two stems send out yearly many blossoms, scenting the air immediately about it with their sweet perfume. It is entirely unprotected by other trees, on a hill.—*Woodstown, N. J., "Register," April 15, '79.*

11. In the pocket of my receptacle-book I find a list of suggested and rejected names for this volume, or parts of it—such as the following:

> As the wild bee hums in May,
> & August mulleins grow,
> & Winter snow-flakes fall,
> & stars in the sky roll round.

> Away from Books—away from Art,
> Now for the Day and Night—the lesson done,
> Now for the Sun and Stars.

Notes of a half-Paralytic,   *As Voices in the Dusk, from Speakers*
Week in and Week out,   *far or hid,*
Embers of Ending Days,   *Autochthons.....Embryons,*
Ducks and Drakes,   *Wing-and-Wing,*
Flood Tide and Ebb,   *Notes and Recallés,*
Gossip at Early Candle-light,   *Only Mulleins and Bumble-Bees,*
Echoes and Escapades,   *Pond-Babble.....Tête-a-Têtes,*
Such as I.....Evening Dews,   *Echoes of a Life in the 19th Century*
Notes after Writing a Book,   *in the New World,*
Far and Near at 63,   *Flanges of Fifty Years,*
Drifts and Cumulus,   *Abandons.....Hurry Notes,*
Maize-Tassels.....Kindlings,   *A Life-Mosaic.....Native Moments,*
Fore and Aft.....Vestibules,   *Types and Semi-Tones,*
Scintilla at 60 and after,   *Oddments.....Sand-Drifts,*
Sands on the Shores of 64,   *Again and Again.*

12. It will be difficult for the future—judging by his books, personal dis-
sympathies, &c.,—to account for the deep hold this author has taken on the
present age, and the way he has color'd its method and thought. I am
certainly at a loss to account for it all as affecting myself. But there could
be no view, or even partial picture, of the middle and latter part of our
Nineteenth century, that did not markedly include Thomas Carlyle. In
his case (as so many others, literary productions, works of art, personal
identities, events,) there has been an impalpable something more effective
than the palpable. Then I find no better text, (it is always important to
have a definite, special, even oppositional, living man to start from,) for
sending out certain speculations and comparisons for home use. Let us
see what they amount to—those reactionary doctrines, fears, scornful analyses of democracy—even from the most erudite and sincere mind of Europe.

13. Not the least mentionable part of the case, (a streak, it may be, of that
humor with which history and fate love to contrast their gravity,) is
that although neither of my great authorities during their lives consider'd
the United States worthy of serious mention, all the principal works of
both might not inappropriately be this day collected and bound up under
the conspicuous title: "*Speculations for the use of North America, and
Democracy there, with the relations of the same to Metaphysics, including Lessons and Warnings (encouragements too, and of the vastest,) from
the Old World to the New.*"

14. I hope I shall not myself fall into the error I charge upon him, of pre-
scribing a specific for indispensable evils. My utmost pretension is probably but to offset that old claim of the exclusively curative power of first-
class individual men, as leaders and rulers, by the claims, and general
movement and result, of ideas. Something of the latter kind seems to me
the distinctive theory of America, of democracy, and of the modern—or
rather, I should say, it *is* democracy, and *is* the modern.

15. I am much indebted to J. Gostick's abstract.

16. I have deliberately repeated it all, not only in offset to Carlyle's ever-
lurking pessimism and world-decadence, but as presenting the most thoroughly *American points of view* I know. In my opinion the above formulas
of Hegel are an essential and crowning justification of New World democracy in the creative realms of time and space. There is that about them
which only the vastness, the multiplicity and the vitality of America would

seem able to comprehend, to give scope and illustration to, or to be fit
for, or even originate. It is strange to me that they were born in Germany,
or in the old world at all. While a Carlyle, I should say, is quite the legitimate European product to be expected.

17. *Samples of my common-place book down at the creek:*

I have—says old Pindar—many swift arrows in my quiver which speak
to the wise, though they need an interpreter to the thoughtless.

Such a man as it takes ages to make, and ages to understand.

H. D. Thoreau.

If you hate a man, don't kill him, but let him live.—*Buddhistic.*

Famous swords are made of refuse scraps, thought worthless.

Poetry is the only verity—the expression of a sound mind speaking after
the ideal—and not after the apparent.—*Emerson.*

The form of oath among the Shoshone Indians is, "The earth hears me.
The sun hears me. Shall I lie?"

The true test of civilization is not the census, nor the size of cities, nor
the crops—no, but the kind of a man the country turns out.—*Emerson.*

The whole wide ether is the eagle's sway:
The whole earth is a brave man's fatherland.—*Euripides.*

Spices crush'd, their pungence yield,
Trodden scents their sweets respire;
Would you have its strength reveal'd?
Cast the incense in the fire.

Matthew Arnold speaks of "the huge Mississippi of falsehood called
History."

The wind blows north, the wind blows south,
The wind blows east and west;
No matter how the free wind blows,
Some ship will find it best.

Preach not to others what they should eat, but eat as becomes you, and
be silent.—*Epictetus.*

Victor Hugo makes a donkey meditate and apostrophize thus:

My brother, man, if you would know the truth,
We both are by the same dull walls shut in;
The gate is massive and the dungeon strong.
But you look through the key-hole out beyond,
And call this knowledge; yet have not at hand
The key wherein to turn the fatal lock.

"William Cullen Bryant surprised me once," relates a writer in a New
York paper, "by saying that prose was the natural language of composition,
and he wonder'd how anybody came to write poetry."

Farewell! I did not know thy worth;
But thou art gone, and now 'tis prized:
So angels walk'd unknown on earth,
But when they flew were recognized.—*Hood.*

John Burroughs, writing of Thoreau, says: "He improves with age—in fact requires age to take off a little of his asperity, and fully ripen him. The world likes a good hater and refuser almost at well as it likes a good lover and accepter—only it likes him farther off."

Louise Michel at the burial of Blanqui, (1881)

Blanqui drill'd his body to subjection to his grand conscience and his noble passions, and commencing as a young man, broke with all that is sybaritish in modern civilization. Without the power to sacrifice self, great ideas will never bear fruit.

> Out of the leaping furnace flame
> A mass of molten silver came;
> Then, beaten into pieces three,
> Went forth to meet its destiny.
> The first a crucifix was made,
> Within a soldier's knapsack laid;
> The second was a locket fair,
> Where a mother kept her dead child's hair;
> The third—a bangle, bright and warm,
> Around a faithless woman's arm.
>
> A mighty pain to love it is,
> And 'tis a pain that pain to miss;
> But of all pain the greatest pain,
> It is to love, but love in vain.

Maurice F. Egan on De Guérin

> A pagan heart, a Christian soul had he,
>   He follow'd Christ, yet for dead Pan he sigh'd,
>   Till earth and heaven met within his breast:
> As if Theocritus in Sicily
>   Had come upon the Figure crucified,
>   And lost his gods in deep, Christ-given rest.
>
> And if I pray, the only prayer
>   That moves my lips for me,
> Is, leave the mind that now I bear,
>   And give me Liberty.—*Emily Brontë.*
>
> I travel on not knowing,
>   I would not if I might;
> I would rather walk with God in the dark,
>   Then go alone in the light;
> I would rather walk with Him by faith
>   Than pick my way by sight.

Prof. Huxley in a late lecture

I myself agree with the sentiment of Thomas Hobbes, of Malmesbury, that "the scope of all speculation is the performance of some action or thing to be done." I have not any very great respect for, or interest in, mere "knowing," as such.

Prince Metternich

Napoleon was of all men in the world the one who most profoundly despised the race. He had a marvellous insight into the weaker sides of human nature, (and all our passions are either foibles themselves, or the cause of foibles.) He was a very small man of imposing character. He was ignorant, as a sub-lieutenant generally is: a remarkable instinct supplied the lack of knowledge. From his mean opinion of men, he never had any anxiety lest he should go wrong. He ventur'd everything, and gain'd thereby an immense step toward success. Throwing himself upon a prodigious arena, he amaz'd the world, and made himself master of it, while others cannot even get so far as being masters of their own hearth. Then he went on and on, until he broke his neck.

18. "Fifty thousand years ago the constellation of the Great Bear or Dipper was a starry cross; a hundred thousand years hence the imaginary Dipper will be upside down, and the stars which form the bowl and handle will have changed places. The misty nebulæ are moving, and besides are whirling around in great spirals, some one way, some another. Every molecule of matter in the whole universe is swinging to and fro; every particle of ether which fills space is in jelly-like vibration. Light is one kind of motion, heat another, electricity another, magnetism another, sound another. Every human sense is the result of motion; every perception, every thought is but motion of the molecules of the brain translated by that incomprehensible thing we call mind. The processes of growth, of existence, of decay, whether in worlds, or in the minutest organisms, are but motion."

-》》》-《《-

Collect

ONE OR TWO INDEX ITEMS

THOUGH the ensuing COLLECT and preceding SPECIMEN DAYS are both largely from memoranda already existing, the hurried peremptory needs of copy for the printers, already referr'd to—(the musicians' story of a composer up in a garret rushing the middle body and last of his score together, while the fiddlers are playing the first parts down in the concert-room)—of this haste, while quite willing to get the consequent stimulus of life and motion, I am sure there must have resulted sundry technical errors. If any are too glaring they will be corrected in a future edition.

A special word about "PIECES IN EARLY YOUTH," at the end. On jaunts over Long Island, as boy and young fellow, nearly half a century ago, I heard of, or came across in my own experience, characters, true occurrences, incidents, which I tried my 'prentice hand at recording—(I was then quite an "abolitionist" and advocate of the "temperance" and "anti-capital-punishment" causes)—and publish'd during occasional visits to New York city. A majority of the sketches appear'd first in the "Democratic Review," others in the "Columbian Magazine," or the "American Review," of that period. My serious wish were to have all those crude and boyish pieces quietly dropp'd in oblivion—but to avoid the annoyance of their surreptitious issue, (as lately announced, from outsiders,) I have, with some qualms, tack'd them on here. *A Dough-Face Song* came out first in the "Evening Post"—*Blood-Money,* and *Wounded in the House of Friends,* in the "Tribune."

Poetry To-Day in America, &c., first appear'd (under the name of *"The Poetry of the Future,"*) in "The North American Review" for February, 1881. *A Memorandum at a Venture,* in same periodical, some time afterward.

Several of the convalescent out-door scenes and literary items, preceding, originally appear'd in the fortnightly "Critic," of New York.

-》》-《《-

DEMOCRATIC VISTAS

As THE greatest lessons of Nature through the universe are perhaps the lessons of variety and freedom, the same present the greatest lessons also in New World politics and progress. If a man were ask'd, for instance, the distinctive points contrasting modern European and American political and other life with the old Asiatic cultus, as lingering-bequeath'd yet in China and Turkey, he might find the amount of them in John Stuart Mill's profound essay on Liberty in the future, where he demands two main constituents, or sub-strata, for a truly grand nationality—1st, a large variety of character—and 2d, full play for human nature to expand itself in numberless and even conflicting directions—(seems to be for general humanity much like the influences that make up, in their limitless field, that perennial health-action of the air we call the weather —an infinite number of currents and forces, and contributions, and temperatures, and cross purposes, whose ceaseless play of counterpart upon counterpart brings constant restoration and vitality.) With this thought—and not for itself alone, but all it necessitates, and draws after it—let me begin my speculations.

America, filling the present with greatest deeds and problems, cheerfully accepting the past, including feudalism, (as, indeed, the present is but the legitimate birth of the past, including feudalism,) counts, as I reckon, for her justification and success, (for who, as yet, dare claim success?) almost entirely on the future. Nor is that hope unwarranted. To-day, ahead, though dimly yet, we see, in vistas, a copious, sane, gigantic offspring. For our New World I consider far less important for what it has done, or what it is, than for results to come. Sole among nationalities, these States have assumed the task to put in forms of lasting power and practicality, on areas of amplitude rivaling the operations of the physical kosmos, the moral political speculations of ages, long, long deferr'd, the democratic republican principle, and the theory of development and perfection by voluntary standards, and self-reliance. Who else, indeed, except the United States, in history, so far, have accepted in unwitting faith, and, as we now see, stand, act upon, and go security for, these things?

But preluding no longer, let me strike the key-note of the following strain. First premising that, though the passages of it have been written at widely different times, (it is, in fact, a collection of memoranda, perhaps for future designers, comprehenders,) and

though it may be open to the charge of one part contradicting another—for there are opposite sides to the great question of democracy, as to every great question—I feel the parts harmoniously
blended in my own realization and convictions, and present them
to be read only in such oneness, each page and each claim and
assertion modified and temper'd by the others. Bear in mind, too,
that they are not the result of studying up in political economy, but
of the ordinary sense, observing, wandering among men, these
States, these stirring years of war and peace. I will not gloss over
the appaling dangers of universal suffrage in the United States. In
fact, it is to admit and face these dangers I am writing. To him or
her within whose thought rages the battle, advancing, retreating,
between democracy's convictions, aspirations, and the people's
crudeness, vice, caprices, I mainly write this essay. I shall use the
words America and democracy as convertible terms. Not an ordinary one is the issue. The United States are destined either to sur-
mount the gorgeous history of feudalism, or else prove the most tremendous failure of time. Not the least doubtful am I on any
prospects of their material success. The triumphant future of their
business, geographic and productive departments, on larger scales
and in more varieties than ever, is certain. In those respects the republic must soon (if she does not already) outstrip all examples
hitherto afforded, and dominate the world.[1]

Admitting all this, with the priceless value of our political institutions, general suffrage, (and fully acknowledging the latest, widest
opening of the doors,) I say that, far deeper than these, what finally
and only is to make of our western world a nationality superior to
any hither known, and outtopping the past, must be vigorous, yet
unsuspected Literatures, perfect personalities and sociologies, original, transcendental, and expressing (what, in highest sense, are not
yet express'd at all,) democracy and the modern. With these, and
out of these, I promulge new races of Teachers, and of perfect
Women, indispensable to endow the birth-stock of a New World.
For feudalism, caste, the ecclesiastic traditions, though palpably retreating from political institutions, still hold essentially, by their
spirit, even in this country, entire possession of the more important
fields, indeed the very subsoil, of education, and of social standards
and literature.

I say that democracy can never prove itself beyond cavil, until it
founds and luxuriantly grows its own forms of art, poems, schools,
theology, displacing all that exists, or that has been produced anywhere in the past, under opposite influences. It is curious to me that
while so many voices, pens, minds, in the press, lecture-rooms, in

our Congress, &c., are discussing intellectual topics, pecuniary dangers, legislative problems, the suffrage, tariff and labor questions, and the various business and benevolent needs of America, with propositions, remedies, often worth deep attention, there is one need, a hiatus the profoundest, that no eye seems to perceive, no voice to state. Our fundamental want to-day in the United States, with closest, amplest reference to present conditions, and to the future, is of a class, and the clear idea of a class, of native authors, literatuses, far different, far higher in grade than any yet known, sacerdotal, modern, fit to cope with our occasions, lands, permeating the whole mass of American mentality, taste, belief, breathing into it a new breath of life, giving it decision, affecting politics far more than the popular superficial suffrage, with results inside and underneath the elections of Presidents or Congresses— radiating, begetting appropriate teachers, schools, manners, and, as its grandest result, accomplishing, (what neither the schools nor the churches and their clergy have hitherto accomplish'd, and without which this nation will no more stand, permanently, soundly, than a house will stand without a substratum,) a religious and moral character beneath the political and productive and intellectual bases of the States. For know you not, dear, earnest reader, that the people of our land may all read and write, and may all possess the right to vote—and yet the main things may be entirely lacking?—(and this to suggest them.)

View'd, to-day, from a point of view sufficiently over-arching, the problem of humanity all over the civilized world is social and religious, and is to be finally met and treated by literature. The priest departs, the divine literatus comes. Never was anything more wanted than, to-day, and here in the States, the poet of the modern is wanted, or the great literatus of the modern. At all times, perhaps, the central point in any nation, and that whence it is itself really sway'd the most, and whence it sways others, is its national literature, especially its archetypal poems. Above all previous lands, a great original literature is surely to become the justification and reliance, (in some respects the sole reliance,) of American democracy.

Few are aware how the great literature penetrates all, gives hue to all, shapes aggregates and individuals, and, after subtle ways, with irresistible power, constructs, sustains, demolishes at will. Why tower, in reminiscence, above all the nations of the earth, two special lands, petty in themselves, yet inexpressibly gigantic, beautiful, columnar? Immortal Judah lives, and Greece immortal lives, in a couple of poems.

Nearer than this. It is not generally realized, but it is true, as the genius of Greece, and all the sociology, personality, politics and religion of those wonderful states, resided in their literature or esthetics, that what was afterwards the main support of European chivalry, the feudal, ecclesiastical, dynastic world over there—forming its osseous structure, holding it together for hundreds, thousands of years, preserving its flesh and bloom, giving it form, decision, rounding it out, and so saturating it in the conscious and unconscious blood, breed, belief, and intuitions of men, that it still prevails powerful to this day, in defiance of the mighty changes of time—was its literature, permeating to the very marrow, especially that major part, its enchanting songs, ballads, and poems.[2]

To the ostent of the senses and eyes, I know, the influences which stamp the world's history are wars, uprisings or downfalls of dynasties, changeful movements of trade, important inventions, navigation, military or civil governments, advent of powerful personalities, conquerors, &c. These of course play their part; yet, it may be, a single new thought, imagination, abstract principle, even literary style, fit for the time, put in shape by some great literatus, and projected among mankind, may duly cause changes, growths, removals, greater than the longest and bloodiest war, or the most stupendous merely political, dynastic, or commercial overturn.

In short, as, though it may not be realized, it is strictly true, that a few first-class poets, philosophs, and authors, have substantially settled and given status to the entire religion, education, law, sociology, &c., of the hitherto civilized world, by tinging and often creating the atmospheres out of which they have arisen, such also must stamp, and more than ever stamp, the interior and real democratic construction of this American continent, to-day, and days to come. Remember also this fact of difference, that, while through the antique and through the mediæval ages, highest thoughts and ideals realized themselves, and their expression made its way by other arts, as much as, or even more than by, technical literature, (not open to the mass of persons, or even to the majority of eminent persons,) such literature in our day and for current purposes, is not only more eligible than all the other arts put together, but has become the only general means of morally influencing the world. Painting, sculpture, and the dramatic theatre, it would seem, no longer play an indispensable or even important part in the workings and mediumship of intellect, utility, or even high esthetics. Architecture remains, doubtless with capacities, and a real future. Then music, the combiner, nothing more spiritual, nothing more sensuous, a god, yet completely human, advances, prevails, holds highest place; supplying in certain wants and quarters what nothing else could supply. Yet in the civilization of to-day it is undeniable that, over all the arts, literature dominates, serves beyond all— shapes the character of church and school—or, at any rate, is capable of doing so. Including the literature of science, its scope is indeed unparallel'd.

Before proceeding further, it were perhaps well to discriminate on certain points. Literature tills its crops in many fields, and some may flourish, while others lag. What I say in these Vistas has its main bearing on imaginative literature, especially poetry, the stock of all. In the department of science, and the specialty of journalism, there appear, in these States, promises, perhaps fulfilments, of highest earnestness, reality, and life. These, of course, are modern. But in the region of imaginative, spinal and essential attributes, something equivalent to creation is, for our age and lands, imperatively demanded. For not only is it not enough that the new blood, new frame of democracy shall be vivified and held together merely by political means, superficial suffrage, legislation, &c., but it is clear to me that, unless it goes deeper, gets at least as firm and as warm a hold in men's hearts, emotions and belief, as, in their days, feudalism or ecclesiasticism, and inaugurates its own perennial sources, welling from the centre forever, its strength will be defective, its growth doubtful, and its main charm wanting. I suggest, therefore, the possibility, should some two or three really original American poets, (perhaps artists or lecturers,) arise, mounting the horizon like planets, stars of the first magnitude, that, from their eminence, fusing contributions, races, far localities, &c., together, they would give more compaction and more moral identity, (the quality to-day most needed,) to these States, than all its Constitutions, legislative and judicial ties, and all its hitherto political, warlike, or materialistic experiences. As, for instance, there could hardly happen anything that would more serve the States, with all their variety of origins, their diverse climes, cities, standards, &c., than possessing an aggregate of heroes, characters, exploits, sufferings, prosperity or misfortune, glory or disgrace, common to all, typical of all—no less, but even greater would it be to possess the aggregation of a cluster of mighty poets, artists, teachers, fit for us, national expressers, comprehending and effusing for the men and women of the States, what is universal, native, common to all, inland and seaboard, northern and southern. The historians say of ancient Greece, with her ever-jealous autonomies, cities, and states, that the only positive unity she ever own'd or receiv'd, was the sad unity of a common subjection, at the last, to foreign conquerors. Subjection, aggregation of that sort, is impossible to America; but the fear of conflicting and irreconcilable interiors, and the lack of a common skeleton, knitting all close, continually haunts me. Or, if it does not, nothing is plainer than the need, a long period to come, of a fusion of the States into the only reliable identity, the moral and artistic one. For, I say, the true nationality of the States, the genuine union, when we come to a mortal crisis, is, and is to be, after all, neither the written law, nor, (as is generally supposed,) either self-interest, or common pecuniary or material objects—but the fervid and tremendous IDEA, melting everything else with resistless heat, and solving all lesser and definite distinctions in vast, indefinite, spiritual, emotional power.

It may be claim'd, (and I admit the weight of the claim,) that common and general worldly prosperity, and a populace well-to-do, and with all life's material comforts, is the main thing, and is enough. It may be argued that our republic is, in performance, really enacting to-day the grandest arts, poems, &c., by beating up the wilderness into fertile farms, and in her railroads, ships, machinery, &c. And it may be ask'd, Are these not better, indeed, for America, than any utterances even of greatest rhapsode, artist, or literatus?

I too hail those achievements with pride and joy: then answer that the soul of man will not with such only—nay, not with such at all—be finally satisfied; but needs what, (standing on these and on all things, as the feet stand on the ground,) is address'd to the loftiest, to itself alone.

Out of such considerations, such truths, arises for treatment in these Vistas the important question of character, of an American stock-personality, with literatures and arts for outlets and return-expressions, and, of course, to correspond, within outlines common to all. To these, the main affair, the thinkers of the United States, in general so acute, have either given feeblest attention, or have remain'd, and remain, in a state of somnolence.

For my part, I would alarm and caution even the political and business reader, and to the utmost extent, against the prevailing delusion that the establishment of free political institutions, and plentiful intellectual smartness, with general good order, physical plenty, industry, &c., (desirable and precious advantages as they all are,) do, of themselves, determine and yield to our experiment of democracy the fruitage of success. With such advantages at present fully, or almost fully, possess'd—the Union just issued, victorious, from the struggle with the only foes it need ever fear, (namely, those within itself, the interior ones,) and with unprecedented materialistic advancement—society, in these States, is canker'd, crude, superstitious, and rotten. Political, or law-made society is, and private, or voluntary society, is also. In any vigor, the element of the moral conscience, the most important, the verteber to State or man, seems to me either entirely lacking, or seriously enfeebled or ungrown.

I say we had best look our times and lands searchingly in the face, like a physician diagnosing some deep disease. Never was there, perhaps, more hollowness at heart than at present, and here in the United States. Genuine belief seems to have left us. The underlying principles of the States are not honestly believ'd in, (for all this hectic glow, and these melo-dramatic screamings,) nor is humanity itself believ'd in. What penetrating eye does not everywhere see through the mask? The spectacle is appaling. We live in an atmosphere of hypocrisy throughout. The men believe not in the women, nor the women in the men. A scornful superciliousness rules in literature. The aim of all the *littérateurs* is to find something to make fun of. A lot of churches, sects, &c., the most dismal phantasms I know, usurp the name of religion. Conversation is a mass of badinage. From deceit in the spirit, the mother of all false deeds, the offspring is already incalculable. An acute and candid person, in the revenue department in Washington, who is led by the course of his employment to regularly visit the cities, north, south and west, to investigate frauds, has talk'd much with me about his discoveries. The depravity of the business classes of our country is not less than has been supposed, but infinitely greater. The official services of America, national, state, and municipal, in all their branches and departments, except the judiciary, are saturated in corruption, bribery, falsehood, mal-administration; and the judiciary is tainted. The great cities reek with respectable as much as non-respectable robbery and scoundrelism. In fashionable life, flippancy, tepid amours, weak infidelism, small aims, or no aims at all, only to kill time. In business, (this all-devouring modern word, business,) the one sole object is, by any means, pecuniary gain. The magician's serpent in the fable ate up all the other serpents; and money-making is our magician's serpent, remaining to-day sole master of the field. The best class we show, is but a mob of fashionably dress'd speculators and vulgarians. True, indeed, behind this fantastic farce, enacted on the visible stage of society, solid things and stupendous labors are to be discover'd, existing crudely and going on in the background, to advance and tell themselves in time. Yet the truths are none the less terrible. I say that our New World democracy, however great a success in uplifting the masses out of their sloughs, in materialistic development, products, and in a certain highly-deceptive superficial popular intellectuality, is, so far, an almost complete failure in its social aspects, and in really grand religious, moral, literary, and esthetic results. In vain do we march with unprecedented strides to empire so colossal, outvying the antique, beyond Alexander's, beyond the proudest sway of Rome. In vain have we annex'd Texas, California, Alaska, and reach north for Canada and south for Cuba. It is as if we were somehow being endow'd with a vast and more and more thoroughly-appointed body, and then left with little or no soul.

Let me illustrate further, as I write, with current observations, localities, &c. The subject is important, and will bear repetition. After an absence, I am now again (September, 1870) in New York city and Brooklyn, on a few weeks' vacation. The splendor, picturesqueness, and oceanic amplitude and rush of these great cities, the unsurpass'd situation, rivers and bay, sparkling sea-tides, costly and lofty new buildings, façades of marble and iron, of original grandeur and elegance of design, with the masses of gay color, the preponderance of white and blue, the flags flying, the endless ships, the tumultuous streets, Broadway, the heavy, low, musical roar, hardly ever intermitted, even at night; the jobbers' houses, the rich shops, the wharves, the great Central Park, and the Brooklyn Park of hills, (as I wander among them this beautiful fall weather, musing, watching, absorbing)—the assemblages of the citizens in their groups, conversations, trades, evening amusements, or along the by-quarters—these, I say, and the like of these, completely satisfy my senses of power, fulness, motion, &c., and give me, through such senses and appetites, and through my esthetic conscience, a continued exaltation and absolute fulfilment. Always and more and more, as I cross the East and North rivers, the ferries, or with the pilots in their pilot-houses, or pass an hour in Wall street, or the gold exchange, I realize, (if we must admit such partialisms,) that not Nature alone is great in her fields of freedom and the open air, in her storms, the shows of night and day, the mountains, forests, seas—but in the artificial, the work of man too is equally great—in this profusion of teeming humanity—in these ingenuities, streets, goods, houses, ships—these hurrying, feverish, electric crowds of men, their complicated business genius, (not least among the geniuses,) and all this mighty, many-threaded wealth and industry concentrated here.

But sternly discarding, shutting our eyes to the glow and grandeur of the general superficial effect, coming down to what is of the only real importance, Personalities, and examining minutely, we question, we ask, Are there, indeed, *men* here worthy the name? Are there athletes? Are there perfect women, to match the generous material luxuriance? Is there a pervading atmosphere of beautiful manners? Are there crops of fine youths, and majestic old persons? Are there arts worthy freedom and a rich people? Is there a great moral and religious civilization—the only justification of a great material one? Confess that to severe eyes, using the moral microscope upon humanity, a sort of dry and flat Sahara appears, these cities, crowded with petty grotesques, malformations, phantoms, playing meaningless antics. Confess that everywhere, in shop, street, church, theatre, barroom, official chair, are pervading flippancy and vulgarity, low cunning, infidelity—everywhere the youth puny, impudent, foppish, prematurely ripe—everywhere an abnormal libidinousness, unhealthy forms, male, female, painted, padded, dyed, chignon'd, muddy complexions, bad blood, the capacity for good motherhood deceasing or deceas'd, shallow notions of beauty, with a range of manners, or rather lack of manners, (considering the advantages enjoy'd,) probably the meanest to be seen in the world.[3]

Of all this, and these lamentable conditions, to breathe into them the breath recuperative of sane and heroic life, I say a new founded literature, not merely to copy and reflect existing surfaces, or pander to what is called taste—not only to amuse, pass away time, celebrate the beautiful, the refined, the past, or exhibit technical, rhythmic, or grammatical dexterity—but a literature underlying life, religious, consistent with science, handling the elements and forces with competent power, teaching and training men—and, as perhaps the most precious of its results, achieving the entire redemption of woman out of these incredible holds and webs of silliness, millinery, and every kind of dyspeptic depletion—and thus insuring to the States a strong and sweet Female Race, a race of perfect Mothers—is what is needed.

And now, in the full conception of these facts and points, and all that they infer, pro and con—with yet unshaken faith in the elements of the American masses, the composites, of both sexes, and even consider'd as individuals—and ever recognizing in them the broadest bases of the best literary and esthetic appreciation—I proceed with my speculations, Vistas.

First, let us see what we can make out of a brief, general, sentimental consideration of political democracy, and whence it has arisen, with regard to some of its current features, as an aggregate, and as the basic structure of our future literature and authorship. We shall, it is true, quickly and continually find the origin-idea of the singleness of man, individualism, asserting itself, and cropping forth, even from the opposite ideas. But the mass, or lump character, for imperative reasons, is to be ever carefully weigh'd, borne in mind, and provided for. Only from it, and from its proper regulation and potency, comes the other, comes the chance of individualism. The two are contradictory, but our task is to reconcile them.[4]

The political history of the past may be summ'd up as having grown out of what underlies the words, order, safety, caste, and especially out of the need of some prompt deciding authority, and of cohesion at all cost. Leaping time, we come to the period within the memory of people now living, when, as from some lair where they had slumber'd long, accumulating wrath, sprang up and are yet active, (1790, and on even to the present, 1870,) those noisy eructations, destructive iconoclasms, a fierce sense of wrongs, amid which moves the form, well known in modern history, in the old world, stain'd with much blood, and mark'd by savage reactionary clamors and demands. These bear, mostly, as on one inclosing point of need.

For after the rest is said—after the many time-honor'd and really true things for subordination, experience, rights of property, &c., have been listen'd to and acquiesced in—after the valuable and well-settled statement of our duties and relations in society is thoroughly conn'd over and exhausted—it remains to bring forward and modify everything else with the idea of that Something a man is, (last precious consolation of the drudging poor,) standing apart from all else, divine in his own right, and a woman in hers, sole and untouchable by any canons of authority, or any rule derived from precedent, state-safety, the acts of legislatures, or even from what is called religion, modesty, or art. The radiation of this truth is the key of the most significant doings of our immediately preceding three centuries, and has been the political genesis and life of America. Advancing visibly, it still more advances invisibly. Underneath the fluctuations of the expressions of society, as well as the movements of the politics of the leading nations of the world, we see steadily pressing ahead and strengthening itself, even in the midst of immense tendencies toward aggregation, this image of completeness in separatism, of individual personal dignity, of a single person, either male or female, characterized in the main, not from extrinsic acquirements or position, but in the pride of himself or herself alone; and, as an eventual conclusion and summing up, (or else the entire scheme of things is aimless, a cheat, a crash,)

the simple idea that the last, best dependence is to be upon humanity itself, and its own inherent, normal, full-grown qualities, without any superstitious support whatever. This idea of perfect individualism it is indeed that deepest tinges and gives character to the
idea of the aggregate. For it is mainly or altogether to serve independent separatism that we favor a strong generalization, consolida-
tion. As it is to give the best vitality and freedom to the rights of
the States, (every bit as important as the right of nationality, the
union,) that we insist on the identity of the Union at all hazards.

The purpose of democracy—supplanting old belief in the necessary absoluteness of establish'd dynastic rulership, temporal, ecclesiastical, and scholastic, as furnishing the only security against chaos,
crime, and ignorance—is, through many transmigrations, and amid
endless ridicules, arguments, and ostensible failures, to illustrate, at
all hazards, this doctrine or theory that man, properly train'd in sanest, highest freedom, may and must become a law, and series of
laws, unto himself, surrounding and providing for, not only his own
personal control, but all his relations to other individuals, and to the
State; and that, while other theories, as in the past histories of nations, have proved wise enough, and indispensable perhaps for their
conditions, *this,* as matters now stand in our civilized world, is the
only scheme worth working from, as warranting results like those
of Nature's laws, reliable, when once establish'd, to carry on themselves.

The argument of the matter is extensive, and, we admit, by no
means all on one side. What we shall offer will be far, far from
sufficient. But while leaving unsaid much that should properly even
prepare the way for the treatment of this many-sided question of
political liberty, equality, or republicanism—leaving the whole history and consideration of the feudal plan and its products, embodying humanity, its politics and civilization, through the retrospect of
past time, (which plan and products, indeed, make up all of the
past, and a large part of the present)—leaving unanswer'd, at least
by any specific and local answer, many a well-wrought argument
and instance, and many a conscientious declamatory cry and warning—as, very lately, from an eminent and venerable person abroad [5]
—things, problems, full of doubt, dread, suspense, (not new to me,
but old occupiers of many an anxious hour in city's din, or night's
silence,) we still may give a page or so, whose drift is opportune.
Time alone can finally answer these things. But as a substitute in
passing, let us, even if fragmentarily, throw forth a short direct or
indirect suggestion of the premises of that other plan, in the new
spirit, under the new forms, started here in our America.

As to the political section of Democracy, which introduces and breaks ground for further and vaster sections, few probably are the minds, even in these republican States, that fully comprehend the aptness of that phrase, "THE GOVERNMENT OF THE PEOPLE, BY THE PEOPLE, FOR THE PEOPLE," which we inherit from the lips of Abraham Lincoln; a formula whose verbal shape is homely wit, but whose scope includes both the totality and all minutiæ of the lesson.

The People! Like our huge earth itself, which, to ordinary scansion, is full of vulgar contradictions and offence, man, viewed in the lump, displeases, and is a constant puzzle and affront to the merely educated classes. The rare, cosmical, artist-mind, lit with the Infinite, alone confronts his manifold and oceanic qualities—but taste, intelligence and culture, (so-called,) have been against the masses, and remain so. There is plenty of glamour about the most damnable crimes and hoggish meannesses, special and general, of the feudal and dynastic world over there, with its *personnel* of lords and queens and courts, so well-dress'd and so handsome. But the People are ungrammatical, untidy, and their sins gaunt and ill-bred.

Literature, strictly consider'd, has never recognized the People, and, whatever may be said, does not to-day. Speaking generally, the tendencies of literature, as hitherto pursued, have been to make mostly critical and querulous men. It seems as if, so far, there were some natural repugnance between a literary and professional life, and the rude rank spirit of the democracies. There is, in later literature, a treatment of benevolence, a charity business, rife enough it is true; but I know nothing more rare, even in this country, than a fit scientific estimate and reverent appreciation of the People—of their measureless wealth of latent power and capacity, their vast, artistic contrasts of lights and shades—with, in America, their entire reliability in emergencies, and a certain breadth of historic grandeur, of peace or war, far surpassing all the vaunted samples of book-heroes, or any *haut ton* coteries, in all the records of the world.

The movements of the late secession war, and their results, to any sense that studies well and comprehends them, show that popular democracy, whatever its faults and dangers, practically justifies itself beyond the proudest claims and wildest hopes of its enthusiasts. Probably no future age can know, but I well know, how the gist of this fiercest and most resolute of the world's war-like contentions resided exclusively in the unnamed, unknown rank and file; and how the brunt of its labor of death was, to all essential purposes, volunteer'd. The People, of their own choice, fighting, dying for their own idea, insolently attack'd by the secession-slave-power, and its very existence imperil'd. Descending to detail, entering any of the armies, and mixing with the private soldiers, we see and have seen august spectacles. We have seen the alacrity with which the American born populace, the peaceablest and most good-natured race in the world, and the most personally independent and intelligent, and the least fitted to submit to the irksomeness and exasperation of regimental discipline, sprang, at the first tap of the drum, to arms—not for gain, nor even glory, nor to repel invasion—but for an emblem, a mere abstraction—for the life, *the safety of the flag.* We have seen the unequal'd docility and obedience of these soldiers. We have seen them tried long and long by hopelessness, mismanagement, and by defeat; have seen the incredible slaughter toward or through which the armies, (as at first Fredericksburg, and afterward at the Wilderness,) still unhesitatingly obey'd orders to advance. We have seen them in trench, or crouching behind breastwork, or tramping in deep mud, or amid pouring rain or thick-falling snow, or under forced marches in hottest summer (as on the road to get to Gettysburg)—vast suffocating swarms, divisions, corps, with every single man so grimed and black with sweat and dust, his own mother would not have known him—his clothes all dirty, stain'd and torn, with sour, accumulated sweat for perfume —many a comrade, perhaps a brother, sun-struck, staggering out, dying, by the roadside, of exhaustion—yet the great bulk bearing steadily on, cheery enough, hollow-bellied from hunger, but sinewy with unconquerable resolution.

We have seen this race proved by wholesale by drearier, yet more fearful tests—the wound, the amputation, the shatter'd face or limb, the slow hot fever, long impatient anchorage in bed, and all the forms of maiming, operation and disease. Alas! America have we seen, though only in her early youth, already to hospital brought. There have we watch'd these soldiers, many of them only boys in years—mark'd their decorum, their religious nature and fortitude, and their sweet affection. Wholesale, truly. For at the front, and through the camps, in countless tents, stood the regimental, brigade and division hospitals; while everywhere amid the land, in or near cities, rose clusters of huge, white-wash'd, crowded, one-story wooden barracks; and there ruled agony with bitter scourge, yet seldom brought a cry; and there stalk'd death by day and night along the narrow aisles between the rows of cots, or by the blankets on the ground, and touch'd lightly many a poor sufferer, often with blessed, welcome touch.

I know not whether I shall be understood, but I realize that it is finally from what I learn'd personally mixing in such scenes that I am now penning these pages. One night in the gloomiest period of the war, in the Patent office hospital in Washington city, as I stood by the bedside of a Pennsylvania soldier, who lay, conscious of quick approaching death, yet perfectly calm, and with noble, spiritual manner, the veteran surgeon, turning aside, said to me, that though he had witness'd many, many deaths of soldiers, and had been a worker at Bull Run, Antietam, Fredericksburg, &c., he had not seen yet the first case of man or boy that met the approach of dissolution with cowardly qualms or terror. My own observation fully bears out the remark.

What have we here, if not, towering above all talk and argument, the plentifully-supplied, last-needed proof of democracy, in its personalities? Curiously enough, too, the proof on this point comes, I should say, every bit as much from the south, as from the north. Although I have spoken only of the latter, yet I deliberately include all. Grand, common stock! to me the accomplish'd and convincing growth, prophetic of the future; proof undeniable to sharpest sense, of perfect beauty, tenderness and pluck, that never feudal lord, nor Greek, nor Roman breed, yet rival'd. Let no tongue ever speak in disparagement of the American races, north or south, to one who has been through the war in the great army hospitals.

Meantime, general humanity, (for to that we return, as, for our purposes, what it really is, to bear in mind,) has always, in every department, been full of perverse maleficence, and is so yet. In downcast hours the soul thinks it always will be—but soon recovers from such sickly moods. I myself see clearly enough the crude, defective streaks in all the strata of the common people; the specimens and vast collections of the ignorant, the credulous, the unfit and uncouth, the incapable, and the very low and poor. The eminent person just mention'd sneeringly asks whether we expect to elevate and improve a nation's politics by absorbing such morbid collections and qualities therein. The point is a formidable one, and there will doubtless always be numbers of solid and reflective citizens who will never get over it. Our answer is general, and is involved in the scope and letter of this essay. We believe the ulterior project of political and all other government, (having, of course, provided for the police, the safety of life, property, and for the basic statute and common law, and their administration, always first in order,) to be among the rest, not merely to rule, to repress disorder, &c., but to develop, to open up to cultivation, to encourage the possibilities of all beneficent and manly outcroppage, and of that aspiration for independence, and the pride and self-respect latent in all characters. (Or, if there be exceptions, we cannot, fixing our eyes on them alone, make theirs the rule for all.)

I say the mission of government, henceforth, in civilized lands, is not repression alone, and not authority alone, not even of law, nor by that favorite standard of the eminent writer, the rule of the best men, the born heroes and captains of the race, (as if such ever, or one time out of a hundred, get into the big places, elective or dynastic)—but higher than the highest arbitrary rule, to train communities through all their grades, beginning with individuals and ending there again, to rule themselves. What Christ appear'd for in the moral-spiritual field for human-kind, namely, that in respect to the absolute soul, there is in the possession of such by each single individual, something so transcendent, so incapable of gradations, (like life,) that, to that extent, it places all beings on a common level, utterly regardless of the distinctions of intellect, virtue, station, or any height or lowliness whatever—is tallied in like manner, in this other field, by democracy's rule that men, the nation, as a common aggregate of living identities, affording in each a separate and complete subject for freedom, worldly thrift and happiness, and for a fair chance for growth, and for protection in citizenship, &c., must, to the political extent of the suffrage or vote, if no further, be placed, in each and in the whole, on one broad, primary, universal, common platform.

The purpose is not altogether direct; perhaps it is more indirect. For it is not that democracy is of exhaustive account, in itself. Perhaps, indeed, it is, (like Nature,) of no account in itself. It is that, as we see, it is the best, perhaps only, fit and full means, formulater, general caller-forth, trainer, for the million, not for grand material personalities only, but for immortal souls. To be a voter with the rest is not so much; and this, like every institute, will have its imperfections. But to become an enfranchised man, and now, impediments removed, to stand and start without humiliation, and equal with the rest; to commence, or have the road clear'd to commence, the grand experiment of development, whose end, (perhaps requiring several generations,) may be the forming of a full-grown man or woman—that *is* something. To ballast the State is also secured, and in our times is to be secured, in no other way.

We do not, (at any rate I do not,) put it either on the ground that the People, the masses, even the best of them, are, in their latent or exhibited qualities, essentially sensible and good—nor on the ground of their rights; but that good or bad, rights or no rights, the democratic formula is the only safe and preservative one for coming times. We endow the masses with the suffrage for their own sake, no doubt; then, perhaps still more, from another point of view, for community's sake. Leaving the rest to the sentimentalists, we present freedom as sufficient in its scientific aspect, cold as ice, reasoning, deductive, clear and passionless as crystal.

Democracy too is law, and of the strictest, amplest kind. Many suppose, (and often in its own ranks the error,) that it means a throwing aside of law, and running riot. But, briefly, it is the superior law, not alone that of physical force, the body, which, adding to, it supersedes with that of the spirit. Law is the unshakable order of the universe forever; and the law over all, and law of laws, is the law of successions; that of the superior law, in time, gradually supplanting and overwhelming the inferior one. (While, for myself, I would cheerfully agree—first covenanting that the formative tendencies shall be administer'd in favor, or at least not against it, and that this reservation be closely construed—that until the individual or community show due signs, or be so minor and fractional as not to endanger the State, the condition of authoritative tutelage may continue, and self-government must abide its time.) Nor is the esthetic point, always an important one, without fascination for highest aiming souls. The common ambition strains for elevations, to become some privileged exclusive. The master sees greatness and health in being part of the mass; nothing will do as well as common ground. Would you have in yourself the divine, vast, general law? Then merge yourself in it.

And, topping democracy, this most alluring record, that it alone can bind, and ever seeks to bind, all nations, all men, of however various and distant lands, into a brotherhood, a family. It is the old, yet ever-modern dream of earth, out of her eldest and her youngest, her fond philosophers and poets. Not that half only, individualism, which isolates. There is another half, which is adhesiveness or love, that fuses, ties and aggregates, making the races comrades, and fraternizing all. Both are to be vitalized by religion, (sole worthiest elevator of man or State,) breathing into the proud, material tissues, the breath of life. For I say at the core of democracy, finally, is the religious element. All the religions, old and new, are there. Nor may the scheme step forth, clothed in resplendent beauty and command, till these, bearing the best, the latest fruit, the spiritual, shall fully appear.

A portion of our pages we might indite with reference toward Europe, especially the British part of it, more than our own land, perhaps not absolutely needed for the home reader. But the whole question hangs together, and fastens and links all peoples. The liberalist of to-day has this advantage over antique or medieval times, that his doctrine seeks not only to individualize but to universalize. The great word Solidarity has arisen. Of all dangers to a nation, as things exist in our day, there can be no greater one than having certain portions of the people set off from the rest by a line drawn—they not privileged as others, but degraded, humiliated, made of no account. Much quackery teems, of course, even on democracy's side, yet does not really affect the orbic quality of the matter. To work in, if we may so term it, and justify God, his divine aggregate, the People, (or, the veritable horn'd and sharp-tail'd Devil, *his* aggregate, if there be who convulsively insist upon it)— this, I say, is what democracy is for; and this is what our America means, and is doing—may I not say, has done? If not, she means nothing more, and does nothing more, than any other land. And as, by virtue of its kosmical, antiseptic power, Nature's stomach is fully strong enough not only to digest the morbific matter always presented, not to be turn'd aside, and perhaps, indeed, intuitively gravitating thither—but even to change such contributions into nutriment for highest use and life—so American democracy's. That is the lesson we, these days, send over to European lands by every western breeze.

And, truly, whatever may be said in the way of abstract argument, for or against the theory of a wider democratizing of institutions in any civilized country, much trouble might well be saved to all European lands by recognizing this palpable fact, (for a palpable fact it is,) that some form of such democratizing is about the only resource now left. *That,* or chronic dissatisfaction continued, mutterings which grow annually louder and louder, till, in due course, and pretty swiftly in most cases, the inevitable crisis, crash, dynastic ruin. Anything worthy to be call'd statesmanship in the Old World, I should say, among the advanced students, adepts, or men of any brains, does not debate to-day whether to hold on, attempting to lean back and monarchize, or to look forward and democratize—but *how,* and in what degree and part, most prudently to democratize.

The eager and often inconsiderate appeals of reformers and revolutionists are indispensable, to counterbalance the inertness and fossilism making so large a part of human institutions. The latter will always take care of themselves—the danger being that they rapidly tend to ossify us. The former is to be treated with indulgence, and even with respect. As circulation to air, so is agitation and a plentiful degree of speculative license to political and moral sanity. Indirectly, but surely, goodness, virtue, law, (of the very

best,) follow freedom. These, to democracy, are what the keel is
to the ship, or saltness to the ocean.

The true gravitation-hold of liberalism in the United States will
be a more universal ownership of property, general homesteads,
general comfort—a vast, intertwining reticulation of wealth. As the
human frame, or, indeed, any object in this manifold universe, is
best kept together by the simple miracle of its own cohesion, and
the necessity, exercise and profit thereof, so a great and varied nationality, occupying millions of square miles, were firmest held and
knit by the principle of the safety and endurance of the aggregate
of its middling property owners. So that, from another point of
view, ungracious as it may sound, and a paradox after what we
have been saying, democracy looks with suspicious, ill-satisfied eye
upon the very poor, the ignorant, and on those out of business. She
asks for men and women with occupations, well-off, owners of
houses and acres, and with cash in the bank—and with some crav-
ings for literature, too; and must have them, and hastens to make
them. Luckily, the seed is already well-sown, and has taken in-
eradicable root.[6]

Huge and mighty are our days, our republican lands—and most
in their rapid shiftings, their changes, all in the interest of the
cause. As I write this particular passage, (November, 1868,) the
din of disputation rages around me. Acrid the temper of the parties,
vital the pending questions. Congress convenes; the President sends
his message; reconstruction is still in abeyance; the nomination and
the contest for the twenty-first Presidentiad draw close, with loudest
threat and bustle. Of these, and all the like of these, the eventuations I know not; but well I know that behind them, and whatever
their eventuations, the vital things remain safe and certain, and all
the needed work goes on. Time, with soon or later superciliousness, disposes of Presidents, Congressmen, party platforms, and
such. Anon, it clears the stage of each and any mortal shred that
thinks itself so potent to its day; and at and after which, (with
precious, golden exceptions once or twice in a century,) all that relates to sir potency is flung to moulder in a burial-vault, and no
one bothers himself the least bit about it afterward. But the People
ever remain, tendencies continue, and all the idiocratic transfers
in unbroken chain go on.

In a few years the dominion-heart of America will be far inland,
toward the West. Our future national capital may not be where
the present one is. It is possible, nay likely, that in less than fifty
years, it will migrate a thousand or two miles, will be re-founded,

and every thing belonging to it made on a different plan, original, far more superb. The main social, political, spine-character of the States will probably run along the Ohio, Missouri and Mississippi rivers, and west and north of them, including Canada. Those regions, with the group of powerful brothers toward the Pacific, (destined to the mastership of that sea and its countless paradises of islands,) will compact and settle the traits of America, with all the old retain'd, but more expanded, grafted on newer, hardier, purely native stock. A giant growth, composite from the rest, getting their contribution, absorbing it, to make it more illustrious. From the north, intellect, the sun of things, also the idea of unswayable justice, anchor amid the last, the wildest tempests. From the south the living soul, the animus of good and bad, haughtily admitting no demonstration but its own. While from the west itself comes solid personality, with blood and brawn, and the deep quality of all-accepting fusion.

Political democracy, as it exists and practically works in America, with all its threatening evils, supplies a training-school for making first-class men. It is life's gymnasium, not of good only, but of all. We try often, though we fall back often. A brave delight, fit for freedom's athletes, fills these arenas, and fully satisfies, out of the action in them, irrespective of success. Whatever we do not attain, we at any rate attain the experiences of the fight, the hardening of the strong campaign, and throb with currents of attempt at least. Time is ample. Let the victors come after us. Not for nothing does evil play its part among us. Judging from the main portions of the history of the world, so far, justice is always in jeopardy, peace walks amid hourly pitfalls, and of slavery, misery, meanness, the craft of tyrants and the credulity of the populace, in some of their protean forms, no voice can at any time say, They are not. The clouds break a little, and the sun shines out—but soon and certain the lowering darkness falls again, as if to last forever. Yet is there an immortal courage and prophecy in every sane soul that cannot, must not, under any circumstances, capitulate. *Vive*, the attack—the perennial assault! *Vive*, the unpopular cause—the spirit that audaciously aims—the never-abandon'd efforts, pursued the same amid opposing proofs and precedents.

Once, before the war, (Alas! I dare not say how many times the mood has come!) I, too, was fill'd with doubt and gloom. A foreigner, an acute and good man, had impressively said to me, that day—putting in form, indeed, my own observations: "I have travel'd much in the United States, and watch'd their politicians, and listen'd to the speeches of the candidates, and read the journals, and gone into the public houses, and heard the unguarded talk of men. And I have found your vaunted America honeycomb'd from top to toe with infidelism, even to itself and its own programme. I have mark'd the brazen hell-faces of secession and slavery gazing defiantly from all the windows and doorways. I have everywhere found, primarily, thieves and scalliwags arranging the nominations to offices, and sometimes filling the offices themselves. I have found the north just as full of bad stuff as the south. Of the holders of public office in the Nation or the States or their municipalities, I have found that not one in a hundred has been chosen by any spontaneous selection of the outsiders, the people, but all have been nominated and put through by little or large caucuses of the politicians, and have got in by corrupt rings and electioneering, not capacity or desert. I have noticed how the millions of sturdy farmers and mechanics are thus the helpless supple-jacks of comparatively few politicians. And I have noticed more and more, the alarming spectacle of parties usurping the government, and openly and shamelessly wielding it for party purposes."

Sad, serious, deep truths. Yet are there other, still deeper, amply confronting, dominating truths. Over those politicians and great and little rings, and over all their insolence and wiles, and over the powerfulest parties, looms a power, too sluggish maybe, but ever holding decisions and decrees in hand, ready, with stern process, to execute them as soon as plainly needed—and at times, indeed, summarily crushing to atoms the mightiest parties, even in the hour of their pride.

In saner hours far different are the amounts of these things from what, at first sight, they appear. Though it is no doubt important who is elected governor, mayor, or legislator, (and full of dismay when incompetent or vile ones get elected, as they sometimes do,) there are other, quieter contingencies, infinitely more important. Shams, &c., will always be the show, like ocean's scum; enough, if waters deep and clear make up the rest. Enough, that while the piled embroider'd shoddy gaud and fraud spreads to the superficial eye, the hidden warp and weft are genuine, and will wear forever. Enough, in short, that the race, the land which could raise such as the late rebellion, could also put it down.

The average man of a land at last only is important. He, in these States, remains immortal owner and boss, deriving good uses, somehow, out of any sort of servant in office, even the basest; (certain universal requisites, and their settled regularity and protection, being first secured,) a nation like ours, in a sort of geological formation state, trying continually new experiments, choosing new delegations, is not served by the best men only, but sometimes more by those that provoke it—by the combats they arouse. Thus national rage, fury, discussion, &c., better than content. Thus, also, the warning signals, invaluable for after times.

What is more dramatic than the spectacle we have seen repeated, and doubtless long shall see—the popular judgment taking the successful candidates on trial in the offices—standing off, as it were, and observing them and their doings for a while, and always giving, finally, the fit, exactly due reward? I think, after all, the sublimest part of political history, and its culmination, is currently issuing from the American people. I know nothing grander, better exercise, better digestion, more positive proof of the past, the triumphant result of faith in human kind, than a well-contested American national election.

Then still the thought returns, (like the thread-passage in overtures,) giving the key and echo to these pages. When I pass to and fro, different latitudes, different seasons, beholding the crowds of the great cities, New York, Boston, Philadelphia, Cincinnati, Chicago, St. Louis, San Francisco, New Orleans, Baltimore—when I mix with these interminable swarms of alert, turbulent, good-natured, independent citizens, mechanics, clerks, young persons—at the idea of this mass of men, so fresh and free, so loving and so proud, a singular awe falls upon me. I feel, with dejection and amazement, that among our geniuses and talented writers or speakers, few or none have yet really spoken to this people, created a single image-making work for them, or absorb'd the central spirit and the idiosyncrasies which are theirs—and which, thus, in highest ranges, so far remain entirely uncelebrated, unexpress'd.

Dominion strong is the body's; dominion stronger is the mind's. What has fill'd, and fills to-day our intellect, our fancy, furnishing the standards therein, is yet foreign. The great poems, Shakspere included, are poisonous to the idea of the pride and dignity of the common people, the life-blood of democracy. The models of our literature, as we get it from other lands, ultra-marine, have had their birth in courts, and bask'd and grown in castle sunshine; all smells of princes' favors. Of workers of a certain sort, we have, indeed, plenty, contributing after their kind; many elegant, many learn'd, all complacent. But touch'd by the national test, or tried by the standards of democratic personality, they wither to ashes. I say I have not seen a single writer, artist, lecturer, or what not, that has confronted the voiceless but ever erect and active, pervading, under-lying will and typic aspiration of the land, in a spirit kindred to itself. Do you call those genteel little creatures American poets? Do you term that perpetual, pistareen, paste-pot work, American art, American drama, taste, verse? I think I hear, echoed as from some mountain-top afar in the west, the scornful laugh of the Genius of these States.

Democracy, in silence, biding its time, ponders its own ideals, not of literature and art only—not of men only, but of women. The idea of the women of America, (extricated from this daze, this fossil and unhealthy air which hangs about the word *lady*,) develop'd, raised to become the robust equals, workers, and, it may be, even practical and political deciders with the men—greater than man, we may admit, through their divine maternity, always their towering, emblematical attribute—but great, at any rate, as man, in all de-partments; or, rather, capable of being so, soon as they realize it, and can bring themselves to give up toys and fictions, and launch forth, as men do, amid real, independent, stormy life.

Then, as towards our thought's finalè, (and, in that, overarching the true scholar's lesson,) we have to say there can be no complete or epical presentation of democracy in the aggregate, or anything like it, at this day, because its doctrines will only be effectually incarnated in any one branch, when, in all, their spirit is at the root and centre. Far, far, indeed, stretch, in distance, our Vistas! How much is still to be disentangled, freed! How long it takes to make this American world see that it is, in itself, the final authority and reliance!

Did you, too, O friend, suppose democracy was only for elections, for politics, and for a party name? I say democracy is only of use there that it may pass on and come to its flower and fruits in man-ners, in the highest forms of interaction between men, and their be-liefs—in religion, literature, colleges, and schools—democracy in all public and private life, and in the army and navy.[7] I have intimated that, as a paramount scheme, it has yet few or no full realizers and believers. I do not see, either, that it owes any serious thanks to noted propagandists or champions, or has been essentially help'd, though often harm'd, by them. It has been and is carried on by all the moral forces, and by trade, finance, machinery, intercommuni-cations, and, in fact, by all the developments of history, and can no more be stopp'd than the tides, or the earth in its orbit. Doubt-less, also, it resides, crude and latent, well down in the hearts of the fair average of the American-born people, mainly in the agricultural regions. But it is not yet, there or anywhere, the fully-receiv'd, the fervid, the absolute faith.

I submit, therefore, that the fruition of democracy, on aught like a grand scale, resides altogether in the future. As, under any profound and comprehensive view of the gorgeous-composite feudal world, we see in it, through the long ages and cycles of ages, the results of a deep, integral, human and divine principle, or fountain, from which issued laws, ecclesia, manners, institutes, costumes, personalities, poems, (hitherto unequall'd,) faithfully partaking of their source, and indeed only arising either to betoken it, or to furnish parts of that varied-flowing display, whose centre was one and absolute—so, long ages hence, shall the due historian or critic make at least an equal retrospect, an equal history for the democratic principle. It too must be adorn'd, credited with its results—then, when it, with imperial power, through amplest time, has dominated mankind—has been the source and test of all the moral, esthetic, social, political, and religious expressions and institutes of the civilized world—has begotten them in spirit and in form, and has carried them to its own unprecedented heights—has had, (it is possible,) monastics and ascetics, more numerous, more devout than the monks and priests of all previous creeds—has sway'd the ages with a breadth and rectitude tallying Nature's own—has fashion'd, systematized, and triumphantly finish'd and carried out, in its own interest, and with unparallel'd success, a new earth and a new man.

Thus we presume to write, as it were, upon things that exist not, and travel by maps yet unmade, and a blank. But the throes of birth are upon us; and we have something of this advantage in seasons of strong formations, doubts, suspense—for then the afflatus of such themes haply may fall upon us, more or less; and then, hot from surrounding war and revolution, our speech, though without polish'd coherence, and a failure by the standard called criticism, comes forth, real at least as the lightnings.

And may-be we, these days, have, too, our own reward—(for there are yet some, in all lands, worthy to be so encouraged.) Though not for us the joy of entering at the last the conquer'd city—not ours the chance ever to see with our own eyes the peerless power and splendid *eclat* of the democratic principle, arriv'd at meridian, filling the world with effulgence and majesty far beyond those of past history's kings, or all dynastic sway—there is yet, to whoever is eligible among us, the prophetic vision, the joy of being toss'd in the brave turmoil of these times—the promulgation and the path, obedient, lowly reverent to the voice, the gesture of the god, or holy ghost, which others see not, hear not—with the proud consciousness that amid whatever clouds, seductions, or heart-wearying postponements, we have never deserted, never despair'd, never abandon'd the faith.

So much contributed, to be conn'd well, to help prepare and brace our edifice, our plann'd Idea—we still proceed to give it in another of its aspects—perhaps the main, the high façade of all. For to democracy, the leveler, the unyielding principle of the average, is surely join'd another principle, equally unyielding, closely tracking the first, indispensable to it, opposite, (as the sexes are opposite,) and whose existence, confronting and ever modifying the other, often clashing, paradoxical, yet neither of highest avail without the other, plainly supplies to these grand cosmic politics of ours, and to the launch'd forth mortal dangers of republicanism, to-day or any day, the counterpart and offset whereby Nature restrains the deadly original relentlessness of all her first-class laws. This second principle is individuality, the pride and centripetal isolation of a human being in himself—identity—personalism. Whatever the name, its acceptance and thorough infusion through the organizations of political commonalty now shooting Aurora-like about the world, are of utmost importance, as the principle itself is needed for very life's sake. It forms, in a sort, or is to form, the compensating balance-wheel of the successful working machinery of aggregate America.

And, if we think of it, what does civilization itself rest upon—and what object has it, with its religions, arts, schools, &c., but rich, luxuriant, varied personalism? To that, all bends; and it is because toward such result democracy alone, on anything like Nature's scale, breaks up the limitless fallows of humankind, and plants the seed, and gives fair play, that its claims now precede the rest. The literature, songs, esthetics, &c., of a country are of importance principally because they furnish the materials and suggestions of personality for the women and men of that country, and enforce them in a thousand effective ways.[8] As the topmost claim of a strong consolidating of the nationality of these States, is, that only by such powerful compaction can the separate States secure that full and free swing within their spheres, which is becoming to them, each after its kind, so will individuality, with unimpeded branchings, flourish best under imperial republican forms.

Assuming Democracy to be at present in its embryo condition, and that the only large and satisfactory justification of it resides in the future, mainly through the copious production of perfect characters among the people, and through the advent of a sane and pervading religiousness, it is with regard to the atmosphere and spaciousness fit for such characters, and of certain nutriment and cartoon-draftings proper for them, and indicating them for New World purposes, that I continue the present statement—an exploration, as of new ground, wherein, like other primitive surveyors, I must do the best I can, leaving it to those who come after me to do much better. (The service, in fact, if any, must be to break a sort of first path or track, no matter how rude and ungeometrical.)

We have frequently printed the word Democracy. Yet I cannot too often repeat that it is a word the real gist of which still sleeps, quite unawaken'd, notwithstanding the resonance and the many angry tempests out of which its syllables have come, from pen or tongue. It is a great word, whose history, I suppose, remains unwritten, because that history has yet to be enacted. It is, in some sort, younger brother of another great and often-used word, Nature, whose history also waits unwritten. As I perceive, the tendencies of our day, in the States, (and I entirely respect them,) are toward those vast and sweeping movements, influences, moral and physical, of humanity, now and always current over the planet, on the scale of the impulses of the elements. Then it is also good to reduce the whole matter to the consideration of a single self, a man, a woman, on permanent grounds. Even for the treatment of the universal, in politics, metaphysics, or anything, sooner or later we come down to one single, solitary soul.

There is, in sanest hours, a consciousness, a thought that rises, independent, lifted out from all else, calm, like the stars, shining eternal. This is the thought of identity—yours for you, whoever you are, as mine for me. Miracle of miracles, beyond statement, most spiritual and vaguest of earth's dreams, yet hardest basic fact, and only entrance to all facts. In such devout hours, in the midst of the significant wonders of heaven and earth, (significant only because of the Me in the centre,) creeds, conventions, fall away and become of no account before this simple idea. Under the luminousness of real vision, it alone takes possession, takes value. Like the shadowy dwarf in the fable, once liberated and look'd upon, it expands over the whole earth, and spreads to the roof of heaven.

The quality of BEING, in the object's self, according to its own central idea and purpose, and of growing therefrom and thereto—

not criticism by other standards, and adjustments thereto—is the lesson of Nature. True, the full man wisely gathers, culls, absorbs; but if, engaged disproportionately in that, he slights or overlays the precious idiocrasy and special nativity and intention that he is, the man's self, the main thing, is a failure, however wide his general cultivation. Thus, in our times, refinement and delicatesse are not only attended to sufficiently, but threaten to eat us up, like a cancer. Already, the democratic genius watches, ill-pleased, these tendencies. Provision for a little healthy rudeness, savage virtue, justification of what one has in one's self, whatever it is, is demanded. Negative qualities, even deficiencies, would be a relief. Singleness and normal simplicity and separation, amid this more and more complex, more and more artificialized state of society—how pensively we yearn for them! how we would welcome their return!

In some such direction, then—at any rate enough to preserve the balance—we feel called upon to throw what weight we can, not for absolute reasons, but current ones. To prune, gather, trim, conform, and ever cram and stuff, and be genteel and proper, is the pressure of our days. While aware that much can be said even in behalf of all this, we perceive that we have not now to consider the question of what is demanded to serve a half-starved and barbarous nation, or set of nations, but what is most applicable, most pertinent, for numerous congeries of conventional, over-corpulent societies, already becoming stifled and rotten with flatulent, infidelistic literature, and polite conformity and art. In addition to establish'd sciences, we suggest a science as it were of healthy average personalism, on original-universal grounds, the object of which should be to raise up and supply through the States a copious race of superb American men and women, cheerful, religious, ahead of any yet known.

America has yet morally and artistically originated nothing. She seems singularly unaware that the models of persons, books, manners, &c., appropriate for former conditions and for European lands, are but exiles and exotics here. No current of her life, as shown on the surfaces of what is authoritatively called her society, accepts or runs into social or esthetic democracy; but all the currents set squarely against it. Never, in the Old World, was thoroughly upholster'd exterior appearance and show, mental and other, built entirely on the idea of caste, and on the sufficiency of mere outside acquisition—never were glibness, verbal intellect, more the test, the emulation—more loftily elevated as head and sample—than they are on the surface of our republican States this day. The writers of a time hint the mottoes of its gods. The word of the modern, say these voices, is the word Culture.

We find ourselves abruptly in close quarters with the enemy. This word Culture, or what it has come to represent, involves, by contrast, our whole theme, and has been, indeed, the spur, urging us to engagement. Certain questions arise. As now taught, accepted and carried out, are not the processes of culture rapidly creating a class of supercilious infidels, who believe in nothing? Shall a man lose himself in countless masses of adjustments, and be so shaped with reference to this, that, and the other, that the simply good and healthy and brave parts of him are reduced and clipp'd away, like the bordering of box in a garden? You can cultivate corn and roses and orchards—but who shall cultivate the mountain peaks, the ocean, and the tumbling gorgeousness of the clouds? Lastly—is the readily-given reply that culture only seeks to help, systematize, and put in attitude, the elements of fertility and power, a conclusive reply?

I do not so much object to the name, or word, but I should certainly insist, for the purposes of these States, on a radical change of category, in the distribution of precedence. I should demand a programme of culture, drawn out, not for a single class alone, or for the parlors or lecture-rooms, but with an eye to practical life, the west, the working-men, the facts of farms and jack-planes and engineers, and of the broad range of the women also of the middle and working strata, and with reference to the perfect equality of women, and of a grand and powerful motherhood. I should demand of this programme or theory a scope generous enough to include the widest human area. It must have for its spinal meaning the formation of a typical personality of character, eligible to the uses of the high average of men—and *not* restricted by conditions ineligible to the masses. The best culture will always be that of the manly and courageous instincts, and loving perceptions, and of self-respect— aiming to form, over this continent, an idiocrasy of universalism, which, true child of America, will bring joy to its mother, returning to her in her own spirit, recruiting myriads of offspring, able, natural, perceptive, tolerant, devout believers in her, America, and with some definite instinct why and for what she has arisen, most vast, most formidable of historic births, and is, now and here, with wonderful step, journeying through Time.

The problem, as it seems to me, presented to the New World, is, under permanent law and order, and after preserving cohesion, (ensemble-Individuality,) at all hazards, to vitalize man's free play of special Personalism, recognizing in it something that calls ever more to be consider'd, fed, and adopted as the substratum for the best that belongs to us, (government indeed is for it,) including the new esthetics of our future.

To formulate beyond this present vagueness—to help line and put before us the species, or a specimen of the species, of the democratic ethnology of the future, is a work toward which the genius of our land, with peculiar encouragement, invites her well-wishers. Already certain limnings, more or less grotesque, more or less fading and watery, have appear'd. We too, (repressing doubts and qualms,) will try our hand.

Attempting, then, however crudely, a basic model or portrait of personality for general use for the manliness of the States, (and doubtless that is most useful which is most simple and comprehensive for all, and toned low enough,) we should prepare the canvas well beforehand. Parentage must consider itself in advance. (Will the time hasten when fatherhood and motherhood shall become a science—and the noblest science?) To our model, a clear-blooded, strong-fibred physique, is indispensable; the questions of food, drink, air, exercise, assimilation, digestion, can never be intermitted. Out of these we descry a well-begotten selfhood—in youth, fresh, ardent, emotional, aspiring, full of adventure; at maturity, brave, perceptive, under control, neither too talkative nor too reticent, neither flippant nor sombre; of the bodily figure, the movements easy, the complexion showing the best blood, somewhat flush'd, breast expanded, an erect attitude, a voice whose sound outvies music, eyes of calm and steady gaze, yet capable also of flashing—and a general presence that holds its own in the company of the highest. (For it is native personality, and that alone, that endows a man to stand before presidents or generals, or in any distinguish'd collection, with *aplomb*—and *not* culture, or any knowledge or intellect whatever.)

With regard to the mental-educational part of our model, enlargement of intellect, stores of cephalic knowledge, &c., the concentration thitherward of all the customs of our age, especially in America, is so overweening, and provides so fully for that part, that, important and necessary as it is, it really needs nothing from us here—except, indeed, a phrase of warning and restraint. Manners, costumes, too, though important, we need not dwell upon here. Like beauty, grace of motion, &c., they are results. Causes, original things, being attended to, the right manners unerringly follow. Much is said, among artists, of "the grand style," as if it were a thing by itself. When a man, artist or whoever, has health, pride, acuteness,

noble aspirations, he has the motive-elements of the grandest style.
The rest is but manipulation, (yet that is no small matter.)

Leaving still unspecified several sterling parts of any model fit
for the future personality of America, I must not fail, again and
ever, to pronounce myself on one, probably the least attended to in
modern times—a hiatus, indeed, threatening its gloomiest consequences after us. I mean the simple, unsophisticated Conscience,
the primary moral element. If I were asked to specify in what quarter lie the grounds of darkest dread, respecting the America of our
hopes, I should have to point to this particular. I should demand
the invariable application to individuality, this day and any day, of
that old, ever-true plumb-rule of persons, eras, nations. Our triumphant modern civilizee, with his all-schooling and his wondrous
appliances, will still show himself but an amputation while this
deficiency remains. Beyond, (assuming a more hopeful tone,) the
vertebration of the manly and womanly personalism of our western
world, can only be, and is, indeed, to be, (I hope,) its all penetrating Religiousness.

The ripeness of Religion is doubtless to be looked for in this
field of individuality, and is a result that no organization or church
can ever achieve. As history is poorly retain'd by what the technists
call history, and is not given out from their pages, except the
learner has in himself the sense of the well-wrapt, never yet written, perhaps impossible to be written, history—so Religion, although
casually arrested, and, after a fashion, preserv'd in the churches and
creeds, does not depend at all upon them, but is a part of the identified soul, which, when greatest, knows not bibles in the old way,
but in new ways—the identified soul, which can really confront Religion when it extricates itself entirely from the churches, and not
before.

Personalism fuses this, and favors it. I should say, indeed, that
only in the perfect uncontamination and solitariness of individuality
may the spirituality of religion positively come forth at all. Only
here, and on such terms, the meditation, the devout ecstasy, the
soaring flight. Only here, communion with the mysteries, the eternal problems, whence? whither? Alone, and identity, and the mood
—and the soul emerges, and all statements, churches, sermons, melt
away like vapors. Alone, and silent thought and awe, and aspiration—and then the interior consciousness, like a hitherto unseen
inscription, in magic ink, beams out its wondrous lines to the sense.
Bibles may convey, and priests expound, but it is exclusively for the

noiseless operation of one's isolated Self, to enter the pure ether of veneration, reach the divine levels, and commune with the unutterable.

To practically enter into politics is an important part of American personalism. To every young man, north and south, earnestly studying these things, I should here, as an offset to what I have said in former pages, now also say, that may-be to views of very largest scope, after all, perhaps the political, (perhaps the literary and sociological,) America goes best about its development its own way—sometimes, to temporary sight, appaling enough. It is the fashion among dillettants and fops (perhaps I myself am not guiltless,) to decry the whole formulation of the active politics of America, as beyond redemption, and to be carefully kept away from. See you that you do not fall into this error. America, it may be, is doing very well upon the whole, notwithstanding these antics of the parties and their leaders, these half-brain'd nominees, the many ignorant ballots, and many elected failures and blatherers. It is the dillettants, and all who shirk their duty, who are not doing well. As for you, I advise you to enter more strongly yet into politics. I advise every young man to do so. Always inform yourself; always do the best you can; always vote. Disengage yourself from parties. They have been useful, and to some extent remain so; but the floating, uncommitted electors, farmers, clerks, mechanics, the masters of parties—watching aloof, inclining victory this side or that side— such are the ones most needed, present and future. For America, if eligible at all to downfall and ruin, is eligible within herself, not without; for I see clearly that the combined foreign world could not beat her down. But these savage, wolfish parties alarm me. Owning no law but their own will, more and more combative, less and less tolerant of the idea of ensemble and of equal brotherhood, the perfect equality of the States, the ever-overarching American ideas, it behooves you to convey yourself implicitly to no party, nor submit blindly to their dictators, but steadily hold yourself judge and master over all of them.

So much, (hastily toss'd together, and leaving far more unsaid,) for an ideal, or intimations of an ideal, toward American manhood. But the other sex, in our land, requires at least a basis of suggestion.

I have seen a young American woman, one of a large family of daughters, who, some years since, migrated from her meagre country home to one of the northern cities, to gain her own support. She soon became an expert seamstress, but finding the employment too confining for health and comfort, she went boldly to work for others, to house-keep, cook, clean, &c. After trying several places, she fell upon one where she was suited. She has told me that she finds nothing degrading in her position; it is not inconsistent with personal dignity, self-respect, and the respect of others. She confers benefits and receives them. She has good health; her presence itself is healthy and bracing; her character is unstain'd; she has made herself understood, and preserves her independence, and has been able to help her parents, and educate and get places for her sisters; and her course of life is not without opportunities for mental improvement, and of much quiet, uncosting happiness and love.

I have seen another woman who, from taste and necessity conjoin'd, has gone into practical affairs, carries on a mechanical business, partly works at it herself, dashes out more and more into real hardy life, is not abash'd by the coarseness of the contact, knows how to be firm and silent at the same time, holds her own with unvarying coolness and decorum, and will compare, any day, with superior carpenters, farmers, and even boatmen and drivers. For all that, she has not lost the charm of the womanly nature, but preserves and bears it fully, though through such rugged presentation.

Then there is the wife of a mechanic, mother of two children, a woman of merely passable English education, but of fine wit, with all her sex's grace and intuitions, who exhibits, indeed, such a noble female personality, that I am fain to record it here. Never abnegating her own proper independence, but always genially preserving it, and what belongs to it—cooking, washing, child-nursing, house-tending—she beams sunshine out of all these duties, and makes them illustrious. Physiologically sweet and sound, loving work, practical, she yet knows that there are intervals, however few, devoted to recreation, music, leisure, hospitality—and affords such intervals. Whatever she does, and wherever she is, that charm, that indescribable perfume of genuine womanhood attends her, goes with her, exhales from her, which belongs of right to all the sex, and is, or ought to be, the invariable atmosphere and common aureola of old as well as young.

My dear mother once described to me a resplendent person, down on Long Island, whom she knew in early days. She was known by the name of the Peacemaker. She was well toward eighty years old, of happy and sunny temperament, had always lived on a farm, and was very neighborly, sensible and discreet, an invariable and welcom'd favorite, especially with young married women. She had numerous children and grandchildren. She was uneducated, but possess'd a native dignity. She had come to be a tacitly agreed upon domestic regulator, judge, settler of difficulties, shepherdess, and reconciler in the land. She was a sight to draw near and look upon, with her large figure, her profuse snow-white hair, (uncoif'd by any head-dress or cap,) dark eyes, clear complexion, sweet breath, and peculiar personal magnetism.

The foregoing portraits, I admit, are frightfully out of line from these imported models of womanly personality—the stock feminine characters of the current novelists, or of the foreign court poems, (Ophelias, Enids, princesses, or ladies of one thing or another,) which fill the envying dreams of so many poor girls, and are accepted by our men, too, as supreme ideals of feminine excellence to be sought after. But I present mine just for a change.

Then there are mutterings, (we will not now stop to heed them here, but they must be heeded,) of something more revolutionary. The day is coming when the deep questions of woman's entrance amid the arenas of practical life, politics, the suffrage, &c., will not only be argued all around us, but may be put to decision, and real experiment.

Of course, in these States, for both man and woman, we must entirely recast the types of highest personality from what the oriental, feudal, ecclesiastical worlds bequeath us, and which yet possess the imaginative and esthetic fields of the United States, pictorial and melodramatic, not without use as studies, but making sad work, and forming a strange anachronism upon the scenes and exigencies around us. Of course, the old undying elements remain. The task is, to successfully adjust them to new combinations, our own days. Nor is this so incredible. I can conceive a community, to-day and here, in which, on a sufficient scale, the perfect personalities, without noise meet; say in some pleasant western settlement or town, where a couple of hundred best men and women, of ordinary worldly status, have by luck been drawn together, with nothing extra of genius or wealth, but virtuous, chaste, industrious, cheerful, resolute, friendly and devout. I can conceive such a community organized in running order, powers judiciously delegated—farming, building, trade, courts, mails, schools, elections, all attended to; and then the rest of life, the main thing, freely branching and blossoming in each individual, and bearing golden fruit. I can see there, in every young and old man, after his kind, and in every woman after hers, a true personality, develop'd, exercised proportionately in body, mind, and spirit. I can imagine this case as one not necessarily rare or difficult, but in buoyant accordance with the municipal and general requirements of our times. And I can realize in it the culmination of something better than any stereotyped *eclat* of history or poems. Perhaps, unsung, undramatized, unput in essays or biographies—perhaps even some such community already exists, in Ohio, Illinois, Missouri, or somewhere, practically fulfilling itself, and thus outvying, in cheapest vulgar life, all that has been hitherto shown in best ideal pictures.

In short, and to sum up, America, betaking herself to formative action, (as it is about time for more solid achievement, and less windy promise,) must, for her purposes, cease to recognize a theory of character grown of feudal aristocracies, or form'd by merely literary standards, or from any ultramarine, full-dress formulas of culture, polish, caste, &c., and must sternly promulgate her own new standard, yet old enough, and accepting the old, the perennial elements, and combining them into groups, unities, appropriate to the modern, the democratic, the west, and to the practical occasions and needs of our own cities, and of the agricultural regions. Ever the most precious in the common. Ever the fresh breeze of field, or hill, or lake, is more than any palpitation of fans, though of ivory, and redolent with perfume; and the air is more than the costliest perfumes.

And now, for fear of mistake, we may not intermit to beg our absolution from all that genuinely is, or goes along with, even Culture. Pardon us, venerable shade! if we have seem'd to speak lightly of your office. The whole civilization of the earth, we know, is yours, with all the glory and the light thereof. It is, indeed, in your own spirit, and seeking to tally the loftiest teachings of it, that we aim these poor utterances. For you, too, mighty minister! know that there is something greater than you, namely, the fresh, eternal qualities of Being. From them, and by them, as you, at your best, we too evoke the last, the needed help, to vitalize our country and our days. Thus we pronounce not so much against the principle of culture; we only supervise it, and promulge along with it, as deep, perhaps a deeper, principle. As we have shown the New World including in itself the all-leveling aggregate of democracy, we show it also including the all-varied, all-permitting, all-free theorem of individuality, and erecting therefor a lofty and hitherto unoccupied framework or platform, broad enough for all, eligible to every farmer and mechanic—to the female equally with the male—a towering selfhood, not physically perfect only—not satisfied with the mere mind's and learning's stores, but religious, possessing the idea of the infinite, (rudder and compass sure amid this troublous voy-

age, o'er darkest, wildest wave, through stormiest wind, of man's
or nation's progress)—realizing, above the rest, that known humanity, in deepest sense, is fair adhesion to itself, for purposes beyond
—and that, finally, the personality of mortal life is most important
with reference to the immortal, the unknown, the spiritual, the only
permanently real, which as the ocean waits for and receives the
rivers, waits for us each and all.

Much is there, yet, demanding line and outline in our Vistas, not
only on these topics, but others quite unwritten. Indeed, we could
talk the matter, and expand it, through lifetime. But it is necessary
to return to our original premises. In view of them, we have again
pointedly to confess that all the objective grandeurs of the world,
for highest purposes, yield themselves up, and depend on mentality
alone. Here, and here only, all balances, all rests. For the mind,
which alone builds the permanent edifice, haughtily builds it to
itself. By it, with what follows it, are convey'd to mortal sense the
culminations of the materialistic, the known, and a prophecy of the
unknown. To take expression, to incarnate, to endow a literature
with grand and archetypal models—to fill with pride and love the
utmost capacity, and to achieve spiritual meanings, and suggest the
future—these, and these only, satisfy the soul. We must not say one
word against real materials; but the wise know that they do not
become real till touched by emotions, the mind. Did we call the
latter imponderable? Ah, let us rather proclaim that the slightest
song-tune, the countless ephemera of passions arous'd by orators
and tale-tellers, are more dense, more weighty than the engines
there in the great factories, or the granite blocks in their foundations.
Approaching thus the momentous spaces, and considering with
reference to a new and greater personalism, the needs and possibilities of American imaginative literature, through the medium-light
of what we have already broach'd, it will at once be appreciated
that a vast gulf of difference separates the present accepted conditions of these spaces, inclusive of what is floating in them, from any
condition adjusted to, or fit for, the world, the America, there sought
to be indicated, and the copious races of complete men and women,
along these Vistas crudely outlined. It is, in some sort, no less a difference than lies between that long-continued nebular state and
vagueness of the astronomical worlds, compared with the subsequent state, the definitely-form'd worlds themselves, duly compacted, clustering in systems, hung up there, chandeliers of the
universe, beholding and mutually lit by each other's lights, serving
for ground of all substantial foothold, all vulgar uses—yet serving

still more as an undying chain and echelon of spiritual proofs and shows. A boundless field to fill! A new creation, with needed orbic works launch'd forth, to revolve in free and lawful circuits—to move, self-poised, through the ether, and shine like heaven's own suns! With such, and nothing less, we suggest that New World literature, fit to rise upon, cohere, and signalize in time, these States.

What, however, do we more definitely mean by New World literature? Are we not doing well enough here already? Are not the United States this day busily using, working, more printer's type, more presses, than any other country? uttering and absorbing more publications than any other? Do not our publishers fatten quicker and deeper? (helping themselves, under shelter of a delusive and sneaking law, or rather absence of law, to most of their forage, poetical, pictorial, historical, romantic, even comic, without money and without price—and fiercely resisting the timidest proposal to pay for it.) Many will come under this delusion—but my purpose is to dispel it. I say that a nation may hold and circulate rivers and oceans of very readable print, journals, magazines, novels, library-books, "poetry," &c.—such as the States to-day possess and circulate —of unquestionable aid and value—hundreds of new volumes annually composed and brought out here, respectable enough, indeed unsurpass'd in smartness and erudition—with further hundreds, or rather millions, (as by free forage or theft aforemention'd,) also thrown into the market—and yet, all the while, the said nation, land, strictly speaking, may possess no literature at all.

Repeating our inquiry, what, then, do we mean by real literature? especially the democratic literature of the future? Hard questions to meet. The clues are inferential, and turn us to the past. At best, we can only offer suggestions, comparisons, circuits.

It must still be reiterated, as, for the purpose of these memoranda, the deep lesson of history and time, that all else in the contributions of a nation or age, through its politics, materials, heroic personalities, military eclat, &c., remains crude, and defers, in any close and thorough-going estimate, until vitalized by national, original archetypes in literature. They only put the nation in form, finally tell anything—prove, complete anything—perpetuate anything. Without doubt, some of the richest and most powerful and populous communities of the antique world, and some of the grandest personalities and events, have, to after and present times, left themselves entirely unbequeath'd. Doubtless, greater than any that have come down to us, were among those lands, heroisms, persons, that have not come down to us at all, even by name, date, or location. Others have arrived safely, as from voyages over wide, century-stretching seas. The little ships, the miracles that have buoy'd them, and by incredible chances safely convey'd them, (or the best of them, their meaning and essence,) over long wastes, darkness, lethargy, ignorance, &c., have been a few inscriptions—a few immortal compositions, small in size, yet compassing what measureless values of reminiscence, contemporary portraitures, manners, idioms and beliefs, with deepest inference, hint and thought, to tie and touch forever the old, new body, and the old, new soul! These! and still these! bearing the freight so dear—dearer than pride—dearer than love. All the best experience of humanity, folded, saved, freighted to us here. Some of these tiny ships we call Old and New Testament, Homer, Eschylus, Plato, Juvenal, &c. Precious minims! I think, if were forced to choose, rather than have you, and the likes of you, and what belongs to, and has grown of you, blotted out and gone, we could better afford, appaling as that would be, to lose all actual ships, this day fasten'd by wharf, or floating on wave, and see them, with all their cargoes, scuttled and sent to the bottom.

Gather'd by geniuses of city, race or age, and put by them in highest of art's forms, namely, the literary form, the peculiar combinations and the outshows of that city, age, or race, its particular modes of the universal attributes and passions, its faiths, heroes, lovers and gods, wars, traditions, struggles, crimes, emotions, joys, (or the subtle spirit of these,) having been pass'd on to us to illumine our own selfhood, and its experiences—what they supply, indispensable and highest, if taken away, nothing else in all the world's boundless storehouses could make up to us, or ever again return.

For us, along the great highways of time, those monuments stand —those forms of majesty and beauty. For us those beacons burn through all the nights. Unknown Egyptians, graving hieroglyphs; Hindus, with hymn and apothegm and endless epic; Hebrew prophet, with spirituality, as in flashes of lightning, conscience like red-hot iron, plaintive songs and screams of vengeance for tyrannies and enslavement; Christ, with bent head, brooding love and peace, like a dove; Greek, creating eternal shapes of physical and esthetic proportion; Roman, lord of satire, the sword, and the codex;—of the figures, some far off and veil'd, others nearer and visible; Dante, stalking with lean form, nothing but fibre, not a grain of superfluous flesh; Angelo, and the great painters, architects, musicians; rich Shakspere, luxuriant as the sun, artist and singer of feudalism in its sunset, with all the gorgeous colors, owner thereof, and using them at will; and so to such as German Kant and Hegel, where they, though near us, leaping over the ages, sit again, impassive, imperturbable, like the Egyptian gods. Of these, and the like of these, is it too much, indeed, to return to our favorite figure, and view them as orbs and systems of orbs, moving in free paths in the spaces of that other heaven, the kosmic intellect, the soul?

Ye powerful and resplendent ones! ye were, in your atmospheres, grown not for America, but rather for her foes, the feudal and the old—while our genius is democratic and modern. Yet could ye, indeed, but breathe your breath of life into our New World's nostrils —not to enslave us, as now, but, for our needs, to breed a spirit like your own—perhaps, (dare we to say it?) to dominate, even destroy, what you yourselves have left! On your plane, and no less, but even higher and wider, must we mete and measure for to-day and here. I demand races of orbic bards, with unconditional uncompromising sway. Come forth, sweet democratic despots of the west!

By points like these we, in reflection, token what we mean by any land's or people's genuine literature. And thus compared and tested, judging amid the influence of loftiest products only, what do our current copious fields of print, covering in manifold forms, the United States, better, for an analogy, present, than, as in certain regions of the sea, those spreading, undulating masses of squid, through which the whale swimming, with head half out, feeds?

Not but that doubtless our current so-called literature, (like an endless supply of small coin,) performs a certain service, and may-be, too, the service needed for the time, (the preparation-service, as children learn to spell.) Everybody reads, and truly nearly everybody writes, either books, or for the magazines or journals. The matter has magnitude, too, after a sort. But is it really advancing? or, has it advanced for a long while? There is something impressive about the huge editions of the dailies and weeklies, the mountain-stacks of white paper piled in the press-vaults, and the proud, crashing, ten-cylinder presses, which I can stand and watch any time by the half hour. Then, (though the States in the field of imagination present not a single first-class work, not a single great literatus,) the main objects, to amuse, to titillate, to pass away time, to circulate the news, and rumors of news, to rhyme and read rhyme, are yet attain'd, and on a scale of infinity. To-day, in books, in the rivalry of writers, especially novelists, success, (so-call'd,) is for him or her who strikes the mean flat average, the sensational appetite for stimulus, incident, persiflage, &c., and depicts, to the common calibre, sensual, exterior life. To such, or the luckiest of them, as we see, the audiences are limitless and profitable; but they cease presently. While this day, or any day, to workmen portraying interior or spiritual life, the audiences were limited, and often laggard—but they last forever.

Compared with the past, our modern science soars, and our journals serve—but ideal and even ordinary romantic literature, does not, I think, substantially advance. Behold the prolific brood of the contemporary novel, magazine-tale, theatre-play, &c. The same endless thread of tangled and superlative love-story, inherited, apparently from the Amadises and Palmerins of the 13th, 14th, and 15th centuries over there in Europe. The costumes and associations brought down to date, the seasoning hotter and more varied, the dragons and ogres left out—but the *thing*, I should say, has not advanced—is just as sensational, just as strain'd—remains about the same, nor more, nor less.

What is the reason our time, our lands, that we see no fresh local courage, sanity, of our own—the Mississippi, stalwart Western men, real mental and physical facts, Southerners, &c., in the body of our literature? especially the poetic part of it. But always, instead, a parcel of dandies and ennuyees, dapper little gentlemen from abroad, who flood us with their thin sentiment of parlors, parasols, piano-songs, tinkling rhymes, the five-hundredth importation—or whimpering and crying about something, chasing one aborted conceit after another, and forever occupied in dyspeptic amours with dyspeptic women. While, current and novel, the grandest events and revolutions, and stormiest passions of history, are crossing to-day with unparallel'd rapidity and magnificence over the stages of our own and all the continents, offering new materials, opening new vistas, with largest needs, inviting the daring launching forth of conceptions in literature, inspired by them, soaring in highest regions, serving art in its highest, (which is only the other name for serving God, and serving humanity,) where is the man of letters, where is the book, with any nobler aim than to follow in the old track, repeat what has been said before—and, as its utmost triumph, sell well, and be erudite or elegant?

Mark the roads, the processes, through which these States have arrived, standing easy, henceforth ever-equal, ever-compact, in their range to-day. European adventures? the most antique? Asiatic or African? old history—miracles—romances? Rather, our own unquestion'd facts. They hasten, incredible, blazing bright as fire. From the deeds and days of Columbus down to the present, and including the present—and especially the late Secession war—when I con them, I feel, every leaf, like stopping to see if I have not made a mistake, and fall'n on the splendid figments of some dream. But it is no dream. We stand, live, move, in the huge flow of our age's materialism—in its spirituality. We have had founded for us the most positive of lands. The founders have pass'd to other spheres—but what are these terrible duties they have left us?

Their politics the United States have, in my opinion, with all their faults, already substantially establish'd, for good, on their own native, sound, long-vista'd principles, never to be overturn'd, offering a sure basis for all the rest. With that, their future religious forms, sociology, literature, teachers, schools, costumes, &c., are of course to make a compact whole, uniform, on tallying principles. For how can we remain, divided, contradicting ourselves, this way? [9] I say we can only attain harmony and stability by consulting ensemble and the ethic purports, and faithfully building upon them. For the New World, indeed, after two grand stages of preparation-strata, I perceive that now a third stage, being ready for, (and without which the other two were useless,) with unmistakable signs appears. The First stage was the planning and putting on record the political foundation rights of immense masses of people—indeed all people—in the organization of republican National, State, and municipal governments, all constructed with reference to each, and each to all. This is the American programme, not for classes, but for universal man, and is embodied in the compacts of the Declaration of Independence, and, as it began and has now grown, with its amendments, the Federal Constitution—and in the State governments, with all their interiors, and with general suffrage; those having the sense not only of what is in themselves, but that their certain several things started, planted, hundreds of others in the same direction duly arise and follow. The Second stage relates to material prosperity, wealth, produce, labor-saving machines, iron, cotton, local, State and continental railways, intercommunication and trade with all lands, steamships, mining, general employment, organization of great cities, cheap appliances for comfort, numberless technical schools, books, newspapers, a currency for money circulation, &c. The Third stage, rising out of the previous ones, to make them and all illustrious, I, now, for one, promulge, announcing a native expression-spirit, getting into form, adult, and through mentality, for these States, self-contain'd, different from others, more expansive, more rich and free, to be evidenced by original authors and poets to come, by American personalities, plenty of them, male and female, traversing the States, none excepted—and by native superber tableaux and growths of language, songs, operas, orations, lectures, architecture—and by a sublime and serious Religious Democracy sternly taking command, dissolving the old, sloughing off surfaces, and from its own interior and vital principles, reconstructing, democratizing society.

For America, type of progress, and of essential faith in man, above all his errors and wickedness—few suspect how deep, how deep it really strikes. The world evidently supposes, and we have evidently supposed so too, that the States are merely to achieve the equal franchise, an elective government—to inaugurate the respectability of labor, and become a nation of practical operatives, law-abiding, orderly and well-off. Yes, those are indeed parts of the task of America; but they not only do not exhaust the progressive conception, but rather arise, teeming with it, as the mediums of deeper, higher progress. Daughter of a physical revolution—mother of the true revolutions, which are of the interior life, and of the arts. For so long as the spirit is not changed, any change of appearance is of no avail.

The old men, I remember as a boy, were always talking of American independence. What is independence? Freedom from all laws or bonds except those of one's own being, control'd by the universal ones. To lands, to man, to woman, what is there at last to each, but the inherent soul, nativity, idiocrasy, free, highest-poised, soaring its own flight, following out itself?

At present, these States, in their theology and social standards, (of greater importance than their political institutions,) are entirely held possession of by foreign lands. We see the sons and daughters of the New World, ignorant of its genius, not yet inaugurating the native, the universal, and the near, still importing the distant, the partial, and the dead. We see London, Paris, Italy—not original, superb, as where they belong—but second-hand here, where they do not belong. We see the shreds of Hebrews, Romans, Greeks; but where, on her own soil, do we see, in any faithful, highest, proud expression, America herself? I sometimes question whether she has a corner in her own house.

Not but that in one sense, and a very grand one, good theology, good art, or good literature, has certain features shared in common. The combination fraternizes, ties the races—is, in many particulars, under laws applicable indifferently to all, irrespective of climate or date, and, from whatever source, appeals to emotions, pride, love, spirituality, common to humankind. Nevertheless, they touch a man closest, (perhaps only actually touch him,) even in these, in their expression through autochthonic lights and shades, flavors, fondnesses, aversions, specific incidents, illustrations, out of his own nationality, geography, surroundings, antecedents, &c. The spirit and the form are one, and depend far more on association, identity and place, than is supposed. Subtly interwoven with the materiality and personality of a land, a race—Teuton, Turk, Californian, or what not—there is always something—I can hardly tell what it is— history but describes the results of it—it is the same as the untellable look of some human faces. Nature, too, in her stolid forms, is full of it —but to most it is there a secret. This something is rooted in the invisible roots, the profoundest meanings of that place, race, or nationality; and to absorb and again effuse it, uttering words and products as from its midst, and carrying it into highest regions, is the work, or a main part of the work, of any country's true author, poet, historian, lecturer, and perhaps even priest and philosoph. Here, and here only, are the foundations for our really valuable and permanent verse, drama, &c.

But at present, (judged by any higher scale than that which finds the chief ends of existence to be to feverishly make money during one-half of it, and by some "amusement," or perhaps foreign travel, flippantly kill time, the other half,) and consider'd with reference to purposes of patriotism, health, a noble personality, religion, and the democratic adjustments, all these swarms of poems, literary magazines, dramatic plays, resultant so far from American intellect, and the formation of our best ideas, are useless and a mockery. They strengthen and nourish no one, express nothing characteristic, give decision and purpose to no one, and suffice only the lowest level of vacant minds.

Of what is called the drama, or dramatic presentation in the United States, as now put forth at the theatres, I should say it deserves to be treated with the same gravity, and on a par with the questions of ornamental confectionery at public dinners, or the arrangement of curtains and hangings in a ball room—nor more, nor less. Of the other, I will not insult the reader's intelligence, (once really entering into the atmosphere of these Vistas,) by supposing it necessary to show, in detail, why the copious dribble, either of our little or well-known rhymesters, does not fulfil, in any respect, the needs and august occasions of this land. America demands a poetry that is bold, modern, and all-surrounding and kosmical, as she is herself. It must in no respect ignore science or the modern, but inspire itself with science and the modern. It must bend its vision toward the future, more than the past. Like America, it must extricate itself from even the greatest models of the past, and, while courteous to them, must have entire faith in itself, and the products of its own democratic spirit only. Like her, it must place in the van, and hold up at all hazards, the banner of the divine pride of man in himself, (the radical foundation of the new religion.) Long enough have the People been listening to poems in which common humanity, deferential, bends low, humiliated, acknowledging superiors. But America listens to no such poems. Erect, inflated, and fully self-esteeming be the chant; and then America will listen with pleased ears.

Nor may the genuine gold, the gems, when brought to light at last, be probably usher'd forth from any of the quarters currently counted on. To-day, doubtless, the infant genius of American poetic expression, (eluding those highly-refined imported and gild-edged themes, and sentimental and butterfly flights, pleasant to orthodox publishers—causing tender spasms in the coteries, and warranted not to chafe the sensitive cuticle of the most exquisitely artificial gossamer delicacy,) lies sleeping far away, happily unrecognized and uninjur'd by the coteries, the art-writers, the talkers and critics of the saloons, or the lecturers in the colleges—lies sleeping, aside, unrecking itself, in some western idiom, or native Michigan or Tennessee repartee, or stump-speech—or in Kentucky or Georgia, or the Carolinas—or in some slang or local song or allusion of the Manhattan, Boston, Philadelphia or Baltimore mechanic—or up in the Maine woods—or off in the hut of the California miner, or crossing the Rocky mountains, or along the Pacific railroad—or on the breasts of the young farmers of the northwest, or Canada, or boatmen of the lakes. Rude and coarse nursing-beds, these; but only from such beginnings and stocks, indigenous here, may haply arrive, be grafted, and sprout, in time, flowers of genuine American aroma, and fruits truly and fully our own.

I say it were a standing disgrace to these States—I say it were a disgrace to any nation, distinguish'd above others by the variety and vastness of its territories, its materials, its inventive activity, and the splendid practicality of its people, not to rise and soar above others also in its original styles in literature and art, and its own supply of intellectual and esthetic masterpieces, archetypal, and consistent with itself. I know not a land except ours that has not, to some extent, however small, made its title clear. The Scotch have their born ballads, subtly expressing their past and present, and expressing character. The Irish have theirs. England, Italy, France, Spain, theirs. What has America? With exhaustless mines of the richest ore of epic, lyric, tale, tune, picture, &c., in the Four Years' War; with, indeed, I sometimes think, the richest masses of material ever afforded a nation, more variegated, and on a larger scale—the first sign of proportionate, native, imaginative Soul, and first-class works to match, is, (I cannot too often repeat,) so far wanting.

Long ere the second centennial arrives, there will be some forty to fifty great States, among them Canada and Cuba. When the present century closes, our population will be sixty or seventy millions. The Pacific will be ours, and the Atlantic mainly ours. There will be daily electric communication with every part of the globe. What an age! What a land! Where, elsewhere, one so great? The individuality of one nation must then, as always, lead the world. Can there be any doubt who the leader ought to be? Bear in mind, though, that nothing less than the mightiest original non-subordinated SOUL has ever really, gloriously led, or ever can lead. (This Soul—its other name, in these Vistas, is LITERATURE.)

In fond fancy leaping those hundred years ahead, let us survey America's works, poems, philosophies, fulfilling prophecies, and giving form and decision to best ideals. Much that is now undream'd of, we might then perhaps see establish'd, luxuriantly cropping forth, richness, vigor of letters and of artistic expression, in whose products character will be a main requirement, and not merely erudition or elegance.

Intense and loving comradeship, the personal and passionate attachment of man to man—which, hard to define, underlies the lessons and ideals of the profound saviours of every land and age, and which seems to promise, when thoroughly develop'd, cultivated and recognized in manners and literature, the most substantial hope and safety of the future of these States, will then be fully express'd.[10]

A strong-fibred joyousness and faith, and the sense of health *al fresco*, may well enter into the preparation of future noble American authorship. Part of the test of a great literatus shall be the absence in him of the idea of the covert, the lurid, the maleficent, the devil, the grim estimates inherited from the Puritans, hell, natural depravity, and the like. The great literatus will be known, among the rest, by his cheerful simplicity, his adherence to natural standards, his limitless faith in God, his reverence, and by the absence in him of doubt, ennui, burlesque, persiflage, or any strain'd and temporary fashion.

Nor must I fail, again and yet again, to clinch, reiterate more plainly still, (O that indeed such survey as we fancy, may show in time this part completed also!) the lofty aim, surely the proudest and the purest, in whose service the future literatus, of whatever field, may gladly labor. As we have intimated, offsetting the material civilization of our race, our nationality, its wealth, territories, factories, population, products, trade, and military and naval strength, and breathing breath of life into all these, and more, must be its moral civilization—the formulation, expression, and aidancy whereof, is the very highest height of literature. The climax of this loftiest range of civilization, rising above all the gorgeous shows and results of wealth, intellect, power, and art, as such—above even theology and religious fervor—is to be its development, from the eternal bases, and the fit expression, of absolute Conscience, moral soundness, Justice. Even in religious fervor there is a touch of animal heat. But moral conscientiousness, crystalline, without flaw, not Godlike only, entirely human, awes and enchants forever. Great is emotional love, even in the order of the rational universe. But, if we must make gradations, I am clear there is something greater. Power, love, veneration, products, genius, esthetics, tried by subtlest comparisons, analyses, and in serenest moods, somewhere fail, somehow become vain. Then noiseless, with flowing steps, the lord, the sun, the last ideal comes. By the names right, justice, truth, we suggest, but do not describe it. To the world of men it remains a dream, an idea as they call it. But no dream is it to the wise—but the proudest, almost only solid lasting thing of all. Its analogy in the material universe is what holds together this world, and every object upon it, and carries its dynamics on forever sure and safe. Its lack, and the persistent shirking of it, as in life, sociology, literature, politics, business, and even sermonizing, these times, or any times, still leaves the abysm, the mortal flaw and smutch, mocking civilization to-day, with all its unquestion'd triumphs, and all the civilization so far known.[11]

Present literature, while magnificently fulfilling certain popular demands, with plenteous knowledge and verbal smartness, is profoundly sophisticated, insane, and its very joy is morbid. It needs tally and express Nature, and the spirit of Nature, and to know and obey the standards. I say the question of Nature, largely consider'd, involves the questions of the esthetic, the emotional, and the religious—and involves happiness. A fitly born and bred race, growing up in right conditions of out-door as much as in-door harmony, activity and development, would probably, from and in those conditions, find it enough merely *to live*—and would, in their relations to the sky, air, water, trees, &c., and to the countless common shows, and in the fact of life itself, discover and achieve happiness—with

Being suffused night and day by wholesome extasy, surpassing all the pleasures that wealth, amusement, and even gratified intellect, erudition, or the sense of art, can give.

In the prophetic literature of these States (the reader of my speculations will miss their principal stress unless he allows well for the point that a new Literature, perhaps a new Metaphysics, certainly a new Poetry, are to be, in my opinion, the only sure and worthy supports and expressions of the American Democracy,) Nature, true Nature, and the true idea of Nature, long absent, must, above all, become fully restored, enlarged, and must furnish the pervading atmosphere to poems, and the test of all high literary and esthetic compositions. I do not mean the smooth walks, trimm'd hedges, poseys and nightingales of the English poets, but the whole orb, with its geologic history, the kosmos, carrying fire and snow, that rolls through the illimitable areas, light as a feather, though weighing billions of tons. Furthermore, as by what we now partially call Nature is intended, at most, only what is entertainable by the physical conscience, the sense of matter, and of good animal health —on these it must be distinctly accumulated, incorporated, that man, comprehending these, has, in towering superaddition, the moral and spiritual consciences, indicating his destination beyond the ostensible, the mortal.

To the heights of such estimate of Nature indeed ascending, we proceed to make observations for our Vistas, breathing rarest air. What is I believe called Idealism seems to me to suggest, (guarding against extravagance, and ever modified even by its opposite,) the course of inquiry and desert of favor for our New World metaphysics, their foundation of and in literature, giving hue to all.[12]

The elevating and etherealizing ideas of the unknown and of unreality must be brought forward with authority, as they are the legitimate heirs of the known, and of reality, and at least as great as their parents. Fearless of scoffing, and of the ostent, let us take our stand, our ground, and never desert it, to confront the growing excess and arrogance of realism. To the cry, now victorious—the cry of sense, science, flesh, incomes, farms, merchandise, logic, intellect, demonstrations, solid perpetuities, buildings of brick and iron, or even the facts of the shows of trees, earth, rocks, &c., fear not, my brethren, my sisters, to sound out with equally determin'd voice, that conviction brooding within the recesses of every envision'd soul—illusions! apparitions! figments all! True, we must not condemn the show, neither absolutely deny it, for the indispensability of its meanings; but how clearly we see that, migrate in soul to what we can already conceive of superior and spiritual points of view, and, palpable as it seems under present relations, it all and several might, nay certainly would, fall apart and vanish.

I hail with joy the oceanic, variegated, intense practical energy, the demand for facts, even the business materialism of the current age, our States. But wo to the age or land in which these things, movements, stopping at themselves, do not tend to ideas. As fuel to flame, and flame to the heavens, so must wealth, science, materialism—even this democracy of which we make so much—unerringly feed the highest mind, the soul. Infinitude the flight: fathomless the mystery. Man, so diminutive, dilates beyond the sensible universe, competes with, outcopes space and time, meditating even one great idea. Thus, and thus only, does a human being, his spirit, ascend above, and justify, objective Nature, which, probably nothing in itself, is incredibly and divinely serviceable, indispensable, real, here. And as the purport of objective Nature is doubtless folded, hidden, somewhere here—as somewhere here is what this globe and its manifold forms, and the light of day, and night's darkness, and life itself, with all its experiences, are for—it is here the great literature, especially verse, must get its inspiration and throbbing blood. Then may we attain to a poetry worthy the immortal soul of man, and which, while absorbing materials, and, in their own sense, the shows of Nature, will, above all, have, both directly and indirectly, a freeing, fluidizing, expanding, religious character, exulting with science, fructifying the moral elements, and stimulating aspirations, and meditations on the unknown.

The process, so far, is indirect and peculiar, and though it may be suggested, cannot be defined. Observing, rapport, and with intuition, the shows and forms presented by Nature, the sensuous luxuriance, the beautiful in living men and women, the actual play of passions, in history and life—and, above all, from those developments either in Nature or human personality in which power, (dearest of all to the sense of the artist,) transacts itself—out of these, and seizing what is in them, the poet, the esthetic worker in any field, by the divine magic of his genius, projects them, their analogies, by curious removes, indirections, in literature and art. (No useless attempt to repeat the material creation, by daguerreotyping the exact likeness by mortal mental means.) This is the image-making faculty, coping with material creation, and rivaling, almost triumphing over it. This alone, when all the other parts of a specimen of literature or art are ready and waiting, can breathe into it the breath of life, and endow it with identity.

"The true question to ask," says the librarian of Congress in a paper read before the Social Science Convention at New York, October, 1869, "The true question to ask respecting a book, is, *has it help'd any human soul?*" This is the hint, statement, not only of the great literatus, his book, but of every great artist. It may be that all works of art are to be first tried by their art qualities, their image-forming talent, and their dramatic, pictorial, plot-constructing, euphonious and other talents. Then, whenever claiming to be first-class works, they are to be strictly and sternly tried by their foundation in, and radiation, in the highest sense, and always indirectly, of the ethic principles, and eligibility to free, arouse, dilate.

As, within the purposes of the Kosmos, and vivifying all meteorology, and all the congeries of the mineral, vegetable and animal worlds—all the physical growth and development of man, and all the history of the race in politics, religions, wars, &c., there is a moral purpose, a visible or invisible intention, certainly underlying all—its results and proof needing to be patiently waited for—needing intuition, faith, idiosyncrasy, to its realization, which many, and especially the intellectual, do not have—so in the product, or congeries of the product, of the greatest literatus. This is the last, profoundest measure and test of a first-class literary or esthetic achievement, and when understood and put in force must fain, I say, lead to works, books, nobler than any hitherto known. Lo! Nature, (the only complete, actual poem,) existing calmly in the divine scheme, containing all, content, careless of the criticisms of a day, or these endless and wordy chatterers. And lo! to the consciousness of the soul, the permanent identity, the thought, the something, before which the magnitude even of democracy, art, literature, &c., dwindles, becomes partial, measurable—something that fully satisfies, (which those do not.) That something is the All, and the idea of All, with the accompanying idea of eternity, and of itself, the soul, buoyant, indestructible, sailing space forever, visiting every region, as a ship the sea. And again lo! the pulsations in all matter, all spirit, throbbing forever—the eternal beats, eternal systole and diastole of life in things—wherefrom I feel and know that death is not the ending, as was thought, but rather the real beginning—and that nothing ever is or can be lost, nor ever die, nor soul, nor matter.

In the future of these States must arise poets immenser far, and make great poems of death. The poems of life are great, but there must be the poems of the purports of life, not only in itself, but beyond itself. I have eulogized Homer, the sacred bards of Jewry, Eschylus, Juvenal, Shakspere, &c., and acknowledged their inestimable value. But, (with perhaps the exception, in some, not all respects, of the second-mention'd,) I say there must, for future and democratic purposes, appear poets, (dare I to say so?) of higher class even than any of those—poets not only possess'd of the religious fire and abandon of Isaiah, luxuriant in the epic talent of Homer, or for proud characters as in Shakspere, but consistent with the Hegelian formulas, and consistent with modern science. America needs, and the world needs, a class of bards who will, now and ever, so link and tally the rational physical being of man, with the ensembles of time and space, and with this vast and multiform show, Nature, surrounding him, ever tantalizing him, equally a part, and yet not a part of him, as to essentially harmonize, satisfy, and put at rest. Faith, very old, now scared away by science, must be restored, brought back by the same power that caused her departure—restored with new sway, deeper, wider, higher than ever. Surely, this universal ennui, this coward fear, this shuddering at death, these low, degrading views, are not always to rule the spirit pervading future society, as it has the past, and does the present. What the Roman Lucretius sought most nobly, yet all too blindly, negatively to do for his age and its successors, must be done positively by some great coming literatus, especially poet, who, while remaining fully poet, will absorb whatever science indicates, with spiritualism, and out of them, and out of his own genius, will compose the great poem of death. Then will man indeed confront Nature, and confront time and space, both with science, and *con amore*, and take his right place, prepared for life, master of fortune and misfortune. And then that which was long wanted will be supplied, and the ship that had it not before in all her voyages, will have an anchor.

There are still other standards, suggestions, for products of high literatuses. That which really balances and conserves the social and political world is not so much legislation, police, treaties, and dread of punishment, as the latent eternal intuitional sense, in humanity, of fairness, manliness, decorum, &c. Indeed, this perennial regulation, control, and oversight, by self-suppliance, is *sine qua non* to democracy; and a highest widest aim of democratic literature may well be to bring forth, cultivate, brace, and strengthen this sense, in individuals and society. A strong mastership of the general inferior self by the superior self, is to be aided, secured, indirectly, but surely, by the literatus, in his works, shaping, for individual or aggregate democracy, a great passionate body, in and along with which goes a great masterful spirit.

And still, providing for contingencies, I fain confront the fact, the need of powerful native philosophs and orators and bards, these States, as rallying points to come, in times of danger, and to fend off ruin and defection. For history is long, long, long. Shift and turn the combinations of the statement as we may, the problem of the future of America is in certain respects as dark as it is vast. Pride, competition, segregation, vicious wilfulness, and license beyond example, brood already upon us. Unwieldy and immense, who shall hold in behemoth? who bridle leviathan? Flaunt it as we choose, athwart and over the roads of our progress loom huge uncertainty, and dreadful, threatening gloom. It is useless to deny it: Democracy grows rankly up the thickest, noxious, deadliest plants and fruits of all—brings worse and worse invaders—needs newer, larger, stronger, keener compensations and compellers.

Our lands, embracing so much, (embracing indeed the whole, rejecting none,) hold in their breast that flame also, capable of consuming themselves, consuming us all. Short as the span of our national life has been, already have death and downfall crowded close upon us—and will again crowd close, no doubt, even if warded off. Ages to come may never know, but I know, how narrowly during the late secession war—and more than once, and more than twice or thrice—our Nationality, (wherein bound up, as in a ship in a storm, depended, and yet depend, all our best life, all hope, all value,) just grazed, just by a hair escaped destruction. Alas! to think of them! the agony and bloody sweat of certain of those hours! those cruel, sharp, suspended crises!

Even to-day, amid these whirls, incredible flippancy, and blind fury of parties, infidelity, entire lack of first-class captains and leaders, added to the plentiful meanness and vulgarity of the ostensible masses—that problem, the labor question, beginning to open like a yawning gulf, rapidly widening every year—what prospect have we? We sail a dangerous sea of seething currents, cross and undercurrents, vortices—all so dark, untried—and whither shall we turn? It seems as if the Almighty had spread before this nation charts of imperial destinies, dazzling as the sun, yet with many a deep intestine difficulty, and human aggregate of cankerous imperfection,— saying, lo! the roads, the only plans of development, long and varied with all terrible balks and ebullitions. You said in your soul, I will be empire of empires, overshadowing all else, past and present, putting the history of old-world dynasties, conquests behind me, as of no account—making a new history, a history of democracy, making old history a dwarf—I alone inaugurating largeness, culminating time. If these, O lands of America, are indeed the prizes, the determinations of your soul, be it so. But behold the cost, and already specimens of the cost. Thought you greatness was to ripen for you like a pear? If you would have greatness, know that you must conquer it through ages, centuries—must pay for it with a proportionate price. For you too, as for all lands, the struggle, the traitor, the wily person in office, scrofulous wealth, the surfeit of prosperity, the demonism of greed, the hell of passion, the decay of faith, the long postponement, the fossil-like lethargy, the ceaseless need of revolutions, prophets, thunderstorms, deaths, births, new projections and invigorations of ideas and men.

Yet I have dream'd, merged in that hidden-tangled problem of our fate, whose long unraveling stretches mysteriously through time —dream'd out, portray'd, hinted already—a little or a larger band— a band of brave and true, unprecedented yet—arm'd and equipt at every point—the members separated, it may be, by different dates and States, or south, or north, or east, or west—Pacific, Atlantic, Southern, Canadian—a year, a century here, and other centuries there—but always one, compact in soul, conscience-conserving, God-inculcating, inspired achievers, not only in literature, the greatest art, but achievers in all art—a new, undying order, dynasty, from age to age transmitted—a band, a class, at least as fit to cope with current years, our dangers, needs, as those who, for their times, so long, so well, in armor or in cowl, upheld and made illustrious, that far-back feudal, priestly world. To offset chivalry, indeed, those vanish'd countless knights, old altars, abbeys, priests, ages and strings of ages, a knightlier and more sacred cause to-day demands, and shall supply, in a New World, to larger, grander work, more than the counterpart and tally of them.

Arrived now, definitely, at an apex for these Vistas, I confess that the promulgation and belief in such a class or institution—a new and greater literatus order—its possibility, (nay certainty,) underlies these entire speculations—and that the rest, the other parts, as superstructures, are all founded upon it. It really seems to me the condition, not only of our future national and democratic development, but of our perpetuation. In the highly artificial and materialistic bases of modern civilization, with the corresponding arrangements and methods of living, the force-infusion of intellect alone, the depraving influences of riches just as much as poverty, the absence of all high ideals in character—with the long series of tendencies, shapings, which few are strong enough to resist, and which now seem, with steam-engine speed, to be everywhere turning out the generations of humanity like uniform iron castings—all of which, as compared with the feudal ages, we can yet do nothing better than accept, make the best of, and even welcome, upon the whole, for their oceanic practical grandeur, and their restless wholesale kneading of the masses—I say of all this tremendous and dominant play of solely materialistic bearings upon current life in the United States, with the results as already seen, accumulating, and reaching far into the future, that they must either be confronted and met by at least an equally subtle and tremendous force-infusion for purposes of spiritualization, for the pure conscience, for genuine esthetics, and for absolute and primal manliness and womanliness—or else our modern civilization, with all its improvements, is in vain, and we are on the road to a destiny, a status, equivalent, in its real world, to that of the fabled damned.

Prospecting thus the coming unsped days, and that new order in them—marking the endless train of exercise, development, unwind, in nation as in man, which life is for—we see, fore-indicated, amid these prospects and hopes, new law-forces of spoken and written language—not merely the pedagogue-forms, correct, regular, familiar with precedents, made for matters of outside propriety, fine words, thoughts definitely told out—but a language fann'd by the breath of Nature, which leaps overhead, cares mostly for impetus and effects, and for what it plants and invigorates to grow—tallies life and character, and seldomer tells a thing than suggests or necessitates it. In fact, a new theory of literary composition for imaginative works of the very first class, and especially for highest poems, is the sole course open to these States. Books are to be call'd for, and supplied, on the assumption that the process of reading is not a half-sleep, but, in highest sense, an exercise, a gymnast's struggle; that the reader is to do something for himself, must be on the alert, must himself or herself construct indeed the poem, argument, history, metaphysical essay—the text furnishing the hints, the clue, the start or frame-work. Not the book needs so much to be the complete thing, but the reader of the book does. That were to make a nation of supple and athletic minds, well-train'd, intuitive, used to depend on themselves, and not on a few coteries of writers.

Investigating here, we see, not that it is a little thing we have, in having the bequeath'd libraries, countless shelves of volumes, records, &c.; yet how serious the danger, depending entirely on them, of the bloodless vein, the nerveless arm, the false application, at second or third hand. We see that the real interest of this people of ours in the theology, history, poetry, politics, and personal models of the past, (the British islands, for instance, and indeed all the past,) is not necessarily to mould ourselves or our literature upon them, but to attain fuller, more definite comparisons, warnings, and the insight to ourselves, our own present, and our own far grander, different, future history, religion, social customs, &c. We see that almost everything that has been written, sung, or stated, of old, with reference to humanity under the feudal and oriental institutes, religions, and for other lands, needs to be re-written, re-sung, re-stated, in terms consistent with the institution of these States, and to come in range and obedient uniformity with them.

We see, as in the universes of the material kosmos, after meteorological, vegetable, and animal cycles, man at last arises, born through them, to prove them, concentrate them, to turn upon them with wonder and love—to command them, adorn them, and carry them upward into superior realms—so, out of the series of the preceding social and political universes, now arise these States. We see that while many were supposing things established and completed, really the grandest things always remain; and discover that the work of the New World is not ended, but only fairly begun.

We see our land, America, her literature, esthetics, &c., as, substantially, the getting in form, or effusement and statement, of deepest basic elements and loftiest final meanings, of history and man—and the portrayal, (under the eternal laws and conditions of beauty,) of our own physiognomy, the subjective tie and expression of the objective, as from our own combination, continuation, and points of view—and the deposit and record of the national mentality, character, appeals, heroism, wars, and even liberties—where these, and all, culminate in native literary and artistic formulation, to be perpetuated; and not having which native, first-class formulation, she will flounder about, and her other, however imposing, eminent greatness, prove merely a passing gleam; but truly having which, she will understand herself, live nobly, nobly contribute, emanate, and, swinging, poised safely on herself, illumin'd and illuming, become a full-form'd world, and divine Mother not only of material but spiritual worlds, in ceaseless succession through time—the main thing being the average, the bodily, the concrete, the democratic, the popular, on which all the superstructures of the future are to permanently rest.

$$\text{⇛⃝⃝}$$

NOTES

1. "From a territorial area of less than nine hundred thousand square miles, the Union has expanded into over four millions and a half—fifteen times larger than that of Great Britain and France combined—with a shore-line, including Alaska, equal to the entire circumference of the earth, and with a domain within these lines far wider than that of the Romans in their proudest days of conquest and renown. With a river, lake, and coastwise commerce estimated at over two thousand millions of dollars per year; with a railway traffic of four to six thousand millions per year, and the annual domestic exchanges of the country running up to nearly ten thousand millions per year; with over two thousand millions of dollars invested in manufacturing, mechanical, and mining industry; with over five hundred millions of acres of land in actual occupancy, valued, with their appurtenances, at over seven thousand millions of dollars, and producing annually crops valued at over three thousand millions of dollars; with a realm which, if the density of Belgium's population were possible, would be vast enough to include all the present inhabitants of the world; and with equal rights guaranteed to even the poorest and humblest of our forty millions of people—we can, with a manly pride akin to that which distinguish'd the palmiest days of Rome, claim," &c., &c., &c.—*Vice-President Colfax's Speech, July 4, 1870.*

LATER—*London "Times," (Weekly,) June 23, '82*

"The wonderful wealth-producing power of the United States defies and sets at naught the grave drawbacks of a mischievous protective tariff, and has already obliterated, almost wholly, the traces of the greatest of modern civil wars. What is especially remarkable in the present development of American energy and success is its wide and equable distribution. North and south, east and west, on the shores of the Atlantic and the Pacific, along the chain of the great lakes, in the valley of the Mississippi, and on the coasts of the gulf of Mexico, the creation of wealth and the increase of population are signally exhibited. It is quite true, as has been shown by the recent apportionment of population in the House of Representatives, that some sections of the Union have advanced, relatively to the rest, in an extraordinary and unexpected degree. But this does not imply that the States which have gain'd no additional representatives or have actually lost some have been stationary or have receded. The fact is that the present tide of prosperity has risen so high that it has overflow'd all barriers, and has fill'd up the back-waters, and establish'd something like an approach to uniform success."

2. See, for hereditaments, specimens, Walter Scott's Border Minstrelsy, Percy's collection, Ellis's early English Metrical Romances, the European continental poems of Walter of Aquitania, and the Nibelungen, of pagan stock, but monkish-feudal redaction; the history of the Troubadours, by Fauriel; even the far-back cumbrous old Hindu epics, as indicating the Asian eggs out of which European chivalry was hatch'd; Ticknor's chapters on the Cid, and on the Spanish poems and poets of Calderon's time. Then always, and, of course, as the superbest poetic culmination-expression of feudalism, the

260

Shaksperean dramas, in the attitudes, dialogue, characters, &c., of the princes, lords and gentlemen, the pervading atmosphere, the implied and express'd standard of manners, the high port and proud stomach, the regal embroidery of style, &c.

3. Of these rapidly-sketch'd hiatuses, the two which seem to me most serious are, for one, the condition, absence, or perhaps the singular abeyance, of moral conscientious fibre all through American society; and, for another, the appalling depletion of women in their powers of sane athletic maternity, their crowning attribute, and ever making the woman, in loftiest spheres, superior to the man.

I have sometimes thought, indeed, that the sole avenue and means of a reconstructed sociology depended, primarily, on a new birth, elevation, expansion, invigoration of woman, affording, for races to come, (as the conditions that antedate birth are indispensable,) a perfect motherhood. Great, great, indeed, far greater than they know, is the sphere of women. But doubtless the question of such new sociology all goes together, includes many varied and complex influences and premises, and the man as well as the woman, and the woman as well as the man.

4. The question hinted here is one which time only can answer. Must not the virtue of modern Individualism, continually enlarging, usurping all, seriously affect, perhaps keep down entirely, in America, the like of the ancient virtue of Patriotism, the fervid and absorbing love of general country? I have no doubt myself that the two will merge, and will mutually profit and brace each other, and that from them a greater product, a third, will arise. But I feel that at present they and their oppositions form a serious problem and paradox in the United States.

5. "Shooting Niagara."—I was at first roused to much anger and abuse by this essay from Mr. Carlyle, so insulting to the theory of America—but happening to think afterwards how I had more than once been in the like mood, during which his essay was evidently cast, and seen persons and things in the same light, (indeed some might say there are signs of the same feeling in these Vistas)—I have since read it again, not only as a study, expressing as it does certain judgments from the highest feudal point of view, but have read it with respect as coming from an earnest soul, and as contributing certain sharp-cutting metallic grains, which, if not gold or silver, may be good hard, honest iron.

6. For fear of mistake, I may as well distinctly specify, as cheerfully included in the model and standard of these Vistas, a practical, stirring, worldly, money-making, even materialistic character. It is undeniable that our farms, stores, offices, dry-goods, coal and groceries, enginery, cash-accounts, trades, earnings, markets, &c., should be attended to in earnest, and actively pursued, just as if they had a real and permanent existence. I perceive clearly that the extreme business energy, and this almost maniacal appetite for wealth prevalent in the United States, are parts of amelioration and progress, indispensably needed to prepare the very results I demand. My theory includes riches, and the getting of riches, and the amplest products, power, activity, inventions, movements, &c. Upon them, as upon substrata, I raise the edifice design'd in these Vistas.

7. The whole present system of the officering and personnel of the army and navy of these States, and the spirit and letter of their trebly-aristocratic rules and regulations, is a monstrous exotic, a nuisance and revolt, and belong here just as much as orders of nobility, or the Pope's council of cardinals. I say if the present theory of our army and navy is sensible and true, then the rest of America is an unmitigated fraud.

8. After the rest is satiated, all interest culminates in the field of persons, and never flags there. Accordingly in this field have the great poets and literatuses signally toil'd. They too, in all ages, all lands, have been creators, fashioning, making types of men and women, as Adam and Eve are made in the divine fable. Behold, shaped, bred by orientalism, feudalism, through their long growth and culmination, and breeding back in return—(when shall we have an equal series, typical of democracy?)—behold, commencing in primal Asia, (apparently formulated, in what beginning we know, in the gods of the mythologies, and coming down thence,) a few samples out of the countless product, bequeath'd to the moderns, bequeath'd to America as studies. For the men, Yudishtura, Rama, Arjuna, Solomon, most of the Old and New Testament characters; Achilles, Ulysses, Theseus, Prometheus, Hercules, Æneas, Plutarch's heroes; the Merlin of Celtic bards; the Cid, Arthur and his knights, Siegfried and Hagen in the Nibelungen; Roland and Oliver; Roustam in the Shah-Nemah; and so on to Milton's Satan, Cervantes' Don Quixote, Shakspere's Hamlet, Richard II., Lear, Marc Antony, &c., and the modern Faust. These, I say, are models, combined, adjusted to other standards than America's, but of priceless value to her and hers.

Among women, the goddesses of the Egyptian, Indian and Greek mythologies, certain Bible characters, especially the Holy Mother; Cleopatra, Penelope; the portraits of Brunhelde and Chriemhilde in the Nibelungen; Oriana, Una, &c., the modern Consuelo, Walter Scott's Jeanie and Effie Deans, &c., &c. (Yet woman portray'd or outlin'd at her best, or as perfect human mother, does not hitherto, it seems to me, fully appear in literature.)

9. Note, to-day, an instructive, curious spectacle and conflict. Science, (twin, in its fields, of Democracy in its)—Science, testing absolutely all thoughts, all works, has already burst well upon the world—a sun, mounting, most illuminating, most glorious—surely never again to set. But against it, deeply entrench'd, holding possession, yet remains, (not only through the churches and schools, but by imaginative literature, and unregenerate poetry,) the fossil theology of the mythic-materialistic, superstitious, untaught and credulous, fable-loving, primitive ages of humanity.

10. It is to the development, identification, and general prevalence of that fervid comradeship, (the adhesive love, at least rivaling the amative love hitherto possessing imaginative literature, if not going beyond it,) that I look for the counterbalance and offset of our materialistic and vulgar American democracy, and for the spiritualization thereof. Many will say it is a dream, and will not follow my inferences: but I confidently expect a time when there will be seen, running like a half-hid warp through all the myriad audible and visible worldly interests of America, threads of manly friendship, fond and loving, pure and sweet, strong and life-long, carried to degrees hitherto unknown—not only giving tone to individual character, and making it unprecedently emotional, muscular, heroic, and refined, but having the deepest relations to general politics. I say democracy infers such loving comradeship, as its most inevitable twin or counterpart, without which it will be incomplete, in vain, and incapable of perpetuating itself.

11. I am reminded as I write that out of this very conscience, or idea of conscience, of intense moral right, and in its name and strain'd construction, the worst fanaticisms, wars, persecutions, murders, &c., have yet, in all lands, in the past, been broach'd, and have come to their devilish fruition. Much is to be said—but I may say here, and in response, that side by side with the unflagging stimulation of the elements of religion and conscience must henceforth move with equal sway, science, absolute reason, and the general proportionate development of the whole man. These scientific facts, deduc-

tions, are divine too—precious counted parts of moral civilization, and, with physical health, indispensable to it, to prevent fanaticism. For abstract religion, I perceive, is easily led astray, ever credulous, and is capable of devouring, remorseless, like fire and flame. Conscience, too, isolated from all else, and from the emotional nature, may but attain the beauty and purity of glacial, snowy ice. We want, for these States, for the general character, a cheerful, religious fervor, endued with the ever-present modifications of the human emotions, friendship, benevolence, with a fair field for scientific inquiry, the right of individual judgment, and always the cooling influences of material Nature.

12. The culmination and fruit of literary artistic expression, and its final fields of pleasure for the human soul, are in metaphysics, including the mysteries of the spiritual world, the soul itself, and the question of the immortal continuation of our identity. In all ages, the mind of man has brought up here —and always will. Here, at least, of whatever race or era, we stand on common ground. Applause, too, is unanimous, antique or modern. Those authors who work well in this field—though their reward, instead of a handsome percentage, or royalty, may be but simply the laurel-crown of the victors in the great Olympic games—will be dearest to humanity, and their works, however esthetically defective, will be treasur'd forever. The altitude of literature and poetry has always been religion—and always will be. The Indian Vedas, the Naçkas of Zoroaster, the Talmud of the Jews, the Old Testament, the Gospel of Christ and his disciples, Plato's works, the Koran of Mohammed, the Edda of Snorro, and so on toward our own day, to Swedenborg, and to the invaluable contributions of Leibnitz, Kant and Hegel—these, with such poems only in which, (while singing well of persons and events, of the passions of man, and the shows of the material universe,) the religious tone, the consciousness of mystery, the recognition of the future, of the unknown, of Deity over and under all, and of the divine purpose, are never absent, but indirectly give tone to all—exhibit literature's real heights and elevations, towering up like the great mountains of the earth. Standing on this ground—the last, the highest, only permanent ground— and sternly criticising, from it, all works, either of the literary, or any art, we have peremptorily to dismiss every pretensive production, however fine its esthetic or intellectual points, which violates or ignores, or even does not celebrate, the central divine idea of All, suffusing universe, of eternal trains of purpose, in the development, by however slow degrees, of the physical, moral, and spiritual kosmos. I say he has studied, meditated to no profit, whatever may be his mere erudition, who has not absorb'd this simple consciousness and faith. It is not entirely new—but it is for Democracy to elaborate it, and look to build upon and expand from it, with uncompromising reliance. Above the doors of teaching the inscription is to appear, Though little or nothing can be absolutely known, perceiv'd, except from a point of view which is evanescent, yet we know at least one permanency, that Time and Space, in the will of God, furnish successive chains, completions of material births and beginnings, solve all discrepancies, fears and doubts, and eventually fulfil happiness—and that the prophecy of those births, namely spiritual results, throws the true arch over all teaching, all science. The local considerations of sin, disease, deformity, ignorance, death, &c., and their measurement by the superficial mind, and ordinary legislation and theology, are to be met by science, boldly accepting, promulging this faith, and planting the seeds of superber laws—of the explication of the physical universe through the spiritual—and clearing the way for a religion, sweet and unimpugnable alike to little child or great savan.

ORIGINS of ATTEMPTED SECESSION

*Not the whole matter, but some side facts worth conning to-day
and any day*

I CONSIDER the war of attempted secession, 1860–65, not as a struggle
of two distinct and separate peoples, but a conflict (often happening,
and very fierce) between the passions and paradoxes of one and the
same identity—perhaps the only terms on which that identity could
really become fused, homogeneous and lasting. The origin and conditions out of which it arose, are full of lessons, full of warnings yet to
the Republic—and always will be. The underlying and principal of
those origins are yet singularly ignored. The Northern States were
really just as responsible for that war, (in its precedents, foundations,
instigations,) as the South. Let me try to give my view. From the age
of 21 to 40, (1840–'60,) I was interested in the political movements of
the land, not so much as a participant, but as an observer, and a regular voter at the elections. I think I was conversant with the springs
of action, and their workings, not only in New York city and Brooklyn, but understood them in the whole country, as I have made leisurely tours through all the middle States, and partially through the
western and southern, and down to New Orleans, in which city I resided for some time. (I was there at the close of the Mexican war—saw
and talk'd with General Taylor, and the other generals and officers,
who were fêted and detain'd several days on their return victorious
from that expedition.)

Of course many and very contradictory things, specialties, developments, constitutional views, &c., went to make up the origin of the war
—but the most significant general fact can be best indicated and stated
as follows: For twenty-five years previous to the outbreak, the controling "Democratic" nominating conventions of our Republic—starting
from their primaries in wards or districts, and so expanding to counties, powerful cities, States, and to the great Presidential nominating
conventions—were getting to represent and be composed of more and
more putrid and dangerous materials. Let me give a schedule, or list,
of one of these representative conventions for a long time before, and
inclusive of, that which nominated Buchanan. (Remember they had
come to be the fountains and tissues of the American body politic,
forming, as it were, the whole blood, legislation, office-holding, &c.)
One of these conventions, from 1840 to '60, exhibited a spectacle such

as could never be seen except in our own age and in these States. The members who composed it were, seven-eighths of them, the meanest kind of bawling and blowing office-holders, office-seekers, pimps, malignants, conspirators, murderers, fancy-men, custom-house clerks, contractors, kept-editors, spaniels well-train'd to carry and fetch, jobbers, infidels, disunionists, terrorists, mail-riflers, slave-catchers, pushers of slavery, creatures of the President, creatures of would-be Presidents, spies, bribers, compromisers, lobbyers, sponges, ruin'd sports, expell'd gamblers, policy-backers, monte-dealers, duellists, carriers of conceal'd weapons, deaf men, pimpled men, scarr'd inside with vile disease, gaudy outside with gold chains made from the people's money and harlots' money twisted together; crawling, serpentine men, the lousy combings and born freedom-sellers of the earth. And whence came they? From back-yards and bar-rooms; from out of the custom-houses, marshals' offices, post-offices, and gambling-hells; from the President's house, the jail, the station-house; from unnamed by-places, where devilish disunion was hatch'd at midnight; from political hearses, and from the coffins inside, and from the shrouds inside of the coffins; from the tumors and abscesses of the land; from the skeletons and skulls in the vaults of the federal alms-houses; and from the running sores of the great cities. Such, I say, form'd, or absolutely control'd the forming of, the entire personnel, the atmosphere, nutriment and chyle, of our municipal, State, and National politics—substantially permeating, handling, deciding, and wielding everything—legislation, nominations, elections, "public sentiment," &c.—while the great masses of the people, farmers, mechanics, and traders, were helpless in their gripe. These conditions were mostly prevalent in the north and west, and especially in New York and Philadelphia cities; and the southern leaders, (bad enough, but of a far higher order,) struck hands and affiliated with, and used them. Is it strange that a thunder-storm follow'd such morbid and stifling cloud-strata?

I say then, that what, as just outlined, heralded, and made the ground ready for secession revolt, ought to be held up, through all the future, as the most instructive lesson in American political history—the most significant warning and beacon-light to coming generations. I say that the sixteenth, seventeenth and eighteenth terms of the American Presidency have shown that the villainy and shallowness of rulers (back'd by the machinery of great parties) are just as eligible to these States as to any foreign despotism, kingdom, or empire—there is not a bit of difference. History is to record those three Presidentiads, and especially the administrations of Fillmore and Buchanan, as so far our topmost warning and shame. Never were publicly display'd more deform'd, mediocre, snivelling, unreliable, false-hearted men.

Never were these States so insulted, and attempted to be betray'd. All the main purposes for which the government was establish'd were openly denied. The perfect equality of slavery with freedom was flauntingly preach'd in the north—nay, the superiority of slavery. The slave trade was proposed to be renew'd. Everywhere frowns and mis-understandings—everywhere exasperations and humiliations. (The slavery contest is settled—and the war is long over—yet do not those putrid conditions, too many of them, still exist? still result in diseases, fevers, wounds—not of war and army hospitals—but the wounds and diseases of peace?)

Out of those generic influences, mainly in New York, Pennsylvania, Ohio, &c., arose the attempt at disunion. To philosophical examina-tion, the malignant fever of that war shows its embryonic sources, and the original nourishment of its life and growth, in the north. I say secession, below the surface, originated and was brought to maturity in the free States. I allude to the score of years preceding 1860. My deliberate opinion is now, that if at the opening of the contest the abstract duality-question of *slavery and quiet* could have been sub-mitted to a direct popular vote, as against their opposite, they would have triumphantly carried the day in a majority of the northern States —in the large cities, leading off with New York and Philadelphia, by tremendous majorities. The events of '61 amazed everybody north and south, and burst all prophecies and calculations like bubbles. But even then, and during the whole war, the stern fact remains that (not only did the north put it down, but) *the secession cause had numeri-cally just as many sympathizers in the free as in the rebel States.*

As to slavery, abstractly and practically, (its idea, and the determi-nation to establish and expand it, especially in the new territories, the future America,) it is too common, I repeat, to identify it exclusively with the south. In fact down to the opening of the war, the whole country had about an equal hand in it. The north had at least been just as guilty, if not more guilty; and the east and west had. The for-mer Presidents and Congresses had been guilty—the governors and legislatures of every northern State had been guilty, and the mayors of New York and other northern cities had all been guilty—their hands were all stain'd. And as the conflict took decided shape, it is hard to tell which class, the leading southern or northern disunionists, was more stunn'd and disappointed at the non-action of the free-state se-cession element, so largely existing and counted on by those leaders, both sections.

So much for that point, and for the north. As to the inception and direct instigation of the war, in the south itself, I shall not attempt interiors or complications. Behind all, the idea that it was from a

resolute and arrogant determination on the part of the extreme slave-
holders, the Calhounites, to carry the states rights' portion of the constitutional compact to its farthest verge, and nationalize slavery, or
else disrupt the Union, and found a new empire, with slavery for its
corner-stone, was and is undoubtedly the true theory. (If successful,
this attempt might—I am not sure, but it might—have destroy'd not
only our American republic, in anything like first-class proportions, in
itself and its prestige, but for ages at least, the cause of Liberty and
Equality everywhere—and would have been the greatest triumph of
reaction, and the severest blow to political and every other freedom,
possible to conceive. Its worst result would have inured to the southern States themselves.) That our national democratic experiment,
principle, and machinery, could triumphantly sustain such a shock,
and that the Constitution could weather it, like a ship a storm, and
come out of it as sound and whole as before, is by far the most signal
proof yet of the stability of that experiment, Democracy, and of those
principles, and that Constitution.

Of the war itself, we know in the ostent what has been done. The
numbers of the dead and wounded can be told or approximated, the
debt posted and put on record, the material events narrated, &c. Meantime, elections go on, laws are pass'd, political parties struggle, issue
their platforms, &c., just the same as before. But immensest results, not
only in politics, but in literature, poems, and sociology, are doubtless
waiting yet unform'd in the future. How long they will wait I cannot
tell. The pageant of history's retrospect shows us, ages since, all
Europe marching on the crusades, those arm'd uprisings of the people,
stirr'd by a mere idea, to grandest attempt—and, when once baffled in
it, returning at intervals, twice, thrice, and again. An unsurpass'd series
of revolutionary events, influences. Yet it took over two hundred years
for the seeds of the crusades to germinate, before beginning even to
sprout. Two hundred years they lay, sleeping, not dead, but dormant
in the ground. Then, out of them, unerringly, arts, travel, navigation,
politics, literature, freedom, the spirit of adventure, inquiry, all arose,
grew, and steadily sped on to what we see at present. Far back there,
that huge agitation-struggle of the crusades stands, as undoubtedly
the embryo, the start, of the high preëminence of experiment, civilization and enterprise which the European nations have since sustain'd, and of which these States are the heirs.

Another illustration—(history is full of them, although the war itself, the victory of the Union, and the relations of our equal States,
present features of which there are no precedents in the past.) The
conquest of England eight centuries ago, by the Franco-Normans—

the obliteration of the old, (in many respects so needing obliteration) —the Domesday Book, and the repartition of the land—the old impedimenta removed, even by blood and ruthless violence, and a new, progressive genesis establish'd, new seeds sown—time has proved plain enough that, bitter as they were, all these were the most salutary series of revolutions that could possibly have happen'd. Out of them, and by them mainly, have come, out of Albic, Roman and Saxon England —and without them could not have come—not only the England of the 500 years down to the present, and of the present—but these States. Nor, except for that terrible dislocation and overturn, would these States, as they are, exist to-day.

It is certain to me that the United States, by virtue of that war and its results, and through that and them only, are now ready to enter, and most certainly enter, upon their genuine career in history, as no more torn and divided in their spinal requisites, but a great homogeneous Nation—free states all—a moral and political unity in variety, such as Nature shows in her grandest physical works, and as much greater than any mere work of Nature, as the moral and political, the work of man, his mind, his soul, are, in their loftiest sense, greater than the merely physical. Out of that war not only has the nationalty of the States escaped from being strangled, but more than any of the rest, and, in my opinion, more than the north itself, the vital heart and breath of the south have escaped us from the pressure of a general nightmare, and are henceforth to enter on a life, development, and active freedom, whose realities are certain in the future, notwithstanding all the southern vexations of the hour—a development which could not possibly have been achiev'd on any less terms, or by any other means than that grim lesson, or something equivalent to it. And I predict that the south is yet to outstrip the north.

—»»‹‹‹—

PREFACE, 1855,

to first issue OF "LEAVES OF GRASS"

Brooklyn, N. Y.

AMERICA does not repel the past, or what the past has produced under its forms, or amid other politics, or the idea of castes, or the old religions—accepts the lessons with calmness—is not impatient because the slough still sticks to opinions and manners and literature, while the life which served its requirements has passed into the new life of the new forms—perceives that the corpse is slowly borne from the eating and sleeping rooms of the house—perceives that it waits a little while in the door—that it was fittest for its days—that its action has descended to the stalwart and well-shaped heir who approaches—and that he shall be fittest for his days.

The Americans of all nations at any time upon the earth, have probably the fullest poetical nature. The United States themselves are essentially the greatest poem. In the history of the earth hitherto, the largest and most stirring appear tame and orderly to their ampler largeness and stir. Here at last is something in the doings of man that corresponds with the broadcast doings of the day and night. Here is action untied from strings, necessarily blind to particulars and details, magnificently moving in masses. Here is the hospitality which for ever indicates heroes. Here the performance, disdaining the trivial, unapproach'd in the tremendous audacity of its crowds and groupings, and the push of its perspective, spreads with crampless and flowing breadth, and showers its prolific and splendid extravagance. One sees it must indeed own the riches of the summer and winter, and need never be bankrupt while corn grows from the ground, or the orchards drop apples, or the bays contain fish, or men beget children upon women.

Other states indicate themselves in their deputies—but the genius of the United States is not best or most in its executives or legislatures, nor in its ambassadors or authors, or colleges or churches or parlors, nor even in its newspapers or inventors—but always most in the common people, south, north, west, east, in all its States, through all its mighty amplitude. The largeness of the nation, however, were monstrous without a corresponding largeness and generosity of the spirit of the citizen. Not swarming states, nor streets and steamships, nor prosperous business, nor farms, nor capital, nor learning, may suffice for the ideal of man—nor suffice the poet. No reminiscences may suffice either. A live nation can always cut a deep mark, and can have the best authority the cheapest—namely, from its own soul. This is the sum of the profitable uses of individuals or states, and of present action and grandeur, and of the subjects of poets. (As if it were necessary to trot back generation after generation to the eastern records! As if the beauty and sacredness of the demonstrable must fall behind that of the mythical! As if men do not make their mark out of any times! As if the opening of the western continent by discovery, and what has transpired in North and South America, were less than the small theatre of the antique, or the aimless sleep-walking of the middle ages!) The pride of the United States leaves the wealth and finesse of the cities, and all returns of commerce and agriculture, and all the magnitude of geography or shows of exterior victory, to enjoy the sight and realization of full-sized men, or one full-sized man unconquerable and simple.

The American poets are to enclose old and new, for America is the race of races. The expression of the American poet is to be transcendent and new. It is to be indirect, and not direct or descriptive or epic. Its quality goes through these to much more. Let the age and wars of other nations be chanted, and their eras and characters be illustrated, and that finish the verse. Not so the great psalm of the republic. Here the theme is creative, and has vista. Whatever stagnates in the fiat of custom or obedience or legislation, the great poet never stagnates. Obedience does not master him, he masters it. High up out of reach he stands, turning a concentrated light—he turns the pivot with his finger—he baffles the swiftest runners as he stands, and easily overtakes and envelopes them. The time straying toward infidelity and confections and persiflage he withholds by steady faith. Faith is the antiseptic of the soul—it pervades the common people and preserves them—they never give up believing and expecting and trusting. There is that indescribable freshness and unconsciousness about an illiterate person, that humbles and mocks the power of the noblest expressive genius. The poet sees for a certainty how one not a great artist may be just as sacred and perfect as the greatest artist.

The power to destroy or remould is freely used by the greatest poet, but seldom the power of attack. What is past is past. If he does not expose superior models, and prove himself by every step he takes, he is not what is wanted. The presence of the great poet conquers—not parleying, or struggling, or any prepared attempts. Now he has passed that way, see after him! There is not left any vestige of despair, or misanthropy, or cunning, or exclusiveness, or the ignominy of a nativity or color, or delusion of hell or the necessity of hell—and no man thenceforward shall be degraded for ignorance or weakness or sin. The greatest poet hardly knows pettiness or triviality. If he breathes into anything that was before thought small, it dilates with the grandeur and life of the universe. He is a seer—he is individual—he is complete in himself—the others are as good as he, only he sees it, and they do not. He is not one of the chorus—he does not stop for any regulation—he is the president of regulation. What the eyesight does to the rest, he does to the rest. Who knows the curious mystery of the eyesight? The other senses corroborate themselves, but this is removed from any proof but its own, and foreruns the identities of the spiritual world. A single glance of it mocks all the investigations of man, and all the instruments and books of the earth, and all reasoning. What is marvellous? what is unlikely? what is impossible or baseless or vague —after you have once just open'd the space of a peach-pit, and given audience to far and near, and to the sunset, and had all things enter with electric swiftness, softly and duly, without confusion or jostling or jam?

The land and sea, the animals, fishes and birds, the sky of heaven and the orbs, the forests, mountains and rivers, are not small themes —but folks expect of the poet to indicate more than the beauty and dignity which always attach to dumb real objects—they expect him to indicate the path between reality and their souls. Men and women perceive the beauty well enough—probably as well as he. The passionate tenacity of hunters, woodmen, early risers, cultivators of gardens and orchards and fields, the love of healthy women for the manly form, seafaring persons, drivers of horses, the passion for light and the open air, all is an old varied sign of the unfailing perception of beauty, and of a residence of the poetic in out-door people. They can never be assisted by poets to perceive—some may, but they never can. The poetic quality is not marshal'd in rhyme or uniformity, or abstract addresses to things, nor in melancholy complaints or good precepts, but is the life of these and much else, and is in the soul. The profit of rhyme is that it drops seeds of a sweeter and more luxuriant rhyme, and of uniformity that it conveys itself into its own roots in the ground out of sight. The rhyme and uniformity of perfect poems show the free growth of metrical laws, and bud from them as unerringly and loosely as lilacs and roses on a bush, and take shapes as compact as the shapes of chestnuts and oranges, and melons and pears, and shed the perfume impalpable to form. The fluency and ornaments of the finest poems or music or orations or recitations, are not independent but dependent. All beauty comes from beautiful blood and a beautiful brain. If the greatnesses are in conjunction in a man or woman, it is enough—the fact will prevail through the universe; but the gaggery and gilt of a million years will not prevail. Who troubles himself about his ornaments or fluency is lost. This is what you shall do: Love the earth and sun and the animals, despise riches, give alms to every one that asks, stand up for the stupid and crazy, devote your income and labor to others, hate tyrants, argue not concerning God, have patience and indulgence toward the people, take off your hat to nothing known or unknown, or to any man or number of men—go freely with powerful uneducated persons, and with the young, and with the mothers of families—re-examine all you have been told in school or church or in any book, and dismiss whatever insults your own soul; and your very flesh shall be a great poem, and have the richest fluency, not only in its words, but in the silent lines of its lips and face, and between the lashes of your eyes, and in every motion and joint of your body. The poet shall not spend his time in unneeded work. He shall know that the ground is already plough'd and manured; others may not know it, but he shall. He shall go directly to the creation. His trust shall master the trust of everything he touches—and shall master all attachment.

The known universe has one complete lover, and that is the greatest poet. He consumes an eternal passion, and is indifferent which chance happens, and which possible contingency of fortune or misfortune, and persuades daily and hourly his delicious pay. What baulks or breaks others is fuel for his burning progress to contact and amorous joy. Other proportions of the reception of pleasure dwindle to nothing to his proportions. All expected from heaven or from the highest, he is rapport with in the sight of the daybreak, or the scenes of the winter woods, or the presence of children playing, or with his arm around the neck of a man or woman. His love above all love has leisure and expanse—he leaves room ahead of himself. He is no irresolute or suspicious lover—he is sure—he scorns intervals. His experience and the showers and thrills are not for nothing. Nothing can jar him—suffering and darkness cannot—death and fear cannot. To him complaint and jealousy and envy are corpses buried and rotten in the earth —he saw them buried. The sea is not surer of the shore, or the shore of the sea, than he is the fruition of his love, and of all perfection and beauty.

The fruition of beauty is no chance of miss or hit—it is as inevitable as life—it is exact and plumb as gravitation. From the eyesight proceeds another eyesight, and from the hearing proceeds another hearing, and from the voice proceeds another voice, eternally curious of the harmony of things with man. These understand the law of perfection in masses and floods—that it is profuse and impartial—that there is not a minute of the light or dark, nor an acre of the earth and sea, without it—nor any direction of the sky, nor any trade or employment, nor any turn of events. This is the reason that about the proper expression of beauty there is precision and balance. One part does not need to be thrust above another. The best singer is not the one who has the most lithe and powerful organ. The pleasure of poems is not in them that take the handsomest measure and sound.

Without effort, and without exposing in the least how it is done, the greatest poet brings the spirit of any or all events and passions and scenes and persons, some more and some less, to bear on your individual character as you hear or read. To do this well is to compete with the laws that pursue and follow Time. What is the purpose must surely be there, and the clue of it must be there—and the faintest indication is the indication of the best, and then becomes the clearest indication. Past and present and future are not disjoin'd but join'd. The greatest poet forms the consistence of what is to be, from what has been and is. He drags the dead out of their coffins and stands them again on their feet. He says to the past, Rise and walk before me that I may realize you. He learns the lesson—he places himself where the future becomes present. The greatest poet does not only dazzle his rays over character and scenes and passions—he finally ascends, and finishes all—he exhibits the pinnacles that no man can tell what they are for, or what is beyond—he glows a moment on the extremest verge. He is most wonderful in his last half-hidden smile or frown; by that flash of the moment of parting the one that sees it shall be encouraged or terrified afterward for many years. The greatest poet does not moralize or make applications of morals—he knows the soul. The soul has that measureless pride which consists in never acknowledging any lessons or deductions but its own. But it has sympathy as measureless as its pride, and the one balances the other, and neither can stretch too far while it stretches in company with the other. The inmost secrets of art sleep with the twain. The greatest poet has lain close betwixt both, and they are vital in his style and thoughts.

The art of art, the glory of expression and the sunshine of the light of letters, is simplicity. Nothing is better than simplicity—nothing can make up for excess, or for the lack of definiteness. To carry on the heave of impulse and pierce intellectual depths and give all subjects their articulations, are powers neither common nor very uncommon. But to speak in literature with the perfect rectitude and insouciance of the movements of animals, and the unimpeachableness of the sentiment of trees in the woods and grass by the roadside, is the flawless triumph of art. If you have look'd on him who has achiev'd it you have look'd on one of the masters of the artists of all nations and times.

You shall not contemplate the flight of the gray gull over the bay, or the mettlesome action of the blood horse, or the tall leaning of sunflowers on their stalk, or the appearance of the sun journeying through heaven, or the appearance of the moon afterward, with any more satisfaction than you shall contemplate him. The great poet has less a mark'd style, and is more the channel of thoughts and things without increase or diminution, and is the free channel of himself. He swears to his art, I will not be meddlesome, I will not have in my writing any elegance, or effect, or originality, to hang in the way between me and the rest like curtains. I will have nothing hang in the way, not the richest curtains. What I tell I tell for precisely what it is. Let who may exalt or startle or fascinate or soothe, I will have purposes as health or heat or snow has, and be as regardless of observation. What I experience or portray shall go from my composition without a shred of my composition. You shall stand by my side and look in the mirror with me.

The old red blood and stainless gentility of great poets will be proved by their unconstraint. A heroic person walks at his ease through and out of that custom or precedent or authority that suits him not. Of the traits of the brotherhood of first-class writers, savans, musicians, inventors and artists, nothing is finer than silent defiance advancing from new free forms. In the need of poems, philosophy, politics, mechanism, science, behavior, the craft of art, an appropriate native grand opera, shipcraft, or any craft, he is greatest for ever and ever who contributes the greatest original practical example. The cleanest expression is that which finds no sphere worthy of itself, and makes one.

The messages of great poems to each man and woman are, Come to us on equal terms, only then can you understand us. We are no better than you, what we inclose you inclose, what we enjoy you may enjoy. Did you suppose there could be only one Supreme? We affirm there can be unnumber'd Supremes, and that one does not countervail another any more than one eyesight countervails another —and that men can be good or grand only of the consciousness of their supremacy within them. What do you think is the grandeur of storms and dismemberments, and the deadliest battles and wrecks, and the wildest fury of the elements, and the power of the sea, and the motion of nature, and the throes of human desires, and dignity and hate and love? It is that something in the soul which says, Rage on, whirl on, I tread master here and everywhere—Master of the spasms of the sky and of the shatter of the sea, Master of nature and passion and death, and of all terror and all pain.

The American bards shall be mark'd for generosity and affection, and for encouraging competitors. They shall be Kosmos, without monopoly or secrecy, glad to pass anything to any one—hungry for equals night and day. They shall not be careful of riches and privilege—they shall be riches and privilege—they shall perceive who the most affluent man is. The most affluent man is he that confronts all the shows he sees by equivalents out of the stronger wealth of himself. The American bard shall delineate no class of persons, nor one or two out of the strata of interests, nor love most nor truth most, nor the soul most, nor the body most—and not be for the Eastern states more than the Western, or the Northern states more than the Southern.

Exact science and its practical movements are no checks on the greatest poet, but always his encouragement and support. The outset and remembrance are there—there the arms that lifted him first, and braced him best—there he returns after all his goings and comings. The sailor and traveler—the anatomist, chemist, astronomer, geologist, phrenologist, spiritualist, mathematician, historian, and lexicographer, are not poets, but they are the lawgivers of poets, and their construction underlies the structure of every perfect poem. No matter what rises or is utter'd, they sent the seed of the conception of it—of them and by them stand the visible proofs of souls. If there shall be love and content between the father and the son, and if the greatness of the son is the exuding of the greatness of the father, there shall be love between the poet and the man of demonstrable science. In the beauty of poems are henceforth the tuft and final applause of science.

Great is the faith of the flush of knowledge, and of the investigation of the depths of qualities and things. Cleaving and circling here swells the soul of the poet, yet is president of itself always. The depths are fathomless, and therefore calm. The innocence and nakedness are resumed—they are neither modest nor immodest. The whole theory of the supernatural, and all that was twined with it or educed out of it, departs as a dream. What has ever happen'd—what happens, and whatever may or shall happen, the vital laws inclose all. They are sufficient for any case and for all cases—none to be hurried or retarded—any special miracle of affairs or persons inadmissible in the vast clear scheme where every motion and every spear of grass, and the frames and spirits of men and women and all that concerns them, are unspeakably perfect miracles, all referring to all, and each distinct and in its place. It is also not consistent with the reality of the soul to admit that there is anything in the known universe more divine than men and women.

Men and women, and the earth and all upon it, are to be taken as they are, and the investigation of their past and present and future shall be unintermitted, and shall be done with perfect candor. Upon this basis philosophy speculates, ever looking towards the poet, ever regarding the eternal tendencies of all toward happiness, never inconsistent with what is clear to the senses and to the soul. For the eternal tendencies of all toward happiness make the only point of sane philosophy. Whatever comprehends less than that—whatever is less than the laws of light and of astronomical motion—or less than the laws that follow the thief, the liar, the glutton and the drunkard, through this life and doubtless afterward—or less than vast stretches of time, or the slow formation of density, or the patient upheaving of strata— is of no account. Whatever would put God in a poem or system of philosophy as contending against some being or influence, is also of no account. Sanity and ensemble characterize the great master—spoilt in one principle, all is spoilt. The great master has nothing to do with miracles. He sees health for himself in being one of the mass—he sees the hiatus in singular eminence. To the perfect shape comes common ground. To be under the general law is great, for that is to correspond with it. The master knows that he is unspeakably great, and that all are unspeakably great—that nothing, for instance, is greater than to conceive children, and bring them up well—that to *be* is just as great as to perceive or tell.

In the make of the great masters the idea of political liberty is indispensable. Liberty takes the adherence of heroes wherever man and woman exist—but never takes any adherence or welcome from the rest more than from poets. They are the voice and exposition of liberty. They out of ages are worthy the grand idea—to them it is confided, and they must sustain it. Nothing has precedence of it, and nothing can warp or degrade it.

As the attributes of the poets of the kosmos concentre in the real body, and in the pleasure of things, they possess the superiority of genuineness over all fiction and romance. As they emit themselves, facts are shower'd over with light—the daylight is lit with more volatile light—the deep between the setting and rising sun goes deeper many fold. Each precise object or condition or combination or process exhibits a beauty—the multiplication table its—old age its—the carpenter's trade its—the grand opera its—the huge-hull'd clean-shap'd New York clipper at sea under steam or full sail gleams with unmatch'd beauty—the American circles and large harmonies of government gleam with theirs—and the commonest definite intentions and actions with theirs. The poets of the kosmos advance through all interpositions and coverings and turmoils and stratagems to first principles. They are of use—they dissolve poverty from its need, and riches from its conceit. You large proprietor, they say, shall not realize or perceive more than any one else. The owner of the library is not he who holds a legal title to it, having bought and paid for it. Any one and every one is owner of the library, (indeed he or she alone is owner,) who can read the same through all the varieties of tongues and subjects and styles, and in whom they enter with ease, and make supple and powerful and rich and large.

These American States, strong and healthy and accomplish'd, shall receive no pleasure from violations of natural models, and must not permit them. In paintings or mouldings or carvings in mineral or wood, or in the illustrations of books or newspapers, or in the patterns of woven stuffs, or anything to beautify rooms or furniture or costumes, or to put upon cornices or monuments, or on the prows or sterns of ships, or to put anywhere before the human eye indoors or out, that which distorts honest shapes, or which creates unearthly beings or places or contingencies, is a nuisance and revolt. Of the human form especially, it is so great it must never be made ridiculous. Of ornaments to a work nothing outre can be allow'd—but those ornaments can be allow'd that conform to the perfect facts of the open air, and that flow out of the nature of the work, and come irrepressibly from it, and are necessary to the completion of the work. Most works are most beautiful without ornament. Exaggerations will be revenged in human physiology. Clean and vigorous children are jetted and conceiv'd only in those communities where the models of natural forms are public every day. Great genius and the people of these States must never be demean'd to romances. As soon as histories are properly told, no more need of romances.

The great poets are to be known by the absence in them of tricks, and by the justification of perfect personal candor. All faults may be forgiven of him who has perfect candor. Henceforth let no man of us lie, for we have seen that openness wins the inner and outer world, and that there is no single exception, and that never since our earth gather'd itself in a mass have deceit or subterfuge or prevarication attracted its smallest particle or the faintest tinge of a shade—and that through the enveloping wealth and rank of a state, or the whole republic of states, a sneak or sly person shall be discover'd and despised —and that the soul has never once been fool'd and never can be fool'd —and thrift without the loving nod of the soul is only a fœtid puff— and there never grew up in any of the continents of the globe, nor upon any planet or satellite, nor in that condition which precedes the birth of babes, nor at any time during the changes of life, nor in any stretch of abeyance or action of vitality, nor in any process of formation or reformation anywhere, a being whose instinct hated the truth.

Extreme caution or prudence, the soundest organic health, large hope and comparison and fondness for women and children, large ali-

mentiveness and destructiveness and causality, with a perfect sense
of the oneness of nature, and the propriety of the same spirit applied
to human affairs, are called up of the float of the brain of the world to
be parts of the greatest poet from his birth out of his mother's womb,
and from her birth out of her mother's. Caution seldom goes far
enough. It has been thought that the prudent citizen was the citizen
who applied himself to solid gains, and did well for himself and for
his family, and completed a lawful life without debt or crime. The
greatest poet sees and admits these economies as he sees the economies of food and sleep, but has higher notions of prudence than to
think he gives much when he gives a few slight attentions at the latch
of the gate. The premises of the prudence of life are not the hospitality of it, or the ripeness and harvest of it. Beyond the independence
of a little sum laid aside for burial-money, and of a few clap-boards
around and shingles overhead on a lot of American soil own'd, and
the easy dollars that supply the year's plain clothing and meals, the
melancholy prudence of the abandonment of such a great being as
a man is, to the toss and pallor of years of money-making, with all
their scorching days and icy nights, and all their stifling deceits and
underhand dodgings, or infinitesimals of parlors, or shameless stuffing
while others starve, and all the loss of the bloom and odor of the earth,
and of the flowers and atmosphere, and of the sea, and of the true
taste of the women and men you pass or have to do with in youth or
middle age, and the issuing sickness and desperate revolt at the close
of a life without elevation or naïveté, (even if you have achiev'd a
secure 10,000 a year, or election to Congress or the Governorship,)
and the ghastly chatter of a death without serenity or majesty, is the
great fraud upon modern civilization and forethought, blotching the
surface and system which civilization undeniably drafts, and moisten-
ing with tears the immense features it spreads and spreads with such
velocity before the reach'd kisses of the soul.

Ever the right explanation remains to be made about prudence. The
prudence of the mere wealth and respectability of the most esteem'd
life appears too faint for the eye to observe at all, when little and
large alike drop quietly aside at the thought of the prudence suitable
for immortality. What is the wisdom that fills the thinness of a year,
or seventy or eighty years—to the wisdom spaced out by ages, and
coming back at a certain time with strong reinforcements and rich
presents, and the clear faces of wedding-guests as far as you can look,
in every direction, running gaily toward you? Only the soul is of itself
—all else has reference to what ensues. All that a person does or thinks
is of consequence. Nor can the push of charity or personal force ever
be anything else than the profoundest reason, whether it brings argu-

America prepares with composure and good-will for the visitors that have sent word. It is not intellect that is to be their warrant and welcome. The talented, the artist, the ingenious, the editor, the statesman, the erudite, are not unappreciated—they fall in their place and do their work. The soul of the nation also does its work. It rejects none, it permits all. Only toward the like of itself will it advance half way. An individual is as superb as a nation when he has the qualities which make a superb nation. The soul of the largest and wealthiest and proudest nation may well go half-way to meet that of its poets.

PREFACE, 1872,

to "As a Strong Bird on Pinions Free,"
(now "Thou Mother with thy Equal Brood," in permanent ed'n)

THE impetus and ideas urging me, for some years past, to an utterance, or attempt at utterance, of New World songs, and an epic of Democracy, having already had their publish'd expression, as well as I can expect to give it, in "Leaves of Grass," the present and any future pieces from me are really but the surplusage forming after that volume, or the wake eddying behind it. I fulfill'd in that an imperious conviction, and the commands of my nature as total and irresistible as those which make the sea flow, or the globe revolve. But of this supplementary volume, I confess I am not so certain. Having from early manhood abandon'd the business pursuits and applications usual in my time and country, and obediently yielded myself up ever since to the impetus mention'd, and to the work of expressing those ideas, it may be that mere habit has got dominion of me, when there is no real need of saying any thing further. But what is life but an experiment? and mortality but an exercise? with reference to results beyond. And so shall my poems be. If incomplete here, and superfluous there, *n'importe*—the earnest trial and persistent exploration shall at least be mine, and other success failing shall be success enough. I have been more anxious, anyhow, to suggest the songs of vital endeavor and manly evolution, and furnish something for races of outdoor athletes, than to make perfect rhymes, or reign in the parlors. I ventur'd from the beginning my own way, taking chances—and would keep on venturing.

I will therefore not conceal from any persons, known or unknown to me, who take an interest in the matter, that I have the ambition of devoting yet a few years to poetic composition. The mighty present age! To absorb and express in poetry, anything of it—of its world—America—cities and States—the years, the events of our Nineteenth century—the rapidity of movement—the violent contrasts, fluctuations of light and shade, of hope and fear—the entire revolution made by science in the poetic method—these great new underlying facts and new ideas rushing and spreading everywhere;—truly a mighty age! As if in some colossal drama, acted again like those of old under the open sun, the Nations of our time, and all the characteristics of Civilization, seem hurrying, stalking across, flitting from wing to wing, gathering, closing up, toward some long-prepared, most tremendous denouement. Not to conclude the infinite scenas of the race's life and toil and happiness and sorrow, but haply that the boards be clear'd from oldest, worst incumbrances, accumulations, and Man resume the eternal play anew, and under happier, freer auspices. To me, the United States are important because in this colossal drama they are unquestionably designated for the leading parts, for many a century to come. In them history and humanity seem to seek to culminate. Our broad areas are even now the busy theatre of plots, passions, interests, and suspended problems, compared to which the intrigues of the past of Europe, the wars of dynasties, the scope of kings and kingdoms, and even the development of peoples, as hitherto, exhibit scales of measurement comparatively narrow and trivial. And on these areas of ours, as on a stage, sooner or later, something like an *eclaircissement* of all the past civilization of Europe and Asia is probably to be evolved.

The leading parts. Not to be acted, emulated here, by us again, that role till now foremost in history—not to become a conqueror nation, or to achieve the glory of mere military, or diplomatic, or commercial superiority—but to become the grand producing land of nobler men and women—of copious races, cheerful, healthy, tolerant, free—to become the most friendly nation, (the United States indeed)—the modern composite nation, form'd from all, with room for all, welcoming all immigrants—accepting the work of our own interior development, as the work fitly filling ages and ages to come;—the leading nation of peace, but neither ignorant nor incapable of being the leading nation of war;—not the man's nation only, but the woman's nation—a land of splendid mothers, daughters, sisters, wives.

Our America to-day I consider in many respects as but indeed a vast seething mass of *materials,* ampler, better, (worse also,) than previously known—eligible to be used to carry towards its crowning stage, and build for good, the great ideal nationality of the future, the nation of the body and the soul,[1]—no limit here to land, help, opportunities, mines, products, demands, supplies, &c.;—with (I think) our political organization, National, State, and Municipal, permanently establish'd, as far ahead as we can calculate—but, so far, no social, literary, religious, or esthetic organizations, consistent with our politics, or becoming to us—which organizations can only come, in time, through great democratic ideas, religion—through science, which now, like a new sunrise, ascending, begins to illuminate all—and through our own begotten poets and literatuses. (The moral of a late well-written book on civilization seems to be that the only real foundation-walls and bases—and also *sine qua non* afterward—of true and full civilization, is the eligibility and certainty of boundless products for feeding, clothing, sheltering everybody—perennial fountains of physical and domestic comfort, with intercommunication, and with civil and ecclesiastical freedom—and that then the esthetic and mental business will take care of itself. Well, the United States have established this basis, and upon scales of extent, variety, vitality, and continuity, rivaling those of Nature; and have now to proceed to build an edifice upon it. I say this edifice is only to be fitly built by new literatures, especially the poetic. I say a modern image-making creation is indispensable to fuse and express the modern political and scientific creations—and then the trinity will be complete.)

When I commenced, years ago, elaborating the plan of my poems, and continued turning over that plan, and shifting it in my mind through many years, (from the age of twenty-eight to thirty-five,) experimenting much, and writing and abandoning much, one deep purpose underlay the others, and has underlain it and its execution ever since—and that has been the religious purpose. Amid many changes, and a formulation taking far different shape from what I at first supposed, this basic purpose has never been departed from in the composition of my verses. Not of course to exhibit itself in the old ways, as in writing hymns or psalms with an eye to the church-pew, or to express conventional pietism, or the sickly yearnings of devotees, but in new ways, and aiming at the widest sub-bases and inclusions of humanity, and tallying the fresh air of sea and land. I will see, (said I to myself,) whether there is not, for my purposes as poet, a religion, and a sound religious germenancy in the average human race, at least in their modern development in the United States, and in the hardy common fibre and native yearnings and elements, deeper and larger, and affording more profitable returns, than all mere sects or churches—as boundless, joyous, and vital as Nature itself—a germenancy that has too long been unencouraged, unsung, almost unknown. With science, the old theology of the East, long in its dotage, begins evidently to die and disappear. But (to my mind) science—and may be such will prove its principal service—as evidently prepares the way for One indescribably grander—Time's young but perfect offspring—the new theology—heir of the West—lusty and loving, and wondrous beautiful. For America, and for to-day, just the same as any day, the supreme and final science is the science of God—what we call science being only its minister—as Democracy is, or shall be also. And a poet of America (I said) must fill himself with such thoughts, and chant his best out of them. And as those were the convictions and aims, for good or bad, of "Leaves of Grass," they are no less the intention of this volume. As there can be, in my opinion, no sane and complete personality, nor any grand and electric nationality, without the stock element of religion imbuing all the other elements, (like heat in chemistry, invisible itself, but the life of all visible life,) so there can be no poetry worthy the name without that element behind all. The time has certainly come to begin to discharge the idea of religion, in the United States, from mere ecclesiasticism, and from Sundays and churches and church-going, and assign it to that general position, chiefest, most indispensable, most exhilarating, to which the others are to be adjusted, inside of all human character, and education, and affairs. The people, especially the young men and women of America, must begin to learn that religion, (like poetry,) is something far, far different from what they supposed. It is, indeed, too important to the power and perpetuity of the New World to be consign'd any longer to the churches, old or new, Catholic or Protestant—Saint this, or Saint that. It must be consign'd henceforth to democracy *en masse,* and to literature. It must enter into the poems of the nation. It must make the nation.

The Four Years' War is over—and in the peaceful, strong, exciting, fresh occasions of to-day, and of the future, that strange, sad war is hurrying even now to be forgotten. The camp, the drill, the lines of sentries, the prisons, the hospitals,—(ah! the hospitals!)—all have passed away—all seem now like a dream. A new race, a young and lusty generation, already sweeps in with oceanic currents, obliterating the war, and all its scars, its mounded graves, and all its reminiscences of hatred, conflict, death. So let it be obliterated. I say the life of the present and the future makes undeniable demands upon us each and all, south, north, east, west. To help put the United States (even if only in imagination) hand in hand, in one unbroken circle in a chant—to rouse them to the unprecedented grandeur of the part they are to play, and are even now playing—to the thought of their great future, and the attitude conform'd to it—especially their great esthetic, moral, scientific future, (of which their vulgar material and political present is but as the preparatory tuning of instruments by an orchestra,) these, as hitherto, are still, for me, among my hopes, ambitions.

"Leaves of Grass," already publish'd, is, in its intentions, the song of a great composite *democratic individual,* male or female. And following on and amplifying the same purpose, I suppose I have in my mind to run through the chants of this volume, (if ever completed,) the thread-voice, more or less audible, of an aggregated, inseparable, unprecedented, vast, composite, electric *democratic nationality*.

Purposing, then, to still fill out, from time to time through years to come, the following volume, (unless prevented,) I conclude this preface to the first instalment of it, pencil'd in the open air, on my fifty-third birth-day, by wafting to you, dear reader, whoever you are, (from amid the fresh scent of the grass, the pleasant coolness of the forenoon breeze, the lights and shades of tree-boughs silently dappling and playing around me, and the notes of the cat-bird for undertone and accompaniment,) my true good-will and love.

W. W.

Washington, D. C., May 31, 1872.

>>>-<<<

NOTES

1. The problems of the achievements of this crowning stage through future first-class National Singers, Orators, Artists, and others—of creating in literature an *imaginative* New World, the correspondent and counterpart of the current Scientific and Political New Worlds,—and the perhaps distant, but still delightful prospect, (for our children, if not in our own day,) of delivering America, and, indeed, all Christian lands everywhere, from the thin moribund and watery, but appallingly extensive nuisance of conventional poetry —by putting something really alive and substantial in its place—I have undertaken to grapple with, and argue, in the preceding "Democratic Vistas."

PREFACE, 1876,

*to the two-volume Centennial Edition
of L. of G. and "Two Rivulets"*

AT THE eleventh hour, under grave illness, I gather up the pieces
of prose and poetry left over since publishing, a while since, my
first and main volume, "Leaves of Grass"—pieces, here, some new,
some old—nearly all of them (sombre as many are, making this
almost death's book) composed in by-gone atmospheres of perfect
health—and preceded by the freshest collection, the little "Two
Rivulets," now send them out, embodied in the present melange,
partly as my contribution and outpouring to celebrate, in some
sort, the feature of the time, the first centennial of our New World
nationality—and then as chyle and nutriment to that moral, indissoluble union, equally representing all, and the mother of many
coming cenennials.

And e'en for flush and proof of our America—for reminder, just
as much, or more, in moods of towering pride and joy, I keep my
special chants of death and immortality[1] to stamp the coloring-
finish of all, present and past. For terminus and temperer to all,
they were originally written; and that shall be their office at the
last.

For some reason—not explainable or definite to my own mind,
yet secretly pleasing and satisfactory to it—I have not hesitated to
embody in, and run through the volume, two altogether distinct
veins, or strata—politics for one, and for the other, the pensive
thought of immortality. Thus, too, the prose and poetic, the dual
forms of the present book. The volume, therefore, after its minor
episodes, probably divides into these two, at first sight far diverse,
veins of topic and treatment. Three points, in especial, have become
very dear to me, and all through I seek to make them again and
again, in many forms and repetitions, as will be seen: 1. That the
true growth-characteristics of the democracy of the New World
are henceforth to radiate in superior literary, artistic and religious
expressions, far more than in its republican forms, universal suffrage, and frequent elections, (though these are unspeakably important.) 2. That the vital political mission of the United States is,
to practically solve and settle the problem of two sets of rights—the
fusion, thorough compatibility and junction of individual State pre-

rogatives, with the indispensable necessity of centrality and Oneness —the national identity power—the sovereign Union, relentless, permanently comprising all, and over all, and in that never yielding an inch: then 3d. Do we not, amid a general malaria of fogs and vapors, our day, unmistakably see two pillars of promise, with grandest, indestructible indications—one, that the morbid facts of American politics and society everywhere are but passing incidents and flanges of our unbounded impetus of growth? weeds, annuals, of the rank, rich soil—not central, enduring, perennial things? The other, that all the hitherto experience of the States, their first century, has been but preparation, adolescence—and that this Union is only now and henceforth, (*i.e.* since the secession war,) to enter on its full democratic career?

Of the whole, poems and prose, (not attending at all to chronological order, and with original dates and passing allusions in the heat and impression of the hour, left shuffled in, and undisturb'd,) the chants of "Leaves of Grass," my former volume, yet serve as the indispensable deep soil, or basis, out of which, and out of which only, could come the roots and stems more definitely indicated by these later pages. (While that volume radiates physiology alone, the present one, though of the like origin in the main, more palpably doubtless shows the pathology which was pretty sure to come in time from the other.)

In that former and main volume, composed in the flush of my health and strength, from the age of 30 to 50 years, I dwelt on birth and life, clothing my ideas in pictures, days, transactions of my time, to give them positive place, identity—saturating them with that vehemence of pride and audacity of freedom necessary to loosen the mind of still-to-be-form'd America from the accumulated folds, the superstitions, and all the long, tenacious and stifling anti-democratic authorities of the Asiatic and European past—my enclosing purport being to express, above all artificial regulation and aid, the eternal bodily composite, cumulative, natural character of one's self.[2]

Estimating the American Union as so far, and for some time to come, in its yet formative condition, I bequeath poems and essays as nutriment and influences to help truly assimilate and harden, and especially to furnish something toward what the States most need of all, and which seems to me yet quite unsupplied in literature, namely, to show them, or begin to show them, themselves distinctively, and what they are for. For though perhaps the main points of all ages and nations are points of resemblance, and, even while granting evolution, are substantially the same, there are some vital things in which this Republic, as to its individualities, and as a compacted Nation, is to specially stand forth, and culminate modern humanity. And these are the very things it least morally and mentally knows—(though, curiously enough, it is at the same time faithfully acting upon them.)

I count with such absolute certainty on the great future of the United States—different from, though founded on, the past—that I have always invoked that future, and surrounded myself with it, before or while singing my songs. (As ever, all tends to followings —America, too, is a prophecy. What, even of the best and most successful, would be justified by itself alone? by the present, or the material ostent alone? Of men or States, few realize how much they live in the future. That, rising like pinnacles, gives its main significance to all You and I are doing to-day. Without it, there were little meaning in lands or poems—little purport in human lives. All ages, all Nations and States, have been such prophecies. But where any former ones with prophecy so broad, so clear, as our times, our lands—as those of the West?)

Without being a scientist, I have thoroughly adopted the conclusions of the great savans and experimentalists of our time, and of the last hundred years, and they have interiorly tinged the chyle of all my verse, for purposes beyond. Following the modern spirit, the real poems of the present, ever solidifying and expanding into the future, must vocalize the vastness and splendor and reality with which scientism has invested man and the universe, (all that is called creation,) and must henceforth launch humanity into new orbits, consonant with that vastness, splendor, and reality, (unknown to the old poems,) like new systems of orbs, balanced upon themselves, revolving in limitless space, more subtle than the stars. Poetry, so largely hitherto and even at present wedded to children's tales, and to mere amorousness, upholstery and superficial rhyme, will have to accept, and, while not denying the past, nor the themes of the past, will be revivified by this tremendous innovation, the kosmic spirit, which must henceforth, in my opinion, be the background and underlying impetus, more or less visible, of all first-class songs.

Only, (for me, at any rate, in all my prose and poetry,) joyfully accepting modern science, and loyally following it without the slightest hesitation, there remains ever recognized still a higher flight, a higher fact, the eternal soul of man, (of all else too,) the spiritual, the religious—which it is to be the greatest office of scientism, in my opinion, and of future poetry also, to free from fables, crudities and superstitions, and launch forth in renew'd faith and scope a hundred fold. To me, the worlds of religiousness, of the conception of the divine, and of the ideal, though mainly latent, are just as absolute in humanity and the universe as the world of chemistry, or anything in the objective worlds. To me

> *The prophet and the bard,*
> *Shall yet maintain themselves—in higher circles yet,*
> *Shall mediate to the modern, to democracy—interpret yet to them,*
> *God and eidólons.*

To me, the crown of savantism is to be, that it surely opens the way for a more splendid theology, and for ampler and diviner songs. No year, nor even century, will settle this. There is a phase of the real, lurking behind the real, which it is all for. There is also in the intellect of man, in time, far in prospective recesses, a judgment, a last appellate court, which will settle it.

In certain parts in these flights, or attempting to depict or suggest them, I have not been afraid of the charge of obscurity, in either of my two volumes—because human thought, poetry or melody, must leave dim escapes and outlets—must possess a certain fluid, aerial character, akin to space itself, obscure to those of little or no imagination, but indispensable to the highest purposes. Poetic style, when address'd to the soul, is less definite form, outline, sculpture, and becomes vista, music, half-tints, and even less than half-tints. True, it may be architecture; but again it may be the forest wild-wood, or the best effect thereof, at twilight, the waving oaks and cedars in the wind, and the impalpable odor.

Finally, as I have lived in fresh lands, inchoate, and in a revolutionary age, future-founding, I have felt to identify the points of that age, these lands, in my recitatives, altogether in my own way. Thus my form has strictly grown from my purports and facts, and is the analogy of them. Within my time the United States have emerged from nebulous vagueness and suspense, to full orbic, (though varied,) decision—have done the deeds and achiev'd the triumphs of half a score of centuries—and are henceforth to enter upon their real history—the way being now, (*i.e.* since the result of the Secession War,) clear'd of death-threatening impedimenta, and the free areas around and ahead of us assured and certain, which were not so before—(the past century being but preparations, trial

voyages and experiments of the ship, before her starting out upon
deep water.)

In estimating my volumes, the world's current times and deeds,
and their spirit, must be first profoundly estimated. Out of the hundred years just ending, (1776–1876,) with their genesis of inevitable
wilful events, and new experiments and introductions, and many
unprecedented things of war and peace, (to be realized better,
perhaps only realized, at the remove of a century hence;) out of
that stretch of time, and especially out of the immediately preceding
twenty-five years, (1850–75,) with all their rapid changes, innova-
tions, and audacious movements—and bearing their own inevitable
wilful birth-marks—the experiments of my poems too have found
genesis.

                                                    W. W.

                        ➤➤➤◄◄◄

NOTES

1. PASSAGE TO INDIA.—As in some ancient legend-play, to close the plot and the
   hero's career, there is a farewell gathering on ship's deck and on shore, a
   loosing of hawsers and ties, a spreading of sails to the wind—a starting out
   on unknown seas, to fetch up no one knows whither—to return no more—and
   the curtain falls, and there is the end of it—so I have reserv'd that poem, with
   its cluster, to finish and explain much that, without them, would not be explain'd, and to take leave, and escape for good, from all that has preceded
   them. (Then probably "Passage to India," and its cluster, are but freer vent
   and fuller expression to what, from the first, and so on throughout, more or
   less lurks in my writings, underneath every page, every line, everywhere.)
      I am not sure but the last inclosing sublimation of race or poem is, what it
   thinks of death. After the rest has been comprehended and said, even the
   grandest—after those contributions to mightiest nationality, or to sweetest
   song, or to the best personalism, male or female, have been glean'd from the
   rich and varied themes of tangible life, and have been fully accepted and
   sung, and the pervading fact of visible existence, with the duty it devolves,
   is rounded and apparently completed, it still remains to be really completed
   by suffusing through the whole and several, that other pervading invisible
   fact, so large a part, (is it not the largest part?) of life here, combining the
   rest, and furnishing, for person or State, the only permanent and unitary
   meaning to all, even the meanest life, consistently with the dignity of the
   universe, in Time. As from the eligibility to this thought, and the cheerful
   conquest of this fact, flash forth the first distinctive proofs of the soul, so to
   me, (extending it only a little further,) the ultimate Democratic purports,
   the ethereal and spiritual ones, are to concentrate here, and as fixed stars,
   radiate hence. For, in my opinion, it is no less than this idea of immortality,

above all other ideas, that is to enter into, and vivify, and give crowning religious stamp, to democracy in the New World.

It was originally my intention, after chanting in "Leaves of Grass" the songs of the body and existence, to then compose a further, equally needed volume, based on those convictions of perpetuity and conservation which, enveloping all precedents, make the unseen soul govern absolutely at last. I meant, while in a sort continuing the theme of my first chants, to shift the slides, and exhibit the problem and paradox of the same ardent and fully appointed personality entering the sphere of the resistless gravitation of spiritual law, and with cheerful face estimating death, not at all as the cessation, but as somehow what I feel it must be, the entrance upon by far the greatest part of existence, and something that life is at least as much for, as it is for itself. But the full construction of such a work is beyond my powers, and must remain for some bard in the future. The physical and the sensuous, in themselves or in their immediate continuations, retain holds upon me which I think are never entirely releas'd; and those holds I have not only not denied, but hardly wish'd to weaken.

Meanwhile, not entirely to give the go-by to my original plan, and far more to avoid a mark'd hiatus in it, than to entirely fulfil it, I end my books with thoughts, or radiations from thoughts, on death, immortality, and a free entrance into the spiritual world. In those thoughts, in a sort, I make the first steps or studies toward the mighty theme, from the point of view necessitated by my foregoing poems, and by modern science. In them I also seek to set the key-stone to my democracy's enduring arch. I recollate them now, for the press, in order to partially occupy and offset days of strange sickness, and the heaviest affliction and bereavement of my life; and I fondly please myself with the notion of leaving that cluster to you, O unknown reader of the future, as "something to remember me by," more especially than all else. Written in former days of perfect health, little did I think the pieces had the purport that now, under present circumstances, opens to me.

[As I write these lines, May 31, 1875, it is again early summer—again my birth-day—now my fifty-sixth. Amid the outside beauty and freshness, the sunlight and verdure of the delightful season, O how different the moral atmosphere amid which I now revise this Volume, from the jocund influence surrounding the growth and advent of "Leaves of Grass." I occupy myself, arranging these pages for publication, still envelopt in thoughts of the death two years since of my dear Mother, the most perfect and magnetic character, the rarest combination of practical, moral and spiritual, and the least selfish, of all and any I have ever known—and by me O so much the most deeply loved—and also under the physical affliction of a tedious attack of paralysis, obstinately lingering and keeping its hold upon me, and quite suspending all bodily activity and comfort.]

Under these influences, therefore, I still feel to keep "Passage to India" for last words even to this centennial dithyramb. Not as, in antiquity, at highest festival of Egypt, the noisome skeleton of death was sent on exhibition to the revelers, for zest and shadow to the occasion's joy and light—but as the marble statue of the normal Greeks at Elis, suggesting death in the form of a beautiful and perfect young man, with closed eyes, leaning on an inverted torch—emblem of rest and aspiration after action—of crown and point which all lives and poems should steadily have reference to, namely, the justified and noble termination of our identity, this grade of it, and outlet-preparation to another grade.

2. Namely, a character, making most of common and normal elements, to the superstructure of which not only the precious accumulations of the learning and experiences of the Old World, and the settled social and municipal necessities and current requirements, so long a-building, shall still faithfully contribute, but which at its foundations and carried up thence, and receiving its impetus from the democratic spirit, and accepting its gauge in all departments from the democratic formulas, shall again directly be vitalized by the perennial influences of Nature at first hand, and the old heroic stamina of Nature, the strong air of prairie and mountain, the dash of the briny sea, the primary antiseptics—of the passions, in all their fullest heat and potency, of courage, rankness, amativeness, and of immense pride. Not to lose at all, therefore, the benefits of artificial progress and civilization, but to re-occupy for Western tenancy the oldest though ever-fresh fields, and reap from them the savage and sane nourishment indispensable to a hardy nation, and the absence of which, threatening to become worse and worse, is the most serious lack and defect to-day of our New World literature.

Not but what the brawn of "Leaves of Grass" is, I hope, thoroughly spiritualized everywhere, for final estimate, but, from the very subjects, the direct effect is a sense of the life, as it should be, of flesh and blood, and physical urge, and animalism. While there are other themes, and plenty of abstract thoughts and poems in the volume—while I have put in it passing and rapid but actual glimpses of the great struggle between the nation and the slave-power, (1861–'65,) as the fierce and bloody panorama of that contest unroll'd itself: while the whole book, indeed, revolves around that four years' war, which, as I was in the midst of it, becomes, in "Drum-Taps," pivotal to the rest entire—and here and there, before and afterward, not a few episodes and speculations—*that*—namely, to make a type-portrait for living, active, worldly, healthy personality, objective as well as subjective, joyful and potent, and modern and free, distinctively for the use of the United States, male and female, through the long future—has been, I say, my general object. (Probably, indeed, the whole of these varied songs, and all my writings, both volumes, only ring changes in some sort, on the ejaculation, How vast, how eligible, how joyful, how real, is a human being, himself or herself.)

Though from no definite plan at the time, I see now that I have unconsciously sought, by indirections at least as much as directions, to express the whirls and rapid growth and intensity of the United States, the prevailing tendency and events of the Nineteenth century, and largely the spirit of the whole current world, my time; for I feel that I have partaken of that spirit, as I have been deeply interested in all those events, the closing of long-stretch'd eras and ages, and, illustrated in the history of the United States, the opening of larger ones. (The death of President Lincoln, for instance, fitly, historically closes, in the civilization of feudalism, many old influences—drops on them, suddenly, a vast, gloomy, as it were, separating curtain.)

Since I have been ill, (1873–74–75,) mostly without serious pain, and with plenty of time and frequent inclination to judge my poems, (never composed with eye on the book-market, nor for fame, nor for any pecuniary profit,) I have felt temporary depression more than once, for fear that in "Leaves of Grass" the *moral* parts were not sufficiently pronounc'd. But in my dearest and calmest moods I have realized that as those "Leaves," all and several, surely prepare the way for, and necessitate morals, and are adjusted to them, just the same as Nature does and is, they are what, consistently with my plan, they must and probably should be. (In a certain sense, while the

Moral is the purport and last intelligence of all Nature, there is absolutely nothing of the moral in the works, or laws, or shows of Nature. Those only lead inevitably to it—begin and necessitate it.)

Then I meant "Leaves of Grass," as publish'd, to be the Poem of average Identity, (of *yours*, whoever you are, now reading these lines.) A man is not greatest as victor in war, nor inventor or explorer, nor even in science, or in his intellectual or artistic capacity, or exemplar in some vast benevolence. To the highest democratic view, man is most acceptable in living well the practical life and lot which happens to him as ordinary farmer, sea-farer, mechanic, clerk, laborer, or driver—upon and from which position as a central basis or pedestal, while performing its labors, and his duties as citizen, son, husband, father and employ'd person, he preserves his physique, ascends, developing, radiating himself in other regions—and especially where and when, (greatest of all, and nobler than the proudest mere genius or magnate in any field,) he fully realizes the conscience, the spiritual, the divine faculty, cultivated well, exemplified in all his deeds and words, through life, uncompromising to the end—a flight loftier than any of Homer's or Shakspere's—broader than all poems and bibles—namely, Nature's own, and in the midst of it, Yourself, your own Identity, body and soul. (All serves, helps—but in the centre of all, absorbing all, giving, for your purpose, the only meaning and vitality to all, master or mistress of all, under the law, stands Yourself.) To sing the Song of that law of average Identity, and of Yourself, consistently with the divine law of the universal, is a main intention of those "Leaves."

Something more may be added—for, while I am about it, I would make a full confession. I also sent out "Leaves of Grass" to arouse and set flowing in men's and women's hearts, young and old, endless streams of living, pulsating love and friendship, directly from them to myself, now and ever. To this terrible, irrepressible yearning, (surely more or less down underneath in most human souls)—this never-satisfied appetite for sympathy, and this boundless offering of sympathy—this universal democratic comradeship—this old, eternal, yet ever-new interchange of adhesiveness, so fitly emblematic of America—I have given in that book, undisguisedly, declaredly, the openest expression. Besides, important as they are in my purpose as emotional expressions for humanity, the special meaning of the "Calamus" cluster of "Leaves of Grass," (and more or less running through the book, and cropping out in "Drum-Taps,") mainly resides in its political significance. In my opinion, it is by a fervent, accepted development of comradeship, the beautiful and sane affection of man for man, latent in all the young fellows, north and south, east and west—it is by this, I say, and by what goes directly and indirectly along with it, that the United States of the future, (I cannot too often repeat,) are to be most effectually welded together, intercalated, anneal'd into a living union.

Then, for enclosing clue of all, it is imperatively and ever to be borne in mind that "Leaves of Grass" entire is not to be construed as an intellectual or scholastic effort or poem mainly, but more as a radical utterance out of the Emotions and the Physique—an utterance adjusted to, perhaps born of, Democracy and the Modern—in its very nature regardless of the old conventions, and, under the great laws, following only its own impulses.

>>> <<<

POETRY TO-DAY *in* AMERICA— SHAKSPERE—*the* FUTURE

STRANGE as it may seem, the topmost proof of a race is its own born poetry. The presence of that, or the absence, each tells its story. As the flowering rose or lily, as the ripen'd fruit to a tree, the apple or the peach, no matter how fine the trunk, or copious or rich the branches and foliage, here waits *sine qua non* at last. The stamp of entire and finish'd greatness to any nation, to the American Republic among the rest, must be sternly withheld till it has put what it stands for in the blossom of original, first-class poems. No imitations will do.

And though no *esthetik* worthy the present condition or future certainties of the New World seems to have been outlined in men's minds, or has been generally called for, or thought needed, I am clear that until the United States have just such definite and native expressers in the highest artistic fields, their mere political, geographical, wealth-forming, and even intellectual eminence, however astonishing and predominant, will constitute but a more and more expanded and well-appointed body, and perhaps brain, with little or no soul. Sugar-coat the grim truth as we may, and ward off with outward plausible words, denials, explanations, to the mental inward perception of the land this blank is plain; a barren void exists. For the meanings and maturer purposes of these States are not the constructing of a new world of politics merely, and physical comforts for the million, but even more determinedly, in range with science and the modern, of a new world democratic sociology and imaginative literature. If the latter were not establish'd for the States, to form their only permanent tie and hold, the first-named would be of little avail.

With the poems of a first-class land are twined, as weft with warp, its types of personal character, of individuality, peculiar, native, its own physiognomy, man's and woman's, its own shapes, forms, and manners, fully justified under the eternal laws of all forms, all manners, all times. The hour has come for democracy in America to inaugurate itself in the two directions specified—autochthonic poems and personalities—born expressers of itself, its spirit alone, to radiate in subtle ways, not only in art, but the practical and familiar, in the transactions between employers and employ'd persons, in business and wages, and sternly in the army and navy,

295

and revolutionizing them. I find nowhere a scope profound enough, and radical and objective enough, either for aggregates or individuals. The thought and identity of a poetry in America to fill, and worthily fill, the great void, and enhance these aims, electrifying all and several, involves the essence and integral facts, real and spiritual, of the whole land, the whole body. What the great sympathetic is to the congeries of bones, joints, heart, fluids, nervous system and vitality, constituting, launching forth in time and space a human being—aye, an immortal soul—such relation, and no less, holds true poetry to the single personality, or to the nation.

Here our thirty-eight States stand to-day, the children of past precedents, and, young as they are, heirs of a very old estate. One or two points we will consider, out of the myriads presenting themselves. The feudalism of the British Islands, illustrated by Shakspere —and by his legitimate followers, Walter Scott and Alfred Tennyson —with all its tyrannies, superstitions, evils, had most superb and heroic permeating veins, poems, manners; even its errors fascinating. It almost seems as if only that feudalism in Europe, like slavery in our own South, could outcrop types of tallest, noblest personal character yet—strength and devotion and love better than elsewhere —invisible courage, generosity, aspiration, the spines of all. Here is where Shakspere and the others I have named perform a service incalculably precious to our America. Politics, literature, and everything else, centers at last in perfect *personnel,* (as democracy is to find the same as the rest;) and here feudalism is unrival'd—here the rich and highest-rising lessons it bequeaths us—a mass of foreign nutriment, which we are to work over, and popularize and enlarge, and present again in our own growths.

Still there are pretty grave and anxious drawbacks, jeopardies, fears. Let us give some reflections on the subject, a little fluctuating, but starting from one central thought, and returning there again. Two or three curious results may plow up. As in the astronomical laws, the very power that would seem most deadly and destructive turns out to be latently conservative of longest, vastest future births and lives. We will for once briefly examine the just-named authors solely from a Western point of view. It may be, indeed, that we shall use the sun of English literature, and the brightest current stars of his system, mainly as pegs to hang some cogitations on, for home inspection.

As depicter and dramatist of the passions at their stormiest outstretch, though ranking high, Shakspere (spanning the arch wide enough) is equal'd by several, and excell'd by the best old Greeks, (as Æschylus.) But in portraying mediæval European lords and barons, the arrogant port, so dear to the inmost human heart, (pride! pride! dearest, perhaps, of all—touching us, too, of the States closest of all—closer than love,) he stands alone, and I do not wonder he so witches the world.

From first to last, also, Walter Scott and Tennyson, like Shakspere, exhale that principle of caste which we Americans have come on earth to destroy. Jefferson's verdict on the Waverley novels was that they turn'd and condens'd brilliant but entirely false lights and glamours over the lords, ladies, and aristocratic institutes of Europe, with all their measureless infamies, and then left the bulk of the suffering, down-trodden people contemptuously in the shade. Without stopping to answer this hornet-stinging criticism, or to repay any part of the debt of thanks I owe, in common with every American, to the noblest, healthiest, cheeriest romancer that ever lived, I pass on to Tennyson, his works.

Poetry here of a very high (perhaps the highest) order of verbal melody, exquisitely clean and pure, and almost always perfumed, like the tuberose, to an extreme of sweetness—sometimes not, however, but even then a camellia of the hot-house, never a common flower—the verse of inside elegance and high-life; and yet preserving amid all its super-delicatesse a smack of outdoors and outdoor folk. The old Norman lordhood quality here, too, cross'd with that Saxon fiber from which twain the best current stock of England springs—poetry that revels above all things in traditions of knights and chivalry, and deeds of derring-do. The odor of English social life in its highest range—a melancholy, affectionate, very manly, but dainty breed—pervading the pages like an invisible scent; the idleness, the traditions, the mannerisms, the stately *ennui;* the yearning of love, like a spinal marrow, inside of all; the costumes, brocade and satin; the old houses and furniture—solid oak, no mere veneering—the moldy secrets everywhere; the verdure, the ivy on the walls, the moat, the English landscape outside, the buzzing fly in the sun inside the window pane. Never one democratic page; nay, not a line, not a word; never free and *naïve* poetry, but involv'd, labor'd, quite sophisticated—even when the theme is ever so simple or rustic, (a shell, a bit of sedge, the commonest love-passage between a lad and lass,) the handling of the rhyme all showing the scholar and conventional gentleman; showing the laureate, too, the *attaché* of the throne, and most excellent, too; nothing better through the volumes than the dedication "to the Queen" at the beginning, and the other fine dedication, "these to his memory" (Prince Albert's,) preceding "Idylls of the King."

Such for an off-hand summary of the mighty three that now, by the women, men, and young folk of the fifty millions given these States by their late census, have been and are more read than all others put together.

We hear it said, both of Tennyson and another current leading literary illustrator of Great Britain, Carlyle—as of Victor Hugo in France—that not one of them is personally friendly or admirant toward America; indeed, quite the reverse. *N'importe*. That they (and more good minds than theirs) cannot span the vast revolutionary arch thrown by the United States over the centuries, fix'd in the present, launch'd to the endless future; that they cannot stomach the high-life-below-stairs coloring all our poetic and genteel social status so far—the measureless viciousness of the great radical Republic, with its ruffianly nominations and elections; its loud, ill-pitch'd voice, utterly regardless whether the verb agrees with the nominative; its fights, errors, eructations, repulsions, dishonesties, audacities; those fearful and varied and long-continued storm and stress stages (so offensive to the well-regulated college-bred mind) wherewith Nature, history, and time block out nationalities more powerful than the past, and to upturn it and press on to the future; —that they cannot understand and fathom all this, I say, is it to be wonder'd at? Fortunately, the gestation of our thirty-eight empires (and plenty more to come) proceeds on its course, on scales of area and velocity immense and absolute as the globe, and, like the globe itself, quite oblivious even of great poets and thinkers. But we can by no means afford to be oblivious of them.

The same of feudalism, its castles, courts, etiquettes, personalities. However they, or the spirits of them hovering in the air, might scowl and glower at such removes as current Kansas or Kentucky life and forms, the latter may by no means repudiate or leave out the former. Allowing all the evil that it did, we get, here and to-day, a balance of good out of its reminiscence almost beyond price.

Am I content, then, that the general interior chyle of our republic should be supplied and nourish'd by wholesale from foreign and antagonistic sources such as these? Let me answer that question briefly:

Years ago I thought Americans ought to strike out separate, and have expressions of their own in highest literature. I think so still, and more decidedly than ever. But those convictions are now strongly temper'd by some additional points, (perhaps the results of advancing age, or the reflections of invalidism.) I see that this world of the West, as part of all, fuses inseparably with the East, and with all, as time does—the ever new, yet old, old human race— "the same subject continued," as the novels of our grandfathers had it for chapter-heads. If we are not to hospitably receive and complete the inaugurations of the old civilizations, and change their small scale to the largest, broadest scale, what on earth are we for?

The currents of practical business in America, the rude, coarse, tussling facts of our lives, and all their daily experiences, need just the precipitation and tincture of this entirely different fancy world of lulling, contrasting, even feudalistic, anti-republican poetry and romance. On the enormous outgrowth of our unloos'd individualities, and the rank self-assertion of humanity here, may well fall these grace-persuading, *recherché* influences. We first require that individuals and communities shall be free; then surely comes a time when it is requisite that they shall not be too free. Although to such results in the future I look mainly for a great poetry native to us, these importations till then will have to be accepted, such as they are, and thankful they are no worse. The inmost spiritual currents of the present time curiously revenge and check their own compell'd tendency to democracy, and absorption in it, by mark'd leanings to the past—by reminiscences in poems, plots, operas, novels, to a far-off, contrary, deceased world, as if they dreaded the great vulgar gulf tides of to-day. Then what has been fifty centuries growing, working in, and accepted as crowns and apices for our kind, is not going to be pulled down and discarded in a hurry.

It is, perhaps, time we paid our respects directly to the honorable party, the real object of these preambles. But we must make *reconnaissance* a little further still. Not the least part of our lesson were to realize the curiosity and interest of friendly foreign experts,[1] and how our situation looks to them. "American poetry," says the London "Times," [2] "is the poetry of apt pupils, but it is afflicted from first to last with a fatal want of raciness. Bryant has been long passed as a poet by Professor Longfellow; but in Longfellow, with all his scholarly grace and tender feeling, the defect is more apparent than it was in Bryant. Mr. Lowell can overflow with American humor when politics inspire his muse; but in the realm of pure poetry he is no more American than a Newdigate prizeman. Joaquin Miller's verse has fluency and movement and harmony, but as for the thought, his songs of the sierras might as well have been written in Holland."

Unless in a certain very slight contingency, the "Times" says: "American verse, from its earliest to its latest stages, seems an exotic, with an exuberance of gorgeous blossom, but no principle of reproduction. That is the very note and test of its inherent want. Great poets are tortured and massacred by having their flowers of fancy gathered and gummed down in the *hortus siccus* of an anthology. American poets show better in an anthology than in the collected volumes of their works. Like their audience they have been unable to resist the attraction of the vast orbit of English literature. They may talk of the primeval forest, but it would generally be very hard from internal evidence to detect that they were writing on the banks of the Hudson rather than on those of the Thames. . . . . In fact, they have caught the English tone and air and mood only too faithfully, and are accepted by the superficially cultivated English intelligence as readily as if they were English born. Americans themselves confess to a certain disappointment that a literary curiosity and intelligence so diffused [as in the United States] have not taken up English literature at the point at which America has received it, and carried it forward and developed it with an independent energy. But like reader like poet. Both show the effects of having come into an estate they have not earned. A nation of readers has required of its poets a diction and symmetry of form equal to that of an old literature like that of Great Britain, which is also theirs. No ruggedness, however racy, would be tolerated by circles which, however superficial their culture, read Byron and Tennyson."

The English critic, though a gentleman and a scholar, and friendly withal, is evidently not altogether satisfied, (perhaps he is jealous,) and winds up by saying: "For the English language to have been enriched with a national poetry which was not English but American, would have been a treasure beyond price." With which, as whet and foil, we shall proceed to ventilate more definitely certain no doubt willful opinions.

Leaving unnoticed at present the great masterpieces of the antique, or anything from the middle ages, the prevailing flow of poetry for the last fifty or eighty years, and now at its height, has been and is (like the music) an expression of mere surface melody, within narrow limits, and yet, to give it its due, perfectly satisfying to the demands of the ear, of wondrous charm, of smooth and easy delivery, and the triumph of technical art. Above all things it is fractional and select. It shrinks with aversion from the sturdy, the universal, and the democratic.

The poetry of the future, (a phrase open to sharp criticism, and not satisfactory to me, but significant, and I will use it)—the poetry of the future aims at the free expression of emotion, (which means far, far more than appears at first,) and to arouse and initiate, more than to define or finish. Like all modern tendencies, it has direct or indirect reference continually to the reader, to you or me, to the central identity of everything, the mighty Ego. (Byron's was a vehement dash, with plenty of impatient democracy, but lurid and introverted amid all its magnetism; not at all the fitting, lasting song of a grand, secure, free, sunny race.) It is more akin, likewise, to outside life and landscape, (returning mainly to the antique feeling,) real sun and gale, and woods and shores—to the elements themselves—not sitting at ease in parlor or library listening to a good tale of them, told in good rhyme. Character, a feature far above style or polish—a feature not absent at any time, but now first brought to the fore—gives predominant stamp to advancing poetry. Its born sister, music, already responds to the same influences. "The music of the present, Wagner's, Gounod's, even the later Verdi's, all tends toward this free expression of poetic emotion, and demands a vocalism totally unlike that required for Rossini's splendid roulades, or Bellini's suave melodies."

Is there not even now, indeed, an evolution, a departure from the masters? Venerable and unsurpassable after their kind as are the old works, and always unspeakably precious as studies, (for Americans more than any other people,) is it too much to say that by the shifted combinations of the modern mind the whole underlying theory of first-class verse has changed? "Formerly, during the period term'd classic," says Sainte-Beuve, "when literature was gov-ern'd by recognized rules, he was consider'd the best poet who had composed the most perfect work, the most beautiful poem, the most intelligible, the most agreeable to read, the most complete in every respect,—the Æneid, the Gerusalemme, a fine tragedy. To-day, something else is wanted. For us the greatest poet is he who in his works most stimulates the reader's imagination and reflection, who excites him the most himself to poetize. The greatest poet is not he who has done the best; it is he who suggests the most; he, not all of whose meaning is at first obvious, and who leaves you much to desire, to explain, to study, much to complete in your turn."

The fatal defects our American singers labor under are subordi-nation of spirit, an absence of the concrete and of real patriotism, and in excess that modern æsthetic contagion a queer friend of mine calls the *beauty disease.* "The immoderate taste for beauty and art," says Charles Baudelaire, "leads men into monstrous excesses. In minds imbued with a frantic greed for the beautiful, all the bal-

ances of truth and justice disappear. There is a lust, a disease of
the art faculties, which eats up the moral like a cancer."

Of course, by our plentiful verse-writers there is plenty of service
perform'd, of a kind. Nor need we go far for a tally. We see, in
every polite circle, a class of accomplish'd, good-natured persons,
("society," in fact, could not get on without them,) fully eligible
for certain problems, times, and duties—to mix egg-nog, to mend
the broken spectacles, to decide whether the stew'd eels shall precede the sherry or the sherry the stew'd eels, to eke out Mrs. A. B.'s
parlor-tableaux with monk, Jew, lover, Puck, Prospero, Caliban, or
what not, and to generally contribute and gracefully adapt their
flexibilities and talents, in those ranges, to the world's service. But
for real crises, great needs and pulls, moral or physical, they might
as well have never been born.

Or the accepted notion of a poet would appear to be a sort of
male odalisque, singing or piano-playing a kind of spiced ideas,
second-hand reminiscences, or toying late hours at entertainments,
in rooms stifling with fashionable scent. I think I haven't seen a
new-publish'd, healthy, bracing, simple lyric in ten years. Not long
ago, there were verses in each of three fresh monthlies, from leading
authors, and in every one the whole central *motif* (perfectly serious) was the melancholiness of a marriageable young woman who
didn't get a rich husband, but a poor one!

Besides its tonic and *al fresco* physiology, relieving such as this,
the poetry of the future will take on character in a more important
respect. Science, having extirpated the old stock-fables and superstitions, is clearing a field for verse, for all the arts, and even for
romance, a hundred-fold ampler and more wonderful, with the new
principles behind. Republicanism advances over the whole world.
Liberty, with Law by her side, will one day be paramount—will at
any rate be the central idea. Then only—for all the splendor and
beauty of what has been, or the polish of what is—then only will
the true poets appear, and the true poems. Not the satin and
patchouly of to-day, not the glorification of the butcheries and wars
of the past, nor any fight between Deity on one side and somebody
else on the other—not Milton, not even Shakspere's plays, grand as
they are. Entirely different and hitherto unknown classes of men,
being authoritatively called for in imaginative literature, will certainly appear. What is hitherto most lacking, perhaps most absolutely indicates the future. Democracy has been hurried on through
time by measureless tides and winds, resistless as the revolution of
the globe, and as far-reaching and rapid. But in the highest walks

of art it has not yet had a single representative worthy of it anywhere upon the earth.

Never had real bard a task more fit for sublime ardor and genius than to sing worthily the songs these States have already indicated. Their origin, Washington, '76, the picturesqueness of old times, the war of 1812 and the sea-fights; the incredible rapidity of movement and breadth of area—to fuse and compact the South and North, the East and West, to express the native forms, situations, scenes, from Montauk to California, and from the Saguenay to the Rio Grande—the working out on such gigantic scales, and with such a swift and mighty play of changing light and shade, of the great problems of man and freedom,—how far ahead of the stereotyped plots, or gem-cutting, or tales of love, or wars of mere ambition! Our history is so full of spinal, modern, germinal subjects—one above all. What the ancient siege of Ilium, and the puissance of Hector's and Agamemnon's warriors proved to Hellenic art and literature, and all art and literature since, may prove the war of attempted secession of 1861–'65 to the future æsthetics, drama, romance, poems of the United States.

Nor could utility itself provide anything more practically serviceable to the hundred millions who, a couple of generations hence, will inhabit within the limits just named, than the permeation of a sane, sweet, autochthonous national poetry—must I say of a kind that does not now exist? but which, I fully believe, will in time be supplied on scales as free as Nature's elements. (It is acknowledged that we of the States are the most materialistic and money-making people ever known. My own theory, while fully accepting this, is that we are the most emotional, spiritualistic, and poetry-loving people also.)

Infinite are the new and orbic traits waiting to be launch'd forth in the firmament that is, and is to be, America. Lately, I have wonder'd whether the last meaning of this cluster of thirty-eight States is not only practical fraternity among themselves—the only real *union*, (much nearer its accomplishment, too, than appears on the surface)—but for fraternity over the whole globe—that dazzling, pensive dream of ages! Indeed, the peculiar glory of our lands, I have come to see, or expect to see, not in their geographical or republican greatness, nor wealth or products, nor military or naval power, nor special, eminent names in any department, to shine with, or outshine, foreign special names in similar departments,—but more and more in a vaster, saner, more surrounding Comradeship, uniting closer and closer not only the American States, but all nations,

and all humanity. That, O poets! is not that a theme worth chanting, striving for? Why not fix your verses henceforth to the gauge
of the round globe? the whole race? Perhaps the most illustrious
culmination of the modern may thus prove to be a signal growth
of joyous, more exalted bards of adhesiveness, identically one in
soul, but contributed by every nation, each after its distinctive kind.
Let us, audacious, start it. Let the diplomats, as ever, still deeply
plan, seeking advantages, proposing treaties between governments,
and to bind them, on paper: what I seek is different, simpler. I
would inaugurate from America, for this purpose, new formulas—
international poems. I have thought that the invisible root out of
which the poetry deepest in, and dearest to, humanity grows, is
Friendship. I have thought that both in patriotism and song (even
amid their grandest shows past) we have adhered too long to petty
limits, and that the time has come to enfold the world.

Not only is the human and artificial world we have establish'd in
the West a radical departure from anything hitherto known—not
only men and politics, and all that goes with them—but Nature itself, in the main sense, its construction, is different. The same old
font of type, of course, but set up to a text never composed or issued
before. For Nature consists not only in itself, objectively, but at
least just as much in its subjective reflection from the person, spirit,
age, looking at it, in the midst of it, and absorbing it—faithfully
sends back the characteristic beliefs of the time or individual—takes,
and readily gives again, the physiognomy of any nation or literature
—falls like a great elastic veil on a face, or like the molding plaster
on a statue.

What is Nature? What were the elements, the invisible backgrounds and eidólons of it, to Homer's heroes, voyagers, gods?
What all through the wanderings of Virgil's Æneas? Then to Shakspere's characters—Hamlet, Lear, the English-Norman kings, the
Romans? What was Nature to Rousseau, to Voltaire, to the German
Goethe in his little classical court gardens? In those presentments
in Tennyson (see the "Idyls of the King"—what sumptuous, perfumed, arras-and-gold Nature, inimitably described, better than
any, fit for princes and knights and peerless ladies—wrathful or
peaceful, just the same—Vivien and Merlin in their strange dalliance, or the death-float of Elaine, or Geraint and the long journey
of his disgraced Enid and himself through the wood, and the wife
all day driving the horses,) as in all the great imported art-works,
treatises, systems, from Lucretius down, there is a constantly lurking, often pervading something, that will have to be eliminated, as

not only unsuited to modern democracy and science in America, but insulting to them, and disproved by them.[3]

Still, the rule and demesne of poetry will always be not the exterior, but interior; not the macrocosm, but microcosm; not Nature, but Man. I haven't said anything about the imperative need of a race of giant bards in the future, to hold up high to eyes of land and race the eternal antiseptic models, and to dauntlessly confront greed, injustice, and all forms of that wiliness and tyranny whose roots never die—(my opinion is, that after all the rest is advanced, *that* is what first-class poets are for; as, to their days and occasions, the Hebrew lyrists, Roman Juvenal, and doubtless the old singers of India, and the British Druids)—to counteract dangers, immensest ones, already looming in America—measureless corruption in politics—what we call religion, a mere mask of wax or lace;—for *ensemble*, that most cankerous, offensive of all earth's shows—a vast and varied community, prosperous and fat with wealth of money and products and business ventures—plenty of mere intellectuality too— and then utterly without the sound, prevailing, moral and æsthetic health-action beyond all the money and mere intellect of the world.

Is it a dream of mine that, in times to come, west, south, east, north, will silently, surely arise a race of such poets, varied, yet one in soul—nor only poets, and of the best, but newer, larger prophets —larger than Judea's, and more passionate—to meet and penetrate those woes, as shafts of light the darkness?

As I write, the last fifth of the nineteenth century is enter'd upon, and will soon be waning. Now, and for a long time to come, what the United States most need, to give purport, definiteness, reason why, to their unprecedented material wealth, industrial products, education by rote merely, great populousness and intellectual activity, is the central, spinal reality, (or even the idea of it,) of such a democratic band of native-born-and-bred teachers, artists, *littérateurs*, tolerant and receptive of importations, but entirely adjusted to the West, to ourselves, to our own days, combinations, differences, superiorities. Indeed, I am fond of thinking that the whole series of concrete and political triumphs of the Republic are mainly as bases and preparations for half a dozen future poets, ideal personalities, referring not to a special class, but to the entire people, four or five millions of square miles.

Long, long are the processes of the development of a nationality. Only to the rapt vision does the seen become the prophecy of the unseen.[4] Democracy, so far attending only to the real, is not for the real only, but the grandest ideal—to justify the modern by that, and not only to equal, but to become by that superior to the past. On a comprehensive summing up of the processes and present and hitherto condition of the United States, with reference to their future, and the indispensable precedents to it, my point, below all surfaces, and subsoiling them, is, that the bases and prerequisites of a leading nationality are, first, at all hazards, freedom, worldly wealth and products on the largest and most varied scale, common education and intercommunication, and, in general, the passing through of just the stages and crudities we have passed or are passing through in the United States.

Then, perhaps, as weightiest factor of the whole business, and of the main outgrowths of the future, it remains to be definitely avow'd that the native-born middle-class population of quite all the United States—the average of farmers and mechanics everywhere—the real, though latent and silent bulk of America, city or country, presents a magnificent mass of material, never before equaled on earth. It is this material, quite unexpress'd by literature or art, that in every respect insures the future of the republic. During the Secession War I was with the armies, and saw the rank and file, North and South, and studied them for four years. I have never had the least doubt about the country in its essential future since.

Meantime, we can (perhaps) do no better than to saturate ourselves with, and continue to give imitations, yet awhile, of the æsthetic models, supplies, of that past and of those lands we spring from. Those wondrous stores, reminiscences, floods, currents! Let them flow on, flow hither freely. And let the sources be enlarged, to include not only the works of British origin, as now, but stately and devout Spain, courteous France, profound Germany, the manly Scandinavian lands, Italy's art race, and always the mystic Orient. Remembering that at present, and doubtless long ahead, a certain humility would well become us. The course through time of highest civilization, does it not wait the first glimpse of our contribution to its cosmic train of poems, bibles, first-class structures, perpetuities— Egypt and Palestine and India—Greece and Rome and mediæval Europe—and so onward? The shadowy procession is not a meagre one, and the standard not a low one. All that is mighty in our kind seems to have already trod the road. Ah, never may America forget her thanks and reverence for samples, treasures such as these—that other life-blood, inspiration, sunshine, hourly in use to-day, all days, forever, through her broad demesne!

All serves our New World progress, even the bafflers, head-winds, cross-tides. Through many perturbations and squalls, and much backing and filling, the ship, upon the whole, makes unmistakably for her destination. Shakspere has served, and serves, may-be, the best of any.

For conclusion, a passing thought, a contrast, of him who, in my opinion, continues and stands for the Shaksperean cultus at the present day among all English-writing peoples—of Tennyson, his poetry. I find it impossible, as I taste the sweetness of those lines, to escape the flavor, the conviction, the lush-ripening culmination, and last honey of decay (I dare not call it rottenness) of that feudalism which the mighty English dramatist painted in all the splendors of its noon and afternoon. And how they are chanted— both poets! Happy those kings and nobles to be so sung, so told! To run their course—to get their deeds and shapes in lasting pigments—the very pomp and dazzle of the sunset!

Meanwhile, democracy waits the coming of its bards in silence and in twilight—but 'tis the twilight of the dawn.

⇒»› ‹«⇐

NOTES

1. A few years ago I saw the question, "Has America produced any great poem?" announced as prize-subject for the competition of some university in Northern Europe. I saw the item in a foreign paper and made a note of it; but being taken down with paralysis, and prostrated for a long season, the matter slipp'd away, and I have never been able since to get hold of any essay presented for the prize, or report of the discussion, nor to learn for certain whether there was any essay or discussion, nor can I now remember the place. It may have been Upsala, or possibly Heidelberg. Perhaps some German or Scandinavian can give particulars. I think it was in 1872.
2. In a long and prominent editorial, at the time, on the death of William Cullen Bryant.
3. Whatever may be said of the few principal poems—or their best passages—it is certain that the overwhelming mass of poetic works, as now absorb'd into human character, exerts a certain constipating, repressing, in-door, and artificial influence, impossible to elude—seldom or never that freeing, dilating, joyous one, with which uncramp'd Nature works on every individual without exception.
4. Is there not such a thing as the philosophy of American history and politics? And if so, what is it? . . . Wise men say there are two sets of wills to nations and to persons—one set that acts and works from explainable motives—from teaching, intelligence, judgment, circumstance, caprice, emulation, greed, &c. —and then another set, perhaps deep, hidden, unsuspected, yet often more potent than the first, refusing to be argued with, rising as it were out of

abysses, resistlessly urging on speakers, doers, communities, unwitting to themselves—the poet to his fieriest words—the race to pursue its loftiest ideal. Indeed, the paradox of a nation's life and career, with all its wondrous contradictions, can probably only be explain'd from these two wills, sometimes conflicting, each operating in its sphere, combining in races or in persons, and producing strangest results.

Let us hope there is (indeed, can there be any doubt there is?) this great unconscious and abysmic second will also running through the average nationality and career of America. Let us hope that, amid all the dangers and defections of the present, and through all the processes of the conscious will, it alone is the permanent and sovereign force, destined to carry on the New World to fulfill its destinies in the future—to resolutely pursue those destinies, age upon age; to build, far, far beyond its past vision, present thought; to form and fashion, and for the general type, men and women more noble, more athletic than the world has yet seen; to gradually, firmly blend, from all the States, with all varieties, a friendly, happy, free, religious nationality —a nationality not only the richest, most inventive, most productive and materialistic the world has yet known, but compacted indissolubly, and out of whose ample and solid bulk, and giving purpose and finish to it, conscience, morals, and all the spiritual attributes, shall surely rise, like spires above some group of edifices, firm-footed on the earth, yet scaling space and heaven.

Great as they are, and greater far to be, the United States, too, are but a series of steps in the eternal process of creative thought. And here is, to my mind, their final justification, and certain perpetuity. There is in that sublime process, in the laws of the universe—and, above all, in the moral law—something that would make unsatisfactory, and even vain and contemptible, all the triumphs of war, the gains of peace, and the proudest worldly grandeur of all the nations that have ever existed, or that (ours included) now exist, except that we constantly see, through all their worldly career, however struggling and blind and lame, attempts, by all ages, all peoples, according to their development, to reach, to press, to progress on, and ever farther on, to more and more advanced ideals.

The glory of the republic of the United States, in my opinion, is to be that, emerging in the light of the modern and the splendor of science, and solidly based on the past, it is to cheerfully range itself, and its politics are henceforth to come, under those universal laws, and embody them, and carry them out, to serve them. And as only that individual becomes truly great who understands well that, while complete in himself in a certain sense, he is but a part of the divine, eternal scheme, and whose special life and laws are adjusted to move in harmonious relations with the general laws of Nature, and especially with the moral law, the deepest and highest of all, and the last vitality of man or state—so the United States may only become the greatest and the most continuous, by understanding well their harmonious relations with entire humanity and history, and all their laws and progress, sublimed with the creative thought of Deity, through all time, past, present, and future. Thus will they expand to the amplitude of their destiny, and become illustrations and culminating parts of the cosmos, and of civilization.

No more considering the States as an incident, or series of incidents, however vast, coming accidentally along the path of time, and shaped by casual emergencies as they happen to arise, and the mere result of modern improvements, vulgar and lucky, ahead of other nations and times, I would finally plant, as seeds, these thoughts or speculations in the growth of our republic—that it is the deliberate culmination and result of all the past—that here, too, as in all departments of the universe, regular laws (slow and sure in planting, slow and sure in ripening) have controll'd and govern'd, and will yet control and govern; and that those laws can no more be baffled or steer'd clear of, or vitiated, by chance, or any fortune or opposition, than the laws of winter and summer, or darkness and light.

The summing up of the tremendous moral and military perturbations of 1861–5, and their results—and indeed of the entire hundred years of the past of our national experiment, from its inchoate movement down to the present day (1780–1881)—is, that they all now launch the United States fairly forth, consistently with the entirety of civilization and humanity, and in main sort the representative of them, leading the van, leading the fleet of the modern and democratic, on the seas and voyages of the future.

And the real history of the United States—starting from that great convulsive struggle for unity, the secession war, triumphantly concluded, and *the South* victorious after all—is only to be written at the remove of hundreds, perhaps a thousand, years hence.

A MEMORANDUM at a VENTURE

"All is proper to be express'd, provided our aim is only high enough."
—J. F. Millet.

"The candor of science is the glory of the modern. It does not hide and repress; it confronts, turns on the light. It alone has perfect faith—faith not in a part only, but all. Does it not undermine the old religious standards? Yes, in God's truth, by excluding the devil from the theory of the universe—by showing that evil is not a law in itself, but a sickness, a perversion of the good, and the other side of the good—that in fact all of humanity, and of everything, is divine in its bases, its eligibilities."

SHALL the mention of such topics as I have briefly but plainly and resolutely broach'd in the "Children of Adam" section of "Leaves of Grass" be admitted in poetry and literature? Ought not the innovation to be put down by opinion and criticism? and, if those fail, by the District Attorney? True, I could not construct a poem which declaredly took, as never before, the complete human identity, physical, moral, emotional, and intellectual, (giving precedence and compass in a certain sense to the first,) nor fulfil that *bona fide* candor and entirety of treatment which was a part of my purpose, without comprehending this section also. But I would entrench myself more deeply and widely than that. And while I do not ask any man to indorse my theory, I confess myself anxious that what I sought to write and express, and the ground I built on, shall be at least partially understood, from its own platform. The best way seems to me to confront the question with entire frankness.

There are, generally speaking, two points of view, two conditions of the world's attitude toward these matters; the first, the conventional one of good folks and good print everywhere, repressing any direct statement of them, and making allusions only at second or third hand—(as the Greeks did of death, which, in Hellenic social culture, was not mention'd point-blank, but by euphemisms.) In the civilization of to-day, this condition—without stopping to elaborate the arguments and facts, which are many and varied and perplexing—has led to states of ignorance, repressal, and cover'd over disease and depletion, forming certainly a main factor in the world's woe. A non-scientific, non-æsthetic, and eminently non-religious condition, bequeath'd to us from the past, (its origins diverse, one of them the far-back lessons of benevolent and wise men to restrain the prevalent coarseness and animality of the tribal ages—with Puritanism, or perhaps Protestantism itself for another, and still another specified in the latter part of this memorandum)—to it is probably due most of the ill births, inefficient maturity, snickering pruriency, and of that human pathologic evil and morbidity which is, in my opinion, the keel and reason-why of every evil and morbidity. Its scent, as of something sneaking, furtive, mephitic, seems to lingeringly pervade all modern literature, conversation, and manners.

The second point of view, and by far the largest—as the world in working-day dress vastly exceeds the world in parlor toilette—is the one of common life, from the oldest times down, and especially in England, (see the earlier chapters of "Taine's English Literature," and see Shakspere almost anywhere,) and which our age to-day inherits from riant stock, in the wit, or what passes for wit, of masculine circles, and in erotic stories and talk, to excite, express, and dwell on, that merely sensual voluptuousness which, according to Victor Hugo, is the most universal trait of all ages, all lands. This second condition, however bad, is at any rate like a disease which comes to the surface, and therefore less dangerous than a conceal'd one.

The time seems to me to have arrived, and America to be the place, for a new departure—a third point of view. The same freedom and faith and earnestness which, after centuries of denial, struggle, repression, and martyrdom, the present day brings to the treatment of politics and religion, must work out a plan and standard on this subject, not so much for what is call'd society, as for thoughtfulest men and women, and thoughtfulest literature. The same spirit that marks the physiological author and demonstrator on these topics in his important field, I have thought necessary to be exemplified, for once, in another certainly not less important field.

In the present memorandum I only venture to indicate that plan and view—decided upon more than twenty years ago, for my own literary action, and formulated tangibly in my printed poems—(as Bacon says an abstract thought or theory is of no moment unless it leads to a deed or work done, exemplifying it in the concrete)—that the sexual passion in itself, while normal and unperverted, is inherently legitimate, creditable, not necessarily an improper theme for poet, as confessedly not for scientist—that, with reference to the whole construction, organism, and intentions of "Leaves of Grass," anything short of confronting that theme, and making myself clear upon it, as the enclosing basis of everything, (as the sanity of everything was to be the atmosphere of the poems,) I should beg the question in its most momentous aspect, and the superstructure that follow'd, pretensive as it might assume to be, would all rest on a poor foundation, or no foundation at all. In short, as the assumption of the sanity of birth, Nature and humanity, is the key to any true theory of life and the universe—at any rate, the only theory out of which I wrote—it is, and must inevitably be, the only key to "Leaves of Grass," and every part of it. *That,* (and not a vain consistency or weak pride, as a late "Springfield Republican" charges,) is the reason that I have stood out for these particular verses uncompromisingly for over twenty years, and maintain them to this day. *That* is what I felt in my inmost brain and heart, when I only answer'd Emerson's vehement arguments with silence, under the old elms of Boston Common.

Indeed, might not every physiologist and every good physician pray for the redeeming of this subject from its hitherto relegation to the tongues and pens of blackguards, and boldly putting it for once at least, if no more, in the demesne of poetry and sanity—as something not in itself gross or impure, but entirely consistent with highest manhood and womanhood, and indispensable to both? Might not only every wife and every mother—not only every babe that comes into the world, if that were possible—not only all marriage, the foundation and *sine qua non* of the civilized state—bless and thank the showing, or taking for granted, that motherhood, fatherhood, sexuality, and all that belongs to them, can be asserted, where it comes to question, openly, joyously, proudly, "without shame or the need of shame," from the highest artistic and human considerations—but, with reverence be it written, on such attempt to justify the base and start of the whole divine scheme in humanity, might not the Creative Power itself deign a smile of approval?

To the movement for the eligibility and entrance of women amid new spheres of business, politics, and the suffrage, the current prurient, conventional treatment of sex is the main formidable obstacle. The rising tide of "woman's rights," swelling and every year advancing farther and farther, recoils from it with dismay. There will in my opinion be no general progress in such eligibility till a sensible, philosophic, democratic method is substituted.

The whole question—which strikes far, very far deeper than most people have supposed, (and doubtless, too, something is to be said on all sides,) is peculiarly an important one in art—is first an ethic, and then still more an æsthetic one. I condense from a paper read not long since at Cheltenham, England, before the "Social Science Congress," to the Art Department, by P. H. Rathbone of Liverpool, on the "Undraped Figure in Art," and the discussion that follow'd:

"When coward Europe suffer'd the unclean Turk to soil the sacred shores of Greece by his polluting presence, civilization and morality receiv'd a blow from which they have never entirely recover'd, and the trail of the serpent has been over European art and European society ever since. The Turk regarded and regards women as animals without soul, toys to be play'd with or broken at pleasure, and to be hidden, partly from shame, but chiefly for the purpose of stimulating exhausted passion. Such is the unholy origin of the objection to the nude as a fit subject for art; it is purely Asiatic, and though not introduced for the first time in the fifteenth century, is yet to be traced to the source of all impurity—the East. Although the source of the prejudice is thoroughly unhealthy and impure, yet it is now shared by many pure-minded and honest, if somewhat uneducated, people. But I am prepared to maintain that it is necessary for the future of English art and of English morality that the right of the nude to a place in our galleries should be boldly asserted; it must, however, be the nude as represented by thoroughly trained artists, and with a pure and noble ethic purpose. The human form, male and female, is the type and standard of all beauty of form and proportion, and it is necessary to be thoroughly familiar with it in order safely to judge of all beauty which consists of form and proportion. To women it is most necessary that they should become thoroughly imbued with the knowledge of the ideal female form, in order that they should recognize the perfection of it at once, and without effort, and so far as possible avoid deviations from the ideal. Had this been the case in times past, we should not have had to deplore the distortions effected by tight-lacing, which destroy'd the figure and ruin'd the health of so many of the last generation. Nor should we have had the scandalous dresses alike of society and the stage. The extreme development of the low dresses which obtain'd some years ago, when the stays crush'd up the breasts into suggestive prominence, would surely have been check'd, had the eye of the public been properly educated by familiarity with the exquisite beauty of line of a well-shaped bust. I might show how thorough acquaintance with the ideal nude foot would probably have much modified the foot-torturing boots and high heels, which wring the foot out of all beauty of line, and throw the body forward into an awkward and ungainly attitude.

"It is argued that the effect of nude representation of women upon young men is unwholesome, but it would not be so if such works were admitted without question into our galleries, and become thoroughly familiar to them. On the contrary, it would do much to clear away from healthy-hearted lads one of their sorest trials—that prurient curiosity which is bred of prudish concealment. Where there is mystery there is the suggestion of evil, and to go to a theatre, where you have only to look at the stalls to see one-half of the female form, and to the stage to see the other half undraped, is far more pregnant with evil imaginings than the most objectionable of totally undraped figures. In French art there have been questionable nude figures exhibited; but the fault was not that *they were nude, but that they were the portraits of ugly immodest women."*

Some discussion follow'd. There was a general concurrence in the principle contended for by the reader of the paper. Sir Walter Stirling maintain'd that the perfect male figure, rather than the female, was the model of beauty. After a few remarks from Rev. Mr. Roberts and Colonel Oldfield, the Chairman regretted that no opponent of nude figures had taken part in the discussion. He agreed with Sir Walter Stirling as to the male figure being the most perfect model of proportion. He join'd in defending the exhibition of nude figures, but thought considerable supervision be exercised over such exhibitions.

No, it is not the picture or nude statue or text, with clear aim, that is indecent; it is the beholder's own thought, inference, distorted construction. True modesty is one of the most precious of attributes, even virtues, but in nothing is there more pretense, more falsity, than the needless assumption of it. Through precept and consciousness, man has long enough realized how bad he is. I would not so much disturb or demolish that conviction, only to resume and keep unerringly with it the spinal meaning of the Scriptural text, *God overlook'd all that He had made,* (including the apex of the whole—humanity—with its elements, passions, appetites,) *and behold, it was very good.*

Does not anything short of that third point of view, when you come to think of it profoundly and with amplitude, impugn Creation from the outset? In fact, however overlaid, or unaware of itself, does not the conviction involv'd in it perennially exist at the centre of all society, and of the sexes, and of marriage? Is it not really an intuition of the human race? For, old as the world is, and beyond statement as are the countless and splendid results of its culture and evolution, perhaps the best and earliest and purest intuitions of the human race have yet to be develop'd.

DEATH of ABRAHAM LINCOLN

LECTURE *deliver'd in New York, April 14, 1879—in Philadelphia, '80—in Boston, '81*

How often since that dark and dripping Saturday—that chilly April day, now fifteen years bygone—my heart has entertain'd the dream, the wish, to give of Abraham Lincoln's death, its own special thought and memorial. Yet now the sought-for opportunity offers, I find my notes incompetent, (why, for truly profound themes, is statement so idle? why does the right phrase never offer?) and the fit tribute I dream'd of, waits unprepared as ever. My talk here indeed is less because of itself or anything in it, and nearly altogether because I feel a desire, apart from any talk, to specify the day, the martyrdom. It is for this, my friends, I have call'd you together. Oft as the rolling years bring back this hour, let it again, however briefly, be dwelt upon. For my own part, I hope and desire, till my own dying day, whenever the 14th or 15th of April comes, to annually gather a few friends, and hold its tragic reminiscence. No narrow or sectional reminiscence. It belongs to these States in their entirety—not the North only, but the South—perhaps belongs most tenderly and devoutly to the South, of all; for there, really, this man's birth-stock. There and thence his antecedent stamp. Why should I not say that thence his manliest traits—his universality—his canny, easy ways and words upon the surface—his inflexible determination and courage at heart? Have you never realized it, my friends, that Lincoln, though grafted on the West, is essentially, in personnel and character, a Southern contribution?

And though by no means proposing to resume the Secession war to-night, I would briefly remind you of the public conditions preceding that contest. For twenty years, and especially during the four or five before the war actually began, the aspect of affairs in the United States, though without the flash of military excitement, presents more than the survey of a battle, or any extended campaign, or series, even of Nature's convulsions. The hot passions of the South—the strange mixture at the North of inertia, incredulity, and conscious power—the incendiarism of the abolitionists—the rascality and *grip* of the politicians, unparallel'd in any land, any age. To these I must not omit adding the honesty of the essential bulk of the people everywhere—yet with all the seething fury and contra-

315

diction of their natures more arous'd than the Atlantic's waves in wildest equinox. In politics, what can be more ominous, (though generally unappreciated then)—what more significant than the Presidentiads of Fillmore and Buchanan? proving conclusively that the weakness and wickedness of elected rulers are just as likely to afflict us here, as in the countries of the Old World, under their monarchies, emperors, and aristocracies. In that Old World were everywhere heard underground rumblings, that died out, only to again surely return. While in America the volcano, though civic yet, continued to grow more and more convulsive—more and more stormy and threatening.

In the height of all this excitement and chaos, hovering on the edge at first, and then merged in its very midst, and destined to play a leading part, appears a strange and awkward figure. I shall not easily forget the first time I ever saw Abraham Lincoln. It must have been about the 18th or 19th of February, 1861. It was rather a pleasant afternoon, in New York city, as he arrived there from the West, to remain a few hours, and then pass on to Washington, to prepare for his inauguration. I saw him in Broadway, near the site of the present Post-office. He came down, I think from Canal street, to stop at the Astor House. The broad spaces, sidewalks, and street in the neighborhood, and for some distance, were crowded with solid masses of people, many thousands. The omnibuses and other vehicles had all been turn'd off, leaving an unusual hush in that busy part of the city. Presently two or three shabby hack barouches made their way with some difficulty through the crowd, and drew up at the Astor House entrance. A tall figure step'd out of the centre of these barouches, paus'd leisurely on the sidewalk, look'd up at the granite walls and looming architecture of the grand old hotel— then, after a relieving stretch of arms and legs, turn'd round for over a minute to slowly and good-humoredly scan the appearance of the vast and silent crowds. There were no speeches—no compliments— no welcome—as far as I could hear, not a word said. Still much anxiety was conceal'd in that quiet. Cautious persons had fear'd some mark'd insult or indignity to the President-elect—for he possess'd no personal popularity at all in New York city, and very little political. But it was evidently tacitly agreed that if the few political supporters of Mr. Lincoln present would entirely abstain from any demonstration on their side, the immense majority, who were any thing but supporters, would abstain on their side also. The result was a sulky, unbroken silence, such as certainly never before characterized so great a New York crowd.

Almost in the same neighborhood I distinctly remember'd seeing

Lafayette on his visit to America in 1825. I had also personally seen and heard, various years afterward, how Andrew Jackson, Clay, Webster, Hungarian Kossuth, Filibuster Walker, the Prince of Wales on his visit, and other celebres, native and foreign, had been welcom'd there—all that indescribable human roar and magnetism, unlike any other sound in the universe—the glad exulting thundershouts of countless unloos'd throats of men! But on this occasion, not a voice—not a sound. From the top of an omnibus, (driven up one side, close by, and block'd by the curbstone and the crowds,) I had, I say, a capital view of it all, and especially of Mr. Lincoln, his look and gait—his perfect composure and coolness—his unusual and uncouth height, his dress of complete black, stovepipe hat push'd back on the head, dark-brown complexion, seam'd and wrinkled yet canny-looking face, black, bushy head of hair, disproportionately long neck, and his hands held behind as he stood observing the people. He look'd with curiosity upon that immense sea of faces, and the sea of faces return'd the look with similar curiosity. In both there was a dash of comedy, almost farce, such as Shakspere puts in his blackest tragedies. The crowd that hemm'd around consisted I should think of thirty to forty thousand men, not a single one his personal friend—while I have no doubt, (so frenzied were the ferments of the time,) many an assassin's knife and pistol lurk'd in hip or breast-pocket there, ready, soon as break and riot came.

But no break or riot came. The tall figure gave another relieving stretch or two of arms and legs; then with moderate pace, and accompanied by a few unknown looking persons, ascended the portico-steps of the Astor House, disappear'd through its broad entrance—and the dumb-show ended.

I saw Abraham Lincoln often the four years following that date. He changed rapidly and much during his Presidency—but this scene, and him in it, are indelibly stamped upon my recollection. As I sat on the top of my omnibus, and had a good view of him, the thought, dim and inchoate then, has since come out clear enough, that four sorts of genius, four mighty and primal hands, will be needed to the complete limning of this man's future portrait—the eyes and brains and finger-touch of Plutarch and Eschylus and Michel Angelo, assisted by Rabelais.

And now—(Mr. Lincoln passing on from this scene to Washington, where he was inaugurated, amid armed cavalry, and sharpshooters at every point—the first instance of the kind in our history—and I hope it will be the last)—now the rapid succession of well-known events, (too well known—I believe, these days, we almost hate to hear them mention'd)—the national flag fired on at Sumter—

the uprising of the North, in paroxysms of astonishment and rage—the chaos of divided councils—the call for troops—the first Bull Run —the stunning cast-down, shock, and dismay of the North—and so in full flood the Secession war. Four years of lurid, bleeding, murky, murderous war. Who paint those years, with all their scenes?—the hard-fought engagements—the defeats, plans, failures—the gloomy hours, days, when our Nationality seem'd hung in pall of doubt, perhaps death—the Mephistophelean sneers of foreign lands and attachés—the dreaded Scylla of European interference, and the Charybdis of the tremendously dangerous latent strata of secession sympathizers throughout the free States, (far more numerous than is supposed)—the long marches in summer—the hot sweat, and many a sunstroke, as on the rush to Gettysburg in '63—the night battles in the woods, as under Hooker at Chancellorsville—the camps in winter—the military prisons—the hospitals—(alas! alas! the hospitals.)

The Secession war? Nay, let me call it the Union war. Though whatever call'd, it is even yet too near us—too vast and too closely overshadowing—its branches unform'd yet, (but certain,) shooting too far into the future—and the most indicative and mightiest of them yet ungrown. A great literature will yet arise out of the era of those four years, those scenes—era compressing centuries of native passion, first-class pictures, tempests of life and death—an inexhaustible mine for the histories, drama, romance, and even philosophy, of peoples to come—indeed the verteber of poetry and art, (of personal character too,) for all future America—far more grand, in my opinion, to the hands capable of it, than Homer's siege of Troy, or the French wars to Shakspere.

But I must leave these speculations, and come to the theme I have assign'd and limited myself to. Of the actual murder of President Lincoln, though so much has been written, probably the facts are yet very indefinite in most persons' minds. I read from my memoranda, written at the time, and revised frequently and finally since.

The day, April 14, 1865, seems to have been a pleasant one throughout the whole land—the moral atmosphere pleasant too—the long storm, so dark, so fratricidal, full of blood and doubt and gloom, over and ended at last by the sun-rise of such an absolute National victory, and utter break-down of Secessionism—we almost doubted our own senses! Lee had capitulated beneath the apple-tree of Appomattox. The other armies, the flanges of the revolt, swiftly follow'd. And could it really be, then? Out of all the affairs of this world of woe and failure and disorder, was there really come the confirm'd, unerring sign of plan, like a shaft of pure light—of rightful rule—of God? So the day, as I say, was propitious. Early herbage, early flowers, were out. (I remember where I was stopping at the time, the season being advanced, there were many lilacs in full bloom. By one of those caprices that enter and give tinge to events without being at all a part of them, I find myself always reminded of the great tragedy of that day by the sight and odor of these blossoms. It never fails.)

But I must not dwell on accessories. The deed hastens. The popular afternoon paper of Washington, the little "Evening Star," had spatter'd all over its third page, divided among the advertisements in a sensational manner, in a hundred different places, *The President and his Lady will be at the Theatre this evening.* . . . (Lincoln was fond of the theatre. I have myself seen him there several times. I remember thinking how funny it was that he, in some respects the leading actor in the stormiest drama known to real history's stage through centuries, should sit there and be so completely interested and absorb'd in those human jack-straws, moving about with their silly little gestures, foreign spirit, and flatulent text.)

On this occasion the theatre was crowded, many ladies in rich and gay costumes, officers in their uniforms, many well-known citizens, young folks, the usual clusters of gas-lights, the usual magnetism of so many people, cheerful, with perfumes, music of violins and flutes—(and over all, and saturating all, that vast, vague wonder, *Victory,* the nation's victory, the triumph of the Union, filling the air, the thought, the sense, with exhilaration more than all music and perfumes.)

The President came betimes, and, with his wife, witness'd the play from the large stage-boxes of the second tier, two thrown into one, and profusely draped with the national flag. The acts and scenes of the piece—one of those singularly written compositions which have at least the merit of giving entire relief to an audience engaged in mental action or business excitements and cares during the day, as it makes not the slightest call on either the moral, emotional, esthetic, or spiritual nature—a piece, ("Our American Cousin,") in which, among other characters, so call'd, a Yankee, certainly such a one as was never seen, or the least like it ever seen, in North America, is introduced in England, with a varied fol-de-rol of talk, plot, scenery, and such phantasmagoria as goes to make up a modern popular drama—had progress'd through perhaps a couple of its acts, when in the midst of this comedy, or non-such, or whatever it is to be call'd, and to offset it, or finish it out, as if in Nature's and the great Muse's mockery of those poor mimes, came interpolated that scene, not really or exactly to be described at all, (for on the many hundreds who were there it seems to this hour to have left a passing blur, a dream, a blotch)—and yet partially to be described as I now proceed to give it. There is a scene in the play representing a modern parlor, in which two unprecedented English ladies are inform'd by the impossible Yankee that he is not a man of fortune, and therefore undesirable for marriage-catching purposes; after which, the comments being finish'd, the dramatic trio make exit, leaving the stage clear for a moment. At this period came the murder of Abraham Lincoln. Great as all its manifold train, circling round it, and stretching into the future for many a century, in the politics, history, art, &c., of the New World, in point of fact the main thing, the actual murder, transpired with the quiet and simplicity of any commonest occurrence—the bursting of a bud or pod in the growth of vegetation, for instance. Through the general hum following the stage pause, with the change of positions, came the muffled sound of a pistol-shot, which not one-hundredth part of the audience heard at the time—and yet a moment's hush—somehow, surely, a vague startled thrill—and then, through the ornamented, draperied, starr'd and striped space-way of the President's box, a sudden figure, a man, raises himself with hands and feet, stands a moment on the railing, leaps below to the stage, (a distance of perhaps fourteen or fifteen feet,) falls out of position, catching his boot-heel in the copious drapery, (the American flag,) falls on one knee, quickly recovers himself, rises as if nothing had happen'd, (he really sprains his ankle, but unfelt then)—and so the figure, Booth, the murderer, dress'd in plain black broadcloth, bareheaded, with full, glossy, raven hair, and his eyes like some mad animal's flashing with light and resolution, yet with a certain strange calmness, holds aloft in one hand a large knife—walks along not much back from the footlights—turns fully toward the audience his face of statuesque beauty, lit by those basilisk eyes, flashing with desperation, perhaps insanity—launches out in a firm and steady voice the words *Sic semper tyrannis*—and then walks with neither slow nor very rapid pace diagonally across to the back of the stage, and disappears. (Had not all this terrible scene—making the mimic ones preposterous—had it not all been rehears'd, in blank, by Booth, beforehand?)

A moment's hush—a scream—the cry of *murder*—Mrs. Lincoln leaning out of the box, with ashy cheeks and lips, with involuntary cry, pointing to the retreating figure, *He has kill'd the President*. And still a moment's strange, incredulous suspense—and then the deluge!—then that mixture of horror, noises, uncertainty—(the

sound, somewhere back, of a horse's hoofs clattering with speed)—
the people burst through chairs and railings, and break them up—
there is inextricable confusion and terror—women faint—quite feeble persons fall, and are trampled on—many cries of agony are
heard—the broad stage suddenly fills to suffocation with a dense
and motley crowd, like some horrible carnival—the audience rush
generally upon it, at least the strong men do—the actors and actresses are all there in their play-costumes and painted faces, with
mortal fright showing through the rouge—the screams and calls,
confused talk—redoubled, trebled—two or three manage to pass up
water from the stage to the President's box—others try to clamber
up—&c., &c.

In the midst of all this, the soldiers of the President's guard, with
others, suddenly drawn to the scene, burst in—(some two hundred
altogether)—they storm the house, through all the tiers, especially
the upper ones, inflamed with fury, literally charging the audience
with fix'd bayonets, muskets and pistols, shouting *Clear out! clear
out! you sons of* —— .... Such the wild scene, or a suggestion of it
rather, inside the play-house that night.

Outside, too, in the atmosphere of shock and craze, crowds of
people, fill'd with frenzy, ready to seize any outlet for it, come near
committing murder several times on innocent individuals. One such
case was especially exciting. The infuriated crowd, through some
chance, got started against one man, either for words he utter'd, or
perhaps without any cause at all, and were proceeding at once to
actually hang him on a neighboring lamp-post, when he was rescued by a few heroic policemen, who placed him in their midst,
and fought their way slowly and amid great peril toward the station
house. It was a fitting episode of the whole affair. The crowd rushing and eddying to and fro—the night, the yells, the pale faces,
many frighten'd people trying in vain to extricate themselves—the
attack'd man, not yet freed from the jaws of death, looking like a
corpse—the silent, resolute, half-dozen policemen, with no weapons
but their little clubs, yet stern and steady through all those eddying
swarms—made a fitting side-scene to the grand tragedy of the
murder. They gain'd the station house with the protected man,
whom they placed in security for the night, and discharged him in
the morning.

And in the midst of that pandemonium, infuriated soldiers, the
audience and the crowd, the stage, and all its actors and actresses,
its paint-pots, spangles, and gas-lights—the life blood from those
veins, the best and sweetest of the land, drips slowly down, and
death's ooze already begins its little bubbles on the lips.

Thus the visible incidents and surroundings of Abraham Lincoln's murder, as they really occur'd. Thus ended the attempted secession of these States; thus the four years' war. But the main things come subtly and invisibly afterward, perhaps long afterward—neither military, political, nor (great as those are,) historical. I say, certain secondary and indirect results, out of the tragedy of this death, are, in my opinion, greatest. Not the event of the murder itself. Not that Mr. Lincoln strings the principal points and personages of the period, like beads, upon the single string of his career. Not that his idiosyncrasy, in its sudden appearance and disappearance, stamps this Republic with a stamp more mark'd and enduring than any yet given by any one man—(more even than Washington's;)—but, join'd with these, the immeasurable value and meaning of that whole tragedy lies, to me, in senses finally dearest to a nation, (and here all our own)—the imaginative and artistic senses—the literary and dramatic ones. Not in any common or low meaning of those terms, but a meaning precious to the race, and to every age. A long and varied series of contradictory events arrives at last at its highest poetic, single, central, pictorial denouement. The whole involved, baffling, multiform whirl of the secession period comes to a head, and is gather'd in one brief flash of lightning-illumination—one simple, fierce deed. Its sharp culmination, and as it were solution, of so many bloody and angry problems, illustrates those climax-moments on the stage of universal Time, where the historic Muse at one entrance, and the tragic Muse at the other, suddenly ringing down the curtain, close an immense act in the long drama of creative thought, and give it radiation, tableau, stranger than fiction. Fit radiation—fit close! How the imagination—how the student loves these things! America, too, is to have them. For not in all great deaths, nor far or near—not Cæsar in the Roman senate-house, or Napoleon passing away in the wild night-storm at St. Helena—not Paleologus, falling, desperately fighting, piled over dozens deep with Grecian corpses—not calm old Socrates, drinking the hemlock —outvies that terminus of the secession war, in one man's life, here in our midst, in our own time—that seal of the emancipation of three million slaves—that parturition and delivery of our at last really free Republic, born again, henceforth to commence its career of genuine homogeneous Union, compact, consistent with itself.

Nor will ever future American Patriots and Unionists, indifferently over the whole land, or North or South, find a better moral to their lesson. The final use of the greatest men of a Nation is, after all, not with reference to their deeds in themselves, or their direct bearing on their times or lands. The final use of a heroic-eminent life— especially of a heroic-eminent death—is its indirect filtering into the

nation and the race, and to give, often at many removes, but unerringly, age after age, color and fibre to the personalism of the
youth and maturity of that age, and of mankind. Then there is a
cement to the whole people, subtler, more underlying, than any
thing in written constitution, or courts or armies—namely, the cement of a death identified thoroughly with that people, at its head,
and for its sake. Strange, (is it not?) that battles, martyrs, agonies,
blood, even assassination, should so condense—perhaps only really,
lastingly condense—a Nationality.

I repeat it—the grand deaths of the race—the dramatic deaths of
every nationality—are its most important inheritance-value—in some
respects beyond its literature and art—(as the hero is beyond his
finest portrait, and the battle itself beyond its choicest song or
epic.) Is not here indeed the point underlying all tragedy? the
famous pieces of the Grecian masters—and all masters? Why, if the
old Greeks had had this man, what trilogies of plays—what epics—
would have been made out of him! How the rhapsodes would have
recited him! How quickly that quaint tall form would have enter'd
into the region where men vitalize gods, and gods divinify men!
But Lincoln, his times, his death—great as any, any age—belong
altogether to our own, and are autochthonic. (Sometimes indeed I
think our American days, our own stage—the actors we know and
have shaken hands, or talk'd with—more fateful than any thing in
Eschylus—more heroic than the fighters around Troy—afford kings of
men for our Democracy prouder than Agamemnon—models of character cute and hardy as Ulysses—deaths more pitiful than Priam's.)

When, centuries hence, (as it must, in my opinion, be centuries
hence before the life of these States, or of Democracy, can be really
written and illustrated,) the leading historians and dramatists seek
for some personage, some special event, incisive enough to mark
with deepest cut, and mnemonize, this turbulent Nineteenth century of ours, (not only these States, but all over the political and
social world)—something, perhaps, to close that gorgeous procession of European feudalism, with all its pomp and caste-prejudices,
(of whose long train we in America are yet so inextricably the
heirs)—something to identify with terrible identification, by far the
greatest revolutionary step in the history of the United States, (perhaps the greatest of the world, our century)—the absolute extirpa-
tion and erasure of slavery from the States—those historians will
seek in vain for any point to serve more thoroughly their purpose,
than Abraham Lincoln's death.

Dear to the Muse—thrice dear to Nationality—to the whole human
race—precious to this Union—precious to Democracy—unspeakably
and forever precious—their first great Martyr Chief.

TWO LETTERS

1.—To —— —— —— (*London, England*)
CAMDEN, N. J., U. S. AMERICA, *March 17th, 1876*

DEAR FRIEND:—Yours of the 28th Feb. receiv'd, and indeed welcom'd.
I am jogging along still about the same in physical condition—still
certainly no worse, and I sometimes lately suspect rather better,
or at any rate more adjusted to the situation. Even begin to think
of making some move, some change of base, &c.: the doctors have
been advising it for over two years, but I haven't felt to do it yet.
My paralysis does not lift—I cannot walk any distance—I still have
this baffling, obstinate, apparently chronic affection of the stomachic
apparatus and liver: yet I get out of doors a little every day—write
and read in moderation—appetite sufficiently good—(eat only very
plain food, but always did that)—digestion tolerable—spirits unflagging. I have told you most of this before, but suppose you might
like to know it all again, up to date. Of course, and pretty darkly
coloring the whole, are bad spells, prostrations, some pretty grave
ones, intervals—and I have resign'd myself to the certainty of permanent incapacitation from solid work: but things may continue at
least in this half-and-half way for months, even years.

My books are out, the new edition; a set of which, immediately
on receiving your letter of 28th, I have sent you, (by mail, March
15,) and I suppose you have before this receiv'd them. My dear
friend, your offers of help, and those of my other British friends,
I think I fully appreciate, in the right spirit, welcome and acceptive
—leaving the matter altogether in your and their hands, and to your
and their convenience, discretion, leisure, and nicety. Though poor
now, even to penury, I have not so far been deprived of any physical thing I need or wish whatever, and I feel confident I shall not
in the future. During my employment of seven years or more in
Washington after the war (1865–72) I regularly saved part of my
wages: and, though the sum has now become about exhausted by
my expenses of the last three years, there are already beginning at
present welcome dribbles hitherward from the sales of my new
edition, which I just job and sell, myself, (all through this illness,
my book-agents for three years in New York successively, badly
cheated me,) and shall continue to dispose of the books myself.
And *that* is the way I should prefer to glean my support. In that

324

way I cheerfully accept all the aid my friends find it convenient to proffer.

To repeat a little, and without undertaking details, understand, dear friend, for yourself and all, that I heartily and most affectionately thank my British friends, and that I accept their sympathetic generosity in the same spirit in which I believe (nay, know) it is offer'd—that though poor I am not in want—that I maintain good heart and cheer; and that by far the most satisfaction to me (and I think it can be done, and believe it will be) will be to live, as long as possible, on the sales, by myself, of my own works, and perhaps, if practicable, by further writings for the press.

W. W.

I am prohibited from writing too much, and I must make this candid statement of the situation serve for all my dear friends over there.

2.—To —————— ———— ——— (*Dresden, Saxony*)

CAMDEN, *New Jersey, U. S. A., Dec. 20, '81*

DEAR SIR:—Your letter asking definite endorsement to your translation of my "*Leaves of Grass*" into Russian is just received, and I hasten to answer it. Most warmly and willingly I consent to the translation, and waft a prayerful *God speed* to the enterprise.

You Russians and we Americans! Our countries so distant, so unlike at first glance—such a difference in social and political conditions, and our respective methods of moral and practical development the last hundred years;—and yet in certain features, and vastest ones, so resembling each other. The variety of stock-elements and tongues, to be resolutely fused in a common identity and union at all hazards—the idea, perennial through the ages, that they both have their historic and divine mission—the fervent element of manly friendship throughout the whole people, surpass'd by no other races —the grand expanse of territorial limits and boundaries—the unform'd and nebulous state of many things, not yet permanently settled, but agreed on all hands to be the preparations of an infinitely greater future—the fact that both Peoples have their independent and leading positions to hold, keep, and if necessary, fight for, against the rest of the world—the deathless aspirations at the inmost centre of each great community, so vehement, so mysterious, so abysmic—are certainly features you Russians and we Americans possess in common.

As my dearest dream is for an internationality of poems and poets, binding the lands of the earth closer than all treaties and diplomacy—As the purpose beneath the rest in my book is such hearty comradeship, for individuals to begin with, and for all the nations of the earth as a result—how happy I should be to get the hearing and emotional contact of the great Russian peoples.

To whom, now and here, (addressing you for Russia and Russians, and empowering you, should you see fit, to print the present letter, in your book, as a preface,) I waft affectionate salutation from these shores, in America's name.   W. W.

‐‑≫≪‑‐

NOTES LEFT OVER

NATIONALITY (AND YET)

IT IS more and more clear to me that the main sustenance for highest separate personality, these States, is to come from that general sustenance of the aggregate, (as air, earth, rains, give sustenance to a tree)—and that such personality, by democratic standards, will only be fully coherent, grand and free, through the cohesion, grandeur and freedom of the common aggregate, the Union. Thus the existence of the true American continental solidarity of the future, depending on myriads of superb, large-sized, emotional and physically perfect individualities, of one sex just as much as the other, the supply of such individualities, in my opinion, wholly depends on a compacted imperial ensemble. The theory and practice of both sovereignties, contradictory as they are, are necessary. As the centripetal law were fatal alone, or the centrifugal law deadly and destructive alone, but together forming the law of eternal kosmical action, evolution, preservation, and life—so, by itself alone, the fullness of individuality, even the sanest, would surely destroy itself. This is what makes the importance to the identities of these States of the thoroughly fused, relentless, dominating Union —a moral and spiritual idea, subjecting all the parts with remorseless power, more needed by American democracy than by any of history's hitherto empires or feudalities, and the *sine qua non* of carrying out the republican principle to develop itself in the New World through hundreds, thousands of years to come.

Indeed, what most needs fostering through the hundred years to come, in all parts of the United States, north, south, Mississippi valley, and Atlantic and Pacific coasts, is this fused and fervent identity of the individual, whoever he or she may be, and wherever the place, with the idea and fact of AMERICAN TOTALITY, and with what is meant by the Flag, the stars and stripes. We need this conviction of nationality as a faith, to be absorb'd in the blood and belief of the people everywhere, south, north, west, east, to emanate in their life, and in native literature and art. We want the germinal idea that America, inheritor of the past, is the custodian of the future of humanity. Judging from history, it is some such moral and spiritual ideas appropriate to them, (and such ideas only,) that have made the profoundest glory and endurance of nations in the past. The races of Judea, the classic clusters of Greece and Rome, and the feudal and ecclesiastical clusters of the Middle Ages, were each and all vitalized by their separate distinctive ideas, ingrain'd in them, redeeming many sins, and indeed, in a sense, the principal reason-why for their whole career.

Then, in the thought of nationality especially for the United States, and making them original, and different from all other countries, another point ever remains to be considered. There are two distinct principles—aye, paradoxes—at the life-fountain and life-continuation of the States; one, the sacred principle of the Union, the right of ensemble, at whatever sacrifice—and yet another, an equally sacred principle, the right of each State, consider'd as a separate sovereign individual, in its own sphere. Some go zealously for one set of these rights, and some as zealously for the other set. We must have both; or rather, bred out of them, as out of mother and father, a third set, the perennial result and combination of both, and neither jeopardized. I say the loss or abdication of one set, in the future, will be ruin to democracy just as much as the loss of the other set. The problem is, to harmoniously adjust the two, and the play of the two. [Observe the lesson of the divinity of Nature, ever checking the excess of one law, by an opposite, or seemingly opposite law—generally the other side of the same law.] For the theory of this Republic is, not that the General government is the fountain of all life and power, dispensing it forth, around, and to the remotest portions of our territory, but that THE PEOPLE are, represented in both, underlying both the General and State governments, and consider'd just as well in their individualities and in their separate aggregates, or States, as consider'd in one vast aggregate, the Union. This was the original dual theory and foundation of the United States, as distinguish'd from the feudal and ecclesiastical single idea of monarchies and papacies, and the divine right of kings. (Kings have been of use, hitherto, as representing the idea of the identity of nations. But, to American democracy, *both* ideas must be fulfill'd, and in my opinion the loss of vitality of either one will indeed be the loss of vitality of the other.)

EMERSON'S BOOKS (THE SHADOWS OF THEM)

IN THE regions we call Nature, towering beyond all measurement, with infinite spread, infinite depth and height—in those regions, including Man, socially and historically, with his moral-emotional influences—how small a part, (it came in my mind to-day,) has literature really depicted—even summing up all of it, all ages. Seems at its best some little fleet of boats, hugging the shores of a boundless sea, and never venturing, exploring the unmapp'd—never, Columbus-like, sailing out for New Worlds, and to complete the orb's rondure. Emerson writes frequently in the atmosphere of this thought, and his books report one or two things from that very ocean and air, and more legibly address'd to our age and American polity than by any man yet. But I will begin by scarifying him— thus proving that I am not insensible to his deepest lessons. I will consider his books from a democratic and western point of view. I will specify the shadows on these sunny expanses. Somebody has said of heroic character that "wherever the tallest peaks are present, must inevitably be deep chasms and valleys." Mine be the ungracious task (for reasons) of leaving unmention'd both sunny expanses and sky-reaching heights, to dwell on the bare spots and darknesses. I have a theory that no artist or work of the very first class may be or can be without them.

First, then, these pages are perhaps too perfect, too concentrated. (How good, for instance, is good butter, good sugar. But to be eating nothing but sugar and butter all the time! even if ever so good.) And though the author has much to say of freedom and wildness and simplicity and spontaneity, no performance was ever more based on artificial scholarships and decorums at third or fourth removes, (he calls it culture,) and built up from them. It is always a *make*, never an unconscious *growth*. It is the porcelain figure or statuette of lion, or stag, or Indian hunter—and a very choice statuette too—appropriate for the rosewood or marble bracket of parlor or library; never the animal itself, or the hunter himself. Indeed, who wants the real animal or hunter? What would that do amid astral and bric-a-brac and tapestry, and ladies and gentlemen talking in subdued tones of Browning and Longfellow and art? The least suspicion of such actual bull, or Indian, or of Nature carrying out itself, would put all those good people to instant terror and flight.

Emerson, in my opinion, is not most eminent as poet or artist or teacher, though valuable in all those. He is best as critic, or diagnoser. Not passion or imagination or warp or weakness, or any pronounced cause or specialty, dominates him. Cold and bloodless intellectuality dominates him. (I know the fires, emotions, love, egotisms, glow deep, perennial, as in all New Englanders—but the façade hides them well—they give no sign.) He does not see or take one side, one presentation only or mainly, (as all the poets, or most of the fine writers anyhow)—he sees all sides. His final influence is to make his students cease to worship anything—almost cease to believe in anything, outside of themselves. These books will fill, and well fill, certain stretches of life, certain stages of development—are, (like the tenets or theology the author of them preach'd when a young man,) unspeakably serviceable and precious as a stage. But in old or nervous or solemnest or dying hours, when one needs the impalpably soothing and vitalizing influences of abysmic Nature, or its affinities in literature or human society, and the soul resents the keenest mere intellection, they will not be sought for.

For a philosopher, Emerson possesses a singularly dandified theory of manners. He seems to have no notion at all that manners are simply the signs by which the chemist or metallurgist knows his metals. To the profound scientist, all metals are profound, as they really are. The little one, like the conventional world, will make much of gold and silver only. Then to the real artist in humanity, what are called bad manners are often the most picturesque and significant of all. Suppose these books becoming absorb'd, the permanent chyle of American general and particular character—what a well-wash'd and grammatical, but bloodless and helpless, race we should turn out! No, no, dear friend; though the States want scholars, undoubtedly, and perhaps want ladies and gentlemen who use the bath frequently, and never laugh loud, or talk wrong, they don't want scholars, or ladies and gentlemen, at the expense of all the rest. They want good farmers, sailors, mechanics, clerks, citizens —perfect business and social relations—perfect fathers and mothers. If we could only have these, or their approximations, plenty of them, fine and large and sane and generous and patriotic, they might make their verbs disagree from their nominatives, and laugh like volleys of musketeers, if they should please. Of course these are not all America wants, but they are first of all to be provided on a large scale. And, with tremendous errors and escapades, this, substantially, is what the States seem to have an intuition of, and to be mainly aiming at. The plan of a select class, superfined, (demarcated from the rest,) the plan of Old World lands and literatures, is not so objectionable in itself, but because it chokes the true plan for us, and indeed is death to it. As to such special class, the United States can never produce any equal to the splendid show, (far, far beyond comparison or competition here,) of the principal European nations, both in the past and at the present day. But an immense and distinctive commonalty over our vast and varied area, west and east, south and north—in fact, for the first time in history, a great, aggregated, real PEOPLE, worthy the name, and made of develop'd heroic individuals, both sexes—is America's principal, perhaps only, reason for being. If ever accomplish'd, it will be at least as much, (I lately think, doubly as much,) the result of fitting and democratic sociologies, literatures and arts— if we ever get them—as of our democratic politics.

At times it has been doubtful to me if Emerson really knows or feels what Poetry is at its highest, as in the Bible, for instance, or Homer or Shakspere. I see he covertly or plainly likes best superb verbal polish, or something old or odd—Waller's "Go, lovely rose," or Lovelace's lines "to Lucusta"—the quaint conceits of the old French bards, and the like. Of *power* he seems to have a gentleman's admiration—but in his inmost heart the grandest attribute of God and Poets is always subordinate to the octaves, conceits, polite kinks, and verbs.

The reminiscence that years ago I began like most youngsters to have a touch (though it came late, and was only on the surface) of Emerson-on-the-brain—that I read his writings reverently, and address'd him in print as "Master," and for a month or so thought of him as such—I retain not only with composure, but positive satisfaction. I have noticed that most young people of eager minds pass through this stage of exercise.

The best part of Emersonianism is, it breeds the giant that destroys itself. Who wants to be any man's mere follower? lurks behind every page. No teacher ever taught, that has so provided for his pupil's setting up independently—no truer evolutionist.

VENTURES, ON AN OLD THEME

A DIALOGUE—*One party says*—We arrange our lives—even the best and boldest men and women that exist, just as much as the most limited—with reference to what society conventionally rules and makes right. We retire to our rooms for freedom; to undress, bathe, unloose everything in freedom. These, and much else, would not be proper in society.

Other party answers—Such is the rule of society. Not always so, and considerable exceptions still exist. However, it must be called the general rule, sanction'd by immemorial usage, and will probably always remain so.

First party—Why not, then, respect it in your poems?

Answer—One reason, and to me a profound one, is that the soul of a man or woman demands, enjoys compensation in the highest directions for this very restraint of himself or herself, level'd to the

average, or rather mean, low, however eternally practical, requirements of society's intercourse. To balance this indispensable abnegation, the free minds of poets relieve themselves, and strengthen
and enrich mankind with free flights in all the directions not
tolerated by ordinary society.

First party—But must not outrage or give offence to it.

Answer—No, not in the deepest sense—and do not, and cannot.
The vast averages of time and the race *en masse* settle these things.
Only understand that the conventional standards and laws proper
enough for ordinary society apply neither to the action of the soul,
nor its poets. In fact the latter know no laws but the laws of themselves, planted in them by God, and are themselves the last standards of the law, and its final exponents—responsible to Him directly,
and not at all to mere etiquette. Often the best service that can be
done to the race, is to lift the veil, at least for a time, from these
rules and fossil-etiquettes.

NEW POETRY—*California, Canada, Texas*—In my opinion the time
has arrived to essentially break down the barriers of form between
prose and poetry. I say the latter is henceforth to win and maintain
its character regardless of rhyme, and the measurement-rules of
iambic, spondee, dactyl, &c., and that even if rhyme and those
measurements continue to furnish the medium for inferior writers
and themes, (especially for persiflage and the comic, as there seems
henceforward, to the perfect taste, something inevitably comic in
rhyme, merely in itself, and anyhow,) the truest and greatest
Poetry, (while subtly and necessarily always rhythmic, and distinguishable easily enough,) can never again, in the English language,
be express'd in arbitrary and rhyming metre, any more than the
greatest eloquence, or the truest power and passion. While admitting that the venerable and heavenly forms of chiming versification
have in their time play'd great and fitting parts—that the pensive
complaint, the ballads, wars, amours, legends of Europe, &c., have,
many of them, been inimitably render'd in rhyming verse—that
there have been very illustrious poets whose shapes the mantle of
such verse has beautifully and appropriately envelopt—and though
the mantle has fallen, with perhaps added beauty, on some of our
own age—it is, notwithstanding, certain to me, that the day of such
conventional rhyme is ended. In America, at any rate, and as a
medium of highest æsthetic practical or spiritual expression, present
or future, it palpably fails, and must fail, to serve. The Muse of
the Prairies, of California, Canada, Texas, and of the peaks of
Colorado, dismissing the literary, as well as social etiquette of over-

sea feudalism and caste, joyfully enlarging, adapting itself to comprehend the size of the whole people, with the free play, emotions, pride, passions, experiences, that belong to them, body and soul—to the general globe, and all its relations in astronomy, as the savans portray them to us—to the modern, the busy Nineteenth century, (as grandly poetic as any, only different,) with steamships, railroads, factories, electric telegraphs, cylinder presses—to the thought of the solidarity of nations, the brotherhood and sisterhood of the entire earth—to the dignity and heroism of the practical labor of farms, factories, foundries, workshops, mines, or on shipboard, or on lakes and rivers—resumes that other medium of expression, more flexible, more eligible—soars to the freer, vast, diviner heaven of prose.

Of poems of the third or fourth class, (perhaps even some of the second,) it makes little or no difference who writes them—they are good enough for what they are; nor is it necessary that they should be actual emanations from the personality and life of the writers. The very reverse sometimes gives piquancy. But poems of the first class, (poems of the depth, as distinguished from those of the surface,) are to be sternly tallied with the poets themselves, and tried by them and their lives. Who wants a glorification of courage and manly defiance from a coward or a sneak?—a ballad of benevolence or chastity from some rhyming hunks, or lascivious, glib *roué?*

In these States, beyond all precedent, poetry will have to do with actual facts, with the concrete States, and—for we have not much more than begun—with the definitive getting into shape of the Union. Indeed I sometimes think *it* alone is to define the Union, (namely, to give it artistic character, spirituality, dignity.) What American humanity is most in danger of is an overwhelming prosperity, "business" worldliness, materialism: what is most lacking, east, west, north, south, is a fervid and glowing Nationality and patriotism, cohering all the parts into one. Who may fend that danger, and fill that lack in the future, but a class of loftiest poets?

If the United States havn't grown poets, on any scale of grandeur, it is certain they import, print, and read more poetry than any equal number of people elsewhere—probably more than all the rest of the world combined.

Poetry (like a grand personality) is a growth of many generations—many rare combinations.

To have great poets, there must be great audiences, too.

BRITISH LITERATURE

To AVOID mistake, I would say that I not only commend the study
of this literature, but wish our sources of supply and comparison
vastly enlarged. American students may well derive from all former
lands—from forenoon Greece and Rome, down to the perturb'd
medieval times, the Crusades, and so to Italy, the German intellect
—all the older literatures, and all the newer ones—from witty and
warlike France, and markedly, and in many ways, and at many
different periods, from the enterprise and soul of the great Spanish
race—bearing ourselves always courteous, always deferential, indebted beyond measure to the mother-world, to all its nations dead,
as all its nations living—the offspring, this America of ours, the
daughter, not by any means of the British isles exclusively, but of
the continent, and all continents. Indeed, it is time we should
realize and fully fructify those germs we also hold from Italy,
France, Spain, especially in the best imaginative productions of
those lands, which are, in many ways, loftier and subtler than the
English, or British, and indispensable to complete our service, proportions, educations, reminiscences, &c. . . . The British element
these States hold, and have always held, enormously beyond its fit
proportions. I have already spoken of Shakspere. He seems to me
of astral genius, first class, entirely fit for feudalism. His contributions, especially to the literature of the passions, are immense, forever dear to humanity—and his name is always to be reverenced
in America. But there is much in him ever offensive to democracy.
He is not only the tally of feudalism, but I should say Shakspere is
incarnated, uncompromising feudalism, in literature. Then one
seems to detect something in him—I hardly know how to describe it
—even amid the dazzle of his genius; and, in inferior manifestations,
it is found in nearly all leading British authors. (Perhaps we will
have to import the words Snob, Snobbish, &c., after all.) While of
the great poems of Asian antiquity, the Indian epics, the book of
Job, the Ionian Iliad, the unsurpassedly simple, loving, perfect idyls
of the life and death of Christ, in the New Testament, (indeed
Homer and the Biblical utterances interwine familiarly with us, in
the main,) and along down, of most of the characteristic, imaginative or romantic relics of the continent, as the Cid, Cervantes' Don
Quixote, &c., I should say they substantially adjust themselves to us,
and, far off as they are, accord curiously with our bed and board
to-day, in New York, Washington, Canada, Ohio, Texas, California
—and with our notions, both of seriousness and of fun, and our
standards of heroism, manliness, and even the democratic require-

ments—those requirements are not only not fulfilled in the Shaksperean productions, but are insulted on every page.

I add that—while England is among the greatest of lands in
political freedom, or the idea of it, and in stalwart personal character, &c.—the spirit of English literature is not great, at least is
not greatest—and its products are no models for us. With the exception of Shakspere, there is no first-class genius in that literature—
which, with a truly vast amount of value, and of artificial beauty,
(largely from the classics,) is almost always material, sensual, not
spiritual—almost always congests, makes plethoric, not frees, expands, dilates—is cold, anti-democratic, loves to be sluggish and
stately, and shows much of that characteristic of vulgar persons,
the dread of saying or doing something not at all improper in itself,
but unconventional, and that may be laugh'd at. In its best, the
sombre pervades it; it is moody, melancholy, and, to give it its due,
expresses, in characters and plots, those qualities, in an unrival'd
manner. Yet not as the black thunderstorms, and in great normal,
crashing passions, of the Greek dramatists—clearing the air, refreshing afterward, bracing with power; but as in Hamlet, moping, sick,
uncertain, and leaving ever after a secret taste for the blues, the
morbid fascination, the luxury of wo. . . .

I strongly recommend all the young men and young women of
the United States to whom it may be eligible, to overhaul the well-
freighted fleets, the literatures of Italy, Spain, France, Germany, so
full of those elements of freedom, self-possession, gay-heartedness,
subtlety, dilation, needed in preparations for the future of the
States. I only wish we could have really good translations. I rejoice
at the feeling for Oriental researches and poetry, and hope it will
go on.

DARWINISM—(THEN FURTHERMORE)

Running through prehistoric ages—coming down from them into the
daybreak of our records, founding theology, suffusing literature,
and so brought onward—(a sort of verteber and marrow to all the
antique races and lands, Egypt, India, Greece, Rome, the Chinese,
the Jews, &c., and giving cast and complexion to their art, poems,
and their politics as well as ecclesiasticism, all of which we more or
less inherit,) appear those venerable claims to origin from God
himself, or from gods and goddesses—ancestry from divine beings
of vaster beauty, size, and power than ours. But in current and
latest times, the theory of human origin that seems to have most
made its mark, (curiously reversing the antique,) is that we have

come on, originated, develop't, from monkeys, baboons—a theory more significant perhaps in its indirections, or what it necessitates, than it is even in itself. (Of the twain, far apart as they seem, and angrily as their conflicting advocates to-day oppose each other, are not both theories to be possibly reconciled, and even blended? Can we, indeed, spare either of them? Better still, out of them is not a third theory, the real one, or suggesting the real one, to arise?)

Of this old theory, evolution, as broach'd anew, trebled, with indeed all-devouring claims, by Darwin, it has so much in it, and is so needed as a counterpoise to yet widely prevailing and unspeakably tenacious, enfeebling superstitions—is fused, by the new man, into such grand, modest, truly scientific accompaniments—that the world of erudition, both moral and physical, cannot but be eventually better'd and broaden'd in its speculations, from the advent of Darwinism. Nevertheless, the problem of origins, human and other, is not the least whit nearer its solution. In due time the Evolution theory will have to abate its vehemence, cannot be allow'd to dominate every thing else, and will have to take its place as a segment of the circle, the cluster—as but one of many theories, many thoughts, of profoundest value—and re-adjusting and differentiating much, yet leaving the divine secrets just as inexplicable and unreachable as before—may-be more so.

Then furthermore—What is finally to be done by priest or poet—and by priest or poet only—amid all the stupendous and dazzling novelties of our century, with the advent of America, and of science and democracy—remains just as indispensable, after all the work of the grand astronomers, chemists, linguists, historians, and explorers of the last hundred years—and the wondrous German and other metaphysicians of that time—and will continue to remain, needed, America and here, just the same as in the world of Europe, or Asia, of a hundred, or a thousand, or several thousand years ago. I think indeed *more* needed, to furnish statements from the present points, the added arriere, and the unspeakably immenser vistas of to-day. Only the priests and poets of the modern, at least as exalted as any in the past, fully absorbing and appreciating the results of the past, in the commonalty of all humanity, all time, (the main results already, for there is perhaps nothing more, or at any rate not much, strictly new, only more important modern combinations, and new relative adjustments,) must indeed recast the old metal, the already achiev'd material, into and through new moulds, current forms.

Meantime, the highest and subtlest and broadest truths of modern science wait for their true assignment and last vivid flashes of light—as Democracy waits for its—through first-class metaphysicians and speculative philosophs—laying the basements and foundations for those new, more expanded, more harmonious, more melodious, freer American poems.

"SOCIETY"

I HAVE myself little or no hope from what is technically called "Society" in our American cities. New York, of which place I have spoken so sharply, still promises something, in time, out of its tremendous and varied materials,. with a certain superiority of intuitions, and the advantage of constant agitation, and ever new and rapid dealings of the cards. Of Boston, with its circles of social mummies, swathed in cerements harder than brass—its bloodless religion, (Unitarianism,) its complacent vanity of scientism and literature, lots of grammatical correctness, mere knowledge, (always wearisome, in itself)—its zealous abstractions, ghosts of reforms— I should say, (ever admitting its business powers, its sharp, almost demoniac, intellect, and no lack, in its own way, of courage and generosity)—there is, at present, little of cheering, satisfying sign. In the West, California, &c., "society" is yet unform'd, puerile, seemingly unconscious of anything above a driving business, or to liberally spend the money made by it, in the usual rounds and shows.

Then there is, to the humorous observer of American attempts at fashion, according to the models of foreign courts and saloons, quite a comic side—particularly visible at Washington city—a sort of high-life-below-stairs business. As if any farce could be funnier, for instance, than the scenes of the crowds, winter nights, meandering around our Presidents and their wives, cabinet officers, western or other Senators, Representatives, &c.; born of good laboring mechanic or farmer stock and antecedents, attempting those full-dress receptions, finesse of parlors, foreign ceremonies, etiquettes, &c.

Indeed, consider'd with any sense of propriety, or any sense at all, the whole of this illy-play'd fashionable play and display, with their absorption of the best part of our wealthier citizens' time, money, energies, &c., is ridiculously out of place in the United States. As if our proper man and woman, (far, far greater words than "gentleman" and "lady,") could still fail to see, and presently achieve, not this spectral business, but something truly noble, active, sane, American—by modes, perfections of character, manners, costumes, social relations, &c., adjusted to standards, far, far different from those.

Eminent and liberal foreigners, British or continental, must at times have their faith fearfully tried by what they see of our New World personalities. The shallowest and least American persons seem surest to push abroad, and call without fail on well-known foreigners, who are doubtless affected with indescribable qualms by these queer ones. Then, more than half of our authors and writers evidently think it a great thing to be "aristocratic," and sneer at progress, democracy, revolution, &c. If some international literary snobs' gallery were establish'd, it is certain that America could contribute at least her full share of the portraits, and some very distinguish'd ones. Observe that the most impudent slanders, low insults, &c., on the great revolutionary authors, leaders, poets, &c., of Europe, have their origin and main circulation in certain circles here. The treatment of Victor Hugo living, and Byron dead, are samples. Both deserving so well of America, and both persistently attempted to be soil'd here by unclean birds, male and female.

Meanwhile I must still offset the like of the foregoing, and all it infers, by the recognition of the fact, that while the surfaces of current society here show so much that is dismal, noisome, and vapory, there are, beyond question, inexhaustible supplies, as of true gold ore, in the mines of America's general humanity. Let us, not ignoring the dross, give fit stress to these precious immortal values also. Let it be distinctly admitted, that—whatever may be said of our fashionable society, and of any foul fractions and episodes—only here in America, out of the long history and manifold presentations of the ages, has at last arisen, and now stands, what never before took positive form and sway, *the People*—and that view'd en masse, and while fully acknowledging deficiencies, dangers, faults, this people, inchoate, latent, not yet come to majority, nor to its own religious, literary, or æsthetic expression, yet affords, to-day, an exultant justification of all the faith, all the hopes and prayers and prophecies of good men through the past—the stablest, solidest-based government of the world—the most assured in a future—the beaming Pharos to whose perennial light all earnest eyes, the world over, are tending—and that already, in and from it, the democratic principle, having been mortally tried by severest tests, fatalities of war and peace, now issues from the trial, unharm'd, trebly-invigorated, perhaps to commence forthwith its finally triumphant march around the globe.

THE TRAMP AND STRIKE QUESTIONS

Part of a Lecture proposed, (never deliver'd)

Two grim and spectral dangers—dangerous to peace, to health, to social security, to progress—long known in concrete to the governments of the Old World, and there eventuating, more than once or twice, in dynastic overturns, bloodshed, days, months, of terror—seem of late years to be nearing the New World, nay, to be gradually establishing themselves among us. What mean these phantoms here? (I personify them in fictitious shapes, but they are very real.) Is the fresh and broad demesne of America destined also to give them foothold and lodgment, permanent domicile?

Beneath the whole political world, what most presses and perplexes to-day, sending vastest results affecting the future, is not the abstract question of democracy, but of social and economic organization, the treatment of working-people by employers, and all that goes along with it—not only the wages-payment part, but a certain spirit and principle, to vivify anew these relations; all the questions of progress, strength, tariffs, finance, &c., really evolving themselves more or less directly out of the Poverty Question, ("the Science of Wealth," and a dozen other names are given it, but I prefer the severe one just used.) I will begin by calling the reader's attention to a thought upon the matter which may not have struck you before —the wealth of the civilized world, as contrasted with its poverty— what does it derivatively stand for, and represent? A rich person ought to have a strong stomach. As in Europe the wealth of to-day mainly results from, and represents, the rapine, murder, outrages, treachery, hoggishness, of hundreds of years ago, and onward, later, so in America, after the same token—(not yet so bad, perhaps, or at any rate not so palpable—we have not existed long enough—but we seem to be doing our best to make it up.)

Curious as it may seem, it is in what are call'd the poorest, lowest characters you will sometimes, nay generally, find glints of the most sublime virtues, eligibilities, heroisms. Then it is doubtful whether the State is to be saved, either in the monotonous long run, or in tremendous special crises, by its good people only. When the storm is deadliest, and the disease most imminent, help often comes from strange quarters—(the homœopathic motto, you remember, *cure the bite with a hair of the same dog.*)

The American Revolution of 1776 was simply a great strike, successful for its immediate object—but whether a real success judged by the scale of the centuries, and the long-striking balance of Time, yet remains to be settled. The French Revolution was absolutely a strike, and a very terrible and relentless one, against ages of bad pay, unjust division of wealth-products, and the hoggish monopoly of a few, rolling in superfluity, against the vast bulk of the work-people, living in squalor.

If the United States, like the countries of the Old World, are also to grow vast crops of poor, desperate, dissatisfied, nomadic, miserably-waged populations, such as we see looming upon us of late years—steadily, even if slowly, eating into them like a cancer of lungs or stomach—then our republican experiment, notwithstanding all its surface-successes, is at heart an unhealthy failure.

Feb., '79.—I saw to-day a sight I had never seen before—and it amazed, and made me serious; three quite good-looking American men, of respectable personal presence, two of them young, carrying chiffonier-bags on their shoulders, and the usual long iron hooks in their hands, plodding along, their eyes cast down, spying for scraps, rags, bones, &c.

DEMOCRACY IN THE NEW WORLD,

estimated and summ'd-up to-day, having thoroughly justified itself the past hundred years, (as far as growth, vitality and power are concern'd,) by severest and most varied trials of peace and war, and having establish'd itself for good, with all its necessities and benefits, for time to come, is now to be seriously consider'd also in its pronounc'd and already developt dangers. While the battle was raging, and the result suspended, all defections and criticisms were to be hush'd, and everything bent with vehemence unmitigated toward the urge of victory. But that victory settled, new responsibilities advance. I can conceive of no better service in the United States, henceforth, by democrats of thorough and heart-felt faith, than boldly exposing the weakness, liabilities and infinite corruptions of democracy. By the unprecedented opening-up of humanity en-masse in the United States, the last hundred years, under our institutions, not only the good qualities of the race, but just as much the bad ones, are prominently brought forward. Man is about the same, in the main, whether with despotism, or whether with freedom.

"The ideal form of human society," Canon Kingsley declares, "is democracy. A nation—and were it even possible, a whole world—of free men, lifting free foreheads to God and Nature; calling no man master, for One is their master, even God; knowing and doing their duties toward the Maker of the universe, and therefore to each other; not from fear, nor calculation of profit or loss, but because they have seen the beauty of righteousness, and trust, and peace; because the law of God is in their hearts. Such a nation—such a society—what nobler conception of moral existence can we form? Would not that, indeed, be the kingdom of God come on earth?"

To this faith, founded in the ideal, let us hold—and never abandon or lose it. Then what a spectacle is *practically* exhibited by our American democracy to-day!

FOUNDATION STAGES—THEN OTHERS

THOUGH I think I fully comprehend the absence of moral tone in our current politics and business, and the almost entire futility of absolute and simple honor as a counterpoise against the enormous greed for worldly wealth, with the trickeries of gaining it, all through society our day, I still do not share the depression and despair on the subject which I find possessing many good people. The advent of America, the history of the past century, has been the first general aperture and opening-up to the average human commonalty, on the broadest scale, of the eligibilities to wealth and worldly success and eminence, and has been fully taken advantage of; and the example has spread hence, in ripples, to all nations. To these eligibilities—to this limitless aperture, the race has tended, en-masse, roaring and rushing and crude, and fiercely, turbidly hastening—and we have seen the first stages, and are now in the midst of the result of it all, so far. But there will certainly ensue other stages, and entirely different ones. In nothing is there more evolution than the American mind. Soon, it will be fully realized that ostensible wealth and money-making, show, luxury, &c., imperatively necessitate something beyond—namely, the sane, eternal moral and spiritual-esthetic attributes, elements. (We cannot have even that realization on any less terms than the price we are now paying for it.) Soon, it will be understood clearly, that the State cannot flourish, (nay, cannot exist,) without those elements. They will gradually enter into the chyle of sociology and literature. They will finally make the blood and brawn of the best American individualities of both sexes—and thus, with them, to a certainty, (through these very processes of to-day,) dominate the New World.

GENERAL SUFFRAGE, ELECTIONS, &c.

IT STILL remains doubtful to me whether these will ever secure,
officially, the best wit and capacity—whether, through them, the
first-class genius of America will ever personally appear in the high
political stations, the Presidency, Congress, the leading State offices,
&c. Those offices, or the candidacy for them, arranged, won, by
caucusing, money, the favoritism or pecuniary interest of rings, the
superior manipulation of the ins over the outs, or the outs over the
ins, are, indeed, at best, the mere business agencies of the people,
are useful as formulating, neither the best and highest, but the
average of the public judgment, sense, justice, (or sometimes want
of judgment, sense, justice.) We elect Presidents, Congressmen, &c.,
not so much to have them consider and decide for us, but as surest
practical means of expressing the will of majorities on mooted
questions, measures, &c.

As to general suffrage, after all, since we have gone so far, the
more general it is, the better. I favor the widest opening of the
doors. Let the ventilation and area be wide enough, and all is safe.
We can never have a born penitentiary-bird, or panel-thief, or
lowest gambling-hell or groggery keeper, for President—though
such may not only emulate, but get, high offices from localities—
even from the proud and wealthy city of New York.

WHO GETS THE PLUNDER?

THE protectionists are fond of flashing to the public eye the glittering delusion of great money-results from manufactures, mines, artificial exports—so many millions from this source, and so many from
that—such a seductive, unanswerable show—an immense revenue of
annual cash from iron, cotton, woollen, leather goods, and a hundred other things, all bolstered up by "protection." But the really
important point of all is, *into whose pockets does this plunder
really go?* It would be some excuse and satisfaction if even a fair
proportion of it went to the masses of laboring-men—resulting in
homesteads to such, men, women, children—myriads of actual
homes in fee simple, in every State, (not the false glamour of the
stunning wealth reported in the census, in the statistics, or tables
in the newspapers,) but a fair division and generous average to
those workmen and workwomen—*that* would be something. But the
fact itself is nothing of the kind. The profits of "protection" go
altogether to a few score select persons—who, by favors of Congress, State legislatures, the banks, and other special advantages,

are forming a vulgar aristocracy, full as bad as anything in the British or European castes, of blood, or the dynasties there of the past. As Sismondi pointed out, the true prosperity of a nation is not in the great wealth of a special class, but is only to be really attain'd in having the bulk of the people provided with homes or land in fee simple. This may not be the best show, but it is the best reality.

FRIENDSHIP (THE REAL ARTICLE)

THOUGH Nature maintains, and must prevail, there will always be plenty of people, and good people, who cannot, or think they cannot, see anything in that last, wisest, most envelop'd of proverbs, "Friendship rules the World." Modern society, in its largest vein, is essentially intellectual, infidelistic—secretly admires, and depends most on, pure compulsion or science, its rule and sovereignty—is, in short, in "cultivated" quarters, deeply Napoleonic.

"Friendship," said Bonaparte, in one of his lightning-flashes of candid garrulity, "Friendship is but a name. I love no one—not even my brothers; Joseph perhaps a little. Still, if I do love him, it is from habit, because he is the eldest of us. Duroc? Ay, him, if any one, I love in a sort—but why? He suits me; he is cool, undemonstrative, unfeeling—has no weak affections—never embraces any one —never weeps."

I am not sure but the same analogy is to be applied, in cases, often seen, where, with an extra development and acuteness of the intellectual faculties, there is a mark'd absence of the spiritual, affectional, and sometimes, though more rarely, the highest æsthetic and moral elements of cognition.

LACKS AND WANTS YET

OF MOST foreign countries, small or large, from the remotest times known, down to our own, each has contributed after its kind, directly or indirectly, at least one great undying song, to help vitalize and increase the valor, wisdom, and elegance of humanity, from the points of view attain'd by it up to date. The stupendous epics of India, the holy Bible itself, the Homeric canticles, the Nibelungen, the Cid Campeador, the Inferno, Shakspere's dramas of the passions and of the feudal lords, Burns's songs, Goethe's in Germany, Tennyson's poems in England, Victor Hugo's in France, and many more, are the widely various yet integral signs or landmarks, (in certain respects the highest set up by the human mind and soul, beyond science, invention, political amelioration, &c.,)

narrating in subtlest, best ways, the long, long routes of history, and giving identity to the stages arrived at by aggregate humanity, and the conclusions assumed in its progressive and varied civilizations. . . . Where is America's art-rendering, in any thing like the spirit worthy of herself and the modern, to these characteristic immortal monuments? So far, our Democratic society, (estimating its various strata, in the mass, as one,) possesses nothing—nor have we con- tributed any characteristic music, the finest tie of nationality—to make up for that glowing, blood-throbbing, religious, social, emo- tional, artistic, indefinable, indescribably beautiful charm and hold which fused the separate parts of the old feudal societies together, in their wonderful interpenetration, in Europe and Asia, of love, belief, and loyalty, running one way like a living weft—and pic- turesque responsibility, duty, and blessedness, running like a warp the other way. (In the Southern States, under slavery, much of the same.) . . . In coincidence, and as things now exist in the States, what is more terrible, more alarming, than the total want of any such fusion and mutuality of love, belief, and rapport of interest, between the comparatively few successful rich, and the great masses of the unsuccessful, the poor? As a mixed political and social ques- tion, is not this full of dark significance? Is it not worth considering as a problem and puzzle in our democracy—an indispensable want to be supplied?

RULERS STRICTLY OUT OF THE MASSES

IN THE talk (which I welcome) about the need of men of training, thoroughly school'd and experienced men, for statesmen, I would present the following as an offset. It was written by me twenty years ago—and has been curiously verified since:

I say no body of men are fit to make Presidents, Judges, and Gen- erals, unless they themselves supply the best specimens of the same; and that supplying one or two such specimens illuminates the whole body for a thousand years. I expect to see the day when the like of the present personnel of the governments, Federal, State, municipal, military, and naval, will be look'd upon with derision, and when qualified mechanics and young men will reach Congress and other official stations, sent in their working costumes, fresh from their benches and tools, and returning to them again with dignity. The young fellows must prepare to do credit to this destiny, for the stuff is in them. Nothing gives place, recollect, and never ought to give place, except to its clean superiors. There is more rude and undevel- opt bravery, friendship, conscientiousness, clear-sightedness, and practical genius for any scope of action, even the broadest and highest, now among the American mechanics and young men, than in all the official persons in these States, legislative, executive, judicial, military, and naval, and more than among all the literary persons. I would be much pleased to see some heroic, shrewd, fully-inform'd, healthy-bodied, middle-aged, beard-faced American blacksmith or boatman come down from the West across the Alleghanies, and walk into the Presidency, dress'd in a clean suit of working attire, and with the tan all over his face, breast, and arms; I would certainly vote for that sort of man, possessing the due requirements, before any other candidate.

(The facts of rank-and-file workingmen, mechanics, Lincoln, Johnson, Grant, Garfield, brought forward from the masses and placed in the Presidency, and swaying its mighty powers with firm hand—really with more sway than any king in history, and with better capacity in using that sway—can we not see that these facts have bearings far, far beyond their political or party ones?)

MONUMENTS—THE PAST AND PRESENT

IF YOU go to Europe, (to say nothing of Asia, more ancient and massive still,) you cannot stir without meeting venerable mementos—cathedrals, ruins of temples, castles, monuments of the great, statues and paintings, (far, far beyond anything America can ever expect to produce,) haunts of heroes long dead, saints, poets, divinities, with deepest associations of ages. But here in the New World, while *those* we can never emulate, we have *more* than those to build, and far more greatly to build. (I am not sure but the day for conventional monuments, statues, memorials, &c., has pass'd away—and that they are henceforth superfluous and vulgar.) An enlarged general superior humanity, (partly indeed resulting from those,) we are to build. European, Asiatic greatness are in the past. Vaster and subtler, America, combining, justifying the past, yet works for a grander future, in living democratic forms. (Here too are indicated the paths for our national bards.) Other times, other lands, have had their missions—Art, War, Ecclesiasticism, Literature, Discovery, Trade, Architecture, &c., &c.—but that grand future is the enclosing purport of the United States.

LITTLE OR NOTHING NEW, AFTER ALL

How small were the best thoughts, poems, conclusions, except for a certain invariable resemblance and uniform standard in the final thoughts, theology, poems, &c., of all nations, all civilizations, all centuries and times. Those precious legacies—accumulations! They come to us from the far-off—from all eras, and all lands—from Egypt, and India, and Greece, and Rome—and along through the middle and later ages, in the grand monarchies of Europe—born under far different institutes and conditions from ours—but out of the insight and inspiration of the same old humanity—the same old heart and brain—the same old countenance yearningly, pensively, looking forth. What we have to do to-day is to receive them cheerfully, and to give them ensemble, and a modern American and democratic physiognomy.

A LINCOLN REMINISCENCE

As IS well known, story-telling was often with President Lincoln a weapon which he employ'd with great skill. Very often he could not give a point-blank reply or comment—and these indirections, (sometimes funny, but not always so,) were probably the best responses possible. In the gloomiest period of the war, he had a call from a large delegation of bank presidents. In the talk after business was settled, one of the big Dons asked Mr. Lincoln if his confidence in the permanency of the Union was not beginning to be shaken—whereupon the homely President told a little story: "When I was a young man in Illinois," said he, "I boarded for a time with a deacon of the Presbyterian church. One night I was roused from my sleep by a rap at the door, and I heard the deacon's voice exclaiming, 'Arise, Abraham! the day of judgment has come!' I sprang from my bed and rushed to the window, and saw the stars falling in great showers; but looking back of them in the heavens I saw the grand old constellations, with which I was so well acquainted, fixed and true in their places. Gentlemen, the world did not come to an end then, nor will the Union now."

FREEDOM

IT IS not only true that most people entirely misunderstand Freedom, but I sometimes think I have not yet met one person who rightly understands it. The whole Universe is absolute Law. Freedom only opens entire activity and license *under the law*. To the degraded or undevelopt—and even to too many others—the thought of freedom is a thought of escaping from law—which, of course, is impossible. More precious than all worldly riches is Freedom—freedom from the painful constipation and poor narrowness of ecclesiasticism—freedom in manners, habiliments, furniture, from the silliness and tyranny of local fashions—entire freedom from party rings and mere conventions in Politics—and better than all, a general freedom of One's-Self from the tyrannic domination of vices, habits, appetites, under which nearly every man of us, (often the greatest brawler for freedom,) is enslaved. Can we attain such enfranchisement—the true Democracy, and the height of it? While we are from birth to death the subjects of irresistible law, enclosing every movement and minute, we yet escape, by a paradox, into true free will. Strange as it may seem, we only attain to freedom by a knowledge of, and implicit obedience to, Law. Great—unspeakably great—is the Will! the free Soul of man! At its greatest, understanding and obeying the laws, it can then, and then only, maintain true liberty. For there is to the highest, that law as absolute as any—more absolute than any—the Law of Liberty. The shallow, as intimated, consider liberty a release from all law, from every constraint. The wise see in it, on the contrary, the potent Law of Laws, namely, the fusion and combination of the conscious will, or partial individual law, with those universal, eternal, unconscious ones, which run through all Time, pervade history, prove immortality, give moral purpose to the entire objective world, and the last dignity to human life.

BOOK-CLASSES—AMERICA'S LITERATURE

For certain purposes, literary productions through all the recorded ages may be roughly divided into two classes. The first consisting of only a score or two, perhaps less, of typical, primal, representative works, different from any before, and embodying in themselves their own main laws and reasons for being. Then the second class, books and writings innumerable, incessant—to be briefly described as radiations or offshoots, or more or less imitations of the first. The works of the first class, as said, have their own laws, and may indeed be described as making those laws, and amenable only to them. The sharp warning of Margaret Fuller, unquell'd for thirty years, yet sounds in the air; "It does not follow that because the United States print and read more books, magazines, and newspapers than all the rest of the world, that they really have, therefore, a literature."

OUR REAL CULMINATION

The final culmination of this vast and varied Republic will be the production and perennial establishment of millions of comfortable city homesteads and moderate-sized farms, healthy and independent, single separate ownership, fee simple, life in them complete but cheap, within reach of all. Exceptional wealth, splendor, countless manufactures, excess of exports, immense capital and capitalists, the five-dollar-a-day hotels well fill'd, artificial improvements, even books, colleges, and the suffrage—all, in many respects, in themselves, (hard as it is to say so, and sharp as a surgeon's lance,) form, more or less, a sort of anti-democratic disease and monstrosity, except as they contribute by curious indirections to that culmination—seem to me mainly of value, or worth consideration, only with reference to it.

There is a subtle something in the common earth, crops, cattle, air, trees, &c., and in having to do at first hand with them, that forms the only purifying and perennial element for individuals and for society. I must confess I want to see the agricultural occupation of America at first hand permanently broaden'd. Its gains are the only ones on which God seems to smile. What others—what business, profit, wealth, without a taint? What fortune else—what dollar—does not stand for, and come from, more or less imposition, lying, unnaturalness?

AN AMERICAN PROBLEM

ONE of the problems presented in America these times is, how to combine one's duty and policy as a member of associations, societies, brotherhoods or what not, and one's obligations to the State and Nation, with essential freedom as an individual personality, without which freedom a man cannot grow or expand, or be full, modern, heroic, democratic, American. With all the necessities and benefits of association, (and the world cannot get along without it,) the true nobility and satisfaction of a man consist in his thinking and acting for himself. The problem, I say, is to combine the two, so as not to ignore either.

THE LAST COLLECTIVE COMPACTION

I LIKE well our polyglot construction-stamp, and the retention thereof, in the broad, the tolerating, the many-sided, the collective. All nations here—a home for every race on earth. British, German, Scandinavian, Spanish, French, Italian—papers published, plays acted, speeches made, in all languages—on our shores the crowning resultant of those distillations, decantations, compactions of humanity, that have been going on, on trial, over the earth so long.

Collect (Appendix)

⤜⤚

PIECES IN EARLY YOUTH
1834–'42

DOUGH-FACE SONG

—Like dough; soft; yielding to pressure; pale.—Webster's Dictionary.

We are all docile dough-faces,
    They knead us with the fist,
They, the dashing southern lords,
    We labor as they list;
For them we speak—or hold our tongues,
    For them we turn and twist.

We join them in their howl against
    Free soil and "abolition,"
That firebrand—that assassin knife—
    Which risk our land's condition,
And leave no peace of life to any
    Dough-faced politician.

To put down "agitation," now,
    We think the most judicious;
To damn all "northern fanatics,"
    Those "traitors" black and vicious;
The "reg'lar party usages"
    For us, and no "new issues."

349

Things have come to a pretty pass,
  When a trifle small as this,
Moving and bartering nigger slaves,
  Can open an abyss,
With jaws a-gape for "the two great parties;"
  A pretty thought, I wis!

Principle—freedom!—fiddlesticks!
  We knew not where they 're found.
Rights of the masses—progress!—bah!
  Words that tickle and sound;
But claiming to rule o'er "practical men"
  Is very different ground.

Beyond all such we know a term
  Charming to ears and eyes,
With it we'll stab young Freedom,
  And do it in disguise;
Speak soft, ye wily dough-faces—
  That term is "compromise."

And what if children, growing up,
  In future seasons read
The thing we do? and heart and tongue
  Accurse us for the deed?
The future cannot touch us;
  The present gain we heed.

Then, all together, dough-faces!
  Let's stop the exciting clatter,
And pacify slave-breeding wrath
  By yielding all the matter;
For otherwise, as sure as guns,
  The Union it will shatter.

Besides, to tell the honest truth
  (For us an innovation,)
Keeping in with the slave power
  Is our personal salvation;
We 've very little to expect
  From t' other part of the nation.

Besides it's plain at Washington
  Who likeliest wins the race,
What earthly chance has "free soil"
  For any good fat place?
While many a daw has feather'd his nest,
  By his creamy and meek dough-face.

Take heart, then, sweet companions,
  Be steady, Scripture Dick!
Webster, Cooper, Walker,
  To your allegiance stick!
With Brooks, and Briggs and Phœnix,
  Stand up through thin and thick!

We do not ask a bold brave front;
  We never try that game;
'Twould bring the storm upon our heads,
  A huge mad storm of shame;
Evade it, brothers—"compromise"
  Will answer just the same.   PAUMANOK.

DEATH IN THE SCHOOL-ROOM (*A Fact*)

TING-A-LING-LING-LING! went the little bell on the teacher's desk of a village-school one morning, when the studies of the earlier part of the day were about half completed. It was well understood that this was a command for silence and attention; and when these had been obtain'd, the master spoke. He was a low thick-set man, and his name was Lugare.

"Boys," said he, "I have had a complaint enter'd, that last night some of you were stealing fruit from Mr. Nichols's garden. I rather think I know the thief. Tim Barker, step up here, sir."

The one to whom he spoke came forward. He was a slight, fair-looking boy of about thirteen; and his face had a laughing, good-humor'd expression, which even the charge now preferr'd against him, and the stern tone and threatening look of the teacher, had not entirely dissipated. The countenance of the boy, however, was too unearthly fair for health; it had, notwithstanding its fleshy, cheerful look, a singular cast as if some inward disease, and that a fearful one, were seated within. As the stripling stood before that place of judgment—that place so often made the scene of heartless and coarse brutality, of timid innocence confused, helpless childhood outraged, and gentle feelings crush'd—Lugare looked on him with a frown which plainly told that he felt in no very pleasant mood. (Happily a worthier and more philosophical system is proving to men that schools can be better govern'd than by lashes and tears and sighs. We are waxing toward that consummation when one of the old-fashion'd school-masters, with his cowhide, his heavy birch-rod, and his many ingenious methods of child-torture, will be gazed upon as a scorn'd memento of an ignorant, cruel, and exploded doctrine. May propitious gales speed that day!)

"Were you by Mr. Nichols's garden-fence last night?" said Lugare.

"Yes, sir," answer'd the boy, "I was."

"Well, sir, I'm glad to find you so ready with your confession. And so you thought you could do a little robbing, and enjoy yourself in a manner you ought to be ashamed to own, without being punish'd, did you?"

"I have not been robbing," replied the boy quickly. His face was suffused, whether with resentment or fright, it was difficult to tell. "And I didn't do anything last night, that I am ashamed to own."

"No impudence!" exclaim'd the teacher, passionately, as he grasp'd a long and heavy ratan: "give me none of your sharp speeches, or I'll thrash you till you beg like a dog."

The youngster's face paled a little; his lip quiver'd, but he did not speak.

"And pray, sir," continued Lugare, as the outward signs of wrath disappear'd from his features; "what were you about the garden for? Perhaps you only receiv'd the plunder, and had an accomplice to do the more dangerous part of the job?"

"I went that way because it is on my road home. I was there again afterwards to meet an acquaintance; and—and— But I did not go into the garden, nor take anything away from it. I would not steal,—hardly to save myself from starving."

"You had better have stuck to that last evening. You were seen, Tim Barker, to come from under Mr. Nichols's garden-fence, a little after nine o'clock, with a bag full of something or other over your shoulders. The bag had every appearance of being filled with fruit, and this morning the melon-beds are found to have been completely clear'd. Now, sir, what was there in that bag?"

Like fire itself glow'd the face of the detected lad. He spoke not a word. All the school had their eyes directed at him. The perspiration ran down his white forehead like rain-drops.

"Speak, sir!" exclaimed Lugare, with a loud strike of his ratan on the desk.

The boy look'd as though he would faint. But the unmerciful teacher, confident of having brought to light a criminal, and exulting in the idea of the severe chastisement he should now be justified in inflicting, kept working himself up to a still greater and greater degree of passion. In the meantime, the child seem'd hardly to know what to do with himself. His tongue cleav'd to the roof of his mouth. Either he was very much frighten'd, or he was actually unwell.

"Speak, I say!" again thunder'd Lugare; and his hand, grasping his ratan, tower'd above his head in a very significant manner.

"I hardly can, sir," said the poor fellow faintly. His voice was husky and thick. "I will tell you some—some other time. Please let me go to my seat—I a'n't well."

"Oh yes; that's very likely;" and Mr. Lugare bulged out his nose and cheeks with contempt. "Do you think to make me believe your lies? I've found you out, sir, plainly enough; and I am satisfied that you are as precious a little villain as there is in the State. But I will postpone settling with you for an hour yet. I shall then call you up again; and if you don't tell the whole truth then, I will give you something that'll make you remember Mr. Nichols's melons for many a month to come:—go to your seat."

Glad enough of the ungracious permission, and answering not a sound, the child crept tremblingly to his bench. He felt very strangely, dizzily— more as if he was in a dream than in real life; and laying his arms on his desk, bow'd down his face between them. The pupils turn'd to their accustom'd studies, for during the reign of Lugare in the village-school, they had been so used to scenes of violence and severe chastisement, that such things made but little interruption in the tenor of their way.

Now, while the intervening hour is passing, we will clear up the mystery of the bag, and of young Barker being under the garden fence on the preceding night. The boy's mother was a widow, and they both had to live in the very narrowest limits. His father had died when he was six years old, and little Tim was left a sickly emaciated infant whom no one expected to live many months. To the surprise of all, however, the poor child kept alive, and seem'd to recover his health, as he certainly did his size and good looks. This was owing to the kind offices of an eminent physician who had a country-seat in the neighborhood, and who had been interested in the widow's little family. Tim, the physician said, might possibly outgrow his disease; but everything was uncertain. It was a mysterious and baffling malady; and it would not be wonderful if he should in some moment of apparent health be suddenly taken away. The poor widow was at first in a continual state of uneasiness; but several years had now pass'd, and none of the impending evils had fallen upon the boy's head. His mother seem'd to feel confident that he would live, and be a help and an honor to her old age; and the two struggled on together, mutually happy in each other, and enduring much of poverty and discomfort without repining, each for the other's sake.

Tim's pleasant disposition had made him many friends in the village, and among the rest a young farmer named Jones, who, with his elder brother, work'd a large farm in the neighborhood on shares. Jones very frequently made Tim a present of a bag of potatoes or corn, or some garden vegetables, which he took from his own stock; but as his partner was a parsimonious, high-tempered man, and had often said that Tim was an idle fellow, and ought not to be help'd because he did not work, Jones generally made his gifts in such a manner that no one knew anything about them, except himself and the grateful objects of his kindness. It might be, too, that the widow was loth to have it understood by the neighbors that she received food from anyone; for there is often an excusable pride in people of her condition which makes them shrink from being consider'd as objects of "charity" as they would from the severest pains. On the night in question, Tim had been told that Jones would send them a bag of potatoes, and the place at which they were to be waiting for him was fixed at Mr. Nichols's garden-fence. It was this bag that Tim had been seen staggering under, and which caused the unlucky boy to be accused and convicted by his teacher as a thief. That teacher was one little fitted for his important and responsible office. Hasty to decide, and inflexibly severe, he was the terror of the little world he ruled so despotically. Punishment he seemed to delight in. Knowing little of those sweet fountains which in children's breasts ever open quickly at the call of gentleness and kind words, he was fear'd by all for his sternness, and loved by none. I would that he were an isolated instance in his profession.

The hour of grace had drawn to its close, and the time approach'd at which it was usual for Lugare to give his school a joyfully-receiv'd dismission. Now and then one of the scholars would direct a furtive glance at Tim, sometimes in pity, sometimes in indifference or inquiry. They knew that he would have no mercy shown him, and though most of them loved him, whipping was too common there to exact much sympathy. Every inquiring glance, however, remain'd unsatisfied, for at the end of the hour, Tim remain'd with his face completely hidden, and his head bow'd in his arms, precisely as he had lean'd himself when he first went to his seat. Lugare look'd at the boy occasionally with a scowl which seem'd to bode vengeance for his sullenness. At length the last class had been heard, and the last lesson recited, and Lugare seated himself behind his desk on the platform, with his longest and stoutest ratan before him.

"Now, Barker," he said, "we'll settle that little business of yours. Just step up here."

Tim did not move. The school-room was as still as the grave. Not a sound was to be heard, except occasionally a long-drawn breath.

"Mind me, sir, or it will be the worse for you. Step up here, and take off your jacket!"

The boy did not stir any more than if he had been of wood. Lugare shook with passion. He sat still a minute, as if considering the best way to wreak his vengeance. That minute, passed in death-like silence, was a fearful one to some of the children, for their faces whiten'd with fright. It seem'd, as it slowly dropp'd away, like the minute which precedes the climax of an exquisitely-performed tragedy, when some mighty master of the histrionic art is treading the stage, and you and the multitude around you are waiting, with stretch'd nerves and suspended breath, in expectation of the terrible catastrophe.

"Tim is asleep, sir," at length said one of the boys who sat near him.

Lugare, at this intelligence, allow'd his features to relax from their expression of savage anger into a smile, but that smile look'd more malignant if possible, than his former scowls. It might be that he felt amused at the horror depicted on the faces of those about him; or it might be that he was gloating in pleasure on the way in which he intended to wake the slumberer.

"Asleep! are you, my young gentleman!" said he; "let us see if we can't find something to tickle your eyes open. There's nothing like making the best of a bad case, boys. Tim, here, is determin'd not to be worried in his mind about a little flogging, for the thought of it can't even keep the little scoundrel awake."

Lugare smiled again as he made the last observation. He grasp'd his ratan firmly, and descended from his seat. With light and stealthy steps he cross'd the room, and stood by the unlucky sleeper. The boy was still as unconscious of his impending punishment as ever. He might be dreaming some golden dream of youth and pleasure; perhaps he was far away in the world of fancy, seeing scenes, and feeling delights, which cold reality never can bestow. Lugare lifted his ratan high over his head, and with the true and expert aim which he had acquired by long practice, brought it down on Tim's back with a force and whacking sound which seem'd sufficient to awake a freezing man in his last lethargy. Quick and fast, blow follow'd blow. Without waiting to see the effect of the first cut, the brutal wretch plied his instrument of torture first on one side of the boy's back, and then on the other, and only stopped at the end of two or three minutes from very weariness. But still Tim show'd no signs of motion; and as Lugare, provoked at his torpidity, jerk'd away one of the child's arms, on which he had been leaning over the desk, his head dropp'd down on the board with a dull sound, and his face lay turn'd up and exposed to view. When Lugare saw it, he stood like one transfix'd by a basilisk. His countenance turn'd to a leaden whiteness; the ratan dropp'd from his grasp; and his eyes, stretch'd wide open, glared as at some monstrous spectacle of horror and death. The sweat started in great globules seemingly from every pore in his face; his skinny lips contracted, and show'd his teeth; and when he at length stretch'd forth his arm, and with the end of one of his fingers touch'd the child's cheek, each limb quiver'd like the tongue of a snake; and his strength seemed as though it would momentarily fail him. The boy was dead. He had probably been so for some time, for his eyes were turn'd up, and his body was quite cold. Death was in the school-room, and Lugare had been flogging A CORPSE.

—*Democratic Review, August, 1841.*

ONE WICKED IMPULSE!

THAT SECTION of Nassau street which runs into the great mart of New York brokers and stock-jobbers, has for a long time been much occupied by practitioners of the law. Tolerably well-known amid the class some years since, was Adam Covert, a middle-aged man of rather limited means, who, to tell the truth, gained more by trickery than he did in the legitimate and honorable exercise of his profession. He was a tall, bilious-faced widower; the father of two children; and had lately been seeking to better his fortunes by a rich marriage. But somehow or other his wooing did not seem to thrive well, and, with perhaps one exception, the lawyer's prospects in the matrimonial way were hopelessly gloomy.

Among the early clients of Mr. Covert had been a distant relative named Marsh, who, dying somewhat suddenly, left his son and daughter, and some little property, to the care of Covert, under a will drawn out by that gentleman himself. At no time caught without his eyes open, the cunning lawyer, aided by much sad confusion in the emergency which had caused his services to be called for, and disguising his object under a cloud of technicalities, inserted provisions in the will, giving himself an almost arbitrary control over the property and over those for whom it was designed. This control was even made to extend beyond the time when the children would arrive at mature age. The son, Philip, a spirited and high-temper'd fellow, had some time since pass'd that age. Esther, the girl, a plain, and somewhat devotional young woman, was in her nineteenth year.

Having such power over his wards, Covert did not scruple openly to use his advantage, in pressing his claims as a suitor for Esther's hand. Since the death of Marsh, the property he left, which had been in real estate, and was to be divided equally between the brother and sister, had risen to very considerable value; and Esther's share was to a man in Covert's situation a prize very well worth seeking. All this time, while really owning a respectable income, the young orphans often felt the want of the smallest sum of money—and Esther, on Philip's account, was more than once driven to various contrivances—the pawn-shop, sales of her own little luxuries, and the like, to furnish him with means.

Though she had frequently shown her guardian unequivocal evidence of her aversion, Esther continued to suffer from his persecutions, until one day he proceeded farther and was more pressing than usual. She possess'd some of her brother's mettlesome temper, and gave him an abrupt and most decided refusal. With dignity, she exposed the baseness of his conduct, and forbade him ever again mentioning marriage to her. He retorted bitterly, vaunted his hold on her and Philip, and swore an oath that unless she became his wife, they should both thenceforward become penniless. Losing his habitual self-control in his exasperation, he even added insults such as woman never receives from any one deserving the name of man, and at his own convenience left the house. That day, Philip return'd to New York, after an absence of several weeks on the business of a mercantile house in whose employment he had lately engaged.

Toward the latter part of the same afternoon, Mr. Covert was sitting in his office, in Nassau street, busily at work, when a knock at the door announc'd a visitor, and directly afterward young Marsh enter'd the room. His face exhibited a peculiar pallid appearance that did not strike Covert at all agreeably, and he call'd his clerk from an adjoining room, and gave him something to do at a desk near by.

"I wish to see you alone, Mr. Covert, if convenient," said the newcomer.

"We can talk quite well enough where we are," answer'd the lawyer; "indeed, I don't know that I have any leisure to talk at all, for just now I am very much press'd with business."

"But I *must* speak to you," rejoined Philip sternly, "at least I must say one thing, and that is, Mr. Covert, that you are a villain!"

"Insolent!" exclaimed the lawyer, rising behind the table, and pointing to the door: "Do you see that, sir! Let one minute longer find you the other side, or your feet may reach the landing by quicker method. Begone, sir!"

Such a threat was the more harsh to Philip, for he had rather high-strung feelings of honor. He grew almost livid with suppress'd agitation.

"I will see you again very soon," said he, in a low but distinct manner, his lips trembling as he spoke; and left the office.

The incidents of the rest of that pleasant summer day left little impression on the young man's mind. He roam'd to and fro without any object or destination. Along South street and by Whitehall, he watch'd with curious eyes the movements of the shipping, and the loading and unloading of cargoes; and listen'd to the merry heave-yo of the sailors and stevedores. There are some minds upon which great excitement produces the singular effect of uniting two utterly inconsistent faculties—a sort of cold apathy, and a sharp sensitiveness to all that is going on at the same time. Philip's was one of this sort; he noticed the various differences in the apparel of a gang of wharf-laborers—turn'd over in his brain whether they receiv'd wages enough to keep them comfortable, and their families also—and if they had families or not, which he tried to tell by their looks. In such petty reflections the daylight passed away. And all the while the master wish of Philip's thoughts was a desire to see the lawyer Covert. For what purpose he himself was by no means clear.

Nightfall came at last. Still, however, the young man did not direct his steps homeward. He felt more calm, however, and entering an eating house, order'd something for his supper, which, when it was brought to him, he merely tasted, and stroll'd forth again. There was a kind of gnawing sensation of thirst within him yet, and as he pass'd a hotel, he bethought him that one little glass of spirits would perhaps be just the thing. He drank, and hour after hour wore away unconsciously; he drank not one glass, but three or four, and strong glasses they were to him, for he was habitually abstemious.

It had been a hot day and evening, and when Philip, at an advanced period of the night, emerged from the bar-room into the street, he found that a thunderstorm had just commenced. He resolutely walk'd on, however, although at every step it grew more and more blustering.

The rain now pour'd down a cataract; the shops were all shut; few of the street lamps were lighted; and there was little except the frequent flashes of lightning to show him his way. When about half the length of Chatham street, which lay in the direction he had to take, the momentary fury of the tempest forced him to turn aside into a sort of shelter form'd by the corners of the deep entrance to a Jew pawnbroker's shop there. He had hardly drawn himself in as closely as possible, when the lightning reveal'd to him that the opposite corner of the nook was tenanted also.

"A sharp rain, this," said the other occupant, who simultaneously beheld Philip.

The voice sounded to the young man's ears a note which almost made him sober again. It was certainly the voice of Adam Covert. He made some commonplace reply, and waited for another flash of lightning to show him the stranger's face. It came, and he saw that his companion was indeed his guardian.

Philip Marsh had drank deeply—(let us plead all that may be possible to you, stern moralist.) Upon his mind came swarming, and he could not drive them away, thoughts of all those insults his sister had told him of, and the bitter words Covert had spoken to her; he reflected, too, on the injuries Esther as well as himself had receiv'd, and were still likely to receive, at the hands of that bold, bad man; how mean, selfish, and unprincipled was his character—what base and cruel advantages he had taken of many poor people, entangled in his power, and of how much wrong and suffering he had been the author, and might be again through future years. The very turmoil of the elements, the harsh roll of the thunder, the vindictive beating of the rain, and the fierce glare of the wild fluid that seem'd to riot in the ferocity of the storm around him, kindled a strange sympathetic fury in the young man's mind. Heaven itself (so deranged were his imaginations) appear'd to have provided a fitting scene and time for a deed of retribution, which to his disorder'd passion half wore the semblance of a divine justice. He remember'd not the ready solution to be found in Covert's pressure of business, which had no doubt kept him later than usual; but fancied some mysterious intent in the ordaining that he should be there, and that they two should meet at that untimely hour. All this whirl of influence came over Philip with startling quickness at that horrid moment. He stepp'd to the side of his guardian.

"Ho!" said he, "have we met so soon, Mr. Covert? You traitor to my dead father—robber of his children! I fear to think on *what* I think now!"

The lawyer's natural effrontery did not desert him.

"Unless you'd like to spend a night in the watch-house, young gentleman," said he, after a short pause, "move on. Your father was a weak man, I remember; as for his son, his own wicked heart is his worst foe. I have never done wrong to either—that I can say, and swear it!"

"Insolent liar!" exclaimed Philip, his eye flashing out sparks of fire in the darkness.

Covert made no reply except a cool, contemptuous laugh, which stung the excited young man to double fury. He sprang upon the lawyer, and clutch'd him by the neckcloth.

"Take it, then!" he cried hoarsely, for his throat was impeded by the fiendish rage which in that black hour possess'd him. "You are not fit to live!"

He dragg'd his guardian to the earth and fell crushingly upon him, choking the shriek the poor victim but just began to utter. Then, with monstrous imprecations, he twisted a tight knot around the gasping creature's neck, drew a clasp knife from his pocket, and touching the spring, the long sharp blade, too eager for its bloody work, flew open.

During the lull of the storm, the last strength of the prostrate man burst forth into one short loud cry of agony. At the same instant, the arm of the murderer thrust the blade, once, twice, thrice, deep in his enemy's bosom! Not a minute had passed since that fatal exasperating laugh—but the deed was done, and the instinctive thought which came at once to the guilty one, was a thought of fear and escape.

In the unearthly pause which follow'd, Philip's eyes gave one long searching sweep in every direction, above and around him. *Above!* God of the all-seeing eye! What, and who was that figure there?

"Forbear! In Jehovah's name forbear;" cried a shrill, but clear and melodious voice.

It was as if some accusing spirit had come down to bear witness against the deed of blood. Leaning far out of an open window, appear'd a white draperied shape, its face possess'd of a wonderful youthful beauty. Long vivid glows of lightning gave Philip a full opportunity to see as clearly as though the sun had been shining at noonday. One hand of the figure was raised upward in a deprecating attitude, and his large bright black eyes bent down upon the scene below with an expression of horror and shrinking pain. Such heavenly looks, and the peculiar circumstance of the time, fill'd Philip's heart with awe.

"Oh, if it is not yet too late," spoke the youth again, "spare him. In God's voice, I command, 'Thou shalt do no murder!'"

The words rang like a knell in the ear of the terror-stricken and already remorseful Philip. Springing from the body, he gave a second glance up and down the walk, which was totally lonesome and deserted; then crossing into Reade street, he made his fearful way in a half state of stupor, half-bewilderment, by the nearest avenues to his home.

When the corpse of the murder'd lawyer was found in the morning, and the officers of justice commenced their inquiry, suspicion immediately fell upon Philip, and he was arrested. The most rigorous search, however, brought to light nothing at all implicating the young man, except his visit to Covert's office the evening before, and his angry language there. That was by no means enough to fix so heavy a charge upon him.

The second day afterward, the whole business came before the ordinary judicial tribunal, in order that Philip might be either committed for the crime, or discharged. The testimony of Mr. Covert's clerk stood alone. One of his employers, who, believing in his innocence, had deserted him not in this crisis, had provided him with the ablest criminal counsel in New York. The proof was declared entirely insufficient, and Philip was discharged.

The crowded court-room made way for him as he came out; hundreds of curious looks fixed upon his features, and many a jibe pass'd upon him. But of all that arena of human faces, he saw only *one*—a sad, pale, black-eyed one, cowering in the centre of the rest. He had seen that face twice before—the first time as a warning spectre—the second time in prison, immediately after his arrest—now for the *last* time. This young stranger —the son of a scorn'd race—coming to the court-room to perform an unhappy duty, with the intention of testifying to what he had seen, melted at the sight of Philip's bloodless cheek, and of his sister's convulsive sobs, and forbore witnessing against the murderer. Shall we applaud or condemn him? Let every reader answer the question for himself.

That afternoon Philip left New York. His friendly employer own'd a small farm some miles up the Hudson, and until the excitement of the affair was over, he advised the young man to go thither. Philip thankfully accepted the proposal, made a few preparations, took a hurried leave of Esther, and by nightfall was settled in his new abode.

And how, think you, rested Philip Marsh that night? *Rested* indeed! O, if those who clamor so much for the halter and the scaffold to punish crime, could have seen that sight, they might have learn'd a lesson there! Four days had elapsed since he that lay tossing upon the bed there had slumber'd. Not the slightest intermission had come to his awaken'd and tensely strung sense, during those frightful days.

Disturb'd waking dreams came to him, as he thought what he might do to gain his lost peace. Far, far away would he go! The cold roll of the murder'd man's eye, as it turn'd up its last glance into his face—the shrill exclamation of pain—all the unearthly vividness of the posture, motions, and looks of the dead—the warning voice from above—pursued him like tormenting furies, and were never absent from his mind, asleep or awake, that long weary night. Anything, any place, to escape such horrid companionship! He would travel inland—hire himself to do hard drudgery upon some farm—work incessantly through the wide summer days, and thus force nature to bestow oblivion upon his senses, at least a little while now and then. He would fly on, on, on, until amid different scenes and a new life, the old memories were rubb'd entirely out. He would fight bravely in himself for peace of mind. For peace he would labor and struggle—for peace he would pray!

At length after a feverish slumber of some thirty or forty minutes, the unhappy youth, waking with a nervous start, rais'd himself in bed, and saw the blessed daylight beginning to dawn. He felt the sweat trickling down his naked breast; the sheet where he had lain was quite wet with it. Dragging himself wearily, he open'd the window. Ah! that good morning air—how it refresh'd him—how he lean'd out, and drank in the fragrance of the blossoms below, and almost for the first time in his life felt how beautifully indeed God had made the earth, and that there was wonderful sweetness in mere existence. And amidst the thousand mute mouths and eloquent eyes, which appear'd as it were to look up and speak in every direction, he fancied so many invitations to come among them. Not without effort, for he was very weak, he dress'd himself, and issued forth into the open air.

Clouds of pale gold and transparent crimson draperied the eastern sky, but the sun, whose face gladden'd them into all that glory, was not yet above the horizon. It was a time and place of such rare, such Eden-like beauty! Philip paused at the summit of an upward slope, and gazed around him. Some few miles off he could see a gleam of the Hudson river, and above it a spur of those rugged cliffs scatter'd along its western shores. Nearer by were cultivated fields. The clover grew richly there, the young grain bent to the early breeze, and the air was filled with an intoxicating perfume. At his side was the large well-kept garden of his host, in which were many pretty flowers, grass plots, and a wide avenue of noble trees. As Philip gazed, the holy calming power of Nature—the invisible spirit of so much beauty and so much innocence, melted into his soul. The disturb'd passions and the feverish conflict subsided. He even felt something like envied peace of mind—a sort of joy even in the presence of all the unmarr'd goodness. It was as fair to him, guilty though he had been, as to the purest of the pure. No accusing frowns show'd in the face of the flowers, or in the green shrubs, or the branches of the trees. They, more forgiving than mankind, and distinguishing not between the children of darkness and the children of light—they at least treated him with gentleness. Was he, then a being so accurs'd? Involuntarily, he bent over a branch of red roses, and took them softly between his hands—those murderous, bloody hands! But the red roses neither wither'd nor smell'd less fragrant. And as the young man kiss'd them, and dropp'd a tear upon them, it seem'd to him that he had found pity and sympathy from Heaven itself.

Though against all the rules of story-writing, we continue our narrative of these mainly true incidents (for such they are,) no further. Only to say that *the murderer* soon departed for a new field of action—that he is still living—and that this is but one of thousands of cases of unravel'd, unpunish'd crime—left, not to the tribunals of man, but to a wider power and judgment.

THE LAST LOYALIST

"She came to me last night,
The floor gave back no tread."

THE STORY I am going to tell is a traditional reminiscence of a country place, in my rambles about which I have often passed the house, now unoccupied, and mostly in ruins, that was the scene of the transaction. I cannot, of course, convey to others that particular kind of influence which is derived from my being so familiar with the locality, and with the very people whose grandfathers or fathers were contemporaries of the actors in the drama I shall transcribe. I must hardly expect, therefore, that to those who hear it thro' the medium of my pen, the narration will possess as life-like and interesting a character as it does to myself.

On a large and fertile neck of land that juts out in the Sound, stretching to the east of New York city, there stood, in the latter part of the last century, an old-fashion'd country-residence. It had been built by one of the first settlers of this section of the New World; and its occupant was originally owner of the extensive tract lying adjacent to his house, and pushing into the bosom of the salt waters. It was during the troubled times which mark'd our American Revolution that the incidents occurr'd which are the foundation of my story. Some time before the commencement of the war, the owner, whom I shall call Vanhome, was taken sick and died. For some time before his death he had lived a widower; and his only child, a lad of ten years old, was thus left an orphan. By his father's will this child was placed implicitly under the guardianship of an uncle, a middle-aged man, who had been of late a resident in the family. His care and interest, however, were needed but a little while—not two years elaps'd after the parents were laid away to their last repose before another grave had to be prepared for the son—the child who had been so haplessly deprived of their fostering care.

The period now arrived when the great national convulsion burst forth. Sounds of strife and the clash of arms, and the angry voices of disputants, were borne along by the air, and week after week grew to still louder clamor. Families were divided; adherents to the crown, and ardent upholders of the rebellion, were often found in the bosom of the same domestic circle. Vanhome, the uncle spoken of as guardian to the young heir, was a man who lean'd to the stern, the high-handed and the severe. He soon became known among the most energetic of the loyalists. So decided were his sentiments that, leaving the estate which he had inherited from his brother and nephew, he join'd the forces of the British king. Thenceforward, whenever his old neighbors heard of him, it was as being engaged in the cruelest outrages, the boldest inroads, or the most determin'd attacks upon the army of his countrymen or their peaceful settlements.

Eight years brought the rebel States and their leaders to that glorious epoch when the last remnant of a monarch's rule was to leave their shores —when the last waving of the royal standard was to flutter as it should be haul'd down from the staff, and its place fill'd by the proud testimonial of our warrior's success.

Pleasantly over the autumn fields shone the November sun, when a horseman, of somewhat military look, plodded slowly along the road that led to the old Vanhome farmhouse. There was nothing peculiar in his attire, unless it might be a red scarf which he wore tied round his waist. He was a dark-featured, sullen-eyed man; and as his glance was thrown restlessly to the right and left, his whole manner appear'd to be that of a person moving amid familiar and accustom'd scenes. Occasionally he stopp'd, and looking long and steadily at some object that attracted his attention, mutter'd to himself, like one in whose breast busy thoughts were moving. His course was evidently to the homestead itself, at which in due time he arrived. He dismounted, led his horse to the stables, and then, without knocking, though there were evident signs of occupancy around the building, the traveler made his entrance as composedly and boldly as though he were master of the whole establishment.

Now the house being in a measure deserted for many years, and the successful termination of the strife rendering it probable that the Vanhome estate would be confiscated to the new government, an aged, poverty-stricken couple had been encouraged by the neighbors to take possession as tenants of the place. Their name was Gills; and these people the traveler found upon his entrance were likely to be his host and hostess. Holding their right as they did by so slight a tenure, they ventur'd to offer no opposition when the stranger signified his intention of passing several hours there.

The day wore on, and the sun went down in the west; still the interloper, gloomy and taciturn, made no signs of departing. But as the evening advanced (whether the darkness was congenial to his sombre thoughts, or whether it merely chanced so) he seem'd to grow more affable and communicative, and informed Gills that he should pass the night there, tendering him at the same time ample remuneration, which the latter accepted with many thanks.

"Tell me," said he to his aged host, when they were all sitting around the ample hearth, at the conclusion of their evening meal, "tell me something to while away the hours."

"Ah! sir," answered Gills, "this is no place for new or interesting events. We live here from year to year, and at the end of one we find ourselves at about the same place which we filled in the beginning."

"Can you relate nothing, then?" rejoin'd the guest, and a singular smile pass'd over his features; "can you say nothing about your own place?—this house or its former inhabitants, or former history?"

The old man glanced across to his wife, and a look expressive of sympathetic feeling started in the face of each.

"It is an unfortunate story, sir," said Gills, "and may cast a chill upon you, instead of the pleasant feeling which it would be best to foster when in strange walls."

"Strange walls!" echoed he of the red scarf, and for the first time since his arrival he half laughed, but it was not the laugh which comes from a man's heart.

"You must know, sir," continued Gills, "I am myself a sort of intruder here. The Vanhomes—that was the name of the former residents and owners—I have never seen; for when I came to these parts the last occupant had left to join the red-coat soldiery. I am told that he is to sail with them for foreign lands, now that the war is ended, and his property almost certain to pass into other hands."

As the old man went on, the stranger cast down his eyes, and listen'd with an appearance of great interest, though a transient smile or a brightening of the eye would occasionally disturb the serenity of his deportment.

"The old owners of this place," continued the white-haired narrator, "were well off in the world, and bore a good name among their neighbors. The brother of Sergeant Vanhome, now the only one of the name, died ten or twelve years since, leaving a son—a child so small that the father's will made provision for his being brought up by his uncle, whom I mention'd but now as of the British army. He was a strange man, this uncle; disliked by all who knew him; passionate, vindictive, and, it was said, very avaricious, even from his childhood.

"Well, not long after the death of the parents, dark stories began to be circulated about cruelty and punishment and whippings and starvation inflicted by the new master upon his nephew. People who had business at the homestead would frequently, when they came away, relate the most fearful things of its manager, and how he misused his brother's child. It was half hinted that he strove to get the youngster out of the way in order that the whole estate might fall into his own hands. As I told you before, however, nobody liked the man; and perhaps they judged him too uncharitably.

"After things had gone on in this way for some time, a countryman, a laborer, who was hired to do farm-work upon the place, one evening observed that the little orphan Vanhome was more faint and pale even than usual, for he was always delicate, and that is one reason why I think it possible that his death, of which I am now going to tell you, was but the result of his own weak constitution, and nothing else. The laborer slept that night at the farmhouse. Just before the time at which they usually retired to bed, this person, feeling sleepy with his day's toil, left the kitchen hearth and wended his way to rest. In going to his place of repose he had to pass a chamber—the very chamber where you, sir, are to sleep to-night—and there he heard the voice of the orphan child uttering half-suppress'd exclamations as if in pitiful entreaty. Upon stopping, he heard also the tones of the elder Vanhome, but they were harsh and bitter. The sound of blows followed. As each one fell it was accompanied by a groan or shriek, and so they continued for some time. Shock'd and indignant, the countryman would have burst open the door and interfered to prevent this brutal proceeding, but he bethought him that he might get himself into trouble, and perhaps find that he could do no good after all, and so he passed on to his room.

"Well, sir, the following day the child did not come out among the work-people as usual. He was taken very ill. No physician was sent for until the next afternoon; and though one arrived in the course of the night, it was too late—the poor boy died before morning.

"People talk'd threateningly upon the subject, but nothing could be proved against Vanhome. At one period there were efforts made to have the whole affair investigated. Perhaps that would have taken place, had not every one's attention been swallow'd up by the rumors of difficulty and war, which were then beginning to disturb the country.

"Vanhome joined the army of the king. His enemies said that he feared to be on the side of the rebels, because if they were routed his property would be taken from him. But events have shown that, if this was indeed what he dreaded, it has happen'd to him from the very means which he took to prevent it."

The old man paused. He had quite wearied himself with so long talking. For some minutes there was unbroken silence.

Presently the stranger signified his intention of retiring for the night. He rose, and his host took a light for the purpose of ushering him to his apartment.

When Gills return'd to his accustom'd situation in the large arm-chair by the chimney hearth, his ancient helpmate had retired to rest. With the simplicity of their times, the bed stood in the same room where the three had been seated during the last few hours; and now the remaining two talk'd together about the singular events of the evening. As the time wore on, Gills show'd no disposition to leave his cosy chair; but sat toasting his feet, and bending over the coals. Gradually the insidious heat and the lateness of the hour began to exercise their influence over the old man. The drowsy indolent feeling which every one has experienced in getting thoroughly heated through by close contact with a glowing fire, spread in each vein and sinew, and relax'd its tone. He lean'd back in his chair and slept.

For a long time his repose went on quietly and soundly. He could not tell how many hours elapsed; but, a while after midnight, the torpid senses of the slumberer were awaken'd by a startling shock. It was a cry as of a strong man in his agony—a shrill, not very loud cry, but fearful, and creeping into the blood like cold, polish'd steel. The old man raised himself in his seat and listen'd, at once fully awake. For a minute, all was the solemn stillness of midnight. Then rose that horrid tone again, wailing and wild, and making the hearer's hair to stand on end. One moment more, and the trampling of hasty feet sounded in the passage outside. The door was thrown open, and the form of the stranger, more like a corpse than living man, rushed into the room.

"All white!" yell'd the conscience-stricken creature—"all white, and with the grave-clothes around him. One shoulder was bare, and I saw," he whisper'd, "I saw blue streaks upon it. It was horrible, and I cried aloud. He stepp'd toward me! He came to my very bedside; his small hand almost touch'd my face. I could not bear it, and fled."

The miserable man bent his head down upon his bosom; convulsive rattlings shook his throat; and his whole frame waver'd to and fro like a tree in a storm. Bewilder'd and shock'd, Gills look'd at his apparently deranged guest, and knew not what answer to make, or what course of conduct to pursue.

Thrusting out his arms and his extended fingers, and bending down his eyes, as men do when shading them from a glare of lightning, the stranger stagger'd from the door, and, in a moment further, dash'd madly through the passage which led through the kitchen into the outer road. The old man heard the noise of his falling footsteps, sounding fainter and fainter in the distance, and then, retreating, dropp'd his own exhausted limbs into the chair from which he had been arous'd so terribly. It was many minutes before his energies recover'd their accustomed tone again. Strangely enough, his wife, unawaken'd by the stranger's ravings, still slumber'd on as profoundly as ever.

Pass we on to a far different scene—the embarkation of the British troops for the distant land whose monarch was never more to wield the sceptre over a kingdom lost by his imprudence and tyranny. With frowning brow and sullen pace the martial ranks moved on. Boat after boat was filled, and, as each discharged its complement in the ships that lay heaving their anchors in the stream, it return'd, and was soon filled with another load. And at length it became time for the last soldier to lift his eye and take a last glance at the broad banner of England's pride, which flapp'd its folds from the top of the highest staff on the Battery.

As the warning sound of a trumpet called together all who were laggards—those taking leave of friends, and those who were arranging their own private affairs, left until the last moment—a single horseman was seen furiously dashing down the street. A red scarf tightly encircled his waist. He made directly for the shore, and the crowd there gather'd started back in wonderment as they beheld his dishevel'd appearance and ghastly face. Throwing himself violently from his saddle, he flung the bridle over the animal's neck, and gave him a sharp cut with a small riding whip. He made for the boat; one minute later, and he had been left. They were pushing the keel from the landing—the stranger sprang—a space of two or three feet already intervened—he struck on the gunwale—and the Last Soldier of King George had left the American shores.

WILD FRANK'S RETURN

As THE sun, one August day some fifty years ago, had just pass'd the meridian of a country town in the eastern section of Long Island, a single traveler came up to the quaint low-roof'd village tavern, open'd its half-door, and enter'd the common room. Dust cover'd the clothes of the way-farer, and his brow was moist with sweat. He trod in a lagging, weary way; though his form and features told of an age not more than nineteen or twenty years. Over one shoulder was slung a sailor's jacket, and in his hand he carried a little bundle. Sitting down on a rude bench, he told a female who made her appearance behind the bar, that he would have a glass of brandy and sugar. He took off the liquor at a draught: after which he lit and began to smoke a cigar, with which he supplied himself from his pocket—stretching out one leg, and leaning his elbow down on the bench, in the attitude of a man who takes an indolent lounge.

"Do you know one Richard Hall that lives somewhere here among you?" said he.

"Mr. Hall's is down the lane that turns off by that big locust tree," answer'd the woman, pointing to the direction through the open door; "it's about half a mile from here to his house."

The youth, for a minute or two, puff'd the smoke from his mouth very leisurely in silence. His manner had an air of vacant self-sufficiency, rather strange in one of so few years.

"I wish to see Mr. Hall," he said at length—"Here's a silver sixpence, for any one who will carry a message to him."

"The folks are all away. It's but a short walk, and your limbs are young," replied the female, who was not altogether pleased with the easy way of making himself at home, which mark'd her shabby-looking customer. That individual, however, seem'd to give small attention to the hint, but lean'd and puff'd his cigar-smoke as leisurely as before.

"Unless," continued the woman, catching a second glance at the sixpence; "unless old Joe is at the stable, as he's very likely to be. I'll go and find out for you." And she push'd open a door at her back, stepp'd through an adjoining room into a yard, whence her voice was the next moment heard calling the person she had mention'd, in accents by no means remarkable for their melody or softness.

Her search was successful. She soon return'd with him who was to act as messenger—a little, wither'd, ragged old man—a hanger-on there, whose unshaven face told plainly enough the story of his intemperate habits—those deeply seated habits, now too late to be uprooted, that would ere long lay him in a drunkard's grave. The youth inform'd him what the required service was, and promised him the reward as soon as he should return.

"Tell Richard Hall that I am going to his father's house this afternoon. If he asks who it is that wishes him here, say the person sent no name," continued the stranger, sitting up from his indolent posture, as the feet of old Joe were about leaving the door-stone, and his blear'd eyes turned to catch the last sentence of the mandate.

"And yet, perhaps you may as well," added he, communing a moment with himself: "you may tell him his brother Frank, Wild Frank, it is, who wishes him to come."

The old man departed on his errand, and he who call'd himself Wild Frank, toss'd his nearly smoked cigar out of the window, and folded his arms in thought.

No better place than this, probably, will occur to give a brief account of some former events in the life of the young stranger, resting and waiting at the village inn. Fifteen miles east of that inn lived a farmer named Hall, a man of good repute, well-off in the world, and head of a large family. He was fond of gain—required all his boys to labor in proportion to their age; and his right hand man, if he might not be called favorite, was his eldest son Richard. This eldest son, an industrious, sober-faced young fellow, was invested by his father with the powers of second in command; and as strict and swift obedience was a prime tenet in the farmer's domestic government, the children all tacitly submitted to their brother's sway—all but one, and that was Frank. The farmer's wife was a quiet woman, in rather tender health; and though for all her offspring she had a mother's love, Frank's kiss ever seem'd sweetest to her lips. She favor'd him more than the rest—perhaps, as in a hundred similar instances, for his being so often at fault, and so often blamed. In truth, however, he seldom receiv'd more blame than he deserv'd, for he was a capricious, high-temper'd lad, and up to all kinds of mischief. From these traits he was known in the neighborhood by the name of Wild Frank.

Among the farmer's stock there was a fine young blood mare—a beautiful creature, large and graceful, with eyes like dark-hued jewels, and her color that of the deep night. It being the custom of the farmer to let his boys have something about the farm that they could call their own, and take care of as such, Black Nell, as the mare was called, had somehow or other fallen to Frank's share. He was very proud of her, and thought as much of her comfort as his own. The elder brother, however, saw fit to claim for himself, and several times to exercise, a privilege of managing and using Black Nell, notwithstanding what Frank consider'd his prerogative. On one of these occasions a hot dispute arose, and, after much angry blood, it was referr'd to the farmer for settlement. He decided in favor of Richard, and added a harsh lecture to his other son. The farmer was really unjust; and Wild Frank's face paled with rage and mortification. That furious temper which he had never been taught to curb, now swell'd like an overflowing torrent. With difficulty restraining the exhibition of his passions, as soon as he got by himself he swore that not another sun should roll by and find him under that roof. Late at night he silently arose, and turning his back on what he thought an inhospitable home, in mood in which the child should never leave the parental roof, bent his steps toward the city.

It may well be imagined that alarm and grief pervaded the whole of the family, on discovering Frank's departure. And as week after week melted away and brought no tidings of him, his poor mother's heart grew wearier and wearier. She spoke not much, but was evidently sick in spirit. Nearly two years had elaps'd when about a week before the incidents at the commencement of this story, the farmer's family were joyfully surprised by receiving a letter from the long absent son. He had been to sea, and was then in New York, at which port his vessel had just arrived. He wrote in a gay strain; appear'd to have lost the angry feeling which caused his flight from home; and said he heard in the city that Richard had married, and settled several miles distant, where he wished him all good luck and happiness. Wild Frank wound up his letter by promising, as soon as he could get through the imperative business of his ship, to pay a visit to his parents and native place. On Tuesday of the succeeding week, he said he would be with them.

Within half an hour after the departure of old Joe, the form of that ancient personage was seen slowly wheeling round the locust-tree at the end of the lane, accompanied by a stout young man in primitive homespun apparel. The meeting between Wild Frank and his brother Richard, though hardly of that kind which generally takes place between persons so closely related, could not exactly be call'd distant or cool either. Richard press'd his brother to go with him to the farm house, and refresh and repose himself for some hours at least, but Frank declined.

"They will all expect me home this afternoon," he said, "I wrote to them I would be there to-day."

"But you must be very tired, Frank," rejoin'd the other; "won't you let some of us harness up and carry you? Or if you like—" he stopp'd a moment, and a trifling suffusion spread over his face; "if you like, I'll put the saddle on Black Nell—she's here at my place now, and you can ride home like a lord."

Frank's face color'd a little, too. He paused for a moment in thought—he was really foot-sore, and exhausted with his journey that hot day—so he accepted his brother's offer.

"You know the speed of Nell, as well as I," said Richard; "I'll warrant when I bring her here you'll say she's in good order as ever." So telling him to amuse himself for a few minutes as well as he could, Richard left the tavern.

Could it be that Black Nell knew her early master? She neigh'd and rubb'd her nose on his shoulder; and as he put his foot in the stirrup and rose on her back, it was evident that they were both highly pleased with their meeting. Bidding his brother farewell, and not forgetting old Joe, the young man set forth on his journey to his father's house. As he left the village behind, and came upon the long monotonous road before him, he thought on the circumstances of his leaving home—and he thought, too, on his course of life, how it was being frittered away and lost. Very gentle influences, doubtless, came over Wild Frank's mind then, and he yearn'd to show his parents that he was sorry for the trouble he had cost them. He blamed himself for his former follies, and even felt remorse that he had not acted more kindly to Richard, and gone to his house. Oh, it had been a sad mistake of the farmer that he did not teach his children to love one another. It was a foolish thing that he prided himself on governing his little flock well, when sweet affection, gentle forbearance, and brotherly faith, were almost unknown among them.

The day was now advanced, though the heat pour'd down with a strength little less oppressive than at noon. Frank had accomplish'd the greater part of his journey; he was within two miles of his home. The road here led over a high, tiresome hill, and he determined to stop on the top of it and rest himself, as well as give the animal he rode a few minutes' breath. How well he knew the place! And that mighty oak, standing just outside the fence on the very summit of the hill, often had he reposed under its shade. It would be pleasant for a few minutes to stretch his limbs there again as of old, he thought to himself; and he dismounted from the saddle and led Black Nell under the tree. Mindful of the comfort of his favorite, he took from his little bundle, which he had strapped behind him on the mare's back, a piece of strong cord, four or five yards in length, which he tied to the bridle, and wound and tied the other end, for security, over his own wrist; then throwing himself at full length upon the ground, Black Nell was at liberty to graze around him, without danger of straying away.

It was a calm scene, and a pleasant. There was no rude sound—hardly even a chirping insect—to break the sleepy silence of the place. The atmosphere had a dim, hazy cast and was impregnated with overpowering heat. The young man lay there minute after minute, as time glided away unnoticed; for he was very tired, and his repose was sweet to him. Occasionally he raised himself and cast a listless look at the distant landscape, veil'd as it was by the slight mist. At length his repose was without such interruptions. His eyes closed, and though at first they open'd languidly again at intervals, after a while they shut altogether. Could it be that he slept? It was so indeed. Yielding to the drowsy influences about him, and to his prolong'd weariness of travel, he had fallen into a deep, sound slumber. Thus he lay; and Black Nell, the original cause of his departure from his home—by a singular chance, the companion of his return—quietly cropp'd the grass at his side.

An hour nearly pass'd away, and yet the young man slept on. The light and heat were not glaring now; a change had come over earth and heaven. There were signs of one of those thunderstorms that in our climate spring up and pass over so quickly and so terribly. Masses of vapor loom'd up in the horizon, and a dark shadow settled on the woods and fields. The leaves of the great oak rustled together over the youth's head. Clouds flitted swiftly in the sky, like bodies of armed men coming up to battle at the call of their leader's trumpet. A thick rain-drop fell now and then, while occasionally hoarse mutterings of thunder sounded in the distance; yet the slumberer was not arous'd. It was strange that Wild Frank did not awake. Perhaps his ocean life had taught him to rest undisturbed amid the jarring of elements. Though the storm was now coming on in its fury, he slept like a babe in its cradle.

Black Nell had ceased grazing, and stood by her sleeping master with ears erect, and her long mane and tail waving in the wind. It seem'd quite dark, so heavy were the clouds. The blast blew sweepingly, the lightning flash'd, and the rain fell in torrents. Crash after crash of thunder seem'd to shake the solid earth. And Black Nell, she stood now, an image of beautiful terror, with her fore feet thrust out, her neck arch'd, and her eyes glaring balls of fear. At length, after a dazzling and lurid glare, there came a peal—a deafening crash—as if the great axle was rent. God of Spirits! the startled mare sprang off like a ship in an ocean-storm! Her eyes were blinded with light; she dashed madly down the hill, and plunge after plunge—far, far away—swift as an arrow—dragging the hapless body of the youth behind her!

In the low, old-fashion'd dwelling of the farmer there was a large family group. The men and boys had gather'd under shelter at the approach of the storm; and the subject of their talk was the return of the long absent son. The mother spoke of him, too, and her eyes brighten'd with pleasure as she spoke. She made all the little domestic preparations—cook'd his favorite dishes—and arranged for him his own bed, in its own old place. As the tempest mounted to its fury they discuss'd the probability of his getting soak'd by it; and the provident dame had already selected some dry garments for a change. But the rain was soon over, and nature smiled again in her invigorated beauty. The sun shone out as it was dipping in the west. Drops sparkled on the leaf-tips—coolness and clearness were in the air.

The clattering of a horse's hoofs came to the ears of those who were gather'd there. It was on the other side of the house that the wagon road led; and they open'd the door and rush'd in a tumult of glad anticipations, through the adjoining room to the porch. What a sight it was that met them there! Black Nell stood a few feet from the door, with her neck crouch'd down; she drew her breath long and deep, and vapor rose from every part of her reeking body. And with eyes starting from their sockets, and mouths agape with stupefying terror, they beheld on the ground near her a mangled, hideous mass—the rough semblance of a human form—all batter'd, and cut, and bloody. Attach'd to it was the fatal cord, dabbled over with gore. And as the mother gazed—for she could not withdraw her eyes—and the appalling truth came upon her mind, she sank down without shriek or utterance, into a deep, deathly swoon.

THE BOY LOVER

LISTEN, and the old will speak a chronicle for the young. Ah, youth! thou art one day coming to be old, too. And let me tell thee how thou mayest get a useful lesson. For an hour, *dream thyself old*. Realize, in thy thoughts and consciousness, that vigor and strength are subdued in thy sinews— that the color of the shroud is liken'd in thy very hairs—that all those leaping desires, luxurious hopes, beautiful aspirations, and proud confidences, of thy younger life, have long been buried (a funeral for the better part of thee) in that grave which must soon close over thy tottering limbs. Look back, then, through the long track of the past years. How has it been with thee? Are there bright beacons of happiness enjoy'd, and of good done by the way? Glimmer gentle rays of what was scatter'd from a holy heart? Have benevolence, and love, and undeviating honesty left tokens on which thy eyes can rest sweetly? Is it well with thee, thus? Answerest thou, it is? Or answerest thou, I see nothing but gloom and shatter'd hours, and the wreck of good resolves, and a broken heart, filled with sickness, and troubled among its ruined chambers with the phantoms of many follies?

O, youth! youth! this dream will one day be a *reality*—a reality, either of heavenly peace or agonizing sorrow.

And yet not for all is it decreed to attain the neighborhood of the threescore and ten years—the span of life. I am to speak of one who died young. Very awkward was his childhood—but most fragile and sensitive! So delicate a nature may exist in a rough, unnoticed plant! Let the boy rest;—he was not beautiful, and dropp'd away betimes. But for the cause —it is a singular story, to which let crusted worldlings pay the tribute of a light laugh—light and empty as their own hollow hearts.

Love! which with its cankerseed of decay within, has sent young men and maidens to a long'd-for, but too premature burial. Love! the child-monarch that Death itself cannot conquer; that has its tokens on slabs at the head of grass-cover'd tombs—tokens more visible to the eye of the stranger, yet not so deeply graven as the face and the remembrances cut upon the heart of the living. Love! the sweet, the pure, the innocent; yet the causer of fierce hate, of wishes for deadly revenge, of bloody deeds, and madness, and the horrors of hell. Love! that wanders over battle-fields, turning up mangled human trunks, and parting back the hair from gory faces, and daring the points of swords and the thunder of artillery, without a fear or a thought of danger.

Words! words! I begin to see I am, indeed, an old man, and garrulous! Let me go back—yes, I see it must be many years!

It was at the close of the last century. I was at that time studying law, the profession my father follow'd. One of his clients was an elderly widow, a foreigner, who kept a little ale-house, on the banks of the North River, at about two miles from what is now the centre of the city. *Then* the spot was quite out of town and surrounded by fields and green trees. The widow often invited me to come and pay her a visit, when I had a leisure afternoon—including also in the invitation my brother and two other students who were in my father's office. Matthew, the brother I mention, was a boy of sixteen; he was troubled with an inward illness— though it had no power over his temper, which ever retain'd the most admirable placidity and gentleness. He was cheerful, but never boister- ous, and everybody loved him; his mind seem'd more develop'd than is usual for his age, though his personal appearance was exceedingly plain. Wheaton and Brown, the names of the other students, were spirited, clever young fellows, with most of the traits that those in their position of life generally possess. The first was as generous and brave as any man I ever knew. He was very passionate, too, but the whirlwind soon blew over, and left everything quiet again. Frank Brown was slim, graceful, and handsome. He profess'd to be fond of sentiment, and used to fall regularly in love once a month.

The half of every Wednesday we four youths had to ourselves, and were in the habit of taking a sail, a ride, or a walk together. One of these afternoons, of a pleasant day in April, the sun shining, and the air clear, I bethought myself of the widow and her beer—about which latter article I had made inquiries, and heard it spoken of in terms of high commenda- tion. I mention'd the matter to Matthew and to my fellow-students, and we agreed to fill up our holiday by a jaunt to the ale-house. Accordingly, we set forth, and, after a fine walk, arrived in glorious spirits at our destination.

Ah! how shall I describe the quiet beauties of the spot, with its long, low piazza looking out upon the river, and its clean homely tables, and the tankards of real silver in which the ale was given us, and the flavor of that excellent liquor itself. There was the widow; and there was a sober, stately old woman, half companion, half servant, Margery by name; and there was (good God! my fingers quiver yet as I write the word!) young Ninon, the daughter of the widow.

O, through the years that live no more, my memory strays back, and that whole scene comes up before me once again—and the brightest part of the picture is the strange ethereal beauty of that young girl! She was apparently about the age of my brother Matthew, and the most fascinat- ing, artless creature I had ever beheld. She had blue eyes and light hair, and an expression of childish simplicity which was charming indeed. I have no doubt that ere half an hour had elapsed from the time we en- ter'd the tavern and saw Ninon, every one of the four of us loved the girl to the very depth of passion.

We neither spent so much money, nor drank as much beer, as we had intended before starting from home. The widow was very civil, being pleased to see us, and Margery served our wants with a deal of politeness —but it was to Ninon that the afternoon's pleasure was attributable; for though we were strangers, we became acquainted at once—the manners of the girl, merry as she was, putting entirely out of view the most distant imputation of indecorum—and the presence of the widow and Margery, (for we were all in the common room together, there being no other company,) serving to make us all disembarass'd and at ease.

It was not until quite a while after sunset that we started on our return to the city. We made several attempts to revive the mirth and lively talk that usually signalized our rambles, but they seem'd forced and discordant, like laughter in a sick-room. My brother was the only one who preserved his usual tenor of temper and conduct.

I need hardly say that thenceforward every Wednesday afternoon was spent at the widow's tavern. Strangely, neither Matthew or my two friends, or myself, spoke to each other of the sentiment that filled us in reference to Ninon. Yet we all knew the thoughts and feelings of the others; and each, perhaps, felt confident that his love alone was unsuspected by his companions.

The story of the widow was a touching yet simple one. She was by birth a Swiss. In one of the cantons of her native land, she had grown up, and married, and lived for a time in happy comfort. A son was born to her, and a daughter, the beautiful Ninon. By some reverse of fortune, the father and head of the family had the greater portion of his possessions swept from him. He struggled for a time against the evil influence, but it press'd upon him harder and harder. He had heard of a people in the western world—a new and swarming land—where the stranger was welcom'd, and peace and the protection of the strong arm thrown around him. He had not heart to stay and struggle amid the scenes of his former prosperity, and he determin'd to go and make his home in that distant republic of the west. So with his wife and children, and the proceeds of what little property was left, he took passage for New York. He was never to reach his journey's end. Either the cares that weigh'd upon his mind, or some other cause, consign'd him to a sick hammock, from which he only found relief through the Great Dismisser. He was buried in the sea, and in due time his family arrived at the American emporium. But there, the son too sicken'd—died, ere long, and was buried likewise. They would not bury him in the city, but away—by the solitary banks of the Hudson; on which the widow soon afterwards took up her abode.

Ninon was too young to feel much grief at the sad occurrences; and the mother, whatever she might have suffer'd inwardly, had a good deal of phlegm and patience, and set about making herself and her remaining child as comfortable as might be. They had still a respectable sum in cash, and after due deliberation, the widow purchas'd the little quiet tavern, not far from the grave of her boy; and of Sundays and holidays she took in considerable money—enough to make a decent support for them in their humble way of living. French and Germans visited the house frequently, and quite a number of young Americans too. Probably the greatest attraction to the latter was the sweet face of Ninon.

Spring passed, and summer crept in and wasted away, and autumn had arrived. Every New Yorker knows what delicious weather we have, in these regions, of the early October days; how calm, clear, and divested of sultriness, is the air, and how decently nature seems preparing for her winter sleep.

Thus it was the last Wednesday we started on our accustomed excursion. Six months had elapsed since our first visit, and, as then, we were full of the exuberance of young and joyful hearts. Frequent and hearty were our jokes, by no means particular about the theme or the method, and long and loud the peals of laughter that rang over the fields or along the shore.

We took our seats round the same clean, white table, and received our favorite beverage in the same bright tankards. They were set before us by the sober Margery, no one else being visible. As frequently happen'd, we were the only company. Walking and breathing the keen, fine air had made us dry, and we soon drain'd the foaming vessels, and call'd for more. I remember well an animated chat we had about some poems that had just made their appearance from a great British author, and were creating quite a public stir. There was one, a tale of passion and despair, which Wheaton had read, and of which he gave us a transcript. Wild, startling, and dreamy, perhaps it threw over our minds its peculiar cast.

An hour moved off, and we began to think it strange that neither Ninon or the widow came into the room. One of us gave a hint to that effect to Margery; but she made no answer, and went on in her usual way as before.

"The grim old thing," said Wheaton, "if she were in Spain, they'd make her a premier duenna!"

I ask'd the woman about Ninon and the widow. She seemed disturb'd, I thought; but, making no reply to the first part of my question, said that her mistress was in another part of the house, and did not wish to be with company.

"Then be kind enough, Mrs. Vinegar," resumed Wheaton, good-naturedly, "be kind enough to go and ask the widow if we can see Ninon."

Our attendant's face turn'd as pale as ashes, and she precipitately left the apartment. We laugh'd at her agitation, which Frank Brown assigned to our merry ridicule.

Quite a quarter of an hour elaps'd before Margery's return. When she appear'd she told us briefly that the widow had bidden her obey our behest, and now, if we desired, she would conduct us to the daughter's presence. There was a singular expression in the woman's eyes, and the whole affair began to strike us as somewhat odd; but we arose, and taking our caps, follow'd her as she stepp'd through the door. Back of the house were some fields, and a path leading into clumps of trees. At some thirty rods distant from the tavern, nigh one of those clumps, the larger tree whereof was a willow, Margery stopp'd, and pausing a minute, while we came up, spoke in tones calm and low:

"Ninon is there!"

She pointed downward with her finger. Great God! There was a *grave*, new made, and with the sods loosely join'd, and a rough brown stone at each extremity! Some earth yet lay upon the grass near by. If we had look'd, we might have seen the resting-place of the widow's son, Ninon's brother—for it was close at hand. But amid the whole scene our eyes took in nothing except that horrible covering of death—the oven-shaped mound. My sight seemed to waver, my head felt dizzy, and a feeling of deadly sickness came over me. I heard a stifled exclamation, and looking round, saw Frank Brown leaning against the nearest tree, great sweat upon his forehead, and his cheeks bloodless as chalk. Wheaton gave way to his agony more fully than ever I had known a man before; he had fallen—sobbing like a child, and wringing his hands. It is impossible to describe the suddenness and fearfulness of the sickening truth that came upon us like a stroke of thunder.

Of all of us, my brother Matthew neither shed tears, or turned pale, or fainted, or exposed any other evidence of inward depth of pain. His quiet, pleasant voice was indeed a tone lower, but it was that which recall'd us, after the lapse of many long minutes, to ourselves.

So the girl had died and been buried. We were told of an illness that had seized her the very day after our last preceding visit; but we inquired not into the particulars.

And now come I to the conclusion of my story, and to the most singular part of it. The evening of the third day afterward, Wheaton, who had wept scalding tears, and Brown, whose cheeks had recover'd their color, and myself, that for an hour thought my heart would never rebound again from the fearful shock—that evening, I say, we three were seated around a table in another tavern, drinking other beer, and laughing but a little less cheerfully, and as though we had never known the widow or her daughter—neither of whom, I venture to affirm, came into our minds once the whole night, or but to be dismiss'd again, carelessly, like the remembrance of faces seen in a crowd.

Strange are the contradictions of the things of life! The seventh day after that dreadful visit saw my brother Matthew—the delicate one, who, while bold men writhed in torture, had kept the same placid face, and the same untrembling fingers—him that seventh day saw a clay-cold corpse, carried to the repose of the churchyard. The shaft, rankling far down and within, wrought a poison too great for show, and the youth died.

THE CHILD AND THE PROFLIGATE

JUST AFTER sunset, one evening in summer—that pleasant hour when the air is balmy, the light loses its glare, and all around is imbued with soothing quiet—on the door-step of a house there sat an elderly woman waiting the arrival of her son. The house was in a straggling village some fifty miles from New York city. She who sat on the door step was a widow; her white cap cover'd locks of gray, and her dress, though clean, was exceedingly homely. Her house—for the tenement she occupied was her own—was very little and very old. Trees cluster'd around it so thickly as almost to hide its color—that blackish gray color which belongs to old wooden houses that have never been painted; and to get in it you had to enter a little rickety gate and walk through a short path, border'd by carrot beds and beets and other vegetables. The son whom she was expecting was her only child. About a year before he had been bound apprentice to a rich farmer in the place, and after finishing his daily task he was in the habit of spending half an hour at his mother's. On the present occasion the shadows of night had settled heavily before the youth made his appearance. When he did, his walk was slow and dragging, and all his motions were languid, as if from great weariness. He open'd the gate, came through the path, and sat down by his mother in silence.

"You are sullen to-night, Charley," said the widow, after a moment's pause, when she found that he return'd no answer to her greeting.

As she spoke she put her hand fondly on his head; it seem'd moist as if it had been dipp'd in the water. His shirt, too, was soak'd; and as she pass'd her fingers down his shoulder she felt a sharp twinge in her heart, for she knew that moisture to be the hard wrung sweat of severe toil, exacted from her young child (he was but thirteen years old) by an unyielding task-master.

"You have work'd hard to-day, my son."

"I've been mowing."

The widow's heart felt another pang.

"Not *all day,* Charley?" she said, in a low voice; and there was a slight quiver in it.

"Yes, mother, all day," replied the boy; "Mr. Ellis said he couldn't afford to hire men, for wages are so high. I've swung the scythe ever since an hour before sunrise. Feel of my hands."

There were blisters on them like great lumps. Tears started in the widow's eyes. She dared not trust herself with a reply, though her heart was bursting with the thought that she could not better his condition. There was no earthly means of support on which she had dependence enough to encourage her child in the wish she knew he was forming—the wish not utter'd for the first time—to be freed from his bondage.

"Mother," at length said the boy, "I can stand it no longer. I cannot and will not stay at Mr. Ellis's. Ever since the day I first went into his house I've been a slave; and if I have to work so much longer I know I shall run off and go to sea or somewhere else. I'd as leave be in my grave as there." And the child burst into a passionate fit of weeping.

His mother was silent, for she was in deep grief herself. After some minutes had flown, however, she gather'd sufficient self-possession to speak to her son in a soothing tone, endeavoring to win him from his sorrows and cheer up his heart. She told him that time was swift—that in the course of a few years he would be his own master—that all people have their troubles —with many other ready arguments which, though they had little effect in calming her own distress, she hoped would act as a solace to the disturb'd temper of the boy. And as the half hour to which he was limited had now elaps'd, she took him by the hand and led him to the gate, to set forth on his return. The youth seemed pacified, though occasionally one of those convulsive sighs that remain after a fit of weeping, would break from his throat. At the gate he threw his arms about his mother's neck; each press'd a long kiss on the lips of the other, and the youngster bent his steps towards his master's house.

As her child pass'd out of sight the widow return'd, shut the gate and enter'd her lonely room. There was no light in the old cottage that night— the heart of its occupant was dark and cheerless. Love, agony, and grief, and tears and convulsive wrestlings were there. The thought of a beloved son condemned to labor—labor that would break down a man—struggling from day to day under the hard rule of a soulless gold-worshipper; the knowledge that years must pass thus; the sickening idea of her own poverty, and of living mainly on the grudged charity of neighbors—thoughts, too, of former happy days—these rack'd the widow's heart, and made her bed a sleepless one without repose.

The boy bent his steps to his employer's, as has been said. In his way down the village street he had to pass a public house, the only one the place contain'd; and when he came off against it he heard the sound of a fiddle— drown'd, however, at intervals, by much laughter and talking. The windows were up, and, the house standing close to the road, Charles thought it no harm to take a look and see what was going on within. Half a dozen footsteps brought him to the low casement, on which he lean'd his elbow, and where he had a full view of the room and its occupants. In one corner was an old man, known in the village as Black Dave—he it was whose musical performances had a moment before drawn Charles's attention to the tavern; and he it was who now exerted himself in a violent manner to give, with divers flourishes and extra twangs, a tune very popular among that thick-lipp'd race whose fondness for melody is so well known. In the middle of the room were five or six sailors, some of them quite drunk, and others in the earlier stages of that process, while on benches around were more sailors, and here and there a person dress'd in landsman's attire. The men in the middle of the room were dancing; that is, they were going through certain contortions and shufflings, varied occasionally by exceedingly hearty stamps upon the sanded floor. In short the whole party were engaged in a drunken frolic, which was in no respect different from a thousand other drunken frolics, except, perhaps, that there was less than the ordinary amount of anger and quarreling. Indeed everyone seem'd in remarkably good humor.

But what excited the boy's attention more than any other object was an individual, seated on one of the benches opposite, who, though evidently enjoying the spree as much as if he were an old hand at such business, seem'd in every other particular to be far out of his element. His appearance was youthful. He might have been twenty-one or two years old. His countenance was intelligent, and had the air of city life and society. He was dress'd not gaudily, but in every respect fashionably; his coat being of the finest broadcloth, his linen delicate and spotless as snow, and his whole aspect that of one whose counterpart may now and then be seen upon the pave in Broadway of a fine afternoon. He laugh'd and talk'd with the rest, and it must be confess'd his jokes—like the most of those that pass'd current there—were by no means distinguish'd for their refinement or purity. Near the door was a small table, cover'd with decanters and glasses, some of which had been used, but were used again indiscriminately, and a box of very thick and very long cigars.

One of the sailors—and it was he who made the largest share of the hubbub—had but one eye. His chin and cheeks were cover'd with huge, bushy whiskers, and altogether he had quite a brutal appearance. "Come, boys," said this gentleman, "come, let us take a drink. I know you're all a getting dry;" and he clench'd his invitation with an appalling oath.

This politeness was responded to by a general moving of the company toward the table holding the before-mention'd decanters and glasses. Clustering there around, each one help'd himself to a very handsome portion of that particular liquor which suited his fancy; and steadiness and accuracy being at that moment by no means distinguishing traits of the arms and legs of the party, a goodly amount of the fluid was spill'd upon the floor. This piece of extravagance excited the ire of the personage who gave the "treat;" and that ire was still further increas'd when he discover'd two or three loiterers who seem'd disposed to slight his request to drink. Charles, as we have before mention'd, was looking in at the window.

"Walk up, boys! walk up! If there be any skulker among us, blast my eyes if he shan't go down on his marrow bones and taste the liquor we have spilt! Hallo!" he exclaim'd as he spied Charles; "hallo, you chap in the window, come here and take a sup."

As he spoke he stepp'd to the open casement, put his brawny hands under the boy's arms, and lifted him into the room bodily.

"There, my lads," said he, turning to his companions, "there's a new recruit for you. Not so coarse a one, either," he added as he took a fair view of the boy, who, though not what is called pretty, was fresh and manly looking, and large for his age.

"Come, youngster, take a glass," he continued. And he pour'd one nearly full of strong brandy.

Now Charles was not exactly frighten'd, for he was a lively fellow, and had often been at the country merry-makings, and at the parties of the place; but he was certainly rather abash'd at his abrupt introduction to the midst of strangers. So, putting the glass aside, he look'd up with a pleasant smile in his new acquaintance's face.

"I've no need for anything now," he said, "but I'm just as much obliged to you as if I was."

"Poh! man, drink it down," rejoin'd the sailor, "drink it down—it won't hurt you."

And, by way of showing its excellence, the one-eyed worthy drain'd it himself to the last drop. Then filling it again, he renew'd his efforts to make the lad go through the same operation.

"I've no occasion. Besides, *my mother has often pray'd me not to drink,* and I promised to obey her."

A little irritated by his continued refusal, the sailor, with a loud oath, declared that Charles should swallow the brandy, whether he would or no. Placing one of his tremendous paws on the back of the boy's head, with the other he thrust the edge of the glass to his lips, swearing at the same time, that if he shook it so as to spill its contents the consequences would be of a nature by no means agreeable to his back and shoulders. Disliking the liquor, and angry at the attempt to overbear him, the undaunted child lifted his hand and struck the arm of the sailor with a blow so sudden that the glass fell and was smash'd to pieces on the floor; while the brandy was about equally divided between the face of Charles, the clothes of the sailor, and the sand. By this time the whole of the company had their attention drawn to the scene. Some of them laugh'd when they saw Charles's undisguised antipathy to the drink; but they laugh'd still more heartily when he discomfited the sailor. All of them, however, were content to let the matter go as chance would have it—all but the young man of the black coat, who has been spoken of.

What was there in the words which Charles had spoken that carried the mind of the young man back to former times—to a period when he was more pure and innocent than now? "*My mother has often pray'd me not to drink!*" Ah, how the mist of months roll'd aside, and presented to his soul's eye the picture of *his* mother, and a prayer of exactly similar purport! Why was it, too, that the young man's heart moved with a feeling of kindness toward the harshly treated child?

Charles stood, his cheek flush'd and his heart throbbing, wiping the trickling drops from his face with a handkerchief. At first the sailor, between his drunkenness and his surprise, was much in the condition of one suddenly awaken'd out of a deep sleep, who cannot call his consciousness about him. When he saw the state of things, however, and heard the jeering laugh of his companions, his dull eye lighting up with anger, fell upon the boy who had withstood him. He seized Charles with a grip of iron, and with the side of his heavy boot gave him a sharp and solid kick. He was about repeating the performance—for the child hung like a rag in his grasp —but all of a sudden his ears rang, as if pistols were snapp'd close to them; lights of various hues flicker'd in his eye, (he had but one, it will be remember'd,) and a strong propelling power caused him to move from his position, and keep moving until he was brought up by the wall. A blow, a cuff given in such a scientific manner that the hand from which it proceeded was evidently no stranger to the pugilistic art, had been suddenly planted in the ear of the sailor. It was planted by the young man of the black coat.

He had watch'd with interest the proceeding of the sailor and the boy—two or three times he was on the point of interfering; but when the kick was given, his rage was uncontrollable. He sprang from his seat in the attitude of a boxer—struck the sailor in a manner to cause those unpleasant sensations which have been described—and would probably have follow'd up the attack, had not Charles, now thoroughly terrified, clung around his legs and prevented his advancing.

The scene was a strange one, and for the time quite a silent one. The company had started from their seats, and for a moment held breathless but strain'd positions. In the middle of the room stood the young man, in his not at all ungraceful attitude—every nerve out, and his eyes flashing brilliantly. He seem'd rooted like a rock; and clasping him, with an appearance of confidence in his protection, clung the boy.

"You scoundrel!" cried the young man, his voice thick with passion, "dare to touch the boy again, and I'll thrash you till no sense is left in your body."

The sailor, now partially recover'd, made some gestures of a belligerent nature.

"Come on, drunken brute!" continued the angry youth; "I wish you would! You've not had half what you deserve!"

Upon sobriety and sense more fully taking their power in the brains of the one-eyed mariner, however, that worthy determined in his own mind that it would be most prudent to let the matter drop. Expressing therefore his conviction to that effect, adding certain remarks to the purport that he "meant no harm to the lad," that he was surprised at such a gentleman being angry at "a little piece of fun," and so forth—he proposed that the company should go on with their jollity just as if nothing had happen'd. In truth, he of the single eye was not a bad fellow at heart, after all; the fiery enemy whose advances he had so often courted that night, had stolen away his good feelings, and set busy devils at work within him, that might have made his hands do some dreadful deed, had not the stranger interposed.

In a few minutes the frolic of the party was upon its former footing. The young man sat down upon one of the benches, with the boy by his side, and while the rest were loudly laughing and talking, they two convers'd together. The stranger learn'd from Charles all the particulars of his simple story—how his father had died years since—how his mother work'd hard for a bare living—and how he himself, for many dreary months, had been the servant of a hard-hearted, avaricious master. More and more interested, drawing the child close to his side, the young man listen'd to his plainly told history—and thus an hour pass'd away.

It was now past midnight. The young man told Charles that on the morrow he would take steps to relieve him from his servitude—that for the present night the landlord would probably give him a lodging at the inn—and little persuading did the host need for that.

As he retired to sleep, very pleasant thoughts filled the mind of the young man—thoughts of a worthy action perform'd—thoughts, too, newly awakened ones, of walking in a steadier and wiser path than formerly.

That roof, then, sheltered two beings that night—one of them innocent and sinless of all wrong—the other—oh, to that other what evil had not been present, either in action or to his desires!

Who was the stranger? To those that, from ties of relationship or otherwise, felt an interest in him, the answer to that question was not pleasant to dwell upon. His name was Langton—parentless—a dissipated young man —a brawler—one whose too frequent companions were rowdies, blacklegs, and swindlers. The New York police offices were not strangers to his countenance. He had been bred to the profession of medicine; besides, he had a very respectable income, and his house was in a pleasant street on the west side of the city. Little of his time, however, did Mr. John Langton spend at his domestic hearth; and the elderly lady who officiated as his housekeeper was by no means surprised to have him gone for a week or a month at a time, and she knowing nothing of his whereabouts.

Living as he did, the young man was an unhappy being. It was not so much that his associates were below his own capacity—for Langton, though sensible and well bred, was not highly talented or refined—but that he lived without any steady purpose, that he had no one to attract him to his home, that he too easily allow'd himself to be tempted—which caused his life to be, of late, one continued scene of dissatisfaction. This dissatisfaction he sought to drive away by the brandy bottle, and mixing in all kinds of parties where the object was pleasure. On the present occasion he had left the city a few days before, and was passing his time at a place near the village where Charles and his mother lived. He fell in, during the day, with those who were his companions of the tavern spree; and thus it happen'd that they were all together. Langton hesitated not to make himself at home with any associate that suited his fancy.

The next morning the poor widow rose from her sleepless cot; and from that lucky trait in our nature which makes one extreme follow another, she set about her toil with a lighten'd heart. Ellis, the farmer, rose, too, short as the nights were, an hour before day; for his god was gain, and a prime article of his creed was to get as much work as possible from every one around him. In the course of the day Ellis was called upon by young Langton, and never perhaps in his life was the farmer puzzled more than at the young man's proposal—his desire to provide for the widow's family, a family that could do him no pecuniary good, and his willingness to disburse money for that purpose. The widow, too, was called upon, not only on that day, but the next and the next.

It needs not that I should particularize the subsequent events of Langton's and the boy's history—how the reformation of the profligate might be dated to begin from that time—how he gradually sever'd the guilty ties that had so long gall'd him—how he enjoy'd his own home again—how the friendship of Charles and himself grew not slack with time—and how, when in the course of seasons he became head of a family of his own, he would shudder at the remembrance of his early dangers and his escapes.

LINGAVE'S TEMPTATION

"ANOTHER DAY," utter'd the poet Lingave, as he awoke in the morning, and turn'd him drowsily on his hard pallet, "another day comes out, burthen'd with its weight of woes. Of what use is existence to me? Crush'd down beneath the merciless heel of poverty, and no promise of hope to cheer me on, what have I in prospect but a life neglected, and a death of misery?"

The youth paused; but receiving no answer to his questions, thought proper to continue the peevish soliloquy. "I am a genius, they say," and the speaker smiled bitterly, "but genius is not apparel and food. Why should I exist in the world, unknown, unloved, press'd with cares, while so many around me have all their souls can desire? I behold the splendid equipages roll by—I see the respectful bow at the presence of pride—and I curse the contrast between my own lot, and the fortune of the rich. The lofty air— the show of dress—the aristocratic demeanor—the glitter of jewels—dazzle my eyes; and sharp-tooth'd envy works within me. I hate these haughty and favor'd ones. Why should my path be so much rougher than theirs? Pitiable, unfortunate man that I am! to be placed beneath those whom in my heart I despise—and to be constantly tantalized with the presence of that wealth I cannot enjoy!" And the poet cover'd his eyes with his hands, and wept from very passion and fretfulness.

O, Lingave! be more of a man! Have you not the treasures of health and untainted propensities, which many of those you envy never enjoy? Are you not their superior in mental power, in liberal views of mankind, and in comprehensive intellect? And even allowing you the choice, how would you shudder at changing, in total, conditions with them! Besides, were you willing to devote all your time and energies, you could gain property too: squeeze, and toil, and worry, and twist everything into a matter of profit, and you can become a great man, as far as money goes to make greatness.

Retreat, then, man of the polish'd soul, from those irritable complaints against your lot—those longings for wealth and puerile distinction, not worthy your class. Do justice, philosopher, to your own powers. While the world runs after its shadows and its bubbles, (thus commune in your own mind,) we will fold ourselves in our circle of understanding, and look with an eye of apathy on those things it considers so mighty and so enviable. Let the proud man pass with his pompous glance—let the gay flutter in finery—let the foolish enjoy his folly, and the beautiful move on in his perishing glory; we will gaze without desire on all their possessions, and all their pleasures. Our destiny is different from them. Not for such as we, the lowly flights of their crippled wings. We acknowledge no fellowship with them in ambition. We composedly look down on the paths where they walk, and pursue our own, without uttering a wish to descend, and be as they. What is it to us that the mass pay us not that deference which wealth commands? We desire no applause, save the applause of the good and discriminating—the choice spirits among men. Our intellect would be sullied, were the vulgar to approximate to it, by professing to readily enter in, and praising it. Our pride is a towering, and thrice refined pride.

When Lingave had given way to his temper some half hour, or there-about, he grew more calm, and bethought himself that he was acting a very silly part. He listen'd a moment to the clatter of the carts, and the tramp of early passengers on the pave below, as they wended along to commence their daily toil. It was just sunrise, and the season was summer. A little canary bird, the only pet poor Lingave could afford to keep, chirp'd merrily in its cage on the wall. How slight a circumstance will sometimes change the whole current of our thoughts! The music of that bird abstract-ing the mind of the poet but a moment from his sorrows, gave a chance for his natural buoyancy to act again.

Lingave sprang lightly from his bed, and perform'd his ablutions and his simple toilet—then hanging the cage on a nail outside the window, and speaking an endearment to the songster, which brought a perfect flood of melody in return—he slowly passed through his door, descended the long narrow turnings of the stairs, and stood in the open street. Undetermin'd as to any particular destination, he folded his hands behind him, cast his glance upon the ground, and moved listlessly onward.

Hour after hour the poet walk'd along—up this street and down that—he reck'd not how or where. And as crowded thoroughfares are hardly the most fit places for a man to let his fancy soar in the clouds—many a push and shove and curse did the dreamer get bestow'd upon him.

The booming of the city clock sounded forth the hour twelve—high noon.

"Ho! Lingave!" cried a voice from an open basement window as the poet pass'd.

He stopp'd, and then unwittingly would have walked on still, not fully awaken'd from his reverie.

"Lingave, I say!" cried the voice again, and the person to whom the voice belong'd stretch'd his head quite out into the area in front, "Stop man. Have you forgotten your appointment?"

"Oh! ah!" said the poet, and he smiled unmeaningly, and descending the steps, went into the office of Ridman, whose call it was that had startled him in his walk.

Who was Ridman? While the poet is waiting the convenience of that personage, it may be as well to describe him.

Ridman was a *money-maker*. He had much penetration, considerable knowledge of the world, and a disposition to be constantly in the midst of enterprise, excitement, and stir. His schemes for gaining wealth were vari-ous; he had dipp'd into almost every branch and channel of business. A slight acquaintance of several years' standing subsisted between him and the poet. The day previous a boy had call'd with a note from Ridman to Lingave, desiring the presence of the latter at the money-maker's room. The poet return'd for answer that he would be there. This was the engage-ment which he came near breaking.

Ridman had a smooth tongue. All his ingenuity was needed in the ex-planation to his companion of why and wherefore the latter had been sent for.

It is not requisite to state specifically the offer made by the man of wealth to the poet. Ridman, in one of his enterprises, found it necessary to procure the aid of such a person as Lingave—a writer of power, a master of elegant diction, of fine taste, in style passionate yet pure, and of the delicate imagery that belongs to the children of song. The youth was absolutely startled at the magnificent and permanent remuneration which was held out to him for a moderate exercise of his talents.

But the *nature* of the service required! All the sophistry and art of Ridman could not veil its repulsiveness. The poet was to labor for the advancement of what he felt to be unholy—he was to inculcate what would lower the perfection of man. He promised to give an answer to the proposal the succeeding day, and left the place.

Now during the many hours there was a war going on in the heart of the poor poet. He was indeed *poor;* often, he had no certainty whether he should be able to procure the next day's meals. And the poet knew the beauty of truth, and adored, not in the abstract merely, but in practice, the excellence of upright principles.

Night came. Lingave, wearied, lay upon his pallet again and slept. The misty veil thrown over him, the spirit of poesy came to his visions, and stood beside him, and look'd down pleasantly with her large eyes, which were bright and liquid like the reflection of stars in a lake.

Virtue, (such imagining, then, seem'd conscious to the soul of the dreamer,) is ever the sinew of true genius. Together, the two in one, they are endow'd with immortal strength, and approach loftily to Him from whom both spring. Yet there are those that having great powers, bend them to the slavery of wrong. God forgive them! for they surely do it ignorantly or heedlessly. Oh, could he who lightly tosses around him the seeds of evil in his writings, or his enduring thoughts, or his chance words—could he see how, haply, they are to spring up in distant time and poison the air, and putrefy, and cause to sicken—would he not shrink back in horror? A bad principle, jestingly spoken—a falsehood, but of a word—may taint a whole nation! Let the man to whom the great Master has given the might of mind, beware how he uses that might. If for the furtherance of bad ends, what can be expected but that, as the hour of the closing scene draws nigh, thoughts of harm done, and capacities distorted from their proper aim, and strength so laid out that men must be worse instead of better, through the exertion of that strength—will come and swarm like spectres around him?

"Be and continue poor, young man," so taught one whose counsels should be graven on the heart of every youth, "while others around you grow rich by fraud and disloyalty. Be without place and power, while others beg their way upward. Bear the pain of disappointed hopes, while others gain the accomplishment of their flattery. Forego the gracious pressure of a hand, for which others cringe and crawl. Wrap yourself in your own virtue, and seek a friend and your daily bread. If you have, in such a course, grown gray with unblench'd honor, bless God and die."

When Lingave awoke the next morning, he despatch'd his answer to his wealthy friend, and then plodded on as in the days before.

LITTLE JANE

"Lift up!" was ejaculated as a signal!—and click! went the glasses in the hands of a party of tipsy men, drinking one night at the bar of one of the middling order of taverns. And many a wild gibe was utter'd, and many a terrible blasphemy, and many an impure phrase sounded out the pollution of the hearts of these half-crazed creatures, as they toss'd down their liquor, and made the walls echo with their uproar. The first and foremost in recklessness was a girlish-faced, fair-hair'd fellow of twenty-two or three years. They called him Mike. He seem'd to be look'd upon by the others as a sort of prompter, from whom they were to take cue. And if the brazen wickedness evinced by him in a hundred freaks and remarks to his companions, during their stay in that place, were any test of his capacity—there might hardly be one more fit to go forward as a guide on the road of destruction. From the conversation of the party, it appear'd that they had been spending the early part of the evening in a gambling house.

A second, third and fourth time were the glasses fill'd; and the effect thereof began to be perceiv'd in a still higher degree of noise and loquacity among the revellers. One of the serving-men came in at this moment, and whisper'd the barkeeper, who went out, and in a moment return'd again.

"A person," he said, "wish'd to speak with Mr. Michael. He waited on the walk in front."

The individual whose name was mention'd, made his excuses to the others, telling them he would be back in a moment, and left the room. As he shut the door behind him, and stepp'd into the open air, he saw one of his brothers—his elder by eight or ten years—pacing to and fro with rapid and uneven steps. As the man turn'd in his walk, and the glare of the street lamp fell upon his face, the youth, half-benumb'd as his senses were, was somewhat startled at its paleness and evident perturbation.

"Come with me!" said the elder brother, hurriedly, "the illness of our little Jane is worse, and I have been sent for you."

"Poh!" answered the young drunkard, very composedly, "is that all? I shall be home by-and-by," and he turn'd back again.

"But, brother, she is worse than ever before. Perhaps when you arrive she may be *dead*."

The tipsy one paus'd in his retreat, perhaps alarm'd at the utterance of that dread word, which seldom fails to shoot a chill to the hearts of mortals. But he soon calm'd himself, and waving his hand to the other:

"Why, see," said he, "a score of times at least, have I been call'd away to the last sickness of our good little sister; and each time it proves to be nothing worse than some whim of the nurse or physician. Three years has the girl been able to live very heartily under her disease; and I'll be bound she'll stay on the earth three years longer."

And as he concluded this wicked and most brutal reply, the speaker open'd the door and went into the bar-room. But in his intoxication, during the hour that follow'd, Mike was far from being at ease. At the end of that hour, the words, "perhaps when you arrive she may be *dead*," were not effaced from his hearing yet, and he started for home. The elder brother had wended his way back in sorrow.

Let me go before the younger one, awhile, to a room in that home. A little girl lay there dying. She had been ill a long time; so it was no sudden thing for her parents, and her brethren and sisters, to be called for the witness of the death agony. The girl was not what might be called beautiful. And yet, there is a solemn kind of loveliness that always surrounds a sick child. The sympathy for the weak and helpless sufferer, perhaps, increases it in our own ideas. The ashiness and the moisture on the brow, and the film over the eyeballs—what man can look upon the sight, and not feel his heart awed within him? Children, I have sometimes fancied too, increase in beauty as their illness deepens.

Besides the nearest relatives of little Jane, standing round her bedside, was the family doctor. He had just laid her wrist down upon the coverlet, and the look he gave the mother, was a look in which there was no hope.

"My child!" she cried, in uncontrollable agony, "O! my child!"

And the father, and the sons and daughters, were bowed down in grief, and thick tears rippled between the fingers held before their eyes.

Then there was silence awhile. During the hour just by-gone, Jane had, in her childish way, bestow'd a little gift upon each of her kindred, as a remembrancer when she should be dead and buried in the grave. And there was one of these simple tokens which had not reach'd its destination. She held it in her hand now. It was a very small much-thumbed book—a religious story for infants, given her by her mother when she had first learn'd to read.

While they were all keeping this solemn stillness—broken only by the suppress'd sobs of those who stood and watch'd for the passing away of the girl's soul—a confusion of some one entering rudely, and speaking in a turbulent voice, was heard in an adjoining apartment. Again the voice roughly sounded out; it was the voice of the drunkard Mike, and the father bade one of his sons go and quiet the intruder.

"If nought else will do," said he sternly, "put him forth by strength. We want no tipsy brawlers here, to disturb such a scene as this."

For what moved the sick girl uneasily on her pillow, and raised her neck, and motion'd to her mother? She would that Mike should be brought to her side. And it was enjoin'd on him whom the father had bade to eject the noisy one, that he should tell Mike his sister's request, and beg him to come to her.

He came. The inebriate—his mind sober'd by the deep solemnity of the scene—stood there, and leaned over to catch the last accounts of one who soon was to be with the spirits of heaven. All was the silence of the deepest night. The dying child held the young man's hand in one of hers; with the other she slowly lifted the trifling memorial she had assigned especially for him, aloft in the air. Her arm shook—her eyes, now becoming glassy with the death-damps, were cast toward her brother's face. She smiled pleasantly, and as an indistinct gurgle came from her throat, the uplifted hand fell suddenly into the open palm of her brother's, depositing the tiny volume there. Little Jane was dead.

From that night, the young man stepped no more in his wild courses, but was reform'd.

DUMB KATE

NOT MANY years since—and yet long enough to have been before the abundance of railroads, and similar speedy modes of conveyance—the travelers from Amboy village to the metropolis of our republic were permitted to refresh themselves, and the horses of the stage had a breathing spell, at a certain old-fashion'd tavern, about half way between the two places. It was a quaint, comfortable, ancient house, that tavern. Huge buttonwood trees embower'd it round about, and there was a long porch in front, the trellis'd work whereof, though old and moulder'd, had been, and promised still to be for years, held together by the tangled folds of a grape vine wreath'd about it like a tremendous serpent.

How clean and fragrant everything was there! How bright the pewter tankards wherefrom cider or ale went into the parch'd throat of the thirsty man! How pleasing to look into the expressive eyes of Kate, the landlord's lovely daughter, who kept everything so clean and bright!

Now the reason why Kate's eyes had become so expressive was, that, besides their proper and natural office, they stood to the poor girl in the place of tongue and ears also. Kate had been dumb from her birth. Everybody loved the helpless creature when she was a child. Gentle, timid, and affectionate was she, and beautiful as the lilies of which she loved to cultivate so many every summer in her garden. Her light hair, and the like-color'd lashes, so long and silky, that droop'd over her blue eyes of such uncommon size and softness—her rounded shape, well set off by a little modest art of dress—her smile—the graceful ease of her motions, always attracted the admiration of the strangers who stopped there, and were quite a pride to her parents and friends.

How could it happen that so beautiful and inoffensive a being should taste, even to its dregs, the bitterest unhappiness? Oh, there must indeed be a mysterious, unfathomable meaning in the decrees of Providence which is beyond the comprehension of man; for no one on earth less deserved or needed 'the uses of adversity' than Dumb Kate. Love, the mighty and lawless passion, came into the sanctuary of the maid's pure breast, and the dove of peace fled away forever.

One of the persons who had occasion to stop most frequently at the tavern kept by Dumb Kate's parents was a young man, the son of a wealthy farmer, who own'd an estate in the neighborhood. He saw Kate, and was struck with her natural elegance. Though not of thoroughly wicked propensities, the fascination of so fine a prize made this youth determine to gain her love, and, if possible, to win her to himself. At first he hardly dared, even amid the depths of his own soul, to entertain thoughts of vileness against one so confiding and childlike. But in a short time such feelings wore away, and he made up his mind to become the betrayer of poor Kate. He was a good-looking fellow, and made but too sure of his victim. Kate was lost!

The villain came to New York soon after, and engaged in a business which prosper'd well, and which has no doubt by this time made him what is call'd a man of fortune.

Not long did sickness of the heart wear into the life and happiness of Dumb Kate. One pleasant spring day, the neighbors having been called by a notice the previous morning, the old churchyard was thrown open, and a coffin was borne over the early grass that seem'd so delicate with its light green hue. There was a new made grave, and by its side the bier was rested—while they paused a moment until holy words had been said. An idle boy, call'd there by curiosity, saw something lying on the fresh earth thrown out from the grave, which attracted his attention. A little blossom, the only one to be seen around, had grown exactly on the spot where the sexton chose to dig poor Kate's last resting-place. It was a weak but lovely flower, and now lay where it had been carelessly toss'd amid the coarse gravel. The boy twirl'd it a moment in his fingers—the bruis'd fragments gave out a momentary perfume, and then fell to the edge of the pit, over which the child at that moment lean'd and gazed in his inquisitiveness. As they dropp'd, they were wafted to the bottom of the grave. The last look was bestow'd on the dead girl's face by those who loved her so well in life, and then she was softly laid away to her sleep beneath that green grass covering.

Yet in the churchyard on the hill is Kate's grave. There stands a little white stone at the head, and verdure grows richly there; and gossips, sometimes of a Sabbath afternoon, rambling over that gathering-place of the gone from earth, stop a while, and con over the dumb girl's hapless story.

TALK TO AN ART-UNION
(*A Brooklyn fragment*)

IT IS A beautiful truth that all men contain something of the artist in them. And perhaps it is the case that the greatest artists live and die, the world and themselves alike ignorant what they possess. Who would not mourn that an ample palace, of surpassingly graceful architecture, fill'd with luxuries, and embellish'd with fine pictures and sculpture, should stand cold and still and vacant, and never be known or enjoy'd by its owner? Would such a fact as this cause your sadness? Then be sad. For there is a palace, to which the courts of the most sumptuous kings are but a frivolous patch, and, though it is always waiting for them, not one of its owners ever enters there with any genuine sense of its grandeur and glory.

I think of few heroic actions, which cannot be traced to the artistical impulse. He who does great deeds, does them from his innate sensitiveness to moral beauty. Such men are not merely artists, they are also artistic material. Washington in some great crisis, Lawrence on the bloody deck of the

Chesapeake, Mary Stuart at the block, Kossuth in captivity, and Mazzini
in exile—all great rebels and innovators, exhibit the highest phases of the
artist spirit. The painter, the sculptor, the poet, express heroic beauty better in description; but the others *are* heroic beauty, the best belov'd of art.

Talk not so much, then, young artist, of the great old masters, who but
painted and chisell'd. Study not only their productions. There is a still higher
school for him who would kindle his fire with coal from the altar of the
loftiest and purest art. It is the school of all grand actions and grand virtues,
of heroism, of the death of patriots and martyrs—of all the mighty deeds
written in the pages of history—deeds of daring, and enthusiasm, devotion, and fortitude.

BLOOD-MONEY

"Guilty of the body and the blood of Christ"

I

OF OLDEN time, when it came to pass
That the beautiful god, Jesus, should finish his work on earth,
Then went Judas, and sold the divine youth,
And took pay for his body.

Curs'd was the deed, even before the sweat of the clutching hand grew dry;
And darkness frown'd upon the seller of the like of God,
Where, as though earth lifted her breast to throw him from her, and heaven
          refused him,
He hung in the air, self-slaughter'd.

The cycles, with their long shadows, have stalk'd silently forward,
Since those ancient days—many a pouch enwrapping meanwhile
Its fee, like that paid for the son of Mary.

And still goes one, saying,
"What will ye give me, and I will deliver this man unto you?"
And they make the covenant, and pay the pieces of silver.

II

Look forth, deliverer,
Look forth, first-born of the dead,
Over the tree-tops of Paradise;
See thyself in yet-continued bonds,
Toilsome and poor, thou bear'st man's form again,
Thou art reviled, scourged, put into prison,
Hunted from the arrogant equality of the rest;

With staves and swords throng the willing servants of authority,
Again they surround thee, mad with devilish spite;
Toward thee stretch the hands of a multitude, like vultures' talons,
The meanest spit in thy face, they smite thee with their palms;
Bruised, bloody, and pinion'd is thy body,
More sorrowful than death is thy soul.

Witness of anguish, brother of slaves,
Not with thy price closed the price of thine image:
And still Iscariot plies his trade.

PAUMANOK.

April, 1843.

WOUNDED IN THE HOUSE OF FRIENDS

"And one shall say unto him, What are these wounds in thy hands? Then he shall answer, Those with which I was wounded in the house of my friends."
—*Zechariah*, xiii. 6

If thou art balk'd, O Freedom,
The victory is not to thy manlier foes;
From the house of friends comes the death stab.

Virginia, mother of greatness,
Blush not for being also mother of slaves;
You might have borne deeper slaves—
Doughfaces, crawlers, lice of humanity—
Terrific screamers of freedom,
Who roar and bawl, and get hot i' the face,
But were they not incapable of august crime,
Would quench the hopes of ages for a drink—
Muck-worms, creeping flat to the ground,
A dollar dearer to them than Christ's blessing;
All loves, all hopes, less than the thought of gain,
In life walking in that as in a shroud;
Men whom the throes of heroes,
Great deeds at which the gods might stand appal'd,
The shriek of the drown'd, the appeal of women,
The exulting laugh of untied empires,
Would touch them never in the heart,
But only in the pocket.

Hot-headed Carolina,
Well may you curl your lip;
With all your bondsmen, bless the destiny
Which brings you no such breed as this.

Arise, young North!
Our elder blood flows in the veins of cowards:
The gray-hair'd sneak, the blanch'd poltroon,
The feign'd or real shiverer at tongues
That nursing babes need hardly cry the less for—
Are they to be our tokens always?

SAILING THE MISSISSIPPI AT MIDNIGHT

VAST and starless, the pall of heaven
    Laps on the trailing pall below;
And forward, forward, in solemn darkness,
    As if to the sea of the lost we go.

Now drawn nigh the edge of the river,
    Weird-like creatures suddenly rise;
Shapes that fade, dissolving outlines
    Baffle the gazer's straining eyes.

Towering upward and bending forward,
    Wild and wide their arms are thrown,
Ready to pierce with forked fingers
    Him who touches their realm upon.

Tide of youth, thus thickly planted,
    While in the eddies onward you swim,
Thus on the shore stands a phantom army,
    Lining forever the channel's rim.

Steady, helmsman! you guide the immortal;
    Many a wreck is beneath you piled,
Many a brave yet unwary sailor
    Over these waters has been beguiled.

Nor is it the storm or the scowling midnight,
    Cold, or sickness, or fire's dismay—
Nor is it the reef, or treacherous quicksand,
    Will peril you most on your twisted way.

But when there comes a voluptuous languor,
    Soft the sunshine, silent the air,
Bewitching your craft with safety and sweetness,
    Then, young pilot of life, beware.

->>> <<<-

November Boughs

※

OUR EMINENT VISITORS

Past, present and future

WELCOME to them each and all! They do good—the deepest, widest, most needed good—though quite certainly not in the ways attempted—which have, at times, something irresistibly comic. What can be more farcical, for instance, than the sight of a worthy gentleman coming three or four thousand miles through wet and wind to speak complacently and at great length on matters of which he both entirely mistakes or knows nothing—before crowds of auditors equally complacent and equally at fault?

Yet welcome and thanks, we say, to those visitors we have, and have had, from abroad among us—and may the procession continue! We have had Dickens and Thackeray, Froude, Herbert Spencer, Oscar Wilde, Lord Coleridge—soldiers, savants, poets—and now Matthew Arnold and Irving the actor. Some have come to make money—some for a "good time"—some to help us along and give us advice—and some undoubtedly to investigate, *bona fide*, this great problem, democratic America, looming upon the world with such cumulative power through a hundred years, now with the evident intention (since the Secession War) to stay, and take a leading hand, for many a century to come, in civilization's and humanity's eternal game. But alas! that very investigation—the method of that investigation—is where the deficit most surely and helplessly comes in. Let not Lord Coleridge and Mr. Arnold (to say nothing of the illustrious actor) imagine that when they have met and survey'd the

392

etiquettical gatherings of our wealthy, distinguish'd and sure-to-be-put-forward-on-such-occasions citizens (New York, Boston, Philadelphia, &c., have certain stereotyped strings of them, continually lined and paraded like the lists of dishes at hotel tables—you are sure to get the same over and over again—it is very amusing)—and the bowing and introducing, the receptions at the swell clubs, the eating and drinking and praising and praising back—and the next day riding about Central Park, or doing the "Public Institutions"—and so passing through, one after another, the full-dress coteries of the Atlantic cities, all grammatical and cultured and correct, with the toned-down manners of the gentlemen, and the kid-gloves, and luncheons and finger-glasses—Let not our eminent visitors, we say, suppose that, by means of these experiences, they have "seen America," or captur'd any distinctive clew or purport thereof. Not a bit of it. Of the pulse-beats that lie within and vitalize this Commonweal to-day—of the hard-pan purports and idiosyncrasies pursued faithfully and triumphantly by its bulk of men North and South, generation after generation, superficially unconscious of their own aims, yet none the less pressing onward with deathless intuition—those coteries do not furnish the faintest scintilla. In the Old World the best flavor and significance of a race may possibly need to be look'd for in its "upper classes," its gentries, its court, its *état major*. In the United States the rule is revers'd. Besides (and a point, this, perhaps deepest of all,) the special marks of our grouping and design are not going to be understood in a hurry. The lesson and scanning right on the ground are difficult; I was going to say they are impossible to foreigners—but I have occasionally found the clearest appreciation of all, coming from far-off quarters. Surely nothing could be more apt, not only for our eminent visitors present and to come, but for home study, than the following editorial criticism of the London *Times* on Mr. Froude's visit and lectures here a few years ago, and the culminating dinner given at Delmonico's, with its brilliant array of guests:

"*We read the list," says the* Times, "*of those who assembled to do honor to Mr. Froude: there were Mr. Emerson, Mr. Beecher, Mr. Curtis, Mr. Bryant; we add the names of those who sent letters of regret that they could not attend in person—Mr. Longfellow, Mr. Whittier. They are names which are well known—almost as well known and as much honor'd in England as in America; and yet what must we say in the end? The American people outside this assemblage of writers is something vaster and greater than they, singly or together, can comprehend. It cannot be said of any or all of them that they can speak for their nation. We who look on at this distance are able perhaps on that account to see the more clearly that there are qualities of the American people which find no representation, no voice, among these their spokesmen. And what is true of them is true of the English class of whom Mr. Froude may be said to be the ambassador. Mr. Froude is master of a charming style. He has the gift of grace and the gift of sympathy. Taking any single character as the subject of his study, he may succeed after a very short time in so comprehending its workings as to be able to present a living figure to the intelligence and memory of his readers. But the movements of a nation,* the voiceless purpose of a people which cannot put its own thoughts into words, yet acts upon them in each successive generation—*these things do not lie within his grasp. . . . The functions of literature such as he represents are limited in their action; the influence he can wield is artificial and restricted, and, while he and his hearers please and are pleas'd with pleasant periods, his great mass of national life will flow around them unmov'd in its tides by action as powerless as that of the dwellers by the shore to direct the currents of the ocean."*

A thought, here, that needs to be echoed, expanded, permanently treasur'd by our literary classes and educators. (The gestation, the youth, the knitting preparations, are now over, and it is full time for definite purpose, result.) How few think of it, though it is the impetus and background of our whole Nationality and popular life. In the present brief memorandum I very likely for the first time awake "the intelligent reader" to the idea and inquiry whether there isn't such a thing as the distinctive genius of our democratic New World, universal, immanent, bringing to a head the best experience of the past—not specially literary or intellectual—not merely "good," (in the Sunday School and Temperance Society sense,)—some invisible spine and great sympathetic to these States, resident only in the average people, in their practical life, in their physiology, in their emotions, in their nebulous yet fiery patriotism, in the armies (both sides) through the whole Secession War—an identity and character which indeed so far "finds no voice among their spokesmen."

To my mind America, vast and fruitful as it appears to-day, is even yet, for its most important results, entirely in the tentative state; its very formation-stir and whirling trials and essays more splendid and picturesque, to my thinking, than the accomplish'd growths and shows of other lands, through European history, or Greece, or all the past. Surely a New World literature, worthy the name, is not to be, if it ever comes, some fiction, or fancy, or bit of sentimentalism or polish'd work merely by itself, or in abstraction. So long as such literature is no born branch and offshoot of the Nationality, rooted and grown from its roots, and fibred with its fibre, it can never answer any deep call or perennial need. Perhaps the untaught Republic is wiser than its teachers. The best literature is always a result of something far greater than itself—not the hero, but the portrait of the hero. Before there can be recorded history or poem there must be the transaction. Beyond the old masterpieces, the Iliad, the interminable Hindu epics, the Greek tragedies, even the Bible itself, range the immense facts of what must have preceded them, their *sine qua non*—the veritable poems and masterpieces, of which, grand as they are, the word-statements are but shreds and cartoons.

For to-day and the States, I think the vividest, rapidest, most stupendous processes ever known, ever perform'd by man or nation, on the largest scales and in countless varieties, are now and here presented. Not as our poets and preachers are always conventionally putting it—but quite different. Some colossal foundry, the flaming of the fire, the melted metal, the pounding trip-hammers, the surging crowds of workmen shifting from point to point, the murky shadows, the rolling haze, the discord, the crudeness, the deafening din, the disorder, the dross and clouds of dust, the waste and extravagance of material, the shafts of darted sunshine through the vast open roof-scuttles aloft—the mighty castings, many of them not yet fitted, perhaps delay'd long, yet each in its due time, with definite place and use and meaning—Such, more like, is a symbol of America.

After all of which, returning to our starting-point, we reiterate, and in the whole Land's name, a welcome to our eminent guests. Visits like theirs, and hospitalities, and hand-shaking, and face meeting face, and the distant brought near—what divine solvents they are! Travel, reciprocity, "interviewing," intercommunion of lands—what are they but Democracy's and the highest Law's best aids? O that our own country—that every land in the world—could annually, continually, receive the poets, thinkers, scientists, even the official magnates, of other lands, as honor'd guests. O that the United States, especially the West, could have had a good long visit and explorative jaunt, from the noble and melancholy Tourguéneff, before he died—or from Victor Hugo—or Thomas Carlyle. Castelar, Tennyson, any of the two or three great Parisian essayists—were they and we to come face to face, how is it possible but that the right understanding would ensue?

≫≪

THE BIBLE as POETRY

I SUPPOSE one cannot at this day say anything new, from a literary point of view, about those autochthonic bequests of Asia—the Hebrew Bible, the mighty Hindu epics, and a hundred lesser but typical works; (not now definitely including the Iliad—though that work was certainly of Asiatic genesis, as Homer himself was—considerations which seem curiously ignored.) But will there ever be a time or place—ever a student, however modern, of the grand art, to whom those compositions will not afford profounder lessons than all else of their kind in the garnerage of the past? Could there be any more opportune suggestion, to the current popular writer and reader of verse, what the office of poet was in primeval times—and is yet capable of being, anew, adjusted entirely to the modern?

All the poems of Orientalism, with the Old and New Testaments at the centre, tend to deep and wide, (I don't know but the deepest and widest,) psychological development—with little, or nothing at all, of the mere æsthetic, the principal verse-requirement of our day. Very late, but unerringly, comes to every capable student the perception that it is not in beauty, it is not in art, it is not even in science, that the profoundest laws of the case have their eternal sway and outcropping.

In his discourse on "Hebrew Poets" De Sola Mendes said: "The fundamental feature of Judaism, of the Hebrew nationality, was religion; its poetry was naturally religious. Its subjects, God and Providence, the covenants with Israel, God in Nature, and as reveal'd, God the Creator and Governor, Nature in her majesty and beauty, inspired hymns and odes to Nature's God. And then the checker'd history of the nation furnish'd allusions, illustrations, and subjects for epic display—the glory of the sanctuary, the offerings, the splendid ritual, the Holy City, and lov'd Palestine with its pleasant valleys and wild tracts." Dr. Mendes said "that rhyming was not a characteristic of Hebrew poetry at all. Metre was not a necessary mark of poetry. Great poets discarded it; the early Jewish poets knew it not."

Compared with the famed epics of Greece, and lesser ones since, the spinal supports of the Bible are simple and meagre. All its history, biography, narratives, etc., are as beads, strung on and indicating the eternal thread of the Deific purpose and power. Yet with only deepest faith for impetus, and such Deific purpose for palpable or impalpable theme, it often transcends the masterpieces of Hellas, and all masterpieces. The metaphors daring beyond account, the lawless soul, extravagant by our standards, the glow of love and friendship, the fervent kiss—nothing in argument or logic, but unsurpass'd in proverbs, in religious ecstacy, in suggestions of common mortality and death, man's great equalizers—the spirit everything, the ceremonies and forms of the churches nothing, faith limitless, its immense sensuousness immensely spiritual—an incredible, all-inclusive non-worldliness and dew-scented illiteracy (the antipodes of our Nineteenth Century business absorption and morbid refinement)—no hair-splitting doubts, no sickly sulking and sniffling, no "Hamlet," no "Adonais," no "Thanatopsis," no "In Memoriam."

The culminated proof of the poetry of a country is the quality of its personnel, which, in any race, can never be really superior without superior poems. The finest blending of individuality with universality (in my opinion nothing out of the galaxies of the "Iliad," or Shakspere's heroes, or from the Tennysonian "Idyls," so lofty, devoted and starlike,) typified in the songs of those old Asiatic lands. Men and women as great columnar trees. Nowhere else the abnegation of self towering in such quaint sublimity; nowhere else the simplest human emotions conquering the gods of heaven, and fate itself. (The episode, for instance, toward the close of the "Mahabharata"—the journey of the wife Savitri with the god of death, Yama,

> *One terrible to see—blood-red his garb,*
> *His body huge and dark, bloodshot his eyes,*
> *Which flamed like suns beneath his turban cloth,*
> *Arm'd was he with a noose,*

who carries off the soul of the dead husband, the wife tenaciously following, and—by the resistless charm of perfect poetic recitation! —eventually redeeming her captive mate.)

I remember how enthusiastically William H. Seward, in his last days, once expatiated on these themes, from his travels in Turkey, Egypt, and Asia Minor, finding the oldest Biblical narratives exactly illustrated there to-day with apparently no break or change along three thousand years—the veil'd women, the costumes, the gravity and simplicity, all the manners just the same. The veteran Trelawney said he found the only real *nobleman* of the world in a good average specimen of the mid-aged or elderly Oriental. In the East the grand figure, always leading, is the *old man,* majestic, with flowing beard, paternal, etc. In Europe and America, it is, as we know, the young fellow—in novels, a handsome and interesting hero, more or less juvenile—in operas, a tenor with blooming cheeks, black mustache, superficial animation, and perhaps good lungs, but no more depth than skim-milk. But reading folks probably get their

information of those Bible areas and current peoples, as depicted
in print by English and French cads, the most shallow, impudent,
supercilious brood on earth.

I have said nothing yet of the cumulus of association (perfectly
legitimate parts of its influence, and finally in many respects the
dominant parts,) of the Bible as a poetic entity, and of every portion of it. Not the old edifice only—the congeries also of events and
struggles and surroundings, of which it has been the scene and
motive—even the horrors, dreads, deaths. How many ages and generations have brooded and wept and agonized over this book! What
untellable joys and ecstasies—what support to martyrs at the stake
—from it. (No really great song can ever attain full purport till long
after the death of its singer—till it has accrued and incorporated the
many passions, many joys and sorrows, it has itself arous'd.) To
what myriads has it been the shore and rock of safety—the refuge
from driving tempest and wreck! Translated in all languages, how
it has united this diverse world! Of civilized lands to-day, whose of
our retrospects has it not interwoven and link'd and permeated?
Not only does it bring us what is clasp'd within its covers; nay, that
is the least of what it brings. Of its thousands, there is not a verse,
not a word, but is thick-studded with human emotions, successions
of fathers and sons, mothers and daughters, of our own antecedents,
inseparable from that background of us, on which, phantasmal as it
is, all that we are to-day inevitably depends—our ancestry, our past.

Strange, but true, that the principal factor in cohering the nations, eras and paradoxes of the globe, by giving them a common
platform of two or three great ideas, a commonalty of origin, and
projecting cosmic brotherhood, the dream of all hope, all time—that
the long trains, gestations, attempts and failures, resulting in the
New World, and in modern solidarity and politics—are to be identified and resolv'd back into a collection of old poetic lore, which,
more than any one thing else, has been the axis of civilization and history through thousands of years—and except for which this America
of ours, with its polity and essentials, could not now be existing.

No true bard will ever contravene the Bible. If the time ever
comes when iconoclasm does its extremest in one direction against
the Books of the Bible in its present form, the collection must still
survive in another, and dominate just as much as hitherto, or more
than hitherto, through its divine and primal poetic structure. To
me, that is the living and definite element-principle of the work,
evolving everything else. Then the continuity; the oldest and new-
est Asiatic utterance and character, and all between, holding together, like the apparition of the sky, and coming to us the same.
Even to our Nineteenth Century here are the fountain heads of song.

FATHER TAYLOR (and ORATORY)

I HAVE never heard but one essentially perfect orator—one who satisfied those depths of the emotional nature that in most cases go through life quite untouch'd, unfed—who held every hearer by spells which no conventionalist, high or low—nor any pride or composure, nor resistance of intellect—could stand against for ten minutes.

And by the way, is it not strange, of this first-class genius in the rarest and most profound of humanity's arts, that it will be necessary, (so nearly forgotten and rubb'd out is his name by the rushing whirl of the last twenty-five years,) to first inform current readers that he was an orthodox minister, of no particular celebrity, who during a long life preach'd especially to Yankee sailors in an old fourth-class church down by the wharves in Boston—had practically been a sea-faring man through his earlier years—and died April 6, 1871, "just as the tide turn'd, going out with the ebb as an old salt should"? His name is now comparatively unknown, outside of Boston—and even there, (though Dickens, Mr. Jameson, Dr. Bartol and Bishop Haven have commemorated him,) is mostly but a reminiscence.

During my visits to "the Hub," in 1859 and '60 I several times saw and heard Father Taylor. In the spring or autumn, quiet Sunday forenoons, I liked to go down early to the quaint ship-cabin-looking church where the old man minister'd—to enter and leisurely scan the building, the low ceiling, every thing strongly timber'd (polish'd and rubb'd apparently,) the dark rich colors, the gallery, all in half-light—and smell the aroma of old wood—to watch the auditors, sailors, mates, "matlows," officers, singly or in groups, as they came in—their physiognomies, forms, dress, gait, as they walk'd along the aisles,—their postures, seating themselves in the rude, roomy, undoor'd, uncushion'd pews—and the evident effect upon them of the place, occasion, and atmosphere.

The pulpit, rising ten or twelve feet high, against the rear wall, was back'd by a significant mural painting, in oil—showing out its bold lines and strong hues through the subdued light of the building—of a stormy sea, the waves high-rolling, and amid them an old-style ship, all bent over, driving through the gale, and in great peril —a vivid and effectual piece of limning, not meant for the criticism of artists (though I think it had merit even from that standpoint,) but for its effect upon the congregation, and what it would convey to them.

399

Father Taylor was a moderate-sized man, indeed almost small, (reminded me of old Booth, the great actor, and my favorite of those and preceding days,) well advanced in years, but alert, with mild blue or gray eyes, and good presence and voice. Soon as he open'd his mouth I ceas'd to pay any attention to church or audience, or pictures or lights and shades; a far more potent charm entirely sway'd me. In the course of the sermon, (there was no sign of any MS., or reading from notes,) some of the parts would be in the highest degree majestic and picturesque. Colloquial in a severe sense, it often lean'd to Biblical and oriental forms. Especially were all allusions to ships and the ocean and sailors' lives, of unrival'd power and life-likeness. Sometimes there were passages of fine language and composition, even from the purist's point of view. A few arguments, and of the best, but always brief and simple. One realized what grip there might have been in such words-of-mouth talk as that of Socrates and Epictetus. In the main, I should say, of any of these discourses, that the old Demosthenean rule and requirement of "action, action, action," first in its inward and then (very moderate and restrain'd) its outward sense, was the quality that had leading fulfilment.

I remember I felt the deepest impression from the old man's prayers, which invariably affected me to tears. Never, on similar or any other occasions, have I heard such impassion'd pleading—such human-harassing reproach (like Hamlet to his mother, in the closet)—such probing to the very depths of that latent conscience and remorse which probably lie somewhere in the background of every life, every soul. For when Father Taylor preach'd or pray'd, the rhetoric and art, the mere words, (which usually play such a big part) seem'd altogether to disappear, and the *live feeling* advanced upon you and seiz'd you with a power before unknown. Everybody felt this marvelous and awful influence. One young sailor, a Rhode Islander, (who came every Sunday, and I got acquainted with, and talk'd to once or twice as we went away,) told me, "that must be the Holy Ghost we read of in the Testament."

I should be at a loss to make any comparison with other preachers or public speakers. When a child I had heard Elias Hicks—and Father Taylor (though so different in personal appearance, for Elias was of tall and most shapely form, with black eyes that blazed at times like meteors,) always reminded me of him. Both had the same inner, apparently inexhaustible, fund of latent volcanic passion—the same tenderness, blended with a curious remorseless firmness, as of some surgeon operating on a belov'd patient. Hearing such men sends to the winds all the books, and formulas, and polish'd speaking, and rules of oratory.

Talking of oratory, why is it that the unsophisticated practices often strike deeper than the train'd ones? Why do our experiences perhaps of some local country exhorter—or often in the West or South at political meetings—bring the most definite results? In my time I have heard Webster, Clay, Edward Everett, Phillips, and such *célébrès;* yet I recall the minor but life-eloquence of men like John P. Hale, Cassius Clay, and one or two of the old abolition "fanatics" ahead of all those stereotyped fames. Is not—I sometimes question—the first, last, and most important quality of all, in training for a "finish'd speaker," generally unsought, unreck'd of, both by teacher and pupil? Though maybe it cannot be taught, anyhow. At any rate, we need to clearly understand the distinction between oratory and elocution. Under the latter art, including some of high order, there is indeed no scarcity in the United States, preachers, lawyers, actors, lecturers, &c. With all, there seem to be few real orators—almost none.

I repeat, and would dwell upon it (more as suggestion than mere fact)—among all the brilliant lights of bar or stage I have heard in my time (for years in New York and other cities I haunted the courts to witness notable trials, and have heard all the famous actors and actresses that have been in America the past fifty years) though I recall marvellous effects from one or other of them, I never had anything in the way of vocal utterance to shake me through and through, and become fix'd, with its accompaniments, in my memory, like those prayers and sermons—like Father Taylor's personal electricity and the whole scene there—the prone ship in the gale, and dashing wave and foam for background—in the little old sea-church in Boston, those summer Sundays) just before the Secession War broke out.

※》《《

THE SPANISH ELEMENT *in* OUR NATIONALITY

[Our friends at Santa Fé, New Mexico, have just finish'd their long drawn out anniversary of the 333d year of the settlement of their city by the Spanish. The good, gray Walt Whitman was asked to write them a poem in commemoration. Instead he wrote them a letter as follows:—*Philadelphia Press,* August 5, 1883.]

CAMDEN, NEW JERSEY, *July* 20, 1883

To Messrs. Griffin, Martinez, Prince, and other Gentlemen at Santa Fé:

DEAR SIRS:—Your kind invitation to visit you and deliver a poem for the 333d Anniversary of founding Santa Fé has reach'd me so late that I have to decline, with sincere regret. But I will say a few words off hand.

We Americans have yet to really learn our own antecedents, and sort them, to unify them. They will be found ampler than has been supposed, and in widely different sources. Thus far, impress'd by New England writers and schoolmasters, we tacitly abandon ourselves to the notion that our United States have been fashion'd from the British Islands only, and essentially form a second England only —which is a very great mistake. Many leading traits for our future national personality, and some of the best ones, will certainly prove to have originated from other than British stock. As it is, the British and German, valuable as they are in the concrete, already threaten excess. Or rather, I should say, they have certainly reach'd that excess. To-day, something outside of them, and to counterbalance them, is seriously needed.

The seething materialistic and business vortices of the United States, in their present devouring relations, controlling and belittling everything else, are, in my opinion, but a vast and indispensable stage in the new world's development, and are certainly to be follow'd by something entirely different—at least by immense modifications. Character, literature, a society worthy the name, are yet to be establish'd, through a nationality of noblest spiritual, heroic and democratic attributes—not one of which at present definitely exists— entirely different from the past, though unerringly founded on it, and to justify it.

To that composite American identity of the future, Spanish character will supply some of the most needed parts. No stock shows a grander historic retrospect—grander in religiousness and loyalty, or for patriotism, courage, decorum, gravity and honor. (It is time to dismiss utterly the illusion-compound, half raw-head-and-bloody-bones and half Mysteries-of-Udolpho, inherited from the English writers of the past 200 years. It is time to realize—for it is certainly true—that there will not be found any more cruelty, tyranny, superstition, &c., in the *résumé* of past Spanish history than in the corresponding *résumé* of Anglo-Norman history. Nay, I think there will not be found so much.)

Then another point, relating to American ethnology, past and to come, I will here touch upon at a venture. As to our aboriginal or Indian population—the Aztec in the South, and many a tribe in the North and West—I know it seems to be agreed that they must gradually dwindle as time rolls on, and in a few generations more leave only a reminiscence, a blank. But I am not at all clear about that. As America, from its many far-back sources and current supplies, develops, adapts, entwines, faithfully identifies its own—are we to see it cheerfully accepting and using all the contributions of foreign lands from the whole outside globe—and then rejecting the only ones distinctively its own—the autochthonic ones?

As to the Spanish stock of our Southwest, it is certain to me that we do not begin to appreciate the splendor and sterling value of its race element. Who knows but that element, like the course of some subterranean river, dipping invisibly for a hundred or two years, is now to emerge in broadest flow and permanent action?

If I might assume to do so, I would like to send you the most cordial, heartfelt congratulations of your American fellow-countrymen here. You have more friends in the Northern and Atlantic regions than you suppose, and they are deeply interested in the development of the great Southwestern interior, and in what your festival would arouse to public attention.

Very respectfully, &c., WALT WHITMAN.

WHAT LURKS BEHIND SHAKSPERE'S HISTORICAL PLAYS?

WE ALL KNOW how much *mythus* there is in the Shakspere question as it stands to-day. Beneath a few foundations of proved facts are certainly engulf'd far more dim and elusive ones, of deepest importance—tantalizing and half suspected—suggesting explanations that one dare not put in plain statement. But coming at once to the point, the English historical plays are to me not only the most eminent as dramatic performances (my maturest judgment confirming the impressions of my early years, that the distinctiveness and glory of the Poet reside not in his vaunted dramas of the passions, but those founded on the contests of English dynasties, and the French wars,) but form, as we get it all, the chief in a complexity of puzzles. Conceiv'd out of the fullest heat and pulse of European feudalism—personifying in unparallel'd ways the mediæval aristocracy, its towering spirit of ruthless and gigantic caste, with its own peculiar air and arrogance (no mere imitation)—only one of the "wolfish earls" so plenteous in the plays themselves, or some born descendant and knower, might seem to be the true author of those amazing works—works in some respects greater than anything else in recorded literature.

The start and germ-stock of the pieces on which the present speculation is founded are undoubtedly (with, at the outset, no small amount of bungling work) in "Henry VI." It is plain to me that as profound and forecasting a brain and pen as ever appear'd in literature, after floundering somewhat in the first part of that trilogy—or perhaps draughting it more or less experimentally or by accident—afterward developed and defined his plan in the Second and Third Parts, and from time to time, thenceforward, systematically enlarged it to majestic and mature proportions in "Richard II," "Richard III," "King John," "Henry IV," "Henry V," and even in "Macbeth," "Coriolanus" and "Lear." For it is impossible to grasp the whole cluster of those plays, however wide the intervals and different circumstances of their composition, without thinking of them as, in a free sense, the result of an *essentially controling plan*. What was that plan? Or, rather, what was veil'd behind it?—for to me there was certainly something so veil'd. Even the episodes of Cade, Joan of Arc, and the like (which sometimes seem to me like interpolations allow'd,) may be meant to foil the possible sleuth, and throw any too 'cute pursuer off the scent. In the whole matter I should specially dwell on, and make much of, that inexplicable element of every highest poetic nature which causes it to cover up and involve its real purpose and meanings in folded removes and far recesses. Of this trait—hiding the nest where common seekers may never find it—the Shaksperean works afford the most numerous and mark'd illustrations known to me. I would even call that trait the leading one through the whole of those works.

All the foregoing to premise a brief statement of how and where I get my new light on Shakspere. Speaking of the special English plays, my friend William O'Connor says:

They seem simply and rudely historical in their motive, as aiming to give in the rough a tableau of warring dynasties,—and carry to me a lurking sense of being in aid of some ulterior design, probably well enough understood in that age, which perhaps time and criticism will reveal. . . . Their atmosphere is one of barbarous and tumultuous gloom,—they do not make us love the times they limn, . . . and it is impossible to believe that the greatest of the Elizabethan men could have sought to indoctrinate the age with the love of feudalism which his own drama in its entirety, if the view taken of it herein be true, certainly and subtly saps and mines.

Reading the just-specified play in the light of Mr. O'Connor's suggestion, I defy any one to escape such new and deep utterance-meanings, like magic ink, warm'd by the fire, and previously invisible. Will it not indeed be strange if the author of "Othello" and "Hamlet" is destin'd to live in America, in a generation or two, less as the cunning draughtsman of the passions, and more as putting on record the first full exposé—and by far the most vivid one, immeasurably ahead of doctrinaires and economists—of the political theory and results, or the reason-why and necessity for them which America has come on earth to abnegate and replace?

The summary of my suggestion would be, therefore, that while the more the rich and tangled jungle of the Shaksperean area is travers'd and studied, and the more baffled and mix'd, as so far appears, becomes the exploring student (who at last surmises everything, and remains certain of nothing,) it is possible a future age of criticism, diving deeper, mapping the land and lines freer, completer than hitherto, may discover in the plays named the scientific (Baconian?) inauguration of modern Democracy—furnishing realistic and first-class artistic portraitures of the mediæval world, the feudal personalities, institutes, in their morbid accumulations, deposits, upon politics and sociology,—may penetrate to that hard-pan, far down and back of the ostent of to-day, on which (and on which only) the progressism of the last two centuries has built this Democracy which now holds secure lodgment over the whole civilized world.

Whether such was the unconscious, or (as I think likely) the more or less conscious, purpose of him who fashion'd those marvellous architectonics, is a secondary question.

A THOUGHT on SHAKSPERE

THE MOST distinctive poems—the most permanently rooted and with heartiest reason for being—the copious cycle of Arthurian legends, or the almost equally copious Charlemagne cycle, or the poems of the Cid, or Scandinavian Eddas, or Nibelungen, or Chaucer, or Spenser, or *bona fide* Ossian, or Inferno—probably had their rise in the great historic perturbations, which they came in to sum up and confirm, indirectly embodying results to date. Then however precious to "culture," the grandest of those poems, it may be said, preserve and typify results offensive to the modern spirit, and long past away. To state it briefly, and taking the strongest examples, in Homer lives the ruthless military prowess of Greece, and of its special god-descended dynastic houses; in Shakspere the dragon-rancors and stormy feudal splendor of mediæval caste.

Poetry, largely consider'd, is an evolution, sending out improved and ever-expanded types—in one sense, the past, even the best of it, necessarily giving place, and dying out. For our existing world, the bases on which all the grand old poems were built have become vacuums—and even those of many comparatively modern ones are broken and half-gone. For us to-day, not their own intrinsic value, vast as that is, backs and maintains those poems—but a mountain-high growth of associations, the layers of successive ages. Everywhere—their own lands included—(is there not something terrible in the tenacity with which the one book out of millions holds its grip?)—the Homeric and Virgilian works, the interminable ballad-romances of the middle ages, the utterances of Dante, Spenser, and others, are upheld by their cumulus-entrenchment in scholarship, and as precious, always welcome, unspeakably valuable reminiscences.

Even the one who at present reigns unquestion'd—of Shakspere—for all he stands for so much in modern literature, he stands entirely for the mighty æsthetic sceptres of the past, not for the spiritual and democratic, the sceptres of the future. The inward and outward characteristics of Shakspere are his vast and rich variety of persons and themes, with his wondrous delineation of each and all—not only limitless funds of verbal and pictorial resource, but great excess, superfœtation—mannerism, like a fine, aristocratic perfume, holding a touch of musk (Euphues, his mark)—with boundless sumptuousness and adornment, real velvet and gems, not shoddy nor paste—but a good deal of bombast and fustian—(certainly some terrific mouthing in Shakspere!)

407

Superb and inimitable as all is, it is mostly an objective and physiological kind of power and beauty the soul finds in Shakspere—a style supremely grand of the sort, but in my opinion stopping short of the grandest sort, at any rate for fulfilling and satisfying modern and scientific and democratic American purposes. Think, not of growths as forests primeval, or Yellowstone geysers, or Colorado ravines, but of costly marble palaces, and palace rooms, and the noblest fixings and furniture, and noble owners and occupants to correspond—think of carefully built gardens from the beautiful but sophisticated gardening art at its best, with walks and bowers and artificial lakes, and appropriate statue-groups and the finest cultivated roses and lilies and japonicas in plenty—and you have the tally of Shakspere. The low characters, mechanics, even the loyal henchmen—all in themselves nothing—serve as capital foils to the aristocracy. The comedies (exquisite as they certainly are) bringing in admirably portray'd common characters, have the unmistakable hue of plays, portraits, made for the divertisement only of the élite of the castle, and from its point of view. The comedies are altogether non-acceptable to America and Democracy.

But to the deepest soul, it seems a shame to pick and choose from the riches Shakspere has left us—to criticise his infinitely royal, multiform quality—to gauge, with optic glasses, the dazzle of his sun-like beams.

The best poetic utterance, after all, can merely hint, or remind, often very indirectly, or at distant removes. Aught of real perfection, or the solution of any deep problem, or any completed statement of the moral, the true, the beautiful, eludes the greatest, deftest poet— flies away like an always uncaught bird.

ROBERT BURNS as POET and PERSON

WHAT THE future will decide about Robert Burns and his works—what place will be assign'd them on that great roster of geniuses and genius which can only be finish'd by the slow but sure balancing of the centuries with their ample average—I of course cannot tell. But as we know him, from his recorded utterances, and after nearly one century, and its diligence of collections, songs, letters, anecdotes, presenting the figure of the canny Scotchman in a fullness and detail wonderfully complete, and the lines mainly by his own hand, he forms to-day, in some respects, the most interesting personality among singers. Then there are many things in Burns's poems and character that specially endear him to America. He was essentially a Republican—would have been at home in the Western United States, and probably become eminent there. He was an average sample of the good-natured, warm-blooded, proud-spirited, amative, alimentive, convivial, young and early-middle-aged man of the decent-born middle classes everywhere and any how. Without the race of which he is a distinct specimen, (and perhaps his poems) America and her powerful Democracy could not exist to-day—could not project with unparallel'd historic sway into the future.

Perhaps the peculiar coloring of the era of Burns needs always first to be consider'd. It included the times of the '76-'83 Revolution in America, of the French Revolution, and an unparallel'd chaos development in Europe and elsewhere. In every department, shining and strange names, like stars, some rising, some in meridian, some declining—Voltaire, Franklin, Washington, Kant, Goethe, Fulton, Napoleon, mark the era. And while so much, and of grandest moment, fit for the trumpet of the world's fame, was being transacted—that little tragi-comedy of R. B.'s life and death was going on in a country by-place in Scotland!

Burns's correspondence, generally collected and publish'd since his death, gives wonderful glints into both the amiable and weak (and worse than weak) parts of his portraiture, habits, good and bad luck, ambition and associations. His letters to Mrs. Dunlop, Mrs. McLehose, (Clarinda,) Mr. Thompson, Dr. Moore, Robert Muir, Mr. Cunningham, Miss Margaret Chalmers, Peter Hill, Richard Brown, Mrs. Riddel, Robert Ainslie, and Robert Graham, afford valuable lights and shades to the outline, and with numerous others, help to a touch here, and fill-in there, of poet and poems. There are suspicions, it is true, of "the Genteel Letter-Writer," with scraps and words from "the Manual

409

of French Quotations," and, in the love-letters, some hollow mouth-
ings. Yet we wouldn't on any account lack the letters. A full and true
portrait is always what is wanted; veracity at every hazard. Besides,
do we not all see by this time that the story of Burns, even for its
own sake, requires the record of the whole and several, with nothing
left out? Completely and every point minutely told out its fullest, explains and justifies itself—(as perhaps almost any life does.) He is very
close to the earth. He pick'd up his best words and tunes directly
from the Scotch home-singers, but tells Thompson they would not
please his, T's, "learn'd lugs," adding, "I call them simple—you would
pronounce them silly." Yes, indeed; the idiom was undoubtedly his
happiest hit. Yet Dr. Moore, in 1789, writes to Burns, "If I were to
offer an opinion, it would be that in your future productions you
should abandon the Scotch stanza and dialect, and adopt the measure
and language of modern English poetry"!

As the 128th birth-anniversary of the poet draws on, (January,
1887,) with its increasing club-suppers, vehement celebrations, letters,
speeches, and so on—(mostly, as William O'Connor says, from people
who would not have noticed R. B. at all during his actual life, nor
kept his company, or read his verses, on any account)—it may be opportune to print some leisurely-jotted notes I find in my budget. I take
my observation of the Scottish bard by considering him as an individual amid the crowded clusters, galaxies, of the old world—and fairly
inquiring and suggesting what out of these myriads he too may be
to the Western Republic. In the first place no poet on record so fully
bequeaths his own personal magnetism,[1] nor illustrates more pointedly how one's verses, by time and reading, can so curiously fuse with
the versifier's own life and death, and give final light and shade to all.

I would say a large part of the fascination of Burns's homely, simple
dialect-melodies is due, for all current and future readers, to the
poet's personal "errors," the general bleakness of his lot, his ingrain'd
pensiveness, his brief dash into dazzling, tantalizing, evanescent
sunshine—finally culminating in those last years of his life, his being
taboo'd and in debt, sick and sore, yaw'd as by contending gales,
deeply dissatisfied with everything, most of all with himself—high-
spirited too—(no man ever really higher-spirited than Robert Burns.)
I think it a perfectly legitimate part too. At any rate it has come to
be an impalpable aroma through which only both the songs and their
singer must henceforth be read and absorb'd. Through that view-
medium of misfortune—of a noble spirit in low environments, and of a
squalid and premature death—we view the undoubted facts, (giving,
as we read them now, a sad kind of pungency,) that Burns's were,
before all else, the lyrics of illicit loves and carousing intoxication.

Perhaps even it is this strange, impalpable *post-mortem* comment and influence referr'd to, that gives them their contrast, attraction, making the zest of their author's after fame. If he had lived steady, fat, moral, comfortable, well-to-do years, on his own grade, (let alone, what of course was out of the question, the ease and velvet and rosewood and copious royalties of Tennyson or Victor Hugo or Longfellow,) and died well-ripen'd and respectable, where could have come in that burst of passionate sobbing and remorse which well'd forth instantly and generally in Scotland, and soon follow'd everywhere among English-speaking races, on the announcement of his death? and which, with no sign of stopping, only regulated and vein'd with fitting appreciation, flows deeply, widely yet?

Dear Rob! manly, witty, fond, friendly, full of weak spots as well as strong ones—essential type of so many thousands—perhaps the average, as just said, of the decent-born young men and the early mid-aged, not only of the British Isles, but America, too, North and South, just the same. I think, indeed, one best part of Burns is the unquestionable proof he presents of the perennial existence among the laboring classes, especially farmers, of the finest latent poetic elements in their blood. (How clear it is to me that the common soil has always been, and is now, thickly strewn with just such gems.) He is well-called the *Ploughman.* "Holding the plough," said his brother Gilbert, "was the favorite situation with Robert for poetic compositions; and some of his best verses were produced while he was at that exercise." "I must return to my humble station, and woo my rustic muse in my wonted way, at the plough-tail." 1787, to the Earl of Buchan. He has no high ideal of the poet or the poet's office; indeed quite a low and contracted notion of both:

> *Fortune! if thou'll but gie me still*
> *Hale breeks, a scone, and whiskey gill,*
> *An' rowth o' rhyme to rave at will,*
>   *Tak' a' the rest.*

See also his rhym'd letters to Robert Graham invoking patronage; "one stronghold," Lord Glencairn, being dead, now these appeals to "Fintra, my other stay," (with in one letter a copious shower of vituperation generally.) In his collected poems there is no particular unity, nothing that can be called a leading theory, no unmistakable spine or skeleton. Perhaps, indeed, their very desultoriness is the charm of his songs: "I take up one or another," he says in a letter to Thompson, "just as the bee of the moment buzzes in my bonnet-lug."

Consonantly with the customs of the time—yet markedly inconsistent in spirit with Burns's own case, (and not a little painful as it remains on record, as depicting some features of the bard himself,) the
relation called *patronage* existed between the nobility and gentry on
one side, and literary people on the other, and gives one of the strongest side-lights to the general coloring of poems and poets. It crops out
a good deal in Burns's Letters, and even necessitated a certain flunkeyism on occasions, through life. It probably, with its requirements,
(while it help'd in money and countenance) did as much as any one
cause in making that life a chafed and unhappy one, ended by a premature and miserable death.

Yes, there is something about Burns peculiarly acceptable to the
concrete, human points of view. He poetizes work-a-day agricultural
labor and life, (whose spirit and sympathies, as well as practicalities,
are much the same everywhere,) and treats fresh, often coarse, natural occurrences, loves, persons, not like many new and some old poets
in a genteel style of gilt and china, or at second or third removes, but
in their own born atmosphere, laughter, sweat, unction. Perhaps no
one ever sang "lads and lasses"—that universal race, mainly the same,
too, all ages, all lands—down on their own plane, as he has. He exhibits no philosophy worth mentioning; his morality is hardly more
than parrot-talk—not bad or deficient, but cheap, shopworn, the platitudes of old aunts and uncles to the youngsters (be good boys and
keep your noses clean.) Only when he gets at Poosie Nansie's, celebrating the "barley bree," or among tramps, or democratic bouts and
drinking generally,

(Freedom and whiskey gang thegither,)

we have, in his own unmistakable color and warmth, those interiors
of rake-helly life and tavern fun—the cantabile of jolly beggars in
highest jinks—lights and groupings of rank glee and brawny amorousness, outvying the best painted pictures of the Dutch school, or any
school.

By America and her democracy such a poet, I cannot too often repeat, must be kept in loving remembrance; but it is best that discrim-
inations be made. His admirers (as at those anniversary suppers, over
the "hot Scotch") will not accept for their favorite anything less than
the highest rank, alongside of Homer, Shakspere, etc. Such, in candor,
are not the true friends of the Ayrshire bard, who really needs a different place quite by himself. The Iliad and the Odyssey express
courage, craft, full-grown heroism in situations of danger, the sense
of command and leadership, emulation, the last and fullest evolution

of self-poise as in kings, and god-like even while animal appetites. The Shaksperean compositions, on vertebers and framework of the primary passions, portray (essentially the same as Homer's,) the spirit and letter of the feudal world, the Norman lord, ambitious and arrogant, taller and nobler than common men—with much underplay and gusts of heat and cold, volcanoes and stormy seas. Burns (and some will say to his credit) attempts none of these themes. He poetizes the humor, riotous blood, sulks, amorous torments, fondness for the tavern and for cheap objective nature, with disgust at the grim and narrow ecclesiasticism of his time and land, of a young farmer on a bleak and hired farm in Scotland, through the years and under the circumstances of the British politics of that time, and of his short personal career as author, from 1783 to 1796. He is intuitive and affectionate, and just emerged or emerging from the shackles of the kirk, from poverty, ignorance, and from his own rank appetites—(out of which latter, however, he never extricated himself.) It is to be said that amid not a little smoke and gas in his poems, there is in almost every piece a spark of fire, and now and then the real afflatus. He has been applauded as democratic, and with some warrant; while Shakspere, and with the greatest warrant, has been called monarchical or aristocratic (which he certainly is.) But the splendid personalizations of Shakspere, formulated on the largest, freest, most heroic, most artistic mould, are to me far dearer as lessons, and more precious even as models for Democracy, than the humdrum samples Burns presents. The motives of some of his effusions are certainly discreditable personally—one or two of them markedly so. He has, moreover, little or no spirituality. This last is his mortal flaw and defect, tried by highest standards. The ideal he never reach'd (and yet I think he leads the way to it.) He gives melodies, and now and then the simplest and sweetest ones; but harmonies, complications, oratorios in words, never. (I do not speak this in any deprecatory sense. Blessed be the memory of the warm-hearted Scotchman for what he has left us, just as it is!) He likewise did not know himself, in more ways than one. Though so really free and independent, he prided himself in his songs on being a reactionist and a Jacobite—on persistent sentimental adherency to the cause of the Stuarts—the weakest, thinnest, most faithless, brainless dynasty that ever held a throne.

Thus, while Burns is not at all great for New World study, in the sense that Isaiah and Eschylus and the book of Job are unquestionably great—is not to be mention'd with Shakspere—hardly even with current Tennyson or our Emerson—he has a nestling niche of his own, all fragrant, fond, and quaint and homely—a lodge built near but outside the mighty temple of the gods of song and art—those universal strivers, through their works of harmony and melody and power, to ever show or intimate man's crowning, last, victorious fusion in himself of Real and Ideal. Precious, too—fit and precious beyond all singers, high or low—will Burns ever be to the native Scotch, especially to the working-classes of North Britain; so intensely one of them, and so racy of the soil, sights, and local customs. He often apostrophizes Scotland, and is, or would be, enthusiastically patriotic. His country has lately commemorated him in a statue.[2] His aim is declaredly to be 'a Rustic Bard.' His poems were all written in youth or young manhood, (he was little more than a young man when he died.) His collected works in giving everything, are nearly one half first drafts. His brightest hit is his use of the Scotch patois, so full of terms flavor'd like wild fruits or berries. Then I should make an allowance to Burns which cannot be made for any other poet. Curiously even the frequent crudeness, haste, deficiencies, (flatness and puerilities by no means absent) prove upon the whole not out of keeping in any comprehensive collection of his works, heroically printed, 'following copy,' every piece, every line according to originals. Other poets might tremble for such boldness, such rawness. In 'this odd-kind chiel' such points hardly mar the rest. Not only are they in consonance with the underlying spirit of the pieces, but complete the full abandon and veracity of the farm-fields and the home-brew'd flavor of the Scotch vernacular. (Is there not often something in the very neglect, unfinish, careless nudity, slovenly hiatus, coming from intrinsic genius, and not 'put on,' that secretly pleases the soul more than the wrought and re-wrought polish of the most perfect verse?) Mark the native spice and untranslatable twang in the very names of his songs—"O for ane and twenty, Tam," "John Barleycorn," "Last May a braw Wooer," "Rattlin roarin Willie," "O wert thou in the cauld, cauld blast," "Gude e'en to you, Kimmer," "Merry hae I been teething a Heckle," "O lay thy loof in mine, lass," and others.

The longer and more elaborated poems of Burns are just such as would please a natural but homely taste, and cute but average intellect, and are inimitable in their way. The "Twa Dogs," (one of the best) with the conversation between Cesar and Luath, the "Brigs of Ayr," "the Cotter's Saturday Night," "Tam O'Shanter"—all will be long read and re-read and admired, and ever deserve to be. With nothing profound in any of them, what there is of moral and plot has an inimitably fresh and racy flavor. If it came to question, Literature could well afford to send adrift many a pretensive poem, and even book of poems, before it could spare these compositions.

Never indeed was there truer utterance in a certain range of idiosyncracy than by this poet. Hardly a piece of his, large or small, but has "snap" and raciness. He puts in cantering rhyme (often doggerel) much cutting irony and idiomatic ear-cuffing of the kirk-deacons—drily good-natured addresses to his cronies, (he certainly would not stop us if he were here this moment, from classing that "to the De'il" among them)—"to Mailie and her Lambs," "to auld Mare Maggie," "to a Mouse,"

> *Wee, sleekit, cowrin, tim'rous beastie:*

"to a Mountain Daisy," "to a Haggis," "to a Louse," "to the Tooth-ache," etc.—and occasionally to his brother bards and lady or gentle-man patrons, often with strokes of tenderest sensibility, idiopathic humor, and genuine poetic imagination—still oftener with shrewd, original, sheeny, steel-flashes of wit, home-spun sense, or lance-blade puncturing. Then, strangely, the basis of Burns's character, with all its fun and manliness, was hypochondria, the blues, palpable enough in "Despondency," "Man was made to Mourn," "Address to Ruin," a "Bard's Epitaph," &c. From such deep-down elements sprout up, in very contrast and paradox, those riant utterances of which a super-ficial reading will not detect the hidden foundation. Yet nothing is clearer to me than the black and desperate background behind those pieces—as I shall now specify them. I find his most characteristic, Nature's masterly touch and luxuriant life-blood, color and heat, not in "Tam O'Shanter," "the Cotter's Saturday Night," "Scots who hae," "Highland Mary," "the Twa Dogs," and the like, but in "the Jolly Beg-gars," "Rigs of Barley," "Scotch Drink," "the Epistle to John Rankine," "Holy Willie's Prayer," and in "Halloween," (to say nothing of a cer-tain cluster, known still to a small inner circle in Scotland, but, for good reasons, not published anywhere.) In these compositions, espe-cially the first, there is much indelicacy (some editions flatly leave it out,) but the composer reigns alone, with handling free and broad and true, and is an artist. You may see and feel the man indirectly in his other verses, all of them, with more or less life-likeness—but these I have named last call out pronouncedly in his own voice,

> *I, Rob, am here.*

Finally, in any summing-up of Burns, though so much is to be said in the way of fault-finding, drawing black marks, and doubtless severe literary criticism—(in the present outpouring I have 'kept myself in,' rather than allow'd any free flow)—after full retrospect of his works and life, the aforesaid 'odd-kind chiel' remains to my heart and brain as almost the tenderest, manliest, and (even if contradictory) dearest flesh-and-blood figure in all the streams and clusters of by-gone poets.

NOTES

1. Probably no man that ever lived—a friend has made the statement—was so fondly loved, both by men and women, as Robert Burns. The reason is not hard to find: he had a real heart of flesh and blood beating in his bosom; you could almost hear it throb. "Some one said, that if you had shaken hands with him his hand would have burnt yours. The gods, indeed, made him poetical, but Nature had a hand in him first. His heart was in the right place; he did not pile up cantos of poetic diction; he pluck'd the mountain daisy under his feet; he wrote of field-mouse hurrying from its ruin'd dwelling. He held the plough or the pen with the same firm, manly grasp. And he was loved. The simple roll of the women who gave him their affection and their sympathy would make a long manuscript; and most of these were of such noble worth that, as Robert Chambers says, 'their character may stand as a testimony in favor of that of Burns.' " [As I understand, the foregoing is from an extremely rare book publish'd by M'Kie, in Kilmarnock. I find the whole beautiful paragraph in a capital paper on Burns, by Amelia Barr.]

2. The Dumfries statue of Robert Burns was successfully unveil'd April 1881 by Lord Roseberry, the occasion having been made national in its character. Before the ceremony, a large procession paraded the streets of the town, all the trades and societies of that part of Scotland being represented, at the head of which went dairymen and ploughmen, the former driving their carts and being accompanied by their maids. The statue is of Sicilian marble. It rests on a pedestal of gray stone five feet high. The poet is represented as sitting easily on an old tree root, holding in his left hand a cluster of daisies. His face is turn'd toward the right shoulder, and the eyes gaze into the distance. Near by lie a collie dog, a broad bonnet half covering a well-thumb'd song-book, and a rustic flageolet. The costume is taken from the Nasmyth portrait, which has been follow'd for the features of the face.

A WORD about TENNYSON

BEAUTIFUL as the song was, the original 'Locksley Hall' of half a century ago was essentially morbid, heart-broken, finding fault with everything, especially the fact of money's being made (as it ever must be, and perhaps should be) the paramount matter in worldly affairs;

Every door is barr'd with gold, and opens but to golden keys.

First, a father, having fallen in battle, his child (the singer)

Was left a trampled orphan, and a selfish uncle's ward.

Of course love ensues. The woman in the chant or monologue proves a false one; and as far as appears the ideal of woman, in the poet's reflections, is a false one—at any rate for America. Woman is *not* 'the lesser man.' (The heart is not the brain.) The best of the piece of fifty years since is its concluding line:

For the mighty wind arises roaring seaward and I go.

Then for this current 1886–7, a just-out sequel, which (as an apparently authentic summary says) 'reviews the life of mankind during the past sixty years, and comes to the conclusion that its boasted progress is of doubtful credit to the world in general and to England in particular. A cynical vein of denunciation of democratic opinions and aspirations runs throughout the poem in mark'd contrast with the spirit of the poet's youth.' Among the most striking lines of this sequel are the following:

Envy wears the mask of love, and, laughing sober fact to scorn,
Cries to weakest as to strongest, 'Ye are equals, equal born,'
Equal-born! Oh yes, if yonder hill be level with the flat.
Charm us, orator, till the lion look no larger than the cat:
Till the cat, through that mirage of overheated language, loom
Larger than the lion Demo—end in working its own doom.
Tumble Nature heel o'er head, and, yelling with the yelling street,
Set the feet above the brain, and swear the brain is in the feet.
Bring the old dark ages back, without the faith, without the hope
Beneath the State, the Church, the Throne, and roll their ruins down
  the slope.

I should say that all this is a legitimate consequence of the tone and convictions of the earlier standards and points of view. Then some reflections, down to the hard-pan of this sort of thing.

The course of progressive politics (democracy) is so certain and resistless, not only in America but in Europe, that we can well afford the warning calls, threats, checks, neutralizings, in imaginative literature, or any department, of such deep-sounding and high-soaring voices as Carlyle's and Tennyson's. Nay, the blindness, excesses, of the prevalent tendency—the dangers of the urgent trends of our times —in my opinion, need such voices almost more than any. I should, too, call it a signal instance of democratic humanity's luck that it has such enemies to contend with—so candid, so fervid, so heroic. But why do I say enemies? Upon the whole is not Tennyson—and was not Carlyle (like an honest and stern physician)—the true friend of our age?

Let me assume to pass verdict, or perhaps momentary judgment, for the United States on this poet—a remov'd and distant position giving some advantages over a nigh one. What is Tennyson's service to his race, times, and especially to America? First, I should say—or at least not forget—his personal character. He is not to be mention'd as a rugged, evolutionary, aboriginal force—but (and a great lesson is in it) he has been consistent throughout with the native, healthy, patriotic spinal element and promptings of himself. His moral line is local and conventional, but it is vital and genuine. He reflects the upper-crust of his time, its pale cast of thought—even its *ennui*. Then the simile of my friend John Burroughs is entirely true, 'his glove is a glove of silk, but the hand is a hand of iron.' He shows how one can be a royal laureate, quite elegant and 'aristocratic,' and a little queer and affected, and at the same time perfectly manly and natural. As to his non-democracy, it fits him well, and I like him the better for it. I guess we all like to have (I am sure I do) some one who presents those sides of a thought, or possibility, different from our own—different and yet with a sort of home-likeness—a tartness and contradiction offsetting the theory as we view it, and construed from tastes and proclivities not at all his own.

To me, Tennyson shows more than any poet I know (perhaps has been a warning to me) how much there is in finest verbalism. There is such a latent charm in mere words, cunning collocutions, and in the voice ringing them, which he has caught and brought out, beyond all others—as in the line,

And hollow, hollow, hollow, all delight,

in 'The Passing of Arthur,' and evidenced in 'The Lady of Shalott,' 'The Deserted House,' and many other pieces. Among the best (I often linger over them again and again) are 'Lucretius,' 'The Lotos Eaters,' and 'The Northern Farmer.' His mannerism is great, but it is a noble and welcome mannerism. His very best work, to me, is contain'd in the books of 'The Idyls of the King,' and all that has grown out of them. Though indeed we could spare nothing of Tennyson, however small or however peculiar—not 'Break, Break,' nor 'Flower in the Crannied Wall,' nor the old, eternally-told passion of 'Edward Gray:'

> *Love may come and love may go,*
> *And fly like a bird from tree to tree.*
> *But I will love no more, no more*
> *Till Ellen Adair come back to me.*

Yes, Alfred Tennyson's is a superb character, and will help give illustriousness, through the long roll of time, to our Nineteenth Century. In its bunch of orbic names, shining like a constellation of stars, his will be one of the brightest. His very faults, doubts, swervings, doublings upon himself, have been typical of our age. We are like the voyagers of a ship, casting off for new seas, distant shores. We would still dwell in the old suffocating and dead haunts, remembering and magnifying their pleasant experiences only, and more than once impell'd to jump ashore before it is too late, and stay where our fathers stay'd, and live as they lived.

May-be I am non-literary and non-decorous (let me at least be human, and pay part of my debt) in this word about Tennyson. I want him to realize that here is a great and ardent Nation that absorbs his songs, and has a respect and affection for him personally, as almost for no other foreigner. I want this word to go to the old man at Farringford as conveying no more than the simple truth; and that truth (a little Christmas gift) no slight one either. I have written impromptu, and shall let it all go at that. The readers of more than fifty millions of people in the New World not only owe to him some of their most agreeable and harmless and healthy hours, but he has enter'd into the formative influences of character here, not only in the Atlantic cities, but inland and far West, out in Missouri, in Kansas, and away in Oregon, in farmer's house and miner's cabin.

Best thanks, anyhow, to Alfred Tennyson—thanks and appreciation in America's name.

≫≫ ≪≪

SLANG in AMERICA

VIEW'D FREELY, the English language is the accretion and growth of every dialect, race, and range of time, and is both the free and compacted composition of all. From this point of view, it stands for Language in the largest sense, and is really the greatest of studies. It involves so much; is indeed a sort of universal absorber, combiner, and conqueror. The scope of its etymologies is the scope not only of man and civilization, but the history of Nature in all departments, and of the organic Universe, brought up to date; for all are comprehended in words, and their backgrounds. This is when words become vitaliz'd, and stand for things, as they unerringly and soon come to do, in the mind that enters on their study with fitting spirit, grasp, and appreciation.

Slang, profoundly consider'd, is the lawless germinal element, below all words and sentences, and behind all poetry, and proves a certain perennial rankness and protestantism in speech. As the United States inherit by far their most precious possession—the language they talk and write—from the Old World, under and out of its feudal institutes, I will allow myself to borrow a simile even of those forms farthest removed from American Democracy. Considering Language then as some mighty potentate, into the majestic audience-hall of the monarch ever enters a personage like one of Shakspere's clowns, and takes position there, and plays a part even in the stateliest ceremonies. Such is Slang, or indirection, an attempt of common humanity to escape from bald literalism, and express itself illimitably, which in highest walks produces poets and poems, and doubtless in pre-historic times gave the start to, and perfected, the whole immense tangle of the old mythologies. For, curious as it may appear, it is strictly the same impulse-source, the same thing. Slang, too, is the wholesome fermentation or eructation of those processes eternally active in language, by which froth and specks are thrown up, mostly to pass away; though occasionally to settle and permanently chrystallize.

To make it plainer, it is certain that many of the oldest and solidest words we use, were originally generated from the daring and license of slang. In the processes of word-formation, myriads die, but here and there the attempt attracts superior meanings, becomes valuable and indispensable, and lives forever. Thus the term *right* means literally only straight. *Wrong* primarily meant twisted, distorted. *Integrity* meant oneness. *Spirit* meant breath, or flame. A *supercilious* person was one who rais'd his eyebrows. To *insult* was to leap against. If you *influenc'd* a man, you but flow'd into him. The Hebrew word which is translated *prophesy* meant to bubble up and pour forth as a fountain. The enthusiast bubbles up with the Spirit of God within him, and it pours forth from him like a fountain. The word prophecy is misunderstood. Many suppose that it is limited to mere prediction; that is but the lesser portion of prophecy. The greater work is to reveal God. Every true religious enthusiast is a prophet.

Language, be it remember'd, is not an abstract construction of the learn'd, or of dictionary-makers, but is something arising out of the work, needs, ties, joys, affections, tastes, of long generations of humanity, and has its bases broad and low, close to the ground. Its final decisions are made by the masses, people nearest the concrete, having most to do with actual land and sea. It impermeates all, the Past as well as the Present, and is the grandest triumph of the human intellect. "Those mighty works of art," says Addington Symonds, "which we call languages, in the construction of which whole peoples unconsciously co-operated, the forms of which were determin'd not by individual genius, but by the instincts of successive generations, acting to one end, inherent in the nature of the race—Those poems of pure thought and fancy, cadenced not in words, but in living imagery, fountain-heads of inspiration, mirrors of the mind of nascent nations, which we call Mythologies—these surely are more marvellous in their infantine spontaneity than any more mature production of the races which evolv'd them. Yet we are utterly ignorant of their embryology; the true science of Origins is yet in its cradle."

Daring as it is to say so, in the growth of Language it is certain that the retrospect of slang from the start would be the recalling from their nebulous conditions of all that is poetical in the stores of human utterance. Moreover, the honest delving, as of late years, by the German and British workers in comparative philology, has pierc'd and dispers'd many of the falsest bubbles of centuries; and will disperse many more. It was long recorded that in Scandinavian mythology the heroes in the Norse Paradise drank out of the skulls of their slain enemies. Later investigation proves the word taken for skulls to mean *horns* of beasts slain in the hunt. And what reader had not been exercis'd over the traces of that feudal custom, by which *seigneurs* warm'd their feet in the bowels of serfs, the abdomen being open'd for the purpose? It now is made to appear that the serf was only required to submit his unharm'd abdomen as a foot cushion while his lord supp'd, and was required to chafe the legs of the seigneur with his hands.

It is curiously in embryons and childhood, and among the illiterate, we always find the groundwork and start, of this great science, and its noblest products. What a relief most people have in speaking of a man not by his true and formal name, with a "Mister" to it, but by some odd or homely appellative. The propensity to approach a meaning not directly and squarely, but by circuitous styles of expression, seems indeed a born quality of the common people every where, evidenced by nick-names, and the inveterate determination of the masses to bestow sub-titles, sometimes ridiculous, sometimes very apt. Always among the soldiers during the Secession War, one heard of "Little Mac" (Gen. McClellan), or of "Uncle Billy" (Gen. Sherman.) "The old man" was, of course, very common. Among the rank and file, both armies, it was very general to speak of the different States they came from by their slang names. Those from Maine were call'd Foxes; New Hampshire, Granite Boys; Massachusetts, Bay Staters; Vermont, Green Mountain Boys; Rhode Island, Gun Flints; Connecticut, Wooden Nutmegs; New York, Knickerbockers; New Jersey, Clam Catchers; Pennsylvania, Logher Heads; Delaware, Muskrats; Maryland, Claw Thumpers; Virginia, Beagles; North Carolina, Tar Boilers; South Carolina, Weasels; Georgia, Buzzards; Louisiana, Creoles; Alabama, Lizzards; Kentucky, Corn Crackers; Ohio, Buckeyes; Michigan, Wolverines; Indiana, Hoosiers; Illinois, Suckers; Missouri, Pukes; Mississippi, Tad Poles; Florida, Fly up the Creeks; Wisconsin, Badgers; Iowa, Hawkeyes; Oregon, Hard Cases. Indeed I am not sure but slang names have more than once made Presidents. "Old Hickory," (Gen. Jackson) is one case in point. "Tippecanoe, and Tyler too," another.

I find the same rule in the people's conversations everywhere. I heard this among the men of the city horse-cars, where the conductor is often call'd a "snatcher" (i. e. because his characteristic duty is to constantly pull or snatch the bell-strap, to stop or go on.) Two young fellows are having a friendly talk, amid which, says 1st conductor, "What did you do before you was a snatcher?" Answer of 2d conductor, "Nail'd." (Translation of answer: "I work'd as carpenter.") What is a "boom"? says one editor to another. "Esteem'd contemporary," says the other, "a boom is a bulge." "Barefoot whiskey" is the Tennessee name for the undiluted stimulant. In the slang of the New York common restaurant waiters a plate of ham and beans is known as "stars and stripes," codfish balls as "sleeve-buttons," and hash as "mystery."

The Western States of the Union are, however, as may be supposed, the special areas of slang, not only in conversation, but in names of localities, towns, rivers, etc. A late Oregon traveller says:

On your way to Olympia by rail, you cross a river called the Shookum-Chuck; your train stops at places named Newaukum, Tumwater, and Toutle; and if you seek further you will hear of whole counties labell'd Wahkiakum, or Snohomish, or Kitsar, or Klikatat; and Cowlitz, Hookium, and Nenolelops greet and offend you. They complain in Olympia that Washington Territory gets but little immigration; but what wonder? What man, having the whole American continent to choose from, would willingly date his letters from the county of Snohomish or bring up his children in the city of Nenolelops? The village of Tumwater is, as I am ready to bear witness, very pretty indeed; but surely an emigrant would think twice before he establish'd himself either there or at Toutle. Seattle is sufficiently barbarous; Stelicoom is no better; and I suspect that the Northern Pacific Railroad terminus has been fixed at Tacoma because it is one of the few places on Puget Sound whose name does not inspire horror.

Then a Nevada paper chronicles the departure of a mining party from Reno: "The toughest set of roosters that ever shook the dust off any town left Reno yesterday for the new mining district of Cornucopia. They came here from Virginia. Among the crowd were four New York cock-fighters, two Chicago murderers, three Baltimore bruisers, one Philadelphia prize-fighter, four San Francisco hoodlums, three Virginia beats, two Union Pacific roughs, and two check guerrillas." Among the far-west newspapers, have been, or are, *The Fairplay* (Colorado) *Flume, The Solid Muldoon,* of Ouray, *The Tombstone Epitaph,* of Nevada, *The Jimplecute,* of Texas, and *The Bazoo,* of Missouri. Shirttail Bend, Whiskey Flat, Puppytown, Wild Yankee Ranch, Squaw Flat, Rawhide Ranch, Loafer's Ravine, Squitch Gulch, Toenail Lake, are a few of the names of places in Butte county, Cal.

Perhaps indeed no place or term gives more luxuriant illustrations of the fermentation processes I have mention'd, and their froth and specks, than those Mississippi and Pacific coast regions, at the present day. Hasty and grotesque as are some of the names, others are of an appropriateness and originality unsurpassable. This applies to the Indian words, which are often perfect. Oklahoma is proposed in Congress for the name of one of our new Territories. Hog-eye, Lick-skillet, Rake-pocket and Steal-easy are the names of some Texan towns. Miss Bremer found among the aborigines the following names: *Men's,* Horn-point; Round-Wind; Stand-and-look-out; The Cloud-that-goes-aside; Iron-toe; Seek-the-sun; Iron-flash; Red-bottle; White-spindle; Black-dog; Two-feathers-of-honor; Gray-grass; Bushy-tail; Thunder-face; Go-on-the-burning-sod; Spirits-of-the-dead. *Women's,* Keep-the-fire; Spiritual-woman; Second-daughter-of-the-house; Blue Bird.

Certainly philologists have not given enough attention to this element and its results, which, I repeat, can probably be found working every where to-day, amid modern conditions, with as much life and activity as in far-back Greece or India, under prehistoric ones. Then the wit—the rich flashes of humor and genius and poetry —darting out often from a gang of laborers, railroad-men, miners, drivers or boatmen! How often have I hover'd at the edge of a crowd of them, to hear their repartees and impromptus! You get more real fun from half an hour with them than from the books of all "the American humorists."

The science of language has large and close analogies in geological science, with its ceaseless evolution, its fossils, and its numberless submerged layers and hidden strata, the infinite go-before of the present. Or, perhaps Language is more like some vast living body, or perennial body of bodies. And slang not only brings the first feeders of it, but is afterward the start of fancy, imagination and humor, breathing into its nostrils the breath of life.

->>> <<<-

AN INDIAN BUREAU REMINISCENCE

AFTER THE close of the Secession War in 1865, I work'd several
months (until Mr. Harlan turn'd me out for having written "Leaves
of Grass") in the Interior Department at Washington, in the Indian
Bureau. Along this time there came to see their Great Father an
unusual number of aboriginal visitors, delegations for treaties, settlement of lands, &c.—some young or middle-aged, but mainly old
men, from the West, North, and occasionally from the South—parties
of from five to twenty each—the most wonderful proofs of what Nature can produce, (the survival of the fittest, no doubt—all the
frailer samples dropt, sorted out by death)—as if to show the earth
and woods, the attrition of storms and elements, and the exigencies
of life at first hand, can train and fashion men, indeed *chiefs*, in
heroic massiveness, imperturbability, muscle, and that last and highest
beauty consisting of strength—the full exploitation and fruitage of
a human identity, not from the culmination-points of "culture" and
artificial civilization, but tallying our race, as it were, with giant,
vital, gnarl'd, enduring trees, or monoliths of separate hardiest
rocks, and humanity holding its own with the best of the said trees
or rocks, and outdoing them.

There were Omahas, Poncas, Winnebagoes, Cheyennes, Navahos,
Apaches, and many others. Let me give a running account of what
I see and hear through one of these conference collections at the
Indian Bureau, going back to the present tense. Every head and
face is impressive, even artistic; Nature redeems herself out of her
crudest recesses. Most have red paint on their cheeks, however, or
some other paint. ("Little Hill" makes the opening speech, which
the interpreter translates by scraps.) Many wear head tires of
gaudy-color'd braid, wound around thickly—some with circlets of
eagles' feathers. Necklaces of bears' claws are plenty around their
necks. Most of the chiefs are wrapt in large blankets of the brightest scarlet. Two or three have blue, and I see one black. (A wise
man call'd "the Flesh" now makes a short speech, apparently asking
something. Indian Commissioner Dole answers him, and the interpreter translates in scraps again.) All the principal chiefs have
tomahawks or hatchets, some of them very richly ornamented and
costly. Plaid shirts are to be observ'd—none too clean. Now a tall
fellow, "Hole-in-the-Day," is speaking. He has a copious head-dress
composed of feathers and narrow ribbon, under which appears a

countenance painted all over a bilious yellow. Let us note this young chief. For all his paint, "Hole-in-the-Day" is a handsome Indian, mild and calm, dress'd in drab buckskin leggings, dark gray surtout, and a soft black hat. His costume will bear full observation, and even fashion would accept him. His apparel is worn loose and scant enough to show his superb physique, especially in neck, chest, and legs. ("The Apollo Belvidere!" was the involuntary exclamation of a famous European artist when he first saw a full-grown young Choctaw.)

One of the red visitors—a wild, lean-looking Indian, the one in the black woolen wrapper—has an empty buffalo head, with the horns on, for his personal surmounting. I see a markedly Bourbonish countenance among the chiefs—(it is not very uncommon among them, I am told.) Most of them avoided resting on chairs during the hour of their "talk" in the Commissioner's office; they would sit around on the floor, leaning against something, or stand up by the walls, partially wrapt in their blankets. Though some of the young fellows were, as I have said, magnificent and beautiful animals, I think the palm of unique picturesqueness, in body, limb, physiognomy, etc., was borne by the old or elderly chiefs, and the wise men.

My here-alluded-to experience in the Indian Bureau produced one very definite conviction, as follows: There is something about these aboriginal Americans, in their highest characteristic representations, essential traits, and the ensemble of their physique and physiognomy—something very remote, very lofty, arousing comparisons with our own civilized ideals—something that our literature, portrait painting, etc., have never caught, and that will almost certainly never be transmitted to the future, even as a reminiscence. No biographer, no historian, no artist, has grasp'd it—perhaps could not grasp it. It is so different, so far outside our standards of eminent humanity. Their feathers, paint—even the empty buffalo skull—did not, to say the least, seem any more ludicrous to me than many of the fashions I have seen in civilized society. I should not apply the word savage (at any rate, in the usual sense) as a leading word in the description of those great aboriginal specimens, of whom I certainly saw many of the best. There were moments, as I look'd at them or studied them, when our own exemplification of personality, dignity, heroic presentation anyhow (as in the conventions of society, or even in the accepted poems and plays,) seem'd sickly, puny, inferior.

The interpreters, agents of the Indian Department, or other whites accompanying the bands, in positions of responsibility, were always interesting to me; I had many talks with them. Occasionally I would go to the hotels where the bands were quarter'd, and spend an hour or two informally. Of course we could not have much conversation—though (through the interpreters) more of this than might be supposed—sometimes quite animated and significant. I had the good luck to be invariably receiv'd and treated by all of them in their most cordial manner.

[*Letter to W. W. from an artist, B. H., who has been much among the American Indians:*]

"I have just receiv'd your little paper on the Indian delegations. In the fourth paragraph you say that there is something about the essential traits of our aborigines which 'will almost certainly never be transmitted to the future.' If I am so fortunate as to regain my health I hope to weaken the force of that statement, at least in so far as my talent and training will permit. I intend to spend some years among them, and shall endeavor to perpetuate on canvas some of the finer types, both men and women, and some of the characteristic features of their life. It will certainly be well worth the while. My artistic enthusiasm was never so thoroughly stirr'd up as by the Indians. They certainly have more of beauty, dignity and nobility mingled with their own wild individuality, than any of the other indigenous types of man. Neither black nor Afghan, Arab nor Malay (and I know them all pretty well) can hold a candle to the Indian. All of the other aboriginal types seem to be more or less distorted from the model of perfect human form—as we know it—the blacks, thin-hipped, with bulbous limbs, not well mark'd; the Arabs large-jointed, &c. But I have seen many a young Indian as perfect in form and feature as a Greek statue—very different from a Greek statue, of course, but as satisfying to the artistic perceptions and demand.

"And the worst, or perhaps the best of it all is that it will require an artist—and a good one—to record the real facts and impressions. Ten thousand photographs would not have the value of one really finely felt painting. Color is all-important. No one but an artist knows how much. An Indian is only half an Indian without the blue-black hair and the brilliant eyes shining out of the wonderful dusky ochre and rose complexion."

➽ ⧏

SOME DIARY NOTES at RANDOM

NEGRO SLAVES IN NEW YORK.—I can myself almost remember negro slaves in New York State, as my grandfather and great-grandfather (at West Hills, Suffolk County, New York) own'd a number. The hard labor of the farm was mostly done by them, and on the floor of the big kitchen, toward sundown, would be squatting a circle of twelve or fourteen "pickaninnies," eating their supper of pudding (Indian corn mush) and milk. A friend of my grandfather, named Wortman, of Oyster Bay, died in 1810, leaving ten slaves. Jeanette Treadwell, the last of them, died suddenly in Flushing last Summer (1884,) at the age of ninety-four years. I remember "old Mose," one of the liberated West Hills slaves, well. He was very genial, correct, manly, and cute, and a great friend of my childhood.

CANADA NIGHTS.—*Late in August.*—Three wondrous nights. Effects of moon, clouds, stars, and night-sheen, never surpass'd. I am out every night, enjoying all. The sunset begins it. (I have said already how long evening lingers here.) The moon, an hour high just after eight, is past her half, and looks somehow more like a human face up there than ever before. As it grows later, we have such gorgeous and broad cloud-effects, with Luna's tawny halos, silver edgings—great fleeces, depths of blue-black in patches, and occasionally long, low bars hanging silently a while, and then gray bulging masses rolling along stately, sometimes in long procession. The moon travels in Scorpion to-night, and dims all the stars of that constellation except fiery Antares, who keeps on shining just to the big one's side.

COUNTRY DAYS AND NIGHTS.—*Sept.* 30, '82, 4.30 A. M.—I am down in Camden County, New Jersey, at the farm-house of the Staffords—have been looking a long while at the comet—have in my time seen longer-tail'd ones, but never one so pronounc'd in cometary character, and so spectral-fierce—so like some great, pale, living monster of the air or sea. The atmosphere and sky, an hour or so before sunrise, so cool, still, translucent, give the whole apparition to great advantage. It is low in the east. The head shows about as big as an ordinary good-sized saucer—is a perfectly round and defined disk—the tail some sixty or seventy feet—not a stripe, but quite broad, and gradually expanding. Impress'd with the silent, inexplicably emotional sight, I linger and look till all begins to weaken in the break of day.

October 2.—The third day of mellow, delicious, sunshiny weather. I am writing this in the recesses of the old woods, my seat on a big pine log, my back against a tree. Am down here a few days for a change, to bask in the Autumn sun, to idle lusciously and simply, and to eat hearty meals, especially my breakfast. Warm mid-days— the other hours of the twenty-four delightfully fresh and mild—cool evenings, and early mornings perfect. The scent of the woods, and the peculiar aroma of a great yet unreap'd maize-field near by—the white butterflies in every direction by day—the golden-rod, the wild asters, and sunflowers—the song of the katydid all night.

Every day in Cooper's Woods, enjoying simple existence and the passing hours—taking short walks—exercising arms and chest with the saplings, or my voice with army songs or recitations. A perfect week for weather; seven continuous days bright and dry and cool and sunny. The night splendid, with full moon—about 10 the grandest of star-shows up in the east and south, Jupiter, Saturn, Capella, Aldebaran, and great Orion. Am feeling pretty well—am outdoors most of the time, absorbing the days and nights all I can.

CENTRAL PARK NOTES.—*American Society from a Park Policeman's Point of View.*—Am in New York City, upper part—visit Central Park almost every day (and have for the last three weeks) off and on, taking observations or short rambles, and sometimes riding around. I talk quite a good deal with one of the Park policemen, C. C., up toward the Ninetieth street entrance. One day in particular I got him a-going, and it proved deeply interesting to me. Our talk floated into sociology and politics. I was curious to find how these things appear'd on their surfaces to my friend, for he plainly possess'd sharp wits and good nature, and had been seeing, for years, broad streaks of humanity somewhat out of my latitude. I found that as he took such appearances the inward caste-spirit of European "aristocracy" pervaded rich America, with cynicism and artificiality at the fore. Of the bulk of official persons, Executives, Congressmen, Legislators, Aldermen, Department heads, etc. etc., or the candidates for those positions, nineteen in twenty, in the policeman's judgment, were just players in a game. Liberty, Equality, Union, and all the grand words of the Republic, were, in their mouths, but lures, decoys, chisel'd likenesses of dead wood, to catch the masses. Of fine afternoons, along the broad tracks of the Park, for many years, had swept by my friend, as he stood on guard, the carriages, etc., of American Gentility, not by dozens and scores, but by hundreds and thousands. Lucky brokers, capitalists, contractors, grocery-men, successful political strikers, rich butchers, dry goods' folk, &c. And on a large proportion of these vehicles, on panels or horse-trappings, were conspicuously borne *heraldic family crests.* (Can this really be true?) In wish and willingness (and if that were so, what matter about the reality?) titles of nobility, with a court and spheres fit for the capitalists, the highly educated, and the carriage-riding classes—to fence them off from "the common people"—were the heart's desire of the "good society" of our great cities —aye, of North and South.

So much for my police friend's speculations—which rather took me aback—and which I have thought I would just print as he gave them (as a doctor records symptoms.)

PLATE GLASS NOTES.—*St. Louis, Missouri, November,* '79.—What do you think I find manufactur'd out here—and of a kind the clearest and largest, best, and the most finish'd and luxurious in the world— and with ample demand for it too? *Plate glass!* One would suppose that was the last dainty outcome of an old, almost effete-growing civilization; and yet here it is, a few miles from St. Louis, on a charming little river, in the wilds of the West, near the Mississippi. I went down that way to-day by the Iron Mountain Railroad—was switch'd off on a side-track four miles through woods and ravines, to Swash Creek, so-call'd, and there found Crystal City, and immense Glass Works, built (and evidently built to stay) right in the pleasant rolling forest. Spent most of the day, and examin'd the inexhaustible and peculiar sand the glass is made of—the original whity-gray stuff in the banks—saw the melting in the pots (a wondrous process, a real poem)—saw the delicate preparation the clay material undergoes for these great pots (it has to be kneaded finally by human feet, no machinery answering, and I watch'd the picturesque bare-legged Africans treading it)—saw the molten stuff (a great mass of a glowing pale yellow color) taken out of the furnaces (I shall never forget that Pot, shape, color, concomitants, more beautiful than any antique statue,) pass'd into the adjoining casting-room, lifted by powerful machinery, pour'd out on its bed (all glowing, a newer, vaster study for colorists, indescribable, a pale red-tinged yellow, of tarry consistence, all lambent,) roll'd by a heavy roller into rough plate glass, I should say ten feet by fourteen, then rapidly shov'd into the annealing oven, which stood ready for it. The polishing and grinding rooms afterward—the great glass slabs, hundreds of them, on their flat beds, and the see-saw music of the steam machinery constantly at work polishing them—the myriads of human figures (the works employ'd 400 men) moving about, with swart arms and necks, and no superfluous clothing—the vast, rude halls, with immense play of shifting shade, and slow-moving currents of smoke and steam, and shafts of light, sometimes sun, striking in from above with effects that would have fill'd Michel Angelo with rapture.

Coming back to St. Louis this evening, at sundown, and for over an hour afterward, we follow'd the Mississippi, close by its western bank, giving me an ampler view of the river, and with effects a little different from any yet. In the eastern sky hung the planet Mars, just up, and of a very clear and vivid yellow. It was a soothing and pensive hour—the spread of the river off there in the half-light—the glints of the down-bound steamboats plodding along—and that yellow orb (apparently twice as large and significant as usual) above the Illinois shore. (All along, these nights, nothing can exceed the calm, fierce, golden, glistening domination of Mars over all the stars in the sky.)

As we came nearer St. Louis, the night having well set in, I saw some (to me) novel effects in the zinc smelting establishments, the tall chimneys belching flames at the top, while inside through the openings at the façades of the great tanks burst forth (in regular position) hundreds of fierce tufts of a peculiar blue (or green) flame, of a purity and intensity, like electric lights—illuminating not only the great buildings themselves, but far and near outside, like hues of the aurora borealis, only more vivid. (So that—remembering the Pot from the crystal furnace—my jaunt seem'd to give me new revelations in the color line.)

➤➤➤ ◄◄◄

SOME WAR MEMORANDA

Jotted Down at the Time

"YANKEE DOODLE"

I FIND this incident in my notes (I suppose from "chinning" in hospital with some sick or wounded soldier who knew of it):

When Kilpatrick and his forces were cut off at Brandy Station (last of September, '63, or thereabouts,) and the bands struck up "Yankee Doodle," there were not cannon enough in the Southern Confederacy to keep him and them "in." It was when Meade fell back. K. had his large cavalry division (perhaps 5000 men,) but the rebs, in superior force, had surrounded them. Things look'd exceedingly desperate. K. had two fine bands, and order'd them up immediately; they join'd and play'd "Yankee Doodle" with a will! It went through the men like lightning—but to inspire, not to unnerve. Every man seem'd a giant. They charged like a cyclone, and cut their way out. Their loss was but 20. It was about two in the afternoon.

WASHINGTON STREET SCENES

April 7, 1864.—WALKING DOWN PENNSYLVANIA AVENUE.—Warmish forenoon, after the storm of the past few days. I see, passing up, in the broad space between the curbs, a big squad of a couple of hundred conscripts, surrounded by a strong cordon of arm'd guards, and others interspers'd between the ranks. The government has learn'd caution from its experiences; there are many hundreds of "bounty jumpers," and already, as I am told, eighty thousand deserters! Next (also passing up the Avenue,) a cavalry company, young, but evidently well drill'd and service-harden'd men. Mark the upright posture in their saddles, the bronz'd and bearded young faces, the easy swaying to the motions of the horses, and the carbines by their right knees; handsome and reckless, some eighty of them, riding with rapid gait, clattering along. Then the tinkling bells of passing cars, the many shops (some with large show-windows, some with swords, straps for the shoulders of different ranks, hat-cords with acorns, or other insignia,) the military patrol marching along, with the orderly or second-lieutenant stopping different ones to examine passes—the forms, the faces, all sorts crowded together, the worn and pale, the pleas'd, some on their way to the railroad depot going home, the cripples, the darkeys, the long trains of government wagons, or the sad strings of ambulances conveying wounded—the many officers' horses tied in front of the drinking or oyster saloons, or held by black men or boys, or orderlies.

THE 195TH PENNSYLVANIA

Tuesday, Aug. 1, 1865.—About 3 o'clock this afternoon (sun broiling hot) in Fifteenth street, by the Treasury building, a large and handsome regiment, 195th Pennsylvania, were marching by—as it happen'd, receiv'd orders just here to halt and break ranks, so that they might rest themselves awhile. I thought I never saw a finer set of men—so hardy, candid, bright American looks, all weather-beaten, and with warm clothes. Every man was home-born. My heart was much drawn toward them. They seem'd very tired, red, and streaming with sweat. It is a one-year regiment, mostly from Lancaster County, Pa.; have been in Shenandoah Valley. On halting, the men unhitch'd their knapsacks, and sat down to rest themselves. Some lay flat on the pavement or under trees. The fine physical appearance of the whole body was remarkable. Great, very great, must be the State where such young farmers and mechanics are the practical average. I went around for half an hour and talk'd with several of them, sometimes squatting down with the groups.

LEFT-HAND WRITING BY SOLDIERS

April 30, 1866.—Here is a single significant fact, from which one may judge of the character of the American soldiers in this just concluded war: A gentleman in New York City, a while since, took it into his head to collect specimens of writing from soldiers who had lost their right hands in battle, and afterwards learn'd to use the left. He gave public notice of his desire, and offer'd prizes for the best of these specimens. Pretty soon they began to come in, and by the time specified for awarding the prizes three hundred samples of such left-hand writing by maim'd soldiers had arrived.

I have just been looking over some of this writing. A great many of the specimens are written in a beautiful manner. All are good. The writing in nearly all cases slants backward instead of forward. One piece of writing, from a soldier who had lost both arms, was made by holding the pen in his mouth.

CENTRAL VIRGINIA IN '64

CULPEPER, where I am stopping, looks like a place of two or three thousand inhabitants. Must be one of the pleasantest towns in Virginia. Even now, dilapidated fences, all broken down, windows out, it has the remains of much beauty. I am standing on an eminence overlooking the town, though within its limits. To the west the long Blue Mountain range is very plain, looks quite near, though from 30 to 50 miles distant, with some gray splashes of snow yet visible. The show is varied and fascinating. I see a great eagle up there in the air sailing with pois'd wings, quite low. Squads of red legged soldiers are drilling; I suppose some of the new men of the Brooklyn 14th; they march off presently with muskets on their shoulders. In another place, just below me, are some soldiers squaring off logs to build a shanty—chopping away, and the noise of the axes sounding sharp. I hear the bellowing, unmusical screech of the mule. I mark the thin blue smoke rising from camp fires. Just below me is a collection of hospital tents, with a yellow flag elevated on a stick, and moving languidly in the breeze. Two discharged men (I know them both) are just leaving. One is so weak he can hardly walk; the other is stronger, and carries his comrade's musket. They move slowly along the muddy road toward the depot. The scenery is full of breadth, and spread on the most generous scale (everywhere in Virginia this thought fill'd me.) The sights, the scenes, the groups, have been varied and picturesque here beyond description, and remain so.

I heard the men return in force the other night—heard the shouting, and got up and went out to hear what was the matter. That night scene of so many hundred tramping steadily by, through the mud (some big flaring torches of pine knots,) I shall never forget. I like to go to the paymaster's tent, and watch the men getting paid off. Some have furloughs, and start at once for home, sometimes amid great chaffing and blarneying. There is every day the sound of the wood-chopping axe, and the plentiful sight of negroes, crows, and mud. I note large droves and pens of cattle. The teamsters have camps of their own, and I go often among them. The officers occasionally invite me to dinner or supper at headquarters. The fare is plain, but you get something good to drink, and plenty of it. Gen. Meade is absent; Sedgwick is in command.

PAYING THE 1ST U. S. C. T.

ONE OF my war time reminiscences comprises the quiet side scene of a visit I made to the First Regiment U. S. Color'd Troops, at

THE OLD BOWERY

A Reminiscence of New York Plays and Acting Fifty Years Ago

IN AN article not long since, "Mrs. Siddons as Lady Macbeth," in "The Nineteenth Century," after describing the bitter regretfulness to mankind from the loss of those first-class poems, temples, pictures, gone and vanish'd from any record of men, the writer (Fleeming Jenkin) continues:

If this be our feeling as to the more durable works of art, what shall we say of those triumphs which, by their very nature, last no longer than the action which creates them—the triumphs of the orator, the singer or the actor? There is an anodyne in the words, "must be so," "inevitable," and there is even some absurdity in longing for the impossible. This anodyne and our sense of humor temper the unhappiness we feel when, after hearing some great performance, we leave the theatre and think, "Well, this great thing has been, and all that is now left of it is the feeble print upon my brain, the little thrill which memory will send along my nerves, mine and my neighbors, as we live longer the print and thrill must be feebler, and when we pass away the impress of the great artist will vanish from the world." The regret that a great art should in its nature be transitory, explains the lively interest which many feel in reading anecdotes or descriptions of a great actor.

All this is emphatically my own feeling and reminiscence about the best dramatic and lyric artists I have seen in bygone days—for instance, Marietta Alboni, the elder Booth, Forrest, the tenor Bettini, the baritone Badiali, "old man Clarke"—(I could write a whole paper on the latter's peerless rendering of the Ghost in "Hamlet" at the Park, when I was a young fellow)—an actor named Ranger, who appear'd in America forty years ago in *genre* characters; Henry Placide, and many others. But I will make a few memoranda at least of the best one I knew.

For the elderly New Yorker of to-day, perhaps, nothing were more likely to start up memories of his early manhood than the mention of the Bowery and the elder Booth. At the date given, the more stylish and select theatre (prices, 50 cents pit, $1 boxes) was "The Park," a large and well-appointed house on Park Row, opposite the present Post-office. English opera and the old comedies were often given in capital style; the principal foreign stars appear'd here, with Italian opera at wide intervals. The Park held a large part in

my boyhood's and young manhood's life. Here I heard the English
actor, Anderson, in "Charles de Moor," and in the fine part of
"Gisippus." Here I heard Fanny Kemble, Charlotte Cushman, the
Seguins, Daddy Rice, Hackett as Falstaff, Nimrod Wildfire, Rip Van
Winkle, and in his Yankee characters. (See pages 14, 15, *Specimen
Days.*) It was here (some years later than the date in the headline)
I also heard Maric many times, and at his best. In such parts as
Gennaro, in "Lucrezia Borgia," he was inimitable—the sweetest of
voices, a pure tenor, of considerable compass and respectable
power. His wife, Grisi, was with him, no longer first-class or young
—a fine Norma, though, to the last.

Perhaps my dearest amusement reminiscences are those musical
ones. I doubt if ever the senses and emotions of the future will be
thrill'd as were the auditors of a generation ago by the deep passion
of Alboni's contralto (at the Broadway Theatre, south side, near
Pearl street)—or by the trumpet notes of Badiali's baritone, or Bettini's pensive and incomparable tenor in Fernando in "Favorita," or
Marini's bass in "Faliero," among the Havana troupe, Castle Garden.

But getting back more specifically to the date and theme I started
from—the heavy tragedy business prevail'd more decidedly at the
Bowery Theatre, where Booth and Forrest were frequently to be
heard. Though Booth *pere*, then in his prime, ranging in age from
40 to 44 years (he was born in 1796,) was the loyal child and con-
tinuer of the traditions of orthodox English play-acting, he stood
out "himself alone" in many respects beyond any of his kind on
record, and with effects and ways that broke through all rules and
all traditions. He has been well describ'd as an actor "whose instant
and tremendous concentration of passion in his delineations over-
whelm'd his audience, and wrought into it such enthusiasm that it
partook of the fever of inspiration surging through his own veins."
He seems to have been of beautiful private character, very honorable, affectionate, good-natured, no arrogance, glad to give the other
actors the best chances. He knew all stage points thoroughly, and
curiously ignored the mere dignities. I once talk'd with a man who
had seen him do the Second Actor in the mock play to Charles
Kean's Hamlet in Baltimore. He was a marvellous linguist. He
play'd Shylock once in London, giving the dialogue in Hebrew, and
in New Orleans Oreste (Racine's "Andromaque") in French. One
trait of his habits, I have heard, was strict vegetarianism. He was
exceptionally kind to the brute creation. Every once in a while he
would make a break for solitude or wild freedom, sometimes for a
few hours, sometimes for days. (He illustrated Plato's rule that to
the forming an artist of the very highest rank a dash of insanity or

what the world calls insanity is indispensable.) He was a small-sized man—yet sharp observers noticed that however crowded the stage might be in certain scenes, Booth never seem'd overtopt or hidden. He was singularly spontaneous and fluctuating; in the same part each rendering differ'd from any and all others. He had no stereotyped positions and made no arbitrary requirements on his fellow-performers.

As is well known to old play-goers, Booth's most effective part was Richard III. Either that, or Iago, or Shylock, or Pescara in "The Apostate," was sure to draw a crowded house. (Remember heavy pieces were much more in demand those days than now.) He was also unapproachably grand in Sir Giles Overreach, in "A New Way to Pay Old Debts," and the principal character in "The Iron Chest."

In any portraiture of Booth, those years, the Bowery Theatre, with its leading lights, and the lessee and manager, Thomas Hamblin, cannot be left out. It was at the Bowery I first saw Edwin Forrest (the play was John Howard Payne's "Brutus, or the Fall of Tarquin," and it affected me for weeks; or rather I might say permanently filter'd into my whole nature,) then in the zenith of his fame and ability. Sometimes (perhaps a veteran's benefit night,) the Bowery would group together five or six of the first-class actors of those days—Booth, Forrest, Cooper, Hamblin, and John R. Scott, for instance. At that time and here George Jones ("Count Joannes") was a young, handsome actor, and quite a favorite. I remember seeing him in the title role in "Julius Cæsar," and a capital performance it was.

To return specially to the manager. Thomas Hamblin made a first-rate foil to Booth, and was frequently cast with him. He had a large, shapely, imposing presence, and dark and flashing eyes. I remember well his rendering of the main role in Maturin's "Bertram, or the Castle of St. Aldobrand." But I thought Tom Hamblin's best acting was in the comparatively minor part of Faulconbridge in "King John"—he himself evidently revell'd in the part, and took away the house's applause from young Kean (the King) and Ellen Tree (Constance,) and everybody else on the stage—some time afterward at the Park. Some of the Bowery actresses were remarkably good. I remember Mrs. Pritchard in "Tour de Nesle," and Mrs. McClure in "Fatal Curiosity," and as Millwood in "George Barnwell." (I wonder what old fellow reading these lines will recall the fine comedietta of "The Youth That Never Saw a Woman," and the jolly acting in it of Mrs. Herring and old Gates.)

The Bowery, now and then, was the place, too, for spectacular pieces, such as "The Last Days of Pompeii," "The Lion-Doom'd" and the yet undying "Mazeppa." At one time "Jonathan Bradford, or the Murder at the Roadside Inn," had a long and crowded run; John Sefton and his brother William acted in it. I remember well the Frenchwoman Celeste, a splendid pantomimist, and her emotional "Wept of the Wishton-Wish." But certainly the main "reason for being" of the Bowery Theatre those years was to furnish the public with Forrest's and Booth's performances—the latter having a popularity and circles of enthusiastic admirers and critics fully equal to the former—though people were divided as always. For some reason or other, neither Forrest nor Booth would accept engagements at the more fashionable theatre, the Park. And it is a curious reminiscence, but a true one, that both these great actors and their performances were taboo'd by "polite society" in New York and Boston at the time—probably as being too robustuous. But no such scruples affected the Bowery.

Recalling from that period the occasion of either Forrest or Booth, any good night at the old Bowery, pack'd from ceiling to pit with its audience mainly of alert, well dress'd, full-blooded young and middle-aged men, the best average of American-born mechanics —the emotional nature of the whole mass arous'd by the power and magnetism of as mighty mimes as ever trod the stage—the whole crowded auditorium, and what seeth'd in it, and flush'd from its faces and eyes, to me as much a part of the show as any—bursting forth in one of those long-kept-up tempests of hand-clapping peculiar to the Bowery—no dainty kid-glove business, but electric force and muscle from perhaps 2000 full-sinew'd men—(the inimitable and chromatic tempest of one of those ovations to Edwin Forrest, welcoming him back after an absence, comes up to me this moment)— Such sounds and scenes as here resumed will surely afford to many old New Yorkers some fruitful recollections.

I can yet remember (for I always scann'd an audience as rigidly as a play) the faces of the leading authors, poets, editors, of those times—Fenimore Cooper, Bryant, Paulding, Irving, Charles King, Watson Webb, N. P. Willis, Hoffman, Halleck, Mumford, Morris, Leggett, L. G. Clarke, R. A. Locke and others, occasionally peering from the first tier boxes; and even the great National Eminences, Presidents Adams, Jackson, Van Buren and Tyler, all made short visits there on their Eastern tours.

Awhile after 1840 the character of the Bowery as hitherto described completely changed. Cheap prices and vulgar programmes came in. People who of after years saw the pandemonium of the pit and the doings on the boards must not gauge by them the times and characters I am describing. Not but what there was more or less rankness in the crowd even then. For types of sectional New York those days—the streets East of the Bowery, that intersect Division, Grand, and up to Third Avenue—types that never found their Dickens, or Hogarth, or Balzac, and have pass'd away unportraitured —the young shipbuilders, cartmen, butchers, firemen (the old-time "soap-lock" or exaggerated "Mose" or "Sikesey," of Chanfrau's plays,) they, too, were always to be seen in these audiences, racy of the East River and the Dry Dock. Slang, wit, occasional shirt sleeves, and a picturesque freedom of looks and manners, with a rude good-nature and restless movement, were generally noticeable. Yet there never were audiences that paid a good actor or an interesting play the compliment of more sustain'd attention or quicker rapport. Then at times came the exceptionally decorous and intellectual congregations I have hinted at; for the Bowery really furnish'd plays and players you could get nowhere else. Notably, Booth always drew the best hearers; and to a specimen of his acting I will now attend in some detail.

I happen'd to see what has been reckon'd by experts one of the most marvelous pieces of histrionism ever known. It must have been about 1834 or '35. A favorite comedian and actress at the Bowery, Thomas Flynn and his wife, were to have a joint benefit, and, securing Booth for Richard, advertised the fact many days before-hand. The house fill'd early from top to bottom. There was some uneasiness behind the scenes, for the afternoon arrived, and Booth had not come from down in Maryland, where he lived. However, a few minutes before ringing-up time he made his appearance in lively condition.

After a one-act farce over, as contrast and prelude, the curtain rising for the tragedy, I can, from my good seat in the pit, pretty well front, see again Booth's quiet entrance from the side, as, with head bent, he slowly and in silence, (amid the tempest of boisterous hand-clapping,) walks down the stage to the footlights with that peculiar and abstracted gesture, musingly kicking his sword, which he holds off from him by its sash. Though fifty years have pass'd since then, I can hear the clank, and feel the perfect following hush of perhaps three thousand people waiting. (I never saw an actor who could make more of the said hush or wait, and hold the audience in an indescribable, half-delicious, half-irritating suspense.) And so throughout the entire play, all parts, voice, atmosphere, magnetism, from

Now is the winter of our discontent,

to the closing death fight with Richmond, were of the finest and grandest. The latter character was play'd by a stalwart young fellow named Ingersoll. Indeed, all the renderings were wonderfully good. But the great spell cast upon the mass of hearers came from Booth. Especially was the dream scene very impressive. A shudder went through every nervous system in the audience; it certainly did through mine.

Without question Booth was royal heir and legitimate representative of the Garrick-Kemble-Siddons dramatic traditions; but he vitalized and gave an unnamable *race* to those traditions with his own electric personal idiosyncrasy. (As in all art-utterance it was the subtle and powerful something *special to the individual* that really conquer'd.)

To me, too, Booth stands for much else besides theatricals. I consider that my seeing the man those years glimps'd for me, beyond all else, that inner spirit and form—the unquestionable charm and vivacity, but intrinsic sophistication and artificiality—crystallizing rapidly upon the English stage and literature at and after Shakspere's time, and coming on accumulatively through the seventeenth and eighteenth centuries to the beginning, fifty or forty years ago, of those disintegrating, decomposing processes now authoritatively going on. Yes; although Booth must be class'd in that antique, almost extinct school, inflated, stagy, rendering Shakspere (perhaps inevitably, appropriately) from the growth of arbitrary and often cockney conventions, his genius was to me one of the grandest revelations of my life, a lesson of artistic expression. The words fire, energy, *abandon*, found in him unprecedented meanings. I never heard a speaker or actor who could give such a sting to hauteur or the taunt. I never heard from any other the charm of unswervingly perfect vocalization without trenching at all on mere melody, the province of music.

So much for a Thespian temple of New York fifty years since, where "sceptred tragedy went trailing by" under the gaze of the Dry Dock youth, and both players and auditors were of a character and like we shall never see again. And so much for the grandest histrion of modern times, as near as I can deliberately judge (and the phrenologists put my "caution" at 7)—grander, I believe, than Kean in the expression of electric passion, the prime eligibility of the tragic artist. For though those brilliant years had many fine and even magnificent actors, undoubtedly at Booth's death (in 1852) went the last and by far the noblest Roman of them all.

‒≫≫ ≪≪‒

NOTES to LATE ENGLISH BOOKS

"SPECIMEN DAYS IN AMERICA," LONDON EDITION, JUNE, 1887. PREFACE TO THE READER IN THE BRITISH ISLANDS

IF YOU will only take the following pages, as you do some long and gossippy letter written for you by a relative or friend traveling through distant scenes and incidents, and jotting them down lazily and informally, but ever veraciously (with occasional diversions of critical thought about somebody or something,) it might remove all formal or literary impediments at once, and bring you and me close together in the spirit in which the jottings were collated to be read. You have had, and have, plenty of public events and facts and general statistics of America;—in the following book is a common individual New World *private life*, its birth and growth, its struggles for a living, its goings and comings and observations (or representative portions of them) amid the United States of America the last thirty or forty years, with their varied war and peace, their local coloring, the unavoidable egotism, and the lights and shades and sights and joys and pains and sympathies common to humanity. Further introductory light may be found in the paragraph, "A Happy Hour's Command," and the bottom note belonging to it, at the beginning of the book. I have said in the text that if I were required to give good reason-for-being of "Specimen Days," I should be unable to do so. Let me fondly hope that it has at least the reason and excuse of such off-hand gossippy letter as just alluded to, portraying American life-sights and incidents as they actually occurred —their presentation, making additions as far as it goes, to the simple experience and association of your soul, from a comrade soul;—and that also, in the volume, as below any page of mine, anywhere, ever remains, for seen or unseen basis-phrase, GOOD-WILL BETWEEN THE COMMON PEOPLE OF ALL NATIONS.

ADDITIONAL NOTE, 1887, TO ENGLISH EDITION "SPECIMEN DAYS"

As I write these lines I still continue living in Camden, New Jersey, America. Coming this way from Washington City, on my road to the sea-shore (and a temporary rest, as I supposed) in the early summer of 1873, I broke down disabled, and have dwelt here, as my

445

central residence, all the time since—almost 14 years. In the preceding pages I have described how, during those years, I partially recuperated (in 1876) from my worst paralysis by going down to Timber Creek, living close to Nature, and domiciling with my dear friends, George and Susan Stafford. From 1877 or '8 to '83 or '4 I was well enough to travel around, considerably—journey'd westward to Kansas, leisurely exploring the Prairies, and on to Denver and the Rocky Mountains; another time north to Canada, where I spent most of the summer with my friend Dr. Bucke, and jaunted along the great lakes, and the St. Lawrence and Saguenay rivers; another time to Boston, to properly print the final edition of my poems (I was there over two months, and had a "good time.") I have so brought out the completed "Leaves of Grass" during this period; also "Specimen Days," of which the foregoing is a transcript; collected and re-edited the "Democratic Vistas" cluster—commemorated Abraham Lincoln's death, on the successive anniversaries of its occurrence, by delivering my lecture on it ten or twelve times; and "put in," through many a month and season, the aimless and resultless ways of most human lives.

Thus the last 14 years have pass'd. At present (end-days of March, 1887—I am nigh entering my 69th year) I find myself continuing on here, quite dilapidated and even wreck'd bodily from the paralysis, &c.—but in *good heart* (to use a Long Island country phrase,) and with about the same mentality as ever. The worst of it is, I have been growing feebler quite rapidly for a year, and now can't walk around—hardly from one room to the next. I am forced to stay indoors and in my big chair nearly all the time. We have had a sharp, dreary winter too, and it has pinch'd me. I am alone most of the time; every week, indeed almost every day, write some—reminiscences, essays, sketches, for the magazines; and read, or rather I should say dawdle over books and papers a good deal—spend half the day at that.

Nor can I finish this note without putting on record—wafting over sea from hence—my deepest thanks to certain friends and helpers (I would specify them all and each by name, but imperative reasons, outside of my own wishes, forbid,) in the British Islands, as well as in America. Dear, even in the abstract, is such flattering unction always no doubt to the soul! Nigher still, if possible, I myself have been, and am to-day indebted to such help for my very sustenance, clothing, shelter, and continuity. And I would not go to the grave without briefly, but plainly, as I here do, acknowledging—may I not say even glorying in it?

PREFACE TO "DEMOCRATIC VISTAS" WITH OTHER PAPERS—ENGLISH EDITION

MAINLY I think I should base the request to weigh the following pages on the assumption that they present, however indirectly, some views of the West and Modern, or of a distinctly western and modern (American) tendency, about certain matters.

Then, too, the pages include (by attempting to illustrate it,) a theory herein immediately mentioned. For another and different point of view of the issue, the Enlightenment, Democracy and Fair-show of the bulk, the common people of America (from sources representing not only the British Islands, but all the world,) means, at least, eligibility to Enlightenment, Democracy and Fair-show for the bulk, the common people of all civilized nations.

That positively "the dry land has appeared," at any rate, is an important fact.

America is really the great test or trial case for all the problems and promises and speculations of humanity, and of the past and present.

I say, too, we * are not to look so much to changes, ameliorations, and adaptations in Politics as to those of Literature and (thence) domestic Sociology. I have accordingly in the following melange introduced many themes besides political ones.

Several of the pieces are ostensibly in explanation of my own writings; but in that very process they best include and set forth their side of principles and generalities pressing vehemently for consideration our age.

Upon the whole, it is on the atmosphere they are born in, and, (I hope) give out, more than any specific piece or trait, I would care to rest.

I think Literature—a new, superb, democratic literature—is to be the medicine and lever, and (with Art) the chief influence in modern civilization. I have myself not so much made a dead set at this theory, or attempted to present it directly, as admitted it to color and sometimes dominate what I had to say. In both Europe and America we have serried phalanxes who promulge and defend the political claims: I go for an equal force to uphold the other.

WALT WHITMAN.

CAMDEN, NEW JERSEY,
    April, 1888.

* We who, in many departments, ways, make *the building up of the masses,* by *building up grand individuals,* our shibboleth: and in brief that is the marrow of this book.

447

ABRAHAM LINCOLN

GLAD am I to give—were anything better lacking—even the most brief and shorn testimony of Abraham Lincoln. Everything I heard about him authentically, and every time I saw him (and it was my fortune through 1862 to '65 to see, or pass a word with, or watch him, personally, perhaps twenty or thirty times,) added to and anneal'd my respect and love at the moment. And as I dwell on what I myself heard or saw of the mighty Westerner, and blend it with the history and literature of my age, and of what I can get of all ages, and conclude it with his death, it seems like some tragic play, superior to all else I know—vaster and fierier and more convulsionary, for this America of ours, than Eschylus or Shakspere ever drew for Athens or for England. And then the Moral permeating, underlying all! the Lesson that none so remote—none so illiterate—no age, no class—but may directly or indirectly read!

Abraham Lincoln's was really one of those characters, the best of which is the result of long trains of cause and effect—needing a certain spaciousness of time, and perhaps even remoteness, to properly enclose them—having unequal'd influence on the shaping of this Republic (and therefore the world) as to-day, and then far more important in the future. Thus the time has by no means yet come for a thorough measurement of him. Nevertheless, we who live in his era—who have seen him, and heard him, face to face, and are in the midst of, or just parting from, the strong and strange events which he and we have had to do with—can in some respects bear valuable, perhaps indispensable testimony concerning him.

I should first like to give a very fair and characteristic likeness of Lincoln, as I saw him and watch'd him one afternoon in Washington, for nearly half an hour, not long before his death. It was as he stood on the balcony of the National Hotel, Pennsylvania Avenue, making a short speech to the crowd in front, on the occasion either of a set of new colors presented to a famous Illinois regiment, or of the daring capture, by the Western men, of some flags from "the enemy," (which latter phrase, by the by, was not used by him at all in his remarks.) How the picture happen'd to be made I do not know, but I bought it a few days afterward in Washington, and it was endors'd by every one to whom I show'd it. Though hundreds of portraits have been made, by painters and photographers, (many to pass on, by copies, to future times,) I have never seen one yet that in my opinion deserv'd to be called a perfectly *good likeness;*

nor do I believe there is really such a one in existence. May I not say too, that, as there is no entirely competent and emblematic likeness of Abraham Lincoln in picture or statue, there is not—perhaps cannot be—any fully appropriate literary statement or summing-up of him yet in existence?

The best way to estimate the value of Lincoln is to think what the condition of America would be to-day, if he had never lived—never been President. His nomination and first election were mainly accidents, experiments. Severely view'd, one cannot think very much of American Political Parties, from the beginning, after the Revolutionary War, down to the present time. Doubtless, while they have had their uses—have been and are "the grass on which the cow feeds"—and indispensable economies of growth—it is undeniable that under flippant names they have merely identified temporary passions, or freaks, or sometimes prejudice, ignorance, or hatred. The only thing like a great and worthy idea vitalizing a party, and making it heroic, was the enthusiasm in '64 for re-electing Abraham Lincoln, and the reason behind the enthusiasm.

How does this man compare with the acknowledg'd "Father of his country?" Washington was model'd on the best Saxon, and Franklin—of the age of the Stuarts (rooted in the Elizabethan period)—was essentially a noble Englishman, and just the kind needed for the occasions and the times of 1776–'83. Lincoln, underneath his practicality, was far less European, was quite thoroughly Western, original, essentially non-conventional, and had a certain sort of outdoor or prairie stamp. One of the best of the late commentators on Shakspere, (Professor Dowden,) makes the height and aggregate of his quality as a poet to be, that he thoroughly blended the ideal with the practical or realistic. If this be so, I should say that what Shakspere did in poetic expression, Abraham Lincoln essentially did in his personal and official life. I should say the invisible foundations and vertebra of his character, more than any man's in history, were mystical, abstract, moral and spiritual—while upon all of them was built, and out of all of them radiated, under the control of the average of circumstances, what the vulgar call *horse-sense*, and a life often bent by temporary but most urgent materialistic and political reasons.

He seems to have been a man of indomitable firmness (even obstinacy) on rare occasions, involving great points; but he was generally very easy, flexible, tolerant, almost slouchy, respecting minor matters. I note that even those reports and anecdotes intended to level him down, all leave the tinge of a favorable impression of him.

As to his religious nature, it seems to me to have certainly been of the amplest, deepest-rooted, loftiest kind.

Already a new generation begins to tread the stage, since the persons and events of the Secession War. I have more than once fancied to myself the time when the present century has closed, and a new one open'd, and the men and deeds of that contest have become somewhat vague and mythical—fancied perhaps in some great Western city, or group collected together, or public festival, where the days of old, of 1863 and '4 and '5 are discuss'd—some ancient soldier sitting in the background as the talk goes on, and betraying himself by his emotion and moist eyes—like the journeying Ithacan at the banquet of King Alcinoüs, when the bard sings the contending warriors and their battles on the plains of Troy:

> *So from the sluices of Ulysses' eyes*
> *Fast fell the tears, and sighs succeeded sighs.*

I have fancied, I say, some such venerable relic of this time of ours, preserv'd to the next or still the next generation of America. I have fancied, on such occasion, the young men gathering around; the awe, the eager questions: "What! have you seen Abraham Lincoln—and heard him speak—and touch'd his hand? Have you, with your own eyes, look'd on Grant, and Lee, and Sherman?"

Dear to Democracy, to the very last! And among the paradoxes generated by America, not the least curious was that spectacle of all the kings and queens and emperors of the earth, many from remote distances, sending tributes of condolence and sorrow in memory of one rais'd through the commonest average of life—a railsplitter and flat-boatman!

Consider'd from contemporary points of view—who knows what the future may decide?—and from the points of view of current Democracy and The Union, (the only thing like passion or infatuation in the man was the passion for the Union of These States,) Abraham Lincoln seems to me the grandest figure yet, on all the crowded canvas of the Nineteenth Century.

[*From the New Orleans Picayune, Jan.* 25, 1887]

NEW ORLEANS in 1848

WALT WHITMAN GOSSIPS OF HIS SOJOURN HERE YEARS AGO AS A
NEWSPAPER WRITER. NOTES OF HIS TRIP UP THE MISSISSIPPI AND
TO NEW YORK

AMONG THE letters brought this morning (Camden, New Jersey, Jan.
15, 1887,) by my faithful post-office carrier, J. G., is one as follows:

"NEW ORLEANS, *Jan. 11, '87.—We have been informed that when
you were younger and less famous than now, you were in New
Orleans and perhaps have helped on the* Picayune. *If you have any
remembrance of the* Picayune's *young days, or of journalism in New
Orleans of that era, and would put it in writing (verse or prose) for
the* Picayune's *fiftieth year edition, Jan. 25, we shall be pleased,"* etc.

In response to which: I went down to New Orleans early in 1848
to work on a daily newspaper, but it was not the *Picayune*, though
I saw quite a good deal of the editors of that paper, and knew its
personnel and ways. But let me indulge my pen in some gossipy
recollections of that time and place, with extracts from my journal
up the Mississippi and across the great lakes to the Hudson.

Probably the influence most deeply pervading everything at that
time through the United States, both in physical facts and in sentiment, was the Mexican War, then just ended. Following a brilliant
campaign (in which our troops had march'd to the capital city,
Mexico, and taken full possession,) we were returning after our victory. From the situation of the country, the city of New Orleans had
been our channel and *entrepot* for everything, going and returning.
It had the best news and war correspondents; it had the most to say,
through its leading papers, the *Picayune* and *Delta* especially, and
its voice was readiest listen'd to; from it "Chapparal" had gone out,
and his army and battle letters were copied everywhere, not only in
the United States, but in Europe. Then the social cast and results;
no one who has never seen the society of a city under similar circumstances can understand what a strange vivacity and *rattle* were
given throughout by such a situation. I remember the crowds of
soldiers, the gay young officers, going or coming, the receipt of important news, the many discussions, the returning wounded, and
so on.

I remember very well seeing Gen. Taylor with his staff and other

451

officers at the St. Charles Theatre one evening (after talking with them during the day.) There was a short play on the stage, but the principal performance was of Dr. Colyer's troupe of "Model Artists," then in the full tide of their popularity. They gave many fine groups and solo shows. The house was crowded with uniforms and shoulder-straps. Gen. T. himself, if I remember right, was almost the only officer in civilian clothes; he was a jovial, old, rather stout, plain man, with a wrinkled and dark-yellow face, and, in ways and manners, show'd the least of conventional ceremony or etiquette I ever saw; he laugh'd unrestrainedly at everything comical. (He had a great personal resemblance to Fenimore Cooper, the novelist, of New York.) I remember Gen. Pillow and quite a cluster of other militaires also present.

One of my choice amusements during my stay in New Orleans was going down to the old French Market, especially of a Sunday morning. The show was a varied and curious one; among the rest, the Indian and negro hucksters with their wares. For there were always fine specimens of Indians, both men and women, young and old. I remember I nearly always on these occasions got a large cup of delicious coffee with a biscuit, for my breakfast, from the immense shining copper kettle of a great Creole mulatto woman (I believe she weigh'd 230 pounds.) I never have had such coffee since. About nice drinks, anyhow, my recollection of the "cobblers" (with strawberries and snow on top of the large tumblers,) and also the exquisite wines, and the perfect and mild French brandy, help the regretful reminiscence of my New Orleans experiences of those days. And what splendid and roomy and leisurely bar-rooms! particularly the grand ones of the St. Charles and St. Louis. Bargains, auctions, appointments, business conferences, &c., were generally held in the spaces or recesses of these bar-rooms.

I used to wander a midday hour or two now and then for amusement on the crowded and bustling levees, on the banks of the river. The diagonally wedg'd-in boats, the stevedores, the piles of cotton and other merchandise, the carts, mules, negroes, etc., afforded never-ending studies and sights to me. I made acquaintances among the captains, boatmen, or other characters, and often had long talks with them—sometimes finding a real rough diamond among my chance encounters. Sundays I sometimes went forenoons to the old Catholic Cathedral in the French quarter. I used to walk a good deal in this arrondissement; and I have deeply regretted since that I did not cultivate, while I had such a good opportunity, the chance of better knowledge of French and Spanish Creole New Orleans people. (I have an idea that there is much and of importance about the Latin race contributions to American nationality in the South and Southwest that will never be put with sympathetic understanding and tact on record.)

Let me say, for better detail, that through several months (1848) I work'd on a new daily paper, *The Crescent;* my situation rather a pleasant one. My young brother, Jeff, was with me; and he not only grew very homesick, but the climate of the place, and especially the water, seriously disagreed with him. From this and other reasons (although I was quite happily fix'd) I made no very long stay in the South. In due time we took passage northward for St. Louis in the "Pride of the West" steamer, which left her wharf just at dusk. My brother was unwell, and lay in his berth from the moment we left till the next morning; he seem'd to me to be in a fever, and I felt alarm'd. However, the next morning he was all right again, much to my relief.

Our voyage up the Mississippi was after the same sort as the voyage, some months before, down it. The shores of this great river are very monotonous and dull—one continuous and rank flat, with the exception of a meagre stretch of bluff, about the neighborhood of Natchez, Memphis, etc. Fortunately we had good weather, and not a great crowd of passengers, though the berths were all full. The "Pride" jogg'd along pretty well, and put us into St. Louis about noon Saturday. After looking around a little I secured passage on the steamer "Prairie Bird," (to leave late in the afternoon,) bound up the Illinois River to La Salle, where we were to take canal for Chicago. During the day I rambled with my brother over a large portion of the town, search'd after a refectory, and, after much trouble, succeeded in getting some dinner.

Our "Prairie Bird" started out at dark, and a couple of hours after there was quite a rain and blow, which made them haul in along shore and tie fast. We made but thirty miles the whole night. The boat was excessively crowded with passengers, and had withal so much freight that we could hardly turn around. I slept on the floor, and the night was uncomfortable enough. The Illinois River is spotted with little villages with big names, Marseilles, Naples, etc.; its banks are low, and the vegetation excessively rank. Peoria, some distance up, is a pleasant town; I went over the place; the country back is all rich land, for sale cheap. Three or four miles from P., land of the first quality can be bought for $3 or $4 an acre. (I am transcribing from my notes written at the time.)

Arriving at La Salle Tuesday morning, we went on board a canalboat, had a detention by sticking on a mud bar, and then jogg'd along at a slow trot, some seventy of us, on a moderate-sized boat.

(If the weather hadn't been rather cool, particularly at night, it would have been insufferable.) Illinois is the most splendid agricultural country I ever saw; the land is of surpassing richness; the place par excellence for farmers. We stopt at various points along the canal, some of them pretty villages.

It was 10 o'clock A. M. when we got in Chicago, too late for the steamer; so we went to an excellent public house, the "American Temperance," and I spent the time that day and till next morning, looking around Chicago.

At 9 the next forenoon we started on the "Griffith" (on board of which I am now inditing these memoranda,) up the blue waters of Lake Michigan. I was delighted with the appearance of the towns along Wisconsin. At Milwaukee I went on shore, and walk'd around the place. They say the country back is beautiful and rich. (It seems to me that if we should ever remove from Long Island, Wisconsin would be the proper place to come to.) The towns have a remarkable appearance of good living, without any penury or want. The country is so good naturally, and labor is in such demand.

About 5 o'clock one afternoon I heard the cry of "a woman overboard." It proved to be a crazy lady, who had become so from the loss of her son a couple of weeks before. The small boat put off, and succeeded in picking her up, though she had been in the water 15 minutes. She was dead. Her husband was on board. They went off at the next stopping place. While she lay in the water she probably recover'd her reason, as she toss'd up her arms and lifted her face toward the boat.

Sunday Morning, June 11.—We pass'd down Lake Huron yesterday and last night, and between 4 and 5 o'clock this morning we ran on the "flats," and have been vainly trying, with the aid of a steam tug and a lumbering lighter, to get clear again. The day is beautiful and the water clear and calm. Night before last we stopt at Mackinaw, (the island and town,) and I went up on the old fort, one of the oldest stations in the Northwest. We expect to get to Buffalo by to-morrow. The tug has fasten'd lines to us, but some have been snapt and the others have no effect. We seem to be firmly imbedded in the sand. (With the exception of a larger boat and better accommodations, it amounts to about the same thing as a becalmment I underwent on the Montauk voyage, East Long Island, last summer.) Later.—We are off again—expect to reach Detroit before dinner.

We did not stop at Detroit. We are now on Lake Erie, jogging along at a good round pace. A couple of hours since we were on the river above. Detroit seem'd to me a pretty place and thrifty. I especially liked the looks of the Canadian shore opposite and of the little village of Windsor, and, indeed, all along the banks of the river. From the shrubbery and the neat appearance of some of the cottages, I think it must have been settled by the French. While I now write we can see a little distance ahead the scene of the battle between Perry's fleet and the British during the last war with England. The lake looks to me a fine sheet of water. We are having a beautiful day.

June 12.—We stopt last evening at Cleveland, and though it was dark, I took the opportunity of rambling about the place; went up in the heart of the city and back to what appear'd to be the courthouse. The streets are unusually wide, and the buildings appear to be substantial and comfortable. We went down through Main Street and found, some distance along, several squares of ground very prettily planted with trees and looking attractive enough. Return'd to the boat by way of the lighthouse on the hill.

This morning we are making for Buffalo, being, I imagine, a little more than half across Lake Erie. The water is rougher than on Michigan or Huron. (On St. Clair it was smooth as glass.) The day is bright and dry, with a stiff head wind.

We arriv'd in Buffalo on Monday evening; spent that night and a portion of next day going round the city exploring. Then got in the cars and went to Niagara; went under the falls—saw the whirlpool and all the other sights.

Tuesday night started for Albany; travel'd all night. From the time daylight afforded us a view of the country all seem'd very rich and well cultivated. Every few miles were large towns or villages.

Wednesday late we arriv'd at Albany. Spent the evening in exploring. There was a political meeting (Hunker) at the capitol, but I pass'd it by. Next morning I started down the Hudson in the "Alida;" arriv'd safely in New York that evening.

-»» «««-

SMALL MEMORANDA

Thousands lost—here one or two preserv'd

ATTORNEY GENERAL'S OFFICE, *Washington, Aug. 22, 1865.*—As I write this, about noon, the suite of rooms here is fill'd with southerners, standing in squads, or streaming in and out, some talking with the Pardon Clerk, some waiting to see the Attorney General, others discussing in low tones among themselves. All are mainly anxious about their pardons. The famous 13th exception of the President's Amnesty Proclamation of ——, makes it necessary that every secessionist, whose property is worth $20,000 or over, shall get a special pardon, before he can transact any legal purchase, sale, &c. So hundreds and thousands of such property owners have either sent up here, for the last two months, or have been, or are now coming personally here, to get their pardons. They are from Virginia, Georgia, Alabama, Mississippi, North and South Carolina, and every southern State. Some of their written petitions are very abject. Secession officers of the rank of Brigadier General, or higher, also need these special pardons. They also come here. I see streams of the $20,000 men, (and some women,) every day. I talk now and then with them, and learn much that is interesting and significant. All the southern women that come (some splendid specimens, mothers, &c.) are dress'd in deep black.

Immense numbers (several thousands) of these pardons have been pass'd upon favorably; the Pardon Warrants (like great deeds) have been issued from the State Department, on the requisition of this office. But for some reason or other, they nearly all yet lie awaiting the President's signature. He seems to be in no hurry about it, but lets them wait.

The crowds that come here make a curious study for me. I get along, very sociably, with any of them—as I let them do all the talking; only now and then I have a long confab, or ask a suggestive question or two.

If the thing continues as at present, the property and wealth of the Southern States is going to legally rest, for the future, on these pardons. Every single one is made out with the condition that the grantee shall respect the abolition of slavery, and never make an attempt to restore it.

Washington, Sept. 8, 9, &c., 1865.—The arrivals, swarms, &c., of the

$20,000 men seeking pardons, still continue with increas'd numbers and pertinacity. I yesterday (I am a clerk in the U. S. Attorney General's office here) made out a long list from Alabama, nearly 200, recommended for pardon by the Provisional Governor. This list, in the shape of a requisition from the Attorney General, goes to the State Department. There the Pardon Warrants are made out, brought back here, and then sent to the President, where they await his signature. He is signing them very freely of late.

The President, indeed, as at present appears, has fix'd his mind on a very generous and forgiving course toward the return'd secessionists. He will not countenance at all the demand of the extreme Philo-African element of the North, to make the right of negro voting at elections a condition and *sine qua non* of the reconstruction of the United States south, and of their resumption of co-equality in the Union.

A GLINT INSIDE OF ABRAHAM LINCOLN'S CABINET APPOINTMENTS. *One item of many.*—While it was hanging in suspense who should be appointed Secretary of the Interior, (to take the place of Caleb Smith,) the choice was very close between Mr. Harlan and Col. Jesse K. Dubois, of Illinois. The latter had many friends. He was competent, he was honest, and he was a *man*. Mr. Harlan, in the race, finally gain'd the Methodist interest, and got himself to be consider'd as identified with it; and his appointment was apparently ask'd for by that powerful body. Bishop Simpson, of Philadelphia, came on and spoke for the selection. The President was much perplex'd. The reasons for appointing Col. Dubois were very strong, almost insuperable—yet the argument for Mr. Harlan, under the adroit position he had plac'd himself, was heavy. Those who press'd him adduc'd the magnitude of the Methodists as a body, their loyalty, more general and genuine than any other sect—that they represented the West, and had a right to be heard—that all or nearly all the other great denominations had their representatives in the heads of the government—that they as a body and the great sectarian power of the West, formally ask'd Mr. Harlan's appointment—that he was of them, having been a Methodist minister—that it would not do to offend them, but was highly necessary to propitiate them.

Mr. Lincoln thought deeply over the whole matter. He was in more than usual tribulation on the subject. Let it be enough to say that though Mr. Harlan finally receiv'd the Secretaryship, Col. Dubois came as near being appointed as a man could, and not be. The decision was finally made one night about 10 o'clock. Bishop Simpson and other clergymen and leading persons in Mr. Harlan's behalf, had been talking long and vehemently with the President. A member of Congress who was pressing Col. Dubois's claims, was in waiting. The President had told the Bishop that he would make a decision that evening, and that he thought it unnecessary to be press'd any more on the subject. That night he call'd in the M. C. above alluded to, and said to him: "Tell Uncle Jesse that I want to give him this appointment, and yet I cannot. I will do almost anything else in the world for him I am able. I have thought the matter all over, and under the circumstances think the Methodists too good and too great a body to be slighted. They have stood by the government, and help'd us their very best. I have had no better friends; and as the case stands, I have decided to appoint Mr. Harlan."

NOTE TO A FRIEND

[Written on the fly-leaf of a copy of "Specimen Days," sent to Peter Doyle, at Washington, June, 1883.]

PETE, do you remember—(of course you do—I do well)—those great long jovial walks we had at times for years, (1866–'72) out of Washington City—often moonlight nights—'way to "Good Hope";—or, Sundays, up and down the Potomac shores, one side or the other, sometimes ten miles at a stretch? Or when you work'd on the horse-cars, and I waited for you, coming home late together—or resting and chatting at the Market, corner 7th Street and the Avenue, and eating those nice musk or watermelons? Or during my tedious sickness and first paralysis ('73) how you used to come to my solitary garret-room and make up my bed, and enliven me, and chat for an hour or so—or perhaps go out and get the medicines Dr. Drinkard had order'd for me—before you went on duty? . . . Give my love to dear Mrs. and Mr. Nash, and tell them I have not forgotten them, and never will.   W. W.

WRITTEN IMPROMPTU IN AN ALBUM

GERMANTOWN, PHILA., Dec. 26, '83

IN MEMORY OF these merry Christmas days and nights—to my friends Mr. and Mrs. Williams, Churchie, May, Gurney, and little Aubrey. . . . A heavy snow-storm blocking up everything, and keeping us in. But souls, hearts, thoughts, unloos'd. And so—one and all, little and big—hav'n't we had a good time?   W. W.

From the Philadelphia Press, Nov. 27, 1884, (*Thanksgiving number*)

THE PLACE GRATITUDE FILLS IN A FINE CHARACTER

Scene.—A large family supper party, a night or two ago, with voices and laughter of the young, mellow faces of the old, and a by-and-by pause in the general joviality. "Now, Mr. Whitman," spoke up one of the girls, "what have you to say about Thanksgiving? Won't you give us a sermon in advance, to sober us down?" The sage nodded smilingly, look'd a moment at the blaze of the great wood fire, ran his forefinger right and left through the heavy white moustache that might have otherwise impeded his voice, and began: "Thanksgiving goes probably far deeper than you folks suppose. I am not sure but it is the source of the highest poetry—as in parts of the Bible. Ruskin, indeed, makes the central source of all great art to be praise (gratitude) to the Almighty for life, and the universe with its objects and play of action.

"We Americans devote an official day to it every year; yet I sometimes fear the real article is almost dead or dying in our self-sufficient, independent Republic. Gratitude, anyhow, has never been made half enough of by the moralists; it is indispensable to a complete character, man's or woman's—the disposition to be appreciative, thankful. That is the main matter, the element, inclination—what geologists call the *trend*. Of my own life and writings I estimate the giving thanks part, with what it infers, as essentially the best item. I should say the quality of gratitude rounds the whole emotional nature; I should say love and faith would quite lack vitality without it. There are people—shall I call them even religious people, as things go?—who have no such trend to their disposition."

➤➤➤ ◀◀◀

LAST of the WAR CASES

Memorandized at the time, Washington, 1865–'66

[OF REMINISCENCES *of the Secession War, after the rest is said, I have thought it remains to give a few special words—in some respects at the time the typical words of all, and most definite—of the samples of the kill'd and wounded in action, and of soldiers who linger'd afterward, from these wounds, or were laid up by obstinate disease or prostration. The general statistics have been printed already, but can bear to be briefly stated again. There were over 3,000,000 men (for all periods of enlistment, large and small) furnish'd to the Union army during the war, New York State furnishing over 500,000, which was the greatest number of any one State. The losses by disease, wounds, kill'd in action, accident, &c., were altogether about 600,000, or approximating to that number. Over 4,000,000 cases were treated in the main and adjudicatory army hospitals. The number sounds strange, but it is true. More than two-thirds of the deaths were from prostration or disease. To-day there lie buried over 300,000 soldiers in the various National army Cemeteries, more than half of them (and that is really the most significant and eloquent bequest of the War) mark'd "unknown." In full mortuary statistics of the war, the greatest deficiency arises from our not having the rolls, even as far as they were kept, of most of the Southern military prisons—a gap which probably both adds to, and helps conceal, the indescribable horrors of those places; it is, however, (restricting one vivid point only) certain that over 30,000 Union soldiers died, largely of actual starvation, in them. And now, leaving all figures and their "sum totals," I feel sure a few genuine memoranda of such things—some cases jotted down '64, '65, and '66 —made at the time and on the spot, with all the associations of those scenes and places brought back, will not only go directest to the right spot, but give a clearer and more actual sight of that period, than anything else. Before I give the last cases I begin with verbatim extracts from letters home to my mother in Brooklyn, the second year of the war.—W. W.]*

Washington, Oct. 13, 1863.—There has been a new lot of wounded and sick arriving for the last three days. The first and second days, long strings of ambulances with the sick. Yesterday the worst, many with bad and bloody wounds, inevitably long neglected. I thought I was cooler and more used to it, but the sight of some cases brought tears into my eyes. I had the luck yesterday, however, to do lots of good. Had provided many nourishing articles for the men for another quarter, but, fortunately, had my stores where I could use them, at once for these new-comers, as they arrived, faint, hungry, fagg'd out from their journey, with soil'd clothes, and all bloody. I distributed these articles, gave partly to the nurses I knew, or to those in charge. As many as possible I fed myself. Then I found a lot of oyster soup handy, and bought it all at once.

It is the most pitiful sight, this, when the men are first brought in, from some camp hospital broke up, or a part of the army moving. These who arrived yesterday are cavalry men. Our troops had fought like devils, but got the worst of it. They were Kilpatrick's cavalry; were in the rear, part of Meade's retreat, and the reb cavalry, knowing the ground and taking a favorable opportunity, dash'd in between, cut them off, and shell'd them terribly. But Kilpatrick turn'd and brought them out mostly. It was last Sunday. (One of the most terrible sights and tasks is of such receptions.)

Oct. 27, 1863.—If any of the soldiers I know (or their parents or folks) should call upon you—as they are often anxious to have my address in Brooklyn—you just use them as you know how, and if you happen to have pot-luck, and feel to ask them to take a bite, don't be afraid to do so. I have a friend, Thomas Neat, 2d N. Y. Cavalry, wounded in leg, now home in Jamaica, on furlough; he will probably call. Then possibly a Mr. Haskell, or some of his folks, from western New York: he had a son died here, and I was with the boy a good deal. The old man and his wife have written me and ask'd me my Brooklyn address; he said he had children in New York, and was occasionally down there. (When I come home I will show you some of the letters I get from mothers, sisters, fathers, &c. They will make you cry.)

How the time passes away! To think it is over a year since I left home suddenly—and have mostly been down in front since. The year has vanish'd swiftly, and oh, what scenes I have witness'd during that time! And the war is not settled yet; and one does not see anything certain, or even promising, of a settlement. But I do not lose the solid feeling, in myself, that the Union triumph is assured, whether it be sooner or whether it be later, or whatever roundabout way we may be led there; and I find I don't change that conviction from any reverses we meet, nor delays, nor blunders. One realizes here in Washington the great labors, even the negative ones, of Lincoln; that it is a big thing to have just kept the United States from being thrown down and having its throat cut. I have not waver'd or had any doubt of the issue, since Gettysburg.

8th September, '63.—Here, now, is a specimen army hospital case:
Lorenzo Strong, Co. A, 9th United States Cavalry, shot by a shell
last Sunday; right leg amputated on the field. Sent up here Monday
night, 14th. Seem'd to be doing pretty well till Wednesday noon,
16th, when he took a turn for the worse, and a strangely rapid and
fatal termination ensued. Though I had much to do, I staid and saw
all. It was a death-picture characteristic of these soldiers' hospitals
—the perfect specimen of physique, one of the most magnificent I
ever saw—the convulsive spasms and working of muscles, mouth,
and throat. There are two good women nurses, one on each side.
The doctor comes in and gives him a little chloroform. One of the
nurses constantly fans him, for it is fearfully hot. He asks to be
rais'd up, and they put him in a half-sitting posture. He call'd for
"Mark" repeatedly, half-deliriously, all day. Life ebbs, runs now
with the speed of a mill race; his splendid neck, as it lays all open,
works still, slightly; his eyes turn back. A religious person coming in
offers a prayer, in subdued tones, bent at the foot of the bed; and
in the space of the aisle, a crowd, including two or three doctors,
several students, and many soldiers, has silently gather'd. It is very
still and warm, as the struggle goes on, and dwindles, a little more,
and a little more—and then welcome oblivion, painlessness, death.
A pause, the crowd drops away, a white bandage is bound around
and under the jaw, the propping pillows are removed, the limpsy
head falls down, the arms are softly placed by the side, all composed, all still,—and the broad white sheet is thrown over everything.

April 10, 1864.—Unusual agitation all around concentrated here.
Exciting times in Congress. The Copperheads are getting furious,
and want to recognize the Southern Confederacy. "This is a pretty
time to talk of recognizing such ——," said a Pennsylvania officer in
hospital to me to-day, "after what has transpired the last three
years." After first Fredericksburg I felt discouraged myself, and
doubted whether our rulers could carry on the war. But that had
pass'd away. The war *must* be carried on. I would willingly go in
the ranks myself if I thought it would profit more than as at present, and I don't know sometimes but I shall, as it is. Then there is
certainly a strange, deep, fervid feeling form'd or arous'd in the
land, hard to describe or name; it is not a majority feeling, but it
will make itself felt. M., you don't know what a nature a fellow
gets, not only after being a soldier a while, but after living in the
sights and influences of the camps, the wounded, &c.—a nature he
never experienced before. The stars and stripes, the tune of Yankee

Doodle, and similar things, produce such an effect on a fellow as never before. I have seen them bring tears on some men's cheeks, and others turn pale with emotion. I have a little flag (it belong'd to one of our cavalry regiments,) presented to me by one of the wounded; it was taken by the secesh in a fight, and rescued by our men in a bloody skirmish following. It cost three men's lives to get back that four-by-three flag—to tear it from the breast of a dead rebel—for *the name* of getting their little "rag" back again. The man that secured it was very badly wounded, and they let him keep it. I was with him a good deal; he wanted to give me some keepsake, he said,—he didn't expect to live,—so he gave me that flag. The best of it all is, dear M., there isn't a regiment, cavalry or infantry, that wouldn't do the like, on the like occasion.

April 12.—I will finish my letter this morning; it is a beautiful day. I was up in Congress very late last night. The House had a very excited night session about expelling the men that proposed recognizing the Southern Confederacy. You ought to hear (as I do) the soldiers talk; they are excited to madness. We shall probably have hot times here, not in the military fields alone. The body of the army is true and firm as the North Star.

May 6, '64.—M., the poor soldier with diarrhœa, is still living, but, oh, what a looking object! Death would be a relief to him—he cannot last many hours. Cunningham, the Ohio soldier, with leg amputated at thigh, has pick'd up beyond expectation; now looks indeed like getting well. (He died a few weeks afterward.) The hospitals are very full. I am very well indeed. Hot here to-day.

May 23, '64.—Sometimes I think that should it come when it *must*, to fall in battle, one's anguish over a son or brother kill'd might be temper'd with much to take the edge off. Lingering and extreme suffering from wounds or sickness seem to me far worse than death in battle. I can honestly say the latter has no terrors for me, as far as I myself am concern'd. Then I should say, too, about death in war, that our feelings and imaginations make a thousand times too much of the whole matter. Of the many I have seen die, or known of, the past year, I have not seen or known one who met death with terror. In most cases I should say it was a welcome relief and release.

Yesterday I spent a good part of the afternoon with a young soldier of seventeen, Charles Cutter, of Lawrence City, Massachusetts, 1st Massachusetts Heavy Artillery, Battery M. He was brought to one of the hospitals mortally wounded in abdomen. Well, I thought to myself, as I sat looking at him, it ought to be a relief to his folks if they could see how little he really suffer'd. He lay very placid, in a half lethargy, with his eyes closed. As it was extremely hot, and I sat a good while silently fanning him, and wiping the sweat, at length he open'd his eyes quite wide and clear, and look'd inquiringly around. I said, "What is it, my boy? Do you want anything?" He answer'd quietly, with a good-natured smile, "Oh, nothing; I was only looking around to see who was with me." His mind was somewhat wandering, yet he lay in an evident peacefulness that sanity and health might have envied. I had to leave for other engagements. He died, I heard afterward, without any special agitation, in the course of the night.

Washington, May 26, '63.—M., I think something of commencing a series of lectures, readings, talks, &c., through the cities of the North, to supply myself with funds for hospital ministrations. I do not like to be so beholden to others; I need a pretty free supply of money, and the work grows upon me, and fascinates me. It is the most magnetic as well as terrible sight: the lots of poor wounded and helpless men depending so much, in one ward or another, upon my soothing or talking to them, or rousing them up a little, or perhaps petting, or feeding them their dinner or supper (here is a patient, for instance, wounded in both arms,) or giving some trifle for a novelty or change—anything, however trivial, to break the monotony of those hospital hours.

It is curious: when I am present at the most appalling scenes, deaths, operations, sickening wounds (perhaps full of maggots,) I keep cool and do not give out or budge, although my sympathies are very much excited; but often, hours afterward, perhaps when I am home, or out walking alone, I feel sick, and actually tremble, when I recall the case again before me.

Sunday afternoon, opening of 1865.—Pass'd this afternoon among a collection of unusually bad cases, wounded and sick Secession soldiers, left upon our hands. I spent the previous Sunday afternoon there also. At that time two were dying. Two others have died during the week. Several of them are partly deranged. I went around among them elaborately. Poor boys, they all needed to be cheer'd up. As I sat down by any particular one, the eyes of all the rest in the neighboring cots would fix upon me, and remain steadily riveted as long as I sat within their sight. Nobody seem'd to wish anything special to eat or drink. The main thing ask'd for was postage stamps, and paper for writing. I distributed all the stamps I had. Tobacco was wanted by some.

One call'd me over to him and ask'd me in a low tone what denomination I belong'd to. He said he was a Catholic—wish'd to find some one of the same faith—wanted some good reading. I gave him something to read, and sat down by him a few minutes. Moved around with a word for each. They were hardly any of them personally attractive cases, and no visitors come here. Of course they were all destitute of money. I gave small sums to two or three, apparently the most needy. The men are from quite all the Southern States, Georgia, Mississippi, Louisiana, &c.

Wrote several letters. One for a young fellow named Thomas J. Byrd, with a bad wound and diarrhœa. Was from Russell county, Alabama; been out four years. Wrote to his mother; had neither heard from her nor written to her in nine months. Was taken prisoner last Christmas, in Tennessee; sent to Nashville, then to Camp Chase, Ohio, and kept there a long time; all the while not money enough to get paper and postage stamps. Was paroled, but on his way home the wound took gangrene; had diarrhœa also; had evidently been very low. Demeanor cool, and patient. A dark-skinn'd, quaint young fellow, with strong Southern idiom; no education.

Another letter for John W. Morgan, aged 18, from Shellot, Brunswick county, North Carolina; been out nine months; gunshot wound in right leg, above knee; also diarrhœa; wound getting along well; quite a gentle, affectionate boy; wish'd me to put in the letter for his mother to kiss his little brother and sister for him. [I put strong envelopes on these, and two or three other letters, directed them plainly and fully, and dropt them in the Washington post-office the next morning myself.]

The large ward I am in is used for Secession soldiers exclusively. One man, about forty years of age, emaciated with diarrhœa, I was attracted to, as he lay with his eyes turn'd up, looking like death. His weakness was so extreme that it took a minute or so, every time, for him to talk with anything like consecutive meaning; yet he was evidently a man of good intelligence and education. As I said anything, he would lie a moment perfectly still, then, with closed eyes, answer in a low, very slow voice, quite correct and sensible, but in a way and tone that wrung my heart. He had a mother, wife, and child living (or probably living) in his home in Mississippi. It was long, long since he had seen them. Had he caus'd a letter to be sent them since he got here in Washington? No answer. I repeated the question, very slowly and soothingly. He could not tell whether he had or not—things of late seem'd to him like a dream. After waiting a moment, I said: "Well, I am going to walk down the ward a moment, and when I come back you can tell me. If you have not written, I will sit down and write." A few minutes after I return'd; he said he remember'd now that some one had written for him two or three days before. The presence of this man impress'd me profoundly. The flesh was all sunken on face and arms; the eyes low in their sockets and glassy, and with purple rings around them. Two or three great tears silently flow'd out from the eyes, and roll'd down his temples (he was doubtless unused to be spoken to as I was speaking to him.) Sickness, imprisonment, exhaustion, &c., had conquer'd the body, yet the mind held mastery still, and call'd even wandering remembrance back.

There are some fifty Southern soldiers here; all sad, sad cases. There is a good deal of scurvy. I distributed some paper, envelopes, and postage stamps, and wrote addresses full and plain on many of the envelopes.

I return'd again Tuesday, August 1, and moved around in the same manner a couple of hours.

September 22, '65.—Afternoon and evening at Douglas Hospital to see a friend belonging to 2d New York Artillery (Hiram W. Frazee, Serg't,) down with an obstinate compound fracture of left leg receiv'd in one of the last battles near Petersburg. After sitting a while with him, went through several neighboring wards. In one of them found an old acquaintance transferr'd here lately, a rebel prisoner, in a dying condition. Poor fellow, the look was already on his face. He gazed long at me. I ask'd him if he knew me. After a moment he utter'd something, but inarticulately. I have seen him off and on for the last five months. He has suffer'd very much; a bad wound in left leg, severely fractured, several operations, cuttings, extractions of bone, splinters, &c. I remember he seem'd to me, as I used to talk with him, a fair specimen of the main strata of the Southerners, those without property or education, but still with the stamp which comes from freedom and equality. I liked him; Jonathan Wallace, of Hurd Co., Georgia, age 30 (wife, Susan F. Wallace, Houston, Hurd Co., Georgia.) [If any good soul of that county should see this, I hope he will send her this word.] Had a family; had not heard from them since taken prisoner, now six months. I had written for him, and done trifles for him, before he came here. He made no outward show, was mild in his talk and behavior, but I knew he worried much inwardly. But now all would be over very soon. I half sat upon the little stand near the head of the bed. Wallace was somewhat restless. I placed my hand lightly on his forehead and face, just sliding it over the surface. In a moment or so he fell into a calm, regular-breathing lethargy or sleep, and remain'd so while I sat there. It was dark, and the lights were lit. I hardly know why (death seem'd hovering near,) but I stay'd nearly an hour. A Sister of Charity, dress'd in black, with a broad white linen bandage around her head and under her chin, and a black crape over all and flowing down from her head in long wide pieces, came to him, and moved around the bed. She bow'd low and solemn to me. For some time she moved around there noiseless as a ghost, doing little things for the dying man.

December, '65.—The only remaining hospital is now "Harewood," out in the woods, northwest of the city. I have been visiting there regularly every Sunday, during these two months.

January 24, '66.—Went out to Harewood early to-day, and remain'd all day.

Sunday, February 4, 1866.—Harewood Hospital again. Walk'd out this afternoon (bright, dry, ground frozen hard) through the woods. Ward 6 is fill'd with blacks, some with wounds, some ill, two or three with limbs frozen. The boys made quite a picture sitting round the stove. Hardly any can read or write. I write for three or four, direct envelopes, give some tobacco, &c.

Joseph Winder, a likely boy, aged twenty-three, belongs to 10th Color'd Infantry (now in Texas;) is from Eastville, Virginia. Was a slave; belong'd to Lafayette Homeston. The master was quite willing he should leave. Join'd the army two years ago; has been in one or two battles. Was sent to hospital with rheumatism. Has since been employ'd as cook. His parents at Eastville; he gets letters from them, and has letters written to them by a friend. Many black boys left that part of Virginia and join'd the army; the 10th, in fact, was made up of Virginia blacks from thereabouts. As soon as discharged is going back to Eastville to his parents and home, and intends to stay there.

Thomas King, formerly 2d District Color'd Regiment, discharged soldier, Company E, lay in a dying condition; his disease was consumption. A Catholic priest was administering extreme unction to him. (I have seen this kind of sight several times in the hospitals; it is very impressive.)

Harewood, April 29, 1866.—*Sunday afternoon.*—Poor Joseph Swiers, Company H, 155th Pennsylvania, a mere lad (only eighteen years of age;) his folks living in Reedsburgh, Pennsylvania. I have known him now for nearly a year, transferr'd from hospital to hospital. He was badly wounded in the thigh at Hatcher's Run, February 6, '65.

James E. Ragan, Atlanta, Georgia; 2d United States Infantry. Union folks. Brother impress'd, deserted, died; now no folks, left alone in the world, is in a singularly nervous state; came in hospital with intermittent fever.

Walk slowly around the ward, observing, and to see if I can do anything. Two or three are lying very low with consumption, cannot recover; some with old wounds; one with both feet frozen off, so that on one only the heel remains. The supper is being given out: the liquid call'd tea, a thick slice of bread, and some stew'd apples.

That was about the last I saw of the regular army hospitals.

NOTES *(such as they are) founded on*

ELIAS HICKS

PREFATORY NOTE.—*As myself a little boy hearing so much of E. H., at that time, long ago, in Suffolk and Queens and Kings Counties— and more than once personally seeing the old man—and my dear, dear father and mother faithful listeners to him at the meetings—I remember how I dream'd to write perhaps a piece about E. H. and his look and discourses, however long afterward—for my parents' sake—and the dear Friends too! And the following is what has at last but all come out of it—the feeling and intention never forgotten yet!*

There is a sort of nature of persons I have compared to little rills of water, fresh, from perennial springs—(and the comparison is indeed an appropriate one)—persons not so very plenty, yet some few certainly of them running over the surface and area of humanity, all times, all lands. It is a specimen of this class I would now present. I would sum up in E. H., and make his case stand for the class, the sort, in all ages, all lands, sparse, not numerous, yet enough to irrigate the soil—enough to prove the inherent moral stock and irrepressible devotional aspirations growing indigenously of themselves, always advancing, and never utterly gone under or lost.

Always E. H. gives the service of pointing to the fountain of all naked theology, all religion, all worship, all the truth to which you are possibly eligible—namely in yourself and your inherent relations. Others talk of Bibles, saints, churches, exhortations, vicarious atonements—the canons outside of yourself and apart from man—E. H. to the religion inside of man's very own nature. This he incessantly labors to kindle, nourish, educate, bring forward and strengthen. He is the most democratic of the religionists—the prophets.

I have no doubt that both the curious fate and death of his four sons, and the facts (and dwelling on them) of George Fox's strange early life, and permanent "conversion," had much to do with the peculiar and sombre ministry and style of E. H. from the first, and confirmed him all through. One must not be dominated by the man's almost absurd saturation in cut and dried biblical phraseology, and in ways, talk, and standard, regardful mainly of the one need he dwelt on, above all the rest. This main need he drove home to the soul; the canting and sermonizing soon exhale away to any auditor that realizes what E. H. is for and after. The present paper, (a bro-

ken memorandum of his formation, his earlier life,) is the cross-notch that rude wanderers make in the woods, to remind them afterward of some matter of first-rate importance and full investigation. (Remember too, that E. H. was a thorough believer in the Hebrew Scriptures, *in his way.)*

The following are really but disjointed fragments recall'd to serve and eke out here the lank printed pages of what I commenc'd unwittingly two months ago. Now, as I am well in for it, comes an old attack, the sixth or seventh recurrence, of my war-paralysis, dulling me from putting the notes in shape, and threatening any further action, head or body.

—W. W., Camden, N. J., July, 1888.

To BEGIN with, my theme is comparatively featureless. The great historian has pass'd by the life of Elias Hicks quite without glance or touch. Yet a man might commence and overhaul it as furnishing one of the amplest historic and biography's backgrounds. While the foremost actors and events from 1750 to 1830 both in Europe and America were crowding each other on the world's stage—While so many kings, queens, soldiers, philosophs, musicians, voyagers, littérateurs, enter one side, cross the boards, and disappear—amid loudest reverberating names—Frederick the Great, Swedenborg, Junius, Voltaire, Rousseau, Linneus, Herschel—curiously contemporary with the long life of Goethe—through the occupancy of the British throne by George the Third—amid stupendous visible political and social revolutions, and far more stupendous invisible moral ones—while the many quarto volumes of the Encyclopædia Française are being published at fits and intervals, by Diderot, in Paris—while Haydn and Beethoven and Mozart and Weber are working out their harmonic compositions—while Mrs. Siddons and Talma and Kean are acting—while Mungo Park explores Africa, and Capt. Cook circumnavigates the globe—through all the fortunes of the American Revolution, the beginning, continuation and end, the battle of Brooklyn, the surrender at Saratoga, the final peace of '83—through the lurid tempest of the French Revolution, the execution of the king and queen, and the Reign of Terror—through the whole of the meteor-career of Napoleon—through all Washington's, Adams's, Jefferson's, Madison's, and Monroe's Presidentiads—amid so many flashing lists of names, (indeed there seems hardly, in any department, any end to them, Old World or New,) Franklin, Sir Joshua Reynolds, Mirabeau, Fox, Nelson, Paul Jones, Kant, Fichte, and Hegel, Fulton, Walter Scott, Byron, Mesmer, Champollion—Amid pictures that dart upon me even as I speak, and glow and mix and coruscate and fade like aurora boreales—Louis the 16th threaten'd

by the mob, the trial of Warren Hastings, the death-bed of Robert
Burns, Wellington at Waterloo, Decatur capturing the Macedonian,
or the sea-fight between the Chesapeake and the Shannon—During
all these whiles, I say, and though on a far different grade, running
parallel and contemporary with all—a curious quiet yet busy life
centred in a little country village on Long Island, and within sound
on still nights of the mystic surf-beat of the sea. About this life,
this Personality—neither soldier, nor scientist, nor littérateur—I propose to occupy a few minutes in fragmentary talk, to give some few
melanges, disconnected impressions, statistics, resultant groups, pictures, thoughts of him, or radiating from him.

Elias Hicks was born March 19, 1748, in Hempstead township,
Queens county, Long Island, New York State, near a village bearing
the old Scripture name of Jericho, (a mile or so north and east of
the present Hicksville, on the L. I. Railroad.) His father and mother
were Friends, of that class working with their own hands, and
mark'd by neither riches nor actual poverty. Elias as a child and
youth had small education from letters, but largely learn'd from
Nature's schooling. He grew up even in his ladhood a thorough
gunner and fisherman. The farm of his parents lay on the south or
sea-shore side of Long Island, (they had early removed from
Jericho,) one of the best regions in the world for wild fowl and for
fishing. Elias became a good horseman, too, and knew the animal
well, riding races; also a singer, fond of "vain songs," as he afterwards calls them; a dancer, too, at the country balls. When a boy
of 13 he had gone to live with an elder brother; and when about 17
he changed again and went as apprentice to the carpenter's trade.
The time of all this was before the Revolutionary War, and the locality 30 to 40 miles from New York city. My great-grandfather,
Whitman, was often with Elias at these periods, and at merry-
makings and sleigh-rides in winter over "the plains."

How well I remember the region—the flat plains of the middle
of Long Island, as then, with their prairie-like vistas and grassy
patches in every direction, and the 'kill-calf' and herds of cattle and
sheep. Then the South Bay and shores and the salt meadows, and
the sedgy smell, and numberless little bayous and hummock-islands
in the waters, the habitat of every sort of fish and aquatic fowl of
North America. And the bay men—a strong, wild, peculiar race—
now extinct, or rather entirely changed. And the beach outside the
sandy bars, sometimes many miles at a stretch, with their old history
of wrecks and storms—the weird, white-gray beach—not without its
tales of pathos—tales, too, of grandest heroes and heroisms.

In such scenes and elements and influences—in the midst of Nature and along the shores of the sea—Elias Hicks was fashion'd

through boyhood and early manhood, to maturity. But a moral and mental and emotional change was imminent. Along at this time he says:

My apprenticeship being now expir'd, I gradually withdrew from the company of my former associates, became more acquainted with Friends, and was more frequent in my attendance of meetings; and although this was in some degree profitable to me, yet I made but slow progress in my religious improvement. The occupation of part of my time in fishing and fowling had frequently tended to preserve me from falling into hurtful associations; but through the rising intimations and reproofs of divine grace in my heart, I now began to feel that the manner in which I sometimes amus'd myself with my gun was not without sin; for although I mostly preferr'd going alone, and while waiting in stillness for the coming of the fowl, my mind was at times so taken up in divine meditations, that the opportunities were seasons of instruction and comfort to me; yet, on other occasions, when accompanied by some of my acquaintances, and when no fowls appear'd which would be useful to us after being obtain'd, we sometimes, from wantonness or for mere diversion, would destroy the small birds which could be of no service to us. This cruel procedure affects my heart while penning these lines.

In his 23d year Elias was married, by the Friends' ceremony, to Jemima Seaman. His wife was an only child; the parents were well off for common people, and at their request the son-in-law mov'd home with them and carried on the farm—which at their decease became his own, and he liv'd there all his remaining life. Of this matrimonial part of his career, (it continued, and with unusual happiness, for 58 years,) he says, giving the account of his marriage:

On this important occasion, we felt the clear and consoling evidence of divine truth, and it remain'd with us as a seal upon our spirits, strengthening us mutually to bear, with becoming fortitude, the vicissitudes and trials which fell to our lot, and of which we had a large share in passing through this probationary state. My wife, although not of a very strong constitution, liv'd to be the mother of eleven children, four sons and seven daughters. Our second daughter, a very lovely, promising child, died when young, with the small-pox, and the youngest was not living at its birth. The rest all arriv'd to years of discretion, and afforded us considerable comfort, as they prov'd to be in a good degree dutiful children. All our sons, however, were of weak constitutions, and were not able to take care of themselves, being so enfeebl'd as not to be able to walk after the ninth or tenth year of their age. The two eldest died in the fifteenth year of their age, the third in his seventeenth year, and the youngest was nearly nineteen when he died. But, although thus helpless, the innocency of their lives, and the resign'd cheerfulness of their dispositions to their allotments, made the labor and toil of taking care of them agreeable and pleasant; and I trust we were preserv'd from murmuring or repining, believing the dispensation to be in wisdom, and according to the will and gracious disposing of an all-wise providence, for purposes best known to himself. And when I have observ'd the great anxiety and affliction which many parents have with undutiful children who are favor'd with health, especially their sons, I could perceive very few whose troubles and exercises, on that account, did not far exceed ours. The weakness and bodily infirmity of our sons tended to keep them much out of the way of the troubles and temptations of the world; and we believ'd that in their death they were happy, and admitted into the realms of peace and joy: a reflection, the most comfortable and joyous that parents can have in regard to their tender offspring.

Of a serious and reflective turn, by nature, and from his reading and surroundings, Elias had more than once markedly devotional inward intimations. These feelings increas'd in frequency and strength, until soon the following:

About the twenty-sixth year of my age I was again brought, by the operative influence of divine grace, under deep concern of mind; and was led, through adorable mercy, to see, that although I had ceas'd from many sins and vanities of my youth, yet there were many remaining that I was still guilty of, which were not yet aton'd for, and for which I now felt the judgments of God to rest upon me. This caus'd me to cry earnestly to the Most High for pardon and redemption, and he graciously condescended to hear my cry, and to open a way before me, wherein I must walk, in order to experience reconciliation with him; and as I abode in watchfulness and deep humiliation before him, light broke forth out of obscurity, and my darkness became as the noon-day. I began to have openings leading to the ministry, which brought me under close exercise and deep travail of spirit; for although I had for some time spoken on subjects of business in monthly and preparative meetings, yet the prospect of opening my mouth in public meetings was a close trial; but I endeavor'd to keep my mind quiet and resign'd to the heavenly call, if it should be made clear to me to be my duty. Nevertheless, as I was, soon after, sitting in a meeting, in much weightiness of spirit, a secret, though clear, intimation accompanied me to speak a few words, which were then given to me to utter, yet fear so prevail'd, that I did not yield to the intimation. For this omission, I felt close rebuke, and judgment seem'd for some time, to cover my mind; but as I humbl'd myself under the Lord's mighty hand, he again lifted up the light of his countenance upon me, and enabl'd me to renew covenant with him, that if he would pass by this my offence, I would, in future, be faithful, if he should again require such a service of me.

The Revolutionary War following, tried the sect of Friends more than any. The difficulty was to steer between their convictions as patriots, and their pledges of non-warring peace. Here is the way they solv'd the problem:

A war, with all its cruel and destructive effects, having raged for several years between the British Colonies in North America and the mother country, Friends, as well as others, were expos'd to many severe trials and sufferings; yet, in the colony of New York, Friends, who stood faithful to their principles, and did not meddle in the controversy, had, after a short period at first, considerable favor allow'd them. The yearly meeting was held steadily, during the war, on Long Island, where the king's party had the rule; yet Friends from the Main, where the American army ruled, had free passage through both armies to attend it, and any other meetings they were desirous of attending, except in a few instances. This was a favor which the parties would not grant to their best friends, who were of a warlike disposition; which shows what great advantages would redound to mankind, were they all of this pacific spirit. I pass'd myself through the lines of both armies six times during the war, without molestation, both parties generally receiving me with openness and civility; and although I had to pass over a tract of country, between the two armies, sometimes more than thirty miles in extent, and which was much frequented by robbers, a set, in general, of cruel, unprincipled banditti, issuing out from both parties, yet, excepting once, I met with no interruption even from them. But although Friends in general experienc'd many favors and deliverances, yet those scenes of war and confusion occasion'd many trials and provings in various ways to the faithful. One circumstance I am willing to mention, as it caus'd me considerable exercise and concern. There was a large cellar under the new meeting-house belonging to Friends in New York, which was generally let as a store. When the king's troops enter'd the city, they took possession of it for the purpose of depositing their warlike stores; and ascertaining what Friends had the care of letting it, their commissary came forward and offer'd to pay the rent; and those Friends, for want of due consideration, accepted it. This caus'd great uneasiness to the concern'd part of the Society, who apprehended it not consistent with our peaceable principles to receive payment for the depositing of military stores in our houses. The subject was brought before the yearly meeting in 1779, and engag'd its careful attention; but those Friends, who had been active in the reception of the money, and some few others, were not willing to acknowledge their proceedings to be inconsistent, nor to return the money to those from whom it was receiv'd; and in order to justify themselves therein, they referr'd to the conduct of Friends in Philadelphia in similar cases. Matters thus appearing very difficult and embarrassing, it was unitedly concluded to refer the final determination thereof to the yearly meeting of Pennsylvania; and several Friends were appointed to attend that meeting in relation thereto, among whom I was one of the number. We accordingly set out on the 9th day of the 9th month, 1779, and I was accompanied from home by my beloved friend John Willis, who was likewise on the appointment.

We took a solemn leave of our families, they feeling much anxiety at parting with us, on account of the dangers we were expos'd to, having to pass not only the lines of the two armies, but the deserted and almost uninhabited country that lay between them, in many places the grass being grown up in the streets, and many houses desolate and empty. Believing it, however, my duty to proceed in the service, my mind was so settled and trust-fix'd in the divine arm of power, that faith seem'd to banish all fear, and cheerfulness and quiet resignation were, I believe, my constant companions during the journey. We got permission, with but little difficulty, to pass the outguards of the king's army at Kingsbridge, and proceeded to Westchester. We afterwards attended meetings at Harrison's Purchase, and Oblong, having the concurrence of our monthly meeting to take some meetings in our way, a concern leading thereto having for some time previously attended my mind. We pass'd from thence to Nine Partners, and attended their monthly meeting, and then turn'd our faces towards Philadelphia, being join'd by several others of the Committee. We attended New Marlborough, Hardwick, and Kingswood meetings on our journey, and arriv'd at Philadelphia on the 7th day of the week, and 25th of 9th month, on which day we attended the yearly meeting of Ministers and Elders, which began at the eleventh hour. I also attended all the sittings of the yearly meeting until the 4th day of the next week, and was then so indispos'd with a fever, which had been increasing on me for several days, that I was not able to attend after that time. I was therefore not present when the subject was discuss'd, which came from our yearly meeting; but I was inform'd by my companion, that it was a very solemn opportunity, and the matter was resulted in advising that the money should be return'd into the office from whence it was receiv'd, accompanied with our reasons for so doing: and this was accordingly done by the direction of our yearly meeting the next year.

Then, season after season, when peace and Independence reign'd, year following year, this remains to be (1791) a specimen of his personal labors:

I was from home on this journey four months and eleven days; rode about one thousand five hundred miles, and attended forty-nine particular meetings among Friends, three quarterly meetings, six monthly meetings, and forty meetings among other people.

And again another experience:

In the forepart of this meeting, my mind was reduc'd into such a state of great weakness and depression, that my faith was almost ready to fail, which produc'd great searchings of heart, so that I was led to call in question all that I had ever before experienc'd. In this state of doubting, I was ready to wish myself at home, from an apprehension that I should only expose myself to reproach, and wound the cause I was embark'd in; for the heavens seem'd like brass, and the earth as iron; such coldness and hardness, I thought, could scarcely have ever been experienc'd before by any creature, so great was the depth of my baptism at this time; nevertheless, as I endeavor'd to quiet my mind, in this conflicting dispensation, and be resign'd to my allotment, however distressing, towards the latter part of the meeting a ray of light broke through the surrounding darkness, in which the Shepherd of Israel was pleas'd to arise, and by the light of his glorious countenance, to scatter those clouds of opposition. Then ability was receiv'd, and utterance given, to speak of his marvellous works in the redemption of souls, and to open the way of life and salvation, and the mysteries of his glorious kingdom, which are hid from the wise and prudent of this world, and reveal'd only unto those who are reduc'd into the state of little children and babes in Christ.

And concluding another jaunt in 1794:

I was from home in this journey about five months, and travell'd by land and water about two thousand two hundred and eighty-three miles; having visited all the meetings of Friends in the New England states, and many meetings amongst those of other professions; and also visited many meetings, among Friends and others, in the upper part of our own yearly meeting; and found real peace in my labors.

Another 'tramp' in 1798:

I was absent from home in this journey about five months and two weeks, and rode about sixteen hundred miles, and attended about one hundred and forty-three meetings.

Here are some memoranda of 1813, near home:

First day. Our meeting this day pass'd in silent labor. The cloud rested on the tabernacle; and, although it was a day of much rain outwardly, yet very little of the dew of Hermon appear'd to distil among us. Nevertheless, a comfortable calm was witness'd towards the close, which we must render to the account of unmerited mercy and love.

Second day. Most of this day was occupied in a visit to a sick friend, who appear'd comforted therewith. Spent part of the evening in reading part of Paul's Epistle to the Romans.

Third day. I was busied most of this day in my common vocations. Spent the evening principally in reading Paul. Found considerable satisfaction in his first epistle to the Corinthians; in which he shows the danger of some in setting too high a value on those who were instrumental in bringing them to the knowledge of the truth, without looking through and beyond the instrument, to the great first cause and Author of every blessing, to whom all the praise and honor are due.

Fifth day, 1st of 4th month. At our meeting to-day found it, as usual, a very close steady exercise to keep the mind center'd where it ought to be. What a multitude of intruding thoughts imperceptibly, as it were, steal into the mind, and turn it from its proper object, whenever it relaxes its vigilance in watching against them. Felt a little strength, just at the close, to remind Friends of the necessity of a steady perseverance, by a recapitulation of the parable of the unjust judge, showing how men ought always to pray, and not to faint.

Sixth day. Nothing material occurr'd, but a fear lest the cares of the world should engross too much of my time.

Seventh day. Had an agreeable visit from two ancient friends, whom I have long lov'd. The rest of the day I employ'd in manual labor, mostly in gardening.

But we find if we attend to records and details, we shall lay out an endless task. We can briefly say, summarily, that his whole life was a long religious missionary life of method, practicality, sincerity, earnestness, and pure piety—as near to his time here, as one in Judea, far back—or in any life, any age. The reader who feels interested must get—with all its dryness and mere dates, absence of emotionality or literary quality, and whatever abstract attraction (with even a suspicion of cant, sniffling,) the "Journal of the Life and Religious Labours of Elias Hicks, written by himself," at some Quaker book-store. (It is from this headquarters I have extracted the preceding quotations.) During E. H.'s natural life, continued from fifty to sixty years—while working steadily, earning his living and paying his way without intermission—he makes, as previously memorandised, several hundred preaching visits, not only through Long Island, but some of them away into the Middle or Southern States, or north into Canada, or the then far West—extending to thousands of miles, or filling several weeks and sometimes months. These religious journeys—scrupulously accepting in payment only his transportation from place to place, with his own food and shelter, and never receiving a dollar of money for "salary" or preaching—Elias, through good bodily health and strength, continues till quite the age of eighty. It was thus at one of his latest jaunts in Brooklyn city I saw and heard him. This sight and hearing shall now be described.

Elias Hicks was at this period in the latter part (November or December) of 1829. It was the last tour of the many missions of the old man's life. He was in the 81st year of his age, and a few months before he had lost by death a beloved wife with whom he had lived in unalloyed affection and esteem for 58 years. (But a few months after this meeting Elias was paralyzed and died.) Though it is sixty years ago since—and I a little boy at the time in Brooklyn, New York—I can remember my father coming home toward sunset from his day's work as carpenter, and saying briefly, as he throws down his armful of kindling-blocks with a bounce on the kitchen floor,

"Come, mother, Elias preaches to-night." Then my mother, hastening the supper and the table-cleaning afterward, gets a neighboring young woman, a friend of the family, to step in and keep house for an hour or so—puts the two little ones to bed—and as I had been behaving well that day, as a special reward I was allow'd to go also.

We start for the meeting. Though, as I said, the stretch of more than half a century has pass'd over me since then, with its war and peace, and all its joys and sins and deaths (and what a half century! how it comes up sometimes for an instant, like the lightning flash in a storm at night!) I can recall that meeting yet. It is a strange place for religious devotions. Elias preaches anywhere—no respect to buildings—private or public houses, school-rooms, barns, even theatres—anything that will accommodate. This time it is in a handsome ball-room, on Brooklyn Heights, overlooking New York, and in full sight of that great city, and its North and East Rivers fill'd with ships—is (to specify more particularly) the second story of "Morrison's Hotel," used for the most genteel concerts, balls, and assemblies—a large, cheerful, gay-color'd room, with glass chandeliers bearing myriads of sparkling pendants, plenty of settees and chairs, and a sort of velvet divan running all round the side-walls. Before long the divan and all the settees and chairs are fill'd; many fashionables out of curiosity; all the principal dignitaries of the town, Gen. Jeremiah Johnson, Judge Furman, George Hall, Mr. Willoughby, Mr. Pierrepont, N. B. Morse, Cyrus P. Smith, and F. C. Tucker. Many young folks too; some richly dress'd women; I remember I noticed with one party of ladies a group of uniform'd officers, either from the U. S. Navy Yard, or some ship in the stream, or some adjacent fort. On a slightly elevated platform at the head of the room, facing the audience, sit a dozen or more Friends, most of them elderly, grim, and with their broad-brimm'd hats on their heads. Three or four women, too, in their characteristic Quaker costumes and bonnets. All still as the grave.

At length after a pause and stillness becoming almost painful, Elias rises and stands for a moment or two without a word. A tall, straight figure, neither stout nor very thin, dress'd in drab cloth, clean-shaved face, forehead of great expanse, and large and clear black eyes,[1] long or middling-long white hair; he was at this time between 80 and 81 years of age, his head still wearing the broad-brim. A moment looking around the audience with those piercing eyes, amid the perfect stillness. (I can almost see him and the whole scene now.) Then the words come from his lips, very emphatically and slowly pronounc'd, in a resonant, grave, melodious voice, *What is the chief end of man?* I was told in my early youth, *it was to glorify God, and seek and enjoy him forever.*

I cannot follow the discourse. It presently becomes very fervid, and in the midst of its fervor he takes the broad-brim hat from his head, and almost dashing it down with violence on the seat behind, continues with uninterrupted earnestness. But, I say, I cannot repeat, hardly suggest his sermon. Though the differences and disputes of the formal division of the Society of Friends were even then under way, he did not allude to them at all. A pleading, tender, nearly agonizing conviction, and magnetic stream of natural eloquence, before which all minds and natures, all emotions, high or low, gentle or simple, yielded entirely without exception, was its cause, method, and effect. Many, very many were in tears. Years afterward in Boston, I heard Father Taylor, the sailor's preacher, and found in his passionate unstudied oratory the resemblance to Elias Hicks's— not argumentative or intellectual, but so penetrating—so different from anything in the books—(different as the fresh air of a May morning or sea-shore breeze from the atmosphere of a perfumer's shop.) While he goes on he falls into the nasality and sing-song tone sometimes heard in such meetings; but in a moment or two more, as if recollecting himself, he breaks off, stops, and resumes in a natural tone. This occurs three or four times during the talk of the evening, till all concludes.

Now and then, at the many scores and hundreds—even thousands —of his discourses—as at this one—he was very mystical and radical,[2] and had much to say of "the light within." Very likely this same *inner light*, (so dwelt upon by newer men, as by Fox and Barclay at the beginning, and all Friends and deep thinkers since and now,) is perhaps only another name for the religious conscience. In my opinion they have all diagnos'd, like superior doctors, the real inmost disease of our times, probably any times. Amid the huge inflammation call'd society, and that other inflammation call'd politics, what is there to-day of moral power and ethic sanity as antiseptic to them and all? Though I think the essential elements of the moral nature exist latent in the good average people of the United States of to-day, and sometimes break out strongly, it is certain that any mark'd or dominating National Morality (if I may use the phrase) has not only not yet been develop'd, but that—at any rate when the point of view is turn'd on business, politics, competition, practical life, and in character and manners in our New World— there seems to be a hideous depletion, almost absence, of such moral nature. Elias taught throughout, as George Fox began it, or rather reiterated and verified it, the Platonic doctrine that the ideals of character, of justice, of religious action, whenever the highest is at stake, are to be conform'd to no outside doctrine of creeds, Bibles, legislative enactments, conventionalities, or even decorums, but are to follow the inward Deity-planted law of the emotional soul. In this only the true Quaker, or Friend, has faith; and it is from rigidly, perhaps strainingly carrying it out, that both the Old and New England records of Quakerdom show some unseemly and insane acts.

In one of the lives of Ralph Waldo Emerson is a list of lessons or instructions, ("seal'd orders" the biographer calls them,) prepar'd by the sage himself for his own guidance. Here is one:

Go forth with thy message among thy fellow-creatures; teach them that they must trust themselves as guided by that inner light which dwells with the pure in heart, to whom it was promis'd of old that they shall see God.

How thoroughly it fits the life and theory of Elias Hicks. Then in Omar Khayyam:

> *I sent my soul through the Invisible,*
> *Some letter of that after-life to spell,*
> *And by-and-by my soul return'd to me,*
> *And answer'd, "I myself am Heaven and Hell."*

Indeed, of this important element of the theory and practice of Quakerism, the difficult-to-describe "Light within" or "Inward Law, by which all must be either justified or condemn'd," I will not undertake where so many have fail'd—the task of making the statement of it for the average comprehension. We will give, partly for the matter and partly as specimen of his speaking and writing style, what Elias Hicks himself says in allusion to it—one or two of very many passages. Most of his discourses, like those of Epictetus and the ancient peripatetics, have left no record remaining—they were extempore, and those were not the times of reporters. Of one, however, deliver'd in Chester, Pa., toward the latter part of his career, there is a careful transcript; and from it (even if presenting you a sheaf of hidden wheat that may need to be pick'd and thrash'd out several times before you get the grain,) we give the following extract:

"I don't want to express a great many words; but I want you to be call'd home to the substance. For the Scriptures, and all the books in the world, can do no more; Jesus could do no more than to recommend to this Comforter, which was the light in him. 'God is light, and in him is no darkness at all; and if we walk in the light, as he is in the light, we have fellowship one with another.' Because the light is one in all, and therefore it binds us together in the bonds of love; for it is not only light, but love—that love which casts out all fear. So that they who dwell in God dwell in love, and they are constrain'd to walk in it; and if they 'walk in it, they have fellowship one with another, and the blood of Jesus Christ his Son cleanseth us from all sin.'

"But what blood, my friends? Did Jesus Christ, the Saviour, ever have any material blood? Not a drop of it, my friends—not a drop of it. That blood which cleanseth from the life of all sin, was the life of the soul of Jesus. The soul of man has no material blood; but as the outward material blood, created from the dust of the earth, is the life of these bodies of flesh, so with respect to the soul, the immortal and invisible spirit, its blood is that life which God breath'd into it.

"As we read, in the beginning, that 'God form'd man of the dust of the ground, and breath'd into him the breath of life, and man became a living soul.' He breath'd into that soul, and it became alive to God."

Then, from one of his many letters, for he seems to have delighted in correspondence:

"Some may query, What is the cross of Christ? To these I answer, It is the perfect law of God, written on the tablet of the heart, and in the heart of every rational creature, in such indelible characters that all the power of mortals cannot erase nor obliterate it. Neither is there any power or means given or dispens'd to the children of men, but this inward law and light, by which the true and saving knowledge of God can be obtain'd. And by this inward law and light, all will be either justified or condemn'd, and all made to know God for themselves, and be left without excuse, agreeably to the prophecy of Jeremiah, and the corroborating testimony of Jesus in his last counsel and command to his disciples, not to depart from Jerusalem till they should receive power from on high; assuring them that they should receive power, when they had receiv'd the pouring forth of the spirit upon them, which would qualify them to bear witness of him in Judea, Jerusalem, Samaria, and to the uttermost parts of the earth; which was verified in a marvellous manner on the day of Pentecost, when thousands were converted to the Christian faith in one day.

"By which it is evident that nothing but this inward light and law, as it is heeded and obey'd, ever did, or ever can, make a true

and real Christian and child of God. And until the professors of
Christianity agree to lay aside all their non-essentials in religion, and
rally to this unchangeable foundation and standard of truth, wars
and fightings, confusion and error, will prevail, and the angelic
song cannot be heard in our land—that of 'glory to God in the highest, and on earth peace and good will to men.'

"But when all nations are made willing to make this inward law
and light the rule and standard of all their faith and works, then we
shall be brought to know and believe alike, that there is but one
Lord, one faith, and but one baptism; one God and Father, that is
above all, through all, and in all.

"And then will all those glorious and consoling prophecies recorded in the scriptures of truth be fulfill'd—'He,' the Lord, 'shall
judge among the nations, and shall rebuke many people; and they
shall beat their swords into ploughshares, and their spears into prun-
ing-hooks; nation shall not lift up the sword against nation, neither
shall they learn war any more. The wolf also shall dwell with the
lamb; and the cow and the bear shall feed; and the lion shall eat
straw like the ox; and the sucking child shall play on the hole of the
asp, and the wean'd child put his hand on the cockatrice's den. They
shall not hurt nor destroy in all my holy mountain; for the earth,'
that is our earthly tabernacle, 'shall be full of the knowledge of the
Lord, as the waters cover the sea.'"

The exposition in the last sentence, that the terms of the texts are
not to be taken in their literal meaning, but in their spiritual one,
and allude to a certain wondrous exaltation of the body, through
religious influences, is significant, and is but one of a great number
of instances of much that is obscure, to "the world's people," in the
preachings of this remarkable man.

Then a word about his physical oratory, connected with the preceding. If there is, as doubtless there is, an unnameable something
behind oratory, a fund within or atmosphere without, deeper than
art, deeper even than proof, that unnameable constitutional something Elias Hicks emanated from his very heart to the hearts of his
audience, or carried with him, or probed into, and shook and arous'd
in them—a sympathetic germ, probably rapport, lurking in every
human eligibility, which no book, no rule, no statement has given
or can give inherent knowledge, intuition—not even the best speech,
or best put forth, but launch'd out only by powerful human magnetism:

*Unheard by sharpest ear—unform'd in clearest eye, or cunningest
    mind,*

Nor lore, nor fame, nor happiness, nor wealth,
And yet the pulse of every heart and life throughout the world,
　　incessantly,
Which you and I, and all, pursuing ever, ever miss;
Open, but still a secret—the real of the real—an illusion;
Costless, vouchsafed to each, yet never man the owner;
Which poets vainly seek to put in rhyme—historians in prose;
Which sculptor never chisel'd yet, nor painter painted;
Which vocalist never sung, nor orator nor actor ever utter'd.

That remorse, too, for a mere worldly life—that aspiration towards the ideal, which, however overlaid, lies folded latent, hidden, in perhaps every character. More definitely, as near as I remember (aided by my dear mother long afterward,) Elias Hicks's discourse there in the Brooklyn ball-room, was one of his old never-remitted appeals to that moral mystical portion of human nature, *the inner light.* But it is mainly for the scene itself, and Elias's *personnel,* that I recall the incident.

Soon afterward the old man died:

On the first day morning, the 14th of 2d month (February, 1830,) he was engaged in his room, writing to a friend, until a little after ten o'clock, when he return'd to that occupied by the family, apparently just attack'd by a paralytic affection, which nearly deprived him of the use of his right side, and of the power of speech. Being assisted to a chair near the fire, he manifested by signs, that the letter which he had just finish'd, and which had been dropp'd by the way, should be taken care of; and on its being brought to him, appear'd satisfied, and manifested a desire that all should sit down and be still, seemingly sensible that his labours were brought to a close, and only desirous of quietly waiting the final change. The solemn composure at this time manifest in his countenance, was very impressive, indicating that he was sensible the time of his departure was at hand, and that the prospect of death brought no terrors with it. During his last illness, his mental faculties were occasionally obscured, yet he was at times enabled to give satisfactory evidence to those around him, that all was well, and that he felt nothing in his way.

His funeral took place on fourth day, the 3d of 3d month. It was attended by a large concourse of Friends and others, and a solid meeting was held on the occasion; after which, his remains were interr'd in Friends' burial-ground at this place (Jericho, Queens County, New York.)

I have thought (even presented so incompletely, with such fearful hiatuses, and in my own feebleness and waning life) one might well memorize this life of Elias Hicks. Though not eminent in literature or politics or inventions or business, it is a token of not a few, and is significant. Such men do not cope with statesmen or soldiers —but I have thought they deserve to be recorded and kept up as a sample—that this one specially does. I have already compared it to a little flowing liquid rill of Nature's life, maintaining freshness. As if, indeed, under the smoke of battles, the blare of trumpets, and the madness of contending hosts—the screams of passion, the groans of the suffering, the parching of struggles of money and politics, and all hell's heat and noise and competition above and around—should come melting down from the mountains from sources of unpolluted snows, far up there in God's hidden, untrodden recesses, and so rippling along among us low in the ground, at men's very feet, a curious little brook of clear and cool, and ever-healthy, ever-living water.

Note.—The Separation.—The division vulgarly call'd between Orthodox and Hicksites in the Society of Friends took place in 1827, '8 and '9. Probably it had been preparing some time. One who was present has since described to me the climax, at a meeting of Friends in Philadelphia crowded by a great attendance of both sexes, with Elias as principal speaker. In the course of his utterance or argument he made use of these words: "The blood of Christ— the blood of Christ—why, my friends, the actual blood of Christ in itself was no more effectual than the blood of bulls and goats—not a bit more—not a bit." At these words, after a momentary hush, commenced a great tumult. Hundreds rose to their feet. . . . Canes were thump'd upon the floor. From all parts of the house angry mutterings. Some left the place, but more remain'd, with exclamations, flush'd faces and eyes. This was the definite utterance, the overt act, which led to the separation. Families diverg'd—even husbands and wives, parents and children, were separated.

Of course what Elias promulg'd spread a great commotion among the Friends. Sometimes when he presented himself to speak in the meeting, there would be opposition—this led to angry words, gestures, unseemly noises, recriminations. Elias, at such times, was deeply affected—the tears roll'd in streams down his cheeks—he silently waited the close of the dispute. "Let the Friend speak; let the Friend speak!" he would say when his supporters in the meeting tried to bluff off some violent orthodox person objecting to the new doctrinaire. But he never recanted.

A reviewer of the old dispute and separation made the following comments on them in a paper ten years ago: "It was in America, where there had been no persecution worth mentioning since Mary Dyer was hang'd on Boston Common, that about fifty years ago differences arose, singularly enough upon doctrinal points of the divinity of Christ and the nature of the atonement. Whoever would know how bitter was the controversy, and how much of human infirmity was found to be still lurking under broad-brim hats and drab coats, must seek for the information in the Lives of Elias Hicks and of Thomas Shillitoe, the latter an English Friend, who visited us at this unfortunate time, and who exercised his gifts as a peacemaker with but little success. The meetings, according to his testimony, were sometimes turn'd into mobs. The disruption was wide, and seems to have been final. Six of the ten yearly meetings were divided; and since that time various sub-divisions have come, four or five in number. There has never, however, been anything like a repetition of the excitement of the Hicksite controversy; and Friends of all kinds at present appear to have settled down into a solid, steady, comfortable state, and to be working in their own way without troubling other Friends whose ways are different."

Note.—Old persons, who heard this man in his day, and who glean'd impressions from what they saw of him, (judg'd from their own points of view,) have, in their conversation with me, dwelt on another point. They think Elias Hicks had a large element of personal ambition, the pride of leadership, of establishing perhaps a sect that should reflect his own name, and to which he should give especial form and character. Very likely. Such indeed seems the means, all through progress and civilization, by which strong men and strong convictions achieve anything definite. But the basic foundation of Elias was undoubtedly genuine religious fervor. He was like an old Hebrew prophet. He had the spirit of one, and in his later years look'd like one. What Carlyle says of John Knox will apply to him:

He is an instance to us how a man, by sincerity itself, becomes heroic; it is the grand gift he has. We find in him a good, honest, intellectual talent, no transcendent one;—a narrow, inconsiderable man, as compared with Luther; but in heartfelt instinctive adherence to truth, in sincerity as we say, he has no superior; nay, one might ask, What equal he has? The heart of him is of the true Prophet cast. 'He lies there,' said the Earl of Morton at Knox's grave, 'who never fear'd the face of man.' He resembles, more than any of the moderns, an old Hebrew Prophet. The same inflexibility, intolerance, rigid, narrow-looking adherence to God's truth.

A Note yet. The United States to-day.—While under all previous conditions (even convictions) of society, Oriental, Feudal, Ecclesiastical, and in all past (or present) Despotisms, through the entire past, there existed, and exists yet, in ally and fusion with them, and frequently forming the main part of them, certain churches, institutes, priesthoods, fervid beliefs, &c., practically promoting religious and moral action to the fullest degrees of which humanity there under circumstances was capable, and often conserving all there was of justice, art, literature, and good manners—it is clear I say, that, under the Democratic Institutes of the United States, now and henceforth, there are no equally genuine fountains of fervid beliefs, adapted to produce similar moral and religious results, according to our circumstances. I consider that the churches, sects, pulpits, of the present day, in the United States, exist not by any solid convictions, but by a sort of tacit, supercilious, scornful sufferance. Few speak openly—none officially—against them. But the ostent continuously imposing, who is not aware that any such living fountains of belief in them are now utterly ceas'd and departed from the minds of men?

A Lingering Note.—In the making of a full man, all the other consciences, (the emotional, courageous, intellectual, esthetic, &c.,) are to be crown'd and effused by the religious conscience. In the higher structure of a human self, or of community, the Moral, the Religious, the Spiritual, is strictly analogous to the subtle vitalization and antiseptic play call'd Health in the physiologic structure. To person or State, the main verteber (or rather *the* verteber) is Morality. That is indeed the only real vitalization of character, and of all the supersensual, even heroic and artistic portions of man or nationality. It is to run through and knit the superior parts, and keep man or State vital and upright, as health keeps the body straight and blooming. Of course a really grand and strong and beautiful character is probably to be slowly grown, and adjusted strictly with reference to itself, its own personal and social sphere—with (paradox though it may be) the clear understanding that the conventional theories of life, worldly ambition, wealth, office, fame, &c., are essentially but glittering mayas, delusions.

Doubtless the greatest scientists and theologians will sometimes find themselves saying, It isn't only those who know most, who contribute most to God's glory. Doubtless these very scientists at times stand with bared heads before the humblest lives and personalities. For there is something greater (is there not?) than all the science and poems of the world—above all else, like the stars shining eternal —above Shakspere's plays, or Concord philosophy, or art of Angelo or Raphael—something that shines elusive, like beams of Hesperus at evening—high above all the vaunted wealth and pride—prov'd by its practical outcropping in life, each case after its own concomitants—the intuitive blending of divine love and faith in a human emotional character—blending for all, for the unlearn'd, the common, and the poor.

I don't know in what book I once read, (possibly the remark has been made in books, all ages,) that no life ever lived, even the most uneventful, but, probed to its centre, would be found in itself as subtle a drama as any that poets have ever sung, or playwrights fabled. Often, too, in size and weight, that life suppos'd obscure. For it isn't only the palpable stars; astronomers say there are dark, or almost dark, unnotic'd orbs and suns, (like the dusky companion of Sirius, seven times as large as our own sun,) rolling through space, real and potent as any—perhaps the most real and potent. Yet none recks of them. In the bright lexicon we give the spreading heavens, they have not even names. Amid ceaseless sophistications all times, the soul would seem to glance yearningly around for such contrasts—such cool, still offsets.

⫸⫷

NOTES

1. In Walter Scott's reminiscences he speaks of Burns as having the most eloquent, glowing, flashing, illuminated dark-orbed eyes he ever beheld in a human face; and I think Elias Hicks's must have been like them.
2. The true Christian religion, (such was the teaching of Elias Hicks,) consists neither in rites or Bibles or sermons or Sundays—but in noiseless secret ecstasy and unremitted aspiration, in purity, in a good practical life, in charity to the poor and toleration to all. He said, "A man may keep the Sabbath, may belong to a church and attend all the observances, have regular family prayer, keep a well-bound copy of the Hebrew Scriptures in a conspicuous place in his house, and yet not be a truly religious person at all." E. believ'd little in a church as organiz'd—even his own—with houses, ministers, or with salaries, creeds, Sundays, saints, Bibles, holy festivals, &c. But he believ'd always in the universal church, in the soul of man, invisibly rapt, ever-waiting, ever-responding to universal truths.—He was fond of pithy proverbs. He said, "It matters not where you live, but how you live." He said once to my father, "They talk of the devil—I tell thee, Walter, there is no worse devil than man."

»»» ««‹

GEORGE FOX (and SHAKSPERE)

WHILE we are about it, we must almost inevitably go back to the origin of the Society of which Elias Hicks has so far prov'd to be the most mark'd individual result. We must revert to the latter part of the 16th, and all, or nearly all of that 17th century, crowded with so many important historical events, changes, and personages. Throughout Europe, and especially in what we call our Mother Country, men were unusually arous'd—(some would say demented.) It was a special age of the insanity of witch-trials and witch-hangings. In one year 60 were hung for witchcraft in one English county alone. It was peculiarly an age of military-religious conflict. Protestantism and Catholicism were wrestling like giants for the mastery, straining every nerve. Only to think of it—that age! its events, persons—Shakspere just dead, (his folios publish'd, complete)—Charles 1st, the shadowy spirit and the solid block! To sum up all, it was *the age of Cromwell!*

As indispensable foreground, indeed, for Elias Hicks, and perhaps *sine qua non* to an estimate of the kind of man, we must briefly transport ourselves back to the England of that period. As I say, it is the time of tremendous moral and political agitation; ideas of conflicting forms, governments, theologies, seethe and dash like ocean storms, and ebb and flow like mighty tides. It was, or had been, the time of the long feud between the Parliament and the Crown. In the midst of the sprouts, began George Fox—born eight years after the death of Shakspere. He was the son of a weaver, himself a shoemaker, and was "converted" before the age of 20. But O the sufferings, mental and physical, through which those years of the strange youth pass'd! He claim'd to be sent by God to fulfil a mission. "I come," he said, "to direct people to the spirit that gave forth the Scriptures." The range of his thought, even then, cover'd almost every important subject of after times, anti-slavery, women's rights, &c. Though in a low sphere, and among the masses, he forms a mark'd feature in the age.

And how, indeed, beyond all any, that stormy and perturb'd age! The foundations of the old, the superstitious, the conventionally poetic, the credulous, all breaking—the light of the new, and of science and democracy, definitely beginning—a mad, fierce, almost crazy age! The political struggles of the reigns of the Charleses, and of the Protectorate of Cromwell, heated to frenzy by theological struggles. Those were the years following the advent and practical working of the Reformation—but Catholicism is yet strong, and yet seeks supremacy. We think our age full of the flush of men and doings, and culminations of war and peace; and so it is. But there could hardly be a grander and more picturesque and varied age than that.

Born out of and in this age, when Milton, Bunyan, Dryden and John Locke were still living—amid the memories of Queen Elizabeth and James First, and the events of their reigns—when the radiance of that galaxy of poets, warriors, statesmen, captains, lords, explorers, wits and gentlemen, that crowded the courts and times of those sovereigns still fill'd the atmosphere—when America commencing to be explor'd and settled commenc'd also to be suspected as destin'd to overthrow the old standards and calculations—when Feudalism, like a sunset, seem'd to gather all its glories, reminiscences, personalisms, in one last gorgeous effort, before the advance of a new day, a new incipient genius—amid the social and domestic circles of that period—indifferent to reverberations that seem'd enough to wake the dead, and in a sphere far from the pageants of the court, the awe of any personal rank or charm of intellect, or literature, or the varying excitement of Parliamentarian or Royalist fortunes—this curious young rustic goes wandering up and down England.

George Fox, born 1624, was of decent stock, in ordinary lower life—as he grew along toward manhood, work'd at shoemaking, also at farm labors—loved to be much by himself, half-hidden in the woods, reading the Bible—went about from town to town, dress'd in leather clothes—walk'd much at night, solitary, deeply troubled ("the inward divine teaching of the Lord")—sometimes goes among the ecclesiastical gatherings of the great professors, and though a mere youth bears bold testimony—goes to and fro disputing—(must have had great personality)—heard the voice of the Lord speaking articulately to him, as he walk'd in the fields—feels resistless commands not to be explain'd, but follow'd, to abstain from taking off his hat, to say *Thee* and *Thou,* and not bid others Good morning or Good evening—was illiterate, could just read and write—testifies against shows, games, and frivolous pleasures—enters the courts and warns the judges that they see to doing justice—goes into public houses and market-places, with denunciations of drunkenness and money-making—rises in the midst of the church-services, and gives his own explanations of the ministers' explanations, and of Bible passages and texts—sometimes for such things put in prison, sometimes struck fiercely on the mouth on the spot, or knock'd down, and lying there beaten and bloody—was of keen wit, ready to any question with the most apropos of answers—was sometimes press'd for a soldier, (*him* for a soldier!)—was indeed terribly buffeted; but goes, goes, goes—often sleeping out-doors, under hedges, or hay stacks— forever taken before justices—improving such, and all occasions, to *bear testimony,* and give good advice—still enters the "steeple-houses," (as he calls churches,) and though often dragg'd out and whipt till he faints away, and lies like one dead, when he comes-to —stands up again, and offering himself all bruis'd and bloody, cries out to his tormenters, "Strike—strike again, here where you have not yet touch'd! my arms, my head, my cheeks."—Is at length arrested and sent up to London, confers with the Protector, Cromwell,—is set at liberty, and holds great meetings in London.

Thus going on, there is something in him that fascinates one or two here, and three or four there, until gradually there were others who went about in the same spirit, and by degrees the Society of Friends took shape, and stood among the thousand religious sects of the world. Women also catch the contagion, and go round, often shamefully misused. By such contagion these ministerings, by scores, almost hundreds of poor travelling men and women, keep on year after year, through ridicule, whipping, imprisonment, &c.—some of the Friend-ministers emigrate to New England—where their treatment makes the blackest part of the early annals of the New World. Some were executed, others maim'd, par-burnt, and scourg'd—two hundred die in prison—some on the gallows, or at the stake.

George Fox himself visited America, and found a refuge and hearers, and preach'd many times on Long Island, New York State. In the village of Oysterbay they will show you the rock on which he stood, (1672,) addressing the multitude, in the open air—thus rigidly following the fashion of apostolic times.—(I have heard myself many reminiscences of him.) Flushing also contains (or contain'd—I have seen them) memorials of Fox, and his son, in two aged white-oak trees, that shaded him while he bore his testimony to people gather'd in the highway.—Yes, the American Quakers were much persecuted—almost as much, by a sort of consent of all the other sects, as the Jews were in Europe in the middle ages. In New England, the cruelest laws were pass'd, and put in execution against them. As said, some were whipt—women the same as men. Some had their ears cut off—others their tongues pierc'd with hot irons—others their faces branded. Worse still, a woman and three men had been hang'd, (1660.)—Public opinion, and the statutes, join'd together, in an odious union, Quakers, Baptists, Roman Catholics and Witches.—Such a fragmentary sketch of George Fox and his time—and the advent of 'the Society of Friends' in America.

Strange as it may sound, Shakspere and George Fox, (think of them! compare them!) were born and bred of similar stock, in much the same surroundings and station in life—from the same England—and at a similar period. One to radiate all of art's, all literature's splendor—a splendor so dazzling that he himself is almost lost in it, and his contemporaries the same—his fictitious Othello, Romeo, Hamlet, Lear, as real as any lords of England or Europe then and there—more real to us, the mind sometimes thinks, than the man Shakspere himself. Then the other—may we indeed name him the same day? What is poor plain George Fox compared to William Shakspere—to fancy's lord, imagination's heir? Yet George Fox stands for something too—a thought—the thought that wakes in silent hours—perhaps the deepest, most eternal thought latent in the human soul. This is the thought of God, merged in the thoughts of moral right and the immortality of identity. Great, great is this thought—aye, greater than all else. When the gorgeous pageant of Art, refulgent in the sunshine, color'd with roses and gold—with all the richest mere poetry, old or new, (even Shakspere's)—with all that statue, play, painting, music, architecture, oratory, can effect, ceases to satisfy and please—When the eager chase after wealth flags, and beauty itself becomes a loathing—and when all worldly or carnal or esthetic, or even scientific values, having done their office to the human character, and minister'd their part to its development—then, if not before, comes forward this over-arching thought, and brings its eligibilities, germinations. Most neglected in life of all humanity's attributes, easily cover'd with crust, deluded and abused, rejected, yet the only certain source of what all are seeking, but few or none find—in it I for myself clearly see the first, the last, the deepest depths and highest heights of art, of literature, and of the purposes of life. I say whoever labors here, makes contributions here, or best of all sets an incarnated example here, of life or death, is dearest to humanity—remains after the rest are gone. And here, for these purposes, and up to the light that was in him, the man Elias Hicks—as the man George Fox had done years before him—lived long, and died, faithful in life, and faithful in death.

—>>> <<<—

Good-Bye My Fancy

⇛⇚

AN OLD MAN'S REJOINDER

In the domain of Literature loftily consider'd (an accomplish'd and veteran critic in his just out work * now says,) 'the kingdom of the Father has pass'd; the kingdom of the Son is passing; the kingdom of the Spirit begins.' Leaving the reader to chew on and extract the juice and meaning of this, I will proceed to say in melanged form what I have had brought out by the English author's essay (he discusses the poetic art mostly) on my own, real, or by him supposed, views and purports. If I give any answers to him, or explanations of what my books intend, they will be not direct but indirect and derivative. Of course this brief jotting is personal. Something very like querulous egotism and growling may break through the narrative (for I have been and am rejected by all the great magazines, carry now my 72d annual burden, and have been a paralytic for 18 years.)

No great poem or other literary or artistic work of any scope, old or new, can be essentially consider'd without weighing first the age, politics (or want of politics) and aim, visible forms, unseen soul, and current times, out of the midst of which it rises and is formulated: as the Biblic canticles and their days and spirit—as the Homeric, or Dante's utterance, or Shakspere's, or the old Scotch or Irish ballads, or Ossian, or Omar Khayyam. So I have conceiv'd and launch'd, and work'd for years at, my 'Leaves of Grass'—personal emanations only at best, but with specialty of emergence and back-

* Two new volumes, 'Essays Speculative and Suggestive,' by John Addington Symonds. One of the Essays is on 'Democratic Art,' in which I and my books are largely alluded to and cited and dissected. It is this part of the vols. that has caused the off-hand lines above—(first thanking Mr. S. for his invariable courtesy of personal treatment).

492

ground—the ripening of the nineteenth century, the thought and fact and radiation of individuality, of America, the Secession war, and showing the democratic conditions supplanting everything that insults them or impedes their aggregate way. Doubtless my poems illustrate (one of novel thousands to come for a long period) those conditions; but 'democratic art' will have to wait long before it is satisfactorily formulated and defined—if it ever is.

I will now for one indicative moment lock horns with what many think the greatest thing, the question of art, so-call'd. I have not seen without learning something therefrom, how, with hardly an exception, the poets of this age devote themselves, always mainly, sometimes altogether, to fine rhyme, spicy verbalism, the fabric and cut of the garment, jewelry, *concetti*, style, art. To-day these adjuncts are certainly the effort, beyond all else. Yet the lesson of Nature undoubtedly is, to proceed with single purpose toward the result necessitated, and for which the time has arrived, utterly regardless of the outputs of shape, appearance or criticism, which are always left to settle themselves. I have not only not bother'd much about style, form, art, etc., but confess to more or less apathy (I believe I have sometimes caught myself in decided aversion) toward them throughout, asking nothing of them but negative advantages—that they should never impede me, and never under any circumstances, or for their own purposes only, assume any mastery over me.

From the beginning I have watch'd the sharp and sometimes heavy and deep-penetrating objections and reviews against my work, and I hope entertain'd and audited them; (for I have probably had an advantage in constructing from a central and unitary principle since the first, but at long intervals and stages—sometimes lapses of five or six years, or peace or war.) Ruskin, the Englishman, charges as a fearful and serious lack that my poems have no humor. A profound German critic complains that, compared with the luxuriant and well-accepted songs of the world, there is about my verse a certain coldness, severity, absence of spice, polish, or of consecutive meaning and plot. (The book is autobiographic at bottom, and may-be I do not exhibit and make ado about the stock passions: I am partly of Quaker stock.) Then E. C. Stedman finds (or found) mark'd fault with me because while celebrating the common people *en masse*, I do not allow enough heroism and moral merit and good intentions to the choicer classes, the college-bred, the *état-major*. It is quite probable that S. is right in the matter. In the main I myself look, and have from the first look'd, to the bulky democratic *torso* of the United States even for esthetic and moral attributes of serious account—and refused to aim at or accept anything less. If America is only for the rule and fashion and small typicality of other lands (the rule of the *état-major*) it is not the land I take it for, and should to-day feel that my literary aim and theory had been blanks and misdirections. Strictly judged, most modern poems are but larger or smaller lumps of sugar, or slices of toothsome sweet cake—even the banqueters dwelling on those glucose flavors as a main part of the dish. Which perhaps leads to something: to have great heroic poetry we need great readers—a heroic appetite and audience. Have we at present any such?

Then the thought at the centre, never too often repeated, Boundless material wealth, free political organization, immense geographic area, and unprecedented 'business' and products—even the most active intellect and 'culture'—will not place this Commonwealth of ours on the topmost range of history and humanity—or any eminence of 'democratic art'—to say nothing of its pinnacle. Only the production (and on the most copious scale) of loftiest moral, spiritual and heroic personal illustrations—a great native Literature headed with a Poetry stronger and sweeter than any yet. If there can be any such thing as a kosmic modern and original song, America needs it, and is worthy of it.

In my opinion to-day (bitter as it is to say so) the outputs through civilized nations everywhere from the great words Literature, Art, Religion, etc., with their conventional administerers, stand squarely in the way of what the vitalities of those great words signify, more than they really prepare the soil for them—or plant the seeds, or cultivate or garner the crop. My own opinion has long been, that for New World service our ideas of beauty (inherited from the Greeks, and so on to Shakspere—*query*—perverted from them?) need to be radically changed, and made anew for to-day's purposes and finer standards. But if so, it will all come in due time— the real change will be an autochtonic, interior, constitutional, even local one, from which our notions of beauty (lines and colors are wondrous lovely, but character is lovelier) will branch or offshoot.

So much have I now rattled off (old age's garrulity,) that there is not space for explaining the most important and pregnant principle of all, *viz.,* that *Art is one,* is not partial, but includes all times and forms and sorts—is not exclusively aristocratic or democratic, or oriental or occidental. My favorite symbol would be a good font of type, where the impeccable long-primer rejects nothing. Or the old Dutch flour-miller who said, 'I never bother myself what road the folks come—I only want good wheat and rye.'

The font is about the same forever. Democratic art results of democratic development, from tinge, true nationality, belief, in the one setting up from it.

OLD POETS

Poetry (I am clear) is eligible of something far more ripen'd and ample, our lands and pending days, than it has yet produced from any utterance old or new. Modern or new poetry, too, (viewing or challenging it with severe criticism,) is largely a-void—while the very cognizance, or even suspicion of that void, and the need of filling it, proves a certainty of the hidden and waiting supply. Leaving other lands and languages to speak for themselves, we can abruptly but deeply suggest it best from our own—going first to oversea illustrations, and standing on them. Think of Byron, Burns, Shelley, Keats, (even first-raters, "the brothers of the radiant summit," as William O'Connor calls them,) as having done only their precursory and 'prentice work, and all their best and real poems being left yet unwrought, untouch'd. Is it difficult to imagine ahead of us and them, evolv'd from them, poesy completer far than any they themselves fulfill'd? One has in his eye and mind some very large, very old, entirely sound and vital tree or vine, like certain hardy, ever-fruitful specimens in California and Canada, or down in Mexico, (and indeed in all lands) beyond the chronological records—illustrations of growth, continuity, power, amplitude and *exploitation*, almost beyond statement, but proving fact and possibility, outside of argument.

Perhaps, indeed, the rarest and most blessed quality of transcendent noble poetry—as of law, and of the profoundest wisdom and æstheticism—is, (I would suggest,) from sane, completed, vital, capable old age. The final proof of song or personality is a sort of matured, accreted, superb, evoluted, almost divine, impalpable diffuseness and atmosphere or invisible magnetism, dissolving and embracing all—and not any special achievement of passion, pride, metrical form, epigram, plot, thought, or what is call'd beauty. The bud of the rose or the half-blown flower is beautiful, of course, but only the perfected bloom or apple or finish'd wheat-head is beyond the rest. Completed fruitage like this comes (in my opinion) to a grand age, in man or woman, through an essentially sound continuated physiology and psychology (both important) and is the culminating glorious aureole of all and several preceding. Like the tree or vine just mention'd, it stands at last in a beauty, power and productiveness of its own, above all others, and of a sort and style uniting all criticisms, proofs and adherences.

495

Let us diversify the matter a little by portraying some of the American poets from our own point of view.

Longfellow, reminiscent, polish'd, elegant, with the air of finest conventional library, picture-gallery or parlor, with ladies and gentlemen in them, and plush and rosewood, and ground-glass lamps, and mahogany and ebony furniture, and a silver inkstand and scented satin paper to write on.

Whittier stands for morality (not in any all-accepting philosophic or Hegelian sense, but) filter'd through a Puritanical or Quaker filter—is incalculably valuable as a genuine utterance, (and the finest,)—with many local and Yankee and *genre* bits—all hued with anti-slavery coloring—(the *genre* and anti-slavery contributions all precious—all help.) Whittier's is rather a grand figure, but pretty lean and ascetic—no Greek—not universal and composite enough (don't try—don't wish to be) for ideal Americanism. Ideal Americanism would take the Greek spirit and law, and democratize and scientize and (thence) truly Christianize them for the whole, the globe, all history, all ranks and lands, all facts, all good and bad. (Ah this *bad*—this nineteen-twentieths of us all! What a stumbling-block it remains for poets and metaphysicians—what a chance (the strange, clear-as-ever inscription on the old dug-up tablet) it offers yet for being translated—what can be its purpose in the God-scheme of this universe, and all?)

Then William Cullen Bryant—meditative, serious, from first to last tending to threnodies—his genius mainly lyrical—when reading his pieces who could expect or ask for more magnificent ones than such as "The Battle-Field," and "A Forest Hymn"? Bryant, unrolling, prairie-like, notwithstanding his mountains and lakes—moral enough (yet worldly and conventional)—a naturalist, pedestrian, gardener and fruiter—well aware of books, but mixing to the last in cities and society. I am not sure but his name ought to lead the list of American bards. Years ago I thought Emerson pre-eminent (and as to the last polish and intellectual cuteness may-be I think so still)—but, for reasons, I have been gradually tending to give the file-leading place for American native poesy to W. C. B.

Of Emerson I have to confirm my already avow'd opinion regarding his highest bardic and personal attitude. Of the galaxy of the past—of Poe, Halleck, Mrs. Sigourney, Allston, Willis, Dana, John Pierpont, W. G. Simms, Robert Sands, Drake, Hillhouse, Theodore Fay, Margaret Fuller, Epes Sargent, Boker, Paul Hayne, Lanier, and others, I fitly in essaying such a theme as this, and reverence for their memories, may at least give a heart-benison on the list of their names.

Time and New World humanity having the venerable resemblances more than anything else, and being "the same subject continued," just here in 1890, one gets a curious nourishment and lift (I do) from all those grand old veterans, Bancroft, Kossuth, von Moltke—and such typical specimen-reminiscences as Sophocles and Goethe, genius, health, beauty of person, riches, rank, renown and length of days, all combining and centering in one case.

Above everything, what could humanity and literature do without the mellow, last-justifying, averaging, bringing-up of many, many years—a great old age amplified? Every really first-class production has likely to pass through the crucial tests of a generation, perhaps several generations. Lord Bacon says the first sight of any work really new and first-rate in beauty and originality always arouses something disagreeable and repulsive. Voltaire term'd the Shaksperean works "a huge dunghill"; Hamlet he described (to the Academy, whose members listen'd with approbation) as "the dream of a drunken savage, with a few flashes of beautiful thoughts." And not the Ferney sage alone; the orthodox judges and law-givers of France, such as La Harpe, J. L. Geoffroy, and Chateaubriand, either join'd in Voltaire's verdict, or went further. Indeed the classicists and regulars there still hold to it. The lesson is very significant in all departments. People resent anything new as a personal insult. When umbrellas were first used in England, those who carried them were hooted and pelted so furiously that their lives were endanger'd. The same rage encounter'd the attempt in theatricals to perform women's parts by real women, which was publicly consider'd disgusting and outrageous. Byron thought Pope's verse incomparably ahead of Homer and Shakspere. One of the prevalent objections, in the days of Columbus was, the learn'd men boldly asserted that if a ship should reach India she would never get back again, because the rotundity of the globe would present a kind of mountain, up which it would be impossible to sail even with the most favorable wind.

"Modern poets," says a leading Boston journal, "enjoy longevity. Browning lived to be seventy-seven. Wordsworth, Bryant, Emerson, and Longfellow were old men. Whittier, Tennyson, and Walt Whitman still live." Started out by that item on Old Poets and Poetry for chyle to inner American sustenance—I have thus gossipp'd about it all, and treated it from my own point of view, taking the privilege of rambling wherever the talk carried me. Browning is lately dead; Bryant, Emerson and Longfellow have not long pass'd away; and yes, Whittier and Tennyson remain, over eighty years old—the latter having sent out not long since a fresh volume, which the English-

speaking Old and New Worlds are yet reading. I have already put
on record my notions of T. and his effusions: they are very attractive and flowery to me—but flowers, too, are at least as profound as
anything; and by common consent T. is settled as the poetic cream-
skimmer of our age's melody, *ennui* and polish—a verdict in which I
agree, and should say that nobody (not even Shakspere) goes
deeper in those exquisitely touch'd and half-hidden hints and indirections left like faint perfumes in the crevices of his lines. Of
Browning I don't know enough to say much; he must be studied
deeply out, too, and quite certainly repays the trouble—but I am
old and indolent, and cannot study (and never did.)

Grand as to-day's accumulative fund of poetry is, there is certainly something unborn, not yet come forth, different from anything now formulated in any verse, or contributed by the past in
any land—something waited for, craved, hitherto non-express'd.
What it will be, and how, no one knows. It will probably have to
prove itself by itself and its readers. One thing, it must run through
entire humanity (this new word and meaning Solidarity has arisen
to us moderns) twining all lands like a divine thread, stringing all
beads, pebbles or gold, from God and the soul, and like God's dynamics and sunshine illustrating all and having reference to all.
From anything like a cosmical point of view, the entirety of imaginative literature's themes and results as we get them to-day seems
painfully narrow. All that has been put in statement, tremendous as
it is, what is it compared with the vast fields and values and varieties left unreap'd? Of our own country, the splendid races North
or South, and especially of the Western and Pacific regions, it sometimes seems to me their myriad noblest Homeric and Biblic elements are all untouch'd, left as if ashamed of, and only certain very
minor occasional *delirium tremens* glints studiously sought and put
in print, in short tales, "poetry" or books.

I give these speculations, or notions, in all their audacity, for the
comfort of thousands—perhaps a majority of ardent minds, women's
and young men's—who stand in awe and despair before the im-
mensity of suns and stars already in the firmament. Even in the
Iliad and Shakspere there is (is there not?) a certain humiliation
produced to us by the absorption of them, unless we sound in
equality, or above them, the songs due our own democratic era
and surroundings, and the full assertion of ourselves. And in vain
(such is my opinion) will America seek successfully to tune any
superb national song unless the heart-strings of the people start it
from their own breasts—to be return'd and echoed there again.

SHIP AHOY!

IN DREAMS I was a ship, and sail'd the boundless seas,
Sailing and ever sailing—all seas and into every port, or out upon
 the offing,
Saluting, cheerily hailing each mate, met or pass'd, little or big,
"Ship ahoy!" thro' trumpet or by voice—if nothing more, some
 friendly merry word at least,
For companionship and good will for ever to all and each.

FOR QUEEN VICTORIA'S BIRTHDAY

*An American arbutus bunch to be put in a little vase on the royal breakfast
table, May 24th, 1890.*

LADY, accept a birth-day thought—haply an idle gift and token,
Right from the scented soil's May-utterance here,
(Smelling of countless blessings, prayers, and old-time thanks,)*
A bunch of white and pink arbutus, silent, spicy, shy,
From Hudson's, Delaware's, or Potomac's woody banks.

* NOTE.—Very little, as we Americans stand this day, with our sixty-five or
seventy millions of population, an immense surplus in the treasury, and all that
actual power or reserve power (land and sea) so dear to nations—very little I
say do we realize that curious crawling national shudder when the "Trent
affair" promis'd to bring upon us a war with Great Britain—follow'd unquestionably, as that war would have, by recognition of the Southern Confederacy
from all the leading European nations. It is now certain that all this then inevitable train of calamity hung on arrogant and peremptory phrases in the
prepared and written missive of the British Minister, to America, which the
Queen (and Prince Albert latent) positively and promptly cancell'd; and which
her firm attitude did alone actually erase and leave out, against all the other
official prestige and Court of St. James's. On such minor and personal incidents
(so to call them,) often depend the great growths and turns of civilization.
This moment of a woman and a queen surely swung the grandest oscillation of
modern history's pendulum. Many sayings and doings of that period, from foreign potentates and powers, might well be dropt in oblivion by America—but
never *this*, if I could have my way.   W. W.

➤➤➤ ❰❰❰

AMERICAN NATIONAL LITERATURE

Is there any such thing—or can there ever be?

So you want an essay about American National Literature, (tremendous and fearful subject!) do you? * Well, if you will let me put down some melanged cogitations regarding the matter, haphazard, and from my own points of view, I will try. Horace Greeley wrote a book named "Hints toward Reforms," and the title-line was consider'd the best part of all. In the present case I will give a few thoughts and suggestions, of good and ambitious intent enough anyhow—first reiterating the question right out plainly: American National Literature—is there distinctively any such thing, or can there ever be? First to me comes an almost indescribably august form, the People, with varied typical shapes and attitudes—then the divine mirror, Literature.

As things are, probably no more puzzling question ever offer'd itself than (going back to old Nile for a trope,) What bread-seeds of printed mentality shall we cast upon America's waters, to grow and return after many days? Is there for the future authorship of the United States any better way than submission to the teeming facts, events, activities, and importations already vital through and beneath them all? I have often ponder'd it, and felt myself disposed to let it go at that. Indeed, are not those facts and activities and importations potent and certain to fulfil themselves all through our Commonwealth, irrespective of any attempt from individual guidance? But allowing all, and even at that, a good part of the matter being honest discussion, examination, and earnest personal presentation, we may even for sanitary exercise and contact plunge boldly into the spread of the many waves and cross-tides, as follows. Or, to change the figure, I will present my varied little collation (what is our Country itself but an infinitely vast and varied collation?) in the hope that the show itself indicates a duty getting more and more incumbent every day.

In general, civilization's totality or real representative National Literature formates itself (like language, or "the weather") not from two or three influences, however important, nor from any learned syllabus, or criticism, or what ought to be, nor from any minds or advice of toploftical quarters—and indeed not at all from the influences and ways ostensibly supposed (though they too are

---

* The essay was for the *North American Review*, in answer to the formal request of the editor. It appear'd in March, 1891.

adopted, after a sort)—but slowly, slowly, curiously, from many
more and more, deeper mixings and siftings (especially in America)
and generations and years and races, and what largely appears to
be chance—but is not chance at all. First of all, for future National
Literature in America, New England (the technically moral and
schoolmaster region, as a cynical fellow I know calls it) and the
three or four great Atlantic-coast cities, highly as they to-day suppose they dominate the whole, will have to haul in their horns. *Ensemble* is the tap-root of National Literature. America is become
already a huge world of peoples, rounded and orbic climates, idi-
ocrasies, and geographies—forty-four Nations curiously and irresistibly blent and aggregated in ONE NATION, with one imperial
language, and one unitary set of social and legal standards over all
—and (I predict) a yet to be National Literature. (In my mind
this last, if it ever comes, is to prove grander and more important
for the Commonwealth than its politics and material wealth and
trade, vast and indispensable as those are.)

Think a moment what must, beyond peradventure, be the real
permanent sub-bases, or lack of them. Books profoundly consider'd
show a great nation more than anything else—more than laws or
manners. (This is, of course, probably the deep-down meaning of
that well-buried but ever-vital platitude, Let me sing the people's
songs, and I don't care who makes their laws.) Books too reflect humanity *en masse*, and surely show them splendidly, or the reverse,
and prove or celebrate their prevalent traits (these last the main
things.) Homer grew out of and has held the ages, and holds
to-day, by the universal admiration for personal prowess, courage,
rankness, *amour propre*, leadership, inherent in the whole human
race. Shakspere concentrates the brilliancy of the centuries of feudalism on the proud personalities they produced, and paints the
amorous passion. The books of the Bible stand for the final superiority of devout emotions over the rest, and of religious adoration,
and ultimate absolute justice, more powerful than haughtiest kings
or millionaires or majorities.

What the United States are working out and establishing needs
imperatively the connivance of something subtler than ballots and
legislators. The Goethean theory and lesson (if I may briefly state it
so) of the exclusive sufficiency of artistic, scientific, literary equip-
ment to the character, irrespective of any strong claims of the political ties of nation, state, or city, could have answer'd under the
conventionality and pettiness of Weimar, or the Germany, or even
Europe, of those times; but it will not do for America to-day at all.
We have not only to exploit our own theory above any that has pre-

ceded us, but we have entirely different, and deeper-rooted, and infinitely broader themes.

When I have had a chance to see and observe a sufficient crowd of American boys or maturer youths or well-grown men, all the States, as in my experiences in the Secession War among the soldiers, or west, east, north, or south, or my wanderings and loiterings through cities (especially New York and in Washington,) I have invariably found coming to the front three prevailing personal traits, to be named here for brevity's sake under the heads Good-Nature, Decorum, and Intelligence. (I make Good-Nature first, as it deserves to be—it is a splendid resultant of all the rest, like health or fine weather.) Essentially these lead the inherent list of the high average personal born and bred qualities of the young fellows everywhere through the United States, as any sharp observer can find out for himself. Surely these make the vertebral stock of super-best and noblest nations! May the destinies show it so forthcoming. I mainly confide the whole future of our Commonwealth to the fact of these three bases. Need I say I demand the same in the elements and spirit and fruitage of National Literature?

Another, perhaps a born root or branch, comes under the words *Noblesse Oblige,* even for a national rule or motto. My opinion is that this foregoing phrase, and its spirit, should influence and permeate official America and its representatives in Congress, the Executive Departments, the Presidency, and the individual States—should be one of their chiefest mottoes, and be carried out practically. (I got the idea from my dear friend the democratic Englishwoman, Mrs. Anne Gilchrist, now dead. "The beautiful words *Noblesse Olige*," said she to me once, "are not best for some develop'd gentleman or lord, but some rich and develop'd nation—and especially for your America.")

Then another and very grave point (for this discussion is deep, deep—not for trifles, or pretty seemings.) I am not sure but the establish'd and old (and superb and profound, and, one may say, needed as old) conception of Deity as mainly of moral constituency (goodness, purity, sinlessness, &c.) has been undermined by nineteenth-century ideas and science. What does this immense and almost abnormal development of Philanthropy mean among the moderns? One doubts if there ever will come a day when the moral laws and moral standards will be supplanted as over all: while time proceeds (I find it so myself) they will probably be intrench'd deeper and expanded wider. Then the expanded scientific and democratic and truly philosophic and poetic quality of modernism demands a Deific identity and scope superior to all limitations, and essentially including just as well the so-call'd evil and crime and criminals—all the malformations, the defective and abortions of the universe.

Sometimes the bulk of the common people (who are far more 'cute than the critics suppose) relish a well-hidden allusion or hint carelessly dropt, faintly indicated, and left to be disinterr'd or not. Some of the very old ballads have delicious morsels of this kind. Greek Aristophanes and Pindar abounded in them. (I sometimes fancy the old Hellenic audiences must have been as generally keen and knowing as any of their poets.) Shakspere is full of them. Tennyson has them. It is always a capital compliment from author to reader, and worthy the peering brains of America. The mere smartness of the common folks, however, does not need encouraging, but qualities more solid and opportune.

What are now deepest wanted in the States as roots for their literature are Patriotism, Nationality, Ensemble, or the ideas of these, and the uncompromising genesis and saturation of these. Not the mere bawling and braggadocio of them, but the radical emotion-facts, the fervor and perennial fructifying spirit at fountain-head. And at the risk of being misunderstood I should dwell on and repeat that a great imaginative *literatus* for America can never be merely good and moral in the conventional method. Puritanism and what radiates from it must always be mention'd by me with respect; then I should say, for this vast and varied Commonwealth, geographically and artistically, the puritanical standards are constipated, narrow, and non-philosophic.

In the main I adhere to my positions in "Democratic Vistas," and especially to my summing-up of American literature as far as to-day is concern'd. In Scientism, the Medical Profession, Practical Inventions, and Journalism, the United States have press'd forward to the glorious front rank of advanced civilized lands, as also in the popular dissemination of printed matter (of a superficial nature perhaps, but that is an indispensable preparatory stage,) and have gone in common education, so-call'd, far beyond any other land or age. Yet the high-pitch'd taunt of Margaret Fuller, forty years ago, still sounds in the air: "It does not follow, because the United States print and read more books, magazines, and newspapers than all the rest of the world, that they really have therefore a literature." For perhaps it is not alone the free schools and newspapers, nor railroads and factories, nor all the iron, cotton, wheat, pork, and petroleum, nor the gold and silver, nor the surplus of a hundred or several hundred millions, nor the Fourteenth and Fifteenth Amendments, nor the last national census, that can put this Commonweal high or highest on the cosmical scale of history. Something else is indispensable. All that record is lofty, but there is a loftier.

The great current points are perhaps simple, after all: first, that the highest developments of the New World and Democracy, and probably the best society of the civilized world all over, are to be only reach'd and spinally nourish'd (in my notion) by a new evolutionary sense and treatment; and, secondly, that the evolution-principle, which is the greatest law through nature, and of course in these States, has now reach'd us markedly for and in our literature.

In other writings I have tried to show how vital to any aspiring Nationality must ever be its autochthonic song, and how for a really great people there can be no complete and glorious Name, short of emerging out of and even rais'd on such born poetic expression, coming from its own soil and soul, its area, spread, idiosyncrasies, and (like showers of rain, originally rising impalpably, distill'd from land and sea,) duly returning there again. Nor do I forget what we all owe to our ancestry; though perhaps we are apt to forgive and bear too much for that alone.

One part of the national American literatus's task is (and it is not an easy one) to treat the old hereditaments, legends, poems, theologies, and even customs, with fitting respect and toleration, and at the same time clearly understand and justify, and be devoted to and exploit our own day, its diffused light, freedom, responsibilities, with all it necessitates, and that our New-World circumstances and stages of development demand and make proper. For American literature we want mighty authors, *not* even Carlyle-and Heine-like, born and brought up in (and more or less essentially partaking and giving out) that vast abnormal ward or hysterical sick-chamber which in many respects Europe, with all its glories, would seem to be. The greatest feature in current poetry (perhaps in literature anyhow) is the almost total lack of first-class power, and simple, natural health, flourishing and produced at first hand, typifying our own era. Modern verse generally lacks quite altogether the modern, and is oftener possess'd in spirit with the past and feudal, dressed may-be in late fashions. For novels and plays often the plots and surfaces are contemporary—but the spirit, even the fun, is morbid and effete.

There is an essential difference between the Old and New. The poems of Asia and Europe are rooted in the long past. They celebrate man and his intellections and relativenesses as they have been. But America, in as high a strain as ever, is to sing them all as they are and are to be. (I know, of course, that the past is probably a main factor in what we are and know and must be.) At present

the States are absorb'd in business, money-making, politics, agriculture, the development of mines, intercommunications, and other
material attents—which all shove forward and appear at their
height—as, consistently with modern civilization, they must be and
should be. Then even these are but the inevitable precedents and
providers for home-born, transcendent, democratic literature—to be
shown in superior, more heroic, more spiritual, more emotional, personalities and songs. A national literature is, of course, in one sense,
a great mirror or reflector. There must however be something before—something to reflect. I should say now, since the Secession
War, there has been, and to-day unquestionably exists, that something.

Certainly, anyhow, the United States do not so far utter poetry,
first-rate literature, or any of the so-call'd arts, to any lofty admiration or advantage—are not dominated or penetrated from actual
inherence or plain bent to the said poetry and arts. Other work,
other needs, current inventions, productions, have occupied and
to-day mainly occupy them. They are very 'cute and imitative and
proud—can't bear being left too glaringly away far behind the other
high-class nations—and so we set up some home "poets," "artists,"
painters, musicians, *literati*, and so forth, all our own (thus claim'd.)
The whole matter has gone on, and exists to-day, probably as it
should have been, and should be; as, for the present, it must be. To
all which we conclude, and repeat the terrible query: American
National Literature—is there distinctively any such thing, or can
there ever be?

-»» «««

GATHERING *the* CORN

Last of October.—Now mellow, crisp Autumn days, bright moonlight nights, and gathering the corn—"cutting up," as the farmers call it. Now, or of late, all over the country, a certain green and brown-drab eloquence seeming to call out, "You that pretend to give the news, and all that's going, why not give us a notice?" Truly, O fields, as for the notice,

Take, we give it willingly.

Only we must do it our own way. Leaving the domestic, dietary, and commercial parts of the question (which are enormous, in fact, hardly second to those of any other of our great soil-products), we will just saunter down a lane we know, on an average West Jersey farm, and let the fancy of the hour itemize America's most typical agricultural show and specialty.

Gathering the Corn—the British call it Maize, the old Yankee farmer Indian Corn. The great plumes, the ears well-envelop'd in their husks, the long and pointed leaves, in summer, like green or purple ribands, with a yellow stem-line in the middle, all now turn'd dingy; the sturdy stalks, and the rustling in the breeze—the breeze itself well tempering the sunny noon—The varied reminiscences recall'd—the ploughing and planting in spring—(the whole family in the field, even the little girls and boys dropping seed in the hill)—the gorgeous sight through July and August—the walk and observation early in the day—the cheery call of the robin, and the low whirr of insects in the grass—the Western husking party, when ripe—the November moonlight gathering, and the calls, songs, laughter of the young fellows.

Not to forget, hereabouts, in the Middle States, the old worm fences, with the gray rails and their scabs of moss and lichen—those old rails, weather beaten, but strong yet. Why not come down from literary dignity, and confess we are sitting on one now, under the shade of a great walnut tree? Why not confide that these lines are pencill'd on the edge of a woody bank, with a glistening pond and creek seen through the trees south, and the corn we are writing about close at hand on the north? Why not put in the delicious scent of the "life everlasting" that yet lingers so profusely in every direction—the chromatic song of the one persevering locust (the in-

sect is scarcer this fall and the past summer than for many years)
beginning slowly, rising and swelling to much emphasis, and then
abruptly falling—so appropriate to the scene, so quaint, so racy and
suggestive in the warm sunbeams, we could sit here and look and
listen for an hour? Why not even the tiny, turtle-shaped, yellow-
back'd, black-spotted lady-bug that has lit on the shirt-sleeve of the
arm inditing this? Ending our list with the fall-drying grass, the
Autumn days themselves,

Sweet days; so cool, so calm, so bright.

(yet not so cool either, about noon)—the horse-mint, the wild carrot, the mullein, and the bumble-bee.

How the half-mad vision of William Blake—how the far freer, far
firmer fantasy that wrote "Midsummer Night's Dream"—would have
revell'd night or day, and beyond stint, in one of our American corn
fields! Truly, in color, outline, material and spiritual suggestiveness,
where any more inclosing theme for idealist, poet, literary artist?

What we have written has been at noon day—but perhaps better
still (for this collation,) to steal off by yourself these fine nights,
and go slowly, musingly down the lane, when the dry and green-
gray frost-touch'd leaves seem whisper-gossiping all over the field
in low tones, as if every hill had something to say—and you sit or
lean recluse near by, and inhale that rare, rich, ripe and peculiar
odor of the gather'd plant which comes out best only to the night
air. The complex impressions of the far-spread fields and woods in
the night, are blended mystically, soothingly, indefinitely, and yet
palpably to you (appealing curiously, perhaps mostly, to the sense
of smell.) All is comparative silence and clear-shadow below, and
the stars are up there with Jupiter lording it over westward; sulky
Saturn in the east, and over head the moon. A rare well-shadow'd
hour! By no means the least of the eligibilities of the gather'd corn!

-»> «€-

A DEATH-BOUQUET

Pick'd Noontime, Early January, 1890

DEATH—too great a subject to be treated so—indeed the greatest subject—and yet I am giving you but a few random lines about it— as one writes hurriedly the last part of a letter to catch the closing mail. Only I trust the lines, especially the poetic bits quoted, may leave a lingering odor of spiritual heroism afterward. For I am probably fond of viewing all really great themes indirectly, and by sideways and suggestions. Certain music from wondrous voices or skilful players—then poetic glints still more—put the soul in rapport with death, or toward it. Hear a strain from Tennyson's late "Crossing the Bar":

> *Twilight and evening bell,*
> *And after that the dark!*
> *And may there be no sadness of farewell,*
> *When I embark;*
>
> *For tho' from out our bourne of Time and Place*
> *The floods may bear me far,*
> *I hope to see my Pilot face to face*
> *When I have crost the bar.*

Am I starting the sail-craft of poets in line? Here then a quatrain of Phrynichus long ago to one of old Athens' favorites:

> *Thrice-happy Sophocles! in good old age,*
> *Bless'd as a man, and as a craftsman bless'd,*
> *He died; his many tragedies were fair,*
> *And fair his end, nor knew he any sorrow.*

Certain music, indeed, especially voluntaries by a good player, at twilight—or idle rambles alone by the shore, or over prairie or on mountain road, for that matter—favor the right mood. Words are difficult—even impossible. No doubt any one will recall ballads or songs or hymns (may-be instrumental performances) that have arous'd so curiously, yet definitely, the thought of death, the mystic, the after-realm, as no statement or sermon could—and brought it hovering near.

A happy (to call it so) and easy death is at least as much a physiological result as a psychological one. The foundation of it really begins before birth, and is thence directly or indirectly shaped and affected, even constituted, (the base stomachic) by every thing from that minute till the time of its occurrence. And yet here is something (Whittier's "Burning Driftwood") of an opposite coloring:

> *I know the solemn monotone*
> *Of waters calling unto me;*
> *I know from whence the airs have blown,*
> *That whisper of the Eternal Sea;*
> *As low my fires of driftwood burn,*
> *I hear that sea's deep sounds increase,*
> *And, fair in sunset light, discern*
> *Its mirage-lifted Isles of Peace.*

Like an invisible breeze after a long and sultry day, death sometimes sets in at last, soothingly and refreshingly, almost vitally. In not a few cases the termination even appears to be a sort of ecstasy. Of course there are painful deaths, but I do not believe such is at all the general rule. Of the many hundreds I myself saw die in the fields and hospitals during the Secession War the cases of mark'd suffering or agony *in extremis* were very rare. (It is a curious suggestion of immortality that the mental and emotional powers remain to their clearest through all, while the senses of pain and flesh-volition are blunted or even gone.)

Then to give the following, and cease before the thought gets threadbare:

> *Now, land and life, finalè, and farewell!*
> *Now Voyager depart! (much, much for thee is yet in store;)*
> *Often enough hast thou adventur'd o'er the seas,*
> *Cautiously cruising, studying the charts,*
> *Duly again to port and hawser's tie returning.*
> *—But now obey thy cherish'd, secret wish,*
> *Embrace thy friends—leave all in order;*
> *To port and hawser's tie no more returning,*
> *Depart upon thy endless cruise, old Sailor!*

SOME LAGGARDS YET

THE PERFECT HUMAN VOICE

STATING IT briefly and pointedly I should suggest that the human voice is a cultivation or form'd growth on a fair native foundation. This foundation probably exists in nine cases out of ten. Sometimes nature affords the vocal organ in perfection, or rather I would say near enough to whet one's appreciation and appetite for a voice that might be truly call'd perfection. To me the grand voice is mainly physiological—(by which I by no means ignore the mental help, but wish to keep the emphasis where it belongs.) Emerson says *manners* form the representative apex and final charm and captivation of humanity: but he might as well have changed the typicality to

Of course there is much taught and written about elocution, the best reading, speaking, etc., but it finally settles down to *best* human vocalization. Beyond all other power and beauty, there is something in the quality and power of the right voice (*timbre* the schools call it) that touches the soul, the abysms. It was not for nothing that the Greeks depended, at their highest, on poetry's and wisdom's vocal utterance by *tete-a-tete* lectures—(indeed all the ancients did.)

Of celebrated people possessing this wonderful vocal power, patent to me, in former days, I should specify the contralto Alboni, Elias Hicks, Father Taylor, the tenor Bettini, Fanny Kemble, and the old actor Booth, and in private life many cases, often women. I sometimes wonder whether the best philosophy and poetry, or something like the best, after all these centuries, perhaps waits to be rous'd out yet, or suggested, by the perfect physiological human voice.

SHAKSPERE FOR AMERICA

LET ME send you a supplementary word to that "view" of Shakspere attributed to me, publish'd in your July number,° and so courteously worded by the reviewer (thanks! dear friend.) But you have left out what, perhaps, is the main point, as follows:

"Even the one who at present reigns unquestion'd—of Shakspere —for all he stands for so much in modern literature, he stands entirely for the mighty æsthetic sceptres of the past, not for the spiritual and democratic, the sceptres of the future." (See pp. 55–58 in "November Boughs," and also some of my further notions on Shakspere.)

° This bit was in "Poet-lore" monthly for September, 1890.

The Old World (Europe and Asia) is the region of the poetry of concrete and real things,—the past, the æsthetic, palaces, etiquette, the literature of war and love, the mythological gods, and the myths anyhow. But the New World (America) is the region of the future, and its poetry must be spiritual and democratic. Evolution is not the rule in Nature, in Politics, and Inventions only, but in Verse. I know our age is greatly materialistic, but it is greatly spiritual, too, and the future will be, too. Even what we moderns have come to mean by *spirituality* (while including what the Hebraic utterers, and mainly perhaps all the Greek and other old typical poets, and also the later ones, meant) has so expanded and color'd and vivified the comprehension of the term, that it is quite a different one from the past. Then science, the final critic of all, has the casting vote for future poetry.

"UNASSAIL'D RENOWN"

THE N. Y. *Critic,* Nov: 24, 1889, propounded a circular to several persons, and giving the responses, says, "Walt Whitman's views [as follow] are, naturally, more radical than those of any other contributor to the discussion":

Briefly to answer impromptu your request of Oct : 19—the question whether I think any American poet not now living deserves a place among the thirteen "English inheritors of unassail'd renown" (Chaucer, Spenser, Shakspere, Milton, Dryden, Pope, Gray, Burns, Wordsworth, Coleridge, Byron, Shelley and Keats,)—and which American poets would be truly worthy, &c. Though to me the *deep* of the matter goes down, down beneath. I remember the London *Times* at the time, in opportune, profound and friendly articles on Bryant's and Longfellow's deaths, spoke of the embarrassment, warping effect, and confusion on America (her poets and poetic students) "coming in possession of a great estate they had never lifted a hand to form or earn"; and the further contingency of "the English language ever having annex'd to it a lot of first-class Poetry that would be American, not European"—proving then something precious over all, and beyond valuation. But perhaps that is venturing outside the question. Of the thirteen British immortals mention'd—after placing Shakspere on a sort of pre-eminence of fame not to be invaded yet—the names of Bryant, Emerson, Whittier and Longfellow (with even added names, sometimes Southerners, sometimes Western or other writers of only one or two pieces,) deserve in my opinion an equally high niche of renown as belongs to any on the dozen of that glorious list.

INSCRIPTION FOR A LITTLE BOOK ON GIORDANO BRUNO

As America's mental courage (the thought comes to me to-day) is so indebted, above all current lands and peoples, to the noble army of Old-World martyrs past, how incumbent on us that we clear those martyrs' lives and names, and hold them up for reverent admiration, as well as beacons. And typical of this, and standing for it and all perhaps, Giordano Bruno may well be put, to-day and to come, in our New World's thankfulest heart and memory.   W. W.
    February 24th, 1890.
        Camden, N. J.

SPLINTERS

WHILE I stand in reverence before the fact of Humanity, the People, I will confess, in writing my L of G, the least consideration out of all that has had to do with it has been the consideration of "the public"—at any rate as it now exists. Strange as it may sound for a democrat to say so, I am clear that no free and original and lofty-soaring poem, or one ambitious of those achievements, can possibly be fulfill'd by any writer who has largely in his thought *the public* —or the question, What will establish'd literature—What will the current authorities say about it?

As far as I have sought any, not the best laid out garden or parterre has been my model—but Nature has been. I know that in a sense the garden is nature too, but I had to choose—I could not give both. Besides the gardens are well represented in poetry; while Nature (in letter and in spirit, in the divine essence,) little if at all.

Certainly, (while I have not hit it by a long shot,) I have aim'd at the most ambitious, the best—and sometimes feel to advance that aim (even with all its arrogance) as the most redeeming part of my books. I have never so much cared to feed the esthetic or intellectual palates—but if I could arouse from its slumbers that eligibility in every soul for its own true exercise! if I could only wield that lever!

Out from the well-tended concrete and the physical—and in them and from them only—radiate the spiritual and heroic.

Undoubtedly many points belonging to this essay—perhaps of the greatest necessity, fitness and importance to it—have been left out or forgotten. But the amount of the whole matter—poems, preface and everything—is merely to make one of those little punctures or eye-lets the actors possess in the theatre-curtains to look out upon "the house"—one brief, honest, living glance.

HEALTH (OLD STYLE)

In THAT condition the whole body is elevated to a state by others unknown—inwardly and outwardly illuminated, purified, made solid, strong, yet buoyant. A singular charm, more than beauty, flickers out of, and over, the face—a curious transparency beams in the eyes, both in the iris and the white—the temper partakes also. Nothing that happens—no event, rencontre, weather, etc.—but it is confronted —nothing but is subdued into sustenance—such is the marvellous transformation from the old timorousness and the old process of causes and effects. Sorrows and disappointments cease—there is no more borrowing trouble in advance. A man realizes the venerable myth—he is a god walking the earth, he sees new eligibilities, powers and beauties everywhere; he himself has a new eyesight and hearing. The play of the body in motion takes a previously unknown grace. Merely *to move* is then a happiness, a pleasure—to breathe, to see, is also. All the beforehand gratifications, drink, spirits, coffee, grease, stimulants, mixtures, late hours, luxuries, deeds of the night, seem as vexatious dreams, and now the awakening;—many fall into their natural places, wholesome, conveying diviner joys.

What I append—Health, old style—I have long treasur'd—found originally in some scrap-book fifty years ago—a favorite of mine (but quite a glaring contrast to my present bodily state:)

> On a high rock above the vast abyss,
>   Whose solid base tumultuous waters lave;
> Whose airy high-top balmy breezes kiss,
>   Fresh from the white foam of the circling wave—
>
> There ruddy HEALTH, in rude majestic state,
>   His clust'ring forelock combatting the winds—
> Bares to each season's change his breast elate,
>   And still fresh vigor from th' encounter finds:
>
> With mighty mind to every fortune braced,
>   To every climate each corporeal power,
> And high-proof heart, impenetrably cased,
>   He mocks the quick transitions of the hour.
>
> Now could he hug bleak Zembla's bolted snow,
>   Now to Arabia's heated deserts turn,
> Yet bids the biting blast more fiercely blow,
>   The scorching sun without abatement burn.

There this bold Outlaw, rising with the morn,
  His sinewy functions fitted for the toil,
Pursues, with tireless steps, the rapturous horn,
  And bears in triumph back the shaggy spoil.

Or, on his rugged range of towering hills,
  Turns the stiff glebe behind his hardy team;
His wide-spread heaths to blithest measures tills,
  And boasts the joys of life are not a dream!

Then to his airy hut, at eve, retires,
  Clasps to his open breast his buxom spouse,
Basks in his faggot's blaze, his passions fires,
  And strait supine to rest unbroken bows.

On his smooth forehead, Time's old annual score,
  Tho' left to furrow, yet disdains to lie;
He bids weak sorrow tantalize no more,
  And puts the cup of care contemptuous by.

If, from some inland height, that, skirting, bears
  Its rude encroachments far into the vale,
He views where poor dishonor'd nature wears
  On her soft cheek alone the lily pale;

How will he scorn alliance with the race,
  Those aspin shoots that shiver at a breath;
Children of sloth, that danger dare not face,
  And find in life but an extended death:

Then from the silken reptiles will he fly,
  To the bold cliff in bounding transports run,
And stretch'd o'er many a wave his ardent eye,
  Embrace the enduring Sea-Boy as his son!

Yes! thine alone—from pain, from sorrow free,
  The lengthen'd life with peerless joys replete;
Then let me, Lord of Mountains, share with thee
  The hard, the early toil—the relaxation sweet.

GAY-HEARTEDNESS

WALKING on the old Navy Yard bridge, Washington, D. C., once with a companion, Mr. Marshall, from England, a great traveler and observer, as a squad of laughing young black girls pass'd us—then two copper-color'd boys, one good-looking lad 15 or 16, barefoot, running after—"What *gay creatures* they all appear to be," said Mr. M. Then we fell to talking about the general lack of buoyant animal spirits. "I think," said Mr. M., "that in all my travels, and all my intercourse with people of every and any class, especially the culti- vated ones, (the literary and fashionable folks,) I have never yet come across what I should call a really GAY-HEARTED MAN."

It was a terrible criticism—cut into me like a surgeon's lance. Made me silent the whole walk home.

AS IN A SWOON

As IN a swoon, one instant,
Another sun, ineffable, full-dazzles me,
And all the orbs I knew—and brighter, unknown orbs;
One instant of the future land, Heaven's land.

L OF G

THOUGHTS, suggestions, aspirations, pictures,
Cities and farms—by day and night—book of peace and war,
Of platitudes and of the commonplace.

For out-door health, the land and sea—for good will,
For America—for all the earth, all nations, the common people,
(Not of one nation only—not America only.)

In it each claim, ideal, line, by all lines, claims, ideals, temper'd;
Each right and wish by other wishes, rights.

AFTER THE ARGUMENT

A GROUP of little children with their ways and chatter flow in,
Like welcome rippling water o'er my heated nerves and flesh.

FOR US TWO, READER DEAR

SIMPLE, spontaneous, curious, two souls interchanging,
With the original testimony for us continued to the last.

→≫·≪←

MEMORANDA

*[Let me indeed turn upon myself a little of the light I have been so
fond of casting on others.*

*Of course these few exceptional later mems are far far short of
one's concluding history or thoughts or life-giving—only a hap-hazard
pinch of all. But the old Greek proverb put it, "Any body who really
has a good quality" (or bad one either, I guess) "has all." There's
something in the proverb; but you mustn't carry it too far.*

*I will not reject any theme or subject because the treatment is too
personal. As my stuff settles into shape, I am told (and sometimes
myself discover, uneasily, but feel all right about it in calmer moments) it is mainly autobiographic, and even egotistic after all—
which I finally accept, and am contented so.*

*If this little volume betrays, as it doubtless does, a weakening
hand, and decrepitude, remember it is knit together out of accumulated sickness, inertia, physical disablement, acute pain, and listlessness. My fear will be that at last my pieces show indooredness,
and being chain'd to a chair—as never before. Only the resolve to
keep up, and on, and to add a remnant, and even perhaps obstinately
see what failing powers and decay may contribute too, have produced it.*

*And now as from some fisherman's net hauling all sorts, and dis-
bursing the same.]*

A WORLD'S SHOW

New York, Great Exposition open'd in 1853.—I went a long time
(nearly a year)—days and nights—especially the latter—as it was
finely lighted, and had a very large and copious exhibition gallery
of paintings (shown at best at night, I tho't)—hundreds of pictures
from Europe, many masterpieces—all an exhaustless study—and,
scatter'd thro' the building, sculptures, single figures or groups—
among the rest, Thorwaldsen's "Apostles," colossal in size—and very
many fine bronzes, pieces of plate from English silversmiths, and
curios from everywhere abroad—with woods from all lands of the
earth—all sorts of fabrics and products and handiwork from the
workers of all nations.

NEW YORK—THE BAY—THE OLD NAME

Commencement of a gossipy travelling letter in a New York city paper, May 10, 1879.—My month's visit is about up; but before I get back to Camden let me print some jottings of the last four weeks. Have you not, reader dear, among your intimate friends, some one, temporarily absent, whose letters to you, avoiding all the big topics and disquisitions, give only minor, gossipy sights and scenes—just as they come—subjects disdain'd by solid writers, but interesting to you because they were such as happen to everybody, and were the moving entourage to your friend—to his or her steps, eyes, mentality? Well, with an idea something of that kind, I suppose, I set out on the following hurrygraphs of a breezy early-summer visit to New-York City and up the North River—especially at present of some hours along Broadway.

What I came to New York for.—To try the experiment of a lecture —to see whether I could stand it, and whether an audience could— was my specific object. Some friends had invited me—it was by no means clear how it would end—I stipulated that they should get only a third-rate hall, and not sound the advertising trumpets a bit —and so I started. I much wanted something to do for occupation, consistent with my limping and paralyzed state. And now, since it came off, and since neither my hearers nor I myself really collaps'd at the aforesaid lecture, I intend to go up and down the land (in moderation,) seeking whom I may devour, with lectures, and reading of my own poems—short pulls, however—never exceeding an hour.

Crossing from Jersey City, 5 to 6 p. m.—The city part of the North River with its life, breadth, peculiarities—the amplitude of sea and wharf, cargo and commerce—one don't realize them till one has been away a long time and, as now returning, (crossing from Jersey City to Desbrosses-st.,) gazes on the unrivall'd panorama, and far down the thin-vapor'd vistas of the bay, toward the Narrows—or northward up the Hudson—or on the ample spread and infinite variety, free and floating, of the more immediate views—a countless river series—everything moving, yet so easy, and such plenty of room! Little, I say, do folks here appreciate the most ample, eligible, picturesque bay and estuary surroundings in the world! This is the third time such a conviction has come to me after absence, returning to New-York, dwelling on its magnificent entrances—approaching the city by them from any point.

More and more, too, the *old name* absorbs into me—MANNAHATTA, "the place encircled by many swift tides and sparkling waters." How fit a name for America's great democratic island city! The word itself, how beautiful! how aboriginal! how it seems to rise with tall spires, glistening in sunshine, with such New World atmosphere, vista and action!

A SICK SPELL

Christmas Day, 25th Dec., 1888.—Am somewhat easier and freer to-day and the last three days—sit up most of the time—read and write, and receive my visitors. Have now been in-doors sick for seven months—half of the time bad, bad, vertigo, indigestion, bladder, gastric, head trouble, inertia—Dr. Bucke, Dr. Osler, Drs. Wharton and Walsh—now Edward Wilkins my help and nurse. A fine, splendid, sunny day. My "November Boughs" is printed and out; and my "Complete Works, Poems and Prose," a big volume, 900 pages, also. It is ab't noon, and I sit here pretty comfortable.

TO BE PRESENT ONLY

At the Complimentary Dinner, Camden, New Jersey, May 31, 1889.—Walt Whitman said:

My friends, though announced to give an address, there is no such intention. Following the impulse of the spirit, (for I am at least half of Quaker stock) I have obey'd the command to come and look at you, for a minute, and show myself, face to face; which is probably the best I can do. But I have felt no command to make a speech; and shall not therefore attempt any. All I have felt the imperative conviction to say I have already printed in my books of poems or prose; to which I refer any who may be curious. And so, hail and farewell. Deeply acknowledging this deep compliment, with my best respects and love to you personally—to Camden—to New-Jersey, and to all represented here—you must excuse me from any word further.

F'm Pall-Mall Gazette, London, England, Feb. 8, 1890

"INTESTINAL AGITATION"

MR. ERNEST RHYS has just receiv'd an interesting letter from Walt Whitman, dated "Camden, January 22, 1890." The following is an extract from it:

I am still here—no very mark'd or significant change or happening —fairly buoyant spirits, &c.—but surely, slowly ebbing. At this moment sitting here, in my den, Mickle Street, by the oakwood fire, in the same big strong old chair with wolf-skin spread over back—bright sun, cold, dry winter day. America continues—is generally busy enough all over her vast demesnes (intestinal agitation I call it,) talking, plodding, making money, every one trying to get on—perhaps to get towards the top—but no special individual signalism —(just as well, I guess.)

"WALT WHITMAN'S LAST 'PUBLIC'"

THE GAY and crowded audience at the Art Rooms, Philadelphia, Tuesday night, April 15, 1890, says a correspondent of the Boston *Transcript*, April 19, might not have thought that W. W. crawl'd out of a sick bed a few hours before, crying,

> Dangers retreat when boldly they're confronted,

and went over, hoarse and half blind, to deliver his memoranda and essay on the death of Abraham Lincoln, on the twenty-fifth anniversary of that tragedy. He led off with the following new paragraph:

Of Abraham Lincoln, bearing testimony twenty-five years after his death—and of that death—I am now my friends before you. Few realize the days, the great historic and esthetic personalities, with him in the centre, we pass'd through. Abraham Lincoln, familiar, our own, an Illinoisian, modern, yet tallying ancient Moses, Joshua, Ulysses, or later Cromwell, and grander in some respects than any of them; Abraham Lincoln, that makes the like of Homer, Plutarch, Shakspere, eligible our day or any day. My subject this evening for forty or fifty minutes' talk is the death of this man, and how that death will really filter into America. I am not going to tell you anything new; and it is doubtless nearly altogether because I ardently wish to commemorate the hour and martyrdom and name I am here. Oft as the rolling years bring back this hour, let it again, however briefly, be dwelt upon. For my own part I hope and intend till my own dying day, whenever the 14th or 15th of April comes, to annually gather a few friends and hold its tragic reminiscence. No narrow or sectional reminiscence. It belongs to these States in their entirety—not the North only, but the South—perhaps belongs most tenderly and devoutly to the South, of all; for there really this man's birthstock; there and then his antecedent stamp. Why should I not say that thence his manliest traits, his universality, his canny, easy ways and words upon the surface—his inflexible determination at heart? Have you ever realized it, my friends, that Lincoln, though grafted on the West, is essentially in personnel and character a Southern contribution?

The most of the poet's address was devoted to the actual occurrences and details of the murder. We believe the delivery on Tuesday was Whitman's thirteenth of it. The old poet is now physically wreck'd. But his voice and magnetism are the same. For the last month he has been under a severe attack of the lately prevailing influenza, the grip, in accumulation upon his previous ailments, and, above all, that terrible paralysis, the bequest of Secession War times. He was dress'd last Tuesday night in an entire suit of French Canadian grey wool cloth, with broad shirt collar, with no necktie; long white hair, red face, full beard and moustache, and look'd as though he might weigh two hundred pounds. He had to be help'd and led every step. In five weeks more he will begin his seventy-second year. He is still writing a little.

From the Camden Post, N. J., June 2, 1890

INGERSOLL'S SPEECH

He attends and makes a speech at the celebration of Walt Whitman's birthday.—Walt Whitman is now in his seventy-second year. His younger friends, literary and personal, men and women, gave him a complimentary supper last Saturday night, to note the close of his seventy-first year, and the late curious and unquestionable "boom" of the old man's wide-spreading popularity, and that of his "Leaves of Grass." There were thirty-five in the room, mostly young, but some old, or beginning to be. The great feature was Ingersoll's utterance. It was probably, in its way, the most admirable specimen of modern oratory hitherto delivered in the English language, immense as such praise may sound. It was 40 to 50 minutes long, altogether without notes, in a good voice, low enough and not too low, style easy, rather colloquial (over and over again saying "you" to Whitman who sat opposite,) sometimes markedly impassion'd, once or twice humorous—amid his whole speech, from interior fires and volition, pulsating and swaying like a first-class Andalusian dancer.

And such a critical dissection, and flattering summary! The Whitmanites for the first time in their lives were fully satisfied; and that is saying a good deal, for they have not put their claims low, by a long shot. Indeed it was a tremendous talk! Physically and mentally Ingersoll (he had been working all day in New York, talking in court and in his office,) is now at his best, like mellow'd wine, or a just ripe apple; to the artist-sense, too, looks at his best—not merely like a bequeath'd Roman bust or fine smooth marble Cicero-head, or even Greek Plato; for he is modern and vital and vein'd and American, and (far more than the age knows,) justifies us all.

We cannot give a full report of this most remarkable talk and supper (which was curiously conversational and Greek-like) but must add the following significant bit of it.

After the speaking, and just before the close, Mr. Whitman reverted to Colonel Ingersoll's tribute to his poems, pronouncing it the cap-sheaf of all commendation that he had ever receiv'd. Then, his mind still dwelling upon the Colonel's religious doubts, he went on to say that what he himself had in his mind when he wrote "Leaves of Grass" was not only to depict American life, as it existed, and to show the triumphs of science, and the poetry in common things, and the full of an individual democratic humanity, for the aggregate, but also to show that there was behind all something which rounded and completed it. "For what," he ask'd, "would this life be without immortality? It would be as a locomotive, the greatest triumph of modern science, with no train to draw after it. If the spiritual is not behind the material, to what purpose is the material? What is this world without a further Divine purpose in it all?"

Colonel Ingersoll repeated his former argument in reply.

FEELING FAIRLY

Friday, July 27, 1890.—Feeling fairly these days, and even jovial—sleep and appetite good enough to be thankful for—had a dish of Maryland blackberries, some good rye bread and a cup of tea, for my breakfast—relish'd all—fine weather—bright sun to-day—pleasant north-west breeze blowing in the open window as I sit here in my big rattan chair—two great fine roses (white and red, blooming, fragrant, sent by mail by W. S. K. and wife, Mass.) are in a glass of water on the table before me.

Am now in my 72d year.

OLD BROOKLYN DAYS

IT MUST have been in 1822 or '3 that I first came to live in Brooklyn. Lived first in Front street, not far from what was then call'd "the New Ferry," wending the river from the foot of Catharine (or Main) street to New York City.

I was a little child (was born in 1819,) but tramp'd freely about the neighborhood and town, even then; was often on the aforesaid New Ferry; remember how I was petted and deadheaded by the gatekeepers and deckhands (all such fellows are kind to little children,) and remember the horses that seem'd to me so queer as they trudg'd around in the central houses of the boats, making the water-power. (For it was just on the eve of the steam-engine, which was soon after introduced on the ferries.) Edward Copeland (afterward Mayor) had a grocery store then at the corner of Front and Catharine streets.

Presently we Whitmans all moved up to Tillary street, near Adams, where my father, who was a carpenter, built a house for himself and us all. It was from here I 'assisted' the personal coming of Lafayette in 1824–5 to Brooklyn. He came over the Old Ferry, as the now Fulton Ferry (partly navigated quite up to that day by 'horse boats,' though the first steamer had begun to be used hereabouts) was then call'd, and was receiv'd at the foot of Fulton street. It was on that occasion that the corner-stone of the Apprentices' Library, at the corner of Cranberry and Henry streets—since pull'd down—was laid by Lafayette's own hands. Numerous children arrived on the grounds, of whom I was one, and were assisted by several gentlemen to safe spots to view the ceremony. Among others, Lafayette, also helping the children, took me up—I was five years old, press'd me a moment to his breast—gave me a kiss and set me down in a safe spot. Lafayette was at that time between sixty-five and seventy years of age, with a manly figure and a kind face.

TWO QUESTIONS

An EDITOR of (or in) a leading monthly magazine (Harper's Monthly, July, 1890,) asks: "A hundred years from now will W. W. be popularly rated a great poet—or will he be forgotten?" . . . A mighty ticklish question—which can only be left for a hundred years hence—perhaps more than that. But whether W. W. has been mainly rejected by his own times is an easier question to answer.

All along from 1860 to '91, many of the pieces in L of G, and its annexes, were first sent to publishers or magazine editors before being printed in the L, and were peremptorily rejected by them, and sent back to their author. The "Eidōlons" was sent back by Dr. H., of "Scribner's Monthly" with a lengthy, very insulting and contemptuous letter. "To the Sun-Set Breeze," was rejected by the editor of "Harper's Monthly" as being "an improvisation" only. "On, on ye jocund twain" was rejected by the "Century" editor as being personal merely. Several of the pieces went the rounds of all the monthlies, to be thus summarily rejected.

June, '90.—The ——— rejects and sends back my little poem, so I am now set out in the cold by every big magazine and publisher, and may as well understand and admit it—which is just as well, for I find I am palpably losing my sight and ratiocination.

PREFACE TO A VOLUME OF ESSAYS AND
TALES BY WM. D. O'CONNOR

Pub'd posthumously in 1891

A HASTY memorandum, not particularly for Preface to the following tales, but to put on record my respect and affection for as sane, beautiful, cute, tolerant, loving, candid and free and fair-intention'd a nature as ever vivified our race.

In Boston, 1860, I first met WILLIAM DOUGLAS O'CONNOR.* As I saw and knew him then, in his 29th year, and for twenty-five further years along, he was a gallant, handsome, gay-hearted, fine-voiced, glowing-eyed man; lithe-moving on his feet, of healthy and magnetic atmosphere and presence, and the most welcome company in the world. He was a thorough-going anti-slavery believer, speaker and writer, (doctrinaire,) and though I took a fancy to him from the first, I remember I fear'd his ardent abolitionism—was afraid it would probably keep us apart. (I was a decided and out-spoken anti-slavery believer myself, then and always; but shy'd from the extremists, the red-hot fellows of those times.) O'C. was then correcting the proofs of *Harrington,* an eloquent and fiery novel he had written, and which was printed just before the commencement of the Secession War. He was already married, the father of two fine little children, and was personally and intellectually the most attractive man I had ever met.

Last of '62 I found myself led towards the war-field—went to Washington City—(to become absorb'd in the armies, and in the big hospitals, and to get work in one of the Departments,)—and there I met and resumed friendship, and found warm hospitality from O'C. and his noble New England wife. They had just lost by death their little child-boy, Philip; and O'C. was yet feeling serious about it. The youngster had been vaccinated against the threatening of small-pox which alarm'd the city; but somehow it led to worse results than it was intended to ward off—or at any rate O'C. thought that proved the cause of the boy's death. He had one child left, a fine bright little daughter, and a great comfort to her parents. (Dear Jeannie! She grew up a most accomplish'd and superior young woman—declined in health, and died about 1881.)

On through for months and years to '73 I saw and talk'd with

* Born Jan. 2d, 1832. When grown, lived several years in Boston, and edited journals and magazines there—went about 1861 to Washington, D. C., and became a U. S. clerk, first in the Light-House Bureau, and then in the U. S. Life-Saving Service, in which branch he was Assistant Superintendent for many years—sicken'd in 1887—died there at Washington, May 9th, 1889.

O'C. almost daily. I had soon got employment, first for a short time in the Indian Bureau (in the Interior Department,) and then for a long while in the Attorney General's Office. The Secession War, with its tide of varying fortunes, excitements—President Lincoln and the daily sight of him—the doings in Congress and at the State Capitals—the news from the fields and campaigns, and from foreign governments—my visits to the Army Hospitals, daily and nightly, soon absorbing everything else,—with a hundred matters, occurrences, personalities,—(Greeley, Wendell Phillips, the parties, the Abolitionists, &c.)—were the subjects of our talk and discussion. I am not sure from what I heard then, but O'C. was cut out for a first-class public speaker or forensic advocate. No audience or jury could have stood out against him. He had a strange charm of physiologic voice. He had a power and sharp-cut faculty of statement and persuasiveness beyond any man's else. I know it well, for I have felt it many a time. If not as orator, his forte was as critic, newer, deeper than any: also, as literary author. One of his traits was that while he knew all, and welcom'd all sorts of great *genre* literature, all lands and times, from all writers and artists, and not only tolerated each, and defended every attack'd literary person with a skill or heart-catholicism that I never saw equal'd—invariably advocated and excused them—he kept an idiosyncrasy and identity of his own very mark'd, and without special tinge or undue color from any source. He always applauded the freedom of the masters, whence and whoever. I remember his special defences of Byron, Burns, Poe, Rabelais, Victor Hugo, George Sand, and others. There was always a little touch of pensive cadence in his superb voice; and I think there was something of the same sadness in his temperament and nature. Perhaps, too, in his literary structure. But he was a very buoyant, jovial, good-natured companion.

So much for a hasty melanged reminiscence and note of William O'Connor, my dear, dear friend, and staunch, (probably my staunchest) literary believer and champion from the first, and throughout without halt or demur, for twenty-five years. No better friend—none more reliable through this life of one's ups and downs. On the occurrence of the latter he would be sure to make his appearance on the scene, eager, hopeful, full of fight like a perfect knight of chivalry. For he was a born sample here in the 19th century of the flower and symbol of olden time first-class knighthood. Thrice blessed be his memory!   W. W.

F'm the Engineering Record, New York, Dec. 13, 1890

AN ENGINEER'S OBITUARY

THOMAS JEFFERSON WHITMAN was born July 18, 1833, in Brooklyn, N. Y., from a father of English stock, and mother (Louisa Van Velsor) descended from Dutch (Holland) immigration. His early years were spent on Long Island, either in the country or Brooklyn. As a lad he show'd a tendency for surveying and civil engineering, and about at 19 went with Chief Kirkwood, who was then prospecting and outlining for the great city water-works. He remain'd at that construction throughout, was a favorite and confidant of the Chief, and was successively promoted. He continued also under Chief Moses Lane. He married in 1859, and not long after was invited by the Board of Public Works of St. Louis, Missouri, to come there and plan and build a new and fitting water-works for that great city. Whitman accepted the call, and moved and settled there, and had been a resident of St. Louis ever since. He plann'd and built the works, which were very successful, and remain'd as superintendent and chief for nearly 20 years.

Of the last six years he has been largely occupied as consulting engineer (divested of his cares and position in St. Louis,) and has engaged in public constructions, bridges, sewers, &c., West and Southwest, and especially the Memphis, Tenn., city water-works.

Thomas J. Whitman was a theoretical and practical mechanic of superior order, founded in the soundest personal and professional integrity. He was a great favorite among the young engineers and students; not a few of them yet remaining in Kings and Queens Counties, and New York City, will remember "Jeff," with old-time good-will and affection. He was mostly self-taught, and was a hard student.

He had been troubled of late years from a bad throat and from gastric affection, tending on typhoid, and had been rather seriously ill with the last malady, but was getting over the worst of it, when he succumb'd under a sudden and severe attack of the heart. He died at St. Louis, November 25, 1890, in his 58th year. Of his family, the wife died in 1873, and a daughter, Mannahatta, died two years ago. Another daughter, Jessie Louisa, the only child left, is now living in St. Louis.

[When Jeff was born I was in my 15th year, and had much care of him for many years afterward, and he did not separate from me. He was a very handsome, healthy, affectionate, smart child, and would sit on my lap or hang on my neck half an hour at a time. As he grew a big boy he liked outdoor and water sports, especially boating. We would often go down summers to Peconic Bay, east end of Long Island, and over to Shelter Island. I loved long rambles, and he carried his fowling-piece. O, what happy times, weeks! Then in Brooklyn and New York City he learn'd printing, and work'd awhile at it; but eventually (with my approval) he went to employment at land surveying, and merged in the studies and work of topographical engineer; this satisfied him, and he continued at it. He was of noble nature from the first; very good-natured, very plain, very friendly. O, how we loved each other—how many jovial good times we had! Once we made a long trip from New York City down over the Allegheny Mountains (the National Road) and via the Ohio and Mississippi Rivers, from Cairo to New Orleans.]

God's blessing on your name and memory, dear brother Jeff!

W. W.

OLD ACTORS, SINGERS, SHOWS, &c., IN NEW YORK

Flitting mention—(with much left out)

SEEMS TO ME I ought acknowledge my debt to actors, singers, public speakers, conventions, and the Stage in New York, my youthful days, from 1835 onward—say to '60 or '61—and to plays and operas generally. (Which nudges a pretty big disquisition: of course it should be all elaborated and penetrated more deeply—but I will here give only some flitting mentionings of my youth.) Seems to me now when I look back, the Italian contralto Marietta Alboni (she is living yet, in Paris, 1891, in good condition, good voice yet, considering) with the then prominent histrions Booth, Edwin Forrest, and Fanny Kemble and the Italian singer Bettini, have had the deepest and most lasting effect upon me. I should like well if Madame Alboni and the old composer Verdi, (and Bettini the tenor, if he is living) could know how much noble pleasure and happiness they gave me, and how deeply I always remember them and thank them to this day. For theatricals in literature and doubtless upon me personally, including opera, have been of course serious factors. (The experts and musicians of my present friends claim that the new Wagner and his pieces belong far more truly to me, and I to them. Very likely. But I was fed and bred under the Italian dispensation, and absorb'd it, and doubtless show it.)

As a young fellow, when possible I always studied a play or libretto quite carefully over, by myself, (sometimes twice through)

before seeing it on the stage; read it the day or two days before.
Tried both ways—not reading some beforehand; but I found I
gain'd most by getting that sort of mastery first, if the piece had
depth. (Surface effects and glitter were much less thought of I am
sure those times.) There were many fine old plays, neither tragedies nor comedies—the names of them quite unknown to to-day's
current audiences. "All is not Gold that Glitters," in which Charlotte Cushman had a superbly enacted part, was of that kind. C. C.,
who revel'd in them, was great in such pieces; I think better than in
the heavy popular rôles.

We had some fine music those days. We had the English opera
of "Cinderella" (with Henry Placide as the pompous old father, an
unsurpassable bit of comedy and music.) We had Bombastes Furi-
oso. Must have been in 1844 (or '5) I saw Charles Kean and Mrs.
Kean (Ellen Tree)—saw them in the Park in Shakspere's "King
John." He, of course, was the chief character. She play'd *Queen
Constance.* Tom Hamblin was *Faulconbridge,* and probably the
best ever on the stage. It was an immense show-piece, too; lots of
grand set scenes and fine armor-suits and all kinds of appointments
imported from London (where it had been first render'd.) The
large brass bands—the three or four hundred "supes"—the interviews between the French and English armies—the talk with *Hubert*
(and the hot irons) the delicious acting of *Prince Arthur* (Mrs.
Richardson, I think)—and all the fine *blare* and court pomp—I remember to this hour. The death-scene of the King in the orchard of
Swinstead Abbey, was very effective. Kean rush'd in, gray-pale and
yellow, and threw himself on a lounge in the open. His pangs were
horribly realistic. (He must have taken lessons in some hospital.)

Fanny Kemble play'd to wonderful effect in such pieces as
"Fazio, or the Italian wife." The turning-point was jealousy. It was
a rapid-running, yet heavy-timber'd, tremendous wrenching, passionate play. Such old pieces always seem'd to me built like an
ancient ship of the line, solid and lock'd from keel up—oak and
metal and knots. One of the finest characters was a great court lady,
Aldabella, enacted by Mrs. Sharpe. O how it all entranced us, and
knock'd us about, as the scenes swept on like a cyclone!

Saw Hackett at the old Park many times, and remember him
well. His renderings were first-rate in everything. He inaugurated
the true "Rip Van Winkle," and look'd and acted and dialogued it
to perfection (he was of Dutch breed, and brought up among old
Holland descendants in Kings and Queens counties, Long Island.)
The play and the acting of it have been adjusted to please popular

audiences since; but there was in that original performance certainly something of a far higher order, more art, more reality, more resemblance, a bit of fine pathos, a lofty *brogue*, beyond anything afterward.

One of my big treats was the rendering at the old Park of Shakspere's "Tempest" in musical version. There was a very fine instrumental band, not numerous, but with a capital leader. Mrs. Austin was the *Ariel*, and Peter Richings the *Caliban*; both excellent. The drunken song of the latter has probably been never equal'd. The perfect actor Clarke (old Clarke) was *Prospero*.

Yes; there were in New York and Brooklyn some fine nontechnical singing performances, concerts, such as the Hutchinson band, three brothers, and the sister, the red-cheek'd New England carnation, sweet Abby; sometimes plaintive and balladic—sometimes anti-slavery, anti-calomel, and comic. There were concerts by Templeton, Russell, Dempster, the old Alleghanian band, and many others. Then we had lots of "negro minstrels," with capital character songs and voices. I often saw Rice the original "Jim Crow" at the old Park Theatre filling up the gap in some short bill—and the wild chants and dances were admirable—probably ahead of anything since. Every theatre had some superior voice, and it was common to give a favorite song between the acts. "The Sea" at the bijou Olympic, (Broadway near Grand,) was always welcome from a little Englishman named Edwin, a good balladist. At the Bowery the loves of "Sweet William,"

When on the Downs the fleet was moor'd,

always bro't an encore, and sometimes a treble.

I remember Jenny Lind and heard her (1850 I think) several times. She had the most brilliant, captivating, popular musical style and expression of any one known; (the canary, and several other sweet birds are wondrous fine—but there is something in song that goes deeper—isn't there?)

The great "Egyptian Collection" was well up in Broadway, and I got quite acquainted with Dr. Abbott, the proprietor—paid many visits there, and had long talks with him, in connection with my readings of many books and reports on Egypt—its antiquities, history, and how things and the scenes really look, and what the old relics stand for, as near as we can now get. (Dr. A. was an Englishman of say 54—had been settled in Cairo as physician for 25 years, and all that time was collecting these relics, and sparing no time or money seeking and getting them. By advice and for a change of base for himself, he brought the collection to America. But the whole enterprise was a fearful disappointment, in the pay and commercial part.) As said, I went to the Egyptian Museum many many times; sometimes had it all to myself—delved at the formidable catalogue—and on several occasions had the invaluable personal talk, correction, illustration and guidance of Dr. A. himself. He was very kind and helpful to me in those studies and examinations; once, by appointment, he appear'd in full and exact Turkish (Cairo) costume, which long usage there had made habitual to him.

One of the choice places of New York to me then was the "Phrenological Cabinet" of Fowler & Wells, Nassau street near Beekman. Here were all the busts, examples, curios and books of that study obtainable. I went there often, and once for myself had a very elaborate and leisurely examination and "chart of bumps" written out (I have it yet,) by Nelson Fowler (or was it Sizer?) there.

And who remembers the renown'd New York "Tabernacle" of those days "before the war"? It was on the east side of Broadway, near Pearl street—was a great turtle-shaped hall, and you had to walk back from the street entrance, thro' a long wide corridor to get to it—was very strong—had an immense gallery—altogether held three or four thousand people. Here the huge annual conventions of the windy and cyclonic "reformatory societies" of those times were held—especially the tumultuous Anti-Slavery ones. I remember hearing Wendell Phillips, Emerson, Cassius Clay, John P. Hale, Beecher, Fred Douglas, the Burleighs, Garrison, and others. Sometimes the Hutchinsons would sing—very fine. Sometimes there were angry rows. A chap named Isaiah Rhynders, a fierce politician of those days, with a band of robust supporters, would attempt to contradict the speakers and break up the meetings. But the Anti-Slavery, and Quaker, and Temperance, and Missionary and other conventicles and speakers were tough, tough, and always maintained their ground, and carried out their programs fully. I went frequently to these meetings, May after May—learn'd much from them—was sure to be on hand when J. P. Hale or Cash Clay made speeches.

There were also the smaller and handsome halls of the Historical and Athenæum Societies up on Broadway. I very well remember W. C. Bryant lecturing on Homœopathy in one of them, and attending two or three addresses by R. W. Emerson in the other.

There was a series of plays and dramatic *genre* characters by a gentleman bill'd as Ranger—very fine, better than merely technical, full of exquisite shades, like the light touches of the violin in the hands of a master. There was the actor Anderson, who brought us

Gerald Griffin's "Gisippus," and play'd it to admiration. Among the actors of those times I recall: Cooper, Wallack, Tom Hamblin, Adams (several), Old Gates, Scott, Wm. Sefton, John Sefton, Geo. Jones, Mitchell, Seguin, Old Clarke, Richings, Fisher, H. Placide, T. Placide, Thorne, Ingersoll, Gale (Mazeppa) Edwin, Horncastle. Some of the women hastily remember'd were: Mrs. Vernon, Mrs. Pritchard, Mrs. McClure, Mary Taylor, Clara Fisher, Mrs. Richardson, Mrs. Flynn. Then the singers, English, Italian and other: Mrs. Wood, Mrs. Seguin, Mrs. Austin, Grisi, La Grange, Steffanone, Bosio, Truffi, Parodi, Vestvali, Bertucca, Jenny Lind, Gazzaniga, Laborde. And the opera men: Bettini, Badiali, Marini, Mario, Brignoli, Amodio, Beneventano, and many, many others whose names I do not at this moment recall.

In another paper I have described the elder Booth, and the Bowery Theatre of those times. Afterward there was the Chatham. The elder Thorne, Mrs. Thorne, William and John Sefton, Kirby, Brougham, and sometimes Edwin Forrest himself play'd there. I remember them all, and many more, and especially the fine theatre on Broadway near Pearl, in 1855 and '6.

There were very good circus performances, or horsemanship, in New York and Brooklyn. Every winter in the first-named city, a regular place in the Bowery, nearly opposite the old theatre; fine animals and fine riding, which I often witness'd. (Remember seeing near here, a young, fierce, splendid lion, presented by an African Barbary Sultan to President Andrew Jackson. The gift comprised also a lot of jewels, a fine steel sword, and an Arab stallion; and the lion was made over to a show-man.)

If it is worth while I might add that there was a small but well-appointed amateur-theatre up Broadway, with the usual stage, orchestra, pit, boxes, &c., and that I was myself a member for some time, and acted parts in it several times—"second parts" as they were call'd. Perhaps it too was a lesson, or help'd that way; at any rate it was full of fun and enjoyment.

And so let us turn off the gas. Out in the brilliancy of the footlights—filling the attention of perhaps a crowded audience, and making many a breath and pulse swell and rise—O so much passion and imparted life!—over and over again, the season through—walking, gesticulating, singing, reciting his or her part—But then sooner or later inevitably wending to the flies or exit door—vanishing to sight and ear—and never materializing on this earth's stage again!

SOME PERSONAL AND OLD-AGE
JOTTINGS

ANYTHING like unmitigated acceptance of my *Leaves of Grass* book, and heart-felt response to it, in a popular however faint degree, bubbled forth as a fresh spring from the ground in England in 1876. The time was a critical and turning point in my personal and literary life. Let me revert to my memorandum book, Camden, New Jersey, that year, fill'd with addresses, receipts, purchases, &c., of the two volumes pub'd then by myself—the *Leaves,* and the *Two Rivulets*—some home customers for them, but mostly from the British Islands. I was seriously paralyzed from the Secession war, poor, in debt, was expecting death, (the doctors put four chances out of five against me,)—and I had the books printed during the lingering interim to occupy the tediousness of glum days and nights. Curiously, the sale abroad proved prompt, and what one might call copious: the names came in lists and the money with them, by foreign mail. The price was $10 a set. Both the cash and the emotional cheer were deep medicines; many paid double or treble price, (Tennyson and Ruskin did,) and many sent kind and eulogistic letters; ladies, clergymen, social leaders, persons of rank, and high officials. Those blessed gales from the British Islands probably (certainly) saved me. Here are some of the names, for I w'd like to preserve them: Wm. M. and D. G. Rossetti, Lord Houghton, Edwd. Dowden, Mrs. Ann Gilchrist, Keningale Cook, Edwd. Carpenter, Therese Simpson, Rob't Buchanan, Alfred Tennyson, John Ruskin, C. G. Oates, E. T. Wilkinson, T. L. Warren, C. W. Reynell, W. B. Scott, A. G. Dew Smith, E. W. Gosse, T. W. Rolleston, Geo. Wallis, Rafe Leicester, Thos. Dixon, N. MacColl, Mrs. Matthews, R. Hannah, Geo. Saintsbury, R. S. Watson, Godfrey and Vernon Lushington, G. H. Lewes, G. H. Boughton, Geo. Fraser, W. T. Arnold, A. Ireland, Mrs. M. Taylor, M. D. Conway, Benj. Eyre, E. Dannreather, Rev. T. E. Brown, C. W. Sheppard, E. J. A. Balfour, P. B. Marston, A. C. De Burgh, J. H. McCarthy, J. H. Ingram, Rev. R. P. Graves, Lady Mount-temple, F. S. Ellis, W. Brockie, Rev. A. B. Grosart, Lady Hardy, Hubert Herkomer, Francis Hueffer, H. G. Dakyns, R. L. Nettleship, W. J. Stillman, Miss Blind, Madox Brown, H. R. Ricardo, Messrs. O'Grady and Tyrrel; and many, many more.

Severely scann'd, it was perhaps no very great or vehement success; but the tide had palpably shifted at any rate, and the sluices were turn'd into my own veins and pockets. That emotional, audacious, open-handed, friendly-mouth'd just-opportune English action, I say, pluck'd me like a brand from the burning, and gave me life again, to finish my book, since ab't completed. I do not forget it, and shall not; and if I ever have a biographer I charge him to put it in the narrative. I have had the noblest friends and backers in America; Wm. O'Connor, Dr. R. M. Bucke, John Burroughs, Geo. W. Childs, good ones in Boston, and Carnegie and R. G. Ingersoll in New York; and yet perhaps the tenderest and gratefulest breath of my heart has gone, and ever goes, over the sea-gales across the big pond.

About myself at present. I will soon enter upon my 73d year, if I live—have pass'd an active life, as country school-teacher, gardener, printer, carpenter, author and journalist, domicil'd in nearly all the United States and principal cities, North and South—went to the front (moving about and occupied as army nurse and missionary) during the Secession war, 1861 to '65, and in the Virginia hospitals and after the battles of that time, tending the Northern and Southern wounded alike—work'd down South and in Washington city arduously three years—contracted the paralysis which I have suffer'd ever since—and now live in a little cottage of my own, near the Delaware in New Jersey. My chief book, unrhym'd and unmetrical (it has taken thirty years, peace and war, "a borning") has its aim as once said, "to utter the same old human *critter*—but now in Democratic American modern and scientific conditions." Then I have publish'd two prose works "Specimen Days," and a late one "November Boughs." (A little volume "Good-Bye my Fancy" is soon to be out, wh' will finish the matter.) I do not propose here to enter the much-fought field of the literary criticism of any of those works.

But for a few portraiture or descriptive bits. To-day in the upper of a little wooden house of two stories near the Delaware river, east shore, sixty miles up from the sea, is a rather large 20-by-20 low ceiling'd room something like a big old ship's cabin. The floor, three quarters of it with an ingrain carpet, is half cover'd by a deep litter of books, papers, magazines, thrown-down letters and circulars, rejected manuscripts, memoranda, bits of light or strong twine, a bundle to be "express'd," and two or three venerable scrap books. In the room stand two large tables (one of ancient St. Domingo mahogany with immense leaves) cover'd by a jumble of more papers, a varied and copious array of writing materials, several glass and china vessels or jars, some with cologne-water, others with real honey, granulated sugar, a large bunch of beautiful fresh yellow chrysanthemums, some letters and envelopt papers ready for the post office, many photographs, and a hundred indescribable things besides. There are all around many books, some quite handsome editions, some half cover'd by dust, some within reach, evidently used, (good-sized print, no type less than long primer,) some maps, the Bible, (the strong cheap edition of the English crown,) Homer, Shakspere, Walter Scott, Emerson, Ticknor's "Spanish Literature," John Carlyle's Dante, Felton's Greece, George Sand's Consuelo, a very choice little Epictetus, some novels, the latest foreign and American monthlies, quarterlies, and so on. There being quite a strew of printer's proofs and slips, and the daily papers, the place with its quaint old fashion'd calmness has also a smack of something alert and of current work. There are several trunks and depositaries back'd up at the walls; (one well-bound and big box came by express lately from Washington city, after storage there for nearly twenty years.) Indeed the whole room is a sort of result and storage collection of my own past life. I have here various editions of my own writings, and sell them upon request; one is a big volume of complete poems and prose, 1000 pages, autograph, essays, speeches, portraits from life, &c. Another is a little *Leaves of Grass*, latest date, six portraits, morocco bound, in pocket-book form.

Fortunately the apartment is quite roomy. There are three windows in front. At one side is the stove, with a cheerful fire of oak wood, near by a good supply of fresh sticks, whose faint aroma is plain. On another side is the bed with white coverlid and woollen blankets. Toward the windows is a huge arm-chair, (a Christmas present from Thomas Donaldson's young daughter and son, Philadelphia) timber'd as by some stout ship's spars, yellow polish'd, ample, with rattan-woven seat and back, and over the latter a great wide wolf-skin of hairy black and silver, spread to guard against cold and draught. A time-worn look and scent of old oak attach both to the chair and the person occupying it.

But probably (even at the charge of parrot talk) I can give no more authentic brief sketch than "from an old remembrance copy," where I have lately put myself on record as follows: Was born May 31, 1819, in my father's farm-house, at West Hills, L. I., New York State. My parents' folks mostly farmers and sailors—on my father's side, of English—on my mother's, (Van Velsor's) from Hollandic immigration. There was, first and last, a large family of children; (I was the second.) We moved to Brooklyn while I was still a little one in frocks—and there in B. I grew up out of frocks—then as child and boy went to the public schools—then to work in a printing office. When only sixteen or seventeen years old, and for three years afterward, I went to teaching country schools down in Queens and Suffolk counties, Long Island, and "boarded round." Then, returning to New York, work'd as printer and writer, (with an occasional shy at "poetry.")

1848-'9.—About this time—after ten or twelve years of experiences and work and lots of fun in New York and Brooklyn—went off on a leisurely journey and working expedition (my brother Jeff with me) through all the Middle States, and down the Ohio and Mississippi rivers. Lived a while in New Orleans, and work'd there. (Have lived quite a good deal in the Southern States.) After a time, plodded back northward, up the Mississippi, the Missouri, &c., and around to, and by way of, the great lakes, Michigan, Huron and Erie, to Niagara Falls and Lower Canada—finally returning through Central New York, and down the Hudson. 1852-'54—Occupied in house-building in Brooklyn. (For a little while of the first part of that time in printing a daily and weekly paper.)

1855.—Lost my dear father this year by death. . . . Commenced putting *Leaves of Grass* to press, for good—after many MSS. doings and undoings—(I had great trouble in leaving out the stock "poetical" touches—but succeeded at last.) The book has since had some eight hitches or stages of growth, with one annex (and another to come out in 1891, which will complete it.)

1862.—In December of this year went down to the field of war in Virginia. My brother George reported badly wounded in the Fredericksburg fight. (For 1863 and '64, see *Specimen Days*.) 1865 to '71—Had a place as clerk (till well on in '73) in the Attorney General's Office, Washington. (New York and Brooklyn seem more like *home*, as I was born near, and brought up in them, and lived, man and boy, for 30 years. But I lived some years in Washington, and have visited, and partially lived, in most of the Western and Eastern cities.)

1873.—This year lost, by death, my dear dear mother—and, just before, my sister Martha—the two best and sweetest women I have ever seen or known, or ever expect to see. Same year, February, a sudden climax and prostration from paralysis. Had been simmering inside for several years; broke out during those times temporarily, and then went over. But now a serious attack, beyond cure. Dr. Drinkard, my Washington physician, (and a first-rate one,) said it was the result of too extreme bodily and emotional strain continued at Washington and "down in front," in 1863, '4 and '5. I doubt if a heartier, stronger, healthier physique, more balanced upon itself, or more unconscious, more sound, ever lived, from 1835 to '72. My greatest call (Quaker) to go around and do what I could there in those war-scenes where I had fallen, among the sick and wounded, was, that I seem'd to be *so strong and well*. (I consider'd myself invulnerable.) But this last attack shatter'd me completely. Quit work at Washington, and moved to Camden, New Jersey—where I have lived since, receiving many buffets and some precious caresses—and now write these lines. Since then, (1874–'91) a long stretch of illness, or half-illness, with occasional lulls. During these latter, have revised and printed over all my books—Bro't out "November Boughs" —and at intervals leisurely and exploringly travel'd to the Prairie States, the Rocky Mountains, Canada, to New York, to my birthplace in Long Island, and to Boston. But physical disability and the war-paralysis above alluded to have settled upon me more and more, the last year or so. Am now (1891) domicil'd, and have been for some years, in this little old cottage and lot in Mickle Street, Camden, with a house-keeper and man nurse. Bodily I am completely disabled, but still write for publication. I keep generally buoyant spirits, write often as there comes any lull in physical sufferings, get in the sun and down to the river whenever I can, retain fair appetite, assimilation and digestion, sensibilities acute as ever, the strength and volition of my right arm good, eyesight dimming, but brain normal, and retain my heart's and soul's unmitigated faith not only in their own original literary plans, but in the essential bulk of American humanity east and west, north and south, city and country, through thick and thin, to the last. Nor must I forget, in conclusion, a special, prayerful, thankful God's blessing to my dear firm friends and personal helpers, men and women, home and foreign, old and young.

From the Camden Post, April 16, '91

OUT IN THE OPEN AGAIN

WALT WHITMAN got out in the mid-April sun and warmth of yesterday, propelled in his wheel chair, the first time after four months of imprisonment in his sick room. He has had the worst winter yet, mainly from grippe and gastric troubles, and threaten'd blindness; but keeps good spirits, and has a new little forthcoming book in the printer's hands.

AMERICA'S BULK AVERAGE

IF I were ask'd *persona* to specify the one point of America's people on which I mainly rely, I should say the final average or bulk quality of the whole.

Happy indeed w'd I consider myself to give a fair reflection and representation of even a portion of shows, questions, humanity, events, unfoldings, thoughts, &c. &c. my age in these States.

The great social, political, historic function of my time has been of course the attempted Secession War.

And was there not something grand, and an inside proof of perennial grandeur, in that war! We talk of our age's and the States' materialism—and it is too true. But how amid the whole sordidness —the entire devotion of America, at any price, to pecuniary success, merchandise—disregarding all but business and profit—this war for a bare idea and abstraction—a mere, at bottom, heroic dream and reminiscence—burst forth in its great devouring flame and conflagration quickly and fiercely spreading and raging, and enveloping all, defining in two conflicting ideas—first the Union cause—second *the other*, a strange deadly interrogation point, hard to define—Can we not now safely confess it? with magnificent rays, streaks of noblest heroism, fortitude, perseverance, and even conscientiousness, through its pervadingly malignant darkness.

What an area and rounded field, upon the whole—the spirit, arrogance, grim tenacity of the South—the long stretches of murky gloom—the general National Will below and behind and comprehending all—not once really wavering, not a day, not an hour— What could be, or ever can be, grander?

As in that war, its four years—as through the whole history and development of the New World—these States through all trials, processes, eruptions, deepest dilemmas, (often straining, tugging at society's heart-strings, as if some divine curiosity would find out how much this democracy could stand,) have so far finally and for more than a century best justified themselves by the average impalpable quality and personality of the bulk, the People *en masse.* . . . I am not sure but my main and chief however indefinite claim for any page of mine w'd be its derivation, or seeking to derive itself, f'm that average quality of the American bulk, the people, and getting back to it again.

LAST SAVED ITEMS

f'm a vast batch left to oblivion

In its highest aspect, and striking its grandest average, essential Poetry expresses and goes along with essential Religion—has been and is more the adjunct, and more serviceable to that true religion (for of course there is a false one and plenty of it,) than all the priests and creeds and churches that now exist or have ever existed—Even while the temporary prevalent theory and practice of poetry is merely one-side and ornamental and dainty—a love-sigh, a bit of jewelry, a feudal conceit, an ingenious tale or intellectual *finesse*, adjusted to the low taste and calibre that will always sufficiently generally prevail—(ranges of stairs necessary to ascend the higher.)

The sectarian, church and doctrinal, follies, crimes, fanaticisms, aggregate and individual, so rife all thro' history, are proofs of the radicalness and universality of the indestructible element of humanity's Religion, just as much as any, and are the other side of it. Just as disease proves health, and is the other side of it. . . . The philosophy of Greece taught normality and the beauty of life. Christianity teaches how to endure illness and death. I have wonder'd whether a third philosophy fusing both, and doing full justice to both, might not be outlined.

It will not be enough to say that no Nation ever achiev'd materialistic, political and money-making successes, with general physical comfort, as fully as the United States of America are to-day achieving them. I know very well that those are the indispensable foundations—the *sine qua non* of moral and heroic (poetic) fruitions to come. For if those pre-successes were all—if they ended at that—if nothing more were yielded than so far appears—a gross materialistic prosperity only—America, tried by subtlest tests, were a failure—has not advanced the standard of humanity a bit further than other nations. Or, in plain terms, has but inherited and enjoy'd the results of ordinary claims and preceding ages.

Nature seem'd to use me a long while—myself all well, able, strong and happy—to portray power, freedom, health. But after a while she seems to fancy, may-be I can see and understand it all better by being deprived of most of those.

How difficult it is to add anything more to literature—and how unsatisfactory for any earnest spirit to serve merely the amusement of the multitude! (It even seems to me, said H. Heine, more invigorating to accomplish something bad than something empty.)

The Highest said: Don't let us begin so low—isn't our range too coarse—too gross? . . . The Soul answer'd: No, not when we consider what it is all for—the end involved in Time and Space.

Essentially my own printed records, all my volumes, are doubtless but off-hand utterances f'm Personality, spontaneous, following implicitly the inscrutable command, dominated by that Personality, vaguely even if decidedly, and with little or nothing of plan, art, erudition, &c. If I have chosen to hold the reins, the mastery, it has mainly been to give the way, the power, the road, to the invisible steeds. (I wanted to see how a Person of America, the last half of the 19th century, w'd appear, put quite freely and fairly in honest type.)

Haven't I given specimen clues, if no more? At any rate I have written enough to weary myself—and I will dispatch it to the printers, and cease. But how much—how many topics, of the greatest point and cogency, I am leaving untouch'd!

–》》《《–